IRVING BERLIN'S
AMERICAN
MUSICAL THEATER

Geoffrey Block, Series Editor

Series Board

Stephen Banfield   Jeffrey Magee

Tim Carter   Carol Oja

Kim Kowalke   Larry Starr

"South Pacific": Paradise Rewritten
Jim Lovensheimer

Pick Yourself Up: Dorothy Fields and the American Musical
Charlotte Greenspan

To Broadway, to Life! The Musical Theater of Bock and Harnick
Philip Lambert

Irving Berlin's American Musical Theater
Jeffrey Magee

IRVING BERLIN'S AMERICAN MUSICAL THEATER

Jeffrey Magee

OXFORD
UNIVERSITY PRESS

OXFORD
UNIVERSITY PRESS

Oxford University Press, Inc., publishes works that further
Oxford University's objective of excellence
in research, scholarship, and education.

Oxford   New York
Auckland   Cape Town   Dar es Salaam   Hong Kong   Karachi
Kuala Lumpur   Madrid   Melbourne   Mexico City   Nairobi
New Delhi   Shanghai   Taipei   Toronto

With offices in
Argentina   Austria   Brazil   Chile   Czech Republic   France   Greece
Guatemala   Hungary   Italy   Japan   Poland   Portugal   Singapore
South Korea   Switzerland   Thailand   Turkey   Ukraine   Vietnam

Published by Oxford University Press, Inc.
198 Madison Avenue, New York, NY 10016

www.oup.com

Oxford is a registered trademark of Oxford University Press

Library of Congress Cataloging-in-Publication Data
Magee, Jeffrey, 1961–
Irving Berlin's American musical theater / Jeffrey Magee.
p.   cm. — (Broadway legacies)
Includes bibliographical references and index.
ISBN 978-0-19-539826-7
1. Berlin, Irving, 1888–1989—Criticism and interpretation.
2. Musicals—United States—History and criticism. I. Title.
ML410.B499M34   2012
782.1′4092—dc23   2011025332

Publication of this book was funded in part by the Publications Endowment of the
American Musicological Society, supported through the National Endowment
for the Humanities.

1 3 5 7 9 8 4 6 2

Printed in the United States of America
on acid-free paper

To my parents,

RICHARD AND JOYCE MAGEE

CONTENTS

• • •

FOREWORD

• • •

An acclaimed jazz historian whose book *The Uncrowned King of Swing: Fletcher Henderson and Big Band Jazz* (Oxford, 2004) was the recipient of the Society for American Music's prestigious Irving Lowens Book Award, Jeffrey Magee brings to his latest book an inspiring and multifaceted American success story: how a Russian Jewish immigrant who arrived in New York at the age of five evolved from peddling newspapers and junk on the street into a songwriter and businessman who not only mastered American colloquial speech and popular musical styles from ragtime to jazz to swing, but "profoundly shaped the principal sites of American musical entertainment, from Tin Pan Alley to Broadway and Hollywood."

Throughout his career Berlin never wavered in his conviction that "the mob is always right," a worldview which, although stated with Berlin's characteristic simplicity and brevity, shares the sentiment of Verdi's famous remark that "the box office is the proper thermometer of success." It is no surprise to learn that when asked to name his "favorite songs," the songs included in Berlin's list were "the ones that, through the years, have won the widest acceptance." For the record, Berlin's top ten included four Tin Pan Alley songs ("Alexander's Ragtime Band," "Always," "How Deep Is the Ocean?" "God Bless America"), the Hollywood mega-hit "White Christmas," and five Broadway songs ("Oh! How I Hate to Get Up in the Morning," "Say It with Music," "Blue Skies," "Easter Parade," "There's No Business Like Show Business").

In this wide-ranging survey of Berlin's musical theater Magee offers a lively discussion of the full range of Berlin's felicitous contributions to Broadway, which was far more substantial than simply puttin' on the hits. In his engaging prose style Magee persuasively measures the pulse of important and often complex critical, social, and aesthetic issues, and invariably offers new insights (as well as equanimity) when exploring areas of Berlin's thought now regularly dismissed as outdated, such as the lasting dramatic relevance of the minstrel show and the revue. A lyric from the last-named song in Berlin's list describes this book with characteristic aptness: "Everything about it is appealing."

Three years after his song "Alexander's Ragtime Band" soared to unprecedented popularity in 1911, centenarian-to-be Irving Berlin (1888–1989) debuted on Broadway with his first complete score, *Watch Your Step*, a show described by Magee's illustrious predecessor, Charles Hamm, in *Irving Berlin, Songs from the Melting Pot: The Formative Years, 1907–1914* (Oxford, 1997) as "a seminal work, more so than any other piece from that period." Often characterized, with more than a grain of accuracy, as a ragtime musical, this timely and new stylistic synthesis was a hit. The show featured the dancing sensations Vernon and Irene Castle (who also sang a little) and invocatory songs such as "Syncopated Walk" and "Play a Simple Melody." The latter was the first of Berlin's celebrated counterpoint (or double) songs, which combine a ballad and a rhythm song into one reprise after each one is first heard separately. Popular future examples of this signature of Berlin's style would include "I Wonder Why/You're Just in Love" from *Call Me Madam* and the contrasting lyrical and musical views expressed in "Old Fashioned Wedding," introduced in the 1966 *Annie Get Your Gun* revival. The most discussed moment in the show, however, was the guest appearance of Verdi's ghost, who joined in a ragged version of his quartet from *Rigoletto* in the second act finale.

Berlin's 1914 opening Broadway salvo was a pioneering musical that preceded by five years both George Gershwin's first hit "Swanee" (sung by Al Jolson in *Sinbad*) and Rodgers and Hart's first song in a Broadway show, "Any Old Place with You" (in *A Lonely Romeo*—not a hit). By two years, it beat out fellow lyricist-composer and future friend Cole Porter's short-lived *See America First*. Berlin's *Watch Your Step* even preceded the first of the historically acclaimed Princess Theatre shows, *Nobody's Home*, (with music by Jerome Kern) launched in 1915.

After thirty more years as an iconic songwriter, Berlin created the words and music for his best-remembered show, the perennial favorite *Annie Get Your Gun* (1946), originally starring Ethel Merman, and followed, respectively, by Betty Hutton, Mary Martin, and Bernadette Peters on film, television, and Broadway over the next fifty years. His last hit, *Call Me Madam* (1950), also starring Merman, is a fine show that remains far too little known despite a well-executed movie adaptation starring the rarely filmed Merman herself and a New York City Center *Encores!* production in 1995. Twelve years later *Encores!* presented another underrated Berlin musical, the 1932 political satire, *Face the Music,* from a book by the frequent Berlin collaborator Moss Hart and originally directed by George S. Kaufman. The Broadway career that offered about twenty musicals, more than half of which preceded the arrival of *Show Boat* in 1927, did not come to a close until nearly a half century after *Watch Your Step* with the widely publicized but ultimately unsuccessful *Mr. President* in 1962. Berlin was then seventy-four but still four years away from writing that masterful double song "Old Fashioned Wedding." When Jerome Kern quipped to his biographer Alexander Woollcott in the early 1920s that "Irving Berlin has *no* place in American music, he *is* American music," Berlin had another forty years and ten or so musicals to go. Readers of Jeffrey Magee's *Irving Berlin's American Musical Theater,* after reading chapters on all these shows and many more, may be excused from concluding that Kern's expansive assessment was an understatement.

GEOFFREY BLOCK
Series Editor, Broadway Legacies

PREFACE

* * *

Irving Berlin (1888–1989) is widely recognized as one of the greatest and most pro-lific of American songwriters, but he remains much less well known as a man of the theater, even as those who knew his work ranked him as a theatrical genius. If, as Alan Jay Lerner claimed, "what Berlin did for the modern musical theatre was to make it possible," then we still have a lot to learn about what made the modern mu-sical theater possible.[1] And Joshua Logan's claim that he "never knew anyone who more enjoyed writing for the theater or better understood how to write for it" than Irving Berlin, is a strong statement by a director who worked regularly with Rodgers and Hammerstein.[2] Together, Lerner and Logan, two major figures of Broadway's Golden Age, position Irving Berlin as a kind of founding father of American musical theater.

Indeed, in his seven-decade career, Berlin profoundly shaped the principal sites of American musical entertainment from Tin Pan Alley to Broadway and Hollywood. His enterprising musicianship, lyric craft, industrious work habits, stalwart patri-otism, and irrepressible optimism (despite bouts of severe depression) manifested a Russian Jewish immigrant's hunger to belong in the New World. For his songs and shows, his influential roles in the entertainment industry, and his ability to distill and define the musical, social, and political spirit of his times, Berlin stands as one of the most powerful forces in twentieth-century American music and theater.

Two decades after Berlin's death, we are just beginning to come to grips with his vast legacy. Although since 1925 at least half a dozen biographies have charted the compelling arc of his immigrant success story, there remains ample room for a sus-tained interpretation of the songs and shows.[3] There have been several insightful studies of his songs, yet they tend to emphasize either lyrics or music, thereby de-emphasizing a key point: that Berlin was one of the rare figures between Stephen Foster and Stephen Sondheim to write both.[4] Meanwhile, scholarly studies of Broad-way composers have established critical and analytical approaches that have informed this book—emphasizing, for example, how archival research informs the subject, how musical dramaturgy works in a musical, and how musical theater am-plifies aspects of individual and collective experience.[5] Yet only one scholar, Charles Hamm, has investigated any aspect of Berlin's career in considerable depth. Hamm's research, focused entirely on Berlin's early work to 1914, remains foundational.[6] That Berlin continued to lead an active career well into the 1960s, however, calls for a scholarly account that addresses a broader swath of his work, one that explores a wide range of Berlin's songs with an emphasis on the medium that compelled his attention for more than half a century: the Broadway stage.

This is now possible thanks to a treasure-trove of material available at two venues—the New York Public Library (NYPL) and the Library of Congress (LC)—that is just beginning to make a mark on studies of Berlin's post-1914 musical theater work. The NYPL holds a wide range of material covering Berlin's entire career, but stands particularly strong in his earliest shows. The LC collection, referred to in this book as LC-IBC, contains well over 600 boxes and some 750,000 documents. They include musical manuscripts and lyric sheets, revue sketches, musical comedy scripts, orchestral parts, screenplays, scrapbooks brimming with newspaper clippings, photographs, business papers, financial and legal records, and correspondence—thousands of letters written to and from powerful and lofty figures including presidents and generals, show business personalities, and ordinary citizens expressing appreciation for Berlin's work or good wishes for his family. The single, stunning fact that emerges from that material is that Berlin wrote a lot of music for the theater that has never been published—mostly because it exceeded the bounds of Tin Pan Alley's conventional sheet music format. Along with that, the collections likewise contain unpublished scripts, which allow for a clearer understanding of the context for which Berlin wrote musical numbers. With such a bounty of primary sources, along with the recent publication of key reference books such as his *Complete Lyrics*, we are in a stronger position than ever to assess the scope and quality of Berlin's work for the theater.[7]

Readers should be aware that many copies of that work—in the form of sheet music for individual songs, songbook anthologies, "vocal selections" and piano-vocal scores for shows, and manuscript versions of musical numbers—coexist and sometimes conflict with regard to details such as capitalization, punctuation, and even individual words and notes. *The Complete Lyrics of Irving Berlin* exists, in part, to offer a standardized way to represent Berlin's lyrics in print. Indeed, because of its meticulous attention to the sound and sense of Berlin's lyrics, its treatment of them as a kind of poetry, and its thoroughness in presenting nearly every lyric that Berlin ever wrote (not to mention its illuminating annotations), *Complete Lyrics* is referred to as "The Bible" within the Irving Berlin Music Company. Thus, in order to meet a condition for permission to reprint them, this book reflects the company's wishes by presenting all lyric examples (both lyrics-only and lyrics with music) in accordance with *Complete Lyrics* (abbreviated in this book's endnotes as *CL*). This seemed like an important step to take for a study about a songwriter famously reticent about letting others quote examples from his work. In rare cases where *Complete Lyrics* differs in word choice from other published sources—most notably in the verse to the stage version of "There's No Business Like Show Business"—I have indicated the alternative in a footnote. This book also includes a few never-before-published lyrics uncovered in the process of my research (particularly notable in the case of the *Ziegfeld Follies of 1919*, see chap. 3), and these get special attention, suggesting that "completeness" may continue to prove elusive with respect to a writer as prolific and long-lived as Berlin.

While keeping Berlin's work at its center, this book's overall organization reflects his collaboration with others, the trait that distinguishes theatrical endeavors from more solitary artistic enterprises. After a biographical introduction, chapter 1 explores Berlin's songwriting and theatrical tendencies across his entire career in the context of what I call his "Lower East Side Aesthetic." The remaining chapters take shape according to the work he did with his partners—usually, but not always, the playwrights. Chapter 2 explores Berlin's first two musicals (*Watch Your Step* and *Stop! Look! Listen!*), which reflected his amiable collaboration with the producer Charles Dillingham in the 1910s. Chapter 3 focuses on Berlin's work for two important revues in the late 1910s: his World War I show, *Yip Yip Yaphank*, and the *Ziegfeld Follies of 1919*. Chapter 4 explores his monumental project of the musical-rich 1920s: the *Music Box Revues* (1921–24), developed under the auspices of his business partner and producer, Sam H. Harris. Chapter 5 covers the broadest chronological range, the two decades in which Berlin collaborated with George S. Kaufman (*The Cocoanuts*, 1925) and like-minded collaborators such as Moss Hart (*Face the Music*, 1932, and *As Thousands Cheer*, 1933). Berlin's World War II revue, *This Is the Army* (1942), gets special attention in chapter 6, for Berlin claimed that it was "the best thing I was ever connected with." Chapter 7 presents an in-depth exploration of Berlin's most successful and enduring book musical, *Annie Get Your Gun* (1946), which featured his only collaboration with book writers Herbert and Dorothy Fields and producers Richard Rodgers and Oscar Hammerstein II. Chapter 8 explores the common ground shared by Berlin's last two book musicals, *Call Me Madam* (1950) and *Mr. President* (1962), both co-written with librettists Howard Lindsay and Russel Crouse.

Throughout his nearly half-century stage career, Berlin consistently worked with the top talent on Broadway: five of his writer-collaborators had won—or would go on to win—the Pulitzer Prize: Kaufman, Hart, Robert Sherwood, and Lindsay and Crouse. (Sherwood himself won four Pulitzers, though his script for *Miss Liberty* was considered a poor effort.) It is worth emphasizing what will be obvious to musical theater aficionados and historians: that three-quarters of the history recounted in this book takes place before *Oklahoma!* turned "integration" into a Broadway buzzword and an aesthetic standard by which to measure new works. Exploring Berlin's work thus becomes a way of reclaiming a rich, long history of pre-*Oklahoma!* musical theater.

While the book's structure thus places emphasis on Berlin's writer and producer colleagues, it remains important to bear in mind that he consistently wrote with performers in mind: the Castles, the Marxes, Al Jolson, Ethel Waters, Fred Astaire, Bing Crosby, and Ethel Merman, and himself, to name a few. Unlike his friends and acquaintances in his remarkable peer group of songwriters, Berlin regularly sang his songs in public, on stage. Even gifted performers such as Gershwin and Porter did not sing their songs in the theater, but Berlin did. Berlin's theatrical and musical roots grew from the soil of performance, because for him, performance animated the survival instinct that drove him from the theater of the Lower East Side to Broadway and beyond, and he never forgot that. For Berlin, the life and the work were intimately, if not obviously, connected. There will undoubtedly be more biographies to come, but we actually know quite a bit about Berlin's life. We are just beginning to come to grips with the vastness of his work—the subject of this book. A brief biographical digest, however, is in order first: a quick narrative of a remarkable life that spanned a century.

IRVING BERLIN'S
AMERICAN
MUSICAL THEATER

INTRODUCTION: IRVING BERLIN'S CENTURY

* * *

He celebrated his birthday on May 11, and his birthplace is sometimes cited as Tyu-men in Western Siberia, but the date and place remain uncertain, even though he strove throughout his life to clarify his increasingly mythologized origins.[1] We know that he was born Israel Beilin in Russia in the spring of 1888, the last of eight children of Moses and Leah Beilin. After their house was burned down in a pogrom when Israel was four or five, the Beilins immigrated to the United States without the two eldest children. (The oldest son remained in Russia; the oldest daughter traveled separately with her husband.) After an arduous journey, the two parents and six children ranging in age from five to nineteen arrived in New York on September 13, 1893. The family's last name became Baline after registering at the checkpoint on Ellis Island, where millions of immigrants passed through on their way to a new life in the United States. Settling his family in a teeming immigrant community on the Lower East Side of Manhattan, Moses Baline gave up his prestigious position as a cantor and took up work first as a kosher meat inspector and then as a house painter. Leah supplemented the family income as a midwife. The children worked as well. Israel, known as "Izzy" in the family, hawked newspapers and sold "junk," including the dismantled parts of a family samovar, a prized possession in many Russian households.

When his father died in 1901, Izzy dropped out of school to earn more money, ultimately leaving his family for some time. As a teenager he became a singing waiter and earned a reputation as a sly, bawdy parodist of popular songs issuing from Tin Pan Alley, the city's famous song-publishing district centered on West Twenty-Eighth Street. Although he could not read or write music, he had a keen ear, and with pianist Mike Nicholson he collaborated on his first published song, "Marie from Sunny Italy" (1907). This bright, gently syncopated love song remains unremarkable but for one thing: on the sheet music, whether by accident or design, the publisher printed the lyricist's name as "I. Berlin." Keeping the new surname, Izzy adopted the new first name "Irving" and thereby stripped away the ethnic resonance of his given name. Other songwriters and entertainers of his generation would likewise change their names or have them changed by older family members, including Jacob Gershowitz (George Gershwin), Hymen Arluck (Harold Arlen), Sonia Kalish (Sophie Tucker), Asa Joelson (Al Jolson), Edward Israel Iskowitz (Eddie Cantor), and Fania Borach (Fanny Brice).

Berlin's songwriting career blossomed quickly, with a handful of further publications in 1908 followed by a breakout year in 1909. On the strength of a comic song about a Jewish burlesque dancer called "Sadie Salome (Go Home)"—inspired in part by the scandal created by the recent U.S. premiere of Richard Strauss's opera *Salome*—he got a job as a staff lyricist for the Ted Snyder Company, at $25 per week plus royalties. Meanwhile, he was becoming known on vaudeville and Broadway, where his songs were regularly interpolated into the period's loosely plotted shows. Berlin himself turned out to be a gifted performer and plugger of his own material. In a 1910 revue called *Up and Down Broadway*, for example, Berlin and Snyder performed a few of the songs they had written together and earned critical raves. That same year, the showman Florenz Ziegfeld began using Berlin's songs in his annual *Follies* production, a practice that would continue over the next two decades. Two other events would enlarge Berlin's musical life in 1910: he acquired a transposing piano, later fondly known as his "Buick," which, while he favored the key of F-sharp, allowed him to play in any key with the shift of a lever under the keyboard, and he traveled with Ted Snyder's business partner, Henry Waterson, to England. There, the songwriter met the British publisher Bert Feldman, who helped establish Berlin's reputation overseas by featuring Berlin's songs in his "song annuals." Berlin would continue to win the appreciation of British audiences throughout his career.

In 1911, Berlin's international reputation soared with the publication of "Alexander's Ragtime Band." Although he had already published several ragtime songs, "Alexander's Ragtime Band" secured his fame as the "Ragtime King," with estimated sheet-music sales of two million copies in the first year. It also won him a partnership with his publisher: henceforth the firm would be known as the Waterson, Berlin, and Snyder Company. In February 1912, now at the height of fame and prosperity, Berlin married Dorothy Goetz, the sister of his friend and fellow songwriter E. Ray Goetz. Shortly after the couple's honeymoon in Cuba, however, Dorothy contracted typhoid fever or pneumonia. Her health deteriorated rapidly, and she died on July 17. Berlin paid homage to his deceased wife in a mournful waltz titled "When I Lost You."

The personal loss did not seem to slow his meteoric rise in American entertainment and his association with some of its leading figures. *Watch Your Step* (1914), produced by Charles Dillingham and starring the newly popular dance team of Irene and Vernon Castle, marked the first time Berlin had written a complete Broadway score; this "syncopated musical show" became the hit of the season, and Berlin's parody of opera in the act 2 finale brought down the house. After that, Broadway saw a new Berlin show almost every year for the next decade. *Stop! Look! Listen!* appeared in 1915 with two hit songs, "I Love a Piano" and "The Girl on the Magazine." In 1916 Berlin collaborated with Victor Herbert on a lavish Ziegfeld production called *The Century Girl*. He worked with George M. Cohan on the *Cohan Revue of 1918*. And then he became the chief songwriter for the *Ziegfeld Follies of 1919*, widely regarded as the best in the series, and articulated the show's keynote in the rich ballad "A Pretty Girl Is Like a Melody."

This period also marked the crucial final stage of Berlin's naturalization. He had begun the process of seeking U.S. citizenship by filing a declaration of intention in 1915; he took the oath of allegiance on February 6, 1918. Soon thereafter he was drafted into the U.S. Army and assigned to Camp Upton in Yaphank, Long Island. Berlin's genuine patriotism did not mitigate his distaste for army life, and, with the comic irreverence he had brought to his early work as a singing waiter, he composed "Oh! How I Hate to Get Up in the Morning." Berlin himself introduced the song in his new show, *Yip Yip Yaphank* (1918), a Broadway revue about army life with a cast featuring his fellow soldiers from Camp Upton. Berlin's winning performance—enhanced by his shy, aw-shucks stage persona, Lower East Side accent, and diminutive size (about five feet, six inches, and less than 125 pounds)—helped make the song the hit of the show.

Berlin's business acumen also came to the fore during this period. He had joined with Herbert and others in the music business in the effort that led to the formation of the American Society of Composers, Authors, and Publishers (ASCAP) in 1914, ensuring that they would earn royalties for performances of their songs. In 1914 Berlin confirmed his allegiance to Broadway by opening his own publishing house on West Forty-fifth Street, in the theater district north of Tin Pan Alley. In 1921 he moved his residence as well, buying an entire building a few blocks away on West Forty-sixth Street. That same year he crowned his Broadway success by partnering with the producer Sam H. Harris to build a theater, the Music Box Theatre, down the street from his publishing house. In each of the next four seasons Berlin's theater staged a new edition of his *Music Box Revue*, which launched several hits, including "All Alone," "All By Myself," "Pack Up Your Sins and Go to the Devil," and "What'll I Do?" Two other songs stood out in particular: "Say It with Music," which articulated the distinctive identity of the series, and "Everybody Step," widely recognized at the time as a pioneering example of jazz.

The early 1920s brought significant changes in Berlin's personal and social life. His mother died in 1922, having watched her son's rapid climb from Lower East Side obscurity to international celebrity. The same year Berlin was absorbed into the tight-knit social group of the Round Table of the Algonquin Hotel. This voluble, witty circle of writers, actors, and musicians met regularly under the informal leadership of the rotund theater critic Alexander Woollcott. There Berlin stoked several important professional and personal relationships. The playwright George S. Kaufman, for example, wrote sketches for the Music Box shows, and in 1925 he collaborated with Berlin on a new musical, *The Cocoanuts*, starring the Marx Brothers. Woollcott himself wrote the first biography of the songwriter, published in 1925. By this time, Berlin had befriended Ellin Mackay, daughter of the Postal Telegraph Cable tycoon Clarence Mackay. This upright businessman, a devout Catholic, bitterly opposed the courtship between his daughter and the self-made Jewish entertainer, and the press covered every twist in the romance. Ellin and Irving finally married over Mackay's objections on January 4, 1926. As a wedding gift Berlin presented his new wife with a tender waltz about enduring love, "Always," and assigned its copyright to her.

By the mid-1920s the music industry had witnessed major changes, thanks to the emergence of radio and the proliferation of sound recordings, and Berlin stood in a strong position to benefit from these developments. For example, when the Irish tenor John McCormack sang Berlin's "All Alone" on radio in 1925, orders for both his recording and the sheet music soared. Recording sales had now supplanted sheet-music sales as the chief measure of a song's popularity. The same year Warner Brothers developed the "vitaphone" system, which revolutionized film with synchronized sound. Just two years later the Warner studio scored an international hit with *The Jazz Singer*, featuring the vaudeville star Al Jolson singing Berlin's new song "Blue Skies." With film as a new way to plug his wares, Berlin devoted more attention to Hollywood. From 1928 to 1930, with "talking pictures" in their infancy, eight films featured his music, including a screen adaptation of *The Cocoanuts*, again starring the Marx Brothers; *Mammy*, another Al Jolson vehicle based on a scenario conceived by Berlin; and *Puttin' on the Ritz*, named after its featured Berlin song.

Hollywood did not entirely distract him from the stage, however. Teaming with the Kaufman protégé Moss Hart, Berlin wrote two shows inspired by current events. *Face the Music* (1932), a "musical comedy revue," lampooned corrupt New York policemen, the Depression-era rich, and show business itself in a farce that included songs such as "Let's Have Another Cup of Coffee" and "Soft Lights and Sweet Music." The following year Hart and Berlin delivered a revue titled *As Thousands Cheer*, featuring "Easter Parade," "Heat Wave," and "Supper Time." Berlin's growing family also absorbed him. A daughter, Mary Ellin, was born in 1926, and it was to her that Berlin dedicated his cheerful, optimistic love ballad "Blue Skies." A son, Irving Jr., was born in early December 1928 but died in his crib on Christmas morning. A second daughter, named Linda after the wife of his friend Cole Porter, arrived in 1932, and the last Berlin child, Elizabeth, was born in 1936.

In late 1934 Berlin traveled to California by airplane and signed a contract with RKO Pictures for a film score. The contract granted him a large sum, plus a percentage of the movie's profits and the unusual privilege of retaining the music copyrights. The movie, *Top Hat* (1935), was Berlin's first entry in a successful series featuring Fred Astaire and Ginger Rogers and helped establish a new standard for the Hollywood musical. The film featured just five songs, but two of them became standards, "Cheek to Cheek" and "Top Hat, White Tie, and Tails." Two more Astaire-Rogers pictures followed in close succession: *Follow the Fleet* (1936), featuring "Let Yourself Go" and "Let's Face the Music and Dance"; and *Carefree* (1938), featuring "Change Partners." Berlin and his music thrived in this milieu. He later said that "I'd rather have Fred Astaire introduce one of my songs than any other singer I know—not because he has a great voice, but because his diction and delivery are so good that he can put over a song like nobody else."

Back in New York after a trip to England in September 1938, Berlin declared his interest in writing a "great peace song." His initial attempt failed, so he pulled from his files an unpublished song he had discarded from *Yip Yip Yaphank* two decades earlier, believing it to have been overwrought for the finale of a wartime revue. He changed a few words and published it as "God Bless America." On November 11, 1938, the popular radio singer Kate Smith performed it on an Armistice Day broadcast then sang it again on Thanksgiving Day. By the end of the year she was singing it to sign off her weekly show. Since then it has often been referred to as the unofficial national anthem. Such was its popularity that Berlin felt obliged to deny any attempt to replace "The Star Spangled Banner." In 1940 it was sung at both the Republican and Democratic national conventions, and Berlin established the God Bless America Fund to distribute the song's profits to the Boy and Girl Scouts of America. By this time, Berlin, anticipating U.S. involvement in the war that had broken out in Europe in 1939, "seemed to be spending all his time singing 'God Bless America' at civic events and writing war-related songs," as his daughter Mary Ellin Barrett recalled.

After the Japanese bombed Pearl Harbor on December 7, 1941, and the United States entered the war, Berlin arranged with the Department of War to revive *Yip Yip Yaphank*, newly titled as *This Is the Army*, to benefit Army Emergency Relief. Working at Camp Upton, where he had been a recruit almost a quarter-century earlier, Berlin revised and rehearsed the show with a new generation of soldier-performers. Berlin himself sang "Oh! How I Hate to Get Up in the Morning" again, and the show featured several new hits, including "This Is the Army, Mister Jones" and "I Left My Heart at the Stage Door Canteen." A U.S. tour led to Hollywood, where the cast made a film version starring George Murphy and Ronald Reagan. From fall 1943 through summer 1945, *This Is the Army* played overseas, beginning in England. Then, after General Dwight Eisenhower, the Supreme Allied Commander in Europe, recognized the show's morale-boosting potential, the company continued to Africa, Italy, the Middle East, and the South Pacific, performing for hundreds of thousands of Allied troops. For Berlin's contribution to the war effort, President Harry Truman presented Berlin with the army's Medal for Merit in 1945. Berlin considered *This Is the Army* to be his greatest achievement.

Although the army show was Berlin's principal focus during the war, it barely interrupted his tenure as a leading Hollywood composer. After the three Astaire-Rogers movies, Hollywood continued to issue a string of new films with Berlin's music, including *Alexander's Ragtime Band* (1938), the first of many "song cavalcade" films featuring mostly established hits rather than new songs. Berlin was gold in Hollywood, which issued several more of his musical films in quick succession: *On the Avenue* (1937), *Second Fiddle* (1939), *Louisiana Purchase* (1941, based on the Broadway show of 1940), and *Holiday Inn* (1942). *Holiday Inn* featured Bing Crosby singing "White Christmas," for which Berlin won an Academy Award. After the war came *Blue Skies* (1946), featuring Crosby and Astaire and using Berlin's famous ballad as its title and theme song; *Easter Parade* (1948), starring Astaire and Judy Garland and reviving the lilting holiday song featured fifteen years earlier in *As Thousands Cheer*; and *Annie Get Your Gun* (1950), the film version of Berlin's most popular and enduring Broadway musical (1946). With Ethel Merman, as Annie Oakley, singing Berlin's proud paean to entertainment, "There's No Business Like Show Business," the show had enjoyed a Broadway run of 1,147 performances. *Miss Liberty* (1949) had a much less successful run. Another Broadway hit starring Merman, *Call Me Madam* (1950), became a movie in 1953. The following year *White Christmas* brought back Crosby singing Berlin's award-winning song in a film with a scenario derived from *Holiday Inn*. Published estimates of record sales of "White Christmas" vary, but by all accounts it sold more records than any other song in the era before rock. Berlin called the song "a publishing house in itself."[2]

After *White Christmas*, two more films featured songs by Irving Berlin: *There's No Business Like Show Business* (1954), a cavalcade-style musical starring Ethel Merman, Donald O'Connor, and Marilyn Monroe; and *Sayonara* (1957), originally intended as a stage musical and ultimately featuring just one Berlin song. Dwight Eisenhower, now U.S. president, awarded Berlin the Congressional Gold Medal in 1955. By then, however, Berlin had begun to sink into a severe depression, which led to semiretirement and intermittent hospitalization. In 1962, now recovered, he attempted a comeback in collaboration with Howard Lindsay and Russel Crouse (with whom he had done *Call Me Madam*) on a show about an American president that would prove to be his final Broadway musical, *Mr. President* (1962). The show ran for eight months on the strength of advance ticket sales, but critical reaction suggested that its creators had missed the mark. Among other things, the contrast between the stage president, an old-fashioned Ohioan finishing out his second term, and the real president, a young, glamorous John F. Kennedy less than two years into his first term, made the show seem out of step.

Yet Berlin was far from finished. For a 1966 revival of *Annie Get Your Gun*, he composed "An Old Fashioned Wedding," a show-stopping number featuring two melodies in counterpoint—one of Berlin's favorite theater-song devices since his first show, *Watch Your Step*, had appeared more than a half-century earlier. One last film project, dubbed *Say It with Music* after the theme song of the *Music Box Revues*, percolated through the 1960s but finally fell through in 1969. At that point, as Mary Ellin Barrett has written, "he really did retire." Yet although he no longer went to his office, he continued to dictate song ideas over the telephone to his assistants until two years before his death.

After his retirement Berlin remained a private man, but, ever the performer, he did make a few more public appearances. His last was in 1973, when he sang "God Bless America" at the White House before a group of former prisoners of war back from Vietnam. In 1977 President Gerald Ford gave Berlin the Medal of Freedom. Meanwhile, many of Berlin's songs assumed new lives. In the late 1970s and early 1980s two songs that Berlin had written a half-century earlier once again became hits: Willie Nelson's version of "Blue Skies" and the Dutch pop singer Taco's revival of "Puttin' on the Ritz" with a disco beat. In his last years Berlin became increasingly reclusive, never leaving his townhouse on Beekman Place near the United Nations building and often refusing to receive visitors; he kept in touch with friends by telephone. He turned one hundred years old in 1988, and the occasion was observed throughout the world. ASCAP held a birthday celebration at Carnegie Hall with a diverse array of musicians, including Frank Sinatra, Isaac Stern, Willie Nelson, and Leonard Bernstein; Berlin himself did not appear. Quoting the song that Berlin had given to his wife Ellin six decades earlier, the ASCAP president Morton Gould announced that "Irving Berlin's music will last forever, not for just an hour, not for just a day, not for just a year, but always." A few months later, Ellin passed away at the age of eighty-five. The following year, after a series of strokes, Berlin died on September 22, 1989, and was buried in Woodlawn Cemetery in the Bronx.

In Berlin's obituary in the *New York Times*, Marilyn Berger wrote that "his was a classic rags-to-riches story that he never forgot could have happened only in America." From the beginning, Berlin's work had grown in a context where survival and performance merged. And that context formed the unique circumstances of Berlin's youth. For the rest of his life, theater would nurture and inspire the craft of America's most versatile, prolific, and long-lived songwriter. For that reason, it makes sense to consider the ways in which his youth on the New York's Lower East Side forged a template for his life and career, and how we may continue to bear witness to its impact on his work as a songwriter and showman.

1

IRVING BERLIN'S THEATER

• • •

The mob is always right.
—*Irving Berlin*

In 1901 Izzy Baline, age thirteen and fatherless, dropped out of school and moved out of his family's Lower East Side tenement flat to fend for himself. He lived in cheap lodgings among the Bowery's lowlife, had his few belongings stolen, and once even got stabbed.[1] He was destitute and alone in perhaps the most densely populated neighborhood in the world, a neighborhood transformed by some of the millions of immigrants who had effected perhaps the most massive demographic change in world history. Yet he did not romanticize want. He "never felt poverty," he claimed, because he'd "never known anything else."[2] And he regarded his childhood as ideal, insisting that "everyone should have a Lower East Side in their lives."[3]

He discovered that singing could be a path to distinction in this crowded, some-times dangerous world. As a freelance, he shuttled from one Bowery saloon to an-other, earning tips by "passing the hat" or by picking change out of the sawdust on barroom floors.[4] He grew especially fond of new songs from George M. Cohan, who made a point of getting his material in the hands of buskers like Baline.[5] Berlin would later refer to Cohan as his "favorite songwriter."[6] Gaining confidence, he auditioned for and won a short-lived position as a chorus boy in a musical called *The Show Girl*, in which he performed during out-of-town tryouts before getting cut on the way to Broadway.[7] He then became a publisher's song-plugger and a singing "stooge" on vaudeville, paid to rise from his seat in the audience as if suddenly overcome by the onstage music to repeat the refrain of a new song published by his employer, Harry Von Tilzer. In 1904 he landed a steady job as a singer at a Chinatown saloon, the Pelham Café, where he earned a regular wage plus tips.

The whole neighborhood was a theater for slumming New York sightseers, who "outnumbered the local talent" in their quest to discover "the seamy side of life," according to Berlin's first biographer, Alexander Woollcott.[8] In three years at the Pelham—also known as "Nigger Mike's" after its swarthy, Russian Jewish proprietor Mike Salter—Baline earned local fame as a parodist of current popular songs, taking material that everyone knew and giving it a freshly satiric and often risqué twist that was "seldom printable."[9] He enjoyed the work, but it took a toll. Four decades later when he was a celebrity, he made a return visit with a reporter and recalled that "I did all right working here. I used to come to work at 8 p.m. and stay on until 6 a.m. I was paid $7 a week and did pretty good passing the hat. Some nights I'd take in $7 and that was terrific. I was very happy here, but I finally got bounced for falling asleep behind the bar."[10]

Every job reinforced the teenager's growing awareness that his livelihood depended on making an immediate impact on a live—and sometimes distracted—audience through performance that blended words, music, and a theatrical impulse. His voice had a soft, ingratiating coarseness—the word *raspy* recurs in the Berlin literature, and "whiskey voice" was the term that Berlin himself used.[11] Yet that voice would prove to project well in theaters seating throngs of one thousand or more such as the Palace, Hammerstein's Victoria, the London Hippodrome, his own Music Box, and many makeshift stages in Europe and the South Pacific. His diction had clarity and precision, making every vowel and consonant count. His stage manner, adapted to the songs he sang, ranged from "diffidence" and "charm" to a mischievous sense of humor.[12] He developed, too, a vocabulary of well-timed gestures, all captured in photographs throughout his life: a pointing index finger, an emphatic fist, or arms outstretched as if offering a benedictory embrace. In the era's entertainment lingo it was called "putting over" a song, and Izzy had a unique talent for it. He was, he admitted, a "ham," craving the crowd's approval. Much later, when he was better known as the famous songwriter Irving Berlin, he would claim that "the mob is always right," a mercilessly populist sensibility that had its roots in the life-and-death struggle that charged his formative experiences on the Lower East Side.[13]

Indeed, Berlin's values embodied what might be called a *Lower East Side Aesthetic*, which holds a practical, and even survivalist, view of creativity as a job joining ambition, entrepreneurship, mercantilism, and, not least, craft. The ethic required him to work hard, meet deadlines, create opportunities, heed his audience's reaction, study the competition, and deliver the goods without cutting corners. To some this might sound remarkably reminiscent of what used to be called the Protestant Work Ethic, except that the more ambitious of the mostly non-Protestant Lower East Siders, being excluded from entry into more conventional and respectable enterprises, found entertainment to be among the most welcoming avenues for work. And, for many such newcomers, the impulse was more sharply geared toward earning enough money to eat. If Berlin's later success would soon give him no worries about where the next meal would come from, the drive to finish the work and observe its impact, socially and economically, remained acutely urgent throughout his life.

In this decisively de-romanticized view of creativity, song and performance stand in dialogue with the audience. For Berlin, a song's artistry resided in an audience's desire to hear it and to buy its sheet music, its sound recordings, and theater tickets to witness its performance on stage and screen. He staked his livelihood on the response of the "mob." When Berlin was asked about his favorites among his own songs, he invariably cited the ones that were immensely and enduringly popular. In one statement he equated his "favorite songs" with the ones that have had the "widest acceptance":

> my favorite songs . . . the ones that, through the years, have won the widest acceptance: "Alexander's Ragtime Band," "Oh, How I Hate to Get Up in the Morning," "Say It With Music," "Always," "Blue Skies," "How Deep Is the Ocean," "Easter Parade," "White Christmas," "God Bless America," and "There's No Business Like Show Business."[14]

Lower East Side Street Scene, ca. 1895, soon after the Beilin family arrived.
Museum of the City of New York, Jacob A. Riis Collection.

He never claimed to have written "underappreciated" or "neglected" gems; for him such terms would have been oxymoronic. It is likely he would have greeted with mixed feelings the title and contents of a songbook published posthumously as *Unsung Irving Berlin*, slim though the volume is.[15] He declared: "I've never been able to understand why some writers, whenever they're asked to name their personal favorites, always choose some obscure piece that only a few people have ever heard."[16]

An important discipline in Berlin's view of entertainment was the ability to remove personal taste from one's business and creative work. If the composer-critic Alec Wilder, in his landmark book on American popular song, could detect in Berlin's work no signs of an individual style, it may be because Berlin endeavored to write in all available song styles to reach the largest possible audience. More than any other writer in the fabled Great American Songbook, Berlin was a stylistic omnivore. Wilder praised Berlin's "uncanny ability to adjust to the demands or needs of the moment, the singer, or the shift in popular mood . . . as difficult to define as the color of a chameleon. One searches for stylistic characteristics and is baffled. For the sea of his talent is always in motion. It's mercurial and elusive."

Berlin, Wilder concluded, was "the best all-around, over-all song writer America has ever had."[17]

The impulse to suspend personal taste in order to decipher the public's collective desire places Berlin among other notable entertainers of his generation and background.[18] The early Hollywood film moguls, most of them sharing Berlin's East European Jewish roots and a hardscrabble upbringing, held similar principles. "The public is never wrong," said Samuel Goldwyn, in a claim that comes remarkably close to Berlin's view of the mob.[19] To judge a film's effectiveness Goldwyn did not watch it; he stood with his back to the screen and faced the audience to gauge its reaction. Likewise, Louis B. Mayer was determined to make a wide variety of movies, including ones that violated his own moral compass, because he realized that they pleased his audience.[20]

Related to unshakeable faith in the audience's judgment was a belief in the mercantile and material dimensions of songwriting. Late in life, Berlin spoke of his feelings about his dwindling popularity as if he had been a retailer: "It was as if I owned a store and people no longer wanted to buy what I had to sell."[21] His peers spoke in similarly material terms. Jerome Kern described his role as a "musical clothier," another statement conjuring the image of a shop owner.[22] The Hollywood moguls also viewed their work in this way, in part, because many of them found their footing in film only after retailing in apparel, including Adolph Zukor (furs), Samuel Goldwyn (gloves), and Carl Laemmle (clothing).[23] Although Berlin did not trade in apparel, he did have a "shop": the Irving Berlin Music Company. Like his early Tin Pan Alley peers, he quickly learned that publishers held the upper hand when it came to profiting from sales of sheet music, so he joined the ranks of the songwriters who, like his former employer Harry Von Tilzer, took control of their own businesses. To this day, the Irving Berlin Music Company controls the licensing and distribution of Irving Berlin's "products" (albeit under the auspices of the Rodgers and Hammerstein Organization, which is, in turn, owned by Imagem Music Group, a Dutch publishing conglomerate).

Making such observations and identifying them as aspects of a *Lower East Side Aesthetic* has at least one drawback: it runs the risk of rearticulating anti-Semitic stereotypes. The notion of Berlin as a stylistic omnivore (like a "chameleon" as Wilder put it) is reminiscent of sweeping claims that Jews lack an individual style, revealing a kind of superficial borrowing that leads to a nonsensical jumble. This was the foundation of Richard Wagner's disdain for "Jewish music," especially the music of Meyerbeer and Mendelssohn, and in Berlin's day, it was echoed by Henry Ford's anti-Semitic newspaper the *Dearborn Independent*.[24] Meanwhile, acknowledging that Berlin embraced the material and mercantile dimension of his work conjures the anti-Semitic stereotype of rapacious greed.

In my view, we can rescue the insights from the prejudices that frame them, and try to escape what the historian David A. Hollinger has called the "booster-bigot trap" in discussions of the Jewish impact in American culture.[25] The first of these views has already been examined and analyzed. The notion that Jewish artists and entertainers lack an individual style has been rearticulated more neutrally (and often positively) as a creative phenomenon variously described as "eclecticism,"[26] "a special talent for pastiche,"[27] "bricolage,"[28] and "polyglot stylistic abilities."[29] This quality links up with what Abraham Schwadron, writing on music, has described as the "drama" of Western ("occidental") Jews: "a drama of adaptation, assimilation . . . and survival."[30] It should be emphasized that such qualities are not exclusively Jewish. Ronald Sanders insists, for example, that "pastiche" is the "gift of people who live in culturally ambivalent situations."[31] To pursue a notion of "Jewishness" through "eclecticism," then, it is important to go beyond the recognition of the quality itself and be able to describe and analyze what kind of eclecticism is involved, and what remains is to show how Berlin's actual music demonstrates these qualities.[32]

For Berlin and, I think, for at least two generations of immigrant Jews in the first half of the twentieth century, two kinds of eclecticism are relevant for understanding the work, and they manifest the spirit of artists in a cultural situation in which they fervently embraced disparate elements that more "respectable" people shunned. First, there is a tendency to recognize African American contributions as essential to finding an American sound in song, what the cultural historian Jeffrey Melnick has described as "a tendency to assimilate and repackage blackness."[33] Second, there is a compatible tendency in this generation of Jewish artists and entertainers to shift seamlessly between forms that others distinguish as "high" or "low," or as Irving Howe has put it in his discussion of American Yiddish theater, between *shund* (trash) and *literatur* (literature).[34]

The wellspring of Berlin's contribution engages fundamentally with these impulses. His songwriting grew from a deep engagement with ragtime and a kind of pastiche, and translation, of its rhythmic elements. In his early years, in fact, Berlin was repeatedly charged with having a secret African American collaborator—a "colored boy in the closet"—and felt obliged to defend himself in public about it.[35] This perhaps helps to explain his now shocking insistence that American popular songwriters were of "pure white blood."[36] Long after ragtime per se passed from the American popular scene, Berlin continued to repackage its elements, and to extend them by absorbing the impact of jazz and swing in the 1920s and beyond. In the theater, his great synthesis of *shund* and *literatur* occurred in his acceptance of minstrelsy and opera as musico-theatrical toolboxes and power sources for his imagination. For Berlin minstrelsy and opera did not occupy opposite points on a high-low hierarchy. Rather they stood as two pillars holding up the edifice of his vision of what an American musical theater could look and sound like.

With regard to the material and mercantile dimensions of his work, Berlin was a commercial powerhouse, to be sure. This impulse has not been as thoroughly examined as the supposed lack of individual style. It may be seen as a non-esoteric, non-elitist refusal to see wide public acceptance and commercial success as incompatible with high quality craftsmanship—even artistry. Public appeal is sought without shame or self-consciousness. For Berlin, the artistic and commercial impulses coexisted, flourishing in a symbiotic relationship. Many writers have, at least obliquely, addressed that phenomenon. For example, this is where Berlin's work intersects with what the film scholar Miriam Hansen has termed "vernacular modernism."[37] Hansen lays particular stress on mass dissemination and mass consumption as features of the modern age, features that purveyors of so-called High Modernism shunned. In the American century, however, Jewish entertainers accepted that and pursued it in shaping Tin Pan Alley, Broadway, and Hollywood. Reaching a wide audience was integral to the work; it was a path to acceptance. As the cultural historian Andrea Most has put it in her study of Jewish culture and musical theater, musicals "encode, in both content and form, the concerns of a group intensely eager for acceptance into a new community."[38] Jeffrey Melnick linked that impulse explicitly with Berlin's status as an American Jew when he writes that Berlin's "overt crowd pleasing . . . betrays a certain anxiety about his authority to speak American."[39]

Berlin "spoke American" in song as well as anyone, but success did not seem to allay his anxiety about the quality and market for his work. An audience, of spectators of shows or buyers of sheet music, completed the transaction necessary for the *Lower East Side Aesthetic* to reach fulfillment. For its true goal was social—to achieve the American Dream that allowed anyone to succeed regardless of how lowly and abject his or her birth. Show business was the ultimate meritocracy, the way that many new immigrants understood the fundamental difference between Old Europe and the New World. The entertainment business did not require formal education, family connections, or inherited wealth. When Berlin wrote that there was "no business like show business," he expressed a patriotic embrace of his adopted county and the unique opportunities it offered to someone standing on the lowest rungs of the social ladder. The fundamental unit of that business was the song.

SONGWRITING

Whether Berlin was writing a song for vaudeville, a revue, or for a musical comedy, he sustained a belief in the integrity of individual songs to be able to stand alone outside of whatever original theatrical context for which they may have been conceived. In this view, Berlin's vision linked artistic principle with hardheaded commercialism. In the period when Berlin began to emerge as a major force in the American musical theater, Victor Herbert (who collaborated on a show with Berlin in 1916) noted that new theater songs must work both within a show and be "independent of the play" unlike numbers in "comic opera" in which songs "are woven into the plot and are part of it."[40] This is because, with the advent of ASCAP—the American Society of Composers, Authors, and Publishers—in 1914, songwriters stood to earn much more from their work than ever before in American history. The formation of ASCAP did not so much change the song unit's role in the music industry as to transfer much more of the profit from its sales to the songwriter. The year 1914 was also the year of Berlin's first full score for the stage, so he entered the musical theater with a newly sharpened sense of the power of song in the commercial marketplace.

It makes sense, then, to explore Berlin's songwriting tendencies in their own right. Perhaps the best way to begin to grasp Berlin's distinctive work as a theatrical songwriter is to focus not just on *style* but on *values*. The principle that drove Berlin above all was that a good song is one that many people want to hear, and it was only in the theater where he could measure a number's impact night after night. With his trust in the "mob," Berlin insisted that "a song must reach an audience."[41] Simply put, for Berlin a good song is a hit song, and a hit song is a good song. Berlin claimed that Oscar Hammerstein II (with whom he enjoyed mutual respect) once said that Berlin was interested only in hits. "What's wrong with that?" Berlin replied. "I may think something I've written is the best thing I've ever done. But if the public doesn't understand what I'm trying to say, if the song doesn't communicate an emotion, then it has no value."[42]

Yet Berlin's famously high regard for the "hit" tends to overshadow his belief that a songwriter should not try to write one. In a chapter outline for a book he never wrote called "The Secret of Song Writing," Berlin advised the novice to "Try to write a great song, don't try to write a hit."[43] In other words, a songwriter's commercial impulse can be satisfied only by serving the demands of craft. Indeed, the importance of craft supported by hard work surfaces again and again in Berlin's published interviews. It's revealing that, although he cited "Alexander's Ragtime Band" as one of his favorites (that is, a song that has won wide acceptance), he nevertheless judged its lyrics "terrible" in a 1920 interview.[44] So he removed his personal taste from a notion of quality determined by public favor, and this impulse may support Alec Wilder's perceptive notion that Berlin's stylistic flexibility reveals a "curious absence of ego . . . all he is concerned with is the best possible song for the occasion, for the situation, for the lyric, or for the current fashion."[45] Laser-like focus on the job at hand demanded from Berlin a fiercely uncompromising work ethic (and a healthy ego). He claimed that he wrote most of his songs "literally by the sweat of my brow."[46]

Berlin distinguished the brow-drenching craft of songwriting from musical composition because he wrote both words and music. "As far as I'm concerned," he declared, "I'm a song writer. Other people can call themselves composers. . . . I think in terms of a song as a unit, with the words and music as an indivisible part of that unit."[47] The concept of "unity" was important to Berlin, and it was the title of the second chapter in his outline for "The Secret of Song Writing," undated but probably written in the mid-1910s, soon after he had become a "songwriter." In a telegraphic summary, he identifies "unity" as the mutual dependence of words and music and, ultimately, as the songwriter's "supreme test." The summary emphasizes the distinctiveness of songwriting from musical composition and verse writing, and it highlights both enduring value ("songs likely to live forever") and immediate impact:

> The inter-relation of lyrics and melody—why they depend upon one another— Why few writers successfully produce both—Why expert specialists decrease the opportunities of individual writers to produce both—Good lyric lost with bad melody—Good melody lost with bad lyric—The saving grace of either when unusually good, despite lack-lustre [sic] nature of the other—Overwhelming importance of lyric-writing ability compared to composing ability—Songs likely to live forever—Unity the supreme test of song writing as an art or profession.

The phrases here have distinctly autobiographical undertone when one considers that the 1910s saw Berlin shift away collaborative songwriting and rely increasingly on himself to produce both words and music. It is not coincidental that Berlin became exclusively a "songwriter" (by his definition of someone who writes both words and music) when he was working on the score of his first musical, *Watch Your Step*, in 1914. It was at the same time when Berlin broke off from his publishing partners Henry Waterson and Ted Snyder and, in November 1914, one month before

Watch Your Step opened, established Irving Berlin, Inc., as the exclusive publisher of Irving Berlin's songs.[48] In short, writing a musical comedy score changed Berlin's conception of himself—and of his self-worth—as a songwriter.

Although Berlin's songs from 1914 on are credited to him alone, he remained a collaborator throughout his life, for as commentators never fail to point out, he did not read or write music. To create his songs, he relied on a musical secretary to write down melodies that Berlin often dictated as he paced around the room, or that he picked out on the piano.[49] Writing about Berlin's work with his first secretary, Cliff Hess, in a way that could be applied to his whole career, the musicologist Charles Hamm notes that "it would be impossible to document precisely what Hess contributed to the final versions of Berlin's songs. The piano accompaniments were, in all likelihood, mostly his work. Lyrics and tunes were Berlin's inventions, and various accounts agree that he knew what harmony he wanted as well."[50] We will never know what kind of details or ideas Berlin's secretaries may have brought to songs bearing Berlin's name alone; it is revealing that they were all accomplished songwriters in their own right: Hess (with Berlin to 1918), Harry Ruby (1918, for *Yip Yip Yaphank*), Arthur Johnston (1919–30), and especially Helmy Kresa (1931–88). Yet there is no question that Berlin remained the controlling creative force behind his songs. To observers, song poured from him as if from a bottomless well of imagination.

The foundation and liberation of that imagination was ragtime, which had emerged in the American musical mainstream just before the turn of the century and had taken the country by storm in Berlin's youth, even as controversy raged around it. Some heard in it a long-awaited, distinctively American musical style; others dismissed it, sometimes with racist indignation, as not music at all. Certainly, in the first decade of the twentieth century it was regarded as edgy, socially transgressive, and very exciting (like jazz in the 1920s, rock 'n' roll in the 1950s, and rap in the 1980s). For Berlin, ragtime was more than just an appealing musical style, or the transient fad that many Americans perceived it to be in the early 1900s. Indeed, for Berlin, ragtime formed the musical and linguistic passport to his adopted country.[51] His early songs make that point explicitly, as they were written in an age when songs exploited ethnic stereotypes. In songs such as "Yiddle, on Your Fiddle, Play Some Ragtime" (featuring Jewish characters) and "Sweet Marie Make-a Rag-a-time Dance Wid Me" (Italian), Berlin portrays ragtime as the language of new-world courtship. In "The International Rag," composed in 1913 on the cusp of World War I, "London dropped its dignity, / So has France and Germany," as they find common ground in their love of ragtime. Ragtime, in Berlin's words and music, becomes a means by which a pluralistic population can be united, Americanized, and modernized. But although ragtime, along with Berlin's moniker "ragtime king," had become passé by the end of World War I, Berlin's songs continue to bear traces of ragtime like a kind of musical DNA that reappears, unmistakable but sometimes reinterpreted by its context, throughout his career, even into the 1960s. If he could claim rhythm as "a big part" of the success of his songs, then ragtime is a big part of his rhythmic vocabulary.

Berlin's brand of ragtime had crystallized in "Alexander's Ragtime Band" (1911), which became a palette of devices from which Berlin drew throughout his life, including repetition of the opening lyric and musical phrase; short, punchy phrases ("come on and hear") that push off from a strong bass-defined downbeat; and the restatement of a principal melodic phrase up (sometimes down) the interval of a perfect fourth (ex. 1.1). We hear such features recur throughout Berlin's theater career, from "Everybody Step" (*Music Box Revue*, 1921) through "The Hostess with the Mostes'" (*Call Me Madam*, 1950).

What may have made "Alexander's Ragtime Band" sound like a fresh spin on a popular style that had been around for more than a decade in 1911 is that it actually avoids one of the rhythmic clichés of ragtime song, the cakewalk figure, comprising a short-long-short rhythm followed by two longs. In early Tin Pan Alley song, especially in the decade before Berlin started publishing songs (1897–1907), the cakewalk figure became synecdochical for ragtime on Tin Pan Alley, most famously in songs such as Joseph Howard's "Hello, Ma Baby" (1899), for which the rhythm forms the basis of an entire chorus.

Berlin would take up the cliché and make it sound fresh. In fact, it became a rhythmic trademark of his style and appeared in many guises, including augmentations (rhythmic expansions), diminutions (rhythmic contractions), tied variants, and what might be called *reverse cakewalk*—but always in the same short-long proportions, whether in sixteenth and eighth notes, eighths and quarters, or, perhaps most commonly, quarters and halves. Example 1.2 shows several examples, more of which will appear throughout the book.

In early 1920s, Berlin started taking key elements of ragtime, combined them with elements of a new style called the blues, and created what several of his contemporaries regarded as jazz. Theater became the incubator of Berlin's brand of jazz, which he developed in his *Music Box Revues* of 1921–24. From the mid-1930s on his rag- and blues-based jazz language extended to swing. Songs from this period still manifest traces of ragtime but now also seek to capture some of the flavor of swing in riff-based phrase construction with instrumental fills ("Louisiana Purchase," "Who Do You Love? I Hope"); swing-like eighth notes (often approximated in Tin Pan Alley's dotted rhythms, as in "Heat Wave"); across-the-bar syncopation and chains of syncopation ("Cheek to Cheek" and "I'm Putting All My Eggs in One Basket"); quasi-instrumental phrases ("Louisiana Purchase," the second phrase of "Eggs," and the end of rst phrase of "Isn't This a Lovely Day?"); and even call-and-response patterns ("Anything You Can Do"). The ragtime roots of such figures remain audible in Berlin's writing, but swing seems to have prompted Berlin's rhythmic language to become

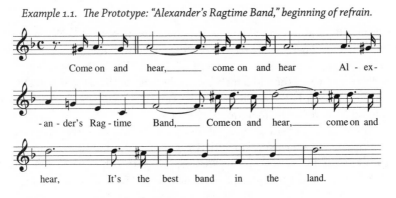

Example 1.1. *The Prototype: "Alexander's Ragtime Band," beginning of refrain.*

Example 1.2. *The cakewalk rhythm and variants in Berlin's songs.*

1.2a. Basic cakewalk rhythm in "The Girl on the Magazine" (1915), "All By Myself" (1921), and "Easter Parade" (1933).

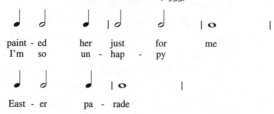

paint - ed her just for me
I'm so un - hap - py

East - er pa - rade

1.2b. "Tied" cakewalk rhythm in "Supper Time" (1933), "Steppin' Out with My Baby" (1947), and "Let Me Sing and I'm Happy" (1928).

Sup - per time__
Step - pin' out__
Let me sing__

1.2c. "Reverse" cakewalk in "White Christmas" (1942) and "I've Got My Love to Keep Me Warm" (1936), and variant in "For Your Country and My Country" (1917).

tree - tops glis - ten And chil - dren lis - ten To
snow is snow - ing, The wind is blow - ing, But

your coun - try, it's my coun - try, with

1.2d. "Reverse tied" cakewalk in "All By Myself" (1921) and "Harlem on My Mind" (1933).

All by my - self___

Har - lem on my mind__

increasingly flexible and varied. For, in the 1930s and beyond, it is leavened with a new penchant for quarter-note triplets and the resulting three-against-two pattern, a device possibly inspired by the songs of his friend Cole Porter. Some of Berlin's most elegant songs of the 1930s make compelling use of that rhythmic feature, including "How Deep Is the Ocean?" (for Tin Pan Alley), "How's Chances" (for the stage), and "Now It Can Be Told" (for the screen).

If ragtime formed the catalytic agent for a modern American style, simplicity was the principal test of a songwriter's mettle. He called it "the first and last rule of writing songs," as he put it in "Secret to Song Writing."[52] In parsing his lyric for one song, he began by saying "In the first place, I consciously strove for simplicity."[53] "Simplicity" rarely carries flattering connotations in accounts of modernity in the Western arts, many of whose innovators—Stravinsky and Schoenberg in music, Picasso and Kandinsky in painting, Chekhov and O'Neill in drama, Joyce and Woolf in fiction, Auden and Eliot in poetry—have earned credit for confronting tradition with new complexity and psychological depth in the very period when Berlin flourished.

Yet in Berlin's world *simplicity* was a difficult, elusive goal that could be reached only through hard work. An eyewitness account makes that vivid. The writer Anita Loos observed Berlin at work, each time with the same outcome:

> I sometimes used to sit beside Irving at his tiny piano and listen while he composed. He would go over and over a lyric until it seemed perfect to my ears. Then he'd scrap the whole thing and begin over again. When I asked Irving what was wrong he invariably said, "It isn't *simple* enough."[54]

It is impossible to substantiate Berlin's biographer Lawrence Bergreen's blunt claim that "his search for musical simplicity was driven by the sublimation of his erotic impulses."[55] It is more fruitful to describe the ways in which his work manifests simplicity. Simplicity permeates Berlin's style, with its preference for monosyllabic words and rhymes, its transparent conversational diction, its melodies based on the musical building blocks of diatonic scales and triads, its long passages and entire songs built on juxtapositions of two or three short rhythmic patterns, and its conventional song forms—the strophic verse-chorus structure whose chorus usually appears in four eight-bar phrases comprising a standard thirty-two bar ABAC or AABA pattern. Such qualities suggest why Richard Rodgers referred to Berlin as America's "folk" songwriter. For Berlin, simplicity carried connotations of discipline and focus. He warned that "would-be writers and some good ones mistake carelessness for simplicity."[56] He illustrated what he meant in an early 1920s interview in which he discussed his song "You'd Be Surprised," in which he noted that he "strove for simplicity by confining my lyric to a description of one surprising and amusing characteristic of one single fictitious person."[57]

Repetition represents a corollary to Berlin's brand of simplicity. "Repetition [is] the soul of a song," he wrote in "The Secret of Song Writing."[58] In a later reflection on his craft he likewise asserted that "I know the importance of repetition, particularly in the title if it's a word or phrase that gains by its being heard over and over."[59] Berlin is easily patronized or mocked for his penchant for simplicity and repetition; his friend Wilson Mizner once cracked, "Irving is a man of few words. But he keeps repeating them."[60] Yet Berlin's belief in the power of repetition deserves closer scrutiny. It emerged from his conception of ragtime, and it is important to recognize it as stemming from a principled songwriting concept and not just a commercial impulse. Berlin explicitly linked textual repetition and musical syncopation. "Syncopation . . . will bear repetition of thought better than other forms," he told an inquiring reporter in 1916. "You can repeat 'I love you' a number of times in syncopated measure very effectively, whereas if you used the ordinary forms it would sound simple."[61] Such an aesthetic runs counter to the values informing what is traditionally viewed as (European) "modern" music, especially the musical language of the modernist icon Arnold Schoenberg, who so abhorred repetition that he would soon create a musical system, the twelve-tone system, to avoid it—in the same period when Berlin cited smart repetition as emblematic of a song's "soul."

For Berlin, however, the value of repetition survived the ragtime era and resurfaced throughout his career, from the threefold repetition of "Manhattan" in "Manhattan Madness" (*Face the Music*, 1932), to the reiterated title phrases of "God Bless America" (1938) and "Happy Holiday" (*Holiday Inn*, 1942), to the rapid-fire repetition to absurdity of the word "money" in "Can You Use Any Money Today?" (*Call Me Madam*, 1950) and several songs in his last stage show (*Mr. President*, 1962). Throughout his career, moreover, Berlin often began a lyric with a key word, then repeated it in a short phrase soon thereafter, as in "Evening, / Lady of the evening" (*Music Box Revue*, 1922), in "Eagles, / American Eagles" (*This Is the Army*, 1942), and "Snow—/ It won't be long before we'll all be there with snow" (*White Christmas*, 1954). He applied this technique most famously in "Cheek to Cheek" (*Top Hat*, 1935) with the lines "Heaven, / I'm in heaven." The extent of repetition in Berlin's lyrics and melodies further confirms Berlin's alertness to writing with an ear tuned to performance—to *oral* delivery and *aural* reception that can bear, and sometimes *requires*, repetition for impact—especially in a bustling marketplace of song, and it further confirms his belief in his distinction between songwriting and composition. As Philip Furia has succinctly put it, Berlin brought "a singer's ear to the craft of songwriting," and repetition stands as evidence of that double gift.[62] In his first *Music Box Revue* (1921), Berlin sought a way to achieve effective repetition of a single song, "Say It with Music," over the course of an entire show.

When Berlin talked about, or deployed, repetition, he had specific standards in mind, for he made a sharp distinction between dynamic repetition founded on disciplined choices, and static repetition that reflected lazy writing and sloppy craftsmanship. "Blue Skies" offers a case in point, for its successful premiere occurred on stage during a musical comedy by Rodgers and Hart, much to their dismay.[63] The lyrics of "Blue Skies" deftly reiterate the word *blue* several times, and almost always on downbeats, from the verse's first line to the last line of the chorus. Yet the word's meaning itself undergoes a dynamic shift from its initial conjuring of sadness ("I was blue / Just as blue as I could be") to its later associations with the narrator's brighter outlook ("Blue skies / Smiling at me"), a change summed up in the song's final line: "Blue days / All of them gone—/ Nothing but blue skies / From now on." He later applied the technique in his film songs. In "Be Careful, It's My Heart," written for *Holiday Inn*, he deploys the word *heart* repeatedly through the refrain to make it the song's keynote—a tender, precious image that forms a stark contrast to quotidian objects: the note "quickly burned" and the book "never returned" ("quickly" and "never" serving as characteristically Berlinian antitheses embedded in the literary parallel of "note" and "book").

Berlin illustrated his notion of the difference between good and bad repetition by discussing a song performed in the legendary *Ziegfeld Follies of 1919*. In an interview, he caricatured how a lazy writer would use the catch-line "You'd Be Surprised" in a "noisy blah" of a chorus:

You'd be surprised! You'd be surprised!
I realized you'd be surprised!
I must say that I recognized
Surprised you'd be—you'd be surprised!

"No punch," was his judgment of that straw man of a lyric. "Just repetition, not *effective*, accentuating repetition. Words, noisy words." He then went on to explain his own method for using that line:

> Every line in the lyric was written with the conscious effort to build it up to a chorus, in which the title was to be repeated again and again, each repetition of "You'd Be Surprised" carrying with it that "punch" of unexpectedness which plays so important a part of humor.[64]

Indeed, Berlin uses the title phrase five times in the refrain, and each reiteration, which follows a silent downbeat creating momentary suspense, carries the "punch" Berlin sought as it punctuates a new view of the subject's romantic method:

> He's not so good in a crowd,
> But when you get him alone,
> [rest] You'd be surprised.
> He isn't much at a dance,
> But when he takes you home,
> [rest] You'd be surprised.

Two other Berlin tendencies help to give that lyric its "punch" and reveal its disciplined craft: monosyllabic language (seen in all words in the passage above but "alone," "surprised," and "isn't"), and description through antithesis, in which the lyric pivots on the conjunction *but* to highlight the contrast between Johnny's behavior in public ("in a crowd" and "at a dance") and private ("alone" and "home").

Antithesis, in fact, marks one of Berlin's stocks-in-trade, though he likely would have shunned the multisyllabic word. In a letter to the musical theater historian Stanley Green, Berlin stated his preference for what he called "opposite images."[65] Whatever we call the device, Berlin relished it. Here are just a few examples of antithesis in songs written across a period of four decades:

> You promised that you'd forget me not, / But you forgot to remember.
> ("Remember," 1925)

> With you, a sunny day; / Without you, clouds in the sky.
> With you, my luck will stay; / Without you, fortune will fly.
> ("With You," 1929)

> The night is cold / But the music's hot;
> ("Let Yourself Go," 1936)

> For while I'm crying for you, / You're / Laughing at me.
> ("You're Laughing at Me," 1937)

> Can't go wrong 'cause I'm in right.
> It's for sure not for maybe . . .
>
> . . .
>
> Can't be bad to feel so good.
>
> . . .
>
> The big day may be tonight.
> ("Steppin' Out with My Baby," 1948)

Business for a Good Girl Is Bad
("Business for a Good Girl Is Bad," 1949)

You love me and I don't doubt it,
But you don't have to shout it;
    Whisper it—
    Whisper it in my ear.
("Whisper It," 1963).

Beyond the individual phrase, antithesis pervades Berlin's songwriting vision for stage and screen. In his shows, Berlin regularly defines a feeling, an image, a musical style, or a way of life by invoking its opposite. In Berlin's first show one character contrasts the "simple melody" that her "mother sang to me" with "your spoony rags and coony drags" that "made my poor heart ache" ("Simple Melody," from *Watch Your Step*, 1914). Likewise, in "The Waltz of Long Ago" (*Music Box Revue of 1923*), Berlin contrasts the "long ago" style of the waltz with the "jazz" of "nowadays." In the witty finale to the revue *As Thousands Cheer*, the chorus and principals exchange opposing views of the value of a reprise; and in the end, all views are heard—as are several brief reprises. In his famous song from the film *Top Hat*, the homely image of a man who loves "to go out fishing" forms a sharp contrast to the elegance of the man "dancing / Cheek to cheek" that we see on the screen. In *Annie Get Your Gun*—a show in which Berlin deploys antithesis regularly—Frank's idealized vision of "The Girl that I Marry" is comically antithetical to the actual girl standing next to him. In a number for *Mr. President* that quotes the title phrase of "The Girl that I Marry," Berlin wrote "Meat and Potatoes" for a young secret service agent who pines for the president's daughter, and he expresses the apparent hopelessness of his love through culinary antithesis (and alliteration): "She'd be yearning for a soufflé; / I'd be longing for a stew." Antithesis became Berlin's way of respecting all tastes, of appealing to the largest possible "mob."

Antithesis pervades Berlin's music as well as his song concepts and lyrics. No songwriting technique proved to be such a perennial favorite in Berlin's theater writing than the counterpoint song, or double song, which presents two contrasting melodies, first separately, then together, in a musical antithesis. For Berlin, such songs were intrinsically theatrical, as they allowed for a musicalization of dialogue, and especially of contrasting points of view. He wrote counterpoint songs throughout his career, from the one he wrote for his first stage show, *Watch Your Step*, in 1914, to the one he wrote more than half a century later for the 1966 revival of *Annie Get Your Gun* (see table 1.1).

Berlin's counterpoint songs often exploit the fundamental stylistic antithesis that marked his songwriting era: the ballad and the rhythm song. The ballad, in Tin Pan Alley's parlance, became a general term for songs emphasizing melodic and harmonic beauty that told a story or elaborated on a feeling. As Charles Hamm has explained at considerable length, through the nineteenth century the term *ballad* had applied more specifically to romantic or nostalgic songs whose lyrics adopted the first-person voice, and they were songs viewed as reflecting a cultivated character and an ennobling force.[66] With Berlin and his contemporaries, the ballad expanded from there to include a more vernacular English diction and a variety of musical styles such as the waltz, the

Table 1.1. Berlin's Counterpoint Songs for Stage and Screen, 1914–66

Simple Melody / Musical Demon (*Watch Your Step*, 1914)
When I Get Back to the USA / America (My Country 'tis of Thee) (*Stop! Look! Listen!*, 1915)
Kiss Me Again / Kiss Me Once More (*Century Girl*, 1916)
Pack Up Your Sins and Go to the Devil (*Music Box Revue of 1922*)
The Call of the South / Swanee River [Old Folks at Home] (*Music Box Revue of 1924*)
Drinking Song / Stars and Stripes Forever (and Dixie) (*Face the Music*, 1932)
Debts / Star Spangled Banner (*As Thousands Cheer*, 1933)
Blue Skies / You Keep Coming Back Like a Song (*Blue Skies*, 1946)
Extra! Extra! (*Miss Liberty*, 1949)
I Wonder Why / You're Just in Love (*Call Me Madam*, 1950)
Dallas / I Like New York ("Sentimental Guy," 1956)
Empty Pockets Filled with Love (*Mr. President*, 1962)
Old-Fashioned Wedding (*Annie Get Your Gun*, 1966)
Wait until You're Married (1966, probably intended for an unfinished show titled "East River")

march, and a rhythmic language that was mostly unsyncopated. The *rhythm song*, in contrast, was marked chiefly by syncopation, absorbed from ragtime in the first two decades of the 1900s, from jazz in the 1920s, and swing in the 1930s and 1940s (and, in Berlin's work, even the 1950s and beyond). The rhythm song also tended to feature more colloquial language, including slang, and well into the 1930s, it sometimes carried racial implications—that is, its subjects or protagonists were sometimes black.

The way in which counterpoint songs grant equal value to the ballad and rhythm song, to the old-fashioned and the new, to gentle lyricism and lively ragtime, is an impulse that charges many Berlin songs that are *not* written in counterpoint. For there is a persistent impulse in Berlin's songwriting that lies beyond what Alec Wilder would call "stylistic characteristics" and might have seemed too obvious for Wilder to mention: the hybridization of rhythm song and ballad, in which Berlin harnesses the short, punchy phrases and rhythmic vitality of ragtime (and, later, of jazz and swing) to the melodic fluency and harmonic richness of the traditional ballad. Berlin had a strong intuitive sense of the borderline between genuine sentiment and mawkishness. And he abhorred maudlin and overwrought expression to an extent that amounted to a moral principle. Ragtime became his way of leavening sentimentality. The 1928 song "How About Me?" offers a vivid example of how Berlin invoked the newly popular torch-song style while cutting the schmaltz with syncopation (ex. 1.3).

The combination of syncopation and affective chromatic harmony that we see in "How About Me?" pervades Berlin's writing for stage and screen. Otherwise lively tunes such as "Let's Have Another Cup of Coffee" and "There's No Business Like

Example 1.3. "How About Me?"

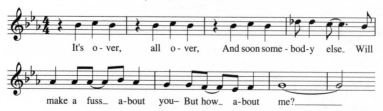

It's o-ver, all o-ver, And soon some-bod-y else_ Will

make a fuss_ a-bout you— But how_ a-bout me?_____

Show Business" feature harmonic progressions marked by a descending chromatic line. Played slowly, they sound even mournful—like straight ballads with the same traits, such as "Blue Skies," "They Say It's Wonderful," "White Christmas," and "The Best Thing for You."

Berlin believed that he had "established" the hybrid song style that he called the "syncopated ballad." In an interview published in late 1913 or early 1914, at a time when he was being celebrated as the great ragtime composer, he took pains to articulate the nature of his contribution in a fascinating statement that carefully avoids denying precisely what it seems to disclaim, that Berlin was the "originator" of ragtime:

> I would not want it said that I claim, by any means, to be the originator of modern ragtime. But I can truthfully say that I have accomplished a number of things which were thought impossible. I have established the syncopated ballad.[67]

To state that he "established the syncopated ballad" may sound like a fairly innocuous claim, but in Tin Pan Alley's early years, insiders had developed a clear taxonomy of song styles, and the ragtime (or "syncopated") song and the ballad stood on opposite ends of the spectrum. Ragtime traded in brisk, peppy moods, rhythmic vitality, and slang. Ballads featured melodic lyricism, slower tempos, and sentiment expressed in more elevated, poetic language. Berlin did not accept the stylistic segregation and thus played a part in redefining the ballad for a modern American audience. He believed that ragtime could effectively channel a variety of moods because he saw it as a distinctively American style. And he was not alone in that view. His contemporary Harry Von Tilzer claimed publicly in 1912 that ragtime was "the distinctive American treatment of song in general."[68] In this view any song, or song style, could be ragged and thus Americanized.

Throughout his career, Berlin gave his ballads a strong rhythmic backbone, and that became his chief means of preserving sentiment without crossing a line into mawkishness. That impulse links disparate songs across the decades spanning a half-century, such as "Always Treat Her Like a Baby" (1914), "All By Myself" (1921), "I've Got My Love to Keep Me Warm" (1936), "Be Careful, It's My Heart (1942), "I Left My Heart at the Stage Door Canteen" (1942), "Count Your Blessings" (1954), and "Whisper It" (1963). Sometimes, rather than simultaneously combining rhythm and ballad elements, Berlin presents them in succession within a single refrain, as we've seen in "How About Me" (1928) but also in "Cheek to Cheek" (1935) and "The Best Things Happen While You're Dancing" (1953), which begin as ballads and deploy a surprising amount of syncopation. Singers, heeding romantic words, understandably tend to smooth out the syncopations, but the syncopated eruptions were integral to Berlin's notion of the ballad.

Given the amount of syncopation Berlin brings to such songs, perhaps the great foil to ragtime for him was not the duple-meter ballad but the waltz. Unlike ragtime, which comprises the dynamic, flexible pulse behind so much of his music in ostensibly different styles, the waltz is a stable, fixed style in Berlin's songwriting orbit and his theatrical imagination. Berlin's waltzes rely on a variety of rhythmic patterns, but, notably, none of them are syncopated. A model he could have easily heeded, but did not, was Scott Joplin's *Bethena* (1905), a syncopated "concert waltz" that fits the cakewalk pattern into triple meter by omitting the pattern's final beat. The waltz had a well-defined role in Berlin's theater. Where Richard Rodgers found in the waltz a foundation for a vast expressive range, expanding on his inheritance from operetta, Berlin used the waltz as a vehicle for a few set themes: nostalgia, loss, regret, domesticity, old-fashioned courtship, and enduring love.

Berlin's idea of the waltz stands in contrast to its nineteenth-century European legacy. For example, Byron's famous "apostrophic hymn" to the waltz had emphasized its seductive intimacy, allowing the possibility for "hands which may freely range in public sight, where ne'er before—but—pray put out the light."[69] That sensibility continued in early Tin Pan Alley, in such songs as "And the Band Played On" (1895), in which a young man named Casey becomes so excited while dancing with a "strawberry blonde" that his "brain . . . nearly exploded." That was not Berlin's style. Berlin wrote plenty of suggestive songs but almost never in waltz style. Far from the flirty suggestiveness that the waltz connoted in the hands of other composers, songwriters, and poets, the waltz for Berlin maintained a strong connection to the values of Victorian America. In this sense he participated in defining the larger shift of the waltz's symbolic and expressive value in American culture.[70] From "When I Lost You" (1912), his first notable waltz written in memory of his deceased first wife, to "Let's Go Back to the Waltz" (1962), a song he wrote fifty years later for his final stage show, the waltz remained a repository of straightforward sincerity and old-fashioned values. On Berlin's Broadway, the waltz regularly appears as one element of a musical and lyrical antithesis. Indeed, the waltz formed one effective dramatic tool in Berlin's multifaceted songwriting arsenal.

DRAMATURGY

Berlin's theater is likewise multifaceted. His stage work chiefly comprises two types of shows: revues and musical comedies, but his theatrical vision was much larger than those two terms suggest. For Berlin's theater, like his songwriting, embraced everything available on the American musical theater scene. Most important was his lifelong belief in minstrelsy as a fundamentally American theatrical style. This fact is hard to square with the equally fundamental notion that Berlin was a songwriter who worked hard to remain current, for he continued to embrace minstrelsy long after it remained a viable theatrical form.

Why is that so? Perhaps the best explanation is that minstrelsy's role in Berlin's theater is analogous to ragtime's role in his songwriting. It was a foundation and a flexible, abundant source from which to construct his vision of a distinctively American musical theater. To the extent that Berlin shaped modern American musical theater, we must confront the ways in which minstrelsy was foundational and persistent in his theatrical imagination.

Berlin engaged with minstrelsy from the beginning of his career, and it is no wonder, since minstrelsy continued to thrive in the early 1900s, in prominent companies such as those of George Primrose and Lou Dockstader, and the troupe led by George M. Cohan and Sam H. Harris (the Cohan and Harris Minstrels)—the latter two being, respectively, Berlin's idol and future partner. As early as 1911, Berlin appeared as an end man in a minstrel number in a George M. Cohan show called *Friar's Frolics*.[71] And in the years before his first musical comedy, Berlin wrote some thirty songs featuring black characters, and some of them were performed in blackface.[72] Many of these songs explored themes and stereotypes common to minstrel songs, including sexual innuendo, exuberant music-making, the awkward but enthusiastic appropriation of cultivated music and literature, and a longing to return to a southern, sometimes rural, home (from an implicitly urban north). Moreover, as Charles Hamm has shown, some numbers with the merest grammatical clues in their sheet music, were performed as minstrel numbers— or "coon songs," as they were known in the early twentieth century. For example, "That Mesmerizing Mendelssohn Tune" features the dropped "g" diction and other language (like "gwine") common to black-dialect song, as in the first phrase:

Honey, listen to that dreamy tune they're playin',
Won't you tell me how on earth you keep from swayin'?

But, as performed by the duo Collins and Harlan, it becomes explicitly minstrelized, with exaggerated diction and interpolated dialogue featuring the name "Liza"—a common name in black-dialect songs of the period and beyond (including Gershwin's "Liza").[73]

Minstrelsy did not appeal simply for its racial masquerade, however. The so-called minstrel first part, with the full troupe seated on risers onstage, and with the formal interlocutor smoothly directing the traffic of solo and group performances of skits and songs, meanwhile exchanging riddles and jokes with the end men who often mocked him: all of this required masterful timing, a sense of pace and seamless flow among varied acts, which fired his imagination.

For three decades, from the 1910s to the 1940s, almost every Berlin stage show features a minstrel number or a number infused with identifiable minstrel elements. Moreover, three shows feature a minstrel-show first part, complete with the familiar stage formation of the chorus on risers, an interlocutor, and end men. End-man– style banter with an authoritative interlocutor remained fundamental to Berlin's theater, even when the more obvious trappings of minstrelsy are absent. It resurfaces, for example, in Groucho Marx's put-ons of Margaret Dumont (in *The Cocoanuts*) and the brash, benighted challenges that Ethel Merman's homespun characters present to show business professionals (in *Annie Get Your Gun*) and to foreign dignitaries (in *Call Me Madam*).

Films provide the most vivid documentation of Berlin's ongoing commitment to minstrelsy—and in each case minstrelsy is depicted as *stage* performance. In other words, the young medium of film became Berlin's means of preserving an old theatrical form that he knew was dying out. The minstrel scenes in the popular later films *This Is the Army* and *White Christmas* had precedents that go back to the earlier years of sound film. The 1930 film *Mammy* starring Al Jolson had its roots in a "play with music" called *Mister Bones* for which Berlin drafted the synopsis in 1927. The main character, performing his stage scenes in blackface, plays the role of an end man in a minstrel show within a plot whose misunderstandings and murderous jealousy recall the Italian verismo one-act opera *I Pagliacci*—providing one case in point of the connection in Berlin's mind between minstrelsy and opera. The film features several numbers performed within the characters' minstrel show world, including an operatic parody that had its origins in the *Music Box Revue of 1923* ("A Bit o' Grand Opera," a.k.a. the "'Yes! We Have No Bananas' Opera Burlesque"). In the 1942 film *Holiday Inn*, Bing Crosby and Marjorie Reynolds perform a number called "Abraham" that embeds swing-style music-making within a nightclub scene rife with the trappings of minstrelsy: including the two main characters in blackface and pseudo-raggedy costumes, plus a black mother (mammy) figure with two young black children acting as pickaninnies.

In the postwar years, Berlin's fascination with minstrelsy had been suppressed by its decline in American entertainment, but his surviving papers reveal that it did not fade from his theatrical imagination. If anything it became more potent. Berlin's original scenario for *White Christmas* is worth quoting in full to reveal how much minstrelsy (and Berlin's own minstrelsy-related songs) played into his original conception of that famous film's opening scene, written for Bing Crosby and Fred Astaire (whose part would eventually be taken by Danny Kaye):

> It is the week before Christmas. Crosby and Astaire are with a minstrel show. This could be an authentic minstrel show—for lack of a better name call it the Georgia Minstrels. We open with the minstrel show finale, done to lyrics and music that was in the *Ziegfeld Follies of 1919*. But instead of finishing up with the song MANDY, which was part of that minstrel show, we will use a number called SOUTHLAND, which was in the Fourth *Music Box Revue*. This is the number that is a counter-melody to "Swanee River." The purpose for this opening is to show Fred Astaire as the interlocutor and Crosby as Mr. Bones, both in blackface, finishing with Astaire and Crosby singing the SOUTHLAND number, and as the entire company do the first chorus of the counter-melody and "Swanee River," Astaire doing a soft-shoe Virginia essence. At the end of this we go to their dressing room. They are taking the cork off their faces and we start our story.[74]

Ultimately, of course, the film's opening scene took place near the front of a European battlefield during World War II, but the minstrel number was preserved, without blackface, by moving it to a rehearsal scene later in the movie.

Likewise, in a typewritten reaction to a script draft for the 1954 film *There's No Business Like Show Business*, Berlin envisions a minstrel scene as his ideal opening for a story of a family of entertainers—specifically in the type of minstrel act known as a "Tom show," featuring characters and scenes drawn from Harriet Beecher Stowe's *Uncle Tom's Cabin*.[75] It is fascinating to watch him offer his "random thoughts" on such scenes:

I have been thinking that maybe we ought to readjust our thinking and start with Mom and Pop and a baby doing an Uncle Tom show—Eliza on the ice pursued by bloodhounds—done with all the simple props and simple stage methods of 1900 travelling Tom show. . . . [ellipsis original] We ought to start with a voice saying "This is show business," and utilize the voice—maybe one of our central characters—throughout, for it would help us over many time lapses. . . . [ellipsis added] Here are a few random thoughts about the possibilities of such a story. I don't cling to any of these but they will give you at least a suggestion of how my mind is working.

1. We start with Mom, Pop, and the baby in the "Uncle Tom's Cabin" somewhere out in the sticks. Small-town audience. Probably should be cold as hell.

2. In the Olio in the same show, Mom, Pop, and their *three kids* do a song and dance routine something like "Mandy."[76]

The scene was not used, but these "thoughts" on a script draft reveal that for Berlin, a minstrel scene was not just a good way to begin a movie but also a way to dramatize the origins and foundations of American show business.

What did minstrelsy mean to Irving Berlin? The cultural historian Eric Lott offers a useful framework in which to answer that question.[77] From one perspective, minstrelsy represents what Lott calls "people's culture," an idealized view of the minstrel show as a common denominator, an unpretentious democratic entertainment accessible to all, which helps to explain its remarkable resilience. The opposite perspective comprises what Lott calls the "cultural domination" view in which minstrelsy is seen as reflecting and reinforcing beliefs in white superiority and the oppression of African Americans. That view helps to explain why minstrelsy as a popular phenomenon did not survive the civil rights era, even though minstrel shows continued long after that and, in recent years, have seen an irony-saturated resurgence in film, hip-hop, and musical theater itself.[78] Berlin's ideology of entertainment, formed early in the twentieth century, clearly stood with the "people's culture" view and blinded him to—or caused him to underestimate—minstrelsy's power to reinforce "cultural domination." Why was Berlin's embrace of minstrelsy so deep and long? I think it was because he believed that minstrelsy's conventions, its structure, and its vitality gave it access to the common denominator in an American audience. It shaped Berlin's notion of a kind of ideal American "common man," the mob for whom all of his work was designed. That it also characterizes his whole generation of immigrant entertainers, especially Jewish ones, has become a common theme in contemporary scholarship. As Melnick has put it, "Berlin's 'contribution,' in essence, was to distill the sights and sounds of minstrelsy into a usable modern musical grammar"—to which he might have added "theatrical" grammar as well.[79]

If minstrelsy forged a connection to what Berlin believed was the common denominator of his audience, opera provided a model for musical dramatization. It did so in two ways: first, it showed how music could carry action and dialogue and develop plot, and second, it showed how conflicting points of view could be presented simultaneously through music and still remain distinctive and intelligible. Opera enjoyed a place in Berlin's theatrical vocabulary partly because of its long presence in minstrel parody, but also because Berlin loved opera and wished to write one, one that would be widely construed as a distinctively American contribution to the genre. He did not do so, but many of his shows reveal the influence of opera on his theatrical imagination. All of his musicals through the mid-1930s include at least one extended, multisectional musical sequence featuring two or more characters in dialogue and action. Such scenes have earned little comment in writings about Berlin's work, first, because most of them survive only in manuscript or in truncated sheet-music versions, and second, because they lack the distilled lyricism that the confined space of the thirty-two bar song form seems to have brought out Berlin's best. Yet when we think of Berlin as a theater composer, such numbers take on great importance as evidence of his interest in carrying story through music, and they clearly convey the impact of opera's legacy on Berlin's conception of theater. What is interesting, too, is that the extended operatic sequence disappears from his later work—in the shows with the most expertly crafted scripts such as *Annie Get Your Gun* and *Call Me Madam*. Improvements in the craft of book writing perhaps obviated the need for extended musical sequences for Berlin, even as better books continued to elicit extended musical sequences from Rodgers and Hammerstein and Leonard Bernstein.

Meanwhile, almost every Berlin show features something else that reveals opera's impact: the counterpoint song. It seems to me not just coincidental that he started writing counterpoint songs for the theater in the same period that he publicly claimed his desire to compose an opera, because in opera two or more characters regularly express conflicting feelings *simultaneously*, as in the famous quartet from Verdi's *Rigoletto*, which Berlin parodied in his first musical comedy, *Watch Your Step*. Even before that Berlin's earliest songs track a love and knowledge of opera, including songs laced with quotations from famous arias and ensembles from the nineteenth-century repertoire that was popular among American audiences, such as *Carmen, Aida,* and *Lucia di Lammermoor*.[80] Even though Berlin's operatic ambitions had faded by the late 1920s, his abiding interest in cultivating the counterpoint song lasted to the end of his career. In short, for Berlin opera formed a deep well from which he drew and distilled a distinctively American theater in musical dialogue, and his counterpoint songs stand out as the singular and persistent legacy of his operatic ambitions.[81]

Minstrelsy and opera, then, form the twin currents that charge the three genres in which he channeled his theatrical energy: vaudeville, revue, and musical comedy.

Berlin proved early in his career to be a master of writing for and performing on vaudeville. Vaudeville, like minstrel shows and revues, tended toward variety rather than unity. Yet unlike any other genre, vaudeville featured separate, independent acts with nothing in common save a spot on the same bill. Behind his attraction to the early revue and musical comedy lay Berlin's knowledge of, love of, and experience of vaudeville. In his study of Berlin's early songs, Charles Hamm places vaudeville at the center of Berlin's universe. Hamm, building on the work of Robert Snyder, further explores the fundamental tension between respectability and expressive release in vaudeville that shaped Berlin's outlook. Berlin, Hamm explains, tended to view vaudeville as a forum for uninhibited, even countercultural, expression.[82] Indeed, vaudeville informed the conception and content of Berlin's earliest musical comedies. On the vaudeville stage a song had to tell a complete story and create a vivid character through which to tell that story. In this context Berlin exploited a savvy trick: what might be called the *reinterpreted refrain*. Songwriting conventions dictated that refrains repeated the same words after every verse. But to avoid stasis or dramatic inertia Berlin found a way to write the verses so that the recurring refrain words took on new meaning with every verse. Excellent examples appear in songs with a protagonist who has multiple lovers. The title of "Call Me Up Some Rainy Afternoon" represents the refrain line that young Nellie Green tells to a young man named Harry Lee with whom she flirts in the first verse. In the second verse, Harry goes to visit Nellie only to hear her through the door giving the same line to another young man.

Berlin was more than a writer for, and observer of, vaudeville. He was also a vaudeville star. He had a distinctive, winning stage persona characterized by modesty, guilelessness, and that soft, "raspy" voice. In September 1911, in the wake of his success with "Alexander's Ragtime Band," he was the headliner on a big-time vaudeville bill at Hammerstein's Victoria.[83] A newspaper headline announced that "Irving Berlin, the Well Known Song Writer, Is Received With Marked Enthusiasm. . . . SINGS TILL HE'S TIRED OUT."

> The audience fairly yelled for more, and Mr. Berlin sang "That Beautiful Rag." At the conclusion he was presented with an immense floral horseshoe. Mr. Berlin started to thrust this into the wings, then remembering his stage training, drew it back and took his bow while standing by the side of it. As the audience still wanted some more, the song writer sang them his masterpiece, "Alexander's Ragtime Band." But still his delighted listeners insisted on more, and he sang them "Ephraim."[84]

One of the audience members at this performance was Charles Dillingham, the producer of Berlin's first musical comedies.

A review of the show *Up and Down Broadway* noted that Berlin and his partner, Ted Snyder, "chopped the biggest chunks of congealed moisture" that night. Snyder played the piano and Berlin sang, and in "That Beautiful Rag," the reviewer noted that "Snyder joined in the chorus . . . and they had to repeat the chorus three times, and then were dragged forth by the applause to bow several times after the next set was under way."[85]

Vaudeville remained a reference point that shaped Berlin's shows in other genres. The order of acts on a vaudeville program had become conventionalized by the early 1900s, and typically the next-to-last position featured the show's headliner, or biggest star. It is interesting to see how that position appears in Berlin's revues: in the 1921 *Music Box Revue*, and in his wartime revues, Berlin himself appeared in that slot. Vaudeville headliners starred in Berlin's revues and musical comedies for decades.

Berlin came of age in the heyday of the revue, so it is no wonder that he thrived as a writer for revues. He contributed to several editions of the *Ziegfeld Follies* and conceived his own revue series, the *Music Box Revues*, which ran for four years (1921–24) and became a source of creative ore that he mined throughout his career. And during the two world wars, Berlin used the revue as a lens through which to focus on the everyday thoughts and experiences of American soldiers and civilians. Although the revue had become passé by the 1940s, it must be understood as central to Berlin's theatrical style. More than merely a subgenre of musical theater, for Berlin the revue was a kind of show of shows, an idiom into which his whole world of theatrical and musical idioms could coexist. It was also the medium that could feature the most stars on one stage. Like the *Ziegfeld Follies*, his own *Music Box Revues* featured Broadway's top-shelf talent. Moreover, the revue was by definition a genre of the here-and-now. It was supposed to *review* current events, current theater, and current music, so it shaped and reinforced Berlin's belief that the musical theater should address the "mob" in the theater, without consideration for enduring value. Revue series like the *Follies* and *Music Box* shows featured new editions every year, and none of them was designed to be revived later. Finally, in the revue, Berlin wrote numbers that addressed a particular theatrical context while being entirely extractable from that context. In the revue (as on vaudeville) Berlin wrote songs designed to have their own integrity outside of their immediate (and ephemeral) theatrical context. Paradoxically, a theater style so relentlessly contemporary, so addressed to the moment, demands to be historicized. Many of Berlin's revue songs that some might now regard as hoary old chestnuts, such as "A Pretty Girl Is Like a Melody" and "Easter Parade," actually spoke directly to contemporary concerns. His artistry as a writer of revues resides in the deft ability to both address his immediate audience and write songs generally enough to endure beyond the contemporary moment.

That perspective also informs his book musicals. They are marked by consistent adherence to the tenets of early musical comedy: to develop a marriage plot within a distinctively American context, with contemporary *American* settings, characters, dialogue, and songs that work both within the plot and may stand alone beyond it. In a major study linking musicals and American national identity, Raymond Knapp has dubbed it the "marriage trope."[86] And the three elements that Stephen Banfield highlights in Jerome Kern's musical comedies often apply to Berlin's as well: the three M's of "marriage, mistaken identity, and money."[87] The marriage-plot archetype, of course, precedes the development of American musical comedy. Some of its most famous theatrical incarnations are Shakespearean and Mozartian. They typically track the romantic arc of two or more relationships, ending either in an actual marriage or in the promise (new or renewed) of romantic commitment.[88] The literary critic Northrup Frye identified the plot archetype as essential to comedy, and argued that the couples' joining in the end represents the creation of a new social order. But it is hardly a revolution, Frye notes, since the new order is one that "the audience has recognized all along to be the proper and desirable state of affairs."[89] The signal difference in American musical comedy is the musical Americanization of the plot archetype, representing the theater's attempt to swerve away from the influence of operetta and opera, to adapt inherited structures to the American situation, and thus to speak to American audiences with unprecedented directness and relevance. European locales and characters, if included at all, served as foils to the essential Americanness of Berlin's shows.

The "Americanizing" element, however, is much more than a matter of simple sets and costumes. The American marriage plot in the shows of Berlin and others often dramatizes the developing love of two people of starkly different backgrounds, representing an idealized vision of a free society, a "more perfect union" than tends to be available in real life. In different ways Andrea Most and Raymond Knapp have viewed the musical's love story as a medium for articulating specifically American values. In the process of working out the romantic configurations, Most uses the language of American Jewish experience to analyze the outcomes: outsiders "get converted, assimilated, or accepted into the group" in a "narrative trajectory from exclusion to acceptance," and in the end, the show's community becomes more "tolerant, egalitarian, or just."[90] From that perspective, musical comedy did nothing less than replicate Irving Berlin's experience of America. Three other stock plot types reinforce that notion: the *Backstager*, featuring a story about the lives of performers on and off the stage; the *Cinderella Story*, featuring a young woman of limited means who finds romance and success with a wealthy male benefactor; and the *Cavalcade Musical*, used most often in film, featuring a romantic plot (often a Backstager) developing through historical time and shaped by the choice of pre-existing songs. Most of Berlin's shows cannot be labeled one thing or another, but the traits of such plot types shape many of his musicals for stage and screen. Berlin's most enduring show, *Annie Get Your Gun*, may be seen as a unique blend of Backstager and Cinderella Story. These were plots that American musical theater writers revisited again and again, for they resonated deeply from the American musical theater's core.

From his first show, *Watch Your Step* (1914) to his last, *Mr. President* (1962), almost all of Berlin's musicals do that as they reveal an impulse to tap into *contemporary* American issues, events, language, cultural style, and popular music. Even the two exceptions—the postwar shows *Annie Get Your Gun* (1946) and *Miss Liberty* (1949)— with their historical settings, reflect a contemporary sensibility. By doing so, Berlin's shows actually echo the thrust and circumstances of so-called Old Comedy in Ancient Greece as described by a recent scholar of comedy: written "for a single, relatively knowable group of spectators, without intent to accommodate the possibilities of later productions or future theatergoers" and with keen awareness "of the people, events, and attitudes 'in the air' during the past year . . . mining this vein of material for comic effect."[91]

In other words, Berlin conceived shows as *events* more than as *works*. As a result, Berlin's shows do not exactly represent the most enduring oeuvre in the American theater: only *Annie Get Your Gun*, the show that least obviously addresses its time, has enjoyed an unbroken string of productions that stretches from its premiere to the present. Yet by engaging with the here-and-now, with no apparent thought of posterity but mainly of the "mob" before him, Berlin distilled and packaged musical comedy conventions that resonated in the theater deep into the twentieth century even as they held to comedy's ancient ideals.

Above all—and this I think manifests the engine that drives all of his work— Berlin seems to have understood and embraced the idea that American musical theater is always, inescapably, about itself. He probably would have scorned the term *metatheater*, but the boot fits. All of his stage shows and films are in some way about theater, about putting on a show, about performing in public, and about the place that tested his mettle and nourished his craft: New York City. This is the case even in shows that are not chiefly set in New York. *Annie Get Your Gun* may be widely considered one of the "Western" musicals of the *Oklahoma!* age, but it is above all a show about "show business," and it all takes place east of (or near to) the Mississippi River and ends up in New York, with plenty of swinging tunes that resonate more with postwar Manhattan than with Annie Oakley's earlier America in Darke County, Ohio. The same may be said of Berlin's films. For example, the plot and protagonists of *White Christmas*—a film conceived by Berlin himself—travel from the European continent to Florida to New England, but when Bob Wallace (Bing Crosby) wants to announce and arrange a benefit show for his former commander, he goes back to his home base, New York City, and imports the entire production to a small Vermont village—an almost allegorical representation of how Broadway's products not only became national phenomena but often strove to serve patriotic ends during peacetime. Berlin's later shows that engage with U.S. political life, *Call Me Madam* and *Mr. President*, displace the earlier New York focus onto the nation's capitol. Yet, like so many earlier shows, they too trace the path by which a public figure, portrayed as an ordinary American, must carve out an identity and a calling through the performance of a public and quasi-theatrical role. In short, those characters reenact what Berlin himself did every time he created a new work for the stage. Thus, coming to grips with Berlin's work in the theater offers more than a slice of the history of musical theater; it offers an angle from which to understand America in the twentieth century. Irving Berlin, at least, saw it that way. As his theater grew from the Lower East Side to the larger world, it was always about defining, reflecting, and proving worthy of his adopted country—in short, it was about *performing* his American citizenship on the musical stage. Berlin's career, like that of many of his theatrical peers, demonstrates a belief in claiming an American identity through *acts*, in every sense of the word.

2

LEGITIMATE VAUDEVILLE
• • •
THE DILLINGHAM SHOWS, 1914–15

All the kind of music there is.
—Variety, *on* Watch Your Step

December 8, 1914: It was the opening night of Irving Berlin's first musical comedy, *Watch Your Step*, and the show came to a halt in the midst of the second act as vaudeville headliner Frank Tinney entered to "thunderous applause." Tinney explained to the audience that his late appearance, as himself, was due to the fact that act 1 had a plot, and he "ruined plots." So Tinney began cracking jokes about the producer, the stars, the show, and himself, and, as the *New York Herald* put it, he "talked freely and familiarly with all the well known first nighters, calling them by their first names and keeping the audience in a roar."[1]

December 25, 1915: On opening night of Berlin's second show, *Stop! Look! Listen!*, the grand finale titled "Everything in America Is Ragtime" took an unexpected and unrehearsed turn. The entire company appeared onstage with the show's star, the ravishing French sensation Gaby Deslys, as they sang and danced on a golden staircase. Suddenly an offstage band began to play along, and then it appeared at the top of the stairs led by none other than the March King himself, John Philip Sousa. Confused by the band's unexpected entrance, Deslys actually stopped singing, but Sousa urged her to continue as he marched his band down the stairs and the swelled ensemble brought the show to a rousing conclusion. The audience loved it. According to the *New York Herald*, the "'Oh's!' and 'Ah's!' which had followed the other innovations for the evening gave way to shouts of pleasure and astonishment at the climax of the performance, and the curtain fell on a 'first night' which Broadway will remember for some time."[2] The show's producer, Charles Dillingham, certainly remembered it. In a memoir he drafted in 1933, the year before he died, Dillingham described the scene in some detail and recalled Sousa's surprise cameo as "a compliment to me," adding: "Sousa was always thinking of nice things to do."[3]

CHARLES DILLINGHAM'S LEGITIMATE VAUDEVILLE

That a comedian would gleefully "ruin" a musical comedy plot and make the audience "roar" with unscripted jokes, and that Sousa's band could invade a Broadway show, upstage its celebrity star, and still be hailed by audience, critics, and producer—all of this points to two fundamental ways in which the musical theater world that Berlin entered in the 1910s differed from the scene he left a half century later. First, the early twentieth-century musical theater was a form of entertainment dominated by two forces: producers and star performers. The writers—composers, lyricists, and librettists—existed to supply the raw material with which these agents added luster to their celebrity and prestige, but their significance ended there. With his first musical comedy, Berlin would help to change that arrangement by making the songwriter—who, with Berlin's unique talent among show composers of the period, wrote *both* music and lyrics—an equal if not greater force, creatively and economically, than the producer and performers. Second, in 1914 and 1915, genre boundaries were conspicuously porous and genre conventions were in flux. Audiences for a show billed as a "musical comedy" did not expect a unified piece featuring songs by a single composer or songwriting team, nor did they expect that the songs, dances, and dialogue would develop the characters and plot. Instead they relished the delightful ebb and flow of elements that worked for and against narrative continuity, one moment sustaining the illusion of reality, the next moment shattering the illusion with a celebrity turn, a conspiratorial wink to the audience, some improvised dialogue referring to the theatrical situation as it unfolded in real time, or even an entire routine imported from another show.[4]

Such moments—call them *vaudevillisms*—constantly bubbled to the surface of early twentieth-century musical comedy, even in shows with a plot and scripted dialogue. This was a theatrical style in which new songs that earned long and loud cheers would be immediately encored, perhaps several times; in which performers interpolated popular songs or routines intended for one show into another; in which a star like Al Jolson—another gleeful ruiner of plots—could come on stage and tell a rapt audience that he would now summarize the remaining story so that he could spend the rest of the evening simply singing his hit songs. And it was a theatrical world where the show's biggest "name"—whether an actor, a singer, a songwriter, a playwright, or a director—might offer a curtain speech, that is, a few impromptu, benedictory words at the end of the opening night's curtain call. In this context, part of the thrill for the audience, in contrast to the experience of the new medium of film, lay in anticipating when the performers would break through theatrical illusion, address the audience directly, and create unforgettably "real" moments—like Frank Tinney's stand-up comedy and the March King's surprise entrance for the grand finale.

Yet Dillingham hardly needed Tinney or Sousa to enhance the appeal of his shows. By 1914 he stood with Florenz Ziegfeld and the Shuberts among Broadway's leading producers. Known for his quiet, polished manner in a loud, rough milieu, Dillingham was said to resemble a banker more than a showman. And although he occupied a position that typically drew grudges and backstabbing, Dillingham seemed to be loved by everyone.[5] Berlin remembered him in 1967 as "one of the kindest and most generous men I ever knew."[6]

Like his rival and sometime partner Florenz Ziegfeld Jr., Dillingham had shaped his career in reaction to a genteel upbringing emphasizing moral and cultural elevation. The son of an Episcopal minister, Dillingham spent his early career as a peripatetic journalist with stints in Hartford, Chicago, Washington, and New York. In 1896, already twenty-eight, Dillingham wrote and produced his own play, *Ten P.M.* Although the show flopped, the influential producer Charles Frohman—who had joined Marc Klaw and Abe Erlanger in the powerful Theatrical Syndicate that had consolidated the theater business in the 1890s—saw something in it that led to an invitation to join his firm, and Dillingham soon became a key figure as a press agent and production assistant. In 1903 he went out on his own and produced *The Office Boy*, the first of a long line of musical shows extending over the next thirty years.[7]

By 1914 Dillingham had been a Broadway producer for more than a decade, and he had enjoyed unprecedented success in the past year—a remarkable feat in the very year that the *New York Dramatic Mirror* had called financially "disastrous" in American theater.[8] Yet, three weeks after *Watch Your Step* opened, the December 25, 1914, issue of *Variety* credited Dillingham as the driving force behind a new fusion of vaudeville and musical comedy. Although the two forms had already witnessed a steady interchange of performers,[9] Dillingham had developed an unusual and systematic method of signing vaudeville headliners for lower than their usual weekly pay with the promise that success in "legitimate" theater could yield unlimited future earnings. In the world of early twentieth-century American theater, the term *legitimate* embraced any kind of theater with a script and plot of some kind in which actors played characters. The distinction was codified in *Variety* itself, which had separate sections for reviews of "legitimate" and "vaudeville" shows. In Dillingham's vision, a legitimate production could thus afford to feature vaudeville stars unencumbered by novices or mediocrities. For Dillingham, the article claimed, the approach opened up "the opportunity to place vaudeville people where their specialties properly introduced would help the play."[10] It would be a musical theater that blended the best of two seemingly incompatible worlds—vaudeville's emphasis on a varied sequence of distinct acts and legitimate theater's tendency toward narrative or thematic coherence. In short, it combined the popularity of vaudeville and the prestige of legitimate theater in a style that might be called *legitimate vaudeville*.

Although the term was not used in the period (or since), it serves here as an apt reminder of the validity and popularity of a musical theater style that did *not* aspire to achieve a tighter connection between song, dialogue, plot, and character, as did the more historically recognized Princess Theatre shows developed by Jerome Kern and his collaborators in the years immediately following Berlin's initial success. Part of the challenge for musical theater historians is that so many other shows of this period, and especially the distinctive shows of Charles Dillingham and Irving Berlin in 1914–15, do not fit easily into the standard rubrics of musical theater, whether vaudeville, revue, melodrama, musical comedy, operetta, opera, or minstrel show. Moreover, their surviving scripts and scores do not lend themselves readily to reconstruction or revival because their performance depended so heavily on the unique qualities of the original cast and on the way the script and songs took shape around several well-known stage personalities. These "problems," however, get exactly to the point. Indeed, the Dillingham-Berlin approach did not aspire to fulfill any one genre's conventions but rather strove to embrace them all. These shows were remarkably successful *because of*, not despite, their generic fluidity. The Dillingham-Berlin musical theater style was a show of shows, a form of theater whose chief subject was itself and its urban milieu. And it was meant to be overtly American, not a British or

Austrian or Italian import (although all of these styles inflect the show); *Watch Your Step*, for example, was billed as "made in America."[11]

The entertainment publication *Variety* threw a spotlight on Dillingham's method because it worked. By the end of 1914, *Variety* noted that he had "two great successes now running in New York": an orientalist "musical fantasy" called *Chin Chin* that had opened in October and would run for 295 performances featuring the vaudeville comedy duo of Dave Montgomery and Fred Stone, and another show, *Watch Your Step*, which had opened December 8 with a score by the twenty-six-year-old Berlin. Dillingham had handpicked Berlin to compose the score in the same way he had cast the show: by trolling vaudeville for talent. Dillingham's impetus for offering the songwriter a contract, the article explained, came from "hearing him sing his own songs" in 1911 at a matinee at Hammerstein's Victoria, which at the time was the leading vaudeville house and a hub of the burgeoning Times Square theater district. Dillingham later wrote that "Alexander's Ragtime Band"—one of the songs Berlin had sung at Hammerstein's—"was the start of 'Watch Your Step.'"[12] In the spirit of Izzy Baline, Irving Berlin had plugged his way to Broadway.

FORTY-SECOND STREET

When Dillingham contracted Berlin to write the score for *Watch Your Step*, Berlin entered the Broadway musical, so to speak, on the ground floor of a building still under construction—both the genre and the physical space in which it developed. Since the Civil War, the musical theater's center of gravity had gradually shifted northward from Fourteenth Street, spreading uptown from the Lower East Side energy that fueled it. In the 1880s and 1890s, the stretch of Broadway between Fourteenth and Forty-first Streets known as the Rialto formed Manhattan's entertainment domain. By the turn of the century, however, ambitious entrepreneurs such as Oscar Hammerstein I, partners Klaw and Erlanger, the Shubert brothers, and David Belasco—most of them Jewish immigrants like Berlin, or their sons—had ventured north of Forty-first Street and built theaters in the Longacre Square neighborhood, also known as "Thieves Lair."[13]

It was not a promising place to establish a theatrical empire. The streets bred pickpockets and prostitutes, and reeked of horse manure, a by-product of the carriage trade that thrived there.[14] But land and construction were cheap, and so, in the century-straddling decade from 1895 to 1904, the area witnessed the rise of several theaters that helped to create the new center of American theater at the intersection of Forty-second Street and Broadway. Among the many venues that arose in this milieu was Klaw and Erlanger's lavish New Amsterdam Theatre (opened 1903), at 214 West Forty-second Street, where audiences would witness the premiere of Berlin's first musical comedy. When the *New York Times* owner Adolph Ochs moved his newspaper into the new, triangular Times Tower in 1904, Longacre became Times Square. That same year saw the completion of Manhattan's first subway line, whose Times Square stop became a choice destination.[15] It is no coincidence that the titles of Berlin's first shows captured the telegraphic cadence of commands in the recently constructed subway line. Passengers stepping off the trains had already been exhorted to "Watch Your Step" and "Stop! Look! Listen!" for their safety.[16] Plucked from the train platform, the titles announced a theatrical style committed to the bustling here-and-now, and signaled a proto-metatheatrical musical comedy style whose subjects were a new kind of city life and theater itself.

THE CULTURE OF CELEBRITY

Dillingham laid the groundwork for his shows with a systematic public relations campaign that included a steady stream of press releases that highlighted the performing talent he was gathering. In the summer of 1914—nearly six months before *Watch Your Step* opened in December—the New York papers began to feature large spreads heralding Dillingham's "new musical comedy" and featuring photographs of stars who had already signed their contracts.[17] The systematic nature of Dillingham's

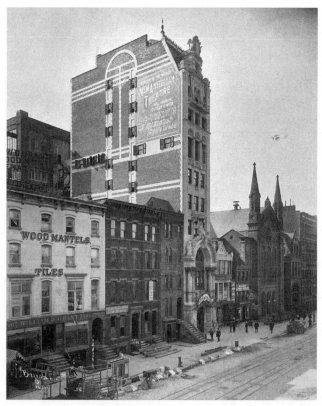

The New Amsterdam Theatre, Forty-second Street, 1903, soon after its construction. The theater would present Berlin's first musical comedy, Watch Your Step *(1914), many editions of the* Ziegfeld Follies, *and Berlin and Hart's* Face the Music *(1932). Museum of the City of New York, Byron Co. Collection.*

campaign can be seen in the way multiple papers report the same entertainment news on the same day. On October 1, 1914, for example, six different newspapers featured brief announcements, in similar language, that "Charles Dillingham yesterday engaged Mr. Frank Tinney for his new Fall review, 'Watch Your Step.'"[18] As the press quotations already reveal, the show's label was in flux even before it opened: it was called both a "musical comedy" and a "review" [sic]. With so many stars signing on, the challenge of deciding who would get top billing became an opportunity for Dillingham to publicize a novel way of giving his headliners equal emphasis. One paper reported that Dillingham had solved his problem "in such form as to please all concerned": to present all the names of the cast members preceded by the conjunction and.[19]

Yet if no one in Watch Your Step got top billing, the show nevertheless had an act that won the most attention: Irene and Vernon Castle. Dillingham recalled first signing the librettist Harry Smith and Berlin, and then pursuing the stars; he found the Castles in Paris.[20] Beginning in 1912, Irene Castle and her husband had become famous for taming and transforming full-body "animal" dances such as the Turkey Trot and Fox Trot that had emerged from African American culture. The Castles made these dances more genteel—and more popular—for the white mainstream. Irene's bobbed hairstyle, slim and petite figure, and elegant wardrobe provided as much material for the press as her dancing, and she became the very model of a modern American woman.[21] In 1913 the couple had appeared in its first musical comedy, The Sunshine Girl, and continued to star in vaudeville.[22] The Sunshine Girl anticipated Watch Your Step in the sense that it featured the Castles in contemporary dances, most famously the tango, which apparently saved the tepidly received show. But The Sunshine Girl was a British import, part of a style that would soon be rendered passé by the kind of brash, explicitly American entertainment that Berlin, Dillingham, and company brought to Broadway in the wake of George M. Cohan's successes.[23] In Watch Your Step, Irene was cast simply as herself, "Mrs. Vernon Castle"—in another instance of blurred boundaries between legitimate and vaudeville, theater and reality. Moreover, as the Castles had worked in vaudeville, they exemplified Charles Dillingham's new approach to signing talent. Variety reported that Dillingham offered them $1,000 weekly for performing in Watch Your Step—a generous sum certainly, yet a steep drop from the $1,600 per week they had made in big-time vaudeville.[24]

Dillingham's public relations campaign seems to have accelerated during the show's out-of-town tryouts in Syracuse and Detroit, and in a way that emphasized the show not just as compelling entertainment but as a kind of arbiter of contemporary urban lifestyle. The Detroit Journal featured one of the show's beautiful stars, Justine Johnstone, in furs and a hat, in an award-winning photograph under the heading "A Prize Beauty."[25] A few days after the show opened, the New York Star published a full-page feature on "Four Beauties in 'Watch Your Step' at the New Amsterdam Theatre," reflecting the era's fascination with chorus girls.[26] Two newspapers, including the New York Times, ran features on the show's "dog star"—including a mock interview with the animal, whose stage role was to remain still and silent while his master commanded him to do various stunts.[27] The show's opening also inspired several feature articles on Irving Berlin as a celebrity songwriter embarking on a new phase of his career.[28] But most of the press stories surrounding the show celebrated the Castles. Nearly every paper in New York, plus *Opera News* and *Vogue* magazine, featured large spreads including photos or drawings of the Castles in action.[29] In consecutive weeks, the *Sun* featured big spreads on "How to Dance the One Step" and "How to Dance the Maxixe," both written "by the Vernon Castles."[30] Together such features solidified the show's gathering reputation for offering everything that was new, contemporary, and exciting in New York: its fashion, its dancing, and its music. *Watch Your Step* was more than a show, more than entertainment; it was a cultural event in which the city saw a comely reflection of itself on the stage and in the media.

Dillingham adopted the same formula for *Stop! Look! Listen!*, casting a celebrity in a starring role, which is chiefly a magnified version of herself—a point brought home in the program that, like the one for *Watch Your Step*, identified the heroine by her real name, Gaby Deslys. In the finale, Berlin even composed her into the song. The lyric uses her name in a rhyming sequence on the long "e" sound: "Composers, just as thick as *bees*, / Writing raggy melod*ies*—/ They're even making Gaby Des*lys* / Sing ragtime."[31]

If Irene Castle embodied one kind of stylish, liberated New Woman, Deslys represented another, the *soubrette*: an attractive, flirtatious, coy, sometimes mischievous young woman featured in many musical comedies. A French singer, dancer, and actress, Deslys had come to New York a few years earlier to star in several Shubert-produced shows, including *Vera Violetta* (1911), which introduced her dance specialty "The Gaby Glide" in a song by that title,[32] and *The Honeymoon Express* (1913). Both shows were glorified vaudeville featuring another emerging star, Al Jolson, and the man who became Deslys's husband, Harry Pilcer, a dancer who made a specialty of

A NOTABLE GROUP IN "WATCH YOUR STEP" AT THE NEW AMSTERDAM THEATRE

Left to right:—Mrs. Vernon Castle, Vernon Castle, Frank Tinney, Elizabeth Brice, Charles King, Sallie Fisher, Harry Kelly and Elizabeth Murray.

"Look at 'em doing it." In Watch Your Step, *Vernon and Irene Castle do the syncopated walk while others, including the blackface comedian Frank Tinney, look on. Billy Rose Theatre Division, The New York Public Library for the Performing Arts, Astor, Lenox and Tilden Foundations.*

falling down steps.[33] Already by 1901, West Forty-third Street was known as Soubrette Row for the concentration of aspiring actresses living there, and Deslys both embodied the type and transcended it with her aura of foreign exoticism.[34] Many commentators singled out her ravishing beauty—and her ever-changing hats—among her chief attributes. "In her simple taste for millinery that soars to the skies," wrote one critic, "this newly-risen star of musical comedy suggests everything from an aeroplane to a Barnum and Bailey parade. . . . Life with her is just one enormous, extraordinary hat after another."[35] Another reviewer led with a description of Deslys's "doll-like features" and "china-blue eyes" while wryly noting, too, her "uncertain top notes" and "agile if not too graceful limbs."[36] Her thick French accent alternately frustrated and charmed her critics, adding yet another angle to the copious commentary on Deslys.

In short, Deslys was a star whose celebrity eclipsed her talent. Her arrival in New York had been heralded by a scandalous liaison with the king of Portugal, Manuel II, which, along with her beauty, may have been her chief claim to fame. In fact, by the

Gaby Deslys and Harry Pilcer in Stop! Look! Listen! *Billy Rose Theatre Division, The New York Public Library for the Performing Arts, Astor, Lenox and Tilden Foundations.*

time she appeared in *Stop! Look! Listen!* Deslys had been as much a topic of shows as an actress in them. Before 1915, *Stop! Look! Listen!*'s librettist Harry B. Smith had never written a show *for* Deslys, but he had written a show *about* her: the "revuette" *Gaby*, a satire, built around the rumored affair of Deslys and Manuel that formed part of a triple bill at the then-new Folies-Bergere theater in spring 1911.[37] Berlin had been involved in the production, writing three new songs for it, including "Down to the Folies-Bergere," "I Beg Your Pardon Dear Old Broadway," and "Spanish Love," a title suggesting the affair, however imprecise it may have been as a description of romance between a French woman and a Portuguese royal. Berlin had likewise referred to Gaby by name in a song called "When I Discovered You" for *Watch Your Step*. So Berlin and Smith were already familiar with their star, as celebrity, long before *Stop! Look! Listen!*

Both *Watch Your Step* and *Stop! Look! Listen!*, then, drew attention for their prominent exhibition of a new kind of woman: publicly liberated, innovative, and a bit risqué. They were magnetic personalities whose striking appearance and activities had already registered in the public eye, even if their theatrical skills were found wanting. Part of the appeal of Berlin's Dillingham shows was that audiences would get a chance to see these celebrities in person, dancing in elegant costumes. That the women would also sing and act went beyond what many audiences needed—or wanted, in light of commentary on Castle's singing voice and Deslys's overall performance.

But it was not just a matter of creating a star vehicle. Both women, in fact, embodied their show's effort to reflect contemporary New York City. In *Watch Your Step* dancing served as the keynote of a larger impulse to parody and celebrate New York's nightlife, where people went out on the town and dancing played a newly significant role.[38] It was a phenomenon that challenged the upper-class, old-money idea that entertaining should be done in the home, not in public.[39] One opening night review noted that the show exceeded the *Ziegfeld Follies* in the way it "epitomizes and satirizes the mad pursuit of gayety which prevails in some circles of this city."[40] So *Watch Your Step*, led by the dancing Castles, addressed the whole culture that the emerging Times Square theater district existed to support.

Stop! Look! Listen! focused on another contemporary New York phenomenon: the cult of the chorus girl. Since the 1890s producers had created shows around groups of beautiful women and marketed them aggressively, making a celebrity of the group. A glamorous aura accrued around such girls, who were avidly sought by "stage-door johnnies" and wealthy men in search of a mistress or a trophy wife. The cult really took off after 1900, when the British import *Florodora* became famous for its scene featuring a number called "Tell Me Pretty Maiden," in which a half dozen beauties are courted and serenaded by an equal number of handsome young men, enticing them to "come along, come along." The "Florodora girls" winked at the audience just before exiting—a newly intimate gesture on Broadway.[41] The song's tuneful vamp and dainty dotted rhythms served as the musical analogs to the lyrics' flirtatious tone. For two decades theater composers, including Berlin, would commemorate the *Florodora* sextet in homage and parody.[42] This archetypal chorus-girl scene resonates in the opening numbers of *Watch Your Step* and *Stop! Look! Listen!* Meanwhile, within the decade after 1900, Florenz Ziegfeld would elevate the chorus-girl show into a new art form, organizing his annual revues chiefly as a means of "glori-fying the American girl," as his advertising would put it. By the time Berlin entered musical comedy, chorus girls had become a fixture. Berlin himself had written (but not published) a lyric some four years earlier that referred specifically to *Florodora* and struck the era's keynote: "Many's the mess was made success / By beautiful cho-rus girls."[43] In *Stop! Look! Listen!*, the profit-driven musical comedy manager, aptly named Hunter Coyne, exclaims that he can do without everything in his show except the chorus girls, identified in the dialogue as "ponies" and "clothes-horses," accord-ing the equine terminology used on Broadway in that era to designate types of cho-rus girls. When the girls, upset about their costumes, threaten to quit en masse, Coyne calls them back, claiming that everything is dispensable, but "leave me my ponies and my clothes-horses, and musical comedy will still go on."[44] The chorus girl's rise to stardom or wealth became the era's archetypal plot and dovetailed nicely (and regularly) with the related plot archetype of the Cinderella story. In the libret-to's cast of characters, "Gaby" is described as "only a chorus girl now, but just wait"—signaling her Cinderella status even before the audience hears a line of dialogue.[45]

PLOT, IF ANY

Star vehicles like *Watch Your Step* and *Stop! Look! Listen!* ran chiefly on what Ethan Mordden has aptly called "the despotism of performing talent" and required min-imal narrative consistency or propulsion.[46] According to generic requirements, mu-sical comedies did not feature coherent scripts with consistent, continuous plots nor did they have characters whose behavior and language departed from stock types. A glimpse of period's conventions emerges in the advertising for Jerome Kern's first show, *The Red Petticoat* (1912), whose narrative consistency inspired un-usual terminology. The Shuberts deliberately avoided the term *musical comedy* and billed it as a "music comedy" [sic] and a "musical play" because the show had a "real plot."[47] Seeking less a plot and characters than a flexible scaffold on which to pre-sent his vaudevillian headliners, Dillingham turned to a frequent collaborator who could be counted on to deliver: Harry B. Smith. Smith duly crafted a script in the required style, and for that he earned credit in the *Watch Your Step* program for the "plot, if any."[48]

The plot, if any, of *Watch Your Step* hinges on a familiar American narrative device popularized by George Barr McCutcheon's novel *Brewster's Millions* (1902) and its adaptations for stage (1906) and screen (1914): a will from a crotchety, wealthy rela-tive with an eccentric restriction. In *Watch Your Step*, the will requires that its heir must not fall in love before the receiving the bequest. This announcement is made in scene 1, in the "Law Office de Danse," and it ignites a family controversy over the inheritance of $2,000,000 from the late curmudgeon Jabez Hardacre. Two naïve cousins, a young woman named Ernesta Hardacre and a young man named Joseph Lilyburn, are revealed as relatives of the deceased, and the scheming family members ally themselves with one or the other in hopes of gaining some of the inheritance. Because the prospective heirs remain unmarried, the other characters conspire to take them out to explore New York's nightlife in hopes of finding them a suitable mate and thus rendering them ineligible for the inheritance. The city "tour" that follows resonates with an earlier model that Harry B. Smith and his collaborators were no doubt familiar: the successful musical farce *A Trip to Chinatown* (1891). Thus Smith presents a series of scenes at familiar contemporary venues: a theater, a ballroom called the "Palais de Fox-Trot," the Metropolitan Opera House, a Pullman Sleeper, and "a Fifth Avenue Cabaret." The stage became a mirror of a new New York City.

In *Stop! Look! Listen!* Smith used another stock scenario, the backstager, as the basis for a Cinderella story in which a shy but ambitious chorus girl volunteers to play the lead in a show when its star unexpectedly backs out. Recognizing that a show without a star will sink, a press agent named Abel Connor (that is, an *able con artist*) insists that the show will not attract an audience if anyone finds out that the new star is a mere chorine who just lives in the neighborhood among the hundreds of aspiring actresses on Soubrette Row. He therefore proposes that she be "discovered" in an exotic place: not Europe, which he claims is overused (a dig at old-world operetta) but Hawai'i. Gaby is duly sent to Hawai'i and the other principal characters follow her. As in *Watch Your Step*, the plot "catch" opens up opportunities for vivid and exotic settings, in this case exploiting the Hawaiian craze then sweeping New York City.[49]

In both shows, Smith gives his characters punning names that reveal something of their position, interests, and motivations, a familiar device in the period's musical farces. In *Stop! Look! Listen!*, for example, in addition to "a manager of musical comedy" named Hunter Coyne and a press agent named Abel Connor, the librettist and composer of the show are named Rob Ayers and Frank Steele, respectively, suggesting their lack of originality. Young women identified as "members of the Frivolity Theatre Co." are given names like Iona Carr, Gladys Canby, May Knott, and Carrie Spear.[50]

Smith's style depended heavily on obvious jokes and puns, sometimes with mild sexual insinuation. In *Stop! Look! Listen!*, the costumer Alphonse is described as the man "who put the chic in chicken."[51] In the opening scene, the chorus girls are having such trouble with their costumes that they threaten to quit. Enter one Gideon Gay, a backer of the show described in the script as "a tired business man." Because he is carrying hat boxes, however, the chorus girls believe him to be Alphonse, so they try to get his attention in the following exchange, typical of Smith's suggestive comedic style:

NORA (*To* GIDEON): Take me first.
GIDEON: Um? (*Looks at her puzzled*)
CARRIE (*Fussing with her dress*): No; you'd better begin with me. I'm the worst.
GIRLS (*Wrangling, ad lib*): No! I am. Me first, etc. (*Several begin to take off their waists,* GIDEON *worried*)
GIDEON: They must think I'm an osteopath.
IONA: This waist is all right, but I'm having trouble with the skirt.
GIDEON: I've had that kind of trouble all my life.[52]

Later, when Abel Connor enters and finds Gaby Deslys (sometimes identified in the script as "Violette") crying, he tries to calm her down with a glass of red wine but, apparently distracted, pours ink into her glass instead. When she discovers what she has imbibed, she says, in Smith's attempt to capture Deslys's famously broken English: "I die—I poison." Connor answers, "What is to be done? I know—swallow some blotting paper. Quick!"[53]

Smith's scripts gave Berlin considerable leeway in composing the score. *Watch Your Step* includes notes that dialogue would be written to suit the spirit and content of a song. The libretto contains several passages that include such phrases as: "cue speeches to duet to be written on whatever the subject of duet may be."[54] Smith's flexibility should not be taken as a lack of pride in his work, however. Take, for example, Dillingham's remarkable story of one of the notable cuts he had insisted upon during the Syracuse tryout, including a star act he had brought back to the United States for the occasion. Note here a rare instance in which a scene is cut because *it did not fit the book*:

I brought W. C. Fields all the way from Australia and as good as his act was it didn't fit in our book . . . [so] I cut out the entire scene. It represented the Automat Restaurant and the machinery in the scene cost $5,000, [from] which we lost also 100 costumes and also W. C. Fields. There was a riot at that rehearsal and nobody'd ever seen practically an entire set thrown into the alley. R. H. Burnside, the producer [recte: director], wept on my shoulder. Harry B. Smith dashed to the box office and asked where he could find a lawyer. It was the first time the cast had agreed on one subject and that was: I was crazy. . . . W. C. Fields soon realized that his act was not for this play and he made a very generous settlement with me. Later on he sent me his photograph with the following inscription: "To Charles B. Dillingham, greatest and kindest of them all, for whom I traveled 39 days and nights to play a one-night stand—and I would do it again." The next season Bill Fields was the biggest hit on Broadway in Ziegfeld's *Follies*.[55]

A Syracuse critic praised Fields's "excellent fifteen minutes of inanimate [*sic*] comedy,"[56] but with or without Fields, reviewers did not so much find Smith's books lacking as simply inconsequential. In its opening night review of *Watch Your Step*, the *New York Times* paid Smith a compliment by claiming that "he was in good form when he did his part, and he was careful not to get in anyone's way."[57] Indeed, the *New York Herald* reported that in resolving the matter of the inheritance—the show's catalytic plot device—Frank Tinney resorted to improvised wisecracks. When Vernon Castle tries to claim the money, Frank Tinney assured the audience that the money did not exist. The *Herald* reported the ensuing dialogue, in which Tinney cracks jokes about Dillingham—who is, of course, not a character in the show:

"Listen, Vernie," says Frank. "There ain't no two million at all. Of course you know Vernon Castle's goin' to get the money, but who's goin' to pay for it? Mr. Dillingham ain't got it. Why, only this morning I asked him for twenty-eight cents to get my laundry, and he said, 'Frank, if I had twenty-eight cents I would send out a number two company.'"[58]

Reviews of *Stop! Look! Listen!* likewise credited Smith for staying out of the show's way. "There isn't a lot to Harry B. Smith's book, and there doesn't need to be," according to one reviewer. "The plot of Harry B. Smith is not important," wrote another. "It serves as a pretext for the introduction of the specialists and chorus ladies."[59] Yet another simply claimed that "Harry B. Smith's book need not disturb any one" because it "did not interfere in the least with Irving Berlin's lilting melodies."[60] And Charles Darnton, of the *New York World*, accepted Smith's "book" (a term he placed in quotation marks) as work that simply "reflected the spirit of the hour so far as Broadway goes."[61]

Smith appears to have been an ideal collaborator in the Dillingham-Berlin shows, although understanding his appeal takes some historical imagination in a genre where the librettist would soon assume increasing importance. Perhaps Dillingham saw in Smith a kindred spirit. Like Dillingham, Smith had roots in journalism, a background that helps account for his unique claim to fame as "the most prolific librettist and lyricist in history."[62] Born in Buffalo, New York, in 1860, Smith grew up in Chicago, where his newspaper career began. Turning to theater writing in his late twenties, Smith cranked out new librettos and lyrics for operettas, musical comedies, and revues and adapted imported European scripts at a pace of more than three per year in a theater career that stretched to 1932.[63] His own estimate put the figures at three hundred librettos (some with collaborators) and about six thousand song lyrics.[64] One early Dillingham production featured Smith's first of several collaborations with Victor Herbert, in *Babette* (1903). In response to it, a *New York Times* review linked Smith pejoratively to the age of mass production: "Mr. Smith is known as one of the largest manufacturers in this country of comic opera librettos, which of late years have been remarkably free from comic spirit in their conception and of wit in their dialogue, and the book of *Babette* has little that will tend to injure the reputation he has established to this effect."[65]

The critical reaction did nothing to stem the tide pouring from Smith's pen, as he would continue to collaborate with, or adapt books with scores by, many leading composers of the era. Victor Herbert was his most frequent collaborator in these years, with at least eight shows between 1903 and 1914, leading to one of his most enduring songs, "Gypsy Love Song." Smith even collaborated simultaneously with Berlin and Herbert: Herbert's *The Debutante*, for which Smith co-wrote the book, opened on December 7, 1914, one day before *Watch Your Step*. Operetta (sometimes billed as "comic opera" then) was Smith's chief focus, and he worked not only with Herbert but also with Reginald De Koven and John Philip Sousa, and adapted Viennese and French librettos for American taste. Among the Viennese operetta composers for whom Smith adapted librettos, some of the leading figures were Franz Lehár, Franz von Suppé, Leo Fall, and Oscar Straus. Smith also collaborated on many revues, most notably with sketches and lyrics for the earliest productions of the *Follies* (before they were called the *Ziegfeld Follies*), including five of the first six (excepting only 1911). Beginning in 1912, he also wrote several lyrics to music by Jerome Kern on the cusp of Kern's landmark Princess Theatre musicals. Kern and Smith wrote the score for the musical comedies *Oh, I Say* (1913) and *90 in the Shade* (1915). Individual lyrics by Smith were also interpolated into *The Girl from Utah* (1914), *Nobody Home* (1915), and *Very Good Eddie* (1915), which opened at the Princess Theatre just two days before Berlin's second show, *Stop! Look! Listen!* For his engagement with operetta, musical comedy, and revue, Smith's work embodies much of early twentieth-century American musical theater in microcosm. His versatility thus made him an apt collaborator for a theatrical style striving to embrace all idioms.

"ALL THE KIND OF MUSIC THERE IS"

Harry B. Smith's role in *Watch Your Step* and *Stop! Look! Listen!*, and the reviewers' response to it, stands as a vivid reminder that writers had little authority in a musical theater driven by producers and star power. Irving Berlin was different. From the start he exerted unusual control over his role as songwriter for the shows, and he became the first musical comedy composer to write a show featuring his own songs exclusively. His contract included a clause restricting interpolations, that is, numbers by other songwriters inserted into the show with the goal of showing off the stars to better advantage (whether or not the number had anything to do with the plot and characters). Interpolations were common practice in early musical comedy, and since the nineteenth-century, even opera stars in America routinely interpolated signature songs in an effort to connect with the audience. "Home, Sweet Home," perhaps the most beloved song in nineteenth-century America, appeared in many an opera for that reason, and Berlin himself commemorated (and parodied) the practice in his 1910 song "That Opera Rag," with its final line (sung to the tune of "Home, Sweet Home"): "Good lord, it's over, they're playin' 'Home Sweet Home.'"

Although Dillingham stood out as unusual for agreeing to limit interpolations, it is clear from his memoir that he intended his shows to be shaped by the style of a single songwriter and that he wanted Berlin to be that songwriter. At first, Berlin was apparently diffident about his ability to write the entire score himself, so he encouraged Harry B. Smith to serve as lyricist so that Berlin could focus solely on the music. As Dillingham recalled in his unpublished memoir:

> When he signed a contract with me to do a score, turning from song writer to composer, he became a little frightened and asked Harry B. Smith who was doing the libretto to write the lyrics. Mr. Smith gave the composer grand advice and encouragement when he said: "Irving Berlin, don't let anybody ever help you with your lyrics."[66]

This would not be the first time that Berlin hesitated to throw himself into writing a score for which he felt unqualified. Three decades later, Rodgers and Hammerstein would have to work hard to convince Berlin that he was the right man for the job of writing the music and lyrics for *Annie Get Your Gun*. And as in the later work, Berlin's diffidence dissolved once he undertook it.

In fact, once Berlin agreed to write the score he became determined to do it right, and there were intense exchanges over how many interpolations might be allowed and the conditions under which they would appear in the show, if Dillingham saw the need. After Berlin had apparently made an oral agreement allowing for up to five interpolations, Dillingham's attorney, Nathan Burkan, told his client that Berlin had changed his mind.[67] On September 9, 1914, Burkan reported that Berlin had decided to write the entire score himself, adding that "I told Mr. Josephson [Berlin's attorney] that this proposition was unfeasible, and that you could not consider it, but in any event I would put it up to you for your consideration."[68] In fact, Berlin had practically written the entire score already. On September 18, *Variety* announced that "Irving Berlin has finished 22 numbers for 'Watch Your Step'"[69]—which is exactly how many numbers appear in the published score. The initially diffident Berlin had now taken over the show with an alacrity that few theater composers of his era shared. *Watch Your Step* would feature no interpolations by other songwriters.

It did not need to. If most people tended to think of Berlin as a "ragtime composer," his *Watch Your Step* score demonstrated, above all, that he commanded an astonishing range of theater styles. *Variety* struck the key note. The show, it claimed, proved that Berlin "is not alone a rag composer, and that he is one of the greatest lyric writers America has ever produced." It went on to note that with its rags, ballads, "trots," a polka, the "grand opera medley," and more, *Watch Your Step* featured "all the kind of music there is."[70]

The claim, though hyperbolic, drew attention to an important point that reflected Berlin's talent, already proven on Tin Pan Alley, for engaging with every available song style. Now Berlin's songwriting versatility came to the theater, and it not only matched the demands of Dillingham's omnivorous theatrical style, it expanded its range as well. Yet that notion has been obscured by emphasis on the show's ragtime elements. Coming to terms with Berlin's score involves both recognizing the ways in which *some* numbers represented ragtime in 1914–15 and the ways in which others explore a variety of other styles.

"A SYNCOPATED MUSICAL SHOW"

As a result of the international success of "Alexander's Ragtime Band" (1911), Berlin was now thoroughly established in the public mind as a ragtime composer, so it was natural for him to distill and extend his particular brand of the style in a Broadway show. The program and publicity of *Watch Your Step* made much of its ragtime associations by billing it as "a syncopated musical show."[71] There was indeed plenty of syncopation to be found in the show.

Berlin's brand of ragtime did not simply depend on syncopation, however. By now, several traits and connotations had clustered around ragtime and given it definition. First, Berlin's ragtime depended not just on any kind of syncopation but on particular patterns that Berlin had already distilled in his earlier Tin Pan Alley and vaudeville songs. These include two basic kinds of syncopation. One is a tied-across-the-bar syncopation producing almost identical passages in *Watch Your Step* and *Stop! Look! Listen!* in songs about going out on the town (ex. 2.1).

Berlin derives such phrases from his earlier songs: an identical pattern, which Charles Hamm describes as a "common musical feature" in ragtime songs, appears in Berlin's 1910 syncopated ballad "Stop, Stop, Stop (Come Over and Love Me Some More)."[72] Aaron Copland, looking for the rhythmic basis of "modern jazz" in 1927,

Example 2.1. Syncopated figures in "on the town" songs.

2.1a. "Let's Go around the Town," Watch Your Step.

Where can we go___ to pass the time a - way?__

2.1b. "When I'm Out with You," Stop! Look! Listen!

Let's take a stroll__ up the av - en - ue___

Example 2.2. Tied variants of cakewalk rhythm in syncopated finales.

2.2a. "The Syncopated Walk," Watch Your Step.

that syn - co - pa - ted walk___

2.2b. "Everything in America Is Ragtime," Stop! Look! Listen!

writ - ing rag - gy mel - o - dies_

identified this "fox trot" rhythm as fundamental, with its alternation of three- and two-note patterns.[73]

A second kind of rhythm features a tied variant of the cakewalk rhythm: the short-long-short-long-long pattern used more overtly and obsessively in the earliest ragtime songs. In these examples from *Watch Your Step* and *Stop! Look! Listen!* the same rhythm appears with similarly rag-oriented lyrics in act-ending numbers (ex. 2.2).

Compared to the intricate syncopation in piano ragtime pieces by composers such as Scott Joplin, such patterns might appear to be rudimentary, yet their power derived from their pervasiveness in a musical show: contemporaries heard in Berlin's score not ragtime as a novelty but as the new normal in show music. More than that, music per se formed just part of the ragtime impulse as it was recognized at the time. Berlin's notion of ragtime also extended to the use of language, including the slang and colloquial expressions that ragtime had normalized in popular song vernacular. A line in a song about publicity in *Stop! Look! Listen!*, for example, exhorts, in syncopated slang: "Blow your horn, / Let 'em know you're comin'; / Blow your horn, / That'll start 'em hummin.'" Above all, the language in Berlin's songs is conversational, a stark contrast to the formal language, inverted syntax, and sometimes strained rhetoric of operetta. Reading the lyrics without line breaks throws that quality into relief. In "Blow Your Horn," for example, Berlin writes:

Barnum and Bailey were wonderful showmen—in the theatrical world, there are no men who would claim to be their equal.

The conversational quality is so smooth that, in reading the words as prose, one may well miss the qualities that make them apt song lyrics, including: rhyme (showmen / no men), assonance (Bailey / claim), alliteration (wonderful / world / who would), and rhythm ("Barnum and Bailey" and "wonderful showmen"). Likewise in "The Syncopated Walk," the act 1 finale of *Watch Your Step*, conversational language coexists easily with rhyming patterns. As a statement and a response the following lines would sound natural in a conversational dialogue:

> Strange, but there's a change in how people walk these days.
> Yes! You must confess that ever since the dancing craze ev'rybody has a syncopated walk.

Presented as *lyrics*, the lines more clearly resonate with multiple rhyming patterns, including pairs of internal rhymes (italicized) and an end rhyme joining two couplets (underlined):

> *Strange,*
> But there's a *change*
> In how people walk these <u>days.</u>
> *Yes!* You must *confess*
> That ever since the dancing <u>craze</u>
> Ev'rybody has a syncopated walk.

An even more compelling example appears in the verse of "I Love a Piano," a song clearly modeled on "Alexander's Ragtime Band," and one of the most popular and enduring songs from *Stop! Look! Listen!*

> As a *child* / I went *wild* / When a <u>band played</u>;
> How I *ran* / To the *man* / When his <u>hand swayed</u>.

Berlin casts the verse in a way that binds together a natural conversational style (all in monosyllables) in two lines with parallel construction (using *when*), a tight rhyme scheme, and internal assonance (on "w" in the first line and on "h" in the second line). Here we can see Berlin's linguistic gift: to match his up-to-date musical style to the way modern Americans actually spoke.

Berlin's ragtime also reveled in sheer repetition. Taking a cue from his own successful model—where his song's persona had called "Oh, ma honey, oh, ma honey" and exhorted listeners to "Come on and hear, come on and hear"—Berlin's songs for *Watch Your Step* and *Stop! Look! Listen!* habitually begin with a repeated lyric phrase at the beginnings of verses and choruses. Although many of these phrases are not matched with musical syncopation, it was in this period when Berlin made his public statement that explicitly linked textual repetition and musical syncopation: "Syncopation . . . will bear repetition of thought better than other forms. You can repeat 'I love you' a number of times in syncopated measure very effectively, whereas if you used the ordinary forms it would sound simple."[74] And it looks simple on the page.

But the examples below capture the "ragtime" flavor of Berlin's lyric-writing and reveal his keen ear for the requirements of a performance-based craft needing to make immediate impact. (The *continuation* of each song, not shown here, also reveals how he could spin out a song beyond the energy of the opening repetition.) (ex. 2.3).

Contemporaries also heard sheer noise as a weapon in Berlin's ragtime arsenal. Several opening night reviews of *Watch Your Step* remarked on the show's clamorous sound and associated it with ragtime. The *New York World* referred to Berlin as "this virtuoso of syncopation who introduced cow bells, tin pans, squawkers, rattles and other election-night musical instruments into the modern dance orchestra."[75] "Madame Critic" of the *New York Dramatic Mirror* also claimed that opening night was "the noisiest affair I have ever attended," and "there was ragtime enough to satisfy the most ardent enthusiast on the subject."[76] When, in spring 1915, the show moved to London, as so many Berlin shows would do in the decades to come, the London *Observer* likewise called the show a "noisy, cheerful, drum-and-cornet succession of rag-time songs and dances."[77] Commentators also linked ragtime to the pace of the action. Several reviews of *Stop! Look! Listen!*, for example, emphasized its brisk tempo. "'Stop! Look! Listen!' Breaks Speed Limit,"[78] announced one headline, and another described it as a "Rapid Musical Review."[79]

Fast, loud, colloquial, repetitive, and syncopated—such traits supported the impulse behind Berlin's ragtime: to capture in words and music the sound of modern America. Berlin was clear about this point. In a 1915 interview, he insisted, rather combatively, that too many other American composers (who remain nameless in the published article) aim to imitate Europe, whereas, "ignorant as I am, from their standpoints, I'm doing something they all refuse to do: I'm writing American music." And for Berlin at this time, "American music" and ragtime were synonymous.[80]

MERGING GRAND OPERA AND THÉ DANSANT

Berlin's notions of ragtime and the future of American music came into focus within his vision for the stage—and specifically in his ideas for a new form of opera. Through 1913, just before writing his first musical comedy scores, Berlin discussed regularly, and publicly, his plans to write an opera in ragtime. While in London in mid-1913, Berlin told the press that "I am writing an opera in ragtime; the whole of the libretto as well as the music"[81]—a remarkably confident statement by a writer who would be hesitant to write both words and music for Dillingham's show the following year. The London *Morning Post* added to the story by reporting that he aimed to write a "*tragic opera in syncopated time*" (emphasis added).[82] When Berlin returned to the United States, his ambitions also attracted the American press, which noted his desire to "write the big American light opera, and an opera in rag-time, if you please."[83]

For Berlin, it was important not just to write an extended musical theater piece using a syncopated style but to show how syncopation could serve as a foundation for a wide range of emotions. He wanted to liberate ragtime from the assumption that it could convey only happy, lively moods. He explained this in an interview published in the *Dramatic Mirror*, in which he argued that his opera would develop "my

Example 2.3. Repetition as a feature of Berlin's ragtime style.

2.3a. *"Office Hours,"* Watch Your Step.

Of-fice hours,   Of-fice hours—

2.3b. *"The Minstrel Parade,"* Watch Your Step.

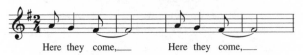

Here they come,___   Here they come,___

2.3c. *"They Always Follow Me Around,"* Watch Your Step.

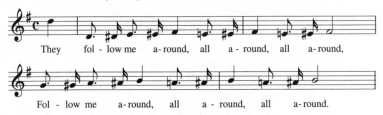

They   fol - low me   a - round, all   a - round, all   a-round,

Fol - low me   a - round,   all   a - round, all   a - round.

2.3d. *"Move Over,"* Watch Your Step.

"Move ov - er,   Move ov- er,   Move ov - er, ov - er,   ov - er.

2.3e. *Act 1 opening,* Stop! Look! Listen!

Show them in here,   Show them in here,   Show them in here, do!

2.3f. *"I Love to Dance,"* Stop! Look! Listen!

I love to   dance,___   I love to dance___

2.3g. *"I Love a Piano,"* Stop! Look! Listen!

I love   a   pian - o,___   I love   a   pian - o._____

idea that beautiful thoughts can best be expressed by syncopation. It alone can catch the sorrow—the pathos—of humanity. That note in ragtime is almost unexplainable—I call it the 'wail' of the syncopated melody."[84] The statement is fascinating not only as a glimpse of Berlin's ragtime aesthetic but also because it reveals his belief that ragtime and opera belong together and that writing a "syncopated" opera would be a worthy ambition. Moreover, it makes an implicit but unmistakable use of the rhetoric with which many commentators would discuss the distinctively Jewish contribution to American music. In his phrase "the 'wail' of the syncopated melody," Berlin joins a common description of Jewish musical expression (the "wail") with a style strongly associated with African Americans. (By the time Berlin was talking about this publicly, Scott Joplin—who was well known as a ragtime composer but not nearly the celebrity that Berlin was—had already written and published his opera *Treemonisha*, which, however, did not aim to be a "ragtime" work and did not reach the stage until the 1970s.)

Berlin's ambition to write a ragtime opera may seem naïve to later generations, but it fit well into contemporaneous notions of the possibilities of opera. Berlin launched his career in an age of operatic populism, a notion promoted by Oscar Hammerstein I in his battle with the elite Metropolitan Opera House, and by the wave of the operatic verismo (or "realism") of Puccini's *La Bohème*, Bizet's *Carmen*, and the popular Italian one-act tragedies—Pietro Mascagni's *Cavalleria Rusticana* and Ruggiero Leoncavallo's *I Pagliacci*—usually presented as a double-bill.[85] The phrase that Hammerstein ascribed to himself—the little man who'll provide grand opera to the masses—might have applied to Berlin as well.[86] So Berlin's notion of writing an opera arose and made sense within Hammerstein's operatic vision. (In 1910, Hammerstein was bought out by the Met, whose board chairman Otto Kahn would publicly declare the possibility of a Berlin opera in the 1920s.[87]) Berlin appears within the immediate context of 1914, and beyond, more than a viable candidate to write such a piece.

The highlight of *Watch Your Step* in many accounts was not a new ragtime song per se, but the second act finale, featuring a "ragtime opera" parody in which Berlin's music and lyrics infuse operatic classics with syncopation and other features of contemporary dance music. Having suffered enough, the "ghost" of Giuseppe Verdi appears (in the person of the tenor Harry Ellis) and condemns the desecration of his music (the famous quartet from *Rigoletto*) and that of his nineteenth-century peers Bizet, Puccini, Gounod, and Leoncavallo. It should be noted that American parodies of nineteenth-century European operas were nothing new. They had roots in blackface minstrelsy and continued in revues and vaudeville, where Berlin himself contributed the pieces that served as models for his *Watch Your Step* act-ender: "Opera Burlesque" and "That Opera Rag." The *New York Dramatic Mirror* critic noted the Berlin difference, however: "as that particular bit of Rigoletto is familiar to almost everybody, since it has so often been murdered in vaudeville and cabaret performances, a ragging was all that it needed to carry it along with other rags into music-loving homes."[88]

Viewed within the larger context of opera in America, *Watch Your Step* gave Berlin a chance to launch a pilot episode of his grand operatic vision. Many critics, in fact, singled out the second act's "ragtime opera" finale, staged in a replica of the Metropolitan

Opera House, as the highlight of the evening. It may not be coincidental that the *Morning Telegraph* critic noted that the "[plot] development is completely lost about the time the characters reach the Metropolitan Opera House." But the critic was not complaining, since he added, "it is well, because by ignoring the story the company is enabled to bring down the curtain on as rousing and as ingeniously an arranged finale as the musical stage of this town has ever known."[89]

The scene does no less than dramatize a conflict between a hallowed European art form (opera) and modern American music and dance in a comic vein that owes much to the minstrel tradition of operatic parodies going back more than half a century. If we are looking for a microcosm of the Berlin-Dillingham theatrical vision of a show-of-shows, we may find it in this number. A typescript page that survives among the show's materials would seem to confirm that notion; at the end of the song appears a revealing phrase in parentheses: "The audience goes wild with enthusiasm. At last society has found the ideal amusement, a combination of grand opera and The [*sic*] Dansant. All join in the final Refrain."[90]

Watch Your Step featured a "ragtime opera" in which the ghost of Giuseppe Verdi appeared, as did operagoers in their boxes. Billy Rose Theatre Division, The New York Public Library for the Performing Arts, Astor, Lenox and Tilden Foundations.

The number appears in three parts. In the first part, five solo singers—different characters from the show—each perform a famous opera melody in the style of some kind of contemporary dance music, each in a different key. The emphasis on the number's "ragtime" quality has been so pervasive that it has obscured the musical variety in this sequence, which includes prominent non-rag passages in waltz and tango style:

Verdi, *Aida*, "Triumphal March," as a rag (Stella) in G major
Puccini, *La Bohème*, "Quando me'n vo," as a hesitation waltz (Ernesta) in E major
Gounod, *Faust*, "Garden Scene," as a maxixe (Algy) in C major
Bizet, *Carmen*, "Votre Toast" (Toreador song), as a tango (Birdie) in E-flat major/ minor
Leoncavallo, *I Pagliacci*, "Vesti la giubba" as a one-step (Chorus) in F major.

A dramatic diminished chord heralds the appearance of Verdi's ghost (in a green spotlight, according to one review[91]). To the tune of the Duke of Mantua's famous melody from the *Rigoletto* quartet, "Verdi" takes the music to a new key, B flat, which bears the same relation to the previous key (F) that the "trio" of a rag or march does to its preceding strain. The following exchange ensues in which "Verdi" (to Verdi's actual music) exhorts the chorus not to "rag" his music, while the chorus answers between phrases in a chastising chatter of responses in a simplified revision of Verdi's original (ex. 2.4). The *Rigoletto* section continues in this manner and rises to a climactic musical shouting match between Verdi, crying out "Please don't," and the

Example 2.4. Watch Your Step, *Act 2 finale, "Old Operas in a New Way (Ragtime Opera Medley)."*

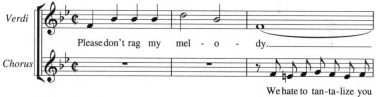

chorus, answering "we will," segueing into quick exchange of "yes" and "no" (shades of the challenge duet "Anything You Can Do" in *Annie Get Your Gun*). In the third and final section, the chorus reprises the "Pagliacci" section in F major, and the orchestra drives to a final cadence, fortissimo and presto.

No wonder the opening night reviews placed more focus on this scene than any other. Not only did the reviews praise the number, they also give glimpses of a fuller picture of the scene than a score, libretto, or photograph alone can provide. They describe a scene in which characters appear on multiple levels, and in which operagoers, shown onstage, claim their seats more for social intercourse than for aesthetic enlightenment. "Verdi" protests "from a balcony." The audience could not care less. Louis Sherwin reported in the *New York Globe* a vivid image of

> the boxes occupied by chattering bored people, some of whom are dancing, some reading the paper, others watching the ticker, telephoning their friends, and otherwise strenuously avoiding the task of listening to the music.[92]

One review notes that some were reading the "war news," a rare reminder that *Watch Your Step* opened just months after Europe (but not yet America) had joined the Great War.[93]

Although clearly a novelty to opening-nighters and critics alike, the staging of audience had precedent in the opening scene of the popular 1909 Weber and Fields musical *The Midnight Sons*.[94] Sherwin's review of *Watch Your Step* even included some dialogue, to show how gossip trumps operatic appreciation among the Met's elite spectators:

> "Were you at the opera last night?" asks one woman.
> "Yes, dear."
> "What did you hear?"
> "I heard the Joneses are getting a divorce."

Louis Sherwin concluded, like many other reviewers, that "the scene is one of the cleverest bits of burlesque that New York has seen in a long while."[95]

Such was the immediate response to the "ragtime opera" that Berlin made a curtain speech, mid-show, at the *end of the act*:

> Slim, young and bashful Irving Berlin . . . was called before the curtain at the end of the second act and compelled to make a speech. He gave the credit to Mr. Dillingham for his splendid production, and he gave the credit to the singers for interpreting his songs so well; but after all it was Mr. Berlin who deserved the honor of speaking for the show.[96]

The audience and critics' response confirmed the scene's importance to Berlin—despite its plot-busting power. Within two weeks of opening night, Berlin recognized the scene's potential as a pilot for his operatic ambitions:

> Isn't there the feeling of a conflict at the end of the second act of "Watch Your Step," when the ghost of Verdi in the stage box protests at the syncopating of his

tunes and there is the alternate "No!" "Yes!" of the chorus and the tenor? There's dramatic value to that music—not much, perhaps, but still enough to suggest what are the possibilities of ragtime.[97]

More than a year later Berlin continued to press this notion by recalling his *Watch Your Step* number, this time emphasizing its seriousness, which clearly escaped audiences and critics at the premiere. Particularly revealing is that, in both statements, he hedges with self-effacing remarks, perhaps anticipating criticism with phrases like "not much, perhaps" and, in the following passage, "the thought was not a great one."

> Syncopation is ordinarily thought of as being comic, but it is not necessarily so. The serious and sentimental can be expressed in terms of syncopation as well as the humorous. In the finale to the first act of "Watch Your Step" I proved that. In that the figure of Verdi appeared and called upon a group of moderns to quit making rags of his masterpieces. The thought was not a great one, but there was an element of seriousness, of pathos, almost, in the ghost of the composer appearing and feeling sad at the treatment his works were receiving.[98]

Berlin explored the scene's "possibilities" further in the act 2 finale in *Stop! Look! Listen!* The show's "Ragtime Melodrama," as it was dubbed, extends for more than twenty-eight pages in the manuscript piano-vocal score for a total of 346 measures, exceeding even *Watch Your Step*'s opera scene, which had also covered more than 300 measures.[99] Unlike the "Ragtime Opera Medley" in *Watch Your Step*, which presented the clash and blend of American dance music and opera but had no real storyline, the melodrama offers a complete plot featuring several stereotyped characters—a "villain," a damsel in distress (the "heroine"), her father, the "hero," a doctor, a police captain, and a chattering chorus.

Critics recognized that Berlin was aiming to recapture the glory of his *Watch Your Step* ragtime opera scene. The "travesty of melodrama, . . ." noted the *Dramatic Mirror*, "is obviously copied after the humorous burlesque of 'Rigoletto' in 'Watch Your Step.'"[100] Still, many critics hailed it as the best thing in the show. *Variety* called it "one of the best laughmakers of the night" and "probably . . . the best thing in comedy ensemble lyric ever written."[101] It conjured "roars of laughter and brought the curtain down to tumultuous applause."[102] Deslys, as the imperiled heroine, drew the most laughs with her French accent. Berlin recalled that on the line, "Just like a cat he crept up those back stairs," Deslys could not help pronouncing "crept" as "crapped." "I could never get her to pronounce the word correctly," Berlin reported, "but it got such a laugh that Dillingham decided to keep it in."[103] Likewise, in the scene's climactic moment, Deslys exclaimed in horror that the villain "has shot my farzer."[104] The father, after being shot to death, rises and dances with the ensemble. Critics and audiences recognized the entire number as a burlesque of stock characters and situations in melodrama. By setting the entire scene to music, however, Berlin gave it continuity and pacing more reminiscent of opera. Much later, however, he dismissed the scene as simply "one of those tapeworms that really wasn't too good."[105]

In the 1910s, *Florodora* still resonated on Broadway, and its famous sextet remained a powerful memory for audiences, critics, and showmen alike. The *Watch Your Step* song "I Love to Have the Boys Around Me" was a case in point. Sung by pretty Elizabeth Brice and featuring an adoring group of "chappies," the song was described by one critic as "almost another 'Florodora' sextet," apparently finding no reason to elaborate on the claim.[106] The critic might well have mentioned the show's opening scene as well. In fact, both of Berlin's Dillingham shows opened with an extended, multisectional ensemble number featuring a *Florodora*-style flirtation between coquettish young women and their suitors.

Florodora's famous sextet itself was not operatic, but Berlin used the model as the basis for long-form musical scenes. In *Watch Your Step*, the curtain opens on a team of secretaries at their typewriters bewailing the stress of having "office hours" after a night of dancing and dining on the town. The scene immediately strikes a distinctively contemporary note: an image of young, single, female middle-class New Yorkers struggling to balance the allure of "steppin' out" and the need to hold a job. They sing about their plight with an oblique reference to another recent popular theater song, "Heaven Will Protect the Working Girl,"[107] which is ironic; whereas the original song had warned of the dangers of New York's nightlife, Berlin's number claims that the working girl's true challenge lies in the workplace:

> In the dizzy business world
> Heaven help the working girl
> After having such a wonderful night.

A matching set of office boys—like the young swains in the famous *Florodora* sextet—enter to dictate a letter, which, as it gradually unfolds, turns out to be a love letter to the secretaries themselves. Then, with characteristic repetition, the boys insist that their love be requited:

> GIRLS: Now will you give me the address?
> BOYS: Address it to yourself, dear.
> GIRLS: This is quite sudden, I confess.
> BOYS: Say yes, say yes, say yes, dear.

By the end of the song, the girls have agreed to marry the boys, and they sing together an onomatopoetic phrase that Berlin would recycle many times (most enduringly in his 1924 torch song waltz, "All Alone") to conjure the sound of bells:

> GIRLS: I can hear the choir singing.
> BOYS: Bells will soon be ringing,
> ALL: Ting-a-ling-a-linging away!

The musical setting features a steady patter of quarter and eighth notes interrupted now and then by the cakewalk figure, an apt musical symbol for the rhythms of contemporary nightlife.

Out of theatrical context, the number looks unremarkable, but it was well designed as an opening scene that established the style and spirit of the show and rooted it firmly in present-day Manhattan. More than that, for a relative novice in the theater, Berlin presents a remarkable demonstration of how to develop a scene musically. For "Office Hours" is far more than a static set piece that establishes the show's mood, style, and look; it forms a microcosm of an entire musical plot: girl meets boy, boy proposes, girl resists then relents, and the wedding is planned. Before the audience's eyes and ears, the scene transforms the modern workplace from a place of business to a place for flirtation and romance.

In *Stop! Look! Listen!* Berlin aimed to recapture the success of *Watch Your Step*'s opening number with another extended musical scene. Again, it occurs in the work-place—this time, the costume shop of the theater. Again, it features a set of chorus girls—not secretaries this time but actual chorus girls. Like "Office Hours" it opens up opportunities for titillation and flirtation. When the costume designers enter, for example, they sing, "I'm simply mad about the color scheme: / The lines bring out your— you know what I mean." The line's *scheme / mean* assonance reveals a rare instance of Berlin writing an end-rhyme that is not a true rhyme. A few moments later, some pages enter with the message that a group of stage-door johnnies want to see the girls. The girls respond with a repeated phrase in the rhythm reminiscent of the "Oh, ma honey" phrase in "Alexander's Ragtime Band": "Show them in here, / Show them in here, / Show them in here, do!" The echo makes it clear that, for Berlin, this scene, with its operatic musical continuity, was meant to have a distinctively ragtime flavor. The boys appear and flirt with the chorus girls, offering to take them for a ride, which the girls resist, as in *Watch Your Step*, with a dash of cakewalk rhythm and a bit of clever quotation from one of Berlin's earlier songs, "Keep Away from the Fellow Who Owns an Automobile" (1912):

Sir, I couldn't go for a ride,
Because I must be careful,
Mother told me,
To keep away from the fellow
Who owns an automobile.[108]

Extending the joke, the lyrics for the girls quote another current song in which romance develops in an automobile in their line about a breakdown requiring the young man "to get out and get under" to fix the car.[109] Despite their misgivings, the girls ultimately agree to "come along"—another echo of *Florodora*'s famous sextet— as they relent in the number's final line:

GIRLS: Good afternoon!
BOYS: Come along, dear.
GIRLS: Good afternoon!
BOYS: Come along, dear;
GIRLS: Good afternoon!
ALL: Goodbye!

As in *Watch Your Step*, the boys and girls finish the scene with a dance. The opening chorus of *Stop! Look! Listen!*, like that of *Watch Your Step*, dramatizes the romantic possibilities of a public venue where women had increasingly prominent professional roles. More than that, it was also a reflexive scene dramatizing life in the theater itself, a glimpse of backstage drama that would have been familiar to the people acting it out. Meanwhile, like an image projected in two facing mirrors, it was a scene that not only stylized real-life events—the stage-door johnnies swarming around the chorus girls with their impressive roadsters—but that represented another variation on the famous *Florodora* sextet, itself a touchstone for the glorification of the chorus girl both on and off stage.

THE ACT 1 FINALES

The end of act 1 was another place where Berlin saw the advantage of placing an extended number. Unlike the "operatic" act 2 finales, these were more clearly based on conventional song forms. *Watch Your Step*'s first act built to a climactic finale called "The Syncopated Walk." Led by the Castles, all the principals come together on stage to describe a "change / In how the people walk these days," because "ever since the dancing craze / Ev'rybody has a syncopated walk."

The number owes much to the ragtime style Berlin developed in earlier songs, with many figures and devices clearly derived from two songs in particular: "Alexander's Ragtime Band" and "Everybody's Doing It Now." Indeed, the song has most of the distinguishing traits of Berlin's ragtime style, with repetitive lyrics, insistent dotted rhythms, modified cakewalk figures, motoric accompanimental riffs, strong bass lines, short punchy melodic phrases coming off strongly accented downbeats— and allusions to and quotations of other songs.

From the beginning of the refrain of "Alexander's Ragtime Band," Berlin derives the opening phrase of the verse of "Syncopated Walk," with its repeated figure of a long tone and dotted-rhythm pickup (reversed from "Alexander") followed by four quarter notes and a long tone. (To get a sense of this rhythm one could sing "Alexander's" opening phrase as "hear, come on and . . .") It continues like its model by rising up by an interval of a fourth and repeating the melodic pattern (ex. 2.5). The refrain of "Syncopated Walk" likewise grows from a short repeated figure that gets restated up a fourth, even though its character—featuring a triplet and a minor mode—otherwise bears little relationship to the ostensible model (ex. 2.6).

From "Everybody's Doing It Now" Berlin copped the title phrase "doin' it" as well as two other devices: the repeated, rising chromatic figure on that phrase (ex. 2.7a-b) and the fourfold, hortatory "Come, come, come, come" phrase sung on a quarter note that repeats over chords with a chromatically shifting inner voice (ex. 2.8a-b). Yet the phrase's continuation is emblematic of how Berlin does not simply repeat himself but takes the ideas in new directions. Also new is an invocation of operetta during the number's climactic passage. When Vernon Castle sings "Come with me" during the duet, the pitches and rhythms echo Herbert's "Gypsy Love Song" (ex. 2.9).

In *Stop! Look! Listen!* Berlin likewise wrote an extended number for the act 1 finale, but here he strings together a sequence of contrasting song styles that express

Example 2.5. "The Syncopated Walk," verse.

Strange, But there's a change___ In how the peo-ple walk these days.___

Yes!___ You must con - fess___ That ev - er since the danc-ing craze

Example 2.6. "The Syncopated Walk," refrain.

Look at 'em do- in' it, Look at 'em do- in' it, That syn-co - pa-ted walk.

Look at'em do- in' it, Look at'em do- in' it, I know who in-tro-duced it.

Example 2.7

2.7a. "Everybody's Doing It Now" (1912).

Ev - 'ry-bo - dy's do - in' it, Do - in' it, do - in' it,

Ev - 'ry-bo - dy's do - in' it, Do - in' it, do - in' it;

2.7b. "The Syncopated Walk."

Let us get start - ed for a syn-co-pa-ted walk. Come a- long, come a-

long, And while we walk— Hum a song, hum a song.

different points of view: different ways that modern New Yorkers like to spend their time, and different kinds of music that they like to listen to. A couple of sections reprise tunes from earlier in the show, an early example of the *reprise finaletto,* a device Berlin would continue to use into the late 1930s.[110] The first section offers a vision of domestic comfort in which the characters express their distaste for "the

Example 2.8

2.8a. *"Everybody's Doing It Now."*

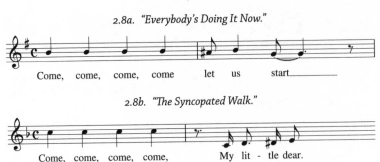

Come, come, come, come let us start_____

2.8b. *"The Syncopated Walk."*

Come, come, come, come, My lit - tle dear.

Example 2.9. *"The Syncopated Walk," quoting "Gypsy Love Song."*

Mr. C.

Come with me_____

Mrs. C.

Don't you he-si-tate, Let us syn-co-pate. What-'ll we do, what-'ll we do?

cabaret throng" in a waltz style. The second section is a romantic song adopting the clichéd romantic spoon-moon motif. In the third section, a character professes disinterest in the movies while singing that he would "rather be list'ning to Sousa." The fourth section counters that view with a celebration of the movies to the tune of "I Love a Piano," a rag-like song heard earlier in the show to great effect. The final section brings together the chorus members in a reprise of "I Love to Dance," reinforcing the show's main theme with a sly reference to Vernon Castle himself in the lyrics. Each section is sung by a different character or characters, suggesting a successive counterpoint of musical and social tastes—an impulse that would find expression in another kind of song that audiences greeted enthusiastically from 1914 to the end of Berlin's career.

SONGS IN COUNTERPOINT

Indeed, Berlin's operatic ambitions had yet another outlet. Opera appealed to his theatrical vision in two ways: it allowed music to carry the action for extended sequences, as in the opening scenes and the act 2 finales, and it provided models for representing contrary points of view simultaneously. In that spirit, Berlin's first musical comedies introduced a new kind of song in which two contrasting melodies first appear separately in succession and then together in counterpoint.

Berlin's opera parodies are themselves incipient exercises in counterpoint songs. In *Watch Your Step*, Berlin's rapid-fire choral patter stands in dialogue with—and in contrast to—Verdi's lyrical *Rigoletto* melody. But the two melodies have little substantive overlap; the choral chatter mostly fits *in between* Verdi's phrases. Part of the unique appeal of the counterpoint songs is the way in which the two opposing voices present important melodic phrases at the same time.

In *Watch Your Step*, Berlin created such a song, titled "Simple Melody," which, like the opera parody, offers a conflict between musical styles. But the conflict presents a paradox, since at the same time that Berlin's lyrics claim stylistic incompatibility, his music exhibits a perfect match: the melodies interlock over a shared harmonic foundation. The first phrase gives a glimpse of Berlin's dialogic method in a number for the characters Algy and Ernesta (ex. 2.10). Algy echoes Ernesta's question "won't you play . . ." but fits in his request before she completes hers. There is a further conflict in these lyrics. Ernesta's verse contrasts songs of "nowadays"—the "spoony rags and coony drags"—with "dear old songs" of her mother's era. Algy's song, however, does not address such songs but rather contrasts "long-haired musicians with their classy melodies" and "high-toned ambitions" with "something snappy and popular the kind that darkies play." Although both associate ragtime with African Americans—in the period's common parlance of "coon songs" and "darkies"—only Algy invokes classical music. So, as the musicologist Larry Hamberlin points out, the argument is "asymmetrical," because one favors ragtime and the other does not, and the styles against which ragtime are contrasted differ.[111]

Adding to the song's impact, the production divided the chorus between the two melodies and staged what critic Charles Darnton called a "sentimental competition" in which the chorus girls sang with Algy (Charles King) and the chorus boys sang with Ernesta (Sallie Fisher). Next to the opera parody, the critic Burns Mantle found

Example 2.10. "Simple Melody."

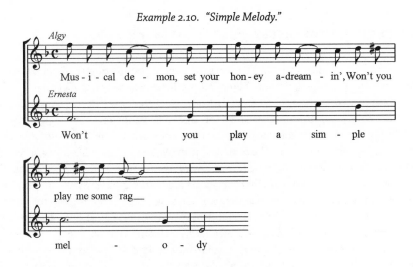

the choral division for "Simple Melody" to be "one of the cleverest things the young composer has done."[112]

In a book on the ways in which opera inflected American popular song, Hamberlin views this piece as emblematic of nothing less than the "paradoxical condition of America's musical life early in the twentieth century":

> Although the lyrics describe irreconcilable differences, the music says that those differences are merely surface features of an underlying unity. Berlin the lyricist portrays Americans whose tastes are divided along class and racial lines; Berlin the composer paints a picture of inclusive musical pluralism.[113]

Heeding the numbers that made a hit in *Watch Your Step*, Berlin wrote another counterpoint song for *Stop! Look! Listen!* Titled "When I Get Back to the U.S.A.," it was performed on an ocean liner set to bring the characters back to New York after their Hawai'ian adventure (this being decades before Hawai'i would become part of the United States). Joseph Santley, who sang it, played the role of Van Cortland Parke (after Van Cortlandt Park in the Bronx, another one of the script's punning names) described in the script as a man "who wants to do people good." He is really the Prince to Deslys's Cinderella. Berlin sets his sprightly melody against "America" ("My Country 'tis of Thee"), sung in long tones by the ensemble. If this number lacked the impact of "Simple Melody," it may have been because the fundamental musical and cultural opposition, between modern ragtime and old-fashioned ballad, was missing. One reviewer seems to have recognized a similarity to the theatrical context and lyric-writing style of "Yankee Doodle Boy" and "Give My Regards to Broadway," and claimed the song was "calculated to make George M. Cohan bitterly envious."[114] Yet few other critics mentioned the song, as they were preoccupied with Gaby Deslys and her hats. When they discussed the music, they gravitated to the "Ragtime Melodrama" and a few other numbers, including minstrel songs and a "girl" song that would become one of Berlin's early show hits.

BLACKFACE, MINSTRELSY, PRETTY GIRLS, AND OPERETTA

Blackface performance and minstrelsy are overlapping but distinctive modes of theater, and they both appear in the Dillingham-Berlin shows. In *Watch Your Step*, Frank Tinney appeared, and reappeared, in blackface in several different roles, including a Pullman porter, a coat-room boy, and a carriage caller at the opera. (The chameleon comic playing multiple roles would become a standard feature of 1920s musical comedy.) In *Stop! Look! Listen!* the comedy duo of Doyle and Dixon likewise appear in several different roles, using blackface at key moments such as their number titled "An Ordinary Pair of Coons." That song's strange, and apparently comic, conceit rested on the notion that because the two characters represented "a race of dusky face / And kinky, inky hair," they could pass as natives of almost any place in the world whose population has "dark-brown face," including Hawai'i, Argentina, India, and "Araby." Yet once in Arabia, they "tried to pass and failed; . . . / And soon we both were jailed"—only to be released by a jailer who happened to be from Georgia, and "that was southern hospitality." Blackface here serves both as mask and as passport to global citizenship.

Watch Your Step also included an entire minstrel number, "The Minstrel Parade." None of the critics mention blackface in this number, but it almost certainly featured at least some blacked-up performers. But makeup did not define the scene's debt to minstrelsy, which lay chiefly in the stage picture, the musical number, and several other features. A Detroit critic recognized the emblematic staging, with "the gorgeously dressed chorus [in] the half-circle of a regulation first part." "Jolly Elizabeth Murray," the Detroit reviewer continued, sings the song "while the men work the tambourines and bones on the end."[115] In the London production, the "infectious and exhilarating" minstrel scene—with its "extremely funny corner men" and "the excited chorusing and tambourining of numerous male and female visitors in the wildest Futurist costumes"—was encored "half a dozen times"[116] and "literally brings down the house."[117]

The song is a kind of Berlin rag number. Like "Alexander's Ragtime Band," it is sung from the perspective of an enthusiastic observer, and the refrain's opening line ("here they come, here they come") repeats a short, syncopated phrase related to the cakewalk figure (ex. 2.11). Between those phrases appears an energetic triplet fill with a resemblance to such figures in "The Syncopated Walk" and Berlin's later "jazz" song, "Everybody Step." Such details are consequential in that they reveal how in Berlin's mind ragtime and jazz bore a family relationship to minstrelsy.

Far from minstrelsy stood "The Girl on the Magazine" (sometimes "The Girl on the Magazine Cover"), Berlin's first attempt at a number referred to in the business as a "girlie song." It featured a male ballad singer and a select group of chorus girls linked thematically by the song's lyrics. In this case, the girls each represented the cover girl of one issue of a quarterly publication. Thus they were dubbed the "Four Seasons" and wore seasonally appropriate attire for spring, summer, autumn, and

Example 2.11

2.11a. "The Minstrel Parade," accompanimental texture.

2.11b. "The Syncopated Walk," accompanimental texture.

winter. (In this quartet of beauties, Marion Davies, as Summer and still a teenager in 1914, would go on to fame as a movie star and longtime mistress of William Randolph Hearst.) In the music, like its more famous successor, "A Pretty Girl Is Like a Melody," the refrain begins with three pickups to a long note supported by dainty figuration in the accompaniment (ex. 2.12). And as in "A Pretty Girl" its bridge spins a gently gliding phrase based on the cakewalk rhythm—a rhythm so transformed by its genteel context that its ragtime roots are almost inaudible (see chap. 1, ex. 1.2a). The song lived a long life beyond the show and would reappear in Berlin's 1948 film, *Easter Parade*.

Yet another song style with no connection to minstrelsy or ragtime plays a role in Berlin's early shows. Early in *Watch Your Step*, the ingénue Ernesta sings a number that sounds imported from operetta. The song "What Is Love?" is a romantic waltz, one of the stock-in-trade styles of American and Viennese operetta. Ernesta apostrophizes Love as an elusive force whose "hidden face" lurks in a "hiding place" and thus remains "wrapped in your mantle of mystery," as she sings in the first verse. The refrain offers a series of questions growing from the title phrase, leading to rhyming sequences such as "Is it gladness? Or a form of sadness? / Or a sign of madness?" and "I keep guessing whether it's a blessing / Or a thing distressing." As in operetta-style waltzes by Victor Herbert such as "Kiss Me Again" (*Mlle. Modiste*, 1905), for example, and as in Jerome Kern's later "You Are Love" (*Show Boat*, 1927), chromatic neighbor notes appear on downbeats, offering poignant if fleeting dissonances against the supporting harmony, as in the opening phrase (ex. 2.13). For the sake of a rhyme, Berlin even includes a touch of the archaic diction ("thee") favored in operetta but long gone from the new American song styles typically heard on Tin Pan Alley and Broadway, as in the second verse:

> Love, love, / Out of the darkness, I call to thee;
> Won't you let me see what you hold for me?

Such language, along with its music, sets the song off from the musical landscape around it, suggesting again how, in the 1910s, Berlin was striving to create an unusually inclusive musical theater style.

Example 2.12. "The Girl on the Magazine," beginning of refrain.

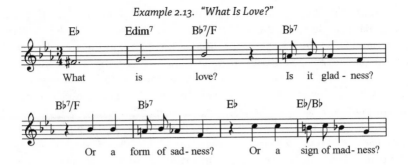

Example 2.13. "What Is Love?"

GENRE IMPLICATIONS

The American musical theater milieu that Berlin entered in 1914 comprised a kind of lawless Wild West in which some shows were sui generis. Gerald Bordman aptly notes that we "[cannot] always classify the period's musicals with total assurance," and that the period's shows often "cavalierly" mix styles.[118] Whereas that observation hits a keynote of the era, it also obscures the possibility that the shows' creators may have deliberately wished to resist classification. Interestingly, in a book called *American Musical Comedy*, Bordman does not even mention Berlin's Dillingham shows. Yet in a paradox emblematic of the period about which he writes, Bordman does mention them in his book about the revue, where he refers to *Watch Your Step* as a show that "must probably go down in the books as musical comedy."[119] Adding to the confusion is none other than Leonard Bernstein. In *his* statement about "American musical comedy," Bernstein famously referred to *Watch Your Step* as an "unforgettable revue"—"unforgettable," although it appeared before his birth.[120] (It is not hard to imagine Bernstein's first musical comedy, *On the Town*, as a wartime update of *Watch Your Step*.)

Watch Your Step epitomized its era, and few critics, even then, could settle on how it might be most aptly labeled. Perhaps it did not matter. The terminological ambiguity that began during the pre-show publicity continued during the out-of-town tryout in Syracuse, and it can be summed up in one sentence of *Variety's* commentary, which referred to the show as "a musical comedy classed as a 'review.'"[121] At least two New York City reviews invoked specific comparisons with the *Ziegfeld Follies*, partly at least because *Watch Your Step* was produced in the New Amsterdam Theatre, where the *Follies* had begun to play annually (and on whose roof, a midnight show regularly played). "Even the most novel of the famous Follies presented in this theatre," claimed the *New York Telegram*, "seems to pale before the glowing, rhythmic vitality of 'Watch Your Step.'"[122] The *Morning Telegraph* noted that the show is "built somewhat upon the lines of the 'Ziegfeld Follies' without any palpable imitation thereof."[123] Neither review elaborated on the claim.

Meanwhile, a local Syracuse paper, noting that the show "starts out with a story," highlighted the show's vaudevillian elements.[124] Reviews of opening night hardly settled the matter. The *New York World* referred both to the Berlin's "musical comedy score" and to the whole show as "a huge vaudeville entertainment."[125] Another critic, Charles Darnton, described the show as "very cleverly" combining "George M. Cohan and vaudeville."[126] The *Sun*, perhaps reflecting the impact of the second-act finale, called the entire show "Mr. Berlin's ragtime opera."[127] And in the most genre-bending discussion of all, in the course of a single article, the *New York Times* used five different terms to define the show: "revue," "musical comedy," "syncopated musical show," "vaudeville done handsomely," and "a large and expensive variety show."[128] Likewise, *Stop! Look! Listen!* was baptized in the press as "a great big bouncing musical comedy that is just vaudeville grown grand."[129] And there is yet one more genre label that has attached to these shows. In a richly informed account of the period, Armond Fields and L. Marc Fields refer to *Watch Your Step* as "one of the direct descendants of the musical burlesque-cum-revues" of Lew Fields and Joe Weber.[130] Indeed the phrase "glorified vaudeville," with which one critic had described the Weber and Fields show *The Midnight Sons*, would also be a perfect fit for Berlin's Dillingham shows.[131]

This can be called genre *confusion* only in retrospect; it would be better to call it genre *profusion*. The shows met the criterion for revues by addressing contemporary themes, personalities, and show business. The shows met the criteria for musical comedy not because they had scripts (at least partial ones) but because they literally used music in a prevailingly comic context where plot regularly gave way to deliberate interruption. The shows were also a kind of all-star vaudeville, as reviews repeatedly recognized. And they featured numbers that explicitly tapped (and parodied) other theatrical conventions, including opera, operetta, and minstrelsy, and set them against one another in a pointed debate that ultimately conveyed the message that all could co-exist and remain viable. Berlin and his collaborators relished this approach because it was bigger than anything and ruled out nothing. Broadway musicals would soon become more interested in storytelling and character development, and their songs would reveal a more consistently high level of craftsmanship, but one would be hard pressed to find a theatrical style flexing its muscles and testing its boundaries more boldly than the American musical theater of the 1910s. The omnivorous impulse that inspired Berlin's diverse early song catalog had now found its realization on stage, and it helped to make "legitimate" the merger of a variety of contrasting, even conflicting, musical and theatrical styles from which American musical theater would draw for decades to come.

3

BERLIN'S FOLLIES, 1918–19

• • •

The best I have ever produced.
—*Florenz Ziegfeld, on the 1919* Follies

The omnivorous theatrical style of the Dillingham shows informed Berlin's revues in the years ahead, and that emerges clearly in his next two important projects: the soldier revue *Yip Yip Yaphank* and the *Ziegfeld Follies of 1919*. *Yip Yip Yaphank* reached the stage toward the end of the Great War and gave Berlin a taste of total control of show from the ground up—from initial conception to producing, writing, and performing—but the talent was limited to the soldiers in his army camp. The *Follies* presented an entirely different scenario. For it, Berlin wrote musical numbers to order, yet his work flourished under the particular demands and values of the producer Florenz Ziegfeld. In both shows Berlin found creative freedom under tight restrictions imposed by external circumstances—something that would shape his work hereafter. Both shows, too, inspired superlatives from observers. Together the two shows established musical numbers, and number types, that would become canonic in Berlin's theatrical style (and be re-created in movies), and they set the stage for an even more ambitious revue project in the 1920s.

"A MILITARY MESS"

Berlin became a U.S. citizen on February 6, 1918, and he was drafted into the army soon thereafter, just shy of his thirtieth birthday. He was stationed at Camp Upton, in Yaphank, Long Island. As he reported later, he hated many aspects of army life, especially reveille. But as Berlin had done before, he was able to turn deprivation into opportunity and convinced his commanding officer that he could best realize his patriotic duty by writing a camp show featuring the soldiers around him. For that he was given the rank of sergeant—and the right to sleep as late as he wished.

    Yip Yip Yaphank,[1] conceived and developed at Camp Upton in the summer of 1918, established the style and structure of a show that he would create for the second war, and his catalyst was the challenge of fusing army content with show business conventions. Hatched in the heyday of the revue, the World War I show reflected the revue's impulse to adopt and parody aspects of current music and theater, while being unified around a central topical theme: the U.S. Army and the common soldier's experience. In this show Berlin discovered the musical theater in army life.

Billed as "A Military 'Mess' Cooked up by the Boys of Camp Upton (In Aid of the Fund to Establish a Community House at Camp Upton For the Wives, Mothers, and Sweethearts Who Visit Their Boys at Camp),"[2] *Yip Yip Yaphank* ran for just thirty-two performances at two different theaters: the Century (Aug. 19–31, 1918) and the Lexington (Sept. 2–14, 1918). Although a brief stint by Broadway standards, it actually had to be extended from the limited eight-performance run that had been planned.[3] This was a remarkable achievement for a show in the Century Theatre, a massive house with more than 2,300 seats. The show succeeded beyond expectation—earning a reported $50,000 from its packed houses by September 1—and had to be moved because the Century was scheduled to host a popular Al Jolson vehicle called *Sinbad* that had moved there from the Winter Garden.[4] Sime Silverman of *Variety*, after witnessing opening night and the "admiration" of the "over-seasoned Broadwayites" in the theater, predicted that the show could run for "a couple of months."[5] The *New York Times* likewise mused, after reflecting on the opening-week crowds, that the show "probably could go ahead for seven or eight more [weeks] if the members of its cast were not required to become soldiers again."[6]

The show had come together quickly. Berlin's inscription on the bound manuscript piano-vocal score indicates that it was written in August 1918, and most of the copyright dates of the show's numbers share that date.[7] There are at least three exceptions that point to a longer development. The opening number ("We Live at Upton") was written "on or just before May 10, 1918."[8] The show's big hit "Oh! How I Hate to Get Up in the Morning," bears a copyright date of July 23, 1918; and "Kitchen Police (Poor Little Me)" was introduced in the *Ziegfeld Follies*, which had opened in June. The cast and crew moved to Manhattan during dress rehearsals. Every day they marched in formation from their quarters to the theater, which Berlin surely knew would drum up interest in the show the way a minstrel parade did.[9] And when the show opened, guards stood near the entrance to impart the aura of an official military function, but as *Variety* reported, the guards made a point of smiling. The spectacle on the street, then, broadcast the show's savvy synthesis of military protocol and musical theater.

Military camp shows were nothing new. Indeed, thousands of soldiers created and performed in ad hoc minstrel shows, vaudevilles, revues, and musical comedies in both wars.[10] But for the most part such shows never went beyond their home camps. The notion of staging a soldier show on Broadway required an imaginative leap, for it would be inevitably compared with the genre's paradigms. Indeed, an all-soldier revue might have seemed a contradiction in terms in the genre's heyday. Unlike most revues, notably the *Ziegfeld Follies*, about which the show features an entire number, *Yaphank* could not depend on stars or feminine display. Yet the *New York Times* viewed that as an "immeasurable advantage over the commercial musical show, for the fact that it is being played by men in service can never be lost sight of."[11] Moreover, two shows staged earlier in 1918 had paved the way for Berlin's undertaking: a musical comedy called *Good-Bye, Bill*, created and performed by the U.S. Army Ambulance Corps, and *Biff-Bang!*, a revue staged by the Pelham (New York) Naval Training Camp.[12] Both shows received strong reviews, and the *Times* even went so far as to claim in spring 1918—in a report that might well have spurred Berlin's vision—that "these 'service' shows . . . are the high spot in the past year of musical entertainment."[13] Still, most of Berlin's cast members were amateurs. Sime Silverman noted with awe that "of all these 350 boys not over 20 ever appeared on the professional stage before. . . . It's only show people who can fully appreciate what that means."[14]

The *Yaphank* cast members were amateurs in more than theater. They were young recruits and had never seen combat. The servicemen were thus performing multiple roles at once: civilians acting as soldiers, and soldiers acting like many other people. Indeed, much of the show's impact and humor depended on masquerade. With its all-male, all-white (with a notable exception), and mostly amateur cast, Berlin's show opened up opportunities for the performers to act like anyone but who they were: white women, black men, black women, black children, and celebrities, both male and female. Some of the privates impersonated officers, and Berlin—a real celebrity who had been made an officer—got to portray a lowly private in one of the scenes that audiences found most humorous and memorable.

The masquerading took forms familiar to theatergoers, for the show parodied show business and musical clichés at every turn. The first several scenes and musical numbers comprised the first act of a minstrel show. Nearly three hundred soldiers sat on steep risers in conventional minstrel-show fashion. A sergeant played the role of interlocutor, the master of ceremonies who moves the show along, announces individual performances, and banters with the end men—the wisecracking privates seated on the stage at either end of the risers. (Only the end men appeared in blackface; the rest of the soldiers were "in the conventional khaki."[15]) In the beginning the sergeant-interlocutor calls the troops/troupe to attention. A captain enters and delivers a rousing speech, telling the soldier-actors that their "enemies" were in front "and to show them no quarter," according to Silverman, who wrote an unusually detailed account of the show that helps to clarify what happened on stage.[16] Silverman failed to note that, by equating the audience with the "enemy," the show played off of the theatrical slang that a successful performance is one that "kills."

Silverman reported a typical comic exchange that bridged military and theatrical impulses. The comedian Bobby Higgins had been trying to tell a joke, wrote Silverman, "but could not secure permission."

> When finally allowed, it was: "Why are the legitimate theatres losing business to the picture houses?" "Because," said Mr. Higgins, "it is easier to fil-um." For that he was ordered before a court martial. When told he would be shot at four in the morning, Higgins replied he did not get up that early. And again, for that one, he was ordered executed immediately.

Higgins won a reprieve, apparently, because he then sang a song. The scene encapsulated an ingenious merger of minstrel-show repartee and military regimentation.

The musical numbers also took off from minstrel conventions. A "Tambourine Drill" exhibited some fancy work with one of minstrelsy's stock instruments instead of rifles, demonstrating the company's collective choreographic precision. For it, Berlin wrote a vigorous, syncopated march tune that he would strategically spot twice more in the show—the last time with words for the stirring grand finale. As in a typical minstrel-show first part, a quartet sang a sentimental old favorite in four-part harmony, with Berlin changing the words to suit the occasion, like many minstrel lyricists before him. The song was the nineteenth-century parlor ballad "Silver Threads among the Gold," about growing old and gray in an enduring romance. Berlin wrote: "Darling I am not too old; / I am only twenty-three. / There's no silver 'mongst the gold, / And the draft is after me." The number went over so well with the opening-night audience that the quartet repeated it several times, according to Silverman.

A courtship number ("Mandy [Sterling Silver Moon]") and a wedding number ("Ding Dong") also made predictable appearances, allowing for the minstrel show's double masquerade of blackfaced white men in drag.[17] Accounts of the show sometimes conflate the two numbers, but "Mandy" featured lyrics, melody, and performers distinct from the later wedding song "Ding Dong." In "Mandy" the singer hears a "familiar tune" sung by a young suitor to his would-be bride: "My pretty Mandy, / Don't you know the parson is handy, / Come and talk it over with Andy / Neath the sterling silver moon." The comedian Danny Healy played Mandy as a dozen other men portrayed "girls" and "boys" in the chorus. The "girls" are described in the program as "pickaninnies," theatrical lingo for little black girls often sporting stiff, Topsy-style braids sticking out from the head in all directions.[18] In the wedding scene, Bobby Higgins—having avoided execution in the previous scene—sang "Ding Dong" with a chorus, while "real colored picks" (not blacked-up men in drag) as Silverman put it, held up the bride's train. (The bride was played by Private Howard Friend—who won claim to fame as the soldier who earned the dedication of "Oh! How I Hate to Get Up in the Morning" because he occupied the cot next to Berlin's at Camp Upton.[19]) The appearance of "real" African Americans—three boys and one girl—must have come as a surprise to the audience led to expect an all-white-male show.[20] More than that, two critics singled out the little girl for special praise. Silverman noted that she won "a riot of applause with her mannerisms and sense of rhythm." And *Theatre Magazine* made the racially pointed observation that "the only real lady in the cast [was] a colored baby-vampire, who acted as flower-girl, and fairly stopped proceedings with a pair of eyes that would be worth a million dollars in the movies if they were topped with Pickford curls instead of Topsy pigtails."[21] The final section of the song, featuring the wedding vows, forms a three-way musical dialogue among the minister, the bride, and the groom, with the groom in a hurry to get to the end, where he sings: "And now I'll kiss the bride." It remains unclear whether the two men then proceeded to kiss, but that was clearly the line's comic implication. Either way, "Ding Dong" struck Silverman as one of the three from the show that "will be popular hits." (That it actually enjoyed only modest success beyond the show only serves to suggest its effectiveness on stage.)

Between the courtship and wedding numbers Berlin inserted a musical number that put a contemporary spin on another old minstrel cliché. In "The Ragtime Razor Brigade" Berlin tapped into a well of late-nineteenth century imagery connected with so-called coon songs—a stage stereotype of the aggressive razor-wielding black bully—while updating it for a time when African American troops had seen combat in modern war. The song avoids the stage dialect spellings common to such songs, perhaps because the refrain presents the words of an officer giving the orders, but its pairing of the terms *ragtime* and *razor* in the context of a minstrel-show sequence leaves no doubt about its racial implications. These troops, the song offers, leave their guns behind and do their most effective work with the "blade" that makes "those German lads afraid," for when they meet the "Hun," they "cut off his retreat" (a suggestive line reminiscent of the phrase "amputate his reveille" in Berlin's already-popular "Oh! How I Hate to Get Up in the Morning"). Silverman described it as a "comedy scene, with . . . a lively melody."

The minstrel sequence also offered two topical songs that link soldier and civilian interests. In "What a Difference a Uniform Will Make," a soldier relates how an army uniform has increased his romantic possibilities in an early exemplar of a Berlin song in which clothes make the man: "Before the war they never noticed me, / But now I've got 'em sitting on my knee—/ Isn't it wonderful, simply remarkable, / What a uniform will do?"[22] The principal melody features a slinky chromatic descent with a slightly syncopated lilt—an astute mix of lust and levity. Silverman reported that the singer, Private Hughie L. Clark won "a big chunk of applause for himself," "especially" in this number.

Another topical number, "Bevo," focused on the closest thing to alcohol that a soldier could drink during wartime. Here is a perfect example of Berlin's knack for zeroing in on a current topic that both soldiers and civilians could laugh about. Bevo was a nonalcoholic malt beverage introduced by Anheuser-Busch after the U.S. armed forces prohibited alcoholic beverages in 1916. It was probably the most widely known of many such drinks called "cereal beverages" and "near beer" that were on the market in the wartime period, as breweries came to grips with the inevitability of Prohibition.[23] Anheuser-Busch advertised Bevo widely and prominently in newspapers, targeting both the civilian family and the military as potential customers with emphasis on the drink's versatility and its "wholesomeness." One ad called Bevo a beverage that "has found a welcome place in the home. A family beverage . . . that goes perfectly with all food. . . . Pure, wholesome and nutritious."[24] Another ad, featuring a soldier carrying a rifle and walking between boxes of Bevo, emphasized that Bevo was "a beverage for the boys in khaki." The ad continued: "After a drill or a march, you are sure to see a long line of hot and dusty-throated soldier boys making a bee-line for Bevo. They know that there lies complete satisfaction, full refreshment and pure wholesomeness."[25] The key word in both ads was *wholesome*, for both civilian and soldier, and that opened up a window for Berlin's amiable musical sarcasm.

The song offers up a new kind of drinking song, for Berlin's lyrics constitute a kind of anti-advertisement. The song's verse creates a list of tame things: "a vicious looking dog that wouldn't bite," "a dangerous looking man who couldn't fight," and then sets up the refrain with the lines:

My brother has wild animals, / But they were really tame;
And I have tasted of a drink / That strikes me just the same.

The chorus then focuses on the drink itself as "the only drink that a soldier can pick" and addresses Bevo itself: "You taste like lager, but you haven't got the kick." The second refrain offers the backhanded compliment that Bevo is "the grandest imitation that we know," and, playing on the phrase *near beer*, it continues: "You may be near it but you ain't near enough." The song would appear again in the 1919 *Follies*, but the main phrase of its chorus had even greater staying power. Berlin recycled it in two songs that would become much better known: the patter melody of "Everybody Step," and a phrase from "God Bless America" (ex. 3.1). "Bevo" represents a rare early example of product placement.[26] With Prohibition on the horizon,

Anheuser-Busch surely understood that any publicity was good publicity, and the company reportedly offered Berlin $10,000 for this particular "advertisement." Berlin donated the money to help build Camp Upton's Community House.[27]

The minstrel sequence excited the opening night crowd. While noting lapses of memory and nerve among the performers, Silverman raved about it and its impact on the audience. "In the opening scene, a minstrel first part, 277 were on stage at the finale—and not a miss. . . . The unison . . . was near perfection. 'Bones' and 'banjos' always in accord without a blemish. There were 32 'bones' in the front line and the 'banjos' extended high up into the flies almost." Every individual act within the minstrel show earned his praise. The audience, which included "army and navy dignitaries" as well as celebrities such as Al Jolson, Irene Castle, and George M. Cohan, was also demonstrative.[28] During the minstrel sequence, Silverman perceived a shift in the audience's collective attitude, from benevolent tolerance to true enjoyment:

> [T]he first part woke up the house. Their early attitude of forebearance [sic] because "it's for the Service" gave way to pleasure, then admiration, and as the show progressed the house realized it was watching one of the best and most novel entertainments Broadway has ever witnessed.

That Silverman could claim that a revue with a prominent and extended minstrel-show component could be one of the "most novel" Broadway shows may seem hyperbolic. But it is more understandable if we consider the fundamental creative insight, a fundamentally American one, embodied in the show's opening scene: the realization that the army and the minstrel show shared several qualities. Both were all-male preserves, and both required their members to be highly trained and operate with precision as a collective body. Both, moreover, depended on a rigid hierarchy that featured a single man in charge of concerted action; the minstrel show's interlocutor is an officer leading the men through a show. The end men and other comedians drawn from the ensemble are the common soldiers who make jokes within a system in which they must perform their jobs on orders.

Example 3.1. Similar phrases in "Bevo" (top staff) and "God Bless America" (bottom staff).

Act 1 featured four more numbers, all of which took off from current musical theater tropes while adhering to the army theme. When the curtain closed on the minstrel sequence, a pair of song-and-dance "Page Boys" emerged for a sequence that offered a series of diversions while the scene changed behind them. The scene functioned in the spirit of the minstrel show's olio (and of vaudeville)—a mini-variety show, played in front of the curtain. This particular olio featured a cyclist imitating the vaudevillian Joe Jackson (known for his bicycling clown act), a juggler, and a troupe of acrobats. The difference is that these performers break the theater's fourth wall, directly address the audience, and openly admit the scene's purpose: "Ladies and Gentlemen, / In a revue ev'ry now and then / It's necessary to change the scene—/ You know very well what I mean." Before the acrobats appear, the Page Boys explain that the reason the scene change is taking so long is that some of the soldiers must effect a double transformation for the ensuing number, from black-faced men to white "ladies":

Ladies and Gentlemen,
Some of the boys must appear again,
Dressed up like ladies, and that's some job—
They were part of the minstrel mob.
Changing from black to white
Isn't a cinch if you do it right;
So while they don their skirts and hats,
We'll introduce a troupe of acrobats.

The "ladies" who appeared in the ensuing scene presented a parody of the *Florodora* sextet, whose memory had persisted in Broadway legend since its premiere in 1900. (In two years, Broadway would see a revival of *Florodora* along with another parody of it in the 1920 *Ziegfeld Follies* to mark the twentieth anniversary of its premiere.) In Berlin's hands, the number becomes a reflexive commentary on the proliferation of *Florodora* numbers in the theater (to which Berlin himself had added in his first two musical comedies) and on the awkwardness of rough-hewn men dressed as dainty ladies: "It's a terrible job to be a dame, / . . . Before it's over / We will all be lame. / For we've been rehearsing nightly, / And it has been no cinch, / We're squeezed in corsets tightly, / And lordy how they pinch!" It continues like a roll call in which each of four "Girls" steps forward to introduce himself and to explain his usual (manly) job—plumber, printer, stoker, and longshoreman—in an incongruous waltz. Several "Boys" then enter and flirt with them, as they all sing in dialogue, culminating in the famous *Florodora* phrase "Come along, come along, come along," to which they add in Berlin's reflexive poke: "That's all they ever say in this kind of a song." Silverman named this number among the ones he believed would become popular. The *New York Times* referred to the scene as "one long laugh" since "no one can forget that these chorus maidens are soldiers."[29]

The next number brought out a "couple" to comment on yet another Broadway cliché: the "love interest." Like the *Florodora* number, the song comprises a reflexive send-up of the clichés of its type. In the verse, the "boy" offers an almost clinical description of the song and its role in a conventional musical comedy:

You and I are very important
In a musical play,
For we represent the love int'rest,
As the managers say.
It's very necessary
To have a sweet melodious lay
For the boy and girl in the plot;
It always helps a lot
To have them sing
A pretty thing
Of which the chorus goes this way:

The refrain, shifting to waltz time, offers a string of clichés, from its straightforward declaration ("I love you"), to a spelling for coy emphasis ("Y-O-U"), to the "cozy spot" where the couple will "bill and coo." Bobby Higgins (the comedian who had almost been "executed" before singing "Ding Dong" in the wedding scene) played the role of the "dame," and the number "got over easily," according to Silverman.

The act 1 finale, "Send a Lot of Jazz Bands over There" merged the country's newly exportable musical style and its army's mission. The past year of 1917–18 had seen Tin Pan Alley's eager embrace of all things jazz not long after the Original Dixieland Jazz Band's appearances at Reisenweber's restaurant on West Fifty-eighth Street, in early 1917. Berlin, as usual, had been among the first songwriters to embrace the jazz fad, with his summer 1917 publication of "Mr. Jazz Himself."[30] Berlin's act 1 finale also played on current Broadway trends. Silverman called it a "Jazzland number" that featured "the words and music costumes [sic] from several of the shows that have employed that scheme." What was the "scheme" and what other shows employed it? Silverman does not say, but he may be referring to the *Ziegfeld Follies*. As early as 1914, the act 1 finale of the *Follies* had featured A. Seymour Brown's number "When the Ragtime Army Goes Away to War."[31] Much closer at hand was the 1918 *Follies*, whose finale featured a spectacular ensemble number called "I Want to Learn to Jazz Dance," which Sime Silverman himself had reviewed just two months earlier.[32] *The Passing Show of 1918*, which had just opened on July 25, also featured an elaborate finale for large ensemble called "Trombone Jazz."[33]

It seems quite possible that Berlin's act 1 finale was an extended number that included a medley of other songs—as suggested in a line of his refrain: "make 'em play a lot of snappy airs." Certainly the scene's spectacle invited a much longer musical exhibition than the song's verse and chorus indicate. Silverman reported that "it finished off with the drops going up showing a dozen or more pianos and players perched up on a high platform, and made a striking spectacle," a description that matches a photograph of the scene that appeared in *Theatre Magazine*, above the caption: "The 'Yip, Yip, Yaphank' boys all together for the super jazz band ensemble."[34] The photograph also helps to demystify Silverman's awkward locution "words and music costumes": in it, the members of the large ensemble sport elaborate costumes bedecked with musical clefs, staves, and notes (but no words are visible).

The rhetoric of the song's music and lyrics also deserve scrutiny, for in them Berlin deploys the words and sounds of *ragtime* and *jazz* as synonyms referring to a distinctive American style that Berlin himself developed. To signal that fusion, and Berlin's role in it, he launches the verse with phrases that are clearly modeled on the analogous passage in "Alexander's Ragtime Band" (ex. 3.2). The four-note repeated phrase on the president's name ("Mister Wilson") nearly echoes its model's opening ("Oh, ma honey"), with slight differences in pitch and rhythm. The continuation likewise follows "Alexander" in the two-bar phrase starting a perfect fourth higher and then descending through a measure of four quarter notes.

The chorus cements the conflation of jazz and ragtime as agents of morale building—specifically the Berlin brand of ragtime embodied in his most famous song to date (and with a nod to George M. Cohan's famous war song, "Over There"):

Send a lot of jazz bands over there
To make the boys feel glad.
Send a troupe of Alexanders
With a ragtime band to Flanders.

It would be easy to claim that this lyric simply reflects the period's widespread confusion about the difference between ragtime and jazz.[35] Yet, given the verbal exactitude that was the hallmark of Berlin's writing, it might be more accurate to suggest that the lyric aims to capitalize on that confusion and to offer clarity by implicating his own work in the discourse—as if to claim "Alexander's Ragtime Band" (a metonym for all of Berlin's other "ragtime" songs) as the wellspring of jazz. That theme, implied here, would become explicit two decades later in the 1938 film *Alexander's Ragtime Band*—where the violinist-bandleader (played by Tyrone Power) who established ragtime with the title song becomes the featured performer in the climactic "jazz" concert at Carnegie Hall. That the film includes a scene depicting the original production of *Yip Yip Yaphank* adds yet another layer to the complex network of reflexivity that Berlin relished.[36]

Act 2 re-set the scene in Camp Upton to set up the show's hit number. In the midst of a show in which so many musical numbers spoofed and echoed musical theater conventions and trends, one song stood out as entirely grown from the army camp experience. The story of "Oh! How I Hate to Get Up in the Morning" has been

Example 3.2

3.2a. "Alexander's Ragtime Band," verse.

3.2b. "Send a Lot of Jazz Bands over There," verse.

told many times, by Berlin himself and his many biographers. "There were a lot of things about army life I didn't like," Berlin later recalled in an oft-quoted statement,

> and the thing I didn't like most of all was reveille. I hated it. I hated it so much that I used to lie awake nights thinking about how much I hated it. To make things worse I had this assignment that kept me working late into the evening, so I didn't get too much sleep. But I wanted to be a good soldier. So every morning when the bugle blew I'd jump right out of bed just as if I liked getting up early. The other soldiers thought I was a little too eager about it and they hated me. That's why I finally wrote a song about it.[37]

If, as Charles Hamm has claimed, many of Berlin's early songs may be heard as "biographical documents,"[38] then we could well extend that claim to Berlin's musical complaint about reveille. His comically hyperbolic plans for vengeance may be the easiest to trace directly to his experience. Berlin wrote the song on June 18, 1918, and published it before the show opened. Thus from the beginning, it had a life apart from the show. One of his biographers, Edward Jablonski, notes that soon after Berlin wrote it, "the song spread through his barracks and then around the rest of his camp, raising his status in the eyes of his fellow draftees. This was subversive stuff, considering the tenor of the patriotic Tin Pan Alley outpouring typified by Cohan's 'Over There.'"[39]

If not quite "subversive," the song nevertheless had the effect of cutting closer to the truth of army camp life than other popular songs depicting soldiers as rugged, manly, and proudly patriotic. Reviews of opening night reveal that the song actually had spread well beyond camp before the show opened. Silverman referred to it as "already popular among war songs," and the *New York Times* even called it a "classic bugler lyric" and an "old" number that was the "most appreciated" by the opening night audience.[40]

Part of the number's appeal lay in Berlin's inspired choice to set the lyrics in the style of a quickstep march. That is, instead of the heavy two-beat tread of earnest march tunes like Cohan's "Over There" (or Cohan's earlier hit, "Yankee Doodle Boy"), Berlin opted for a skipping triplet pattern known from Sousa marches such as "The Washington Post." The verse quickly sets up a lightly ironic tone, claiming that army life "is simply wonderful," the "food is great," and it's all "very lovely." Pivoting on an emphatic "but," Berlin then launches the refrain, including its catchy wake-up line "You've got to get up, You've got to get up, / You've got to get up this morning!" set to a paraphrase of "Reveille" in that lilting 6/8 meter. What really lends the song its humor, however, is its hyperbolic plans for revenge on the bugler, including the line "amputate his *reveille* / And step upon it *heavily*," with its unique three-syllable rhyme, and the second refrain's double-rhyming claim that he'll then "get that oth*er pup* / The one who wakes the bug*ler up*."[41]

The number also demonstrated keen theatrical sense by marking the first appearance of the show's creator and star, a gifted and proven vaudevillian headliner. Up to this point, Berlin himself had not been seen onstage, so when an officer came to Berlin's tent calling for him to get up, the show created a great deal of anticipation that its creator was about to emerge—not quite yet in full uniform, as it turned out. As *Theatre Magazine* reported:

Of course, there was a welcome that rocked the theatre, but to his credit as a good actor, there he stood, while his friends waited for a nod of recognition, staring dreamily ahead, and buttoning up his coat.[42]

Although not about theater or music, for once, "Oh! How I Hate to Get Up in the Morning" did ultimately lead the show back to Broadway. For the next number featured a series of revue stars visiting the camp to show their appreciation in an extended piece titled "Down from the Follies" that deftly mixes comedy and pathos. First the chorus girls—cross-dressed men—came on to sing and dance "for the boys who are going to France." Then several *Follies* stars—impersonated by soldiers wearing costumes donated by the stars themselves—also appeared, including a bevy of headliners from that summer's production: Lillian Lorraine, W. C. Fields, Will Rogers, Marilyn Miller, Eddie Cantor, (Joe) Frisco, and Ann Pennington. (Coincidentally, that *Follies* edition would close on the same day as *Yip Yip Yaphank*, September 14, 1918).[43] Such imitations were standard fare in revues: Marilyn Miller herself had done a string of "Impressions" in the *Passing Show of 1914* and parodies of current stage performers, and of shows on stage and screen, were regular features of the *Follies* itself from its inception.[44] Berlin's *Follies* parody therefore mirrors the source of its inspiration—a parody of a parody.

The scene continued with a format that Berlin often favored in multisectional numbers: groups of actors identifying their roles in the scene. The "boys" offer thanks in a song, followed by a sequence of appearances by army personnel, each presented in song: military police, cooks, doctors, prisoners, and finally the buglers. The buglers deftly turn the scene back to Berlin, as they concede that "the hardest job of all is waking Irving Berlin." Berlin reenters, now in overalls and large apron, carrying a pail and mop, singing about his lowly "Kitchen Police" job, which he earned by sleeping too late. After Berlin sings, the chorus and orchestra continue as "Berlin walks to Follies Girls. Business of shaking hands, saying hello, etc.," according to stage directions preserved among his papers. An offstage sergeant breaks in with a line that sends Berlin "back to the kitchen," and "Berlin exits slowly" as the chorus sings the refrain's final quatrain again.[45] Here we have a clever and poignant moment of role reversal: Berlin portrays a lowly private getting a chance to meet Broadway stars, but those "stars" are mostly rank-and-file soldiers impersonating the stars. The real star of the scene was Berlin himself.

In the midst of act 2, after "Kitchen Police," the "Page Boys" returned for "More Killing Time," this time posing as the vaudevillian team of Savoy and Brennan, known for their drag act.[46] According to Silverman, Sergeant-Major William Bauman, as Savoy, gave "the prize impersonation of the evening . . . with Private Fitzpatrick not doing Jay Brennan at all." Again, here the show featured a double impersonation, with at least one soldier-actor imitating another actor who dressed up as a woman. Like the other headliners imitated in the Follies sequence, their models—the real Brennan and Savoy—were appearing just blocks away in the *Ziegfeld Follies of 1918* at the New Amsterdam Theatre.

The show shifted to a quiet moment at the Y.M.C.A., where a soldier was writing a letter home to his mother, in song. Lawrence Bergreen claims that it was the only song that "fell flat," yet reviews singled out the number as exceptional. Silverman named it among three that would become "popular," and *Theatre Magazine* called it "a really beautiful song," noting that "I have heard soldiers singing it already, not carelessly, as they sing the average popular song, but as if it really meant something to them."[47] Twenty-five years later, during the second war, another reviewer would remember it fondly as a "touching little ballad."[48]

"Around the hour of 11," according to the *New York Times*, the Y.M.C.A. sequence continued with an exhibition by the lightweight champion Benny Leonard boxing two soldiers, first separately then together. Leonard, who had grown up as Benny Leiner on the Lower East Side, was the athletic image of Irving Berlin, a Jewish entertainer known as the "Ghetto Wizard" and standing at the top of his game in 1918. For a show that reinterpreted minstrelsy's meaning in wartime and that parodied *Florodora*, it was quite a show-business coup to feature one of the nation's dominant boxers as well. At some point, toward the end or just after the Y.M.C.A. sequence, "the boys were alerted that they were going overseas," Berlin recalled.[49]

Then came the *coup de theatre*. The ensuing finale trumped all that preceded it by slicing through the show's layers of theatrical reflexivity and conjuring the reality of war. The vigorous syncopated music that had accompanied the well-synchronized "drill dances" in both acts now reappeared with lyrics (ex. 3.3), as the men marched down ramps and into the aisles singing the stirring march-style refrain: "We're on Our Way to France."

In some accounts the final performance introduced a novel twist of making it appear that the soldiers were actually going straight from the theater to a boat that would take them to France. As the biographer Edward Jablonski put it:

> For that last night. . . . As the cast, in full uniform, with rifles and other military regalia, sang 'We're on Our Way to France,' Berlin led them not into the wings but offstage, down the aisle, and out of the theater. The audience, in midcheer, was stunned: clearly, the men were literally demonstrating the lyric of the song. According to reports, there were gasps, muffled outcries, sobs—the soldiers were, it seemed, bound for a troopship, the trenches, possibly death.[50]

Yet *Variety*, and Berlin himself, indicated that the notion of marching down the aisles had been part of the show's original conception. *Variety*'s review of opening night noted that "many troopers marched down the aisle and onto the boat in full equipment." And Berlin himself remembered that

Example 3.3. "We're on Our Way to France," verse.

All is rea-dy, so just hold stea-dy; we'll soon be leav-ing for the

pier.   No more wait-ing or hes-i-tat-ing— the time to sail is here.

they marched through the Theater, went out to the street and backstage where they boarded a transport, and as the lights lowered, the transport, on wheel, slowly moved offstage. It was a very touching and emotional scene.

This was not just a description of the last performance, for Berlin goes on to suggest that he had "that finale in mind" before the show even opened.[51]

Jablonski's source for his description of the audience's reaction to the number—with "gasps, muffled outcries, sobs"—remains unclear (he refers to unspecified "reports"), but it does match a later re-creation of the scene in the film *Alexander's Ragtime Band*. This is where the line between film legend and theatrical fact blur, but that may be appropriate for a scene in which Berlin strove to break down the theater's "fourth wall" and bring the ensemble into the audience for a moment in which they appeared transformed from actors to soldiers. A show that had at once sustained and parodied theater's conventions through masquerade and reflexivity now appeared to strip away all artifice and remind the audience of dangers in the larger world.

One thing that we know did *not* happen in the finale of *Yip Yip Yaphank*: the musical number originally intended for the scene was not used. Berlin had written "God Bless America" as the number the men would sing while striding down the aisles, but, as he recalled, "having that finale in mind, it seemed painting the lily to have solders sing 'God Bless America' in that situation, so I didn't use it."[52] Yet he seems to have come close to using it. In a letter to Harry Ruby, who was his musical secretary at Camp Upton, Berlin noted that "I did let the boys hear it and decided that 350 soldiers in overseas outfits marching down the aisle of the Century Theater going off

"*We're on Our Way to France,*" *the finale of* Yip Yip Yaphank. *Courtesy of Rodgers & Hammerstein, on behalf of the Estate of Irving Berlin.*

to war, singing 'God Bless America,' was wrong."[53] Ruby himself believed that he might have been "partly responsible" for the song's omission from the show. "There were so many patriotic songs coming out everywhere at that time . . . when he brought in 'God Bless America,' I took it down for him, and I said, 'Geez, another one?' And I guess Irving took me seriously. He put it away."[54]

Whether or not Ruby influenced Berlin's choice, the accounts of its deletion from the show indicates a finely tuned sense of theater. "We're on Our Way to France" was more tightly focused on the immediate situation, whereas "God Bless America" was deliberately timeless, abstract, and hymnlike—a style that held less weight in a revue striving for immediate appeal to the "mob."

Despite its short run, *Yip Yip Yaphank* had long resonance on stage and screen. At the advent of American engagement in World War II, Berlin would thoroughly revise the show and dub it *This Is the Army* (sometimes abbreviated *TITA.*). From its opening night on July 4, 1942, to its final performance in October 1945, that show would be seen by millions of soldiers and civilians, in the United States and far beyond. After its final performance Berlin started a book about the experience. "No story of T.I.T.A. would be complete," he wrote, "without beginning at the beginning and the beginning is *Yip Yip Yaphank*."[55] The show would also be a reference point in later movies, not just *Alexander's Ragtime Band* but the 1943 film version of *This Is the Army*, a popular Warner Brothers production in the war years, which features a sequence showing rehearsals and performances of several songs from *Yip Yip Yaphank*—including the famous finale again. More importantly for the next phase of his career, however, *Yip Yip Yaphank* brought out another dimension of Berlin's theatrical talent: producing. Up to now he had been signed on to help create someone else's show (Dillingham's, Ziegfeld's) and served as one member on a collaborative team. Now he was his own producer—the officer in charge of the theatrical troupe/troops. And the taste of that experience would bear fruit in an unprecedented theatrical venture in the decade ahead. Yet *Yip Yip Yaphank* was still a one-off, largely amateur production. Equally important to the enterprise he would undertake in the 1920s was his long experience in the flagship revue series of the 1910s: Ziegfeld's *Follies*.

THE ZIEGFELD FOLLIES OF 1919

Berlin stood in a unique position to absorb and define Ziegfeld's style because he had been part of it almost from the start. With all the resources of the theater at his disposal, including pretty girls instead of cross-dressed men, the *Follies* became an important incubator of Berlin's ideas about the revue genre as he would develop it in the 1920s (in the *Music Box Revues*) and early 1930s (in *As Thousands Cheer*)—even if, in those shows, it became clear that the *Follies* sometimes stood as a model of what Berlin would *not* do.[56] Beginning in 1911, Berlin wrote several numbers for the *Follies*. At first, however, his work did not help to glorify the girls so much as it stoked the shows' all-important, if less celebrated, comedy. As such Berlin's songs suited Ziegfeld's chief usage of musical numbers.[57] In the 1911 edition, at least three of Berlin's songs were introduced by comic headliners.[58] Fanny Brice became a frustrated lover in "Doggone That Chilly Man" and related the story of an untutored black pianist in "Ephraham Played upon the Piano"; Bert Williams introduced "Woodman, Woodman, Spare that Tree!"—a henpecked husband's twist on a nostalgic nineteenth-century parlor ballad.[59] Berlin contributed more comic material for the *Follies* of 1912 ("A Little Bit of Everything") and 1916 ("In Florida among the Palms"). For the war-themed 1918 edition he wrote "I'm Gonna Pin a Medal on the Girl I Left Behind," "The Blue Devils of France," and, for Ziegfeld's emerging star, Marilyn Miller, "Poor Little Me," which Berlin himself would soon thereafter perform in *Yip Yip Yaphank*.

Then came the 1919 *Follies*, widely regarded as the best and most memorable of the whole series. Critics greeted it as "an historic achievement in the theatre" and "the biggest and brightest of the 'Follies.'" Ziegfeld himself called it "the best I have ever produced."[60] Berlin was that show's principal songwriter. For it, Berlin, typically, contributed a variety of songs that covered a vast stylistic and topical range, from a crowd-pleasing minstrel-show scene to a number that intoned Ziegfeld's promise of "glorifying the American girl" better than any other song in *Follies* history.

Several recurring themes wove together in the 1919 *Follies*: modern romance, postwar civilian life, Prohibition, and, not surprisingly, music and theater themselves. Songs about modern romance typically revealed one or both members of a couple with multiple lovers—the Tin Pan Alley equivalent of the bedroom farce, a staple of the period's popular theater. Berlin had explored the topic many times in his early songs, as in "Call Me Up Some Rainy Afternoon," where a young woman named Nellie Green meets an admirer at a party and gives him the instruction that forms the title phrase. When he arrives at the door of her house, he overhears her saying the same thing to another admirer. In the 1919 *Follies*, Eddie Cantor sang Berlin's latest version of serial romance, "You'd Be Surprised" (added during the show's Broadway run). The song tells the story of a young man named Johnny whose girlfriend Mary finds that his passions may only be aroused in private, while he remains rather bland "in a crowd." As in "Call Me Up," Berlin writes the second verse to set up a reinterpreted refrain. Having learned from Mary that they'd "be surprised" by Johnny's romantic behavior in private, the girlfriends seek him out and discover the same thing, and thus the second refrain voices *their* findings.

The show's take on modern love also featured a pair of Harem numbers—a typical orientalist conceit striving to put a contemporary comic spin on the image of a man with multiple wives. It was a rather hoary cliché by 1919, but the critical response suggests that Berlin's musical numbers refreshed it by offering the perspective of the wives and of the harem's guard.[61] The first number, "Harem Life," presented eight "beautiful harem girls," who sing "eight of the Sultan's wives are we"—an echo of the 1888 *Mikado*'s three little girls from school that would recur in one of his 1920s revues. Each of them describes her particular job in turn before the final line in which they join together to sing that at the end of the day "we all dance the vision of Salome"— an in-joke about the plethora of Salome impersonations on the American musical stage since the Richard Strauss's opera had scandalized New York a decade earlier.[62] The second number throws a spotlight on an ordinary "guy" on the sidelines. "I'm the Guy Who Guards the Harem" relates that while the Sultan is gone, "I keep them happy," noting that "If the Sultan ever saw the way I guard the harem, / He would go out and engage someone / To stand guard over me." If harem scenes were wearing out their welcome on the American stage, Berlin's songs welcomed them back by reinterpreting them from an unexpected angle—inviting audiences to identify with the kept women and average guy who covets them.

Berlin also wrote at least two songs for the 1919 *Follies* dealing with the Great War's residual impact on civilian life, one a comic march, the other a sentimental ballad. The jocular march featured Eddie Cantor as a former private who enjoys turning the tables on an officer in civilian life—"I've Got My Captain Working for Me Now." "I'm gonna have him *wrapped in* work up to his brow," Cantor sang in Berlin's fresh rhyme on *captain*. The ballad, titled "My Tambourine Girl," featured the tenor John Steel in a "girl" number in which he recalls a "Salvation lassie" who came to his aid on a battlefield in Flanders. In the song's novel twist, the young man claims he had actually met and fell in love with the "beautiful maid" on Broadway—long before "we thought of going to war"—where she beat a tambourine in a street-level effort to save souls. But he did not tell her his feelings, he reports in the refrain, until he met her in "no-man's land." For Cantor's ex-private and John Steel's wounded veteran, the postwar world invited reflection on the unexpected benefits of war's privations. Such numbers reassured American audiences that the former soldiers among them could find a sort of redemption.

That reassurance had to be a solace for audiences that also faced another privation: Prohibition. The *Follies* songwriters found several ways to deal with the looming impact of the Volstead Act. Berlin was chief among them with an "extended sequence" on the subject, which Kimball and Emmet claim "does not survive."[63] Although the music cannot be located, the entire scene actually appears in the show's script at the Library of Congress. It begins "in one" (before the curtain) set in Times Square as offstage chimes stroke midnight. "Father Time," played by the comedian Eddie Dowling, introduces a funeral in what the script calls "recitative"—a hint that Berlin conceived the number operatically. The deceased is "John Barleycorn," the personification of alcohol, who died on July 1, the day Prohibition went into effect. From there, Berlin constructed the scene in a fashion similar to the "Down from the Follies" sequence in *Yip Yip Yaphank*. Several groups enter and exit in turn, representing different perspectives on Prohibition: the Mourners express sadness for themselves and the country ("Place us in a padded cell, / For the country's going to hell"), the Bartenders (played by the singing duo Van and Schenck) fear they will be out of work; Chorus Girls worry that they will no longer receive sumptuous gifts from inebriated sugar daddies; the Working Man, holding a tin can, longs for his daily beer; and the Soldiers, just back from the war, "cannot help from thinking / That I should have stayed in Paree / Where no one dares to interfere with what you're drinking."[64] Vaudeville headliner Bert Williams then takes center stage, still in one, for his comic number "You Cannot Make Your Shimmy Shake on Tea," in which the singer claims that you cannot do the new shimmy dance without "scotch or rye to lubricate your knee." In what the script dubs "scene 2" of the number, the curtains open to reveal "a saloon of the future," starring John Steel as a customer and Eddie Cantor as a waiter discussing what Steel may order to drink. The scene becomes a "girl number," as chorus girls enter one by one, dressed in costumes suggesting various beverages: Coca Cola, sarsaparilla, grape juice, lemonade, and Bevo—in which Berlin quotes his own song from *Yip Yip Yaphank*. Steel laments his choices in a recurring refrain based on the tune "How Dry I Am." The "Spirit of Alcohol," embodied by yet another Ziegfeld girl, then emerges to reassure him that "I don't want you to weep . . . I'm not dead, I'm only asleep." In the meantime, she offers "to give to you a little cocktail that is new." Enter Marilyn Miller for the scene's finale, "A Syncopated Cocktail," which links the pleasures of jazz with the newly illegal pleasures of alcohol. Sixteen chorus girls dressed as "China Dolls" dance while Miller sings. The song is richly allusive. It conjures *Florodora* yet again in its recurring line "come along, oh come along," and it conflates jazz and ragtime again as Berlin deploys the terms "jazzy melody" and "raggy melody" as synonyms. Even without an extant score, the script contains plenty of evidence that Berlin conceived the entire scene as a continuous musical number with operatic aspirations, an impulse he would develop to new heights in the 1920s.

The operatic impulse emerges again in a sequence built around several classical melodies, presented with Berlin's song "A Pretty Girl Is Like a Melody," and structured to resemble one particular opera that American audiences knew well: Jacques Offenbach's *The Tales of Hoffmann*. Although, as Berlin recalled, each *Follies* to date had featured a "so-called Ziegfeld Girl number,"[65] the 1919 *Follies* established several traits that would adhere to such numbers for decades. They grew from the particular circumstances of the 1919 production. It started with costumes. Berlin recalled that, after he had already written his quota of songs for the show, Ziegfeld called him in and said "I have to have another song! Look at these costumes."[66] Berlin took home the costume plates and thought about the number. He knew he was writing for a classically trained tenor making his *Ziegfeld Follies* debut: John Steel, who would come to be known as "Everyman's McCormack" after the famous Irish tenor. Steel wanted a feature that would bring out his particular talents. "[H]aving him in mind I thought of an idea to have each girl represent a classical number," recalled Berlin.

> There were five of these melodies, each representing a girl. I wrote a special lyric for each classic so Steel could sing it. I then found it necessary to have some kind of springboard for these old classics. The result was "A Pretty Girl Is Like a Melody." It is interesting to note that the last thing I thought of was this song. In other words, I had no idea that it would be anything more than a "special material" song.[67]

A fifteen-year-old special dancer named Doris Eaton, working underage and thus under the pseudonym Lucille Levant (taking the last name of her sister's husband Oscar Levant), witnessed the scene and recalled it more than eight decades later in her memoir, *The Days We Danced*. Her description reveals two things that have been forgotten in later accounts and portrayals of this ostensibly sentimental and grandiose number: humor and intimacy.

> Most people think of that scene as beautiful girls descending a white marble staircase, another of those lavish, embellished production numbers—a conception based on the movie version [*The Great Ziegfeld* (1936)]. In fact, no number ever had such a simple, exquisite presentation, the antithesis of flair and ostentation.
> The curtain parted on an empty, dark stage. As the music started, the spotlight picked up John Steel walking slowly to center stage from the backdrop. John had a beautiful, clear tenor voice, and he sang the verse and a chorus of the Berlin

John Steel, who sang "A Pretty Girl Is Like a Melody" and would star in Berlin's Music Box Revues. *He was the avatar of many tenors who sang "beautiful girl" numbers in the succeeding decades. Harry Ransom Center, University of Texas at Austin.*

song. Then as each girl appeared—one at a time—the music switched to refrains of well-known classical compositions, such as Mendelssohn's "Song of Spring" and Offenbach's "Barcarolle." With each "haunting refrain," the spotlight picked up a showgirl, dressed to match the mood of the music. She walked toward John, flirted a bit, and continued past him, fading into the darkness of the stage, while he sang the humorous lyrics of love found and love lost to one of those classic melodies. After all five girls had appeared, John sang "A Pretty Girl Is Like a Melody," as the five beauties surrounded him. . . .

At the conclusion of that historic scene, the applause was spontaneous and generous, but it always seemed to me that the audience initially seemed somewhat taken aback, still absorbing the loveliness in sound and sight and simplicity that they had just experienced. There was a brief hush in the theater before the explosion of applause. It was a special moment in *Follies* history.[68]

Doris Eaton—writing under her married name Doris Eaton Travis—had much to say about the classical interludes, whose lyrics were long believed to be lost. But first, the "special material" song deserves attention as an exemplar of Berlin's theatrical writing. "A Pretty Girl Is Like a Melody" stands among Berlin's most well-crafted songs, with a tight weave of music and lyrics. The lyrics comprise an extended simile comparing feminine and musical beauty. The verse establishes the singer as an authority, one who has both "an ear for music" and "an eye for a maid." The parallel placement of "e" and "m" on the key words helps to set up the simile. To cement the connection in the verse, Berlin introduces a compound simile in the line "They go together like sunny weather / Goes with the month of May," which combines internal rhyme (*together* / *weather*) and alliteration with a reverberant "th" sound and decisive "m" that concludes the phrase. The verse also serves to foreshadow the title phrase, with the keywords *girl* and *pretty*, each appearing twice. The refrain then announces the title phrase and develops the idea in language striking for its vividness, simplicity, and conversational naturalness. In the refrain's bridge, for example, Berlin states an elegant variation on the song's basic simile—

> Just like the strain of a haunting refrain,
> She'll start upon a marathon
> And run around your brain.

That couplet embodies the song's message in a perfect blend of sound and sense. It includes alliteration—on *strain* and *start* and on a recurring "n" sound that hums under the surface. It also features a network of internal rhymes and end rhymes: *strain* / *refrain* / *brain* and *upon* / *marathon*.

Berlin's music, written with John Steel's voice in mind, matches the elegance and subtlety of his lyrics (ex. 3.4). The verse is tuneful but mostly defers lyricism until the refrain. Its most lyrical moment highlights the compounded simile on "They go together like sunny weather / Goes with the month of May," reaching a melodic peak on F-sharp, which receives vivid support with a sonority very rare in pre-1920s popular song: a ninth chord with a suspended fourth.[69] The F-sharp will return to play an important role in the refrain. In fact, this verse returns to the tonic (G major) just before the refrain, retracing the D-B-G tonic triad. That tonic triad will also return to play an important role in the refrain.

The refrain itself features a remarkable melodic and harmonic architecture. It begins with a pickup gesture and opening bar steering the music into richer, more chromatic harmonic terrain, recalling Berlin's earlier "girl" song, "The Girl on the Magazine." The first eight bars, moving through the dominant of the dominant (A) and the dominant (D) defer a firm tonic triad until the end of the phrase. But the unusual harmonic plan, and some chromaticism in the melody, serve artfully to disguise the fact that the melody basically outlines a tonic triad—G, B, and D—reversing the triadic descent in the verse's principal phrase. Throughout the refrain, the melody continues to reach upward—one step higher in the bridge emphasizing E. The E reappears as the climactic pitch of the second "A" section (on "noon"), where the melody then rises one step more to the melodic climax on F-sharp in the final section (on "leave"). That F-sharp marks a striking fusion of words and music. The lyrics pine that "She will *leave* you and then . . .," as the melody and harmony together veer to F-sharp major, far from the home key of G. From there—"and then"—the song returns "home" through a circle of fifths progression: F-sharp–B–E–A-minor–D–G. The expected resolution to the upper-register tonic, as elusive as the "pretty girl" herself, remains out of reach for the voice. The song represents an uncanny integration of words, music, and scenic purpose.

The song, however, was conceived only as a musical frame in which to present the classical melodies, the girls, and most importantly for Ziegfeld, the costumes they wore. Each melody accompanied a girl, literally enacting the verse's line "I link a pretty girlie with each pretty tune that's played." Later in the refrain, the phrase "she

Example 3.4. *"A Pretty Girl Is Like a Melody," a facsimile of the original sheet music.*

A Pretty Girl Is Like A Melody

Words and Music by
IRVING BERLIN

I have an ear for mu - sic, And I have an eye for a

maid I link a pret - ty girl - ie, With

(continued)

will leave you / and then / come back again" also saw its reflection on stage, as all of the girls returned and surrounded Steel during the reprise. The melodies are listed in table 3.1 (see p. 92) in the order in which they appear in the script—a source, however, that may not be a fully dependable document of what happened in the scene.[70]

All of these tunes were widely known in early twentieth-century America, holding appeal to traditional music lovers with a strong fragrance of nineteenth-century

each pret-ty tune that's played. They go to-geth-er,

like sun-ny weath-er, Goes with the month of May

I've stu-died girls and mu-sic, So I'm qual-i-fied to say:

A Pretty Girl 4

(*continued*)

Mitteleuropa. All of them qualified for what in this period was commonly referred in the United States as "good music," and most of them could have been found on sheet music in the domestic parlor piano bench.[71] Berlin could have counted on Ziegfeld's audiences to recognize them.

Long believed lost, the lyrics that Berlin wrote for those "classical" melodies survive in the show's unpublished script. For years, they also survived in the memory of Doris Eaton Travis (1904–2010), who, at the age of 105 when I interviewed her in

A Pretty Girl 4

(continued)

2009, was able to match words and music, from memory, with incredible precision—in a few cases, with slight, but telling, differences from the script that more often cast doubt on the script's typist than on Travis's memory.[72] Those words and music are here reunited with the melodies, in the order in which they appear in the script. The lyrics open up new perspectives on a song known for linking beautiful women and music in an extended simile.

A Pretty Girl 4

The "Humoresque" lyrics establish the pattern, as the tune itself becomes a medium facilitating the suitor's romance (ex. 3.5). He "met a maid" when the "orchestra played this lovely tune," and now the tune "reminds" him of the long-lost girl. (The script version begins *"while the string* orchestra" played; whereas Travis sang *"when the sweet* orchestra played," shown here.) The way Travis sang the final phrase—"for it reminds me of that certain girl"—with wide leaps, suggests that Berlin set the lyrics to the last phrase of the principal melody of Dvořák's piece (shown above the main staff in the example).

Table 3.1. Melodies to which Berlin wrote new lyrics for the scene featuring "A Pretty Girl Is Like a Melody" in the *Ziegfeld Follies of 1919*, in script order

Composer	Full Title and Date	Common American Title
Antonín Dvořák	Humoresque in G-flat major, op. 101, no. 7 (1894)	"Humoresque"
Felix Mendelssohn	"Frühlingslied" (1842) from *Lieder ohne Worte* (*Songs without Words*, 1844)	"Spring Song"
Jules Massenet	"Élégie," for cello and orchestra, from incidental music to *Les Érinnyes* (1872)	"Elegy"
Jacques Offenbach	"Belle nuit, ô nuit d'amour" (Beautiful night, o night of love), from *Les Contes d'Hoffmann* (*The Tales of Hoffmann*, 1881)	"Barcarolle"
Franz Schubert	"Ständchen," from *Schwanengesang* (*Swan Song*, 1828)	"Serenade"
Robert Schumann	"Träumerei" (Dreaming), from *Kinderszenen* (*Scenes of Childhood*, 1838)	"Träumerei"

Example 3.5. Dvořák, "Humoresque," lyrics by Irving Berlin.

When the sweet or-ches - tra played this love - ly tune, I met a maid and from the start she set my brain a - whirl; But a-las we part-ed soon and now I long to hear this tune, For it re-minds me of that cer-tain girl.

The other five lyrics are more specific about what happens to the elusive girls, and each implicates music—and musicians—deeply into the fabric of the romance. In the "Barcarolle" (ex. 3.6), the suitor woos his lover at the opera (to hear Offenbach's *Tales of Hoffmann*) only to find that her love "grew cold" as the "music died away."[73]

In the four others, she abruptly runs away with another man—or returns to her husband. And Berlin tends to deliver the reversal's comic punch in the final line's rhyme. In the "Spring Song" (ex. 3.7), the man meets a girl in spring and gets her commitment that summer, only to find that, once he bought the wedding ring, she "ran off with the drummer." In the "Elegy" she runs off with the "cello fellow"—in a piece known for its ravishing cello solo (ex. 3.8). The "Serenade" offers the risqué hint of marital infidelity, as the suitor woos a "maid" with that song only to find himself the target of her husband, wielding his "garden spade." (ex. 3.9; the script lacks the

Example 3.6. Offenbach, "Barcarolle," lyrics by Irving Berlin.

Example 3.7. Mendelssohn, "Spring Song," lyrics by Irving Berlin.

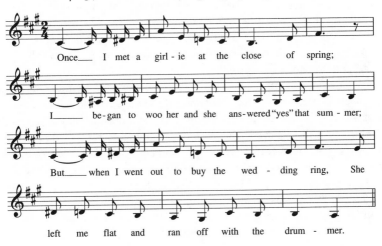

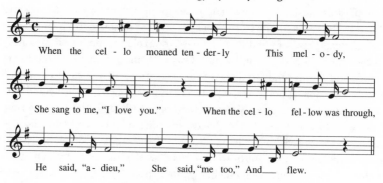

Example 3.8. Massenet, "Elegy," lyrics by Irving Berlin.

When the cel - lo moaned ten - der - ly This mel - o - dy,

She sang to me, "I love you." When the cel - lo fel - low was through,

He said, "a - dieu," She said, "me too," And___ flew.

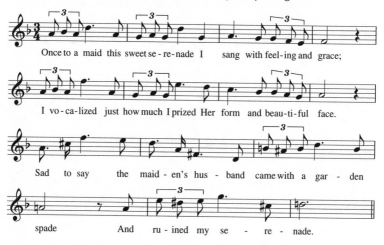

Example 3.9. Schubert, "Serenade," lyrics by Irving Berlin.

Once to a maid this sweet se - re - nade I sang with feel-ing and grace;

I vo - ca - lized just how much I prized Her form and beau - ti - ful face.

Sad to say the maid - en's hus - band came with a gar - den

spade And ru - ined my se - re - nade.

adjective *garden*, sung by Mrs. Travis in the interview, a nice touch that not only fits the music but rings true to Berlin's tendency toward specific imagery.) Finally, in "Träumerei," the music again stokes the man's romantic passions, but for naught, as the girl returns to her "boy in France"—rhymed repeatedly on key words, "dance," "chance," and "romance" (ex. 3.10).

How do these lyrics affect our understanding of this great exemplar of the *Follies* girl number? In some ways, they fundamentally change our view of it. They reveal very clearly how the number illustrates Berlin's verse line about "linking" each girl to "each pretty tune that's played." The lyrics are reflexive, referring to "*this* lovely tune," "*this* melody" and "*this* sweet serenade," for example.[74] More importantly, they show that a scene usually understood as an earnest hymn to feminine pulchritude had an unmistakably comic element. They also reveal that the objective vision of beauty in the "Pretty Girl" song was balanced in the classical interludes by a portrayal of each "girl" as an active, even transgressive, agent in her romantic destiny. That two of the girls rejected the suitor in favor of a *musician* (the drummer and the cellist) adds a

Example 3.10. Schumann, "Träumerei," lyrics by Irving Berlin.

We met_____ one eve - ning at a dance; The band was play- ing, I was say- ing, "Give me just one chance." She told____ me of a boy in France, And then she van- ished, and it ban-ished my ro- mance.

layer of irony to a scene featuring a debonair singer, whom the number implies will continue to have his flings.

Meanwhile, questions remain about the number of the classical interludes. Sources regularly cite six different interludes by title, and the script includes six, but Berlin repeatedly referred to just five, and Doris Travis likewise recalled only five.[75] In our 2009 interview, her blank reaction when I mentioned the sixth, Schumann's "Träumerei," deserves respect in a context where she so precisely recalled the five others. The most likely explanation for the numerical conflict would seem to be *not* that Berlin and Travis forgot the sixth but that it was cut before or during rehearsals, or even after opening night, since the whole number existed to cover an approximately seven-minute scene change. The Offenbach "Barcarolle" stands in the center of Travis's memory of the scene. She told me she stood backstage waiting to go on in the next scene and noted that the "Barcarolle" was the last in the sequence, even though it appears fourth in the script. It was thus closest to her ensuing appearance on stage, and perhaps served for her like a compelling cue line. Thus the number order in the script does not likely reflect the performance order.

Placing the "Barcarolle" last was a sly stroke of theater. For the tales that Hoffmann told, as Berlin and much of his audience knew, were tales about women that he had loved and lost, just like John Steel's "pretty girls." Also, the tales told in Berlin's classical interludes are framed, like Hoffmann's, by a prologue and epilogue (in the form of "A Pretty Girl Is Like a Melody") presented by a reminiscing storyteller.[76] Moreover, both the opera and the *Follies* scene are reflexive, placing music itself in the foreground of their storytelling. It is important to note here that *The Tales of Hoffmann* was no obscure reference of a cultural sophisticate: Berlin and his fellow New Yorkers had ample opportunity to see the opera in the previous decade and a half, a period when the Met and the Manhattan Opera House (before it closed in 1911) had performed the opera more than four dozen times. It was one of the most frequently staged operas in early twentieth-century New York.

The rediscovered lyrics stand in dialogue with more than just Offenbach's opera, however. First, they also show Berlin engaging with the contemporary Tin Pan Alley practice of setting classical tunes to new English-language lyrics. In other words, when Berlin set these melodies to lyrics, he was not just trying to attach classical or operatic prestige to his "girl" number; he was also creating a witty dialogue with the period's lyric-writing conventions. "Spring Song" was an especially popular hook for lyricists seeking to hang their words on an enduring tune. For example, a 1904 sheet music publication of "Spring Song" features the following words by James O'Dea:

Soft the April sun is streaming from the skies,
And from the leafy boughs above the birds once more are calling
Sweet the timid daisy greets with loving eyes,
The day break of the golden year enthralling.

Several other versions of "Spring Song" issued by American publishers in the early twentieth century all feature florid language, earnest sentiment, and idyllic nature imagery typical of what was known in the song industry as a high-class ballad, and the same goes for settings of the other melodies. In contrast to such purple poetry, Berlin's lyrics stand out for their freshness and lack of sentimentality.

Second, the rediscovered interlude lyrics may restore a sense of female agency in the number, but they do little to detract from the number's treatment of women as spectacle and as the romantic partners of men, nor from the masculine authority embodied by John Steel, the paradigm of the tuxedoed, classically trained tenor. He alone sings, the women are not given voice, and we learn of their actions only through his words. When the five girls surrounded Steel as he sang the final chorus, their formation in effect enhanced his power as the number's musical and visual center of gravity. Members of the opening night audience could not have failed to notice, too, that many of the women in the "Pretty Girl" scene had appeared as Sultan's wives in the earlier "harem" number. From that perspective, the images and sounds of the "Pretty Girl" number may be understood a kind of de-orientalized harem number.

We might also consider the scene for the way it participates in the larger public discourse on women's place in American life in the crucial decade of the 1910s. It was in this period, not the 1920s, when the historian Sara M. Evans identifies the "break-down of Victorianism" as the governing force in American women's lives. By 1916 the cause of women's suffrage had taken its place on the national political agenda, and both the Republican and Democratic conventions of that year were, as Evans puts it, "besieged by women."[77] The Senate would pass the Nineteenth Amendment three years later, on June 4, 1919, just twelve days before that season's *Follies* opened on June 16.

Now, I would not argue that Berlin composed the "pretty girl" number in response to the passage of the Nineteenth Amendment. From that point of view, the number could be reduced to a simple expression of patriarchal backlash. In fact, as we know, Berlin had a much more pragmatic idea in mind: to fulfill Ziegfeld's request for a musical number that would enhance the exhibition of some beautiful costumes. Yet it is interesting to note that, while addressing other contemporary issues very explicitly, such as Prohibition and postwar civilian life, the *1919 Follies* did not feature a single sketch or song that treated the cause of women. Still, contemporary audience members had vivid access to the connection between the onstage display of women and the profound change in their offstage legal status. In this context, Berlin's vignettes about the elusive girls may give voice to larger anxieties about the changing roles of women in American society. In fact, with the rediscovered lyrics to its classical melodies, the "Pretty Girl" scene seems in retrospect to represent a kind of savvy double coding—and another exemplar of Berlinian antithesis. It sings stories of the breakdown of Victorian feminine roles with the "good music" that comprised the soundtrack of the Victorian home. And it at once celebrates female agency while sustaining the singular authority of the male voice and star of the scene. In this sense, it fit into a well-established Ziegfeld pattern of emphasizing feminine beauty *and* treating women as "socially powerful," as Ann Ommen van der Merwe has noted of songs dating back to the first *Follies* production of 1907.[78] And the pattern would inform Berlin's later work as well, perhaps most notably in *Annie Get Your Gun* with its contrasting outcomes of the challenge duet "Anything You Can Do" (which Annie "wins") and the shooting match in the final scene (which Annie loses, on purpose).

However we might choose to view it, "A Pretty Girl Is Like a Melody" remains a crucial song in the American musical theater canon. It became a paradigm for the tenor-and-parade-of-girls number replayed in countless revues, nightclub floor shows, and beauty pageants for decades to come. Berlin himself would re-create the style in several numbers, sung by John Steel, in his *Music Box Revues*. He would parody the number in his 1932 comedy, *Face the Music*. And the number has been refracted in later Broadway musicals by other writers such as Rodgers and Hart's *Pal Joey* ("The Flower Garden of My Heart"), Stephen Sondheim's *Follies* ("Beautiful Girls"), and Mel Brooks's *The Producers* ("Springtime for Hitler"). The number also got reinvented in a recent song by Stephin Merritt and the Magnetic Fields, "A Pretty Girl Is Like a Minstrel Show"—an absurdist title that happens to conflate the two most potent numbers in the 1919 *Follies*.

If "Pretty Girl" came as an afterthought, as some "special material" generated by a Ziegfeldian request, then the act 1 minstrel finale was a different story. Others may have remembered "Pretty Girl" as the most representative *Follies* song, but for overall effect, nothing topped the act 1 finale. *Variety*'s opening night review called it "as handsome a staged scene . . . as Ziegfeld ever put on, or even better."[79] Adapted from the minstrel opening of *Yip Yip Yaphank*, it began with a fresh new Berlin song that, like "A Pretty Girl," serves as a prologue to the scene.

The scene's original *Follies* staging began "in one"—as theater people used to call a performance in front of the traveler curtain—with Eddie Cantor singing the verse and chorus of "I'd Rather See a Minstrel Show."[80] The song is an up-tempo, march-style number, which, in the spirit of "Alexander's Ragtime Band," "Everybody's Doing It," and *Watch Your Step*'s "Minstrel Parade," aims to create excitement about a musical style or performance. In the song's verse, the singer derides other theatrical forms, including "the drama" (an off-rhyme with the ensuing "hammer") and the revue, a self-effacing joke that gets lost when the song appears out of its original context. The singer claims to come from Alabama, "home of the minstrel show"—a deliberate historical inaccuracy (to create another off-rhyme with "drama" and "hammer") and perhaps a joke on Cantor, a New York Jew performing in blackface. The chorus celebrates the minstrel show's virtues, especially its "riddles and jokes." As Cantor hits the song's final cadence—almost certainly sung with the kind of climactic descending slide that was almost de rigueur in the period's stage performances[81]—the traveler curtain opens and grants his wish: it reveals the entire company standing in front of chairs in minstrel-show formation and repeating the chorus, as if in a communal confirmation of Cantor's heraldic introduction.

As the song ends, an interlocutor (played by George LeMaire) says, in a gender-inclusive twist on the typically all-male minstrel show first line: "*Ladies and* gentlemen be seated" (italics added). The company sits, and Cantor and Bert Williams assume the roles of the end men Tambo and Bones, respectively. The interlocutor begins some comic banter in riddles with Bones, and the company interjects scripted commentary and laughter. Although no music survives for this dialogue,[82] its rhythmic, rhyming language is clearly conceived for a musical setting. (The film *White Christmas* may provide a clue here to what the dialogue sounded like: it is sung to music—probably, but not necessarily, music that Berlin wrote in 1919—by Bing Crosby, Danny Kaye, and Rosemary Clooney in between the songs "I'd Rather See a Minstrel Show" and "Mandy.")

The interlocutor, continuing in rhyming (and probably sung) verse, announces a ballad—a familiar sentimental interlude in a minstrel show's "first part," as its act was commonly called. A quartet rises from the front row of the company and, as in *Yip Yip Yaphank*, sings the nineteenth-century parlor song "Silver Threads among the Gold." Tambo then resumes the comic banter, leading to the famously punning punch line preserved in *White Christmas*:[83]

TAMBO: Mister Interloc'tor.
INTERLOCUTOR: What is wrong with you?
TAM: I know a doctor.
INT: Tell about him, do.
TAM: Sad to say, one day he fell right into a great big well.
INT: That's too bad.
TAM: It serves him right.
INT: Why speak in such a tone?
TAM: He should have attended to the sick and left the well alone.

Berlin then effects a transition to a new number through a quatrain expressing nostalgia for the minstrel show:

INT: That's a joke that was told,
    By the minstrel men we miss
QUARTET: When Georgie Primrose,
    Danced to a song like this.

On that cue, the vaudeville headliners Gus Van and Joe Schenck then come forward and sing "Mandy," identified in the typescript lyric book as an "old-fashioned song and dance number," for which Ziegfeld's leading lady, Marilyn Miller, appears as famous minstrel man George Primrose. (The song itself was not so old-fashioned, but it had been recycled, and revised, from *Yip Yip Yaphank*'s "Mandy [Sterling Silver Moon].") The script then describes a complex production number featuring Ray Dooley as "Mandy" appearing in blackface as a pickaninny along with "little colored

Alfred Cheney Johnston

Town Country July 20th 1919

"MAURESETTE" AND MARILYN MILLER IN THE "ZIEGFELD FOLLIES"

"Mauresette" is a Lucile model and, in common with all Lucile models, hides her identity behind a fanciful name. She is *Oil* in "The Follies Salad," an orientally degagée lady in the "Harem Number," and *Humoresque* in "A Pretty Girl is Like a Melody." After the music she takes to drink—soft drink—and becomes *Bevo* in "A Saloon of the Future." Marilyn Miller, (Mrs. Frank Carter) at the right, is effervescent as *George Primrose* in the Minstrel number, in which she clogs daintily before Eddie Cantor, Bert Williams and George Lemaire as *Tambo, Bones and Middleman*

Mauresette and Marilyn Miller, two stars of the 1919 Ziegfeld Follies. Mauresette appeared as a sultan's wife in the harem number, as Humoresque in the sequence featuring "A Pretty Girl Is Like a Melody," and as the non-alcoholic beverage Bevo in the operatically conceived spoof on Prohibition. Miller is shown here impersonating the minstrel showman George Primrose in the act 1 finale. Courtesy of Rodgers & Hammerstein, on behalf of the Estate of Irving Berlin.

children."[84] (Such "pick" routines—featuring black children whose cuteness was meant to arouse patronizing white adoration—were standard fare in the period's musical theater, as *Yip Yip Yaphank* exhibited.) The script continues with a breath-taking telegraphic description of the scene's climax—including further choruses of "Mandy," a "fast buck dance," a "tambourine routine" by the entire company, and a Marilyn Miller soft-shoe dance accompanied by "Swanee River" [*sic*] and one more chorus of "Mandy" "sung 'Piano' by all."[85]

Framed by Eddie Cantor's enthusiastic claims before the traveler, the whole min-strel scene represents a fond historic re-creation of a genre that the song admits is moribund, with its motley succession of old riddles, parlor ballad, stylized wedding, George Primrose impersonation, "Old Folks at Home," tambourine routine, and "picks," along with the interlocutor's reminder of "the minstrel days we miss"—as if to say, "Minstrelsy is dead; long live minstrelsy." Once again, as in the "Pretty Girl" number, Berlin's songs are thoroughly woven into a production number that inte-grates the full resources of the theater—singing, dancing, scenic display, character portrayal, and narrative, which, in this case, comprises a story about the wedding of "Mandy" embedded in a story about minstrelsy's revival—that is, a show within, and *about*, a show. Some thirty-five years into the future, the scene's re-creation in the film *White Christmas*'s "minstrel number" projects a kind of secondary nostalgia—a fond memory not just of minstrelsy but of the *Follies* itself—further distanced from its source style by its transference to film and by its presentation as a rehearsal. As late as 1967, Berlin still recalled the "Mandy" number in the *Follies* as "the high spot" of that show and "one of the thrills of my memory."[86]

With the "Pretty Girl" scene and the minstrel finale, Berlin's score for the 1919 *Follies* rearticulated the vast musical theater territory and stylistic juxtapositions that he had staked out in his early shows with Charles Dillingham: on one hand, embracing classical music, beautiful melody, and quiet elegance; on the other hand, paying homage to the boisterous humor and rhythmic vitality of the minstrel show. As different as they are, however, the two numbers also share the common ground of self-referentiality: the allusions to Offenbach, to "this sweet serenade," "this melody," and "this lovely tune" in the classical interludes; the pretty melody that carries the simile "a pretty girl is like a melody"; and the minstrel number about a minstrel show. The number demonstrates minstrelsy's contradictory position in this period: both a beloved and moribund theatrical form that drew its contemporary energy from nostalgia for its past.

Together "Pretty Girl" and "Minstrel Show," and other Berlin numbers in the 1919 *Follies*, like *Yip Yip Yaphank* before it, anticipate the keynotes of Berlin's four editions of the *Music Box Revues* of 1921 through 1924: reflexivity, musical contrast, a delicate balance of nostalgia and currency, and musical variety embracing opera, musical comedy, minstrelsy, and the revue itself. The *Music Box Revues* would continue to explore Berlin's concept of the revue as a show of shows.

4

"AMERICA'S GREATEST SHOW"

• • •

THE *MUSIC BOX REVUES,* 1921–24

Say it with music.
—Irving Berlin

Jerome Kern's famous comment—"Irving Berlin has *no* place in American music. He *is* American music"—is quoted ad nauseam but never historicized.[1] Kern wrote it in the mid-1920s, just as Berlin had ended a run of four annual revues that claimed music, not sex or comedy, as the shows' unique trademark. The music by Irving Berlin that flowed most freshly in Kern's mind must have been his most recent *theater* music.

For if the 1910s saw an effort to Americanize musical theater, the 1920s saw its proliferation; and Berlin played a key role in making that happen. "Eighteen Prospective New Theatres" ran the headline on a *New York Times* article of June 6, 1920, heralding what would become the most varied, prolific, and prosperous decade Broadway had ever seen. The article connected the new burst in theater construction to a postwar surge of interest in entertainment, noting how "the enforced inactivity of the builders during the war period" had yielded to "a sudden popular passion for almost any kind of entertainment" and "an outbreak of purposed theatre building."[2] Two figures who had dominated New York's entertainment world since the century's early years aimed to stoke the "popular passion" by building one of the new theaters: Berlin and his new business partner, Sam H. Harris. Three weeks before the article appeared, Berlin and Harris had bought a parcel of land at 239–247 West Forty-fifth Street. The theater they envisioned—dubbed the Music Box before they even broke ground—would rise on the north side of the block just west of Broadway, and its unique aim was to feature the music of a single composer: Irving Berlin, of course.[3]

Owners and observers alike saw it as a risky venture, far exceeding its projected costs. The expenses would be regularly reported in the press, as would the resulting ticket prices that raised the bar on Broadway's "top," as *Variety* typically referred to a show's highest priced tickets.[4] Berlin would even write lyrics for his new revue that joked about the financial stress as the "Berlin and Harris Worries of 1922." Yet with a wealth of success in entertainment during the century's first two decades, the partners knew what they were doing. By 1920 Harris, sixteen years Berlin's senior, was a veteran Broadway showman. Early in the century he had partnered with Berlin's idol, George M. Cohan, in leading a popular minstrel troupe, the Cohan and Harris Minstrels, and in producing the landmark musical comedy *Little Johnny Jones* (1904). The Cohan-and-Harris collaboration lasted more than fifteen years; it ended over a

The Music Box. Courtesy of Rodgers & Hammerstein, on behalf of the Estate of Irving Berlin.

disagreement about the Actors Equity strike of 1919 (Harris sided with the actors; Cohan never forgave them), which thus separated two names that were as inextricable as Rodgers and Hammerstein would become in the decades ahead. Their falling out opened up the chance for Harris to work with Berlin.[5]

Harris's producing career had had its rough and humble beginnings as a boxing manager, but he inspired the playwright Moss Hart's lofty tribute to "this ordinary-appearing man, of obviously little education or learning, . . . a man of impeccable taste, with a mind of vigor, clarity and freshness." "Everyone in the theatre adored him," Hart continued, because in a world of selfish tantrums Harris was "the most tranquil human being I have ever known . . . a great gentleman of the theatre and, so far as I am concerned, its last aristocrat."[6] For four decades up to his last musical production (*Lady in the Dark*), in the year of his death (1941), Harris produced shows that helped define the center of American theater.

Harris and Berlin had crossed paths several times in Berlin's early career, beginning about the time that Berlin began publishing songs in 1907.[7] Their contacts continued through the 1910s, but it was not until 1920 that they became business partners in the Music Box project, and it was Harris who produced the theater's first shows: the *Music Box Revues* in 1921 through 1924.

The distinctive intimacy of the Music Box made a strong contribution to the shows it featured. It could seat a little more than one thousand theatergoers, but in

Irving Berlin and Sam H. Harris. Courtesy of Rodgers & Hammerstein, on behalf of the Estate of Irving Berlin.

a neighborhood graced by larger venues such as Winter Garden and Globe Theaters (both with more than 1,500 seats), the New Amsterdam (about 1,800 seats), and vaudeville's Palace (about 1,750 seats), the Music Box stood out for its modest size, designed for the delicate precision of Berlin's marriage of words and music, and for a fast-paced, dialogue-driven comedy. The Music Box was "everybody's dream of a theatre," wrote Moss Hart, whose literary style would flourish there in the 1930s.

> If there is such a thing as a theatre's making a subtle contribution to the play being given on its stage, the Music Box is that theatre.... Even in broad daylight, as we stepped inside its doors and into the darkened auditorium, there was an indefinable sense that here the theatre was always at its best.[8]

Harris and Berlin both understood that they needed a distinctive venue to help create a distinctive style in an increasingly crowded theater scene, especially in their genre of choice, the revue. The context is crucial because the plethora of revues actually became a *subject* of Berlin's revues. In an era that saw more regular theatergoers who kept up with the revues and saw as many as possible, revues had to strike a fine balance between novelty and familiarity. A *New York Times* article of the period noted the "touchy revue public" that brought high standards and firm expectations to new offerings.[9] Matching the boom in theater construction was a profusion of revues with tantalizing titles such as the *Scandals*, the *Frivolities*, the *Gaieties*, the *Hitchy-Koo*, and the *Midnight Whirl*. Some were one-off shows such as Berlin's own *Yip Yip Yaphank*, plus *Peek-A-Boo* (1919), *Tick-Tack-Toe* (1919), *Silks and Satins* (1920), and *Biff! Bing! Bang!* (1921). Other revues hopefully included the year in their titles, as if promising to return the following year, even if—like the *Broadway Brevities of 1920* and the *Snapshots of 1921*—they did not. Meanwhile, the grandest annual revues, routinely billed as "mammoth" and "monster," could be found at the 5,200-seat Hippodrome Theatre, known for its casts of hundreds, aquatic spectacles, and live animal acts, all produced by Charles Dillingham.[10]

Before all of these, the American revue really took on its identity in the glamorous, standard-setting *Follies* of Florenz Ziegfeld (beginning in 1907); it continued with the "more daring" if less visually stunning *Passing Show*, produced by the Shuberts (beginning in 1912); and it flourished in two new revues launched in 1919—the chic, intimate, and "arty" *Greenwich Village Nights* (soon to be called *Greenwich Village Follies* to Ziegfeld's consternation), staged by the debonair John Murray Anderson, and George White's *Scandals*, with what one chronicler has called its "steely, cynical, sixty-mile-an-hour jazz-age tone."[11]

The years from 1919 to 1921 formed the revue's peak. According to historians of the genre, the revue became "the archetype of postwar jazz-and-prohibition entertainment,"[12] and it became crucial in American musical theater's "liberation" from European operetta.[13] In fact, however, the period actually saw about as many shows labeled "musical comedy" (or "musical farce") as "revue,"[14] yet as we have seen in the Berlin-Dillingham shows, the episodic structure and abundant variety of the revue pulled musical comedy into its orbit, so that musical comedies often resembled revues more than book shows.[15]

In the *Music Box Revues*, Berlin realized something he had been reaching toward for several years: composing the complete score of a *professional* Broadway musical revue. He had done the complete score for his first musical comedies; and he had gotten a taste of complete creative control of a revue in his unique, mostly amateur, soldier show *Yip Yip Yaphank*. But writing revues was typically a team effort in which several songwriters tended to share the work, and they ranked far down in the hierarchy of attractions. "Experience has shown that the authors and composers of the 'Follies' are of but secondary importance," noted a *New York Times* article about the 1919 *Follies*, before listing the show's fleet of writers.[16] The *Music Box Revues*, then, would be unique in featuring a single composer and making him, in effect, the star— something that the Shuberts or Ziegfeld would never have done. The notion of a songwriter as the controlling force of a musical show was unheard of until that time.

Berlin and Harris, however, also knew that a revue's success still depended on performing talent. That was reflected in newspaper previews of the shows, undoubtedly fueled by press releases from Harris. The 1921 show established the pattern. It was "news" when a cast member signed on to do the show. The first announced cast member, billed as the show's "principal comedienne," was Florence Moore, known for her flair in bedroom farces.[17] The handsome Joseph Santley and pretty Ivy Sawyer, now a married couple known for musical comedy, were cast several weeks later.[18] In late August just a month before opening, Berlin and Harris signed the veteran stage comics Willie Collier and Sam Bernard, who, according to the *New York Times*, would "introduce travesties of Weber and Fields type."[19] The *Times* also announced that Berlin himself would perform in the show.[20] And then, with opening night less than two weeks away, the *Times* ran down the complete list of the show's stars, a "practically unbelievable cast" now including the operetta singer Wilda Bennett.[21]

If contemporary audiences were drawn to the opening night for its star talent, the 1921 *Music Box Revue* (the year would not be appended to the title until 1923) now compels particular attention for other reasons. It was the first and most deeply admired of the series. *Variety* dubbed it simply "America's greatest show." Moreover, its complete piano-vocal score survives in manuscript, imparting a vivid sense of the structure and flow of musical numbers that has remained inaccessible for decades. That Berlin preserved the first, and no other, *Music Box Revue* in this way further suggests its importance to the composer himself. Although several individual numbers were published separately in standard popular song form with verse and chorus, sheet music can hardly begin to suggest their musical and theatrical lavishness.

Indeed, of the twenty-three scenes in the *Music Box Revue* of 1921, seventeen featured musical numbers, and fully seven of those numbers comprise extended, multi-sectional musical scenes that developed a plot with characters, including the opening scene and the grand finale, as well as several interior numbers: an elegant vision of a couple longing for home while "dining out," a depiction of a man in an easy chair reveling so much in his "little book of poetry" that its characters come alive, a hilarious send-up of contemporary marriage and divorce, and an interview with Irving Berlin himself. These were much more than songs: they were fully musicalized comedy sketches that lasted more than ten minutes in some cases.

Further, Berlin threaded a single tune through the score in multiple numbers, so that its significance exceeds the boundaries of any single song unit. That tune, "Say It with Music," pervades the score to impress upon the listener the keynote of the show and of the theater itself. Several later shows, all book shows, would become better known for deploying the unifying device of a recurring musical theme (*Show Boat*, *Lady in the Dark*, *Cats*, and *Curtains* to name a few). But the only prominent precursor within the American musical theater scene was an operetta: Victor Herbert and Rida Johnson Young's *Naughty Marietta*, whose "dream melody" blossomed into "Ah, Sweet Mystery of Life."

All together, the show's emphasis on music, its multiple musical scenes that range far beyond conventional song forms, and its recurring musical theme "Say It with Music" suggest that Berlin still harbored operatic ambitions and that the revue had become the medium through which to channel those ambitions. Add to that the fact that the theater itself was built to present the music of a single composer, an architectural phenomenon with precedent only in the work of a very different theater composer, Richard Wagner—with whom Jerome Kern would soon unapologetically compare Berlin—and it becomes clear that Berlin was staking a claim as a unique figure in American culture: a songwriter, publisher, and showman without peer.[22] Yet from the opening curtain, he demonstrated that he would stake that claim with a self-effacing and highly reflexive sense of humor.

MUSICAL PROLOGUES

Beginning in the 1921 show, Berlin framed his revues with prologues and finales that comprised extended musical scenes about the show itself. Such prologues were becoming staples of the revue, which, in the roaring traffic of new works, had become an increasingly self-conscious and self-referential genre. The *Ziegfeld Follies of 1919*, for example, had opened with a chef assembling the show's elements in a "Follies Salad," a musical number created not by Berlin but by *Follies* stalwarts Gene Buck and Dave Stamper.[23] Berlin picked up the idea and reconceived it for his own revue while the concept was apparently still fresh. (Within a decade, Brooks Atkinson would complain that the revue's self-referential habits had become "tedious."[24]) The first show opened with a comic allegory about the birth of the *Music Box Revue*, featuring the new show as a "baby girl" emerging from a music box and "Eight Little Notes" embodied by chorus girls. This is the only prologue for which the music and lyrics survive in a piano-vocal score.

Of the 1922 and 1923 prologues we know nothing beyond what programs and reviews reveal, but it is clear that they also featured a reflexive musical sketch, including references by name to the Music Box, and in at least one case (1923) to other revue producers and the general multitude of revues on Broadway. The 1922 show opened in a Park Avenue apartment where a couple of "first nighters" prepared to go to the theater, then it shifted to the Music Box stage where the music director appears with several chorus girls and a dresser.[25] The 1923 show included "an arch with the year in silver figures . . . at the opening and again at the close."[26] The prologue featured a calendar of show girls embodying the months of the year, and an additional girl in the role of "Music Box Revue 1923." A singer explains that "Every Jake and Pat with an office in their hat puts on a revue and calls it, 'This and That of 1923.'" A theatergoing couple appears and attempts to buy tickets for the *Music Box Revue* at the "Fraudway Ticket Office" from the "Gyp Brothers," who attempt to sell them tickets for other revues. "We have tickets for the Shubert and the Carroll by the barrel," they claim—a jab at the Shubert brothers' productions (*The Passing Show* and *Artists and Models*), and *Earl Carroll's Vanities*. The woman, however, won't be dissuaded: she takes off her jewelry to pay for the Music Box tickets.[27]

The 1924 show put a novel yet nostalgic twist on the self-referential prologue. Accenting the vast gulf between contemporary and historic New York, the 1924 *Music Box Revue* opened with a scene featuring Rip Van Winkle, awakened by a Mountain Climber in the Catskills. The Mountain Climber explains that "the man who wrote this melody" sent him to see the *Music Box Revue*. The Mountain Climber escorts Rip to the big city, where he observes a parade of girls from various neighborhoods and boroughs, including a "Broadway stepper" who is "jazzing her life away." Rip then sings "Where is the little old New York, / The one that

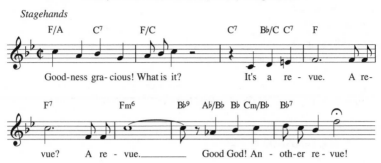

Example 4.1. Music Box Revue, *opening (1921).*

I used to know, / long, long ago?" Proceeding to the Music Box Theatre to see the new revue, he is invited to observe the entire show from the wings until the finale, where he appears as the guest of honor at a banquet hosted by the entire company.[28]

The 1921 show established the pattern with a prologue about the revue and the theater—a kind of comic consecration of the house. The extended, multisectional scene features several characters and several key and tempo changes, all serving to demonstrate the point that this revue emphasizes music and the Music Box itself.[29] The curtain parts to reveal a replica of the theater's roof, with "cats" prowling (an ambiguous reference in the stage directions that is most likely a shorthand reference to cat *burglars*), as the orchestra plays an introductory flourish laced with fragments of "Say It with Music." The "cats" disappear as a stork flies in and drops a bundle to the accompaniment of a gentle rag-like version of "Rock-a-bye Baby" (in four, instead of the usual triple meter, to accommodate the cakewalk syncopation), followed by a full instrumental rendition of the refrain of "Say It with Music." With the bundle in place, the curtain rises to expose a replica of the theater's full exterior, and four stagehands emerge to examine the mysterious package. "What's in the queer-looking bundle?," they sing, as the music segues into a moderate patter style. After asking about the bundle's possible origins, the stagehands begin to ask what it is: A drama? A comedy? A farce? They "look for a clue." As they discover the "baby" revue, they sing in recitative-like dialogue with shock and dismay (ex. 4.1).

The bundle opens and reveals a "baby girl" played by a petite actress named Aleta known for her "dainty, diminutive" fairylike stage presence.[30] She begins a dialogue of two-bar phrases with the stagehands revealing that she is named "The Music Box Revue" and was sent here by her father (implicitly Irving Berlin). She explains that "My father and mother are weary and worn, / They fought each other before I was born." The line hints at the severe financial and artistic pressure under which Berlin and his collaborators worked to prepare the first show in a new theater. The stagehands then ask a series of questions to determine whether she can do all of the things that audiences expect from a revue: dancing, singing, costumes, and comedy. The musical exchange includes a clever quip about the nature of costumes in a typical revue:

STAGEHANDS: Do you know just how to dress?
GIRL: I can dress.
STAGEHANDS: Yes, yes!
GIRL: More or less.
STAGEHANDS: Make it less.

The sequence ends with the Stagehands rocking the girl to the tune of "Rock-a-bye Baby," now with a message more threatening than soothing:

If you behave,
They'll stay till you're through—
But if you're bad,
They'll walk out on you.

Before falling asleep, the girl places an unidentified book in a music box prop, and the music shifts to another instrumental refrain of "Say It with Music," followed by one last phrase of "Rock-a-bye Baby," to round out the sequence on a full cadence. At this point, the number seems complete, and the show could go on with a new song or sketch. But Berlin is far from done with his musical exhibition, for the number has not yet explained why the "cats" appeared on the Music Box roof when the curtains opened.

Enter nine Burglars (all chorus girls) and a "misterioso" musical passage that takes the music to a minor key. Berlin's melody here comes from stock phrases used in silent film: an almost identical theme appears in the 1914 *Remick Folio of Moving Picture Music* (ex. 4.2).[31] After establishing their creepy credentials, the Burglars' song moves to a bright major key as they explain the disadvantages of their illegal trade: "We don't advise young men to take a course in burglary, / For cracking safes is not as safe as it's cracked up to be."

That phrase leads to a remarkably jaunty "chorus" (so labeled in the copyist's piano-vocal score) in which the Burglars further discuss their work, ending with the quip: "Just like a famous patent medicine, / We work while you sleep"—an allusion to an ad line for a popular laxative called Cascarets.[32] The Burglars then do a dance to the tune they have just sung, confirming the distance they have come from their threatening "misterioso" entrance.

Yet for all the singing about their work, the Burglars have not yet *done* their work. At the end of the dance they spot their quarry: the book that the girl left in the music box. When they realize that the book is the plot of a revue, they consider taking it to Ziegfeld or Dillingham. And if neither of them wants it? They'll do what any good gangsters would do: "We'll go and tie it up in knots, / And throw it in the Hudson River / With the rest of the plots." The entire section forms the second verse and chorus of the perky melody they sang before discovering the book. The Burglars exit to the "misterioso" tune to which they entered, rounding off this, the second large section of the musical scene.

The Burglars' exit wakes the baby girl, who cries, in a remarkable eight-bar passage with a lilting melody over a chord progression redolent of the blues (ex. 4.3). Again, Berlin might have ended the opening scene right here, but the music continues. As the baby girl winds up the music box, we hear a new orchestration of "Say It with Music," and eight chorus girls enter as the Eight Little Notes.

Example 4.2

4.2a. Music Box Revue, *opening, Burglars entrance music (1921).*

4.2b. *"Mysterioso Pizzicato" silent-film theme (1914).*

Example 4.3. Music Box Revue, *opening, "baby girl" song (1921).*

The Eight Little Notes, representing each pitch of the standard diatonic scale, return throughout the show, like human analogs to the recurring "Say It with Music" melody. The Eight Little Notes sing their own song, launched by a grammatical inversion ("Eight Little Notes are we") that echoes Gilbert and Sullivan's three little maids from school—an allusion to *The Mikado* that would have been lost on few observers of the New York theater scene, which had witnessed five productions of the show in the 1910–18 period.[33] (For revue audiences, it also conjured more recent memories of "Harem Life" in the 1919 *Follies* with its eight chorus girls singing "Eight of the Sultan's wives are we.") The "Notes" song itself comprises two sections, beginning with a full thirty-six-bar chorus in a new key (now F major) followed by a slower D-major section in which they explain something very important about the show and its distinctiveness from all other revues—in case the audience had not yet gotten the point (ex. 4.4).

Here we have the show's keynote, and its distinction from all other revues. Music—not words, costumes, or legs—is the show's theme. Yet the Eight Little Notes ultimately finish by paying homage not to music but to another key element of the show:

And now before we leave you to let the show advance,
We'll present the little gent who taught us how to dance.

Example 4.4. Music Box Revue, *opening, Eight Little Notes entrance (1921).*

Eight Little Notes

Another allegorical character named "Dance" enters and directs a long nonsinging passage that comprises two thirty-two-bar choruses plus a coda, bringing the opening number at last to a close.

The first *Music Box Revue*'s opening sequence comprises the longest continuous musical number that Berlin had written to date (more than 550 measures, plus repeats). It served to introduce not just a single show but to launch a series, and even more importantly, to initiate a new theater. It linked that theater to the production of revues, and in savvy, self-effacing humor it personified the new revue in the form of a baby girl. By showing the stagehands react in mock horror to the new show's genre ("Good God! Another revue!"), it disarmed potential skepticism about whether it could carve out a distinctive style in a milieu teeming with other revues, some of them well established, including shows produced by Ziegfeld and Dillingham. It also articulated the new revue's values: not chiefly in plot, lyrics, jokes, costumes, or "legs," but in music. It emphasized that point not just in words but by demonstration—an extended *musical* number in which all dialogue occurred through music. The Eight Little Notes articulated and embodied that musical emphasis. And the recurring melody of "Say It with Music," not yet sung to words, reinforced that message.

"SAY IT WITH MUSIC"

Berlin withheld the lyrics until the penultimate number of act 1. The song would appear again in the grand finale, with witty new lyrics serving as a reflexive joke about the show's expenses—and as a musical curtain call. Berlin had copyrighted the song six months before the show opened, and it had gotten plenty of public "plugs" before opening night; thus many theatergoers would have heard it before even entering the theater, and Berlin rewarded their prior knowledge by presenting the tune, wordless, in the prologue.[34] Yet now the complete song appears in its theatrical context for the first time, for it joins musical theater's twin forces, "melody and romance," as the verse puts it. With its satin lyricism, its linkage of music and love, and its allusions to famous nineteenth-century European composers as standard-bearers of musical beauty (in this case Chopin and Liszt), the song conjures memories of "A Pretty Girl Is Like a Melody." The scene even included excerpts from other familiar songs to amplify the song's message that music "never fails" to inspire love.

The song rewards careful scrutiny (ex. 4.5).[35] The verse is a marvel of concision and tightly bonded lyrics and music. It consists of four lines: three eleven-syllable lines followed by a ten-syllable vest leading into the refrain. (*Vest* was Ira Gershwin's term for the phrase that connects the verse and the refrain.) The first three lines rise and fall in gentle arcs, launched by a phrase that Berlin borrowed from the refrain of his 1914 ballad "Always Treat Her Like a Baby" (mm. 5–6 and 9–10, originally set to the words "treat her like a baby."). The vest begins like the other lines, but continues with a string of half notes, floating down the scale to the E-flat tonic on the refrain's downbeat (mm. 17–20). Chromatic inflections add poignancy: the B-natural on "lovers" and "wander" lends sweetness; the G-flat on "tell" casts a shadow. The refrain's melodic breadth, recapitulating the verse's arched contours, is redolent of a Kern ballad, with only whole and half notes for its first ten bars. It also resembles the main theme of Franz Schubert's Quartett-Satz in C Minor, D. 703,[36] adding more resonance to the song's celebration of "beautiful music" by nineteenth-century European composers. But it would be hard to mistake it for a real Kern song—or a Schubert string quartet movement. The accompaniment features the kind of rippling chords that often decorate long-limbed Berlin ballads. The light ragtime lilt that appears, ironically, to reinforce the rhyme on "Chopin or Liszt" (with "rather be kissed") also echoes well-established patterns in Berlin's song galaxy, where rag figures and classical allusions coexist. Moreover, in the refrain Berlin doubles the melody in the bass, a device he would revisit in a small family of romantic ballads, such as "Soft Lights and Sweet Music" and "Change Partners" in the 1930s, and "The Best Thing for You" as late as 1950. The lyric is earnest without pretension, with conversational phrases like "somehow I'd rather . . .," a reference to "Mister Cupid," and a resonating "-el" in the phrase "A melody mellow / Played on a cello / Helps . . ."

Although the refrain falls into a clear ABAC pattern, Berlin ingeniously elides the last sixteen bars with a poetic enjambment (". . . cello / Helps . . .") and a chromatic scalar descent across the conversational phrase linking the "A" and "C" sections: "A melody mellow / Played on a *cello / Helps* Mister Cupid along; / So say it with a beautiful song."

Although "Say It with Music" appears to be among the shorter numbers in the score, it developed into a more elaborate musical scene as Berlin inserted phrases from popular love songs into it: "A Little Love, a Little Kiss" (Lao Silesu and Adrian Ross, 1912), "Kiss Me Again" (Victor Herbert and Henry Blossom, 1905), and "You Made Me Love You (I Didn't Want to Do It)" (Joe McCarthy and James V. Monaco, 1913).[37]

Example 4.5. "*Say It with Music*," *from* Music Box Revue (1921)*, piano-vocal score.*

Moderato con espressione

Mu-sic is a lan - guage lo-vers un-der-stand;

Me - lo - dy and ro - mance wan-der hand in hand;

Cu-pid ne-ver fails as - sis-ted by a band—

(continued)

All three tunes were sentimental favorites by 1921. "Kiss Me Again" had formed the culminating passage of a number titled "If I Were on the Stage" in the operetta *Mlle. Modiste*. Music Box audiences surely understood the reference: the operetta itself had been revived four times within a decade after its original 1905 production, and the song "Kiss Me Again" became one of the era's most familiar romantic waltzes. "A Little Love" had also become a standard. The song makes a telling appearance as a middlebrow chestnut in Stephen Vincent Benet's short story "The King of the Cats": "To a man whose simple Princetonian nature found in 'Just a Little Love, a Little Kiss' the quintessence of musical art, the average symphony was a positive torture."[38] The perfumed language, melodic arabesques, and Old-World ambience of these tunes amplify the number's romantic resonance. "You Made Me Love You" also enjoyed wide popularity, thanks to performances and a recording by Al Jolson. It is a jauntier, more down-to-earth Tin Pan Alley tune than the others but clearly matches the theme of the scene. All three melodies, in short, allow the couple to "say it with music."

The scene was performed as a duet by the young operetta star Wilda Bennett, as "The Girl," and the musical comedy singer Paul Frawley, as "The Man," each of whom sang a full verse and chorus before exchanging phrases in conversational give-and-take. That Berlin cast an operetta singer to introduce the song gives us a clue about his musical values for this number. A singer like Bennett gave beautiful voice—a voice clearly unsuited for ragtime or slang—to the "beautiful song." For the *New York Times* critic Alexander Woollcott, it was the show's "one real song," and he predicted that "by February you will have heard it so often that you will gladly shoot at sunrise anyone who so much as hums it in your hearing."[39]

The scene also looked beautiful. *Variety*'s Jack Lait called it a "typical Berlin knockout . . . staged with rare lightings and harmonies and animated illustrations."[40] The *Herald* claimed it as "one of the best" of Berlin's "tunes" and noted that stage director Hassard Short "framed the scene in an uncommonly effective blend of red and black."[41] The number certainly formed a climactic moment in act 1. It combined scenic opulence with a melody, introduced early and often, that had finally found its full expression in the voice of an operetta singer. As the theme, even thesis, of the show, and as the song blossom of an instrumental melody planted in the first scene, "Say It with Music" might have served as an apt, if unusually calm, act 1 finale. Berlin held a trump card for the real act 1 finale, however. Meanwhile, much of the show developed the basic idea of "Say It with Music"—the idea that music itself would carry an unusual amount of the evening's entertainment.

MUSICAL SKETCHES

The *Music Box Revues* were rich with extended musical sequences that range far beyond the bounds of conventional song forms. None of the shows presented more of them than the 1921 edition. These musical scenes carry action and dialogue, like the openings of Berlin's Dillingham shows. Unlike those shows, however, the musical scenes in the *Music Box Revues* were self-contained numbers, complete mini-comedies in themselves—musical sketches.

Two of them explored the competing desires of stepping out on the town and enjoying the domestic comforts of home. "Dining Out," dubbed in the program as a "word-and-musical meal," presents a scene in which a couple identified as "Boy and Girl Diners" spend an evening in a restaurant. And "spend" is the operative word. At once, a Coatroom Boy and a Coatroom Girl offer to take their accessories (hat, coats, and cane) with the quip that "for a dollar or so you can buy them back again." Attended by the Headwaiter, the Diners then take their seats and order their meal—oysters, chicken, cauliflower, and mushrooms for the main course, a French pastry for dessert, and a cigar. The foods appear in the form of featured chorus members, dancing and singing their brief biographies. The Chicken, for example, tells her story in a way that allows Berlin to quote—or rather paraphrase—one of his earlier songs ("I Want to Go Back to Michigan," 1912):

I was born
Way out in Michigan on a farm;
I'd have sworn
That no one ever would do me harm.
Like a baby I was fed
Till I grew fat; then I was led
Out to the barn,
And in a minute I lost my head.
"Oh, how I wish again
That I was in Michigan
Back on the farm."

But before the food appears, the Diners express through song their longing for a simpler, quieter meal at home. "A Cozy Kitchenette Apartment" comprises a complete song embedded in the middle of a scene marked thus far by quick exchanges of dialogue in a quarter-note patter that was Berlin's default style for developing plot and character through music. Another quotation appears here when the diners imagine listening to "Humoresque" (the same Dvořák tune featured in the "Pretty Girl" number of the 1919 *Follies*) on the phonograph. The "Cozy Kitchenette Apartment" song embodies another recurrent trope in Berlin's theater song palette that would resonate long on Broadway: a young couple imagining the quaint, idealized retreat where they will enjoy the domestic bliss of marriage—whether cottage, country home, or apartment.

Each part of the meal makes its entrance and achieves its exposition—an echo of the "Follies Salad" opening of Ziegfeld's 1919 edition. And, typically, Berlin exploits the culinary variety in order to conjure disparate musical styles: the Oysters appear in a lively ragtime song; the Chicken's song conjures a rube-song style (with its countrified protagonist); the Mushroom and Cauliflower feature a waltz; the French Pastry sings and dances to some saucy can-can music; the cigar appears to the accompaniment of habanera rhythms associated with what is supposed its native Cuba, but the cigar actually reveals itself as a fake—merely a five-cent panatela. Then, heralded by a phrase from the famous Funeral March from Chopin's *Piano Sonata in B-flat Minor*, the "Check" appears, impersonated by yet another chorus member, and explains itself in a slowly rocking, solemn melody in 6/8 time. The Coatroom Boy and Girl then deliver the hat, walking cane, and coats (reprising their earlier melody and the joke that "for a dollar or so you can buy them back again"). The boy and girl begin to leave, but eight chorus girls emerge from trees as the "Tips"—reminding the young man "Don't forget the little Tip, tip, tip, tip." The scene continues "after Boy Diner is cleaned out thoroughly tipping," and the couple sings a reprise of its "cozy kitchenette" song as the scene finally ends.

The "Dining Out" scene was one of the show's most elaborate numbers—featuring more than ten minutes of continuous music with multiple keys, meters, and melodic styles, ranging from speechlike patter and speech itself to lyrical melody. The song "Cozy Kitchenette Apartment" stands out as a melodic jewel placed in the center of its setting. Like the prologue, the entire number reiterated the show's overall theme that music—Irving Berlin's music—was the element that distinguished it from shows putting more emphasis on comedy or beauty. Yet "Dining Out" was also a sight to behold, for it exploited the theater's onstage platform elevators, and many reviewers singled it out for special praise and description. "The scenic effects are a constant delight," wrote one. "In the 'Dining Out' episode, the diners at their table rise slowly into mid-air, and underneath them the various features of the dinner come symbolized in the forms of pretty dancers."[42] Likewise, *Variety*'s reviewer Jack Lait claimed that "the staging is extraordinary. It starts in a café, the floor of which lifts to a balcony, carrying the principals up, while below them in pantomime are enacted the items of their café menu. For a pre-finale, trees come to life with girls in them [the Tips] and there is a blare of animation, when suddenly it is transformed to the bungalow they have been singing about, and they are at home, washing dishes. A smash."[43]

A key figure in the "Dining Out" scene was Joseph Santley, a romantic leading man with matinee-idol looks (which we know not just from photographs but from the fact that he had starred in a 1910 musical comedy called *The Matinee Idol*). Berlin knew him from his leading role in *Stop! Look! Listen!* as Van Cortland Parke, the benefactor and romantic interest of Gaby Deslys's Cinderella-like protagonist. In real life he had married the singer-dancer Ivy Sawyer in 1916, and together they were the "Boy and Girl Diners" in the "Dining Out" scene.

Santley also starred in the next number, which likewise features an uninterrupted flow of continuous music portraying a man enjoying his "Little Book of Poetry." As in "Dining Out," the scene offers a contrast between going out and staying in, but the man, in this case, remains home. Here, the protagonist compares his life of quiet contemplation with its antithesis, the noisy, aimless life of the cabaret crowd:

Some folks who don't know what to do with their evenings,
Up till dawn with their dress clothes on they will roam,
Dancing round in a cabaret,
Homeward bound at the break of day—

The singer proceeds to deliver a refrain about how "Mister Kipling and Poe / Are the best friends I know" in a song style redolent of a genteel parlor ballad. As the number continues, the protagonists of several poems—Poe's Annabel Lee, Kipling's Vampire, and Longfellow's Evangeline and Paul Revere, and Whittier's Maud Muller—come to life and, in the case of the vampire, actually sing.[44] The music launches a rag-like style as Paul Revere and Maud Muller conduct their romance with support from Kipling's Gunga Din, Longfellow's Hiawatha, and Poe's Raven. Then, after Maud—the yearning, unfulfilled rustic maiden of Whittier's poem—agrees to marry Paul, they hear the wedding bells. The passage alludes to the "bells, bells, bells" of another famous Poe verse—a reference that probably doubled as another wink to the revue regulars who could remember Berlin's song "Bells" from the 1920 *Follies*.[45] The fantasy fades and the singer is left alone again, reprising his opening melody about "my little book of poetry."

The number accentuates the musical contrast between the singer's sentimental ballad *about* poetry and the ragtime song that animates the promiscuous mixing of poetry's familiar characters. In other words, the ballad presents poetry as a domestic comfort, while ragtime activates the creative imagination: it makes poetry come alive. Berlin matches the ballad style to the domestic sanctuary and the man's conservative middle-class poetic tastes. Ragtime intrudes upon the scene as a figment of the man's imagination, a disruption and a stylistic aberration that matches the mixing of poetic characters. Thus, the ragtime section does what ragtime had often done in Berlin's work: it puts a modern twist on the familiar, as in Berlin's famous 1911 invitation "to hear the Swanee River played in ragtime" and in the "ragtime opera" of *Watch Your Step*. By 1921 the notion of ragging the classics was passé, but it reappears here in a new guise. The "classics" in this case come from English-language poetry and thus there is no older music to "rag," just words and stories.

The second act features two other musical sketches, each engaging with the kind of topical fads in which revues tended to trade. In "Fair Exchange," Berlin presents a satire on contemporary marriage and divorce. Two couples appear before a judge "waiting at the court around the corner" to grant them divorces. On behalf of both couples, a lawyer makes a convincing case for the breakup in a witty pair of quatrains that sums up a case of spouse swapping:

> The husbands are the best of friends;
> They've been so all through life—
> In fact, when they're not with each other,
> They're with each other's wife.
> And the wives are very clubby,
> As the evidence has shown:
> They adore each other's hubby
> And they share everything they own.

When the jury makes its decision ("Divorce—in the first degree!"), the members of the First Couple and Second Couple look at their newly divorced spouses and exclaim "We're free," and then turn to embrace the others' spouse. The newly reconstituted couples (Man 1 and Woman 2, and Woman 1 and Man 2) leave the courtroom to visit the "parson waiting / At the church around the corner" and immediately remarry. There, the parson asks the couples exactly the same question that the judge had asked—"What do you want?"—and of course their reply this time (marriage) is precisely the opposite of the one they gave to the judge (divorce). The couples then look forward to settling down in the flat "waiting / At the house around the corner," which would seem to bring the scene to closure. But as the chorus rejoices with the newlyweds (in part to the tune of Mendelssohn's famous "Wedding March"), the lawyer notes: "then / We'll change the scenery again / To a Court around the corner," completing the cycle and thus reinforcing this satire on the fragility and transience of contemporary marriage. With the phrase "change the scenery," the lawyer's line also highlights the inherent theatricality of the divorce court and the church wedding.

Music flows through the entire number as it carries action and dialogue, alternating between lyric song and declamatory patter. The recurring "around the corner" tune acts as the main chorus, and its appearance marks key moments in the scene's "plot." Its melody conjures the dainty sway of early Jerome Kern tunes written for the British stage (or for British imports on the American stage) such as "How'd You Like to Spoon with Me" (1905), and recalls the style of the show's earlier number for a couple, "Cozy Kitchenette Apartment." But here Berlin deploys the style ironically: the verse presents the First Couple as a happy pair, but not until the final line of the verse does the audience learn why (ex. 4.6).

Only when the couples enter the courtroom and the church does the music shift to the declamatory style typical of Berlin's extended-number conversations, in a style comparable to recitative in opera. The interactions among the judge, jury, and the two couples, and then among parson, congregation, and the two couples, feature speech-like alternations of more commonplace quarter-note patter. Meanwhile, the number features several key changes, in an almost symmetrical pattern that starts and ends in G major, before ratcheting up a half-step for the final refrain (for the "flat . . . / At the house around the corner"). As in a lot of nineteenth-century Italian opera that Berlin knew, each key change marks a significant dramatic moment.

The scene's attitude toward marriage may strike musical theater aficionados as more redolent of Sondheim than of early Berlin. Yet as Gerald Bordman notes, several early musical comedies traded in marital infidelity and divorce, including *Marrying Mary*, derived from a play titled *My Wife's Husbands*, in which a divorced woman is courted simultaneously by a man and his grown son.[46] It reflected the period's larger fad for bedroom farces, musical and otherwise.[47]

Indeed, the 1921 *Music Box Revue* had already placed that fad at the core of its sketch material in scenes featuring Florence Moore, a comedienne well known for her flair for bedroom farce. In the 1917–18 season, Moore had appeared in a popular play titled *Parlor, Bedroom, and Bath*, and in the 1921 *Music Box Revue* she starred in two sketches parodying the style: "Under the Bed" and "A Play without a Bedroom."

Example 4.6. Music Box Revue, "Fair Exchange" (1921).

Like a cou-ple of child - ren, We're so hap-py and gay,___ For we've been

mar - ried two years now—___ And we're gon-na be di-vorced to - day!

"Under the Bed" rushes quickly through the genre's formulaic plot devices: a series of lovers come to visit Moore and one by one she escorts them to a position under the bed to hide from the next lover who appears.[48] Moore's on-stage escapades became a joke in another musical sketch featuring Berlin himself.

In the show's penultimate number, Berlin appeared for what the program called an "interview," in which the Eight Little Notes (now reporters) ask Berlin how he goes about his work. "I kidded myself," he said. "It was a very tough spot, right next to closing," he recalled fifty years later, using the vaudevillian language for the program position of a show's headliner.[49] With its continuously flowing score and a protagonist who was himself the show's composer, the scene "says it with music" and again reinforces the revue's keynote. At this point in his career, Berlin was as respected a performer as he was a songwriter: Since his 1911 performance in vaudeville that prompted Dillingham to hire him to compose the score for *Watch Your Step*, he had performed two numbers in *Yip Yip Yaphank*, and he had sung in vaudeville again at the Palace as recently as 1919. Yet the composer's appearance on stage was still a novelty for a revue. Just seeing and hearing Berlin perform on stage would have been a major attraction for audiences. Moreover, the number is chock-full of earlier Berlin songs, and if one were searching for a precedent for Berlin's later cavalcade film musicals—movies whose plots took shape around mostly preexisting songs such as *Alexander's Ragtime Band* (1938), *Blue Skies* (1946), *Easter Parade* (1948), and *White Christmas* (1954), for

Berlin and the Eight Little Notes, who joined him onstage for "An Interview" in the first Music Box Revue. Courtesy of Rodgers & Hammerstein, on behalf of the Estate of Irving Berlin.

example—this number might be seen as a pilot for those larger and more famous projects. In the space of 245 bars (perhaps seven or eight minutes in performance), Berlin presents a narrative medley that strings together passages from ten different songs across the past decade in order to tell a whimsical story of his career. It goes back, predictably, to "Alexander's Ragtime Band," which serves as a kind of touchstone of his songwriting career and as a foil, stylistically and chronologically, to the show's say-it-with-music theme. If the number became a seed for future film musicals, however, it too seems to have had roots in an earlier model. In Berlin's 1911 vaudeville appearance, *Variety* had reported that Berlin came on "next to last" and "sang two of his newest songs" in a "medley of his own 'hits,' woven into a story."[50] The description matches almost exactly what Berlin would do a decade later at the Music Box.

Berlin's 1921 medley "story" begins with an orchestral introduction that must have been a musical pun: it is based on Berlin's song "Tell Me Little Gypsy," the most popular number from the previous year's *Follies*. The pun, which may seem forced today, would be that Berlin is the "little gypsy"—perhaps a sly reference both to his small stature and his Jewishness—who will soon "tell" his interviewers about his work. Soon the Eight Little Notes appear, and they explain their "work" through declamatory patter laced with references, in both lyrics and music, to "Say It with Music," reinforcing the show's claim to distinction (ex. 4.7). As the Reporters finish their statement on the phrase "with Irving Berlin," the orchestra begins a brief transitional passage that invokes two more quotations: one from "Alexander's Ragtime Band" and the other in a minor-key vamp introducing Berlin himself that contains another sly in-joke, a one-bar quotation of the musical phrase "look at 'em doin' it" from "The Syncopated Walk." In the next few minutes, the reporters and audience will literally "look at" Berlin "doing" his thing.

The interview begins in the familiar patter style with which Berlin habitually conveys dialogue in his extended scenes. Mostly in the key of F major, the passage gets a lift when Berlin gives a response in A major. The return to F lends freshness to the Reporters' next "Say it with Music" quotation. Meanwhile, Berlin's answer that "I write my songs very easily . . . I go right home and write it," belies his actual statements about writing by the "sweat of my brow." The Reporters repeat Berlin's phrase in a Gilbert-and-Sullivan-style echo: "He goes right home and writes it."

From here on, Berlin takes over the number with a sequence of some of his most famous and popular songs of the previous decade, now set to new words designed to address the interests of the Reporters. He is, of course, practicing what he has been preaching for the whole show: he's saying it with music. He begins by explaining how

Example 4.7. Music Box Revue, *"An Interview"* (1921).

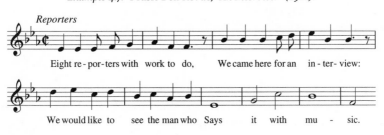

he came to write the 1911 song "Ragtime Violin." He then tells the Reporters about the Berlin-Snyder collaboration "I Want to Be in Dixie," in another a wry joke about the songwriting business:

> I don't know why, but ev'ry guy
> Who has the knack for words and music
> Wants to tell the world he's going to
> D-I-X-I don't know how to spell it.
> But I know there's lots of dough
> In a song of Dixieland.[51]

Berlin then shifts to "Oh! How I Hate to Get up in the Morning." After two lines of the original lyrics, he explains (to the song's next musical phrase): "Let me tell you from the start / That was one came from the heart!" The new lyrics here continue with an allusion to the leading comedienne's particular talent:

> A soldier's life is nice, I'm sure,
> But since I'm out, like Florence Moore,
> I've spent the most of my time in bed.

For later observers, the line's meaning and currency remain inaccessible without the knowledge that theatergoers in 1921 were assumed to possess: that Berlin himself had sung "Oh! How I Hate to Get Up in the Morning" just three years earlier in *Yip Yip Yaphank*; that Broadway was in the midst of a fad for bedroom farces; that Moore herself made a specialty of acting in them; *and*, moreover, that she had mocked that specialty in the Music Box earlier that night.

The next three songs in the sequence focus the interview on finances. When the Reporters ask if "Alexander's Ragtime Band" earned a lot of money, Berlin replies (singing the last section of his famous tune):

> I must admit, 'twas quite a bit,
> But when the Music Box was planned,
> I never knew how many songs it took to build a theatre,
> So ev'ry night, I try to write
> An "Alexander's Ragtime Band."

The music and dialogue segue to a new interview question, sung now to one of Berlin's hits from the 1919 *Follies*, "You'd Be Surprised."

> REPORTERS: And does it cost very much
>   A pretty theatre to build?
> BERLIN: You'd be surprised.
> REPORTERS: And will you lose very much
>   If ev'ry seat isn't filled?
> BERLIN: You'd be surprised.

When the Reporters ask "Who's gonna pay for the losses?" Berlin answers with yet another song, "Nobody Knows and Nobody Seems to Care," which he had sung at the Palace in his 1919 vaudeville appearance.

Example 4.8. Music Box Revue, "All by Myself" in "An Interview" (1921).

At last, the Reporters wind up the interview by asking Berlin to sing his "latest song," and he proceeds to sing a full chorus of "All By Myself" with its original words. The setting reveals something obscured in later performances of the song treating it as a torchy ballad: its syncopated melody (featuring the tied reverse cakewalk pattern, to be precise) and pounding on-the-beat bass conjured elements of a style that contemporaries recognized as Berlin's distinctive brand of jazz (ex. 4.8).

The musical sketches and the prologue in the 1921 Music Box Revue provide a vivid glimpse of what an opera by Berlin would have looked and sounded like: alternately comic and poignant, vividly connected to the current American scene in its topicality and language, and featuring musically declaimed conversation while channeling lyrical melody at key points in order to distill feeling or reflection. If he did not ultimately write the Great American Opera, it may be because he knew both his mastery and his economic interests lay in the song unit, and that the vast canvas of the operatic musical sequence tended to dilute his melodic gifts. Yet opera remained an important force in Berlin's work, and in the Music Box Revues, it also appeared in the guise of musical numbers about opera and its counterpart in dance: ballet.

BALLET AND OPERA

By opening act 2 with a ballet, the first Music Box Revue picked up yet another current trend and set a pattern for subsequent editions of the show. Titled "The Fountain of Youth," its music was likely not composed by Berlin.[52] Yet because Berlin had such a strong hand in shaping the show, it certainly refracts an element of his revue concept and reveals a neglected aspect of the era's musical theater. Ballet had quickly become a fixture of revues after the Ballet Russes's first visit to New York in early 1916. That event may have been seen as an opportunity to bring more classiness to revue dancing, but above all ballet now carried the cachet of topicality and currency that revues relished. Musical theater historians have so far tended, understandably, to focus on the period of the 1930s and 1940s as a peak period for the incorporation of ballets into musical comedies and musical plays, through the work of innovative choreographers such as George Balanchine and Agnes de Mille, but Broadway's ballet fad dates back at least as far as the late 1910s.[53] Indeed, dozens of revue programs reveal that the act 2 opening became the conventional slot for a revue's ballet number.[54] The year 1916—soon after the Ballet Russes's arrival—was the watershed when five different revues featured a ballet, or a parody of one, as in the "Ballet Loose" that appeared in *The Century Girl*, a show on which Berlin had collaborated (see table 4.1).

While de rigueur in the 1916–1917 season, however, ballets seem to have declined in 1918–19. The trendy revues launched in those immediate postwar years—such as the *Greenwich Village Follies* and *George White's Scandals*—did not feature them. So when Berlin included a ballet number in his 1921 revue, it must have appeared to be a traditional, if not passé, choice. Perhaps by the early 1920s ballet attracted less fascination than toleration—or worse. Reviews of the Music Box's first ballet were mixed. When Alexander Woollcott, in his review of opening night, considered ways the show could be cut so that it might end by about 11 p.m., he pointed to "that ugly and fearfully stupid ballet which begins the second act."[55] Other critics were more generous. The *World* claimed that it featured "some of the most graceful dancing of the night."[56] *Variety's* Jack Lait offered the most detailed description of the scene: "The overture glides into a classical [style] and the curtain reveals a mythical garden with a fountain. It is the fountain of youth, Santley playing youth. The allegory takes up but a minute, when girls came up from nowhere and a gorgeous ballet fills the eye."[57]

All three of the remaining *Music Box Revue*'s would include at least one ballet number. For the 1924 show, Berlin enlisted the talents of the petite ballerina Ula Sharon, who was featured in two numbers. Woollcott, proving that he was not a ballet hater, lavished high praise on a scene called "Ballet Dancers at Home," in which a married couple (played by Sharon and Carl Randall) cooks supper then goes to bed to the strains of Carl Maria von Weber's *Invitation to the Dance* and Debussy's *Prelude to the Afternoon of a Faun*. Woollcott called it "the most charming and the most distinguished number I ever saw in a music hall."[58] Berlin offered yet another twist on ballet in "I Want to Be a Ballet Dancer," featuring Fanny Brice as a klutzy Jewish girl aspiring to be "just like Pavlova." The sheet music covers for songs from the 1922 show reinforced the revues' ballet themes by portraying several lithe ballerinas floating *en pointe* from an opened music box.[59]

Opera numbers, operatic themes, and operatic singers also held a prominent place in the *Music Box Revues*. Berlin composed two types of opera-related numbers in them. He derived the ideas from two distinct earlier models: the thematic parade-of-girls number epitomized by "A Pretty Girl Is Like a Melody," and the burlesqued opera style so lauded in the "ragtime opera" number in *Watch Your Step*.

Table 4.1. Ballets and Pantomimes as Act 2 Openers in Broadway Revues, 1916–24

Ballet or Pantomime title	Show
"The Blushing Ballet: Dance"	*Ziegfeld Follies of 1916*
"An Olympian Ballet"	*Passing Show of 1916*
"Anna Pavlova in The Sleeping Beauty"	*The Big Show* (1916)
"A Burmese Ballet"	*The Show of Wonders* (1916)
"The Ballet Loose"	*The Century Girl* (1916)
"Colonial Ballet"	*Doing Our Bit* (1917)
"Falling Leaves: A Poem-Choreographic"	*Miss 1917* (1917)
"The Spider Ballet"	*George White's Scandals* (1920)
"The Kiss"	*Broadway Brevities of 1920*
"Dream Fantasies Ballet"	*The Passing Show of 1921*
"The Fountain of Youth"	*Music Box Revue* (1921)
"Princess Beautiful (A Cleveland Bronner Ballet)"	*Make It Snappy* (1922)
"Farljandio"	*Ziegfeld Follies of 1922*
"La Repetition (after Degas)"	*Michio Itow's Pin Wheel* (1922)
"In Gold: 'A Ballet of Siam'"	*The Passing Show of 1922*
"Cowardice (A Mimodrama by Leon Bakst)"	*Revue Russe* (1922)
"The Fisherman's Dream"	*Music Box Revue of 1923*
"La Marquise"	*Ziegfeld Follies of 1923*
"Ballet of the Winds"	*Earl Carroll's Vanities* (1924)
"Alice in Wonderland"	*Music Box Revue of 1924*

"Diamond Horse-shoe" (1922), forged from the mold of "A Pretty Girl Is Like a Melody," was a delicate ballad linking elusive feminine beauty to familiar strains of "good music" that matched chorus girls masquerading as operatic heroines, including Isolde, Carmen, Aida, Butterfly and several others.[60] The number was singled out for special praise in the *New York Times*, which noted that the "diamond horse-shoe affair . . . fairly takes the breath away."[61] The song's singer was none other than John Steel, whom Berlin hired away from the *Ziegfeld Follies* for the 1922 and 1923 *Music Box Revues*. Those shows featured several other lyrical parade-of-beauties numbers modeled on the "Pretty Girl" urtext, a type of number lacking in the first *Music Box Revue*. In the haunting "Lady of the Evening" (1922), a remarkable song, Steel portrayed the sad clown Pierrot as ten chorus girls played the ladies of the evening. Other numbers followed suit. In "Will She Come from the East?" (1922), the singer wonders where he would find his true love among four women representing the East, West, North, and South of the United States. In "One Girl" (1923), Steel portrayed a "roaming Romeo" who has found his enduring love at last, even as he admits, in a catalog reminiscent of Mozart's *Don Giovanni*, to lingering memories of women he loved in Spain, Holland, Italy, France, and Ireland—each represented by a chorus girl.

Steel's "Diamond Horse-shoe" number had its precedents not just in Berlin's earlier opera songs but in a jewel song from the 1921 show featuring the singer with the voice of Berlin's "beautiful music": Wilda Bennett. In addition to "Say It with Music," Bennett sang "The Legend of the Pearls," in which Berlin took up the old story of what happens to a lovelorn woman's tears. The song idea opened up another opportunity for the stage director Hassard Short, and in fact it launched a fascination with "jewel numbers," which would recur in several notable shows through the ensuing decade.[62] The number also featured the Eight Little Notes, now posing as pearls on a necklace, and a solo dancer. Berlin's lyric tells the sad story of a woman who lost her love "on her wedding day," so "beside the sea she sat and cried, / A most unhappy girl. / And ev'ry tear that fell below / Became a precious pearl." The refrain develops the idea in a musical language by now closely associated with elegant women in Berlin's revue numbers: long melody tones supported by dainty filigree in the accompaniment, and a gentle, subdued syncopated pattern in the bridge. The refrain opens, too, with a clear case of "eye music"—in the score, the melody's whole notes *look* like pearls (ex. 4.9).

Jack Lait wrote two full paragraphs on the scene—especially on Hassard Short's design—an astonishingly large tract of print real estate for a single musical number in a show that ran almost four hours on opening night:

> Never has anything more gorgeous been given to any audience. Miss Bennett appears in a gown that is mad with pearls. She blazes with them for they are soaked in light for hours before she enters, and sings a song, when lo! A drop

Example 4.9. Music Box Revue, *"The Legend of the Pearls," refrain, mm. 1–4 (1921).*

vanishes, and there is a hanging portiere of pearls, from tormentor to floor and the full width of the stage, while against the back wall is a lavelliere of brilliants, flanked with tremendous pearl pendants some ten feet long. From every side come girls dressed in pearls on black. Suddenly the lights flash off and the pearls alone are seen, like a million radium baubles in the dark. The audience, already stunned by the spectacle, is here taken entirely breathless. When the lights go up again and it seems nothing more could be done to enhance what is already miraculous, Miss Bennett re-enters, two pearl-bristling pages holding a train of pearls—more pearls—millions of pearls. The pearl parade is bewildering and no word-picture of it would visualize it.[63]

Bennett would not appear in any other edition of the *Music Box Revues*, but her vocal style represented the operatic end of the spectrum of the show's many voice types. That role would soon be filled by an aspiring opera singer.

In the 1923 show, Berlin included a hilarious send-up of opera, extending his penchant for opera burlesque begun in early songs such as "That Opera Rag" and his "Opera Burlesque" on the sextet from *Lucia di Lammermoor* and continued in his Dillingham shows. In this number, he juxtaposed several operatic quotations with the popular song "Yes! We Have No Bananas," the 1923 hit by Frank Silver and Irving Cohn purporting to be the call of a Greek street vendor. The operatic allusions included several that Berlin had invoked before: the "Triumphal March" from Verdi's *Aida* (quoted in "That Opera Rag"), the quartet from Verdi's *Rigoletto* (the basis for the "ragtime opera" in *Watch Your Step*), the Offenbach "Barcarolle" (from *Tales of Hoffmann*, used in the "Pretty Girl" number), the "Ride of the Valkyries" from Wagner's *Ring*. The number works up to a musical frenzy, growing louder ("fortissimo") and faster ("accel[erando] jazz tempo") at the end, where it returns to the original "Bananas" melody then cadences unexpectedly on the familiar "shave-and-a-haircut-two-bits" melody—like a punch line to an old joke made fresh in a new one.[64] Adding comic incongruity to the scene was the motley sextet of singers it featured, including John Steel, comedian Frank Tinney, leading-man Joseph Santley, actress Lora Sanderson ("not long on voice," according to *Variety*'s critic[65]), comedienne Florence Moore, and the operatic soprano Grace Moore.

Indeed, Grace Moore's presence in the 1923 and 1924 *Music Box Revues* added operatic luster to the shows—and reveals the lengths Berlin would go to add a real prima donna to his theatrical arsenal. Berlin had discovered Moore in Paris and got her to sign a contract written on a tablecloth at the fashionable restaurant Ciro's, for which the waiter ordered Berlin to pay. In her autobiography, Moore admits that her chief reason for accepting the job was to earn money; her real aspirations were to sing on a legitimate operatic stage.[66] Yet Moore's ambitions and abilities helped to steer the ship of Berlin's revue songwriting and the shows' reception in the press. *Variety* hailed her as "the best feminine voice the Music Box has had, and she partly eclipsed the tenor of John Steel." Burns Mantle claimed that "the songs are the best of all, especially when Miss Moore sings."[67] Steel grew "extremely jealous," according to Moore, and other actors also felt outshined by the opera diva, so she became the target of pranks—having her toe stepped on just before hitting a high note, for example, and getting a jolt from a "cute electric-shock chair" courtesy of the "roguish, lovable" Frank Tinney.[68] Yet she recalled her time at the Music Box as "happy, eventful days" because she was "a young star with her first taste of success and fame."[69] Indeed, her presence shaped the music of the last two revues perhaps more than any other single performer: Berlin wrote at least ten numbers that featured Moore.

Those songs tend to strike one of two keynotes: nostalgia and romantic yearning. In "The Waltz of Long Ago," Moore intoned virtues typical of Berlin's waltzes. "I love to dance / The dreamy waltz of long ago, / When Grandmama and Grandpapa / Were girl and beau." Joseph Santley and Ivy Sawyer played the grandparents, and the set reinforced the number's nostalgic theme as it "transformed into a drawingroom of the '70s, with costuming being of that period also."[70] Similarly nostalgic was Moore's presentation of an extended number that traces the growth of a little girl. Titled "Rockabye, Baby," it began as a lullaby in which Moore, in the role of a mother, sings her baby daughter to sleep. The number continued as a medley of songs with new lyrics, each depicting a different stage of the girl's life: as a four-year-old playing in the nursery, as a school girl with "books and slate, / Standing alone at the school-house gate," then as a young woman in her "first romance," followed by a wedding. The medley ends as the singer envisions the bride standing "over a cradle," as the medley segues back to the refrain, now portrayed as the song the grown girl sings to her new baby. The song movingly traces the circle of life, musically returning to the image of mother and baby with which it began. Except for the reference to "School Days," and a quotation of "here comes the bride" (Wagner's wedding march from *Lohengrin*), it remains unclear what tunes comprised the medley, as only the refrain appears to survive.[71]

Moore also brought romance to her Music Box numbers. "An Orange Grove in California" featured Moore in a duet with John Steel portraying a couple separated by a great distance and longing to reunite in the setting described in the title. The song impressed theatergoers as a complete sensory experience of sight, sound, and even scent, with what *Variety*'s critic hailed as an "outstanding scenic effect":

> What looked like real oranges hung from the trees and filled baskets. At the finale all glowed with light, dimly at first and brilliantly when the curtains were drawn . . . the house being flooded with the perfume of oranges by means of an idea credited to William Norton, the Music Box's (theatre) manager. So subtle was the scent effect that it could not but create a buzz throughout the house.[72]

More than any other performer, Oscar Shaw, the handsome leading man of the 1924 revue, appeared with Moore in duets. One duet added in 1925 for that show's tour marks the most enduring Berlin melody of their collaboration: "All Alone." On one side of the stage stood the suave Shaw in a black dinner jacket; on the other side stood the charming Moore in a black velvet evening dress. Each held a 1920s model telephone whose mouthpiece projected a small light that illuminated their faces.[73] In the otherwise dark theater, they sang of their loneliness in one of Berlin's most poignant and unusual waltzes—a song that flows from one phrase to the next without repeating itself and that descends, like a solitary falling leaf, in a disarming series of parallel phrases with but a single rhyme:

I'm all alone ev'ry evening,
All alone feeling blue,
Wond'ring where you are
And how you are
And if you are
All alone too.

The scene, added during the run of the fourth and final *Music Box Revue*, epitomized the whole series, distinguished above all by "class"—the single word with which it was most often identified during its run and by which it is still remembered.[74]

Moore also sang in a sequence leading into the 1924 show's act 1 finale that one critic singled out as "worthy of a popular opera." But the number had little to do with the genre that most operagoers knew. Straining to categorize it, the critic called it "classical jazz."[75]

BERLIN'S JAZZ

The Music Box, in fact, was where Berlin incubated his brand of jazz, and the style reveals a potent intersection of musical, linguistic, theatrical, and social currents in the early 1920s.[76] One critic referred to several of his numbers as "jazz creation[s]."[77] The critic was not alone: many of his contemporaries linked jazz to Berlin. An account of the 1922 show, for example, acknowledged Berlin, revealingly, as "*still* the single-handed master of syncopes and jazz" (emphasis added).[78] In 1925 Berlin's first biographer Alexander Woollcott noted "the preposterous fashion of using the word 'jazz' and the word 'Berlin' as interchangeable terms"—and devoted most of the book's final chapter to reinforcing the association.[79] By the mid-1920s press reports regularly describe Berlin as a "jazz composer" and even "king of jazz";[80] they further link him with efforts to stage a "jazz opera" at the Metropolitan Opera House,[81] and to develop (with Sergei Diaghilev) "a new ballet to express the effect of modern jazz music."[82] Such projects never materialized, and Berlin's status as jazz "king" evaporated with the Jazz Age. Since then Berlin hardly ranks a mention in jazz history writing—except as the writer of standards taken up by bona fide jazz musicians.[83] One biographer, Laurence Bergreen, has even insisted that Berlin "despised" jazz.[84] Berlin's work contradicts that notion. Yet his identification as a jazz composer at a time when, as Mark Tucker has written, jazz was "a fluid, unstable construct," raises the question of why and how the Berlin's *jazz* label made sense to so many observers at the time.[85]

The song "Everybody Step" established the paradigm. After its premiere in the 1921 *Music Box Revue*, at least three prominent commentators identified it as an exemplar of jazz. These included composers John Alden Carpenter, who cited "Everybody Step" as one of the "ten great masterpieces" in music history,[86] and George Gershwin, who more modestly pointed to "Everybody Step" as the single best exercise for singers trying to learn jazz. Unfortunately, even Gershwin was vague in defining his terms and applying them to the song, beyond his reference to what he called its "rhythmical variation."[87] Yet looking at the song and others related to it gives us strong clues about its jazz credentials.

In "Everybody Step," Berlin constructs a playful collage of then-familiar figures in a way that suggests he wanted the seams to show. The crucial passage is the principal phrase of the refrain (ex. 4.10). Here Berlin combines disparate features associated with ragtime and blues with concision unprecedented in American popular song: *secondary rag* rhythm (mm. 2–4),[88] marked by patterns of three eighth notes against an explicit duple-meter beat; a related figure called two-note secondary rag (mm. 5–6 and 7–8)[89]; *blue notes*, especially the melodically and harmonically prominent flat seventh (in mm. 1–3); a pattern that I call *blues bass*, with its pounding four-beat chords in contrast to the oom-pah alternating bass of ragtime and rag-inflected song (mm. 2–7),[90] and a truncated *blues chord progression* (through the first half of m. 7)— all packed into an eight-bar phrase comprising the "A" section of an A A′ B A″ song form.

To an ear attuned to Tin Pan Alley, blues, and ragtime in the first two decades of the twentieth century, the passage comprises a collage of features that had currency and strong African American resonance—while also holding its African American sources at some distance, as if placing them in quotation marks. Heard in this way, the passage does conform to later notions that jazz represented a fusion of ragtime and blues. But such recognition does not otherwise bring the example closer to jazz as it has been construed by later jazz musicians and historians. It still privileges notated composition, omitting most of the very features that would later come to define the idiom. Yet Berlin's juxtaposition of distinctive blues and ragtime features within the refrain's principal phrase may help to explain why so many 1920s commentators pointed to "Everybody Step" as a paradigm for the new style.

Beyond its principal phrase, Berlin reinforces the song's rich resonance with unmistakable allusions to—and, in one phrase, a near quotation of—three of his own songs that had accrued strong ragtime associations since their appearance in sheet music, stage performances, and sound recordings in the early 1910s: "Alexander's Ragtime Band" (1911), "Everybody's Doing It Now" (1911),[91] and "The Syncopated Walk" (1914). Freely deploying elements derived from these songs, Berlin creates, in effect, a lineage for "jazz" that leads back to his own earlier songs. The opening phrase of "Everybody Step," for example, clearly derives from that of "The Syncopated Walk" (ex. 4.11a and 4.11b). Both feature a repeated one-bar idea marked by a strong downbeat chord, a chromatic fill, and a dotted-rhythm pickup to the next bar. The roots of both phrases extend back to "Alexander's Ragtime Band," whose famous refrain introduces the rhythmic pattern (ex. 4.11c).

In "Everybody Step," however, Berlin draws an unmistakable connection to "The Syncopated Walk," as he actually quotes a phrase of words and music from its refrain: "Look at 'em doin' it"—which, like the opening bars of "Everybody Step," features an ascending chromatic triplet (ex. 4.12a and 4.12b). A year earlier, moreover, Berlin had already reused that phrase from "Syncopated Walk" in a song that evokes jazz, a song for the *Ziegfeld Follies of 1920* called "The Syncopated Vamp" (see the piano part in the second measure of ex. 4.13). That song celebrates a "jazzy Cleopatra" from whose "stylish clothes / A little bit of her ankle shows," and whose vigorous dancing and bold flirtations make her, like jazz itself, both dangerous and irresistible. The song abetted the widespread linkage of jazz and promiscuous femininity—here, exoticized in the familiar and safely distant image of Cleopatra—supporting a

Example 4.10. "Everybody Step," refrain, mm. 1–8 (1921).

Example 4.11

4.11a. "Everybody Step," verse, beginning.

Soon_____ You'll hear a tune_____ That's gon-na lift

4.11b. "The Syncopated Walk," verse, beginning.

Strange,_____ But there's a change_____ In how the peo-

4.11c. "Alexander's Ragtime Band," refrain, beginning.

Come on and hear,_____ come on and hear_____ Al - ex-

gender-charged rhetoric that quickly developed into discussions of whether anyone could make a "lady" or "honest woman" out of jazz.[92] "Everybody Step" also deploys a figure that could be called the *Alexander break*, which includes a melodic rest on a downbeat articulated by a bass accent, followed by a dotted-rhythm figure, which is then repeated or sequenced. The model, again, appears in "Alexander's Ragtime Band" (ex. 4.14). Such breaks recur in songs throughout Berlin's post-"Alexander" ragtime vein.

Berlin implicates "Everybody Step" even more deeply with his brand of ragtime through links to yet another song for "everybody": "Everybody's Doing It Now," the song

Example 4.12

Example 4.12a. "Everybody Step," refrain, mm. 21–22

They sim-ply ru-in it;   Look at'em do-in' it.

Example 4.12b. "The Syncopated Walk, refrain, beginning.

Look at 'em do-in' it,   Look at 'em do-in' it,

Example 4.13. "The Syncopated Vamp," refrain, mm. 6–7 (1920).

mer-i-can shoul-der shak-ers she's the champ

that planted the phrase "doin' it" [*sic*] in popular-song vernacular by repeating it no fewer than thirteen times in its refrain. The exhortation to "Come, come don't hesitate," in "Everybody Step," also recalls the earlier song's "Come, come, come, come let us start." At the same time, the word "hesitate" recalls its use in "The Syncopated Walk" with a pun on "hesitate" referring both to its denotative meaning ("to hold back") and to its connotative allusion to the Hesitation waltz—a dance implicitly rendered passé by the more vigorous duple-meter ragtime- and jazz-related dances that became popular in the 1910s. Once again, however, these passages derive from the famous exhortations to "come on and hear" and "come on along" that Berlin had introduced in "Alexander's Ragtime Band." Berlin's effort to press controversial idioms such as ragtime and jazz into the musical mainstream seems to require the hortatory tone, calling on "everybody" to "come on and hear" the new style. All of these musical and linguistic features from Berlin's earlier songs become additional referents that fuel the musical associations conjured in "Everybody Step." Having established a network of connections through music, Berlin could leave it to others to interpret them as signs of jazz. At least one composer had already taken the cue: a short piano piece called "Jazzy," written in summer 1921 by the young Aaron Copland, uses Berlin's "come on and hear" motif in its principal theme.[93]

If "Everybody Step" drew heavily on earlier Berlin songs, it, in turn, became a wellspring of ideas for Berlin's subsequent "jazz creations" in the *Music Box Revues*. In "Pack Up Your Sins and Go to the Devil" (ex. 4.15), Berlin develops and extends the

Example 4.14. The "Alexander" break.

4.14a. "Alexander's Ragtime Band," verse, mm. 7–8.

4.14b. "Everybody Step," verse, mm. 5–6.

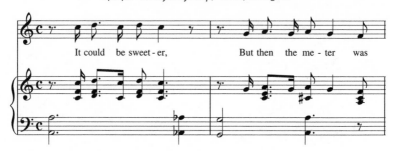

4.14c. "Everybody Step," refrain, mm. 15–16.

two-note secondary rag figure that had appeared in "Everybody Step." The song, however, places the figure in a new stylistic world by setting it to the gutty blues bass pattern. Here, too, Berlin once again invokes blues harmony but recontextualizes it, for the refrain begins not on the tonic (F) but on the dominant of the dominant (G), which then moves to the dominant (C). In the bridge, Berlin takes the song's rhythmic language a step further by reiterating its principal rhythm against an accompaniment marked by an augmented (three-note) secondary-rag pattern, which leads to an Alexander break (ex. 4.16). He ultimately crowns the number with a patter based on a new secondary-rag melody, first sung alone then presented in counterpoint to the principal tune (ex. 4.17). The patter melody itself—with its rising four-eighths-and-a-quarter figure covering three beats—bears a striking resemblance to the second strain of Zez Confrey's piano novelty "Stumbling" (1922), which Henry O. Osgood and Aaron Copland would soon identify as an exemplary jazz melody.[94]

Example 4.15. "Pack Up Your Sins and Go to the Devil," refrain, mm. 1–4.

Example 4.16. "Pack Up Your Sins," refrain, mm. 16–23.

Still other songs combine Berlin's jazz elements in a fresh way. "When You Walked Out Someone Else Walked Right In" features a melody based on the reverse tied cakewalk rhythm played over a blues bass (ex. 4.18). When the principal phrase returns, Berlin gives it a stronger blues inflection, adding the flat seventh to the harmony, and moving not to the dominant of the dominant but to the subdominant, as if he is writing a blues progression (ex. 4.19). The refrain of "Learn to Do the Strut" sustains a blues progression for almost eight bars, supported by flat sevenths and thirds, before swerving to the major submediant, as Berlin had done in "Everybody Step" (ex. 4.20). "Bring on the Pepper" combines blues bass, blue notes, secondary rag, and cakewalk rhythms, making it an obvious a sequel to "Everybody Step."

Beyond all of their musical resemblances, the songs also draw from a common well of themes linked by implications or descriptions of risqué or illicit behavior: vigorous dancing, drinking (this, during Prohibition), sexual freedom, and a carefree attitude

Example 4.17. "Pack Up Your Sins," secondary rag rhythms in patter section (mm. 1–4).

Example 4.18. "When You Walked Out Someone Else Walked Right In" (1923), refrain, mm. 1–4.

about eternal damnation—all things that jazz was thought to inspire in the 1920s. "Everybody Step," "Bring on the Pepper," and "Learn to Do the Strut" all celebrate fast dancing whose accompaniment is variously described as a "jazzy fiddle" ("Everybody Step"), "a peppy jingle / That the jazz bands love to play" ("Bring on the Pepper"), and "a jazzy tune" ("Learn to Do the Strut"). In "Pack Up Your Sins," the singer reports a message from a deceased friend who enjoys an afterlife in Hades with "the finest of gentlemen / And the finest of ladies," all of whom would "Rather be down below than up above—" because there "You'll hear a heavenly tune / That went to the Devil / Because the jazz bands, / They started pickin' it, / Then put a trick in it / A jazzy kick in it."[95] In the song "When You Walked Out Someone Else Walked Right In," the singer

Example 4.19. "When You Walked Out," refrain, mm. 17–24.

does not pine for her departed lover, but instead blithely celebrates a quick change in her romantic fortunes in the suggestive line "Off with the old love and on with the new!" Whether or not the prominent and repeated use of the word "walked" also conjures the sexual resonance that Charles Hamm found in a few of Berlin's songs dating from a decade earlier, "When You Walked Out" nevertheless suggests that sexual freedom has become a domain of gender equality.[96] Although those lyrics do not mention jazz, the music abets the message with its ragtime and blues references. The lyrics of "Tokio [sic] Blues" add an orientalizing element to references in Berlin's jazz vein and relocate the exotic femininity evoked in "The Syncopated Vamp." In a musical setting stocked with now-familiar devices such as secondary rag, blue notes, and blues bass, the lyrics evoke a girl's plaintive desire to return to her Japanese home. In early Tin Pan Alley and vaudeville song, homesickness has its most common expression in the "back-to-Dixie" number, in which the song's persona longs for the simple, idyllic world of the old South. In "Tokio Blues" Berlin uses his by now well-established jazz markers to fuse the "back-to-Dixie" number and *Japonisme* in a kind of orientalized minstrelsy that reached a peak of popularity in the years just before the *Music Box Revues*.[97]

Although musical and linguistic elements in the sheet music may go a long way to reveal features that contemporaries heard as jazz, no analysis of the phenomenon can stop there. In the case of Berlin's jazz, several elements of performance style and context framed and defined the idiom in ways that are hidden from view in the sheet music. Early performances amplify the generic implications of what Berlin wrote. Indeed, to Berlin's audiences of the early 1920s, a rich network of theatrical contexts reinforced the familial relationship of the songs and their jazz associations.

First, Berlin wrote most of his Music Box jazz songs for a sister act, most often the Brox Sisters, a close-harmony trio who embodied the suggestive image of the

Example 4.20. "Learn to Do the Strut," refrain, mm. 1–9.

newly faddish flapper—the petite, short-haired, boyishly shaped girl-woman, who wore makeup and no corset, and whose dresses tended to show some ankle and maybe more. Berlin, jazz, and sister acts had formed a bond in Berlin's first song using the word *jazz*: "Mr. Jazz Himself" (1917), whose cover featured a cameo photograph of two women and the caption "as introduced by the Watson Sisters."[98] It was the Broxes, however, who became most closely identified with Berlin's brand of jazz on stage and on sound recordings. For them, Berlin wrote "Everybody Step" and "The Schoolhouse Blues" for the 1921 show; "When You Walked Out" and "Learn to Do the Strut" for the 1923 revue; and "Tokio Blues" and "Who" for the 1924 show—all part of the song family related to "Everybody Step." (Although the Broxes did not appear in the 1922 edition of the series, Berlin had written in the same vein for a comparable sister act, the McCarthy Sisters, who premiered "Pack Up Your Sins" and "Bring on the Pepper.") In his review of the *Music Box Revue of 1924*, Alexander Woollcott described the Broxes as "the sidling trio who seem to have been expressly created to sing Irving Berlin's songs."[99]

Table 4.2. "Jazz" in Irving Berlin's *Music Box Revues*

1921	**Everybody Step** (Brox Sisters and ensemble)
	The Schoolhouse Blues* (Brox Sisters)
1922	**Pack Up Your Sins and Go to the Devil** (Margaret and Dorothy McCarthy and ensemble)
	Bring on the Pepper* (Margaret and Dorothy McCarthy, with Sylvia Jocelyn and the Eight Music Box Dancers)
1923	When You Walked Out Someone Else Walked Right In (Brox Sisters)
	Learn to Do the Strut* (Brox Sisters and ensemble)
1924	Tokio Blues* (Brox Sisters and ensemble)
	Who* (Brox Sisters)
	Call of the South / Old Folks at Home and **Bandanna Ball** (ensemble)

Bold indicates act 1 finale

* recorded by the Brox Sisters (available on *The Ultimate Irving Berlin*, vol. 2 [Pearl Gem 0117], 2002)

The Brox Sisters, who appeared in the Music Box Revues *of 1921, 1923, and 1924 and who became closely associated with Berlin's brand of jazz. Courtesy of Rodgers & Hammerstein, on behalf of the Estate of Irving Berlin.*

The Brox Sisters recorded five songs from the *Music Box Revues* around the time that the songs had their premieres in the show. The recordings reveal a standardized approach to the material that helped to stabilize the sound of Berlin's jazz and homogenize a style whose notated versions, as we have seen, evoke stylistic heterogeneity.[100] It should be noted that although the recordings are valuable documents of contemporary performance practice, they do not necessarily replicate the sounds that audiences heard from the Music Box stage. Three songs that the Brox Sisters recorded—"Bring on the Pepper," "Learn to Do the Strut," and "Tokio Blues"—were staged with a larger ensemble of performers who do not appear on the recordings. Moreover, of the act-one finales, the Broxes recorded only "Learn to Do the Strut," and that is likely a truncated version of the stage performance because Berlin's finales lasted longer than the approximately three-minute limit of a 78-r.p.m. record.

Yet the records do provide a vivid glimpse of the Broxes' singing, and thus a useful document of Berlin's jazz in performance. On record, the Broxes sang as one in tight, lockstep harmony—never once venturing even a short phrase of solo or duet. The sisters' singing style featured a high range and a coy nasality that anticipated Helen Kane and the animated character she inspired, Betty Boop. That style also had a deliberate rhythmic rigidity in a period before swing became the crucible of jazz performance, a quality especially apparent when they deliver the streams of eighth notes in secondary-rag passages, as in their 1923 recording of "Bring on the Pepper." The Broxes' approach conveyed an affect that might be characterized as innocent naughtiness, teasing the border between wholesome and risqué. In "Schoolhouse Blues" that becomes especially clear when they sing the phrase: "Now if we don't pass our exam / Ooh-woo-woo we're going to be in a jam / Mother's going to spank us, / But we don't give a——"—replacing Berlin's rhyming oath with a conspicuous silence, as if saying "damn" would be worse than academic failure and corporal punishment.[101]

In visual presentation and musical style, the singers' act seems to have been calculated to go against newly popular models of black jazz and blues performance. Indeed, they formed a stark contrast to the hefty, dark-skinned, matriarchal, and lower-voiced African American vaudeville blues singers such as Mamie Smith and Ma Rainey who had come to New York around 1920 to perform and record on the newly popular "race" records. (Bessie Smith, who would soon be dubbed "Empress of the Blues," made her first records in 1923.) Berlin's jazz, then, appears to be intricately bound up with public images of body shape, skin color, and voice type, and the Brox Sisters embodied it.[102] Berlin's songs and the Broxes' performances of them form a blatant early example of how the sounds and images of jazz developed within a framework that intersects gender and race.[103]

The staging of "Everybody Step" also became a model for Berlin's later jazz efforts. In each of the first three revues, a jazz number highlighted the act 1 finale. It began with the Brox Sisters in "one"—that is, in front of the traveler curtain, which concealed all but the front of the stage during scene changes—and then the traveler opened to reveal the full company. Under the headline "America's Greatest Show," Jack Lait identified "Everybody Step" as the show's "best number," and noted that "When the girls get it swinging the curtains part and the whole stage is in Alice blue and the whole company enters, dressed alike for a stunning effect and a work-up of hysterical enthusiasm in front."[104] Subsequent productions strove for equally "stunning effects" and further linked jazz to feminine power and allure as dangerous forces, albeit with a strong dose of humor. The 1922 production staged "Pack Up Your Sins" as a comic vision of hell, with the Devil and *her* jazz band accepting a parade of historic and contemporary "sinners" into the underworld, including Cleopatra, Don Juan, Salome, the jazz clarinetist Ted Lewis, and the dancer Gilda Gray. The presence of Cleopatra and Salome, in particular, further dramatizes the era's associations of jazz and exoticized and eroticized femininity, here embodied by historical figures. Gilda Gray represents their contemporary heir. She had committed her most recent "sin" just three months earlier, during the summer of 1922, when she had danced the risqué shimmy in the *Ziegfeld Follies* while singing the topical racially charged song "It's Getting Dark on Old Broadway."[105] The staging of "When You Walked Out Someone Else Walked In," though not a finale, added a racial implication to the song's message of sexual freedom. *Variety* noted that the Brox Sisters performed it in "high yallow"—in other words, in a light shade of blackface makeup.[106]

Berlin's revues further defined jazz through antithesis, that is, with numbers whose musical qualities, lyric sensibility, and performance style stood in stark contrast to the jazz songs. "Everybody Step" appeared in the scene immediately following its musical opposite, "Say it With Music," with its smooth ballad style and its reference to "the strains of Chopin or Liszt" as models of "beautiful music." In other songs, Berlin even creates a dialogue with the jazz songs by denying the attraction of jazz altogether. In "The Waltz of Long Ago," Berlin writes that "Jazz dancing nowadays does not appeal to me; / I never cared about the jazzy melody. / I'd love to dance around a while, / But my kind of dance is out of style." By idealizing the waltz, the song directly contradicts "Learn to Do the Strut" from earlier in the same show, which had urged dancers to move beyond "the waltz and the lancers" and learn this "brand-new step."[107] In the *Music Box Revues*, the nostalgic and sentimental songs, like many others that conjured the past or a genteel way of life, tended to be performed by classically trained singers, such as John Steel and Grace Moore.

Berlin and his collaborators embedded the jazz / non-jazz opposition into the structure of the show. Recall the 1924 show's prologue featuring Rip Van Winkle, who, after seeing a "Broadway stepper" who is "jazzing her life away," sings "Where is the little old New York, / The one that I used to know, long, long ago?" Rip Van Winkle appears as a quaint vision of a stable, idealized past—a fictionalized and *white* nineteenth-century past, a past that must be "honored" by a banquet at show's end, even as that past now appears obliterated by Jazz Age cultural miscegenation. No matter that nineteenth-century New York itself had been riven by ethnic and class tensions.[108] The show's version of the city's past downplayed conflict in order to evoke a picture of racial homogeneity and social stability. The *Music Box Revue* had conjured that past before and not just in its theme song's allusion to the "beautiful music" of Chopin and Liszt. The 1921 revue created a strong association between middle-class domestic comforts and reassuringly familiar nineteenth-century cultural icons: as in the reference to "the tuneful 'Humoresque'" in the "Dining Out" scene, and the "little book of poetry" featuring works of Kipling, Poe, and Longfellow. In the 1922 revue, Berlin's song "Crinoline Days" harkened "Back to the olden / Days that were golden" and, particularly, to "eighteen seventy-four / [When] Rosy complexions weren't bought in a store"—a lyric that, despite its "rosy" imagery, implicitly conjures a white face. In a review highlighting Grace Moore's performance of "The Waltz of Long Ago," a critic noted that the setting and costumes for the number recalled "the 70's."[109]

Berlin's choice of decade merits attention. Conjuring "the 70's" suggests a strategic decision to invoke not just a pre-jazz New York but also a New York that existed before new waves of south- and east-European immigration—especially Russian-Jewish immigration—accelerated in the half-century since. Between 1881 (when anti-Semitic violence began to escalate in Russia, ultimately driving out the Berlin family) and 1921 (when Congress acted to restrict European immigration), New York City witnessed a population influx unprecedented in the nation's history. The same period saw a wave of African American migration from the rural South to the urban North that transformed Harlem from a "genteel community" of established white upper-class citizens to the capital of black America.[110] The 1921–24 period—precisely the years of Berlin's *Music Box Revues*—marked a peak of nativist reaction across the country. Harbingers of decline, books such as Madison Grant's *The Passing of the Great Race* (1916), Lothrop Stoddard's *The Rising Tide of Color* (1920), and articles in the *Saturday Evening Post* by Kenneth Roberts reflected and articulated a widely felt sense of threat to Anglo-Saxon stock and that something needed to be done about it.[111] In 1921, when the country's principal immigration gateway, Ellis Island, began to overflow, ships carrying newcomers detoured to Boston. In response, Congress reinforced its Emergency Immigration Act of 1921 with the National Origins Act of 1924, further limiting immigration. Berlin alluded to the event in the 1924 *Music Box Revue* with an unusual serio-comic song for Fanny Brice called "Don't Send Me Back to Petrograd," in which a Russian immigrant pleads to remain "in the land of the free." "I'll promise to work the best I can," she continues, "I'll even wash sheets for the Ku Klux Klan."[112] The *Music Box Revue* years saw a peak in the membership and national profile of the Klan, culminating in its 1925 parade of 40,000 members down Pennsylvania Avenue in Washington, DC.[113] Berlin's references to the 1870s in distinctly non-jazz songs stood as poignant symbols of an era when the city's demographic profile had been comparatively stable and homogeneous.

The notion that Berlin's shows purposefully idealized an era that preceded the waves of immigration in which Berlin and his family had participated may sound like a contradiction. Yet at a time when the term *jazz* and its musical signs were increasingly coded "Jewish" in contemporary discourse, it made sense for Berlin and his collaborators to evoke alternative, and distinctly non-Jewish, sounds and images of New York. The effort corresponds to entertainment forms in which the theater historian Henry Bial has identified the impulse of "active vanishing"—a deliberate effort to strip away connotations of Jewishness in order to attract the widest possible audience.[114] Events in Berlin's personal life only encouraged that impulse, as he courted the daughter of a wealthy Catholic businessman who saw the Jewish entertainer as an unwelcome intruder in his family.

In this context, Rip Van Winkle, nineteenth-century music and poetry, and images of 1870s New York thus formed perfect foils for Berlin's "jazz creations," which may be heard as the aural analog to the cultural miscegenation driven by European immigration, black migration, and urbanization. As in the Broxes' use of "high yellow" makeup, the racial mixture sometimes also had visual reinforcement. The act 1 finale of the 1924 show made that as explicit as possible. Here, Berlin conflated jazz and minstrelsy in a particularly dramatic way. A small group, led by Oscar Shaw and Grace Moore, began "in one" singing a song called "Call of the South," which grew into a double number with Stephen Foster's "Old Folks at Home" as its counterpoint. The traveler then parted to reveal the whole company, featuring Fanny Brice, singing a song called "Bandanna Ball." Few critics mentioned the music this time, but many remarked on the seemingly miraculous lighting and makeup effect that transformed the entire ensemble from whiteface to blackface. An opening-night critic marveled that the actors "are at one moment white and at the next negro. Every one last night grew feverish over that chemical accomplishment; and it alone is enough to establish the revue as a popular destination."[115] The *New York Times* critic called it "the outstanding moment."[116] And yet another critic saw such artistry in the number that he found it "worthy of inclusion in a popular opera." Yet, the same critic invoked revealing terms when straining to describe the show's overall musical style: "Here is jazz—," he wrote, "but it is classical jazz."[117] The scene, in effect, parts the curtain that had obscured what Berlin had been striving for in the preceding years. Despite having stripped away the trappings of traditional minstrelsy he had brought the minstrel spirit into the jazz age. Jeffrey Melnick has described "Berlin's talent" the 1910s and 1920s as the ability "to reconfigure the minstrel stance and defuse its most offensive elements . . . to distill the sights and sounds of minstrelsy into a usable modern musical grammar."[118] We can now hear that "grammar" develop—or, from another perspective, *devolve*—from "Everybody Step" through "Bandanna Ball." The final *Music Box Revue*'s nineteenth-century, Rip Van Winkle theme allowed Berlin to restore minstrelsy's nineteenth-century roots in this climactic number, which, by appearing as the act 1 finale, draws an unmistakable link to the more overtly jazz-oriented interior finales of the previous three years—and to the act 1 finales of *Yip Yip Yaphank* and the *Ziegfeld Follies of 1919*.

Only a few months before the 1924 show, Paul Whiteman had introduced Gershwin's *Rhapsody in Blue* as the ultimate refinement of jazz, and Otto Kahn had just announced his view that the Met should produce a "jazz opera," so the notion of jazz as a potentially new vein of "classical" music was in the air. With Gershwin and Berlin in the forefront, such views also developed within an intellectual context in which racial mixing had begun to loom large as a theme in discussions of jazz. Several scholars have recently highlighted the ways in which the period's public discourse constructed a close relationship between jazz and Jewish Americans, especially Russian and East European immigrants.[119] In 1925, Samson Raphaelson wrote in the preface to his play *The Jazz Singer* that "Jazz is Irving Berlin, Al Jolson, George Gershwin, Sophie Tucker," and that "Jews are determining the nature and scope of jazz more than any other race—more than the negroes, from whom they have stolen jazz and given it a new color and meaning."[120] By 1927, the writer Isaac Goldberg, who would go on to write the first Gershwin biography and many other books, had constructed a historical narrative that conflates a black-to-Jewish ethnic transference with a South-to-North geographical move: "In the course of its filtration from the South to a small but noisy point called Manhattan Island, it [jazz] has undergone something decidedly more than a sea change. It reaches from the black South to the black North, but in between it has been touched by the commercial wand of the Jew." He identifies Gershwin, Berlin, and Kern as the key figures in the process.[121]

This problematic narrative of Jewish immigrants as cultural mediators, a view advanced by Jews and Gentiles alike, with both philo-Semitic and anti-Semitic implications, received wide circulation in the 1920s. Understandably, it lost favor for several decades in writings on music, but it has recently been revived for critical analysis.[122] While confronting the political and economic asymmetries in what Melnick calls "black-Jewish relations," these scholars find in Jewish blackface, Jewish jazz, and theatrical performance the channeling of elements and perceptions of black culture that few other ethnic groups—certainly not the increasingly nativist white Anglo-Saxon mainstream—were willing to acknowledge or confront. If Berlin's brand of jazz now seems naïve or inappropriate in a historical narrative that places African American improvisers at its center, it is because it has been heard within a limited historical perspective. Under its genial surface, Berlin's jazz was defiantly heterogeneous and synthetic, mixing black and white signs—themselves multilayered and complex—with a distinctively assimilative Jewish sensibility in a period when racial boundaries in the public sphere were being policed more intensively, and sometimes more violently, than ever.

Later jazz writers would identify jazz's defining qualities in precisely the things that Berlin's sheet music could not represent: improvisation; subtle pitch inflections such as scoops, slides, and blue notes that lie between the flat and neutral third; a variety of timbral and textural devices including growls, grunts, and wah-wah effects, which in the case of brass instruments could be enhanced through the artful use of plunger mutes; and the rhythmic flexibility that would later come to be recognized as swing. If Berlin had not yet fathomed such qualities or found a way to capture them in print and on stage, he nevertheless played a crucial role in defining jazz—while invoking its critics through a kind of staged musical debate—as a powerful cultural symbol, an exciting, modern, and democratic common ground on which, ideally, *everybody* could step.

THE GRAND FINALE

If Berlin tended to use jazz as the catalyst for the act 1 finale, he saw the grand finale as an opportunity to finish the frame around the show with another long and highly self-referential musical scene. We know little of the finales of the 1922–24 shows beyond what programs and reviews report, but it is clear enough that they tended to comment on the show, to reprise several numbers, and to bring on the stars and ensemble. The 1921 show again established the pattern. It begins "in one" before the traveler curtain. In the reflexive style that the show had conjured in the opening, the Eight Reporters address the audience members about the show they are watching and place it in the context of revue conventions. In a sing-songy waltz style, they begin:

> Ladies and Gentlemen, every revue
> Has a finale, and we have one too.

Berlin then proceeds to set up a joke on the audience. The Reporters describe the kind of singer who must deliver the final song: a "tenor who's handsome and young," "who reaches a clear high C," and who sings like the great John McCormack. For audiences in 1921 who knew Berlin's previous work with Ziegfeld, only one man fit that description: John Steel, "everyman's McCormack" (who was not in the 1921 show).

Enter one half of the show's famous comic duo Collier and Bernard. Willie Collier met none of the criteria in the job description, as everyone in the house would have known. Collier, it turns out, has come on to explain—in a continuation of the sing-songy waltz tune—that the tenor "handsome and bold," with a "voice made of gold," cannot be there, because "he has an awful cold." But, Collier claims, since he has "a voice that can reach high C . . . they gave the finale to me." Continuing Berlin's waltz, Collier takes another of the show's many jabs at contemporary revue conventions, including the *Ziegfeld Follies of 1919*—for which Berlin had written a couple of memorable Prohibition songs:

> We thank you all for your kindness
> And you ought to thank us too:
> We have three hundred jokes on Prohibition
> That we might have told to you.

Then Collier delivers another joke about the revue's cost as he promises to bring on the show's stars for a final appearance:

> I would like to present to you
> The payroll of this revue,
> Harris and Berlin's *Worries of 1922.*

Collier continues with what amounts to a sung curtain call, naming fifteen cast members, pausing only to note, in rhyme, that the names do not rhyme: "Berlin claims / The principals haven't got rhymable names."

Then, still performing in one, Collier sets up a sequence of brief reprises of several of the show's numbers that will be sung on the full stage. Collier, not yet having named himself or his partner, Sam Bernard, continues the curtain-call routine on the line "Now for the greatest of all in the play," and Bernard interrupts him: "If you point to yourself there'll be murder to pay!" and Collier quickly continues "I was speaking about the girls, / The Tips and the Notes and the Pearls / We must admit that the girls are a hit / Now we'll raise up the curtain a bit, / And we'll start the Finale and bring on the . . ."

An abrupt shift of tempo, meter, and key accompanies the parting curtain that reveals the Tips from the "Dining Out" scene doing their dainty Allegretto ditty. The Pearls immediately follow in a new key and tempo, singing "The Legend of Pearls," but Florence Moore interrupts—still singing "Pearls"—with another self-referential line: "When a pearl disappears, / Hassard Short is in tears." The Notes follow, again in a new key, singing the eight notes of the scale on whole notes, followed by a rapid reprise (marked "Vivo" in the score) of the Eight Little Notes's song from the opening. Wilda Bennett then commands attention—and we can imagine here that the whole cast comes together around her, as she sings:

> And now before you leave us
> To go upon your way,
> Kindly tell your friends about us,
> And whate'er you say, won't you
> Say It With Music.

A full chorus of the show's theme song ensues (with repeat marks in the score!), with new words reinforcing Bennett's take-home message about recouping the show's tremendous expense (pronouncing BER-lin with an accent on the first syllable, as Cole Porter would do in "You're the Top"):

> Say it with music,
> Beautiful music—
> Somehow we're hoping that soon
> You'll be buying this little tune:
> The sale of each copy
> When times are choppy
> Helps Irving Berlin along,
> So say it with a beautiful song.

Thus, the finale ends by reinforcing the centrality of music and its composer and making a joke of his commercial ambitions—all while plugging his hit song yet one more time. Befitting Berlin's expert theatrical sense, however, this finale, with its curtain call *written into the score*, does not call for the composer himself to appear on stage—despite two references to Berlin by name.

The 1921 *Music Box Revue* fulfilled the expectations and aesthetics of a revue of the period: it fit hand-in-glove with its time and place so perfectly that it was unrepeatable. A professional revival would be fascinating and logistically possible, but no matter how expertly and expensively done, it would fail utterly to deliver the special and unique effect that it delivered in its initial run in the Music Box: a sense of intimate connection between the score, the composer, the performers, the theater, and the audience.

That first *Music Box Revue* ran for 440 performances in New York before going on the road. Subsequent *Music Box Revues* drew great interest, but each successive show ran for fewer performances: 330, 273, and 184. By the end, Berlin confessed in a letter to his fiancée, Ellin Mackay: "As I told you so many times, the thrill of the Music Box has gone and now it has become a job that I love most when it's finished."[123]

If Berlin grew weary of staging the revues, the results nevertheless fired his imagination for decades. "They would take on a deep nostalgic color for him, from the first to the last," Barrett writes, "and he would vow to do another before he cooled."[124] In the early summer of 1938, Berlin conceived a new *Music Box Revue*, and the idea percolated almost continuously for three decades.[125] The few surviving materials from that show's original conception include a lyric for an extended opening number in which a couple attempts to enter the Music Box with tickets for the *Music Box Revue of 1923*—except that it's 1938 and a sign in the theater's lobby clearly reveals that the show now playing is *Of Mice and Men*. The couple explains that they were held up by traffic, and they "don't want to see a drama—we came here to see a revue." The theater manager promises to "see what I can do," and he steps forward as the curtains close behind him. He then addresses the audience directly, apologizing to the audience who has come to see *Of Mice and Men* but feeling obliged to show the revue for which the couple has tickets. Therefore, he explains, the Music Box will stage a revue in three acts: "A first act, a second, and a last—the present, the future, and the past."

The scene shows that, a decade and a half after the last *Music Box Revue*, Berlin continued to view the reflexive prologue as an essential feature of his show, now with a sense of its history.

That history, it turned out, did not have much of a future, but it spawned more ideas that give us compelling glimpses of Berlin's theatrical vision. Later in 1939, Berlin drafted several scenarios and song lists for a proposed film that he titled "Say It with Music," clearly modeled on his 1938 Hollywood success, *Alexander's Ragtime Band*. Most of the scenarios include a substantial scene depicting the *Music Box Revue* and songs that were featured in it. Berlin's first attempt at the scenario reveals several things. Notably the *Music Box Revues*, and the Music Box itself, are portrayed as a transitional stage in a young woman's career that gets launched in vaudeville (the Palace) and reaches its peak in opera (the Met). In other words, the revue implicitly forms the middle, common ground that connects all points on the theatrical spectrum. Berlin conceived the show as a backstager about a sister act, with the twist that the two sisters represent distinct spheres of the musical world, and they embodied the kind of musical oppositions that he built into many of his shows and counterpoint songs:

> They are two different types of singers; one with a beautiful soprano voice, and the other a blues singer. The ideal casting would be Jeanette MacDonald and Alice Faye. The character of MacDonald goes from the Palace Theatre to the Music Box to the Metropolitan Opera House. Faye, her sister, makes all the sacrifices, not in an obvious ham way, but subtly helps her sister get to the top. The songs will be distributed between these two girls; one doing the ballad type, the other the rhythm and novelty numbers.[126]

Since that film never came to fruition, Berlin used the title again and again for other musical film projects in the 1950s and 1960s, all of which saw the same fate. As late as the 1950s he conceived a film about "a songwriter, a producer, and a theater" to commemorate the early years of his partnership with Sam Harris. The scenario, never developed, survives among Berlin's papers at the Library of Congress.[127] And in the 1960s, Berlin's final project, again titled "Say It with Music," saw more extensive development, including several songs, plus scripts drafted by Arthur Laurents (1963) and Betty Comden and Adolph Green (1966). Julie Andrews, then at a peak of her career in musical films (*The Sound of Music, Mary Poppins*), was considered for a spot in the cast. But the film never materialized.[128] Like Berlin's earlier cavalcade film musicals, this one was conceived to cover a span of American history (approximately fifty years), cutting back and forth across that period, using Berlin songs representative of the times. The years of that film's development, which ended in 1969, track a sea change of interest in musical film—from a high in the mid-1960s with *My Fair Lady* (1964), *Mary Poppins* (1964), and *The Sound of Music* (1965) to a decline of audience by the decade's end. "Say It with Music" was one more attempt to tell a story using the Berlin song catalog. Like popular music and Broadway, however, Hollywood had moved on to other things. Yet in the mid-1920s, the Music Box experience would yield more immediate dividends in Berlin's theatrical career: collaborations with some of Broadway's most skilled comedic writers.

5

"AN IDEAL COMBINATION"
• • •
BERLIN, KAUFMAN AND CO., 1920S–30S

A lot of satin songs . . . with an acid, cruel sense of humor.
—*Percy Hammond*

In the final scene of the 1929 comedy *June Moon*, two songwriters create a song with a lyric derived from one of Tin Pan Alley and Broadway's prized conceits, the image of an innocent young couple settling "In a bungalow for two, / Where we can bill and coo—." The playwrights punctuate this final line with a gratuitously opinionated stage direction: "Mercifully, the curtain is down."[1]

From title to curtain, *June Moon* adopts a lightly satirical attitude toward the popular song industry. And that industry's leading figure—judging by the number of references to him in the script—was Irving Berlin.[2] In fact, just four years earlier Berlin had written a song called "A Little Bungalow" that may well have been the target of *June Moon*'s final jab. Eschewing the "bill and coo" cliché, Berlin's song nevertheless tapped a common well of imagery, with "shady trees," "birds and bees," "clouds . . . drifting by," and a "moon above."[3]

That song was designed for the romantic leads in a 1925 musical comedy called *The Cocoanuts*, with a script by the very man who would spoof the style in *June Moon*: George S. Kaufman, a habitual collaborator working in this case with Morrie Ryskind. Intermittently over a span of three decades, Berlin would join forces with Kaufman and his cohorts on a series of musical comedies that bear the stamp of the creative tension between Berlin's songwriting style, which embraced romance and sentimentality, and Kaufman's witty, satirical, and decisively unsentimental comedic style.[4] Kaufman and Berlin formed an odd couple indeed, for Kaufman held a long-standing cynicism about songs and songwriters—suggesting to Berlin, for example, that the last word of his famous lyric phrase "I'll be loving you / Always," would better confront the reality of modern romance if changed to "Thursday."[5] Almost proudly nonmusical, Kaufman famously quipped that "I don't know the difference between Handel's *Largo* and–well, Largo's *Handel*."[6] According to Berlin, "George hated music so much that if I'd written 'Rock of Ages' he'd have thrown it out."[7]

Claiming tone-deafness did not keep Kaufman from working on musicals with Broadway's leading composers. His writing and directing credits for musicals exceed the resumes of many who loved them more. It began with a celebrated gender-bending sketch for the *Music Box Revue of 1923* called "If Men Played Cards as Women Do," followed by *The Cocoanuts* (with Berlin, 1925); *Strike Up the Band* (with George and Ira Gershwin, 1927, revised by Morrie Ryskind in 1930); *Of Thee I Sing* (with the Gershwins and Ryskind, 1931); *Let 'Em Eat Cake* (Gershwins and Ryskind, 1933); and *I'd Rather Be Right* (with Rodgers and Hart, 1937). His script for *Of Thee I Sing* earned the first Pulitzer Prize ever given to a musical comedy. Just as Richard Rodgers claimed that his collaboration with Lorenz Hart during the same period thrived on the tension between "unsentimental lyrics and sentimental melody," Berlin and Kaufman, and Kaufman's similar-minded collaborators such as Moss Hart, struck a fruitful balance between innocent earnestness and streetwise parody that helped define musical comedy in the interwar period before the Rodgers and Hammerstein era.[8] In response to Berlin and Moss Hart's *Face the Music*, Percy Hammond wrote that the creators formed an "ideal combination": "Mr. Berlin contributes a lot of satin songs. But, perhaps fearful that his efforts might be too mellifluous, he collaborates with Moss Hart, a sarcastic chap with an acid, cruel sense of humor."[9] The critic Brooks Atkinson, having witnessed both *Of Thee I Sing* and *Face the Music* in what he regarded as an otherwise barren musical theater landscape by early 1932, saw in Kaufman and Hart Broadway's "most brilliant satirists" and looked to them for "a concrete program for the rejuvenation of a moribund quarter of the theatre."[10]

Kaufman and Hart differed in at least one important respect: although Kaufman did not like music, Hart did.[11] Yet it makes sense to consider these authors and shows together because the writers formed an informal collaborative network that began in the mid-1920s, peaked during the 1930s, and continued into the 1950s (see table 5.1). Kaufman, the senior member of the group, had come to New York in the early 1920s as a newspaper writer. His penchant for collaboration on scripts reportedly stemmed from diffidence about his ability to write for the theater, an activity that turned into lifelong occupation when his emerging stage work posed inevitable conflicts of interest with his work as drama editor of the *New York Times*. Perhaps sorry he could not travel both paths, Kaufman ultimately left the *Times* and chose the theater after a string of successes.

A writer of Kaufman's talent could hardly avoid Broadway's bursting scene in the 1920s, a decade that saw the construction of more than two dozen new theaters to help launch an average of 225 new productions per year, including more than four hundred musicals.[12] Such were the various threads that bound Kaufman, Berlin, and cohorts together in this milieu that in 1939 Kaufman and Moss Hart wrote a play— *The Man Who Came To Dinner*—whose grumpily rotund protagonist was modeled on Alexander Woollcott, the theater critic notable for writing the first biography of Irving Berlin. Many of those in Kaufman's circle, including Woollcott, had been members of the informal society of wits who formed the so-called Algonquin Round Table in the 1920s. Berlin himself was an occasional visitor to the group.

The shows of Berlin, Kaufman, and Co. sported a lighthearted but pointed skepticism about contemporary characters and events. The collaborators did not see the theater as an engine for real social change, but they certainly saw it as a democratic force, a great leveler of overweening ambition, pretension, and hypocrisy in the realms of society, politics, the press, and entertainment—including theater itself. Drawing from life, they freely mixed fact and fiction—a device that allowed for insider jokes between the writers and their savvy urban audiences. In their habitual name-dropping, their oblique allusions to the here-and-now, the scripts and songs contain abundant clues to an ongoing intimacy between Broadway's writers and audiences that would dissipate in years to come. Meanwhile, the dialogue features witty repartee and a brisk

1923	***Music Box Revue of 1923***, including Kaufman sketch "If Men Played Cards as Women Do," produced by Sam H. Harris
1925	**The Cocoanuts**, book by Kaufman (with "uncredited assist from journalist Morrie Ryskind"[1]), produced by Harris
1927	*Strike Up the Band*, book by Kaufman, music and lyrics by George and Ira Gershwin; book revised in 1930 by Ryskind
1928	*Animal Crackers*, play by Kaufman and Ryskind, produced by Harris (film, 1930)
1929	*June Moon*, play by Kaufman and Ring Lardner, produced by Harris
1930	**Once in a Lifetime*, play by Kaufman and Hart, produced by Harris
1931	**Of Thee I Sing*, musical with book by Kaufman and Ryskind, music and lyrics by George and Ira Gershwin, produced by Harris
1932	**Face the Music**, musical comedy with book by Moss Hart with "uncredited assist by Morrie Ryskind,"[2] book directed by Kaufman, produced by Harris
1932	**Dinner at Eight*, play by Kaufman and Edna Ferber, produced by Harris
1933	***As Thousands Cheer**, revue with sketches by Moss Hart, produced by Harris *Let 'Em Eat Cake*, musical with book by Kaufman and Ryskind; music and lyrics by George and Ira Gershwin, produced by Harris
1934	*Merrily We Roll Along*, play by Kaufman and Hart, produced by Harris *Bring on the Girls*, play by Kaufman and Ryskind (closed out of town)
1935	*A Night at the Opera*, film with screenplay by Kaufman and Ryskind **First Lady*, play by Kaufman and Katharine Dayton, produced by Harris

(continued)

Table 5.1. *(continued)*

1936	*Stage Door, play by Kaufman and Ferber, produced by Harris* *You Can't Take It with You*, play by Kaufman and Hart, produced by Harris (film, 1938) *A Day at the Races*, screenplay revised by Kaufman
1937	*I'd Rather Be Right*, musical comedy by with book by Kaufman and Hart, music and lyrics by Richard Rodgers and Lorenz Hart, produced by Harris
1938	*Sing Out the News*, Harold Rome revue co-produced by Kaufman and Hart, who also contributed sketch material *The Fabulous Invalid*, play by Kaufman and Hart, produced by Harris
1939	*The American Way*, play by Kaufman and Hart, produced by Harris *The Man Who Came to Dinner*, play by Kaufman and Hart, produced by Harris
1940	**Louisiana Purchase**, musical comedy with book by Ryskind *George Washington Slept Here*, play by Kaufman and Hart, produced by Harris
1941	*Lady in the Dark*, musical with book by Hart (with "advice" from Kaufman), music and lyrics by Kurt Weill and Ira Gershwin, produced by Harris
1955	**"Sentimental Guy,"** unfinished musical comedy with book by S. L. Behrman (and brief assist from Kaufman)

*staged at the Music Box Theatre

1. Kaufman, *Kaufman and Co.*, 855.

2. *CL*, 273.

pace. The plots create comedic climaxes of maximum confusion and hilarity, as they typically track the ups and downs of an underdog who wins in the end—or, in the musicals, a marriage plot sabotaged then resolved. At its best, the Kaufman style had what Moss Hart called "wonderful economy"[13]—lean, spare, edited to the bone.

The dialogue, songs, and situations are relentlessly contemporary, loaded with allusions that heightened their appeal to first-run audiences, yet they were so precisely situated in their time and place as to render them resistant to revival. The rampant, unscrupulous nature of the Florida land speculation that drives the loosely structured plot of *The Cocoanuts* (1925) would become old news by the Depression era. Yet the contrast between its stars, the disruptive, irreverent Marx Brothers, and stuffy "official" society, embodied by the grand dame Margaret Dumont—who in this role established herself as the ideal foil to Groucho that she would continue to play in films—exhibits a familiar class-based opposition rooted in minstrelsy and fundamental to American comedy. In *Face the Music* (1932), corrupt New York City politics, Depression-era satire, and self-referential songwriting and show-business clichés fuel the comedy and musical numbers, and remain remarkably fresh even if they do not touch today's audiences with the audacity and currency that struck first-nighters. The newspaper headlines on which Moss Hart and Berlin based the sketches and songs of *As Thousands Cheer* (1933) soon lost their currency as well, yet the dialogue and music are so artfully crafted that they impart a vivid slice of life in the early Depression period. In *Louisiana Purchase* (1940), the lonely Republican in a Democratically controlled government of the prewar period would not claim the same empathy from postwar, post-FDR era audiences, yet the alternately farcical and sentimental dialogue, situations, and songs forged a state-of-the-art musical comedy in its day.

Another key figure linked Berlin, Kaufman, and their associates in this network: the producer Sam H. Harris. Harris produced many shows by Kaufman and Co., including: Kaufman and Moss Hart's first collaboration, *Once in a Lifetime* (1930); Kaufman and Ryskind's *Of Thee I Sing*, with the Gershwins (1931); *Face the Music* (1932); Kaufman and Edna Ferber's *Dinner at Eight* (1932); *As Thousands Cheer* (1933); Kaufman and Hart's *You Can't Take It With You* (1936); Kaufman and Ferber's *Stage Door* (1936); and Kaufman and Hart's *The Man Who Came to Dinner* (1939).

Sam H. Harris, then, was the catalyst in bringing the collaborators together, and the bond that ensured a long-term association among them. In fact, it was Harris who approached Kaufman about writing a musical comedy with Berlin for the Marx Brothers, a show that became *The Cocoanuts*. The show launched three decades of on-and-off collaboration between Berlin and what might be loosely, and whimsically, called the Kaufman School of musical comedy writing.

THE COCOANUTS

By all accounts, including Berlin's, *The Cocoanuts* was not vintage Berlin. "He never talked about *The Cocoanuts*," according to his daughter, "except to say it wasn't the best score he ever wrote." Stanley Green pronounced it "one of his lesser efforts."[14] But the show compels attention for many reasons. It was Berlin's sole book show of the musical-comedy rich 1920s, his first full-length collaboration with Kaufman (and with the uncredited co-author Morrie Ryskind), and the first book show for the Marx Brothers—and thus a launching pad for their more famous films.[15] Ryskind, who claimed some of the credit for originating the Marxes' comic style, called it a "turning point in the art of comedy" with echoes extending to Woody Allen and beyond.[16] From a perspective focusing on Berlin's contribution, it represents another prime example of how his theater strove to incorporate everything on the American stage. Billed "musical comedy," *The Cocoanuts* embraced minstrelsy, vaudeville, revue, and opera.

It was another case of *legitimate vaudeville*—except that in the 1920s the quality of musical comedy scripts had risen thanks to writers like Kaufman. Still, like Berlin's Dillingham shows, *The Cocoanuts* was conceived as a vehicle for performers, who up to now had been vaudeville headliners. Kaufman, already a deft writer of situation comedy, ended up creating less a plot with dialogue than a framework for the manic verbal and physical humor of the Marxes, led by Groucho. Kaufman understood that Groucho did not play a character: he *was* the character. The final script identifies Groucho's character as "Groucho" or "Julius" (his real name) although the character had a name: Henry W. Schlemmer, hotel manager.[17]

One of the show's scripts is even published—a rare feat for a 1920s musical. And a footnote supplied by its editor, Donald Oliver, informs the reader that the published version of the script "was prepared as a documentation of the show as it played on its opening night in New York in 1925."[18] As Oliver acknowledges, however, no script can claim to offer the show's definitive, or even authoritative, text; it can present the by-product of a performance and its original production circumstances, which comprise the show's truly original and unrecoverable text.

Much of it could not have been written down because of the show's allowance for improvisation. A scene that hinged on a malapropism (a "Chicoism," as Ryskind called it) emerged from the typewriter, after opening night, as a draft of the "Viaduct" (or "Why a Duck?") scene between Groucho and Chico that would became a classic bit in their repertoire.[19] The Marxes also added a lot of physical humor, indicated in the script only with the term *business*—a single word that for the Marxes amounted to a license for comic mayhem.[20] More than that, the show underwent significant changes during its run, including the substitution of at least three numbers. Like so many star-driven shows of the period, then, the extant material from *The Cocoanuts* is a reminder that much of what gave the original production its vitality does *not* survive.

Yet what *does* survive gives us a valuable glimpse of Berlin's musical comedy style of the 1920s. The plot has the conventional farcical features of the period: a distinctively contemporary American setting, a young couple wrapped in a marriage plot, deception and confusion that upset the couple's hopes and plans, a haughty aristocrat (a Mrs. Potter, played by Dumont) who objects to the romantic attachment and whose wealth forms a catalyst for the action, and a clutch of petty criminals deployed to disrupt the plans of the others. In the act 1 finale, the romantic male lead, Bob, gets accused of stealing Mrs. Potter's $100,000 diamond necklace. Mrs. Potter, who never liked Bob, announces her daughter Polly's engagement to another man, Harvey. Yet Harvey, it turns out, was the man who had plotted to steal the necklace. In short, the deception and resulting confusion end act 1 in familiar musical comedy fashion with all principals on stage, with the temporary break-up of the principal couple, and with the impending nuptials of one member of the couple and someone else—the "wrong" man. And the reprise finaletto includes several songs stitched together, including Polly's wistful rendition of "A Little Bungalow" with Harpo leaning sympathetically on her shoulder.

Groucho Marx and Margaret Dumont began their legendary collaboration in The Cocoanuts.
Courtesy of Rodgers & Hammerstein, on behalf of the Estate of Irving Berlin.

In the 1920s, Florida was all the rage as a topic for songs and as a locale for comedy, thanks to the real-estate explosion there.[21] In a typical grammatical inversion Groucho/Schlemmer asks, "Do you know that property values have increased 1924 since one thousand percent?"[22] He sums up the guiding philosophy of the Cocoanut Manor building project—and by extension, Florida's real-estate boom, and by further extension, American capitalism—with a Ziegfeldian twist as "glorifying the American sucker."[23]

None of Berlin's songs for *The Cocoanuts* had staying power, which Ryskind attributes in part to Marxian madcap.[24] Yet certain numbers reinforce our understanding of patterns in his theatrical writing. The opening, for example, comprises a zany extended musical sequence featuring the hotel guests and Zeppo Marx (the brothers' straight man) as front-desk manager fielding a variety of requests while also flirting with female guests. The scene then shifts to a chorus of bellboys, who describe their demanding jobs, all in music. The whole number has a clear stylistic relationship to the lengthy ensemble scenes with which Berlin liked to launch his musicals since *Watch Your Step* a decade earlier, and it looks ahead to the bustling opener of *Face the Music* in 1932.

Current dance music plays an important role in the score, another mark of 1920s musical comedy. "The Monkey-Doodle-Doo," an invented animal dance, features many of Berlin's jazz trademarks, including secondary-rag figures, accented blue notes, and a pounding blues bass—and what surely must be the first-ever rhyme of *mangoes* and *gang goes*. Following the template of so many of the period's dance songs, the song's patter section offers a list of popular dances (Turkey Trot, Grizzly Bear, Bunny Hug, and many more), only to reject them since "they don't compare with what we're calling the Monkey-Doodle-Doo." Berlin also wrote a Charleston number with a title reminiscent of his 1912 hit "Everybody's Doing It": "Everyone in the World (Is Doing the Charleston)." He wrote a tango song titled simply "Tango Melody."

Minstrelsy also makes a prominent appearance. A number called "Minstrel Days" resonates with the reflexive nostalgia of his 1919 *Follies* song "I'd Rather See a Minstrel Show":

Those good old minstrel days—
My heart is yearning
For those minstrel days.
My thoughts are turning
To those old-fashioned scenes,
Semicircles and tambourines.

Few of these songs fit into the plot. Indeed, the dialogue surrounding them suggests that many serve a deliberately disruptive function, yet they are also tightly woven into the script. The minstrel number, for example, overwhelms an earnest investigation into Mrs. Potter's stolen jewelry by a pompous detective named Hennessy. Kaufman tropes minstrelsy by having Hennessy begin his inquiry like an interlocutor: "Ladies and Gentlemen be seated." Hennessy's sober line of questioning gets nowhere as Groucho and Chico crack jokes. When Hennessy asks "Why did you cross from Miss Martyn's room into Mrs. Potter's room?" Groucho answers, "That's an old one. To get on the other side." In the dialogue leading into the song, the script starts dubbing Groucho (a.k.a. Julius) and Chico the "end men" as they nonsensically quote lyrics from a new Tin Pan Alley song published by none other than Irving Berlin, Inc. ("Yes Sir, That's My Baby," by Walter Donaldson and Gus Kahn, 1925). The sequence also adumbrates an idea that will later shape *Face the Music*: the inherent theatricality of courtroom procedures.

HENNESSY (*To* MRS. POTTER): Now then, Mrs. Potter, that jewel case was opened
    with your key. Is that right?
MRS. POTTER: Yes sir.
END MAN: That's my baby.
HENNESSY: And that key has not been returned.
MRS. POTTER: No sir.
END MAN: Don't mean maybe.
HENNESSY: It was stolen from your bag.
MRS. POTTER: Yes sir.
ALL: That's my baby doll. (GROUCHO *starts to dance*)

HENNESSY (*To* GROUCHO): Stop that. (*To* HARPO) Cut that out. Now then, there is one important witness who hasn't said anything else. (HARPO *stands*) We will now hear from Miss Penelope Martyn.

JULIUS: You bet you will. Miss Penelope Martyn. Dixie's darling song-bird will now render that popular song success—Minstrel Days. (*Number "Minstrel Days" Penelope and Others.*)[25]

The scene continues with an opera parody, in which Hennessy's self-importance again becomes the target of the musical diversion. Mocking the investigation of the stolen jewels, Chico steals Hennessy's shirt and Groucho begins an inquiry into the missing garment, which launches Hennessy's song "The Tale of the Shirt" based on the Habanera melody from Bizet's *Carmen*. Even on paper, the whole scene is hilarious, and it proves that Berlin and Kaufman did not need blackface or racial caricature to exploit minstrelsy's conventions in a musical comedy scene.

If the mini-minstrel show won laughs, the musical number that seems to have been intended as a potential hit was the quaintly earnest "A Little Bungalow." The song taps the conventional imagery of the "cozy cottage" number so beloved by Broadway and Tin Pan Alley writers, set to a melody whose dainty dotted rhythms suggest a familial relationship with the previous year's hit, "Tea for Two." Kaufman later claimed that he had thought the spot would feature "Always," the tune he had recently heard Berlin create in an Atlantic City hotel room, but returning to New York for rehearsals he found that "in its place in *The Cocoanuts* was a song called *A Little Bungalow*, which we never could reprise in Act Two because the actors couldn't remember it that long."[26] Morrie Ryskind told a different story: that Kaufman had judged "Always" too sentimental and axed it from the show.[27]

The Cocoanuts ran for a respectable 276 performances, closed in August 1926, then went on tour. The *New York Times* typified the critical reaction to the show by focusing chiefly on the antics of the Marx Brothers. It described Berlin's music as "always pleasing" and singled out "A Little Bungalow" as "especially melodious."[28] A "summer edition" added the Brox Sisters to the cast along with several new songs by Berlin. Although a popular entry in the season's musical comedies, *The Cocoanuts* took a decidedly second place among the newsworthy events in Berlin's life that year. Just four weeks after the show opened, Berlin married Ellin Mackay, and the *New York Times* ran a page-one article headlined "Ellin Mackay Wed to Irving Berlin; Surprises Father." The article reported the hastily arranged ceremony at Manhattan's Municipal Building, from which the couple ostensibly departed on their honeymoon.[29] The show, meanwhile, took on new life in 1929, when it was made into a film—the film debuts of the Marx Brothers and Margaret Dumont. It also featured *Ziegfeld Follies* and musical comedy star Mary Eaton, sister of Doris Eaton Travis, and Oscar Shaw, a romantic leading man who had appeared in the *Music Box Revue of 1924* and, more recently, in the Gershwin musical comedy *Oh, Kay!* opposite Gertrude Lawrence. The Marxes remained at the center of the plot, but the film included many of Berlin's songs. For decades it appeared that the film would be the sole surviving performance document of a long-forgotten stage show. That is, until 1988, when *The Cocoanuts* was revived and raved—and videotaped with the approval of its centenarian composer.[30]

When the film of *The Cocoanuts* came out, Berlin had been away from Broadway for two years, and it would be two more years before he returned. When he did, he formed a short but compelling collaboration with George S. Kaufman's protégé, Moss Hart. Hart had just recently arrived on Broadway when Sam H. Harris partnered him with Berlin. Among the most memorable scenes in Hart's classic memoir, *Act One*, occurs in 1930 when the twenty-six-year-old Hart looks down from a tenth-floor window of the Astor Hotel at the Music Box Theatre's marquee and glimpses his name next to Kaufman's and the title of their new play, *Once in a Lifetime*, a satire of Hollywood's transition from silence to sound. This is the moment when, in the memoir's Horatio Alger trajectory, Hart arrived as a major Broadway talent.[31]

He had cultivated that talent since childhood, a difficult childhood marked by near-poverty and emotional friction from which theater became his only escape. "Theatre," he famously wrote in *Act One*, "is an inevitable refuge of the unhappy child."[32] Hart may have come from uptown, in the Bronx, but his background was similar enough to Berlin's to give him a share of the Lower East Side sensibility for which performance and theater appeared to offer a one-way ticket to the American dream. Like Berlin, he worked extraordinarily hard to perfect his craft, heeded the audience's response and its bottom line at the box office, and developed an attitude described by one of his biographers as "audience-friendly" and "posterity-be-damned."[33] It may seem as if Hart's theater was indifferent to or lighthearted about Depression-era conditions, when compared with the more directly engaged theater of his peers. For a more politically activist theater in the 1930s, one would have to look elsewhere, at the work of the Group Theater and the Federal Theater Project. Harold Clurman, a director of the idealistic Group Theater, reflected that "the theatre of the thirties attempted to make the stage an instrument of public enlightenment through a passionate involvement with the national scene."[34] Hart's social engagement was never so earnest. Youthful privations conditioned his response to the country's. Hart's contemporaries in American theater, the biographer Stephen Bach notes, "were wakened to social conditions they had never considered before but that Moss had known from birth and was happy now to ignore. . . . He viewed himself as a connoisseur of hard knocks and was more than ready to move on."[35] No wonder Hart and Berlin formed a vital, if brief, collaboration in the early 1930s.

In his memoir, which is marked by both candor and a penchant for taking liberty with the facts, Hart claimed that he once told the theater manager Max Siegel that "I do not write musical comedies. I'm a playwright. I write plays—*only* plays."[36] Yet from the start, Hart had been inspired by musical theater even as he idolized playwrights such as Eugene O'Neill and George Bernard Shaw (whose *Pygmalion* got musicalized for a show Hart would later famously direct). Hart's first playwriting effort in 1922, in fact, had been a revue modeled in part on Berlin's state-of-the-art Music Box annuals.[37] And in 1930, a few months before *Once in a Lifetime* opened, a musical comedy called *Jonica*, with a script that Hart had co-written with Dorothy Heyward, became Hart's Broadway debut and saw forty performances—although he does not even mention it in his autobiography.[38]

Berlin and Moss Hart. Courtesy of Rodgers & Hammerstein, on behalf of the Estate of Irving Berlin.

By the time he teamed up with Berlin in 1931, then, Hart had not only written both musical comedy and legitimate theater, he had seen his efforts in both areas produced on the Broadway stage—no small accomplishment for a man of twenty-seven. Although Hart described the disciplined focus and long hours required to work with Berlin as "tantamount to entering a monastery," the result of their first collaboration could hardly have been further from monastic.[39] Working through numerous drafts, at one point in collaboration with Morrie Ryskind, Hart and Berlin created and discarded several titles—including "Off the Beat," "This Town of Ours," and "Curtain Going Up"—as they strove for contemporary resonance and tried to strike some of the show's keynotes and satirical targets. (Musical numbers for various versions of the show appear in table 5.2.) At last, under the title *Face the Music*, the show opened at the New Amsterdam on February 17, 1932, and ran for a modest 165 performances. It was billed as "a musical comedy revue," another confusingly hybridized label of Berlin's work that nevertheless indicated two important things about the show. Like a revue, it was about contemporary people, places, events, and theater, and it featured elaborate production numbers. Like a musical comedy, it had

Table 5.2. *Face the Music*, Musical Numbers from 1931 Draft to 2007 Revival

Off the Beat (1931 draft of act 1)	Opening Night[1] (1932)	Piano-vocal score (LC-IBC)	Encores! Revival (2007)
Automat Opening	Lunching at the Automat	Automat Opening	Lunching at the Automat
Let's Have Another Cup of Coffee	Let's Have Another Cup of Coffee	Let's Have Another Cup o' Coffee	Let's Have Another Cup of Coffee
Two Cheers Instead of Three			Two Cheers Instead of Three (1931, intended for act 1 after "Coffee")[2]
			The Police of New York (1931, originally intended as act 1 finale)
Reisman's Doing a Show	[Reisman's Doing a Show]	Riseman's [sic] Doing a Show	Reisman's Doing a Show
	Torch Song	Torch Song	Torch Song
You Must Be Born with It	You Must Be Born with It	You Must Be Born with It	You Must Be Born with It
A Roof in Manhattan	(On) A Roof in Manhattan	A Roof in Manhattan	(Castles in Spain) On a Roof in Manhattan
What Chance Have I with Love "(Note for Mr. Harris. This song was not finished in time to be included in the script.)"			[Dear Old] Crinoline Days
My Beautiful Rhinestone Girl	My Beautiful Rhinestone Girl	My Beautiful Rhinestone Girl	My Beautiful Rhinestone Girl
The Police of New York			
	Soft Lights and Sweet Music	Soft Lights and Sweet Music	Soft Lights and Sweet Music

(continued)

Table 5.2. (continued)

Off the Beat (1931 draft of act 1)	Opening Night[1] (1932)	Piano-vocal score (LC-IBC)	Encores! Revival (2007)
			If You Believe (1930, intended for Reaching for the Moon; introduced in There's No Business . . ., 1954)
	[act 2] Opening [Of All the Rotten Shows]	Opening –second act [Of All the Rotten Shows]	Well, Of All the Rotten Shows
	I Say It's Spinach	I Say It's Spinach	I Say It's Spinach (and the Hell with It)
			How Can I Change My Luck? (1931, "probably" intended for Face the Music)
	Drinking Song	Drinking Song	A Toast to Prohibition
	Dear Old Crinoline Days	Dear Old Crinoline Days	
	I Don't Want To Be Married	I Don't Want To Be Married	I Don't Wanna Be Married
	Manhattan Madness	Manhattan Madness	Manhattan Madness
	(Finale)	Investigation	Investigation

1. From Norton 2:666.

2. Parenthetical notes on deleted songs that were reinstated for the 2007 Encores! production are drawn from CL, 279–81.

a book—which, in this case, was directed by George S. Kaufman with his signature fast pace.

The curtain opens on the kind of vigorous ensemble scene that often launched acts in the Kaufman and Co. farcical style, musical or not: brisk entrances and exits, rapid-fire snippets of overlapping dialogue from conversations in progress, and an overall sense of a "bustling throng converging upon the place," as the stage directions put it.[40] The "place" is the automat, a kind of self-service restaurant where putting a nickel or two in a coin slot and turning a knob opened a glass window to a

The New Amsterdam Theatre, Forty-second Street, 1932, advertising its current show, Face the Music. *Billy Rose Theatre Division, The New York Public Library for the Performing Arts, Astor, Lenox and Tilden Foundations.*

plate of macaroni and cheese, a chicken potpie, a sandwich, a piece of cake or pie, or a perfectly measured cup of coffee—with cream, if requested—from a dolphin-head spout. The automat proved a perfect microcosm for Hart and Berlin's Depression-era Manhattan. The 1920s had seen a voracious expansion of the automat's presence in the city. By 1931, when Berlin and Hart began collaborating on their new musical, the automat had become a popular symbol for thrift, quality, efficiency, and modernity. As such it thrived while other businesses collapsed in the early Depression years.[41]

In this replica of an automat, Hart's script conjures "a hungry and garrulous humanity" having its lunch. Hovering in its midst, at the center of the wall hangs a large picture of President Hoover, in case anyone mistakes the time and place: the United States of America, 1932. Brooks Atkinson's review of opening night singled out the scene as a comedic highpoint, emblematic of the entire show: "Nothing in this bountiful merry-go-round of Irving Berlin tunes and Moss Hart gibes is quite so hilarious as the first stinging scene in the Automat, where the captains of industry of another day are feeding off the regular five-cent dinner. . . . a brilliant opening scene."[42]

"Times are not so sweet," Berlin's chorus begins, as the "bluebloods"—the Morgans, the Whitneys, the Rockefellers, and many other actual Manhattan aristocrats (Berlin's lyrics name names, as Atkinson's opening night review noted)—have to spend a few of their remaining nickels in the only restaurant they can still afford. In their midst emerges a pretty, perky soubrette named Kit Baker and the renowned Broadway producer Hal Reisman, a thinly disguised Ziegfeld.[43] Kit longs to return to the stage. "You wouldn't want to glorify me again, would you, Mr. Reisman?," Kit pleads, reminding him that she is "the biggest box-office draw in musical comedy." Reisman *does* want to put on a show, he tells her, but he lacks the means to finance it. A few moments later, as if in answer to the question "Who can bankroll our show?," Kit bumps into a young man and spills her coffee on him. "Thanks for the coffee," he quips, "but I ordered sardines." They look at each other and laugh: it is Pat Mason Jr., Kit's friend and, conveniently, the son of a banker. Pat's father, however, has no money to back a show, so Pat proposes that Reisman put it on at Woolworths. Everyone's shopping at five-and-dime stores for bargains these days, Pat reasons, so they would have a captive audience.

The conversation builds up to a song that will develop Kit and Pat's relationship through the coffee image that sparked their meeting just minutes earlier. Reisman at first can't accept the absurdity of Pat's proposal, but he soon warms to the idea, and the three continue to make plans with gathering excitement. After Reisman exits,

The critic Brooks Atkinson called the opening number of Face the Music *a "hilarious [and] . . . stinging scene in the Automat." Courtesy of Rodgers & Hammerstein, on behalf of the Estate of Irving Berlin.*

two lines hint at blossoming romance (which is more assumed than developed) and lead crisply into a scene-ending song that confirms our growing suspicion that Kit and Pat will most likely accomplish two things that so many musical comedy couples have done before: fall in love and put on a show.

REISMAN: Me? Hal Reisman—do a show out of Woolworths?

KIT: Why not? Glorifying the American Dime. What have you got to lose?. . . .

REISMAN: All right, I'll take a chance.

KIT: Great! (*Rise*)

REISMAN (*To* PAT): Go and see 'em. See what you can do.

PAT: All right.

REISMAN: Better than no show at all I guess. Gee, I never thought I'd come to this.

PAT: Kit and I'll go see 'em this afternoon.

REISMAN: Right! And if they say yes we'll start things going.

PAT: All right. I'll phone you the minute we find out.

REISMAN: Great! I'm going right over to the office and clear the decks. See you later, Kit. (*exit L*)

KIT: Whee! A job!

PAT: Am I wonderful or am I wonderful?

KIT: Both! (*Both sit*)

SONG: "Let's Have Another Cup of Coffee"
  CURTAIN

The song "Let's Have Another Cup of Coffee" fit the situation perfectly: it was too soon for a real love duet, especially in the wise-cracking 1930s. Yet a number here, even without romantic implications, helps to place firm focus on the couple. The song, of course, became one of Berlin's hits and a hopeful anthem of the Depression era. But the show's plot gives it a richer context than its lyric alone admits, for the song becomes a way to toast the prospect of putting on a show with the modest beverage for which the automats were beloved: the five-cent cup of coffee.[44]

More than that, however, contemporary audiences had access to another dimension of the number: its collage-like parody of a kind of song that had become a Tin Pan Alley specialty in recent years. The song's verse signals that dimension in self-referential lines: "Songwriters say the storm quickly passes; / That's their philosophy. / They see the world through rose-colored glasses; / Why shouldn't we?" The verse and chorus contain quotations and paraphrases of lyrics from at least eight songs of the past decade and a half—"a litany of Pollyanna weather songs," as Philip Furia put it, in which images of fair weather reflect an optimistic outlook that may not be justified by the facts.[45] (Table 5.3) Herbert Hoover, the thoroughly discredited president, comes in for ridicule as well. Besides being named in a line citing his Pollyanna advice that "now's the time to buy," he is also invoked in a line that quotes a statement widely attributed to him: that "prosperity is *just around the corner*." In this light, "Let's Have Another Cup of Coffee" becomes less an expression of Depression-era optimism than an ironic representation of it, deploying shards of songs from an earlier, less troubled time. Indeed, the entire refrain is so chock full of quotations

Table 5.3. "Let's Have Another Cup of Coffee" lyrics, and source of key phrases

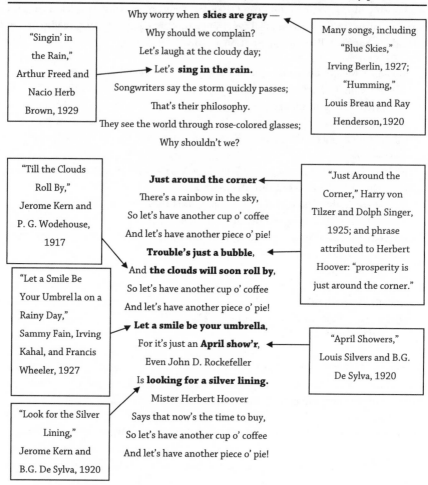

Why worry when **skies are gray** —
Why should we complain?
Let's laugh at the cloudy day;
Let's **sing in the rain.**
Songwriters say the storm quickly passes;
That's their philosophy.
They see the world through rose-colored glasses;
Why shouldn't we?

"Singin' in the Rain," Arthur Freed and Nacio Herb Brown, 1929

Many songs, including "Blue Skies," Irving Berlin, 1927; "Humming," Louis Breau and Ray Henderson, 1920

"Till the Clouds Roll By," Jerome Kern and P. G. Wodehouse, 1917

Just around the corner
There's a rainbow in the sky,
So let's have another cup o' coffee
And let's have another piece o' pie!
Trouble's just a bubble,
And **the clouds will soon roll by**,
So let's have another cup o' coffee
And let's have another piece o' pie!
Let a smile be your umbrella,
For it's just an **April show'r**,
Even John D. Rockefeller
Is **looking for a silver lining.**
Mister Herbert Hoover
Says that now's the time to buy,
So let's have another cup o' coffee
And let's have another piece o' pie!

"Just Around the Corner," Harry von Tilzer and Dolph Singer, 1925; and phrase attributed to Herbert Hoover: "prosperity is just around the corner."

"Let a Smile Be Your Umbrella on a Rainy Day," Sammy Fain, Irving Kahal, and Francis Wheeler, 1927

"April Showers," Louis Silvers and B.G. De Sylva, 1920

"Look for the Silver Lining," Jerome Kern and B.G. De Sylva, 1920

that the refrain's tag line "So let's have another cup of coffee, / And let's have another piece of pie" is the longest sequence of words that Berlin himself wrote for it.

The next several scenes reveal excitement and complications that come with efforts to put on a show in a cash-strapped city teeming with corruption. The plot develops as Hart presents more caricatures of the Depression's impact. We see store managers in formal dress standing before Fifth Avenue's "gilt-edged store fronts" such as Tiffany and Cartier, calling out two-for-one bargains, and getting no takers.[46] We see a Palace Theatre marquee featuring a motley list of current attractions that include entertainers such as Ethel Barrymore, Al Jolson, and the Marx Brothers, and other newsmakers such as Albert Einstein,[47] the celebrity evangelist Aimee Semple McPherson, and the stallion film star named Rex the Wonder Horse.[48] An absurd sign advertises "free sandwiches" costing between a dime and a quarter. A street vendor enters with a pushcart full of entertainers calling: "first-class actors, singers, good actors. Who wants any actors?"[49] The Depression, in short, is a farce, and everyone is a member of the cast.

The show-business plot thickens as such gags duck in and out. Walking down Fifth Avenue toward Woolworth, Pat and Kit spot a richly dressed woman on a shopping spree, and realizing that getting her attention might lead to good things for the show Pat asks her for the time. The gaudily bejeweled woman consults one of her many watches and announces that "on a clear day you can see me from Yonkers." Further conversation reveals that unlike almost everyone else in the city she and her husband are "lousy with money," and that, what's more, he longs to get into show business. Startled by their good fortune, Pat and Kit agree to meet with him, and, as the woman exits, they sing a four-line reprise of "Let's Have Another Cup of Coffee."

It turns out that the woman is the wife of the police chief Martin Van Buren Meshbesher, and the next scene takes place in his "elaborate" office in the Empire State Building, which was at this time a newly finished building that was still seeking tenants and thus dubbed by some the "Empty State Building."[50] For the show's original audience, the very sight of New York's finest in an "elaborate" office would have signaled the familiar target of the Seabury Commission investigating the corrupted police, who, in league with other city officials, had made false arrests and extorted cash in exchange for dropping charges. In offstage reality, one sheriff had become notorious when his testimony describing his "wonderful tin box" of cash became public, and the stage picture magnified the image by showing every officer with his own little tin box.[51]

In this world, Kit, Pat, and Reisman hardly need to make a pitch: Meshbesher not only has a lot of money, he needs to find a way to launder it—and keep it out of sight of the "reformers." The dialogue between Meshbesher, Reisman, and the police "boys" has touches of absurdity that sound like echoes of a Marx Brothers routine:

> MESHBESHER: We've been making a lot of money and the reformers are out after us. Now then, if they ever open our tin boxes, what are they going to find? Money—that's what they're going to find. Therefore: (a) we've got to get rid of the money; (b) we've got to get rid of the tin boxes; and (j) [sic] we're in a hell of a fix (sits).
>
> REISMAN (Rises): Gentlemen, as I see it, your problem is how to get rid of a lot of money.
>
> BOYS: That's right.
>
> REISMAN: And I don't know any better way you could do it than back one of my shows. If that doesn't take care of you, nothing will (sits).[52]

The police see Reisman's point and agree to back the show (and we have the spark for a plot engine that would later run The Producers). Soon the showman is on the phone exhorting his secretary, Goldie (who happens to share the name of Florenz Ziegfeld's secretary, Goldie Clough), to notify the press that "Reisman's doing a show." Several characters repeat the phrase in an incantatory echo that becomes the basis for a perky ensemble number conjuring the redemptive joy of theater. Putting on a show is the cure for all of the Depression's ills.

The original production segued directly into a number called "Torch Song." "Torch Song" is set in a police station, where a young woman, likely costumed so that her identity as a prostitute would have been clear at first sight, is being brought in for incarceration by one Sergeant O'Rourke.[53] "I'm just one of those women," she sings, and goes on to tell the story of how she deliberately sought out heartbreak so that she could sing the genre convincingly:

> I wanted to sing a torch song,
> So I got a man to break my heart,
> And though I soon became a tart,
> I did it for the sake of art
> And a torch song.

Berlin's triple rhyme (heart-tart-art) brings out the number's burlesque qualities, reinforced by an accented va-va-va-voom triplet figure between vocal phrases.

It is burlesque in both senses: lewd and broadly satirical. As with many songs in the show, "Torch Song" taps a satiric vein at the intersection of show business clichés and hard news. The term *torch song* refers to a kind of lament over lost love; the singer "carries the torch" for her absent lover, despite his departure, infidelity, or death. But Berlin's song is less a torch song per se than a send-up of the genre, complete with references to the singer Helen Morgan, recognized in her time as the ultimate torch singer, and noted especially for her trademark pose on or near a piano. The lyrics also cite another song heard recently on the Broadway stage, Cole Porter's "Love for Sale" (1930), a streetwalker's woeful tale of having "every love but true love." In its reflexive, parodistic allusiveness—another song about a type of song—the number thus bears a familial resemblance to "Let's Have Another Cup of Coffee."

More than just a spoof of torch songs and singers, however, Berlin's "Torch Song" addresses, however obliquely, the real victims of the widespread and systematic graft among New York City police and judges. When Berlin and Hart were hard at work on the show through 1931, New Yorkers could not avoid daily exposure to news about the investigations by the man appointed by then-governor Franklin Roosevelt to get to the bottom of the problem: Samuel Seabury.

The Seabury Investigation uncovered a specific pattern of corruption that pertains to "Torch Song," and that tends to be overlooked in historical summaries of the investigation: that the police had been arresting innocent, and usually working-class, young women by the dozens on false "morals" charges and putting them in jail if they did not buy back their innocence and freedom. A series of page-one *New York Times* headlines summarize the story's development:

> "Innocent Girls Arrested" (November 27, 1930)
> "Girls Accuse Police at Ouster Hearing" (December 18, 1930)
> "Roosevelt Pardons Six Women 'Framed' by Police" (December 23, 1930)
> "77 Minor Girls Imprisoned Unlawfully by 7 Judges" (January 9, 1931)
> "Mayor Acts to Free 71 Imprisoned Girls" (January 14, 1931)
> "Jailed Minor Girls to Get New Trials by Bennett Order" (January 15, 1931)
> "Woman of Standing Framed in Vice Case" (January 16, 1931).

A year later in February 1932, when the show opened, this issue had almost become old news. So with the matter largely exposed by others, Berlin and Hart—like their latter-day counterparts on *Saturday Night Live* or *The Daily Show*—felt perhaps freer to bring some levity to it. In this case, the woman buys her freedom through song instead of cash. Instead of a jail sentence, she is given a chance to audition for Reisman's show. For opening night audiences, there was no mistaking the resonance between the show on stage and the news from the New York streets just outside the theater. Many critics praised "Torch Song" and its singer, Jean Sargent, making her Broadway debut.[54] Yet the song was cut from the show—perhaps because it was more of a revue-number than a plot-number and thus the most easily excised piece in a show that ran long. In retrospect, however, it stands out as an ingenious song that channels an array of contemporary social, theatrical, and musical currents.

In contrast to the torch-song singer, two characters in the next scene believe that success in show business comes not through experience but through inborn talent. Unlike most other characters in the show, Pickles and Joe are performers and *they know it*, so they are introduced here in the song "You Must Be Born with It"—an implicit jab at the police and other show business wannabes who are in it for money rather than for talent. Hereafter, Pickles and Joe become a familiar musical-comedy duo: the comic secondary couple that serves as the foil to the more romantic relationship emerging between Pat and Kit. But later we learn they are not a conventional couple headed down the usual road of domestic stability. In act 2, a police detective brings them into the station ("both in underwear," according to the handwritten stage directions next to the crossed-out "pajamas"), because they were found in the same hotel room together without evidence of being married. Joe claims it is Pickles's fault because she refuses to marry him, which leads Pickles to sing "I Don't Wanna Be Married": "Don't speak of wedding chimes," she sings in the verse, "Because we mustn't be behind the times; / Besides, a wedding isn't necessary at all." The two duets of Pickles and Joe are perky, syncopated tunes well designed to identify their roles in the plot—even if they form an unconventional couple in which the young woman eschews the marriage plot's conventional goal.

Pat and Kit not only have more songs, they have more musical variety. After conferring with the police chief about the new show, they appear on the terrace of the Meshbesher penthouse apartment envisioning a life together. Typical of the Kaufman and Co. style, however, the dialogue does little to prepare the song's romantic developments. In "On a Roof in Manhattan," Kit and Pat sing a vision of domestic bliss that rejects clichés. As in the "Coffee" and "Torch" songs, Berlin puts a new twist on songwriting and musical-comedy conventions of a more innocent time. In the verse, they sing about how "A cottage by the sea / Is not for you and me," and, pointedly the lyric continues: "A little bungalow / Would never do, I know"—a line that may reflect Berlin's reaction to the final lines of Kaufman and Ryskind's *June Moon*. Instead they envision "a castle in Spain" on an urban summit, recalling a line from the verse of Rodgers and Hart's recent hit "My Heart Stood Still" (1927), in which "castles rise in Spain."

The music of "On a Roof in Manhattan" also taps another wellspring of popular song. With its pulsating habanera rhythm and mariachi-style harmonizing in sixths, the song captures some of the flavor of the new Latin music fad that was sweeping the musical world in the early 1930s. As John Storm Roberts notes in a seminal study of Latin music in the United States, Don Azpiazu had brought "authentic Cuban dance music" to American audiences for the first time and popularized the sound with a hit record, "The Peanut Vendor," released in November 1930, and the song's sheet music published by Berlin's competitor E. B. Marks.[55] The following year, as Berlin and Hart developed *Face the Music*, the record was a national hit, and other Latin American songs flooded Tin Pan Alley and the record industry. Meanwhile, in New York, Xavier Cugat's band further stoked the so-called Rumba Craze with its high profile residency at the Waldorf-Astoria Hotel. That Berlin copyrighted the song in July 1931, more than six months before the show opened, reveals a familiar impulse to strike when the time is right.

Berlin was not the first Broadway songwriter to adopt the new style, however. Just a month earlier, in June, Broadway had seen a rumba novelty in a show called *Third Little Show*—which had opened at the Music Box Theatre.[56] The fad resonates through other popular music, too, as in several later songs of Cole Porter ("The Gypsy in Me" [1934], "Begin the Beguine" [1935], "My Heart Belongs to Daddy" [1938]) and compositions such as Gershwin's *Cuban Overture* (originally titled *Rumba*, 1932) and Copland's *El Salón México* (1932–36). But Berlin, as he so often did, stood among the very first songwriters to exploit the new style.[57] That he applied it to an updated version of Broadway's hackneyed "cozy cottage" motif comprises a remarkably astute gesture. The number's staging clinched its impact. Hassard Short used his signature revolving stage to captivating effect. A reviewer noted how "the penthouse terrace swings around to reveal the dancers of the castle in Spain." Brooks Atkinson called the number "a work of art."[58]

The penultimate scene of act 1 reveals backstage chaos during a rehearsal for show-within-a-show bearing a clichéd revue title, *The Rhinestones of 1932*, and marked by the kind of spitfire dialogue that Hart learned at Kaufman's side. It also contains another echo of Groucho Marx, as when Reisman finds himself confronted by reporters eager to follow up on a recent newspaper story announcing that "Bankers Agree to Finance City on Strength of Reisman Proportion."[59] Surrounded by jostling reporters, Reisman pontificates:

> Boys, I love this city. I was born and raised in one of our city's gutters. I watched this city grow, boys. Saw it grow from a struggling little New England fishing village. Was I the man to turn my back when the city was on the brink of disaster? No. For a mere 75% of the profits I stepped in and saved it. My only regret is that I have but one show to give for my city.[60]

Show business, it appears, has saved the entire city of New York, and since the city is backing the show, various departments of the city government, including the police, want to host parties for the chorus girls.

So the financing is in place, but the show itself leaves something to be desired. The Stage Manager has reported that the rhinestone gondola will not fit through the door, and the narcissistic tenor Rodney St. Clair is having terrible trouble with his rhinestone-studded tuxedo. This leads to a reflexive show-within-a-show number called "My Beautiful Rhinestone Girl," sung by St. Clair, who had been purchased by Reisman from the pushcart carrying out-of-work actors. Set as a flowing, through-composed waltz, the song sends up the Ziegfeld "girl" number and aptly recasts it for the Depression era. It does so by starting off with an unusual sequence of *negative* similes in list-song format before arriving at a deliberate anticlimax suggested by the title:

Not like a glittering diamond,
Not like a pearl from the sea,
Not like the greenest of emeralds,
Are you my darling to me.
Not like a beautiful topaz,
Not like a sapphire of blue,
Not like a rosy red ruby,
But like a rhinestone are you.

The satire here is partly self-inflicted. By deploying the simile, Berlin recalls a lyric-writing device he used to great effect in "A Pretty Girl Is Like a Melody." Meanwhile, his gem imagery also recalls "Diamond Horse-shoe" from the 1922 *Music Box Revue*, in which the singer imagines the Metropolitan Opera audience as "a horseshoe set with diamonds, / A diamond horseshoe set with girls." The joke further implicates two of Berlin's accomplices in the revue, namely the tuxedoed tenor John Steel (for whom he wrote both "Pretty Girl" and "Diamond Horse-shoe"), and the designer Hassard Short, whose jewel numbers became a stylistic calling card in the 1920s and were widely imitated to the point of cliché.[61] The larger joke, of course, is that the rhinestone is both the most affordable gem in a time of financial crisis and the least precious of the ones named in the song's verse.

With production values intended to be "as foolishly opulent as possible," as Hart put it, the collaborators conspired to present a jewel number to end all jewel numbers.[62] After a typical opening "in one," with the tenor before a rhinestone-studded velvet curtain, the curtain opened to reveal an exotic Venetian scene with the Piazza San Marco, St. Mark's Cathedral, and the Doge's Palace outlined in rhinestones. A chorus wearing rhinestoned costumes awaits the arrival of a gondola with bride (played by Mrs. Meshbesher) and groom—all drenched in rhinestones that glittered with shades of blue light. At the number's climax, "a flock of rhinestone doves—with flapping rhinestone wings—lower a huge rhinestone wedding bell onto the happy couple."[63]

The joke is double-edged, mocking both the overwrought production values of the pre–Depression-era revue and the extravagant waste of money from the police force's little tin boxes. Yet the scenic wonders inspired more awe than laughter. Although some of the in-the-know revue regulars chuckled at the number's satirical intent, many audience members simply murmured admiration and offered sincere applause for an opulence that appeared more ravishing than foolish. "All the Audience Refuse to Take his Rhinestone Burlesque as a Joke," read the sub-headline of a newspaper report focusing the scene's impact.[64] Nevertheless, as our first glimpse of the *Rhinestones of 1932*, "My Beautiful Rhinestone Girl" is meant to fail —justifying the revised show that will be conceived and staged in act 2. Berlin succeeded in doing a rare thing: writing a good exemplar of a bad song. The only rivals that come immediately to mind are two other tenor-and-girls song spoofs that came later: Rodgers and Hart's "Flower Garden of My Heart" in *Pal Joey* and Mel Brooks's "Springtime for Hitler" in *The Producers*.

In the midst of all of these song parodies Berlin wrote one sincere romantic ballad that stands out from the surrounding farce and serves as the act 1 finale: "Soft Lights and Sweet Music." Here is where Hart's "acid" humor gets most pointedly juxtaposed with Berlin's "satin" elegance. Hart's scene is farcical: a ball at the Central Park Casino where we see chorus girls in evening gowns each entering on the arm of a uniformed police officer. The ball serves as a backdrop for further machinations by Meshbesher, who reveals that he has held back one of his little tin boxes of cash. With the traveler curtain still closed, Pat sings the melody and Kit ultimately joins in.[65] As the couple begins to dance, other couples enter and dance in pairs in such a way as to create the illusion of dancers reflected in a mirror. Staged by Hassard Short, the "mirror" number expanded on an effect introduced in a sketch from the 1922 *Music Box Revue*.[66]

"Soft Lights and Sweet Music" stands among the most elegant theater songs Berlin ever wrote. The lyrics develop in a series of parallel statements in which Berlin pairs each phrase about light with a matching phrase about music:

I can't resist the moan of a cello:	I can't resist the light of the moon.
So place me in a light that is mellow	And let me hear a beautiful tune.
The music must flow;	The lights must be low.

The refrain continues the parallel construction, now with the element of romance added as the outcome of pairing lights and music:

Soft lights	and	sweet music	and you in my arms;
Soft lights	and	sweet melody	will bring you closer to me.
Chopin	and	pale moonlight	reveal all your charms;
So give me velvet lights and		sweet music	and you in my arms.

The lyric reflects Berlin's sensitivity to sound. The title phrase's soft, sweet "s" whispers throughout the song. The mood of soft sensuality gets further support from a recurring "l" sound in key words (*cello, light(s), flow, low, pale, velvet*) and a humming "m" (*moan, moon, mellow, music, must, arms, charms*).

Berlin's music reinforces his well-crafted lyric. The verse's series of phrase pairs [4 + 4] + [4 + 4] + [2 + 2] supports the schematically paired lyric phrases (ex. 5.1). But its supple rhythms obscure the square-cut design with a quasi-rubato effect conjured by quarter-note triplets. Such across-the-beat triplet patterns appear increasingly in Berlin's work in the 1930s and beyond, and allow his rhythmic language to become more flexible and less obviously indebted to ragtime.

Example 5.1. "Soft Lights and Sweet Music," verse, beginning.

Example 5.2. "Soft Lights and Sweet Music," refrain, mm. 1–8.

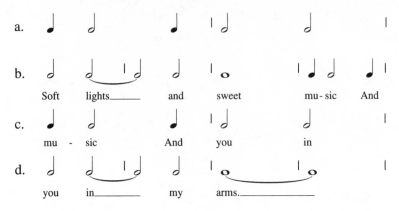

Example 5.3. Basic cakewalk rhythm (5.3a) and its manifestations in "Soft Lights and Sweet Music," refrain (5.3b, 5.3c, and 5.3d).

Example 5.4. "Soft Lights and Sweet Music," bridge.

The verse, moreover, creates a haunting effect through its prevailing F-minor mood, estranged by the prominent B-natural half-notes on downbeats (the sharp-4th degree of an F-minor scale) on the first syllable of "cello" and "mellow." Although the B-natural's harmonic support simply turns out to be the dominant of the dominant (G), the local harmonic shift from F-minor to G-major produces a rich and strange effect.

Berlin shifts to F major for the refrain, but here too, modal complications develop immediately, as the harmony features a sequence of parallel seventh chords that obscure the tonic and conjure an uncanny mood (ex. 5.2). Yet the mood is grounded in a familiar rhythmic language, two patterns whose ragtime roots Berlin masks by augmentation. The first of them clearly derives from the cakewalk rhythm of early ragtime song (ex. 5.3a shows the basic cakewalk pattern and exx. 5.3b, 5.3c, and 5.3d show its overlapping augmentations in "Soft Lights"). The second features a kind of tied syncopation also common in the ragtime era (ex. 5.4).

Act 1 encompassed the planning and presentation of the show-within-a-show. Act 2 reveals the show's impact and consequences, onstage and off. First Berlin depicts the response of the audience and critics as they leave the theater, singing:

The "1st lead sheet . . . by Irving Berlin" appears to have been the product of a lesson in music notation for which Berlin wrote down the melody of "Soft Lights and Sweet Music"—several months after the Face the Music *opened and the song was published.*
Library of Congress, Music Division.

Well, of all the rotten shows!
Why it opened, heaven knows.
Did you ever see such scenery?
Did you ever see such clothes?
What a reminiscent score—
And the book was such a bore!
And that awful rhinestone number—
That was done before the war.

When they sing "Any wonder why / The theatre's going to hell?" Berlin comments on the conventional wisdom about Broadway's decline, thanks to talking pictures, the Depression, and overall mediocrity in the writing. (But *Face the Music* itself appears to have been critic proof; as one noted, Sam Harris had two hits in a "subnormal" theatrical season.[67]) In a sequence analogous to the beginning of act 1, Kit and Pat emerge from the crowd and sing an optimistic duet with a bouncy dotted rhythm that recalls "Let's Have Another Cup of Coffee." Hart's dialogue sets up the number in a few snappy lines:

KIT: Pat, what's the worst that can happen?
PAT: The show'll close.

KIT: And we'll be right back where we were.

PAT: But are we downhearted?

KIT: Well, what about you?

The song is "I Say It's Spinach (and the Hell with It)," a kind of throwaway phrase by which Pat and Kit insist that losing the show doesn't mean much, "Long as I'm yours, / Long as you're mine, / Long as there's love and a moon to shine." Contemporary New Yorkers would have caught a resonance in the title line that is lost to later observers— yet another indication of the show's up-to-dateness in 1932. In 1928, the *New Yorker* published a cartoon featuring a well-dressed woman and her petite, curly-haired little girl sitting at a carefully set table, covered with a table cloth. The woman says, "It's broccoli, dear," and the daughter replies, "I say it's spinach, and I say the hell with it."[68] The original program acknowledged the *New Yorker* for the borrowed phrase.[69]

Later in act 2, Rodney St. Clair goes to a speakeasy for a post-performance drink, and a group of barflies threatens to beat him up unless he promises never to sing the rhinestone song again. St. Clair makes the promise and further appeases his would-be assailants by ordering a round of drinks and launching yet another song spoof: "Drinking Song." Such songs had a long history on the musical stage, most notably in the popular waltz number of the same title from Sigmund Romberg's 1924 operetta, *The Student Prince*.[70] As an opera lover in his early years, Berlin no doubt had seen productions featuring a *brindisi*, a type of number in many nineteenth-century Italian operas (and a few earlier) in which a character offers a toast and exhorts a party of guests to drink. Many of them appear in operas that had long been popular in America.[71] The twist, of course, is that America is in the midst of Prohibition. Good-natured irony flows freely here, as St. Clair toasts the Eighteenth Amendment for the financial windfall it has provided for bootleggers. Berlin turns the number into a counterpoint song, as St. Clair's repeats the refrain as the other men hum "Stars and Stripes Forever" (and phrases from "Dixie"), reinforcing the number's ironic flag-waving patriotism (ex. 5.5).

Before St. Clair arrived, Kit and Pat had joined the Meshbeshers at the speakeasy, reading the early newspaper reviews, which do not bode well ("the dullest show of even this dull season"). Pat advises that the show needs one thing to turn its fortunes: sex. Meshbesher, who lacks show business instincts as well as a sex drive (according to an authority, his wife), tries to imagine the show revised in this way:

MESHBESHER: What would you do with the crinoline number?

PAT: Take the crinoline *off* the girls!

MESHBESHER: But that's all they wear.

PAT: That's just the idea!

MESHBESHER: Oh, I get it.[72]

After Meshbesher at last agrees to the changes, Mrs. Meshbesher muses that "I've been telling him for years that sex is a wonderful thing. (*To Pat and Kit*) But he won't give in. He always argues with me."

The "crinoline number"—sung in act 2 when the crinoline is "off the girls"—conjures still another earlier song type that Berlin himself had used, and the result is another many-layered joke that is entertaining in its own right but rewards audience members

Example 5.5. "Drinking Song."

who had followed Berlin's stage career closely. In the 1922 *Music Box Revue*, Berlin had written a nostalgic ballad called "Crinoline Days" that fondly recalled nineteenth-century manners, referring to a specific year "back in eighteen seventy-four" and the era's modest dress styles—"before anyone could gaze / At Molly's and May's / Little ankle displays." (Many audience members would have remembered not just the song but Hassard Short's remarkable staging of it, in which an elevator lifted the lead singer, Grace La Rue, and her surrounding ground cloth "twenty feet in the air and the huge thing made a skirt"[73]—thus anticipating by some eight decades a memorable moment in the number "Defying Gravity" in *Wicked*.)

In style and tone, Berlin's new number for the 1932 show, "Dear Old Crinoline Days," matches the one from a decade earlier—now pointedly referring to a specific year a decade earlier: "back in eighteen *sixty*-four." The new crinoline number had replaced Berlin's original idea for the scene, a "nudist" song in the style of "A Pretty Girl Is Like a Melody," which describes what the audience sees.[74] Berlin apparently realized just in time that once again an antithesis would better serve the scene—producing a comic cognitive dissonance between what the audience hears (a song about old-fashioned dresses) and sees (a faux-nude chorus in flesh-toned body suits).[75] For 1932 theatergoers the scene also conjured the infamously risqué Earl Carroll revues, which, as everyone in the theater would have known, had been raided by the police. In fact, Hart's police react in the same way: they arrest the culprits. But in *Face the Music* the police raid is staged. In other words, the police realize that raids stoke box offices. So they have it both ways: boosting ticket sales while enforcing the law.

But the Seabury investigation is closing in. Back in her swanky apartment, Mrs. Meshbesher is having her hair done by a personal assistant when a stranger appears, asking to speak with Mr. Meshbesher. As Meshbesher is not in, the stranger agrees to wait for a while, but finally decides to leave. Mrs. Meshbesher says goodbye but realizes she has not learned the stranger's name: "The name is Seabury," notes the stranger, and Mrs. Meshbesher exclaims "Oh!" and promptly faints. Blackout. In the darkness, Hart launches a Kaufmanesque sequence of chaos and noise, with newsboys shouting "extra!," sirens blaring, orchestra wailing.[76] Out of this emerges "Manhattan Madness," a song that blithely captures contemporary New York's bustle and disorder with a title phrase that may have been borrowed from a newspaper column—something Berlin and Hart's next show would do more systematically.[77] To reinforce the number's (and the show's) connections to contemporary New York, the scene featured a simulated Times Square news ticker; the program even acknowledged the Motogram Corporation for its "moving letter sign."[78]

The curtain parts as the "madness" (conjured in part to cover a scene change) yields to a "very swanky resort" where we find the police, actors, the Meshbeshers, and Reisman himself in hiding from the Seabury investigators. The police sheriff poses as a man named "Smith," and Reisman himself, also named "Smith," acts as a waiter in the resort restaurant where the principals have gathered. After a discussion, Reisman hits upon the idea for the thespian fugitives to return to Manhattan and turn themselves in so that he may stage the investigation himself.

REISMAN: I've been watching those investigations for years, and they always peter out. And you know why, don't you? They don't know how to put 'em on. What they need is a showman!

MRS. MESHBESHER: Why, what do you mean?

REISMAN: Look! They've got the greatest natural attraction in the world right in their hands and what do they do with it? Just throw it away! They've got something that gets on the front page of every paper in the country, and they don't even charge for it. I'd like to handle one of those things once I'd just show them—I'd give 'em an investigation and clean up, too.

MRS. MESHBESHER: Why—what would you do?

REISMAN: What wouldn't I do? Who do they get for their leading man? Max Steuer. I don't say he's a bad lawyer, but where's the sex appeal? I'd give them Bing Crosby and get every woman in town.

MRS. MESHBESHER: Mr. Reisman, why don't you do it?

REISMAN: What?

MRS. MESHBESHER: Put the investigation on for us.

. . .

REISMAN: Say, I begin to see it. Hal Reisman presents "Investigations of 1932,"
glorifying the American Policeman. An all-star cast produced under the
personal supervision of Hal Reisman.

MRS. MESHBESHER: You see! Reisman's putting it on!

The line leads into a reprise of "Reisman's Doing a Show," and the scene changes to a
courtroom in Manhattan, where Reisman's new "show" begins and the characters
recapitulate the plot—entirely in music. The "Investigation" scene, which occupies
more than one-third of the piano-vocal score, stands out as one of Berlin's longest continuous musical scenes since the opening of the 1921 *Music Box Revue*, and it suggests he was
still channeling his operatic ambitions into musical comedy. The scene weaves together
new patter melodies with reprises of several numbers, including "My Beautiful Rhinestone Girl," "Of All the Rotten Shows," "Dear Old Crinoline Days," and "I Say It's Spinach."

In the sensational finale of Face the Music, *Mrs. Meshbesher (Mary Boland), the bejeweled
wife of the corrupt police chief, enters on a papier-mâché elephant. Courtesy of Rodgers &
Hammerstein, on behalf of the Estate of Irving Berlin.*

Reisman begins by announcing he has staged the ensuing courtroom scene. And three witnesses appear before a jury of lovely chorus girls—"probably the most attractive jury ever seen on or off stage," according to one review.[79] Kit Baker appears as Lady Godiva, admitting she appeared naked on stage because she "needed the job." Then Meshbesher himself appears in a Gilbert-and-Sullivanesque sequence where the jury echoes his words. And finally Mrs. Meshbesher enters on a papier mâché elephant purchased from Ziegfeld. And since this is a musical comedy, the investigation finds guilt but ultimately grants reprieves to the accused, because in the theater the demands of musical comedy trump the law. Led by Pat and Kit, the ensemble comes together to close the show with a reprise of "Soft Lights and Sweet Music."

The show received enthusiastic, if qualified, reviews. Most critics compared *Face the Music* to the Gershwin/Kaufman show *Of Thee I Sing*, and usually ranked it a notch below that other Sam Harris production. But their judgments tended to be based more on the book than the music. What they generally failed to note was the extent to which Berlin, more than the Gershwins, had stuffed his score with pointed parodies and allusions to—or fresh twists on—a cornucopia of pre-Depression popular song styles: the Pollyanna weather song ("Let's Have Another Cup of Coffee"), the torch song ("Torch Song"), the cozy-cottage number ("A Roof in Manhattan"), the tenor-and-parade-of-girls jewel number ("My Beautiful Rhinestone Girl"), the counterpoint song, in this case also a *brindisi* ("Drinking Song"), and a nostalgic crinoline number ("Dear Old Crinoline Days"). Although each addressed a plot point, the numbers were above all *songs about songs*. Berlin spiked other numbers with references to the world just outside the theater's lobby: the automat, the Times Square news ticker, a *New Yorker* cartoon, the revue itself. Alec Wilder even speculated that Berlin may have taken the phrase "Soft Lights and Sweet Music" from ads for a nightclub since the song was originally published with quotation marks around its title.[80] The show held a funhouse mirror up to contemporary New York, its people, places, music, and theater.

Although the show never named the particular culprits of widespread corruption and graft, the audience knew who they were. Mayor Jimmy Walker, who had to testify before the Seabury Commission, was even glimpsed on opening night by at least two critics, one of whom wrote that he sported "a grin with reservations,"[81] and the other reporting that "shafts of barbed wit at the expense of the local municipal administration caused much craning of necks in the direction of Mayor Walker."[82] Walker would resign in disgrace a few months later, just two months after the show closed. In that light, the show's title itself could have been seen as having a chip on its shoulder—a phrase that one critic used to describe the next year's offering by Berlin and Hart.[83]

"THE SMART NEW REVUE": *AS THOUSANDS CHEER*

A Depression-era revue might have seemed a contradiction in terms, since Ziegfeld's lavish productions had set a standard for spectacle and abundance that defined the genre in the century's first three decades. By 1933, Broadway had seen just two new *Follies* editions in the past six years. The brand had become faded and nostalgic, and now Ziegfeld was dead. "The public had wearied of ever-increasing lavishness," Lehman Engel writes, "and the growing cost of this lavishness made the future for producers an impossibility."[84] But if the revue's economic foundation had evaporated, its format still proved irresistible, as even a quick skim of Broadway seasons in the early 1930s reveals: the genre continued to flourish, even if attendance was down and runs were shorter.[85] In fact, a few key figures on Broadway—many of them in George S. Kaufman's orbit—were determined to reinvent the genre. The goal now was to feature up-to-the-minute topicality, satire, brisk pace, sparkling dialogue, and songs and sketches closely linked, with limited reliance on Ziegfeldian extravagance in sets, costumes, and feminine exhibition—one template for later television variety comedy from Sid Caesar's *Your Show of Shows* to *The Daily Show*. Revues titled *The Little Show* (1929), *Three's a Crowd* (1930) and *The Band Wagon* (1931) set the tone.[86] The historians Lehman Engel and Ethan Mordden, writing much later, would refer to such shows as exemplars of "the new revue," characterized as "knowing, facetious, and chic"—and rather arch about its own conventions and clichés.[87] All of which is a fair description of Berlin's *Music Box Revues* a decade earlier. More recently, *The Band Wagon*, unusually for a non–Irving Berlin revue, had featured songs from one creative source, the team of Arthur Schwartz and Howard Dietz, and it also took its style from two key figures in Berlin's world: Kaufman, who wrote several sketches, and Hassard Short, who directed. *The Band Wagon* "may well have been the most sophisticated, imaginative, and musically distinguished revue ever mounted on Broadway," according to Stanley Green, an encyclopedic chronicler of musical theater's history.[88]

Berlin and Hart's contribution to the "new revue" was titled *As Thousands Cheer*. Arriving two years after *The Band Wagon*, it did not produce the innovation but, as Berlin had done since the ragtime era, it capitalized on a new trend and gave it unique focus. The show opened in September 1933 and ran for four hundred performances, in what would turn out to be one of the longest runs of a Depression-era musical.[89] The unique focus came from the concept of an "animated newspaper," in which every song and sketch derived from a news item. "Mr. Berlin and Mr. Hart have seized upon a technical device that simplifies the revue form enormously," wrote Brooks Atkinson.[90]

"Unity"—a word rarely uttered by creators of revues—became a calling card for this approach. As Berlin told an interviewer just after the show opened: "We made up our mind to evolve a musical show around all the various episodes of which partook of a common unity. A revue of deliberately selected limitations which would give it cohesiveness and character instead of merely rambling through a number of more or less topical acts as has been the rule until now."[91] Hart likewise told an interviewer that "we had no desire to do a conventional sort of revue."[92] The critics responded positively. Hammond called it "the smart new revue"; *Variety* called it "ultra-smart" and noted that it "doesn't go in for heavy scenic production features and certainly doesn't emphasize girls."[93] For Brooks Atkinson, it was not so much "new" as a return to the "genuine meaning" of revue—to refract the contemporary world in comedy and song.[94]

To enhance the newspaper theme, each sketch and song played out under a headline presented to the audience on a slide projected into an oblong, gilt-framed blank space on a curtain above the stage.[95] The original plan had been to present lighted headlines that moved across a screen in the manner of the Times Square news ticker, described at the time as an "electric bulletin board"—the device used during "Manhattan Madness" in *Face the Music*. That vision, though unrealized in *As Thousands Cheer*, would have enhanced the show's currency: it had been launched with much fanfare just five years earlier on election night, 1928.[96] The "electric bulletin board" itself was news.

All of the sketches and characterizations were based on real events and impersonations of real people. A kind of double celebrity took effect: the show's stars—including former *Follies* star Marilyn Miller, the comedienne Helen Broderick (featured in *Three's a Crowd*), the debonair singer-actor dancer Clifton Webb (featured in *The Band Wagon*), and the singer Ethel Waters, known for investing racial pathos in recent hits such as "Am I Blue?" and "Stormy Weather"—took on roles of equally well-known, or even better-known figures in the news, including Joan Crawford and Douglas Fairbanks Jr., Woolworth heiress Barbara Hutton, Mahatma Gandhi, Aimee Semple McPherson, ex-President Hoover and his wife, Noël Coward, John D. Rockefeller, Josephine Baker, and many others. Many reviewers focused on impersonations as the show's chief appeal. The *New Yorker* was typical in gravitating toward the show's star power, noting that "Clifton Webb's talented libeling of almost everybody you ever heard of makes 'As Thousands Cheer' by far the funniest thing in town."[97]

The topicality of the impersonations proved evanescent, but for Berlin, the show produced several hits that endured as standards, including "How's Chances," "Heat Wave," "Supper Time," "Harlem on My Mind," and one song that would become a holiday anthem, "Easter Parade." That shows a remarkable balance of durable craftsmanship and savvy engagement with contemporary America. These numbers and others deserve close scrutiny for how they connect to contemporaneous events and people—for the songs and sketches comprise distilled, stylized expressions of late 1933 America, representing "frozen moments" in a revue concept that by its nature depended on events very much in flux. By taking its themes and structure from a newspaper, the show ensured that it would be both up-to-date and soon passé. That it ran even four hundred performances is testimony to its effectiveness as theater of the moment.

Although Berlin insisted that he and Hart had no political agenda in mind, one recurring theme that emerges from the sketches and songs is the desire to portray the rich and/or powerful behind the scenes at a time of economic collapse. In short, the show found the comedy and pathos in funhouse mirror glimpses of the rich and powerful when they are beyond the public eye. "Whatever satire there may be in the piece was really implicit in the news items themselves," Berlin claimed soon after the opening.

> It wasn't preconceived and we didn't have any editorial attitude at all when we started out to write the words and music . . . the satirical emphasis that may be present just came itself. There are some persons, you know, who need no distortion to caricature and the same is true with much of the world's news. It is satire in itself and only has to be photographically reproduced to be the most gorgeous kind of irony. It is the result of the closest sort of collaboration . . . George S. Kaufman told us, when we were in the throws [sic] of composition, to stick right to our theme. And that's what we've done.[98]

The show begins with a sketch and song illustrating the inherent theatricality of the newspaper industry itself—attracted to trivial incidents among the rich. And what better way to dramatize that fact than by taking up a cliché of the business, most commonly attributed to the nineteenth-century American journalist and editor, Charles A. Dana: "If a dog bites a man, that's not news. But if a man bites a dog, that's news."[99] Thus, the show's opening headline: "Man Bites Dog."

The scene opens on a "well-appointed [dining] room of a duplex apartment in the east 70s." (The opening night program identified the location as "Park Avenue."[100]) The butler sets the table for two, George and Emily Andrews, while "a particularly offensive looking Pekingese" named Gertrude faces the audience from a perch in a highchair. We learn that George spent the day at the doctor's getting a wound, a dog bite, "cauterized." It is also revealed that the Andrews's last butler, Wilson, left because Gertrude bit him, too. George and Emily argue about whether Gertrude should continue to sleep on their bed, since every time George turns over he gets bitten, and if he tries to get up she growls. When Emily is called away to the phone, George talks to Gertrude in her chair, and the line leads to a blackout and song as follows:

MR. ANDREWS: (*Sweetly*) Hello, Gertrude! Good old Gertrude. (*Coyly*) See all these bandages, Gertrude? That's what *you* did—last night, and the night before and the night before that. For seven years you've been biting me, Gertrude. There isn't an inch of me that you don't know! (*He extends his hand toward Gertrude—then quickly draws it away.*) Ah, no! You've had your last bite out of *me*, Gertrude! From now on, it's an eye for an eye, a tooth for a tooth, and a bite for a bite!

MRS. ANDREWS (*Re-entering*): George![101]

The blackout segued quickly to Berlin's first number, the kind of extended quasi-operatic action piece with which he had opened all of his shows since *Watch Your Step*.[102] It begins with a scurrying orchestral introduction, allowing for a curtain and quick set change. The number appears in two parts. In the first, set in an office, a reporter tries to get the attention of his editor, who is on the phone planning a big "spread" about Roosevelt's latest speech. The reporter sings in a rapid-fire patter style:

I've got a headline—oh, what a headline,
Off the beaten track:
A dog bit a man and the man bit the dog right back.

The editor, at first distracted and resistant to the reporter's manic chatter, finally gets it and tells his phone caller:

Never mind that Roosevelt speech—
I've a headline now that's a peach.
It's a most important story
That'll set the town agog.
Kill the Roosevelt spread;

"Man Bites Dog!" The opening number of As Thousands Cheer, *Berlin and Hart's revue based on newspaper headlines. Courtesy of Rodgers & Hammerstein, on behalf of the Estate of Irving Berlin.*

Print this instead:
MAN—BITES—DOG.

Berlin sets the last phrase on three accented long tones, the musical equivalent of large, boldface type. Suddenly, in the dark, we hear newsboys calling out the head-line, as the scurrying orchestral passage returns, and the scene changes to Times Square ("Columbus Circle" in the program). A full chorus of "boys and girls with newspapers" proclaims the headline in a frenzied effort to sell papers. "At last," they cry, "something else in the news / Besides that the drys will lose / Besides that we'll soon have booze"—a reference to the Twenty-first Amendment, which would become law just weeks after the show opened—and thus probably caused the line to be changed. "At last," they go on, "a man bit a dog at last." In reality it was not the first time: a 1925 *New York Times* headline had announced "Man Bites a Dog, So Gets into the News," followed by the subhead: "dog retaliates in kind, and police decide it acted in self-defense."[103] More recently, Broadway had seen a farce on the subject. It ran for just seven performances in the spring of 1933, but the title, *Man Bites Dog*, may well have caught the attention of Berlin and Hart, since that short-lived show had been set in "the News Room of 'The Daily Tab' in an American City."[104] All of this makes the opening scene even more current than it claims.

The chorus continues, in typical Hart and Berlin style, to name names: renowned columnists (all New York based) Arthur Brisbane, Walter Lippmann, and Hey-wood Broun, and publisher "Mister [William Randolph] Hearst." When the newsboys and girls reveal that Lippmann interviewed the dog and discovered that the dog was female, Berlin finds a rhyme with "rich," leading to the scene's edgy punch-line:

> He says 'twas a dog you hate to be with,
> The kind you see with the rich—
> Not a great big manly he-dog,
> A little she-dog—a bitch—which
> Gives us a headline off the beaten track:
> A bitch bit a man and the man bit the bitch right back.

In addition to being a line that could never have been sung in the new mass media such as radio and film, the scene cuts several ways, not just at the newspaper industry but at the kind of people who can afford an Upper East Side townhome and a butler—in other words, some of the very people who attend shows at the Music Box. For all of the scene's satire, however, it ultimately expressed affection for newspapers, for their history, for their writers, editors, publishers, and for the people who appear in—and read—them. Newspapers had been Kaufman's métier, after all. And it was the Kaufman and Hart style to skewer with a smile.

In Berlin's numbers such smiles could even be warm and sincere. Two songs envision the poignant gap between public persona and private feeling in two of the period's most prominent women: Barbara Hutton and Josephine Baker. Scene 2 appeared under the headline "Woolworth Declares Regular Dividend—Barbara Hutton to Wed Prince Mdivani." Hutton, played by Marilyn Miller in the original production, was then the twenty-year-old woman "Woolworth heiress" who on her next birthday would inherit about one-third of the fortune bequeathed by her late grandfather, founder of the five-and-dime store chain. Her various affairs were considered news: earlier that year, on a ship's dock, she had abandoned an Italian count who declared his belief that he had been engaged to her.[105] In spring 1933, rumors of her wedding plans had circulated for at least a few weeks in the press; she married Alexis Mdivani from the Russian Republic of Georgia on June 20, 1933.[106] Berlin captured the news quickly, for he copyrighted a song about it less than three weeks later, on July 6.[107]

Remarkably, although a wealthy heiress of the nickel-and-dime fortune should have been a sitting duck for satire in the early Depression years, Berlin's song captures the solitary longing of a woman who can never be sure that a man is interested in anything more than her money. Titled "How's Chances," the song reminds the listener, with an uncanny balance that might be called breezy poignancy, that the rich and famous yearn for true love as much as anyone—and perhaps more so, because a woman worth millions of dollars may not be able to know whether the love is true or mixed with visions of prosperity. As the husband of Clarence Mackay's daughter, Berlin surely had an intimate knowledge of that feeling.

Typically, Berlin crafted the song both to fit the scene and to be easily extractable and sold on Tin Pan Alley with a few alterations. The stage version of the song's verse begins with an oblique reference to her Woolworth fortune: "The nickels and dimes I got / Have bought me an awful lot." (The published version changes the verse so that the woman simply seeks love with no reference to her inherited wealth.) The verse of the stage version continues to portray the persona as a rich woman, but the rest of the song resists specificity. In fact, the song's persona bears a family resemblance to those of other Berlin songs sung by people who care less for material wealth than for true love and modest comforts (as in "I Say It's Spinach" and at least three others in his future: "Plenty to be Thankful For," "I Got the Sun in the Morning," and "Count Your Blessings").

The refrain of "How's Chances" begins with Berlin at his most conversational, with a halting delivery: "How's chances, / Say, how are the chances / Of making you love me / The way I love you?" As if the would-be lover remains in doubt about the answer, the crucial question is delayed by the colloquial solecism of the title phrase, followed by the studied faux-casual "say" and the near-repetition ("how are the chances"). And it does all that without a single rhyme.

The music conjures a spirit of longing and wistfulness only distantly implicit in the scene's spirit of lighthearted satire—another instance where Berlin's "satin songs" serve as foils to Hart's wit. That comes out especially in the refrain's opening phrase. At first, the melody features sighing leaps and supple rhythms marked by Berlin's newly favored quarter-note triplets, but it all happens over a gentle, static tonic harmony flavored by an added sixth. Then Berlin leads the song into richer harmonic territory, with poignant ninth chords on the melodic peaks and key words "love me" (E) and "you" (F-natural, a blue note) emphasizing the personal, intimate nature of the love (ex. 5.6). The harmony's chromatic richness and the melody's lyricism serve to obscure (as so many of Berlin's ballads do) that the rhythmic language of the refrain's final section derives entirely from the cakewalk rhythm, leavened by a quarter-note triplet that decorates the pattern's second long beat (ex. 5.7).

Example 5.6. "How Chances," refrain, mm. 1–8.

Example 5.7. "How Chances," refrain, mm. 25–32.

As it turned out, the number captured a fleeting moment. A few weeks after the show's opening, Barbara, now also known as Princess Mdivani, made news again when she turned twenty-one and became about $20 million richer. Within two years, she and Mdivani were divorced, and, on the day after the divorce was final, she married a Danish count. Mdivani died in a car accident a few months later.

In another song about celebrity, Berlin takes a similar approach: he finds the common humanity in a very different woman whose life had been dramatized in the newspapers. By 1932 Josephine Baker had spent seven years in Europe, based in Paris, but she performed all over the Continent. Her semi-nude performances aroused both excitement and outrage, and everywhere she made news. In Zagreb, Yugoslavia, for example, her performances were banned after she had sparked "considerable public indignation."[108] In Paris she lived the glamorous life of a celebrity, but Hart and Berlin's sketch and song envision her as suffused with ennui. The sketch takes place in a busy Parisian restaurant, as Baker enters and causes a stir in the crowd. Her personal secretary starts reviewing her schedule for the following day, including a rehearsal, tea with a countess, cocktails with a marquis, and a party with Coco Chanel after the show. Baker orders her to cancel all of the social engagements, and the secretary takes her cigarette (in a long holder), as the song launches the unspoken cause of Baker's dissatisfaction: nostalgia for Harlem, where the St. Louis native had briefly performed before moving to Paris.

The music to "Harlem on My Mind," marked "slow blues tempo," does not use the blues form and includes just a few blue notes. In fact, its principal phrase deploys the reverse cakewalk pattern, an essential tool in Berlin's rhythmic kit. But Berlin signifies blues early in the verse. He sets the words "and I'm blue, so blue" to a series of blues-drenched seventh chords (F–D♭–C), pounded out in the blues-bass pattern that Berlin had used widely in the 1920s. (The D-flat represents a chord that jazz musicians would later dub a *tritone substitution* for the dominant, G7.) As Ethel Waters sang that line, theatergoers and popular song aficionados could have heard echoes of her famous recording (and film performance) of the song "Am I Blue?"[109] The falling leap on "so blue" retraces the rising phrase that she had sung on the title words (a major sixth)—as if answering the earlier song's question (ex. 5.8).[110]

The lyrics are laced with other allusions befitting Berlin's relentlessly contemporary revue-writing style. In the refrain's bridge, Berlin conjures Cab Calloway's signature expression "hi-de-ho" (popularized following his 1931 hit "Minnie the Moocher") to cap the antithesis-sharpened contrast between her adopted land and her longed-for home: "My lips begin to whisper 'mon cheri,' / But my heart keeps singing hi-de-ho." (Her *lips whisper* French, but her *heart sings* Harlemese.) In the first chorus Baker laments that "at night I hate to go down / To that highfalutin flat / That Lady Mendl designed"—a reference to the flamboyant interior designer Elsie De Wolfe, who would be mentioned again a year later in a line of Cole Porter's "Anything Goes." In the same spot of the second refrain, Berlin uses the phrase "fifty-million Frenchmen"—the title of a 1929 Porter musical, and before that, a popular song of 1927.

I've become too damned refined,
And at night I hate to go down
To my flat with fifty-million

Example 5.8

5.8a. *"Harlem on My Mind," verse.*

5.8b. *"Am I Blue?," refrain, beginning, as sung by Ethel Waters.*

Frenchmen tagging behind
With Harlem on my mind.

In fact, contemporary audiences had access to a perspective on this number as a kind of answer-song to "Fifty Million Frenchman (Can't Be Wrong)"—in which American culture's restraints (notably in the form of Prohibition) stand up poorly to the freewheeling lifestyle imagined in France. It may have helped, of course, that by the time the show opened in September 1933, the Twenty-first Amendment, repealing Prohibition, had been proposed and was in the process of being ratified by the states.

The number's title resonates with yet another current song: Hoagy Carmichael's "Georgia on My Mind," published in 1930 and popular on records and radio in the years thereafter.[111] Whereas Carmichael's song can be read as a paean to a southern place *or* to a beloved woman (whose name happens to be Georgia),[112] Berlin's title refers to a specific section of New York City that had become the black entertainment center of Manhattan. Yet by voicing Baker's alleged nostalgia for a place associated with an idealized African American life, Berlin invokes a link not so much a specific song as to a song *type* that harks back to Stephen Foster standards such as "My Old Kentucky Home" and "Old Folks at Home." The "home" song with a back-to-Dixie accent had continued to flourish well into the twentieth century, as in Berlin's own "When the Midnight Choo-Choo Leaves for Alabam'" (1912) and George Gershwin and Irving Caesar's "Swanee" (1919). In "Harlem on My Mind" Berlin subtly yet unmistakably replaces the rural Dixie ideal with an exotic urban locale—both strongly associated with African American life. There were precedents for this in Berlin's work. In the *Music Box Revue of 1924*, Berlin had already shifted the back-to-Dixie impulse to an exotic orientalized urban milieu, in a faux-blues style, in "Tokio Blues." Just six years earlier he had written, in the original "Harlem" version of "Puttin' on the Ritz" (1927; published 1929), of "the well-to-do / Up on Lenox Avenue" and, in a more pointed reference to black migration from the rural south to the urban north, of "Spangled gowns upon a bevy / Of high browns from down the levee, / All misfits / Puttin' on the Ritz." Rather than a site of African American "misfits," Harlem now represents a comfortable home for the sophisticated Baker, who feels like a "misfit" in Paris. That, in turn, offers a counternarrative to the period's story of American expatriate writers and artists who found their muse in Paris, as Philip Furia has noted.[113] In sum, "Harlem on My Mind" forms a nexus of ideas, themes, and phrases (musical and linguistic) that had percolated in American popular music over the past decade. In other words, it is another exemplar of Berlin's distinctive songwriting gift.

Berlin had selected Ethel Waters for the cast after hearing her sing a new song by Harold Arlen and Ted Koehler at Harlem's Cotton Club: "Stormy Weather." An African American singer in an otherwise all-white cast, Waters was to be a "featured" performer, a rung under the headliner status of Clifton Webb, Helen Broderick, and Marilyn Miller. As such she received four musical numbers, including "Harlem on My Mind," and claimed that "I never had better material work with."[114] In one of the songs, she injected a tragic tone so foreign to revues that some reviewers—and cast members—thought it should be cut.

Waters's first appearance in the show, however, was a suggestive comic number, and it had nothing to do with celebrity. "Heat Wave Hits New York" was the headline. The lyric develops an extended double-entendre on the meaning of "hot" and on the convention of designating storms with feminine qualities (and names). In the verse, Berlin begins with a smart couplet that hints at, but withholds, his true goal: "A heat wave / Blew right into town last week; / She came from / The island of Martinique." It's only in the verse's second (and final) couplet that "she" is revealed as a real woman who dances the "cancan," a name that Berlin uses to introduce yet another pun as the punch-line of the refrain's principal phrase. There he uses a tie to delay that punch line so that it comes out: "She certainly can [beat] cancan."[115]

The song's music and lyrics suggest some ethnomusicological confusion—the notion that the cancan came from Martinique (instead of France), and that its rhythm features habanera-like syncopation, do not hold up well upon further investigation. To point that out, of course, misses the word play and suggestive humor that make the song a minor masterpiece for the theater. The righteous custodians of the newly networked and commercialized medium of radio, however, did not miss the song's suggestive humor. A revised, unpublished, lyric in Berlin's Library of Congress papers reveals that Berlin thoroughly laundered the lyric for the airwaves. On a lyric sheet labeled "new lyric for radio," one of Berlin's most evocative refrain lines—"She started the heat wave / By letting her seat wave"—was changed to "By letting her feet wave." The radio version also lost the "can" pun when the dance became, inexplicably, "yam-yam." There is no evidence that Berlin resisted making such changes but rather accepted them as a means to reach the mob. The changes also serve as a reminder of the vast gap that existed between the level of erotic suggestiveness allowable in a Broadway theater and that on the radio.

Berlin's papers also reveal an early draft that was less suggestive than the one that Ethel Waters ultimately sang. The witty bridge, with its resonating rhyme on the long "e" sound (each sustained by a long tone)—"*Gee!* / Her anato*my* / Made the mercu*ry* / Jump to ninety-*three*"—was written in an earlier draft as "Gee! / Watch the mercury / Jumping a degree, / Up to ninety-three." The revised version is tighter—"jumping" becomes simply "jump"—allowing for the critical inclusion of the word *anatomy*.[116] The song's patter section—a kind of emphatic interlude between refrains—features verbal riffs on the phrase "it's so hot that . . .," and it also underwent a telling revision. One of Berlin's drafts features the following pair of phrases:

> It's so hot,
> To keep your hat on
> Makes you as warm as a bride;
> It's so hot,
> The lady sat on
> Top of an egg—and it fried!

In the same spot, the revised (stage) version reads:

> It's so hot,
> The coldest maiden
> Feels just as warm as a bride;
> It's so hot,
> A chicken laid an
> Egg on the street—and it fried!

In both versions, the "bride" / "fried" rhyme seems to have been a compass guiding the patter lyric's direction, but the "maiden" / "laid an" double rhyme sharpens the humor. The revision is tighter, funnier, and bawdier thanks to the word "feels" and the crisp double antithesis between "coldest maiden" and "warm . . . bride." The whole patter gains vitality, too, from its musical setting: an irregular syncopated pattern that begins in the same rhythm as the principal phrase of "Puttin' on the Ritz" and continues with a spiky chain of syncopation copped from the emerging swing style (ex. 5.9).

Several other songs developed current news items and newspaper conventions without recourse to celebrity. "Debts" lampoons the politics of American loans

Example 5.9. "Heat Wave," patter section.

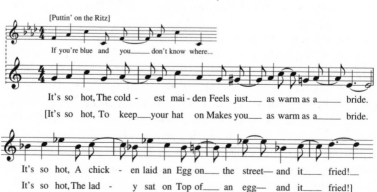

abroad during the Depression. Representatives of England, Germany, Italy, and France prepare to board a ship back across the sea as they sing a counterpoint song with the Statue of Liberty (played by Helen Broderick), who forgets the words to *her* song, "The Star Spangled Banner," the country's newly minted national anthem.[117] "Lonely Heart," is a wistful ballad told from the perspective of an advice-column reader seeking help to find her true love. "The Funnies" captures the point-of-view of an enthusiastic average reader for whom comic-strip characters come alive on stage (like the characters from the "Little Book of Poetry" in the first *Music Box Revue*). It was sung by Marilyn Miller—whose fairylike beauty and innocence had made her one of Hart's favorite stage personalities. (Hart told a reporter that he had seen her no fewer than thirty-seven times in Ziegfeld's 1920 musical comedy *Sally*.[118])

Few Berlin shows went without a minstrel number, and *As Thousands Cheer* was no exception. In "To Be or Not to Be" Hart and Berlin approached a popular play from an unusual angle, from the perspective of the neglected wife of a self-important actor who had a single line in a then-popular play, *The Green Pastures*. This Pulitzer Prize– winner by Marc Connelly, which portrayed biblical stories from the perspective of African American children, had become a staple of the contemporary American the-ater since its premiere in 1930, running for more than six hundred performances on Broadway and five annual tours. Its disarming expressions of innocence, sincerity, and faith through suffering appealed to Broadway audiences in the early Depression years. A *New York Times* announcement in May 1933 noted that it would play its 1,300th overall performance, end its current road season, and look ahead to another tour in 1934—this just two months before Berlin wrote a song to be coupled with the headline "Green Pastures Starts Third Road Season."[119] Inspired by his bit part, the man aspires to Shakespearean artistry, while his wife tries to force him into deciding between the marriage and the career. The refrain's melody is based on an augmented secondary-rag rhythm, a legacy of Berlin's jazz style of the 1920s. And the scene taps into minstrel-show conventions that go back decades: a benighted, pompous black actor aspiring to classical theater stardom in a way reminiscent of a character in Berlin's 1912 "Opera Burlesque" on the sextet from *Lucia di Lammer-moor*. Ethel Waters sang the song, a nagging wife's effort to bring her pretentious, distracted husband down to earth, and if she had any qualms about the scene's racial stereotypes—still common fare on stage and screen—she never voiced them. In her memoir she simply called it "a take-off which I did with Hamtree Harrington, a perfect man to work with."[120]

Yet Waters's real passion in the show was the tragic "Supper Time." The scene's headline—"Unknown Negro Lynched by Frenzied Mob"—allowed Berlin to write a lament without specifying its cause. Indeed, it can (and has) served as a kind of torch song. Berlin's lyric finds the common denominator that links the agonized, newly widowed mother on stage with everyday table-setting scenes in the homes of his audience. With apt precision, he set blue notes to the key words "table," "able," and "man," linking the action she must perform ("set the <u>table</u>"), her paralysis in grief ("somehow I'm not <u>able</u>"), and the object of her grief ("'Cause that <u>man</u> of mine / Ain't comin' home no more.") The extended bridge and its transition back to the principal phrase at the climax marks a stroke of songwriting genius. At the end of the bridge, Berlin pivots on the word "Lord," first used as a reference to God, then repeats "Lord" as a horrific wail of lament before restating the title line that forms the song's melodic peak and climactic moment. (The manuscript piano-vocal score, however, shows "God!" in place of the second "Lord!"[121]) (ex. 5.10).

"Supper Time" presents a stark contrast to the Upper East Side dinner-table scene that opened the show. In her memoir, Waters implied that Clifton Webb and Marilyn Miller, who had to come on next in "a flippant bedroom dance"—a humorous and suggestive number in which a couple awakes in bed on the morning of their wedding (typical revue fare)—wanted "Supper Time" to be cut as it troubled them to follow such a tragic scene.[122] And at least two critics claimed that it did not even belong in a revue. John Mason Brown wrote, in a final paragraph designated "P.S.": "I do wish Miss Waters could find another number to take the place of 'Supper Time,' which neither fits her gifts nor fits into the general scheme of things at the Music Box."[123] The *New Yorker*'s anonymous critic noted that "I was only mildly distressed by one item—Miss Ethel Waters is supposed to be a Negress whose husband has been

Example 5.10. "Supper Time," refrain, mm. 29–33.

How can I be thank-ful When they start to thank the Lord? Lord! Sup-per time_
[God!]

Ethel Waters, as the widow of a lynched man, sang Berlin's "Supper Time" in As Thousands Cheer. *Courtesy of Rodgers & Hammerstein, on behalf of the Estate of Irving Berlin.*

lynched, and she sings a song about it, which definitely seemed to belong somewhere else. In Mr. Harris's safe, possibly."[124] Ethan Mordden has suggested that the song was more radical than bona fide leftist theater of the era because it was presented as mainstream entertainment.[125] Sam Harris, having witnessed the audience's fervid reaction in Philadelphia, simply said, "It stays in."[126] Harris was not chiefly trying to make a social statement; he was recognizing good theater when he saw it. It was all about the audience's reaction.

The act 1 finale and the act 2 opener both portrayed aspects of that audience. In the breathtaking act 1 finale, Berlin introduced "Easter Parade," a number to animate a headline representing a throwback to newspapers of old: "Rotogravure Section—Easter Parade on Fifth Avenue—1883." The origins of the scene concept and musical number grew out of earlier work by both collaborators. Hart had written a screenplay including newsreels from historical (pre-film) people and events. One of his ideas that never made it to film, according to Steven Bach, was a scene featuring an Easter parade on Fifth Avenue.[127] For it, Berlin reached into his own trunk and found his principal phrase and rhythm in his 1917 song "Smile and Show Your Dimple," a song coaxing a "little girlie" to cheer up after a broken romance.[128]

Many commentators claim that the song secularizes the Christian holiday—no mention of God, Jesus, resurrection, or even church. It serves chiefly as an excuse for a man (Clifton Webb) to go strolling about in public with the "grandest lady" (Marilyn Miller), bedecked in a "bonnet, with all the frills upon it." As Philip Roth has famously claimed about Berlin's "Jewish genius" in a characteristically Jewish grammatical inversion: "Easter he turns into a fashion show."[129] But Roth (or his fictional alter ego) is wrong: Berlin did not do this. What he did was distill into song something that well-to-do Christian New Yorkers had been doing already for decades.[130] The Easter parade, not churchgoing, had marked the single most public and visible collective recognition of the holiday since the 1880s. Hart and Berlin thus

"Easter Parade" comprised the act 1 finale of As Thousands Cheer. *Courtesy of Rodgers & Hammerstein, on behalf of the Estate of Irving Berlin.*

set the scene back a half-century to 1883, but their audience had ready access to memories of much more recent Easter parades on Fifth Avenue. For years the annual event had received detailed coverage in the newspapers, as New Yorkers exchanged Lenten "sack cloth" (as some articles reported it) for holiday finery and walked down the street. A 1914 spread, for example, showed "Great Throngs of Easter Paraders on Fifth Avenue," a crowd so thick that it is difficult to discern the clothing of any individual. But six insets feature close-ups of prominent New Yorkers promenading in formal dress, the men in top hats and tails, the women in elaborate gowns, topped off by hats—none of which, in 1914, are bonnets. So if, as Berlin's clever rhyme puts it, "you're in the rotogravure," that means you had attained a special status among New York's elite. (Among the elites pictured in the 1914 spread, incidentally, were Clarence Mackay and his eldest daughter, Katherine, two of Berlin's future in-laws.)

The scene and song also offer another loving picture of New York City itself—as Berlin had done in many other shows. The finale was like nothing Berlin had presented before, yet it functions like the 1919 *Follies* minstrel finale, conjuring nostalgia for times and styles gone by in an awe-inspiring blend of music, words, and spectacle. The lyric also belongs to a song style that Berlin had already cultivated. In spirit, though not in musical or linguistic style, it is connected to Berlin's "steppin' out" song type portraying characters going out on the town in fancy dress (as in "Puttin' on the Ritz," and the later songs "Top Hat, White Tie, and Tails" and "Steppin' Out with My Baby"). For Berlin, as his songs remind us, clothes heralded the public performance of self.

For all its fond nostalgia, even "Easter Parade" had a newsworthy angle. Rotogravures had reached a peak in popularity in the early 1930s, with eighty Sunday papers featuring them.[131] In 1932 a George Gallup poll found that rotogravures were the most popular sections of newspapers.[132]

Act 2 presents yet another intersection of social class, news, and theater itself. Berlin's song "Metropolitan Opening" introduces the scene by focusing on how the nouveau riche had assumed the roles—and the exclusive theater boxes—of the old aristocracy. This act 2 opener marks a sharp contrast to the act 1 finale. It wrenches the news back to the present and shifted focus to another medium: the radio. At the onset of the Depression, the Metropolitan Opera faced a crisis, as Joseph Horowitz succinctly states: "in 1929–30 the company posted its first deficit in two decades. In 1930–31, subscriptions sank, tours were lost, costs soared."[133] An agreement with NBC radio helped to save the Met, which made its first operatic broadcast in 1931. The *New York Times* reported on its first page the outpouring of positive response to a Christmas Day broadcast of 1931 and the Met's unprecedented direct appeal to listeners for donations. As the Met's president and chairman Paul D. Cravath noted, the Met "could no longer rely . . . upon a small group of rich men," noting that regular patrons and radio audiences would have to contribute for its survival.[134] The sketch and song identify and satirize a pivotal moment in the Met's history; Berlin's song brings levity to that paradigm shift in the Met's clientele.

The radio historian Susan Smulyan has documented the "backlash against broadcast advertising" in the early 1930s, and Hart and Berlin's scene comically demonstrated why that would be, as commercials continually interrupt—and play over—an opera performance.[135] Listeners and newspapers found common cause in attacking the ever-present advertising on commercial radio that forms one of the targets of the song and sketch: "Asserts Radio 'Ads' Disgust Listeners," ran an early 1931 article in the *New York Times*.[136] The scene exploits that response to the new phenomenon of radio advertising. And yet, the scene actually anticipates the news in this case: the first commercial announcement within a Met broadcast occurred after *As Thousands Cheer* opened, on December 30, 1933.[137] And the scene's roots go back even further: Hart had derived the opera sketch from an earlier camp-show sketch about radio, while the number also connects to Berlin's even earlier send-ups of opera and its audiences of two decades earlier.[138]

For the act 2 finale, Hart and Berlin exploited the tension between revue conventions in general and the newspaper theme of this particular show, and they did it to great comic effect. The grand finale in musical comedy and revue conventionally featured a sequence of reprises of earlier numbers. But the newspaper theme demanded more than a rehash of already-heard songs. Under the headline, "Supreme Court Hands Down Important Decision," the chorus emerges to sing that the show would not include a reprise (pronounced with a long "e" to rhyme with "if you please," "same old wheeze," and "melodies"). The reason is that "The finest legal minds have met / And everyone agrees / That when we reach the Finale, / We don't have to sing a reprise." Presenting the finale-reprise convention as a kind of legal precedent that has been overturned by the Supreme Court allows Berlin to treat it as "news" in the finale of *As Thousands Cheer*. "Here's a show that'll end at last / Without a reprise—/ And that's news!" sings the chorus.

Yet soon after the chorus makes this declaration, the principals step forward and sing eight-bar phrases from the show's key songs: "Easter Parade," "Heat Wave," and "Debts." To each of them, the chorus responds angrily that they may not do that. Then Marilyn Miller and Clifton Webb step forward as the orchestra plays the melody of "How's Chances." As the chorus protests, Miller sings:

> Never mind that introduction,
> For we don't intend to sing
> The chorus of "How's Chances,"
> As it wouldn't mean a thing.

Then Webb adds:

> We'd like to sing a song
> That wasn't written for the score,
> A simple little chorus
> That they haven't heard before.

He then launches a new song that Berlin had written but later admitted he could not link to a headline[139]—"Not for All the Rice in China," a romantic number in list-song style. The song had no news content, but it was *theatrical* news: a new song *introduced* in a revue's finale. Like his finale for the first *Music Box Revue*, this one is reflexive, commenting not only on the show itself but on musical theater clichés, and engaging directly with the audience in a kind of conspiratorial wink that helped to re-create the temporary community that characterizes effective theatrical ritual.

Ultimately, *As Thousands Cheer* had a homogenizing effect: the news turns everyone into a celebrity, and by extension, all of the celebrities become theatrical figures, performing their lives on the national or world stage. The humor, for all but one anomalously tragic scene, comes from imagining each figure in a behind-the-scenes moment, offering a satiric glimpse of their lives out of the spotlight, beyond the reach of the media. The show also has a self-congratulatory element. At almost every turn, it reinforces the cultural centrality of New York City, even when it leaves New York, as *Face the Music* had briefly done. And it turned all human action into show business. In this show, the theater itself is like a powerful sun within the city's galaxy, and all of the news events and celebrities orbit around it. As Brooks Atkinson wrote, *As Thousands Cheer* "finds Broadway motives in every person it satirizes."[140]

Yet the show proved to be remarkably resilient beyond Broadway. From Boston to Chicago, reviewers of the touring production widely praised the show. A Chicago critic called it "the most national of the modern cycle of smart Broadway revues" and claimed that "even its sketches which deal with subjects peculiar to New York . . . are done with enough elemental comedy to make them genuinely amusing to inlanders." It helped, he added, that many of Berlin's songs were already well known from frequent radio play—the advent of network radio being a new boon to Broadway—including "The Easter Bonnet" (the program's title for the musical number "Easter Parade"), "Heat Wave," "Not for All the Rice in China" and "How's Chances."[141] It might have seemed impossible to bring back the two Berlin-Hart shows, so deeply woven were they into the fabric of the people and places of early 1930s America. But both reappeared on Broadway decades later in the "Encores!" series, designed to bring long-dormant shows back to life for short runs. Both revivals, too, saw cast albums preserving most of the musical numbers from the original productions.

In retrospect, however, Berlin's best known and most enduring projects of the 1930s appeared not on stage but on screen, in a string of five film musicals in four years: three Astaire-Rogers films, *Top Hat* (1935), *Follow the Fleet* (1936), and *Carefree* (1938); along with *On the Avenue* (1937), starring Dick Powell and Alice Faye; and *Alexander's Ragtime Band* (1938), featuring Faye, Tyrone Power, Don Ameche, and Ethel Merman. Berlin quickly proved to be a master of the new medium, and he particularly relished working with Fred Astaire.[142] The 1930s, after all, were the decade when Broadway composers began a cross-country exchange between New York and Hollywood. Alone or in pairs, Berlin, Rodgers and Hart, Cole Porter, the Gershwins, Jerome Kern, Dorothy Fields, and many others shifted their sights and talents to Hollywood, where the "talking picture" allowed for song to be heard from the screen. Berlin, as usual, had been there at the start. His new song "Blue Skies" had been sung by Al Jolson in *The Jazz Singer* (1927), launching the international popularity of talkies and effecting a paradigm shift in the film industry. Many songwriters delivered the goods, earned their pay, and walked away, not knowing how their creations would be used on the screen.

Berlin was unusual in insisting on creative control in an industry where songwriters (as in early Broadway) were seen as makers of raw material that producers and directors used as they saw fit. Even so, his love of the theater could not keep him away from Broadway—and from the mob whose reaction he could uniquely gauge when his songs were performed on the stage. He stated publicly his preference for the immediate exchange between creator and spectator on Broadway,[143] and also claimed that "there was quite a difference" between writing for Broadway and Hollywood: "In the case of 'Annie Get Your Gun,' after four months I heard the songs in New Haven and knew through the audience's reaction what we had."[144] In other words, he needed to witness the unique interaction of performers and audience that only the stage could provide.

So the Kaufman and Hart style continued to shape Berlin's ideas for the theater even after more than half a dozen successes in Hollywood. The one that was most characteristic, a revue titled *Happy Holiday*, never reached the stage, but, greatly transformed, it did reach the screen. Another did reach the stage—*Louisiana Purchase* (with Morrie Ryskind, 1940). If it lacked the sharp satirical edge of *The Cocoanuts*, *Face the Music*, and *As Thousands Cheer*, it did enjoy a longer Broadway run, the longest, in fact, of any Berlin show before *Annie Get Your Gun*.

LOUISIANA PURCHASE

Louisiana Purchase belongs in the orbit of Kaufman and Co. because its libretto was by Morrie Ryskind, Kaufman's sometime collaborator on Marx Brothers projects (*The Cocoanuts* and *Animal Crackers*) and Gershwin operettas (*Of Thee I Sing* and *Let 'Em Eat Cake*).

Thanks mostly to his successful sojourn in Hollywood, Berlin had been away from Broadway for seven years before *Louisiana Purchase* opened in May 1940. Its 444-performance run was longer than any Berlin show to date. Undoubtedly, part of its audience appeal was the show's sheer star power: William Gaxton and Victor Moore brought with them a "star text" defined by their appearance as the president and vice-president, respectively, in *Of Thee I Sing*.[145] They had appeared together again in *Anything Goes*, and their co-star in that show, Ethel Merman, called them simply "the finest comedy team that ever worked."[146] Gaxton's handsome straight-man persona formed a marked contrast to Moore's bumbling naïf, and everyone on 1940's Broadway would have heard the resonance between his new role as Senator Oliver Loganberry—a clueless milquetoast who drinks only hot water and does not know what a girdle is—and his already legendary characterization of Vice President Alexander Throttlebottom.

The show also featured two notable female stars with character names almost echoing their real names: Irene Bordoni, as Madame Bordelaise, a friendly restaurateur; and the young ballerina Zorina as Marina, Gaxton's love interest. By 1940 Bordoni was a Broadway musical veteran, having appeared in shows since 1912. With her coquettish style and French accent—exploited in shows with titles like *The French Doll* and *Naughty Cinderella*—she cut a figure similar to Gaby Deslys. But she had more talent than Deslys, and her performance of Cole Porter's suggestive "Let's Do It" in the 1928 show *Paris* stood among her best-known moments on stage. At sixty-five and near the end of her career, Bordoni was now more of a motherly figure, and her role as Madame Bordelaise bears more than a passing resemblance to the matronly advisors who would soon populate the world of Rodgers and Hammerstein: beloved and benevolent community-builders like Aunt Eller (*Oklahoma!*), Nettie Fowler (*Carousel*), and even Mother Abbess (*The Sound of Music*).[147] In contrast to Bordoni, the monomial Zorina was a relative newcomer to Broadway. A Norwegian ballerina, formerly with the Ballet Russes, she had recently discovered her comedic gifts in Rodgers and Hart's 1938 musical *I Married an Angel*. According to a feature story in *Stage* magazine, Broadway was now "passionately and collectively in love with her" thanks to her "willowy, lithe" figure coupled with a "wide, limpid smile" that trailed off "into a thoughtful little laugh."[148]

The show opens with a reflexive "Apologia"—a partly sung, partly spoken number by Berlin—featuring an attorney named Sam Leibowitz who disclaims any connection between plot and characters and real life—although the show's inspiration came from the real, everyday corruption in post–Huey Long Baton Rouge. The lawyer declares that he represents the firm of "Rafferty, Driscoll, and O'Brien," which is a sly and inverted reference to the firm that actually represented Berlin: O'Brien, Driscoll, and Raftery.

The story proper begins with key figures in the Louisiana Purchasing Company (including William Gaxton, as the handsome young Jim Taylor) trying to figure out how to compromise the Republican senator Oliver Loganberry (Victor Moore), who has been assigned to investigate a federal corruption case involving their firm. Although Loganberry is a "confirmed bachelor" and appears to be incorruptible, Taylor insists that when all else fails, "Sex Marches On." So the men conceive a plot to catch Loganberry in a scandal. Loganberry arrives in New Orleans and gets a bite to eat at one of the city's most popular restaurants, run by the beloved Madame Bordelaise, known to regulars as "Bordy" (Irene Bordoni). When Jim approaches her to do the job, she turns him down, saying she's only selling New Orleans, not herself ("Louisiana Purchase"). An Austrian émigré named Marina van Linden (Zorina) has arrived seeking help from Bordelaise, an old friend whom she knew in Europe. Marina needs $500 to help her mother get out of Austria and safely to America. Jim realizes that Marina would be the perfect candidate to do his dirty work. Marina reluctantly takes the job to compromise the senator, but she grows to like Loganberry so much she can't follow through with her charge—even for the $500 she needs to pay for her mother's emigration from Nazi-controlled Austria—and they sing an innocent duet of their mutual regard called "You're Lonely and I'm Lonely." She does, however, get the senator in a mildly intimate moment where they can be photographed together—and the exposure means that the senator "must" marry Marina.

After innumerable plot complications, Loganberry's investigation—and his presidential ambitions—are thwarted not by a conventional personal scandal but by the simple gesture of accidentally crossing a picket line created by the Louisiana Purchasing Company. As Jim points out in the Finale Ultimo: "You know that it's a fact / That since the Wagner Act / The head of labor says / That a candidate for Prez / Mustn't cross a picket line." (The pickets echo the phrase "Mustn't cross a picket line" in Gilbert-and-Sullivan style.) Loganberry winds up in a happy romance with Bordelaise, as Jim Taylor and Marina come together in the end.

Perhaps owing to Ryskind's Hollywood experience, the Jim-Marina romance is a classic screwball comedy affair with initial attraction suppressed by animosity that grows when Marina sides with Loganberry, revealing (untruthfully) that by the time they were photographed together, she was already engaged to marry Loganberry. Berlin captures their attraction-repulsion tension in the song "Outside of That I Love You," a list song expressing what they dislike about each other. In act 2, Jim forgives Marina and sings "Fools Fall in Love." Meanwhile, the show also features musical comedy's familiar secondary, naïve comic couple consisting of Lee Davis, son of a retired army colonel involved in the scandal, and Emmy-Lou, niece of Jim Taylor. Their subplot develops around thwarted plans to get married, because as long as their father and uncle are being investigated by Loganberry, the wedding gets postponed. In act 2, when their wedding plans seem hopeless, Emmy-Lou sings "You Can't Brush Me Off," joined by Lee and a singing quartet, famous at the time, called the Martins.

Although sometimes viewed as anticipating the "integrated" musical of the Rodgers and Hammerstein era soon to come, *Louisiana Purchase* is best understood as a continuation of mainstream musical comedy as it had been established since the 1920s—with a script crafted to show off the stars, songs, scenes, and costumes. In fact, but for its references to contemporary politics and its swing-inflected numbers, the show would not have been out of place more than a decade earlier, with its marriage plot for multiple couples, deception, confusion, and petty mischief disrupting people's romantic (and other) hopes and plans, and even a scene right out of bedroom farce that had been so popular in the late teens and early 1920s. Berlin's numbers also take their places alongside familiar models: a pseudo-spiritual called "The Lawd Done Fixed Up My Soul" in the tradition of the Gershwins' "Clap Yo' Hands" (*Oh, Kay!*, 1926) and Porter's "Blow, Gabriel, Blow" (*Anything Goes*, 1934), a Pollyanna weather song ("It's a Lovely Day Tomorrow"), two duets that track the romance of the principal couple ("Outside of That I Love You" and "Fools Fall in Love"), and a good old reprise finaletto for act 1 that features the ensemble in a scene of surprise over pending nuptials of the "wrong" couple (Loganberry and Marina), brought together more by circumstance than by true love.

Ryskind even included a minstrel-style scene "in one" between a black butler (Abner) and a French butler (Alphonse) who exchange linguistic styles in the midst of a discussion about the impending Mardi Gras. Clearly intended to cover a major set change, the scene begins in stereotyped stage dialect that matches the characters. (Abner: "I'se goin to take my gal to the Mardi Gras and do some mellow jivin'." Alphonse: "kess-ke-say, jive?") The scene ends with the butlers speaking the other's language. (Abner: "C'est la vie." Alphonse: "Damn if it ain't. Evening Abner." Abner: "Bon soir.")

Meanwhile, the show's style of political humor resonates with the ongoing impact of the Kaufman and Co. musicals with Gershwin—*Of Thee I Sing* and *Let 'Em Eat Cake*—as both of them had books co-written by Ryskind and featured Victor Moore playing the role of a hapless, naïve politician thrust into circumstances beyond his control or understanding, and for whom everything nevertheless turns out okay. In *Louisiana Purchase*, Ryskind's script attempts to strike a delicate political balance by turning the jokes on both Republicans and Democrats. Yet it reveals some decisively Republican leanings in its jokes about the power of labor unions and about the political suicide of crossing picket lines. The Austrian émigré Marina, who has just left her Nazi-occupied country, even imagines her American life on welfare and says "Heil Roosevelt." Marina's circumstances also provide a perspective on pre–World War II America, for she emigrated from Austria after the Anschluss that led to the Nazi confiscation of her mother's property. When Irene Bordoni sang the soaring, long-limbed ballad "It's a Lovely Day Tomorrow" for 1940 audiences, the song had particular poignancy. The show had yet one more thing that the snappiest musical comedies exhibited in the 1930s: a ballet number choreographed by George Balanchine. Indeed, the scene that Balanchine staged foreshadowed the famous dream ballet of *Oklahoma!*, for it portrays a young woman (Zorina) torn between two men, embodied in the dance as the "spirit of Jim Taylor" and the "spirit of Senator Loganberry."

The book may be more coherent and streamlined than *Face the Music*, but it is more conventional and not nearly as sharp in its social satire. This may be because Morrie Ryskind was on the cusp of a political conversion. An FDR supporter in 1932, and a pro-union activist in his 1930s Hollywood crowd, he grew tired of what he viewed the administration's philosophy of "something for everyone for nothing," and when Roosevelt decided to run for an unprecedented third term, Ryskind registered as a Republican for the first time.[149] After testifying against Communist sympathizers in Hollywood before the House Un-American Activities Committee in 1947, he never worked in Hollywood again. He went on to become a noted conservative columnist, helping William Buckley establish the *National Review*, and he lived to toast the presidential election of his old Hollywood friend Ronald Reagan, which he viewed as a "vindication."[150]

Louisiana Purchase, like all of Berlin's stage shows to this point, was so thoroughly of its time that it was un-revivable in its original form, but it does survive in two forms. For one, it became a notable 1941 film—lacking several of Berlin's songs—starring Bob Hope in the Gaxton role of Jim Taylor, and with Moore, Bordoni, and Zorina reprising their Broadway roles. Much later, it came back to Broadway for a short run in the 1990s with a thoroughly revised script, excising the dated political humor and the minstrelized character of Abner—and a cast album.

HAPPY HOLIDAY

In the years between *As Thousands Cheer* and *Louisiana Purchase*, Hart and Berlin discussed other projects. In one of the great "what ifs" in Hollywood musical history, Hart was invited to write the screenplay for a musical film based on Frank L. Baum's novel *The Wizard of Oz*, and said he would do it only if Berlin wrote the songs.[151] They considered at least one other project, but it came to fruition a different form than they had initially envisioned it, and by then Hart was no longer involved. That Berlin internalized the irreverent skepticism of the Kaufman and Hart style comes out in a rough draft of a revue called "Happy Holiday," which he had discussed with Hart but never finished—at least not for the stage. It's a fascinating document, perhaps the only one of its kind, of Berlin working out an entire revue concept on paper. (To judge from the surviving materials, he would do such scenarios for films quite often.) Dated February 16, 1939, the four-page typescript summarizes a revue in sixteen scenes "to be done entirely with lyrics and music," with some numbers described as "sketches" (suggesting extended musical sequences) in the typescript.[152] Berlin appears to have planned it as a solo project. Yet its model is clearly *As Thousands Cheer*, which Berlin cites several times in the typescript. Instead of using newspaper headlines as the basis for the individual scenes, however, this scenario proposes to proceed through a complete year of American holidays. "The point of view," Berlin writes in a comment that would surprise people who know Berlin as the writer of earnest holiday paeans such as "Easter Parade" and "White Christmas," "will be the debunking of the holiday spirit." Berlin continued:

> Through some mechanical device such as a calendar, an hour glass, or anything denoting time, the important holidays in a year will be shown in rotation as they naturally fall; each holiday as an individual item in the revue. . . . Each holiday will be announced through whatever medium we have a la the headline announcements in AS THOUSANDS CHEER.

Some of the numbers are thoroughly described, others just suggested. A prologue sets the tone—what Berlin in a related, but undated, document described as the "keynote of the revue"—showing two busy clerks in a flower shop whimsically inventing new holidays, such as "Dog Day—send a posey to your doggie, etc." In typical Berlin style, the scene focuses on a couple of ordinary people doing an ordinary activity in order to represent a larger idea—that American holidays exist chiefly to support American capitalism.

The first number evokes the kind of busy, chattering ensemble scene that typified act-openers in the Kaufman-Hart style. Its target is the breathtaking hypocrisy of New York's privileged social cliques. It is two minutes to midnight on New Year's Eve in a boisterous New York café. Members of the ensemble are gossiping about extramarital affairs:

> These cracks become quite vicious and when they reach an almost censurable point, lights go out, bells ring and ensemble goes into "A Happy New Year to Everybody." Much kissing and "best wishes" and a complete opposite to what we heard before. This finishes with the entire chorus down in one, singing a "New Year's Resolution" finale.

For the next "holiday" Berlin peered seventeen years into the future to Inauguration Day 1956. Berlin writes that "the Republicans have finally elected a new president, but the Roosevelts won't get out of the White House. They have barricaded themselves in." Written toward the end of Roosevelt's second term, it reveals that Berlin perceived, along with many Americans, the likelihood that Roosevelt would be re-elected again for an unprecedented third term in 1940. For Broadway regulars, the scene also would have been perceived as a witty response to the sketch from *As Thousands Cheer* that comically portrayed the Hoovers on the day before Roosevelt's first inauguration.

"Lincoln's Birthday" followed with what Berlin envisioned as "a number done by a colored choir or an Ethel Waters. Some angle on emancipation day. Not too heavy, but a sincere emancipation number—a tentative title 'FATHER ABRAHAM.'" Proceeding by the calendar, Berlin offered no specific ideas for "Valentine's Day" and "Washington's Birthday" except to claim that they should each present a fresh "angle" on the holiday.

For St. Patrick's Day, Berlin conceived a scene more reminiscent of early vaudeville than of late 1930s Broadway. In a set that Berlin describes as "a row of apartment houses in an Irish neighborhood" he envisions

> A male character dressed ultra-Irish and with a brogue singing "When Irish Eyes are Smiling." A woman, his wife, also dressed Irish to the teeth, picking up the coins that are being dropped from the windows. At the finish of his song she goes into an Irish reel. They then start counting the silver that she collected and do it in pure, unadulterated Yiddish.

Like a vaudeville sketch from three decades earlier, the scene relies on fixed, and by 1939, hoary, ethnic stereotypes. Indeed, the scenario derives from Berlin's 1913 song "Abie Sings an Irish Song," in which a Jewish tailor sets up shop in an Irish neighborhood and sustains his business by singing Irish melodies as his customers walk in. Performing Irish, apparently, is good for Jewish business. Berlin may have held some doubts about whether the sketch would work, for he adds that "if it is impossible to cast the man in this act, we can cut out the song and let him play an Irish reel on the organ while his wife dances. This should be very short and is only good, if at all, as a black-out."

For number seven, "Easter," Berlin recognized a special challenge: creating a number that would not be overshadowed by memories of the act 1 finale of *As Thousands Cheer*. Acknowledging that in his typescript, he also mused that "there is possibly a good angle in an egg-hunt or in a Mr. & Mrs. Bunny duet, finishing with 32 children before the chorus is over." But he offered no further development of the idea.

One of Berlin's most developed and inspired numbers was conceived for Mother's Day, whose humor depends on a sharp contrast between a stereotyped image of traditional motherhood and a hardboiled cougar:

> The returning black sheep is singing a heart-breaking Mother song written along the lines of "M is for the different [sic] things she gave me, etc."[153] This is done in front of the little white gate leading into the cottage where he knows Mother is waiting to kill the fatted calf. When he enters, we find a very sophisticated mother with platinum hair, polished fingernails, a long cigarette holder and a young gigolo. She is sore as hell at being surprised by a middle-aged son.

For "Decoration Day" (what would later become Memorial Day) Berlin imagined a counterpoint number featuring an original melody sung against the "Marseillaise." Comparing the conception to the "Debts" number in *As Thousands Cheer*, Berlin envisioned a light satire on an apparent tendency of the French government to bestow awards on Americans.

> The French Ambassador is decorating four great Americans with the Legion of Honor. We will choose four types and show how promiscuous France is in handing

out these decorations. It will be done very seriously and part of the song given over to some ridiculous service that each of our types has rendered to France. This will be a patter chorus against the French national anthem, "Marseillaise," which the four Americans sing very reverently while the Ambassador repeats his part of the lyric enumerating their deeds and how proud France is to honor them. For this scene it may be a good idea to have the words "Decoration Day" somewhere prominently shown in the scene.

Two of the numbers—for Independence Day and Halloween—Berlin conceived as potential ballets, a legacy from his earlier revues. As he writes parenthetically, "this kind of a revue done completely with words and music can stand two ballets— one in each act, especially if you can get Balanchine to do something very arty and good." His vision for Independence Day was more specific than for Halloween. Independence Day, he wrote, "suggests a peppy, colorful, firecracker ballet." In the later, undated, partial scenario he requested "a Balanchine or Fokine, if possible just as good as it would be done in the Russian Ballet." In this Berlin was tapping into a contemporary New York phenomenon: the impulse to fuse classical ballet and American vernacular dance. Balanchine had recently choreographed a ballet number for Rodgers and Hart's musical *On Your Toes* (1937); a film of the same year, *Shall We Dance*, featured Fred Astaire and Ginger Rogers enacting the merger of dance styles that reaches fruition in a the final number confirming their romantic merger.

Three other holidays inspired scenes of social commentary, somewhat resonating with scenes from his earlier shows with Moss Hart. Labor Day conjured a vision of social class crossing, with named aristocrats, recalling the automat opening of *Face the Music*. This time the number is tinged with an attitude toward labor unions, which had developed unprecedented power and influence during the 1930s, an influence that would figure in the plot of the same year's *Louisiana Purchase* as well:

> A sit-down strike of the Capitalists showing their point of view, including the Duponts, Morgans, Rockefellers, Fords, Chryslers, etc. They refuse to make any more money and demand the same privileges that Labor has today. They will no longer be sent off on their yachts to Palm Beach while Labor is given the chance to make speeches and have fun. Let Labor eat those rich French dishes and get indigestion for a change. Let them drink Magnums of Vintage champagne and have a terrible hangover the next day and see how they like it. In a nut-shell, this is the legitimate squawk of the so-called privileged, proclaiming the hardships of the Capitalists.

Another scene with which Berlin spiked social commentary was the Columbus Day number picturing "a communist meeting in Columbus Circle in front of the statue of Christopher Columbus. In the midst of fighting among themselves the statue comes to life and asks 'Where are those peaceful Indians I left here in 1492?'"—an echo of Rip Van Winkle's "Where is the little old New York . . .?" in the *Music Box Revue of 1924*. The joke allows Columbus to represent a kind of centrist American, though its intended targets are all of the above: Columbus, Communists, and Indians. It is in part a play on the stereotype, the cliché, of warlike Indians, and of communists as an ineffectual and marginalized group. Like the Mother's Day scene, this one depends on recognition of a cognitive dissonance between past and present.

Berlin's most pointed social commentary came out in his conception of the Armistice Day scene. Its final stinging image reveals Berlin at his sharpest and most poignant in a moment reminiscent of the famous "Supper Time" number in *As Thousands Cheer*.

> This will be a number in one sung in front of a moving picture screen done by male voices. During the number, different newsreel shots will be thrown on the screen. The number will be a stirring, patriotic Armistice Day song, sung as it might have been on Armistice Day in 1918, beginning something like "A war to end all wars has been fought, hurray, hurray, At last a world with one single thought, Armistice Day." The lyric will continue and in turn mention all the warring nations predicting peace from now on and good will to all men. "The world has learned its lesson, hurray, hurray, And every heart is singing Armistice Day." As the song goes on a series of newsreel shots will be thrown on the screen of what's happening in Europe today, finishing with that pathetic newsreel of a little wounded Chinese baby, after the Japanese had bombed the town.

Thanksgiving, Christmas, and the "Finale" followed this shocking scene with unanticipated levity. The rest of the scenario was very concise. For Thanksgiving, Berlin simply noted that it should feature "a love duet with a new angle on the 'look what I have to be thankful for' idea," but he crossed out the phrase "with a new angle on the 'look what I have to be'" and wrote in pencil, simply, "PLENTY." The "Christmas and Finale," he wrote, "will sum up our whole idea and point of view." He continued, "An enormous Christmas tree in back of the stage with Santa Claus handing out presents to the cast."

He finished the typescript with a self-effacing but firm reflection typical of Berlin's typescript scenarios: "All this is a rough draft and many of the items can be improved on. However, the structure of the revue will have to remain as is. There will be an advantage of being confined to the holidays in their rotation."

Of course, "Happy Holiday" never made it to the stage, but Berlin soon developed it into the 1942 film *Holiday Inn*, in which the revue concept was embedded into a narrative plot featuring Bing Crosby as retired stage star who opens a New England inn, which is open only on holidays—each one marked by a song. "Father Abraham" became simply "Abraham," a swinging number featuring Bing Crosby and Marjorie Reynolds in blackface. "Plenty to be Thankful For" became the film's Thanksgiving song, and the finale's image of a large Christmas tree and Santa Claus handing out presents would be replicated at the end of the film spun off from the *Holiday Inn* scenario, *White Christmas*. Thus, it could be justifiably claimed that the concept and plot framework, if not the melody and lyrics, of one of Berlin's most enduring holiday film songs had its roots in this stage scenario conceived with a notably edgier, Kaufman-and-Hart based, aesthetic—a style that would seem out of step as the storm clouds gathered for another world war.

6

MUSICAL THEATER OF WAR

• • •

THIS IS THE ARMY, 1942–45

The story behind "This is the Army" is as good as the show itself.
—*Irving Berlin*

On the evening of April 20, 1944, in Italy's Santa Maria Opera House, Berlin put on a show for an audience like none he had ever encountered in more than four decades of public entertaining, not even in the rough Lower East Side saloons where he had gotten his start. The audience comprised one thousand men of the U.S. Fifth Army who had come "straight from the front wearing combat boots and helmets, faces drained of expression, eyes unfocused. . . . Once seated they just waited, staring."[1] "It was startling," recalled Alan Anderson, the show's stage manager. After the overture "came to a crashing end," Anderson continued, "there was a moment—maybe half a moment—of silence . . . then it started like a wave. First applause, then whistling, stamping, yelling. It felt almost like hysteria."[2] From there the show continued to build to the moment when its creator came on stage, dressed in his vintage World War I uniform, and sang his popular soldier's lament, "Oh! How I Hate to Get Up in the Morning." "They cheered and cheered until he quieted them again, walking right down to the edge of the stage," Anderson recalled. "It was time for his new song."[3] Like so many before it, the new Berlin song spoke directly to the mob before him: "The Fifth Army Is Where My Heart Is."

Anderson's anecdote encapsulates what Berlin was about: finding a way to rivet spectators with other things on their mind; writing and singing material to fit the situation; using entertainment as a force of hope and optimism against desperate reality, all in service of his country. As Anderson put it, "they came to us right from the rim of hell and were plunged into the revelry of a big Broadway revue."[4] Bluntly dubbed *This Is the Army*, the show held enduring force in Berlin's memory as his most important work, perhaps because Anderson's words—"from the rim of hell" to "a big Broadway revue"—come close to summing up the trajectory of Berlin's own life, from his pogrom-scorched shtetl to the Great White Way.

This Is the Army tends to escape historical memory because, aside from a handful of hit songs—such "This Is the Army, Mister Jones" and "I Left My Heart at the Stage Door Canteen"—it disappeared after the war and did not lend itself to revival. It falls under the radar of most musical theater historians for many reasons: because of its short Broadway run (113 performances), because no Broadway script survives, because Berlin continually changed the show to suit his far-flung audiences, and because it was a revue designed for contemporary audiences living through a global war. *This Is the Army* opened less than a year before Rodgers and Hammerstein's *Oklahoma!*, and the comparison is telling. *TITA* (as its company tended to abbreviate it) harkened back to an earlier form of musical theater while addressing the here-and-now directly, whereas *Oklahoma!* arrived as a new paradigm for musical theater with a plot set in the past.[5] Both benefited from a wartime Broadway that was starved for young talent and fresh entertainment and was awash in nostalgia, from revivals of older musical comedies and operettas to hybrid variety shows billed as "vaudeville revues" featuring veteran entertainers to "farewell" vehicles for aging stars like Al Jolson and Eddie Cantor.[6]

Cultural historians and film historians tend to treat *This Is the Army* entirely as a product of Hollywood.[7] No wonder: the 1943 film became the Warner Brothers biggest grossing movie to date, second only to MGM's *Gone with the Wind* in that era.[8] But the film overlaid a sentimental and overtly patriotic plot starring Ronald Reagan and George Murphy onto a revue whose creator had striven to avoid maudlin sentiments, star power, and direct expressions of patriotism. For a musical theater aficionado, the film's value is chiefly documentary, for its show-within-a-show motif allows it to preserve some of the songs, sketches, and staging of the original Broadway production.

The stage show deserves center stage in Berlin's work for several reasons, most notably its extended tours of the United States, Europe, North Africa, the Middle East, and the South Pacific, through almost the entire span of U.S. involvement in World War II. The show played a central role in the morale-boosting efforts promoted from the very top of American military command, with 1,264 performances for more than 2.5 million military and civilian spectators from its Broadway opening on July 4, 1942, through its final, postwar, performance in Hawai'i in late October 1945. Small wonder that Berlin called it "the best thing I've ever been connected with."[9]

The show succeeded not through flag-waving and sentiment but, like its predecessor *Yip Yip Yaphank*, by focusing instead on the ordinary experiences of the common soldier to which civilians could readily relate: getting wrenched out of bed too early, having to clean the kitchen, finding solace in a safe haven for R & R, facing rigid rules with nimble wit, and dreaming of the girl he left behind. Striving to reflect the shared preoccupations of soldiers and civilians, Berlin's new army show again steered clear of war's violence and chaos, tragedy and loss. It did not need to remind its audience of life's brutality, as Berlin knew from long experience. His entertainment impulse arose from a fervent effort to create a space for levity and pathos in a dangerous, unstable world. As a result, he helped to normalize the American experience of an abnormal event: a world at war.

Although *Yip Yip Yaphank* served as his template, Berlin grasped that the new war required a new kind of show. In an interview he made a pointed contrast between the two wars: "Today we're fighting a war all over the globe. There is no longer an 'Over There' . . . It's 'Over Here' too. . . . Our feelings have changed about war. It's become more personal to all of us and less sentimental."[10] Likewise, he told a reporter visiting Camp Upton that "the boys are different from those who served in 1918. . . . They are more serious and grim. They know what they are up against. There is only one thing about them that is old-fashioned—one thing they have in common with the boys in the other war—that's their patriotism."[11] The war and feelings about it may have

The premiere of This Is the Army *on July 4, 1942, was a major event in wartime New York City. The show ran in the Broadway Theatre for less than three months before going on the road, to Hollywood to be adapted for film, and then to Allied military outposts around the world. Courtesy of Rodgers & Hammerstein, on behalf of the Estate of Irving Berlin.*

been different, but Berlin's compass, as ever, remained pointed at the American Everyman. He would walk around Camp Upton, talking to the soldiers, overhearing conversations, longings, and complaints: he wanted to grow the show from deep engagement with the soldiers' ordinary feelings in an extraordinary situation.

Berlin's focus on the ordinary citizen, whether soldier or civilian, meshed well with the widespread American notion of World War II as the "people's war" to be fought by and for the "common man."[12] And it developed at a time when the War Department's ideal for sustaining morale had shifted from didactic lectures and pamphlets on war aims to lively entertainment focusing on Americans as ordinary people with a decent system of government and an attractive way of life that stood in sharp contrast with that of totalitarian regimes.[13] But the shift from dry pedagogy to lively entertainment came slowly—and not without resistance.

Like American war mobilization itself, the revival of *Yip Yip Yaphank* needed the catalyst of Pearl Harbor to get under way. Certainly the film version of *This Is the Army* presents Pearl Harbor as the thrust that launched the show. The *idea* of reviving it, however, appears to have been first floated publicly long before that—soon after the peacetime draft began in September 1940. The front-page headline in *Variety* on October 2, 1940, announced "Revive 1918 Soldier Show" and in smaller print: "'Yip, Yip, Yaphank' for Conscripts." The article claimed that the show "is slated to be revived and played in the draftee camps where conscriptionists are being trained," and went on to describe the original show and *Variety*'s review of it. Interestingly, the article cites no source for the information, so a reader is left to wonder whether it was floating a rumor or thinking wishfully.

Indeed, despite the draft, the military was a long way from embracing camp shows for the purpose of boosting morale, and Berlin's World War II show was still more than a year away from being written. Articles in *Variety* document the slow process by which entertainment moved from the margins to the center of the military's morale project. Soon after the draft got under way in September 1940, *Variety* began to print articles about camp shows regularly. A front-page article in the November issue reported that Camp [*sic*] Dix in New Jersey (re-named Fort Dix the previous year) had built ten theaters for films and stage shows and that a producer interviewed for the story predicted the development of a vaudeville-like circuit for performing at camps.[14] In February 1941, even as such entertainment continued to flourish, however, *Variety* noted that the War Department appeared to lack interest in supporting it.[15] The paper reported that Berlin himself spoke at a February 6 meeting about camp shows, but it did not indicate any comments that he made.[16]

Perhaps he made an impact, however, because the following month saw a shift in tone about the military's interest in entertainment. Three *Variety* headlines in March and April track decisive moments in the story:

"Army's New Morale Dept. to Probe Problems of Camp Entertainment"[17]
"Army Stage Shows Gain Momentum in U.S. Desire to Build Morale"[18]
"Army Could Use Showfolk: Cites Chance for Draftees"[19]

The following month saw the first mention of reviving Berlin's show since the previous October. On May 21, the notion captured a headline—"Berlin Huddles on '41 Yaphank"—with a report on meetings to plan the revival, on a discussion of blending new and old material into the show, and on potential cast members and a possible tour.[20] *Variety* continued to give the War Department and its Morale Division occasional prods for lack of follow-through.[21] But on August 27, 1941, *Variety* ran a front-page story with a bigger-than-usual all-caps headline "U.S. ARMY AS NO. 1 BARNUM," with the subheading "More Shows to Bolster Morale" and smaller subhead: "War Dept., Severely Scored for Lack of Proper Entertainment, Under New Plan Will Become the Greatest Employer of Talent—All Types for All Camps." The key to the turnaround appears to have been money. As *Variety* put it, "After a week of confabs, budgets for the big-scale entertainment program this winter are being drawn up on a 'don't-worry-about-the-cost' basis."[22]

Pressure from the theatrical community can only have gone so far, however. The War Department's dawning recognition of entertainment's value also got an indirect and unexpected boost from an article in the *Atlantic Monthly* in June 1941: Cleveland Amory's "What We Fight For." Although it did not mention entertainment per se, the article shaped the thinking of two men who would be key military supporters of Berlin's show: General George Marshall and his aide, Frank McCarthy. Amory's article, written in response to an earlier article arguing that Americans needed a new "faith to fight for," claimed a more pragmatic view of Americans as a "plain, ordinary people" who did not need a faith because they had everything they needed: they had worked out "a better government than has ever been worked out for any people in any country." Marshall and McCarthy seized upon Amory's article as a platform for a vision of entertainment that would offer appealing treatments of the American way of life and of decent "plain, ordinary" Americans.[23] The War Department's March 1942 letter to Berlin, inviting him to revive *Yip Yip Yaphank*, came out under Marshall's auspices; Berlin answered, "nothing could be closer to my heart."[24] McCarthy was assigned as a military supervisor of *This Is the Army* to make sure that Berlin and his company got everything they needed to ensure the show's success. It was a good match; McCarthy had already met Ezra Stone, who would become the stage director of *This Is the Army*, during a production at the Virginia Military Institute. Stone later described McCarthy as a "good friend" with a penchant for show business that would culminate in an Academy Award for producing the 1970 film *Patton*.[25]

Much more than *Yip Yip Yaphank*, then, *This Is the Army* was part of a larger, systematic enterprise to entertain the troops and sustain morale, a phenomenon that developed at the same time that many performers toured under the auspices of the United Services Organization, formed in early 1941. Yet Berlin's show was uniquely prominent and successful in tandem with the large network of "Soldiers in Greasepaint," or Camp Shows, Inc., launched in October 1941 and sponsored by the USO.[26] A 1943 *Theatre Arts* article called TITA "the granddaddy of all contemporary soldier shows" in a wide-ranging survey of military theatricals, noting that "the theatre, which often seems to have reached a stalemate on Broadway, may be going through a process of rebirth and rediscovery in this new world of men thrown together in all sorts of amazing combinations, in all sorts of remote and lonely places in the world."[27]

Several features of the show made it unique: it was an army camp show that drew talent not from a single camp but from a national search; its touring company was designated an official detachment of the U. S. Army; its actors and backstage staff were given an assortment of military ranks; and its platoon of black talent made it the only racially integrated military unit before the army was officially desegregated in 1948. Moreover, *This Is the Army, Inc.*, was set up as a charitable corporation[28] that donated all net earnings from ticket sales for the stage and screen versions, from sheet music sales, and from song performance royalties, to Army Emergency Relief, a service agency organized to provide short-term financial aid and other support to soldiers and their dependents.[29] After the war, President Truman presented Berlin with the Medal for Merit for sustaining military and civilian morale during wartime and raising more than $6 million for the relief effort.[30]

This morale-raising stage show, far from a distraction from the serious business of war, rather must be seen as a keystone of the war since, as the historian Paul Fussell has claimed, morale was "one of the unique obsessions of the Allies" during World War II.[31] That obsession gave rise to a multifarious entertainment system sustained by the Special Services Division. And within that system, which included what one wartime theater commentator referred to as "probably the largest single theatrical producing organization, with the exception of the Federal Theatre, that has ever existed,"[32] *This Is the Army* holds a unique place. If World War II was America's "good war," as Studs Terkel dubbed it (with quotation marks signaling some irony), then

This Is the Army was the good war's greatest show.[33] Its sustained international success during World War II—spanning almost the entire period of America's engagement in the war—suggests that it offers a revealing glimpse of Berlin's values and contradictions, and by extension those of wartime America.

Nowhere are those values and contradictions more apparent than in Berlin's ongoing and unapologetic reliance on the conventions of minstrelsy he had deployed in *Yip Yip Yaphank*. This first racially integrated army unit reproduced racial images and sounds that had roots in nineteenth-century entertainment. Race forms the show's basic paradox, onstage and offstage, just as (in many ways) it lies at the heart of the nation. Berlin's theatrical approach should not be surprising, for it was not unique, or even unusual. In its encouragement of military camp shows, the Special Services Division, which oversaw all soldier entertainment, had even published a manual including two full-length minstrel shows with music.[34] For Berlin, as for many of his generation, racial masquerade and stereotyping comprised just one element of a rich theatrical legacy. For him, minstrelsy still served as an apt theatrical medium for the new war with its "serious and grim" soldiers. That was evident from the show's first scene.

Billed on the program as a "Military Minstrel Show," the opening sequence used several post–Civil War minstrel devices, echoing their use in *Yip Yip Yaphank*: a large, uniformed male ensemble on risers; rapid-fire dialogue between characters of unequal status in the manner of minstrelsy's end man–interlocutor banter; a tenor spotlighted in the role of a romantic balladeer. Later scenes would also offer elements inherited from minstrelsy: a hefty dose of female impersonation, and the integration of contemporary references and nostalgia for the past. Minstrelsy offered Berlin a broad, flexible vocabulary of theatrical and musical conventions that helped to rein in two tendencies he wanted to avoid, especially for his soldier audiences—maudlin sentiments and overt patriotism.

While Berlin preserved *Yaphank*'s minstrel-show framework, he renovated its interior. The first scene sets the tone with the image of 150-uniformed men in minstrel formation on risers, in front of which a motley crew of selectees enters and begins to sing the song "This Is the Army, Mister Jones." The scene creates a sharp contrast between the minstrel-soldiers—whom Berlin had initially hoped to present in blackface—with their matching uniforms, straight posture, lockstep movements, and stentorian singing; and the selectees, who dress in mismatched underclothes, stumble around and slouch, and sing in weak, shallow tones. After the selectees sing the song, the minstrel-soldiers repeat the chorus while the selectees change into uniform—which, according to a typescript stage direction, "are hardly a perfect fit"—and they march off the stage.[35] Before our eyes, civilians have been transformed into soldiers, and minstrelsy serves as the crucible of that transformation.

The minstrel first part features a run of banter and boasting between the end man Dick Bernie and the interlocutor, who has summoned him "front and center." We cannot know exactly what happened in stage performances, but the film at least preserves the spirit of the scene, as does the British script.[36] In classic end man fashion, Bernie acts as a disruptive figure who trades rapid-fire dialogue with the interlocutor on his left as he tries to crack the stony façade of the guard on his right, which he succeeds in doing with the line: "You heard of the March of Time? There's his brother,

Waste of Time." As the scene progresses, Bernie's pace quickens and the boasts grow. In the end of the scene as filmed, he willingly surrenders to the guard for his verbal trespassing, an act that reinforces the interlocutor's superiority even as it gets Dick Bernie the end man's ultimate reward: the last laugh.[37]

A minstrel show typically offered contrast in the form of a tenor singing a romantic ballad. The romantic balladeer was the musical star of the minstrel first part. This, too, fit well into a wartime show, for it allowed Berlin to develop an impulse he viewed as universal to the common soldier: yearning for the girl he left behind. To satisfy this convention Berlin wrote "I'm Getting Tired So I Can Sleep," a song in the form of a love letter in which a soldier looks forward to dreaming as the best way to reunite with his faraway loved one.

The romantic ballad's "girl-I-left-behind" trope also stands behind two later numbers, including a song that became the show's hit ballad, "I Left My Heart at the Stage Door Canteen." Here, a soldier pines for the hostess he met at the famous army nightclub, whose rules forbade hostesses from leaving the venue with a soldier. Berlin keeps overblown sentimentality in check by using the mundane act of dunking doughnuts as a way to convey the soldier's longing:

I kept her serving doughnuts / Till all she had were gone;
I sat there dunking doughnuts / Till she caught on.

The other "girl-I-left-behind" song, "With My Head in the Clouds," appears within a pair of numbers in tribute to the U.S. Army Air Forces, but its lyrics strike a jarring note, as Berlin invokes the yearning of distant lovers as bombs fall on the enemy:

When the night is clear
And the bombardier
Drops a bomb that's wired for sound,
How I yearn to return
With my head in the clouds
To the one I love on the ground.

Beyond yearning for women, the men in *This Is the Army* also impersonate them. Berlin's show uses two kinds of female impersonation. One features a group of men embodying a generic stereotyped femininity.[38] This is the minstrel type evoked in the number "Ladies of the Chorus," which Berlin recycled from *Yip Yip Yaphank*. Here, the humor arises from the contrast between a dainty female ideal and the ungainly, hairy masculinity it cannot conceal. Another kind of female impersonation became a minstrel art form. Robert Toll has noted that female impersonation emerged in the post–Civil War era as "minstrelsy's most important new specialty role,"[39] whose performers "excited more interest than any other minstrel specialist."[40] Earlier in the "Stage Door Canteen" sequence, fascination vies with humor as a soldier does a striking parody of a specific woman, the actress Lynn Fontanne, then breaks the illusion with a masculine shout.

The minstrel first part culminates in the mock-wedding number heard in the *Ziegfeld Follies of 1919* (as modified from *Yip Yip Yaphank*): "Mandy." As portrayed on film, the version for *This Is the Army* features the soldier's chorus on risers, plus several performers in blackface. Five of them stand in the back encircled by a large banjo image on a backdrop, and others dance in the foreground, where we see the double masquerade of white men in both drag *and* a light shade of blackface that used to be called "high yellow," often featured in minstrelsy's female impersonations.[41]

Racial stereotypes also surface in a number for the African American performers called "What the Well-Dressed Man in Harlem Will Wear." As in the opening number "This Is the Army, Mister Jones," Berlin presents the conversion from civilian to soldier as a matter of dressing up, as the Harlem "dude" sheds his "Lenox Avenue clothes" for a uniform marked by a "suntan shade of cream / Or an olive-drab color scheme." A reference to Berlin's earlier song "Top Hat, White Tie, and Tails" notes what the civilian has given up. The last line evokes an image of the boxing legend Joe Louis as "Brown Bomber Joe," and the film (but not the stage version) matches it with the appearance of Louis himself. The number begins with a contemporary musical signifier of Harlem nightlife: a phrase of scat followed by a swing-style melody and band arrangement.

Focusing chiefly on American soldiers and their concerns and feelings, *This Is the Army* largely defined the enemy by its absence, yet Berlin wrote a few songs that appeared briefly in various versions of the show to define what the Americans and their Allies were fighting against, and here, too, it is possible to detect the minstrel impulse at work. For example, the Broadway opening included a number titled "Aryans under the Skin." In it, eight men—four dressed up as "German Fräuleins" and four dressed as "Japs"—play a coy game of flirtation whose chorus (in published form) begins with the lines—

Japs: Six [*sic*] little Japanese from Tokyo—
Germans: Six [*sic*] little German Fräuleins from Berlin—[42]

yet another echo of the famous trio from Gilbert and Sullivan's *The Mikado*, "Three Little Maids from School Are We," and also of Berlin's own "Eight Little Notes" number from the first *Music Box Revue* ("Eight little notes are we, / Useful as we can be").

An early version of the song under the title "Welcome Yellow Aryans," which exists among hundreds of documents related to the show in the Library of Congress, includes musical stereotyping with roots in early Tin Pan Alley as well: the verse (sung by "Moto") features parallel fourth intervals over a dronelike D-minor accompaniment—both stock icons of Tin Pan Alley's hoary old orientalist vein. The chorus (sung by a representative of German femininity named "Gretchen") features a hymnlike tune and harmony in F major in a "slow march tempo," perhaps in emulation of "Deutschland über alles."[43]

In both versions, Berlin dramatizes the Axis alliance of Japan and Germany made vivid in propaganda minister Josef Goebbels's claim that the Japanese were a "pure race" and thus qualified as "Yellow Aryans," a fact about which Berlin wrote to the Hollywood director Mark Sandrich during preparation for the film *Holiday Inn*.[44] And in both versions, Berlin chose to depict the Germans as women. Perhaps because they lacked the non-Caucasian racial markers of the Japanese, the Germans needed to be marked by gender instead of race for the purpose of parody, following a wartime pattern of feminizing the enemy as a way to project domination and strength.[45]

Berlin wrote the piece in late December 1941 and initially intended it as a mock-holiday number ("Aryan Day") for *Holiday Inn*. Once *This Is the Army* began to develop, however, he decided to use it for that show. Either way, the song brings the minstrel impulse to a sharp-edged caricature of a united and threatening enemy force less than three weeks after the Pearl Harbor attack. It was cut during the show's Broadway run. A song called "That Russian Winter" captures the ways in which Mother Nature had a role in deflating Hitler's boasts. It too was cut before the show went overseas. For a radio show, Berlin mocked Goebbels again in a song called "Ve Don't Like It," which invokes the radio itself and a pun on Berlin's own name: "Herr Doktor Goebbels / Is on the air today. / Let's tune in and get Berlin / And hear what he has to say."[46]

Later theater programs indicate that references about the Axis powers diminished.[47] A song called "The Kick in the Pants," added during the overseas tour, takes off from the old "do-the-brand-new-dance" type of song popular in the 1920s. The tone of most of these songs is more evocative of a sports rivalry than a war.

Ultimately, *This Is the Army* was, above all, about the *American* army. Berlin seems to have intuitively understood something that Studs Terkel later noted about the ordinary soldier: "for the typical American soldier, despite the perverted film sermons, it was not 'getting another Jap' or 'getting another Nazi' that impelled him up front. 'The reason you storm the beaches is not patriotism or bravery,' reflects the tall rifleman. 'It's that sense of not wanting to fail your buddies. There's sort of a special sense of kinship.'"[48] By keeping its focus on the "typical" soldier's concerns, *This Is the Army* stoked that kinship.

Finally, like a minstrel show, *This Is the Army* combined nostalgia and contemporaneity. Minstrel nostalgia tends to point to minstrelsy's own past, and so it is that Berlin adopts his World War I hit, "Oh! How I Hate to Get Up in the Morning," for use in the new war. Here, the show's creator, dressed in his uniform from the first war, again lends his raspy, impish voice to a common army gripe of the ordinary soldier. The ensuing finale jolts the audience back into the present, suggesting that the first war's business has not yet been completed. In a number called "This Time," the uniformed minstrels of scene 1 have now become full-fledged combat soldiers with rifles. For the film, Berlin added a verse featuring the lines "dressed up to kill," a phrase he would change in response to a controversy within the company's ranks that spilled out into the public.

The critics hailed the show with lockstep praise in print—preceded by an unusually public show of enthusiasm within the theater itself. As Berlin's daughter Mary Ellin (then fifteen years old) recalled, "the whole evening had the critics on their feet applauding. This was something that never happened, so someone remarked, the gentlemen and ladies of the press putting themselves publicly on the line."[49]

African American newspapers tended to feature mostly positive stories on the show—usually emphasizing its quality, its black performers, and the potential of its mixed-race cast to herald a more democratic army.[50] From black newspapers, indeed, a few criticisms emerged only after the film appeared, but they were rare amid reports of Joe Louis's involvement and the ongoing sense of a need to support the

In This Is the Army, *Berlin donned his World War I uniform and sang "Oh! How I Hate to Get Up in the Morning," earning long ovations. Courtesy of Rodgers & Hammerstein, on behalf of the Estate of Irving Berlin.*

war effort. For example, while the *Pittsburgh Courier*'s critic called it "one of the greatest films to come out of Hollywood," he chided its emphasis on "the grinning, tap-dancing, Harlemesque jitterbug fashion too long associated with the race."[51] Toward the end of the war, a reporter in Guam revealed that black soldiers had been expressing increasingly open disdain toward black stereotypes in films, and with reference to *TITA*'s still-touring stage production he noted that "even the comparatively innocuous 'This Is the Army' came in for a round of criticism from GI's on this island, who are currently voicing resentment against the clowning of Sgt. James

Cross. . . . Negro servicemen have not failed to note that the big soldier chorus in the production is composed entirely of whites, and that Negro participation in the 'Stage Door Canteen' scene is limited to a single Negro soldier stationed near the wings."[52]

Only one review of the stage production, while generous in praise, took *TITA* to task for the racial masquerading and stereotyping of its minstrel elements. In the socialist paper the *Daily Worker* Ralph Warner noted that the show reflects "one of the ancient weaknesses of that song-writing alley in the heart of Broadway—in its out-moded treatment of Negroes." He went on to describe the blackface routine of "Mandy" in the midst of the opening scene's "white-face minstrel show." He also pointed to "What the Well-Dressed Man in Harlem Will Wear" as an example of a similarly outmoded number. Then he noted that the finale is the only time the white and black performers appear together on stage, connecting the show with the nation's military: "this virtual segregation in the production is merely a reflection of the policy of the Army in building segregated units."[53]

One additional feature, outside the theater, links *This Is the Army* to minstrel traditions and reveals its unresolved racial attitudes. In New York and on tour in the United States, the company paraded through city streets in full costume as an elaborate ballyhoo to raise excitement about the show.[54] As far back as *Watch Your Step* Berlin had celebrated the phenomenon of "The Minstrel Parade," and in *TITA* he got to have one—now transformed by military pageantry. The parades became a widely noted feature of the show's fall 1942 tour. Alan Anderson recalled how "cheering sidewalk crowds" greeted the company's "energetic marches from the railroad station to the theater in every city," adding that in some cities "these marches were augmented by local Army installations who added military rolling stock to the parade. These varied from jeeps to half tracks, to tanks, to field guns."[55] Some newspaper accounts of the touring production described these parades. A Pittsburgh paper, for example, carried a photograph of the parade as a news item in itself and described how "320 khaki clad soldiers marched from the Pennsylvania Railroad Station to the Nixon Theater yesterday for the opening tonight."[56] The film tries to capture the flavor of these parades in a brief montage that helps build excitement for the final scenes dramatizing the Washington, D.C., performance.

The parades offered an offstage but very public view of the show's racial dynamics. The initial plan was to feature the company in integrated ranks, organized by theatrical skills. And in fact, this is what happened at first; soon after the opening the *Pittsburgh Courier* even published a photo of black and white soldiers marching together in Manhattan, with the caption "No segregated ranks here."[57] On tour, however, the company's black members marched in a separate platoon. Published accounts differ about why that happened. According to Ezra Stone, he and Anderson had planned the integrated approach, but a colonel insisted on segregating the ranks.[58] According to Anderson (writing several years later), two black sergeants requested the segregated formation in order to display the platoon's talents.[59] Neither Stone nor Anderson describes what the black platoon did, but they agree that its "crack precision" (Stone) "raised the level of the entire company" (Anderson).

Other instances of offstage segregation did not come by request. At the Washington, D.C., Red Cross, where the company had arranged lodging, the Red Cross manager began directing the black troops to segregated accommodations. But Berlin saw the company as an impregnable unit, and the executive officer Marc Daniels insisted that the entire company would stay together, on orders from General Marshall: "there is no designation of race on the roster," Daniels told the manager. The entire company was permitted to stay in the "white" Red Cross facility.[60] St. Louis would be the only other place where the black performers faced discrimination in lodging.[61] Yet racism kept creeping into the company's experiences. George Murphy, starring in a Berlin-like role in the film, described its director Michael Curtiz as a "wild Hungarian" who could not understand the racist nature of his directions when he yelled "Bring on the nigger troops!" When Murphy tried to correct him by using the phrase "colored troops," Curtiz responded: "Bring on the colored niggers!"[62]

As for Berlin, his actions suggest that his penchant for minstrelsy, and his show's on-stage segregation, could coexist with racial empathy. Three days before the scheduled opening of *TITA* in Washington, the *Baltimore Afro-American* ran a story titled "Irving Berlin Cracks D.C.'s Jim-Crow Law," which explained that the National Theatre's manager had announced that African Americans may purchase "any seat in the house" for Berlin's show thanks to Berlin himself. "Mr. Berlin's action," the paper reported, was a response to a letter about a recent refusal of admission to an African American woman who had purchased a ticket.[63] On tours to war zones, he performed in (segregated) hospitals for wounded black soldiers. Fifty years after the show closed, a *New York Times* reporter interviewed two of *TITA*'s black platoon members at a reunion of the surviving company members. Both sustained fond memories of the show: "The old man was fantastic," recalled dancer Bill Smith.[64] When all of the racially charged incidents surrounding *TITA* are accounted for, what the historian Benjamin Alpers has written about the film applies to the show onstage and off: "*This Is the Army* neatly embodied the ambivalence toward the black troops" that characterized the military, and the nation, in general.[65]

If the show's racial dynamics looked both forward and backward, so did Berlin's song styles. While minstrelsy formed the show's theatrical core, Berlin filled out the score with a variety of song styles that spanned three decades. "I Left My Heart at the Stage Door Canteen" is a syncopated ballad with a fresh, supple melody that might have found a home in an earlier era of Tin Pan Alley, as might the sturdy, marchlike Air Force tribute "With My Head in the Clouds." "What the Well-Dressed Man in Harlem Will Wear" stands out as a swing number whose up-to-date musical style couples with racial imagery that goes back to the original Harlem version of "Puttin' on the Ritz." Berlin also retooled his *Yaphank* "Florodora" spoof for the cross-dressing number "Ladies of the Chorus." The minstrel show's romantic balladeer number, "I'm Getting Tired So I Can Sleep," is also a syncopated ballad with a rhythmic pulse that resonates with Cole Porter's Latin-tinged beguine numbers. The act 1 finale broke the fourth wall, like the grand finale of *Yaphank*, in a manner that reversed the trajectory of the earlier show. Here, uniformed navy men break into the theater from the back, interrupt the stage action, and demand their own number, which turns into a welcoming quickstep march called "How About a Cheer for the Navy." (The show's programs simply indicated "Finale Act 1" to ensure the element of surprise.) Berlin spotted his own quickstep march, "Oh! How I Hate to Get Up in the Morning," in the time-honored, next-to-last program position—where he won a ten-minute ovation on opening night before even opening his mouth.[66]

In *TITA* Berlin conceived a way for the number to expand into a ballet—a *dream ballet*—and his papers preserve an unusual document of his vision of the scene. It captures his acute sense of theater and ends with a characteristically modest shrug, an unexpected bolt of modesty in an otherwise confident and vivid statement.[67] Writing in the third person, he began: "this comes immediately after the Irving Berlin rendition of 'Oh, How I Hate to Get Up in the Morning' as a flashback to 1919 as it was done in 'Yip Yip Yaphank.'" Then he continued with a sly send-up of military regimentation and deprivation that portrayed the soldier's life as one of elegance, comfort, and leisure:

When the curtains are drawn at the end of this number, the quartette come out and in "one" and sing 16 bars of lyrics and music to the effect that

> That was the case in Berlin's day
> When they hated to get up somehow
> But bugle calls are all passé
> It's a different Army now!

The curtains part disclosing a typical Army barracks, its drabness is exaggerated, but must be a literal reproduction. 16 regulation Army cots are on stage each occupied by a soldier covered by an Army blanket. Dawn begins to rise and we hear bird effects from the orchestra, etc. As the scene gradually lights up a string quartette in gay Hungarian costumes headed by a gypsy violinist, also gaily dressed, enters and very schmaltzy starts playing Reveille as though it were Ave Maria. The quartette place themselves on the side of the scene, possibly on a platform, and the violinist leaves the group and works around the different beds as though he were playing to individual tables in a Hungarian restaurant. The boys gradually rise and when the blankets are uncovered they are revealed in very snappy loud pajamas. After a very kind (*not sissy*) Sergeant puts them through a mild setting up exercise routine they return to bed in a sitting up position as 16 maids with breakfast trays dance on a serve the soldiers. After the maids enter with the breakfast trays 16 valets, dressed conventionally British in cutaway coats, morning striped trousers, dance on and lay out each uniform at the foot of each bed and exit quickly. Into a dance with the girls finishing with the boys back in bed, the girls sitting on the side of the bed, as the string quartette and gypsy violinist come back and in the same schmaltzy manner play Taps and lulls them back to sleep—as the girls go into the finish. For this ballet the music is the tune of "Hate to Get Up in the Morning" reconstructed of course to fit the different moods.

This is just a rough outline as a guide to whoever stages the number and of course is subject to change.[68]

The unsentimental man of the theater cut this cherished ballet vision when the show went overseas.

Clothes play a key role in the scenario (with its "gay Hungarian costumes," "very snappy loud pajamas," and "cutaway coats, morning striped trousers"), and, in fact, sartorial imagery stands at the center of Berlin's wartime vision. From the opening minstrelized transformation of civilian conscripts to enlisted soldiers, to the Harlem "dudes" changing from their "Lenox Avenue clothes" to their crisp uniforms, to the verse added to the Hollywood finale ("dressed up to win"), Berlin regularly reminds the audience that costuming forms a key link between theater and war. That theme emerges again and again in songs he continued to write during wartime and beyond. For example, in the spring of 1945 he wrote a series of lyrics expressing the soldier's longing to return to civilian clothes: "Oh, to emerge again / In a blue serge again" and, for the Army Nurse Corps, "Oh, for a dress again, / To caress again."[69] After the war, he conjured "just a blue serge suit" in an image, he wrote, that "seems to me to be the symbol of civilian life and everything that goes with peace."[70] He also wrote a song asking the question: "For what is a soldier? Cool or warm, / He's just a civilian / In uniform!"[71]

In keeping with his desire to capture the pulse of the soldier's life, Berlin drew inspiration from actual documents of the war effort. Among the massive materials that survive from *This Is the Army*, there are two in particular that he seems to have exploited to make his songs sound more authentic. The Stage Door Canteen number, for example, shows the clear influence of a two-page list of twenty-one "Rules for Hostesses" distributed to the young women hired to dance and socialize with servicemen in the military-approved social venues. The "Rules" coexist among Berlin's papers with a handwritten list of selected rules (almost certainly in Berlin's hand), which correlate closely to the lyrics that Berlin wrote for the scene (see table 6.1).[72] In another example of how electronic mass media (radio and film) had a tendency to launder even slightly risqué material (cf. "Heat Wave"), a key line of Berlin's original lyric was too explicit for Hollywood's Hays Office, guardian of the Production Code. The Hayes Office asked Berlin to change the final phrase of Hostesses's line "We can go and have a fling / With some guy in the Theatre Wing / *But never give all to a soldier*," and Berlin obliged with the less suggestive—and uncharacteristically multisyllabic—"But *never be found / Canoodling around* with a soldier."[73]

Another document that appears to have served as source material for Berlin's songwriting is the War Department's *Technical Manual of Field Music*, published in September 1940 when the peacetime draft was announced.[74] Berlin had already quoted "Reveille" in "Oh! How I Hate to Get Up in the Morning" back in 1918. The manual, found among surviving materials for *This is the Army*, may have served as a reminder that field music tended to be simple and triadic, focusing chiefly on the three pitches of the major triad, a trait shared by bugle calls such as "Reveille" and "The Call to Assembly," for example. Such similarities to existing music are nothing new in Berlin's songwriting style: they have their roots in the myriad quotations and allusions he wove into his earliest songs. Here they have the effect of integrating his songwriting style with the military culture it served (exx. 6.1–6.2). The refrain of "The Army's Made a Man Out of Me" begins by tracing a tonic triad and continues with short phrases (repeating "a man out of me") that reinforce the key pitches (ex. 6.2d). In this tune, Berlin also conjures a relationship with another well-known wartime song outside of the field manual: "Don't Sit under the Apple Tree (with Anyone Else but Me)," which also repeats its title's last phrase, "anyone else but me."

If minstrel conventions and songs inspired by bugle calls represent two ways in which Berlin grasped a potent force for the theater of war, another lies in his flexible

Table 6.1. Source material from Berlin's lyric for the "Stage Door Canteen" number, act 2, *This Is the Army*

"Rules for Hostesses"	*Berlin's handwritten list*	*Berlin's lyric*
6. Hostesses are not to spend too much time with any one group of service men, and the girls are requested not to dance too long with any one man. This must be left to the discretion of the girls themselves. But—realize that we have many more guests than hostesses—and try to divide your favors evenly.	[Do not] Dance too long with one man	A hostess mustn't dance too long / With any one man
8. Hostesses should not congregate in groups—and talk among themselves while on duty.	Do not congregate in groups	Don't congregate in groups
10. The food that is served at the CANTEEN has been donated by the merchants of New York for the exclusive use of the service men. No worker in the CANTEEN is permitted to eat this food.	Do not eat the food	You mustn't eat the food
14. NO HOSTESS IS TO LEAVE THE CANTEEN AT ANY TIME—UNDER ANY CIRCUMSTANCES WITH A SERVICE MAN—OR TO MEET HIM OUTSIDE IN THE VICINITY OF THE CANTEEN.	Above all—no intimacy	We mustn't be seen / Outside the canteen with a soldier.

conception of the show. When it became clear that the company would be going overseas, Berlin embraced the idea of changing the show in order to reach new audiences. He recognized immediately that the large company would have to be significantly reduced, that the show had to be streamlined, made less elaborate, with new dialogue and musical numbers added and others omitted. By all accounts, Berlin relished the changes because his audience-centered values precluded any notion of a single ideal version of the show. He reduced the 310-member company by more than half to a streamlined organization of 150. Anderson remembered Berlin calling a meeting in which he spoke like a military commander: "Cutting down to one hundred fifty guys is going to be tough and after we do that, we've got to do some rewriting—make changes, new songs, new sketches. We're going to play for soldier audiences in war zones. It's a different audience—even the emotions will be different . . . keep in mind it's going to be rugged a lot of time. We need healthy guys."[75]

Example 6.1. *Bugle calls in* Technical Manual of Field Music.

6.1a. *"Reveille."*

6.1b. *"Call to Assembly."*

Example. 6.2. *Triadic melodies in* This Is the Army.

6.2a. *"This Is the Army, Mister Jones."*

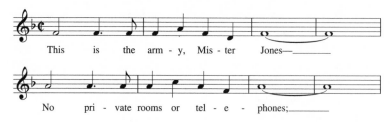

This   is   the   arm - y,   Mis - ter   Jones—_____

No   pri - vate rooms or   tel - e - phones;_____

6.2b. *"What the Well Dressed Man in Harlem Will Wear."*

Sun - tan__   shade of   cream   Or   an o - live drab col - or scheme

6.2c. *"How About a Cheer for the Navy."*

Hip,   hip, hoo - ray!____   We have-n't got long to   stay,____   So

how a - bout one bou - quet   for   the   Na - vy?

6.2d. *"The Army's Made a Man Out of Me."*

The   Arm - y's   made   a   man out   of   me,   A

man   out   of   me,   A   man   out   of   me.

The plan worked. As Anderson wrote, "in rehearsal the orchestra of twenty-four men (instead of forty-six) and the chorus of sixty men (instead of one hundred seventy-one), seemed not to lose any of their effectiveness."[76] In fact, several observers, including company members and audience members who saw both the Broadway and overseas versions of the show, judged the streamlined overseas version to be superior. One commentary, written for *Variety* but apparently too dated to run by the time it passed the military censors, noted that in Leyte, Philippines, "on a makeshift stage in a mosquito-infested and mud-ridden village, the show ran even faster and smoother than it did in New York."[77]

Because the show was constantly on the move, it was constantly changing. Berlin liked to write at least one new song for each new place and for performances on radio and film (see table 6.2)—from the United Kingdom (where it played in London, Glasgow, Manchester, Liverpool, Birmingham, Bristol, and Bournemouth) to Italy (Rome, Santa Maria, Foggia), Egypt, Iran, India, New Guinea, the Philippines, and other locales in the South Pacific. All told, the new songs inserted for specific locales over a twenty-seven month period add up to a full show's worth of music. Added to that are several songs that he included more or less spontaneously, as in a performance in Italy, where he sang Italian songs he remembered from his Lower East Side days, and performances in the Philippines in spring 1945 when he included "God Bless America" as the finale (at last). The show's publicist, Ben Washer, kept a diary dotted with telegraphic summaries of happenings on tour. In the diary's only detailed account of Berlin performing for an overseas audience, Washer wrote an entry titled "Rome Civilian Perf[ormance]" on January 17, 1944:

> Finally Irving Berlin is on after a brief introduction in Italian. They know him and his music and do not wait for the introduction to be finished before applauding. After "Oh! How I Hate to Get Up in the Morning" he asks them if they know any of his songs. They call for them by name. Remember. Always. All Alone. + Alexander. Then he says that he has sung his songs for them, now he would like to sing one of their songs. He says that when he first came to America many years ago, he lived in an Italian neighborhood, where he played with the Italian children. "They taught us their songs in Italian," he explains, "and we taught them our Jewish songs. Now I'd like to sing one of the songs they taught me, 'Oi Marie." And he sings, first as he had been taught so many years ago, the entire song in Italian, and then he asks them to sing it with him. He leaves the stage and the audience is as wet eyed as audible.

Whereas later pop stars might shout a localized greeting to their audiences ("Hello Milwaukee!") and proceed with the same songs they would perform everywhere else, Berlin channeled that impulse into specific songs designed for specific audiences and places. Songs like "My British Buddy," "The Fifth Army Is Where My Heart Is" (in Italy), and "Heaven Watch over the Philippines" were highly site-specific, did not travel well, and lacked any hit potential back in the states—but they made their immediate audiences feel almost blessed.

Table 6.2. Post-Broadway additions to *This Is the Army*, 1943–45

Song title	Place introduced	Date written or introduced
Ve Don't Like It	ABC Lux Radio Theater	February 1943
What Does He Look Like (That Boy of Mine)?	Hollywood (film)	March 1943
Dressed Up to Kill / Dressed Up to Win	Hollywood (film)	1943
Don't Sing—Go Into Your Dance	London	November 1943
The Kick in the Pants[1]	London	November 1943
My British Buddy	London	November 1943
Daddy's Coming Home on a Furlough	London	November 1943
The Fifth Army Is Where My Heart Is	Italy	April 1944
What Are We Going to Do with All the Jeeps	Italy	May 1944
There Are No Wings on a Foxhole	Italy	June 1944
"air corps song"[2]	Italy	June 1944
Misses the Army[3]	[Italy]	July 1944
Cozy Little Foxhole by the Sea	Italy	July 1944

I Get Along with the Aussies	[never performed]	December 1944
I'm Getting Old in New Guinea	New Guinea (radio)	January 1945
Heaven Watch Over the Philippines	Philippines	March (?) 1945 [Berlin left show at end of March—see TITA daily log]
Oh, To Be Home Again	Philippines (?)	April-May 1945 [used in place of "Oh! How I Hate to Get Up in the Morning" after Berlin left the show—see "TITA programs" file, LC-IBC Box 279, Folder 1]

1. Berlin wrote a new lyric for the song in Italy in late May 1944 (Ben Washer diary, LC-IBC Box 509, Folder 1).

2. Ben Washer's diary refers to an "air corps song" that Berlin wrote in late May 1944 and introduced at a show in Italy on June 6, 1944 (at which the D-Day invasion was announced during intermission). But a month later, on July 4, 1944, Washer recorded that Berlin did not like the song and announced it publicly: "B. sings Air Corps song—but no gd & in curtain speech about 2nd anniversary says he will not sing it again." It is unclear what song Washer is referring to, as the song does not appear to survive.

3. "Misses the Army" represents a new lyric for the women's army corps, set to the tune of "This Is the Army, Mister Jones."

While Berlin insisted on complete authority over the show, he also remained deeply engaged as a performer. Throughout the overseas tour, Berlin performed constantly for groups of soldiers and officers who could not otherwise see the show. He regularly went to hospitals to perform for injured soldiers. That his assistants kept records of these visits is just one example of scattered evidence that Berlin intended to chronicle his experiences in a book about *This Is the Army* after the war ended. A list of hospitals and Red Cross units where Berlin performed includes twenty-eight venues visited in the spring and early summer of 1944, plus estimates of audience size, ranging from two hundred to five thousand spectators. Another typescript lists "appearances by Irving Berlin other than those in 'This is the Army' in the South West Pacific Theater December 23, 1944–April 1, 1945." Berlin did seventy-five additional performances in this three-month period—almost one per day. The list includes mostly hospitals but also radio stations, mess halls, officers' clubs, and parties where he performed right up to his final departure from the company in late March 1945.[78] Whenever Berlin left the show, so did "Oh! How I Hate to Get Up in the Morning." That was his song, and his alone.

Further testimony to Berlin's intense dedication to the show was his determination to write letters to the family members of every company member during the two periods when he returned to the states while the show was still running. These letters, of which copies exist in his files of correspondence, were form letters, but each one was individualized with the company member's name, and many of them inspired expressions of gratitude from the recipients.[79] That Berlin relished his letter-writing campaign emerges in a letter preserved between the pages of Washer's diary. Berlin reported the project as if it were part of the show itself: "I only have three more letters to write for the boys. The answers keep coming in, and apparently the idea is a hit."[80]

The men never saw the front, but they had so many close calls that Alan Anderson came to believe that a "special angel" followed the show.[81] It began even before they came anywhere near a war zone. In Boston, for example, several cast and crew went to the Cocoanut Grove nightclub having been promised drinks on the house, but when the manager failed to deliver the goods, the *TITA* members left, only to learn the following morning of the 1942 fire that killed hundreds.[82] In London, their furlough was cancelled and the show shipped out earlier than planned to Africa and Italy on General Eisenhower's orders. Soon after that, London was bombed and "the buildings we had been living in for seventeen days" were destroyed.[83] In Liverpool, "an undetonated parachute bomb broke through a theater's ceiling and hung by its strings above the startled—but still dancing—performers on the stage."[84] Later, in Italy, the company just missed getting bombed in the Naples harbor.[85]

The show faced other dangers from within its ranks, two conflicts affecting prominent members of the company and the show itself. Both incidents reflected a clash of military discipline and theatrical values. And both of them involved Berlin directly. Throughout the U.S. tour leading up to the company's stint in Hollywood, a conflict had been brewing between Berlin and the show's only other notable theatrical personality, the young actor and director Ezra Stone. At twenty-two, Stone already had two Broadway directing credits to his name and was widely known for his performance in the title role of the radio sitcom *Henry Aldrich*, from its premiere in 1939 to 1942 when he left the show and entered the army.[86] There were other experienced theater people in the show but none with Stone's *wunderkind* luster. So when the show proved successful, Stone began to chafe under Berlin's orders that no one in the company but Berlin himself could talk to the press about the show. The army, he said, wanted it that way, wanted it to be seen as strictly a Berlin show.[87]

The conflict reached a crisis in a very public way. The curtain call had been staged so that Stone, as director, was to salute Berlin, as creator and star, and Berlin was to return the salute, acting out the show's creative hierarchy in a military gesture. But on the night of a command performance for President Roosevelt, despite an "order" from Berlin to do the show no differently for its illustrious audience member, Stone broke ranks during the curtain call, snubbed Berlin, and directed his salute to Roosevelt instead. Berlin summoned Stone immediately after the curtain closed and told him he would never trust him again. Stone remained with the company for several months, and he continued to be featured in the number "The Army Has Made a Man Out of Me," in which Berlin may well have been playing off the adolescent persona of Stone's Henry Aldrich portrayal.

But tensions mounted as the adversaries escalated their conflict with Jewish slurs—Berlin referring to Stone's lackluster "Jewish cronies" in the chorus, and Stone to "kikes in the music division."[88] In this account, Stone's use of the verbal dagger "kikes" was unforgivable, yet it was Berlin who first defined the conflict in Jewish terms, as if to say that Stone and his friends were not "assimilated" enough to serve the larger cause. The conflict escalated further in Hollywood. Stone joined together with another member of the ensemble and petitioned Los Angeles–area clergy to protest Berlin's use of the phrase "dressed up to kill" in the film's finale. The pressure came in and Berlin ultimately relented, changing the line to "dressed up to win"—but this happened only after the number had been filmed, so the new word had to be dubbed. Careful observation of the film reveals one soldier clearly mouthing the word "kill" while we hear the word "win."

Much later, Stone described another conflict with Berlin even before the show reached the stage. He had objected to Berlin's desire to use blackface makeup in the opening minstrel scene. In a 1987 letter to the editor of the *Journal of American History* (while Berlin was still alive), Stone praised an article that had confronted the ways in which Hollywood participated in wartime propaganda and fostered stereotypical images of African Americans, something the authors, Clayton R. Koppes and Gregory D. Black, had highlighted in their discussion of *This Is the Army*.[89] Stone wrote of his discussions with Berlin that "the sinful, stereotype factor and tastelessness did not sway him. . . . I finally won the battle. Only because I convinced him that I'd never have the time to get all those guys out of the black face paint for the rest of the show. It was bad enough having the dancers in black face for the *Mandy* number which was also in *Yip Yip Yaphank*."[90]

The conflict between Berlin and Stone grew toxic, then, over a variety of fundamental values, involving authority, recognition, and representation on and off stage. Berlin, it might be said, represented a conservative, assimilationist American view that accepted minstrelsy as a viable form of entertainment—the "people's culture" view—and that rallied American unity as it drew stark lines between America and its enemies.

Stone represented a progressive, liberal ideology for whom minstrelsy represented "cultural domination" and for whom killing was not an acceptable topic about which to boast from the stage, no matter how good the war cause. Stone's means of dealing with these issues in the face of Berlin's unchallengeable authority was either to subvert that authority in a public forum (on the Washington, D.C., stage or through contacts in the religious community) or to use show-business logistics to persuade Berlin to make certain choices (like his reasoning that actors could not change out of blackface makeup fast enough to keep the show moving.) There was never any doubt about who would win this conflict. Berlin assumed the show's leadership like a military commander (e.g., his pre-show "order" in Washington), and many members of the company viewed him as a "father figure."[91] The show went overseas without Ezra Stone.

The Berlin-Stone conflict illuminates fundamental ideological rifts within the show's concept and structure. On a basic level the disagreement was an ego conflict familiar in show business. Berlin's insistence that no one besides himself should receive prominent billing and that no one but himself should do interviews about the show with the media rankled Stone, a radio star in his own right. In that Washington performance for the president, Stone had violated a basic principle of show business—disregarding the creator and director, and adding something not intended for the show. For Stone, it was the only way to vent his frustration at what he felt to be Berlin's suffocating authority. Anderson, in his book, also offered the plausible theory that Berlin knew "from experience that to have a show done your own way you've got to be in charge. He doesn't want stars and he doesn't want commissioned officers. He wants enlisted men so that nobody will pull rank. No Broadway stars, no Pentagon stars, either."[92] In other words, Berlin acted as the general of the production; thus Stone's infraction amounted to an offense worthy of court-martial.

On the overseas tour, another incident almost led to an actual court-martial, and it exposed a fundamental conflict over military hierarchy and show business values. Early on, Lieutenant Marc Daniels had been assigned to the *TITA* company as an executive officer to oversee its operations but to remain aloof from management of the actual show. (Daniels had been the one who neutralized the Washington Red Cross manager's bigotry.) Daniels brought real theatrical experience as well as military training to the job.[93] As Anderson relates, one day in Italy, when Berlin was away from the company, Daniels posted a sign calling for a rehearsal of a particular number.[94] When the director-choreographer Bob Sidney objected and took down the sign, Daniels ordered the sign back up and insisted on rehearsing the number. Sidney continued to protest, and Daniels ultimately ordered him to be sequestered in his quarters and to remain there. Both men pushed the issue to the point where Sidney was charged with "insubordination," which almost led to court-martial when another officer reported the incident outside the company. By then Berlin had returned—and ultimately resolved the matter by calling General Marshall and getting Sidney to deliver an apology to the lieutenant in front of the company. Berlin soothed the feelings of all involved, except for the officer who had reported the matter outside the company. That officer had violated one of Berlin's core principles: that *TITA* had autonomy within the military. Anderson called the whole incident "a dramatic reminder of the potency of his protection and the delicate balance of authority in the outfit when he was away."[95]

Berlin's authority in this production exceeded any other theatrical project he was ever involved in. Perhaps that's why he really wanted its story told. Years later, Alan Anderson set out to write such a book and contacted Berlin about it, but Berlin did not show interest in the project. "Why do you want to write a book about the show?" Anderson remembered him saying. "Nobody cares about that anymore. You'd be wasting your time."[96] Anderson published the book in 2004, and it remains an invaluable document of the show behind the scenes. Berlin himself had made several attempts to write the story of *This Is the Army*. His papers preserve a two-page mimeographed typescript titled "Proposed Outline for Book on Irving Berlin's 'This Is the Army,'" which was to include sixteen chapters plus a complete score of the show. The outline dates from the period of the overseas tour, for it bears the stamp: "Reviewed and Passed / U.S. Army / Feb. 1944 / Press Censor / E.T.O / U.S.A."[97] In one draft he began: "The story behind 'This is the Army' is as good as the show itself—that story should be written and I wish I could do it."[98]

Of course he never did it. For Berlin, the next project was always more important than remembering the one that came before. And his next project proved to be the one that most theatergoers remember him for. Moreover, instead of the all-male preserve of his army show, it was a compelling portrait of a unique American woman.

7

SOMETHING FOR THE GIRLS

• • •

ANNIE GET YOUR GUN, 1945–PRESENT

I hate that term "integrated score." . . . If you have a great song,
you can always integrate it into any show.
—Irving Berlin[1]

Although still sore from the Caesarean section that had brought her son into the world two days earlier, Ethel Merman took the call in her hospital bed. On the line was Dorothy Fields, who wanted just a few minutes to summarize a new musical comedy that she had conceived to bring Merman back to Broadway after a year's hiatus. Richard Rodgers and Oscar Hammerstein II, whom the Fieldses had approached to produce the show, were already excited about staging it. Fields herself was too excited to wait until Merman left the hospital. So Merman invited her up, adding a quip that she would repeat many times when recounting the story: "After all, I'm in stitches, and not with laughing." Fields hurried to Merman's side and summed up her vision of a musical based on the life of the sharpshooter Annie Oakley, who had earned world renown performing in Buffalo Bill's Wild West shows from 1885 to 1901.[2]

Fields had thought up the idea in "a flash" one recent August evening after hearing a woman describe a recent encounter with a soldier on leave. (In another version of the story, Fields hears it secondhand from her own husband.) The soldier had had a swath of medals across his chest for sharpshooting on Coney Island.[3] Dorothy's mind must have conjured one of the several famous photographs of Annie Oakley sporting a similar array across her blouse. Dorothy and her brother Herbert had honed their craft on several Merman vehicles in recent years, and Dorothy was already on the lookout for another—thus: Merman as Oakley. It was the only time, she recalled, that an idea came to her as if "from God."[4]

From a later vantage point, it seems like a strange time for such an epiphany. In the week of the meeting in Merman's hospital room, the world was changing profoundly in ways that Merman, the Fieldses, and Rodgers and Hammerstein could not avoid confronting daily on radio and in newspapers. "New Age Ushered" ran the *New York Times* front page headline on August 7, reporting the bombing of Hiroshima. "Nagasaki Flames Rage for Hours—Smoke Rises to 20,000 Feet Long After Atomic Bombing—Blast Visible Many Miles," announced the headline on August 10. Then, on August 12, the day after Merman gave birth, amid more news, a more reflective story appeared under the headline "The Past Four Months: Unequalled in History." Three days later, as Merman pondered Dorothy Fields's proposal, the *Times* front page showed a photo of President Truman surrounded by his cabinet under a banner headline announcing the Japanese surrender.[5] It is perhaps revealing that none of the key figures—Fields, Merman, or Rodgers—mentions these events when recalling "Annie Oakley"'s origins and early development. Yet the show that would be called *Annie Get Your Gun* was conceived in the midst of birth and death and the dramatic resolution of World War II. Indeed, dated from its conception, the show may be viewed as the first postwar musical comedy. And its songs would be written by a genuine war hero. But none of the key players knew it yet.

For if, in retrospect, some might be inclined to ask how a musical comedy could have meaning in the atomic age, the librettists and producers pondered a more pressing and pragmatic question: Who would compose the score? Rodgers himself did not want to do it, and in fact there was never a question that this would be another Rodgers and Hammerstein show. "The idea of our writing the score was never brought up," Rodgers recalled, "because neither Oscar nor I thought we were the right ones for it. We had been going in a certain direction with *Oklahoma!* and *Carousel*, and this did not seem to be along the same path."[6] (Ironically, *Oklahoma!* was the show to which the critics would compare *Annie Get Your Gun* most frequently.) The Fieldses envisioned a traditional musical comedy, a domain in which they had worked regularly with another songwriter, Cole Porter. Indeed, Porter's songs had helped define Merman's brassy stage persona, but his urbane and polysyllabic style would not be suitable for a rube like Annie, and, moreover, Dorothy planned to write the lyrics. Under the circumstances, the obvious candidate was Jerome Kern, whom Rodgers, Hammerstein, and Fields all esteemed, and with whom Hammerstein and Fields had worked closely in the past.[7] A month after Fields met Merman in the hospital, the *New York Times* announced that Kern, persuaded by Hammerstein, "one of his closest friends," would indeed compose the score.[8]

As it happened, Kern never had a chance to begin it. On November 2 he returned to New York from Hollywood to start work on "Annie Oakley" and to witness the revival of *Show Boat*, opening in January. On the morning of November 5, however, after reminding his wife of a lunch meeting with Dorothy Fields, he was walking down a Manhattan street and collapsed on the sidewalk. For the next few days he went in and out of a coma. He died of a cerebral hemorrhage on November 11, with Hammerstein at his side—in the same hospital where Fields had met with Merman three months earlier.[9] A private funeral service was quickly arranged for next day.[10] With a strong sense that the show must go on, however, Rodgers, Hammerstein, and Fields cast about for a new composer. Although Fields had planned to write the lyrics for the show's songs, she quickly relented when the collaborators mentioned the name of a show composer who always wrote both words and music. So the first call, probably within forty-eight hours of Kern's funeral, went to Irving Berlin.[11]

Berlin did not jump at the opportunity. He claimed he was "tired."[12] For more than two years, he had been zigzagging the globe, touring with *This Is the Army* and making occasional visits to Hollywood and New York. He had, in fact, just returned to New York from Hawai'i in late October, where he had appeared in the final performance of *This Is the Army*. Moreover, Berlin was by now an official war hero; he had received the Army Medal of Merit on September 1.[13] Now he was being asked to apply himself to a major project that was strikingly different from anything he had ever attempted.

Rodgers and Hammerstein laid out the plan with alacrity and conviction—a Merman show with a Fields script and Berlin's songs would be a surefire hit. Yet, as Rodgers recalled, "our enthusiasm barely made a dent."[14] Berlin had several reasons for begging off. Besides being tired, he was planning a new revue at the Music Box, tentatively titled "Tea Leaves," which the *Times* dubbed his "pet project."[15] Also, according to Rodgers, he resisted writing songs for a "book show" in the new era of musical theater that *Oklahoma!* had launched, feeling that a book would restrict his songwriting range.[16] He also said he did not feel qualified to write songs for the kind of "hillbilly" and "period" songs that the show would require.[17] On that point, Hammerstein cajoled the reluctant songwriter by saying all he had to do to summon the proper style was drop the "g's" on words ending in "-ing."[18] The producers sent Berlin a draft of the script and waited for him to think it over. Having voiced his doubts, Berlin let the matter drop. But on a Friday, as Berlin recalled, Rodgers called with another nudge: Joshua Logan would direct the show if Berlin wrote the score.[19] Logan, whom the savvy Rodgers and Hammerstein knew Berlin respected, could list several Rodgers shows to his credit and, more importantly, had been called in as a trusted advisor, and, briefly, a director, for *This Is the Army*.[20] With Rodgers and Hammerstein, the Fieldses, Merman, and Logan on board, the show was already accruing blockbuster potential.

So over a weekend, Berlin went to Atlantic City, one of his creative refuges over the past three decades. What happened next has become the stuff of legend, and accounts of Berlin's sweatshop exercise vary as to how many and what songs he drafted that weekend. Berlin himself cited two songs, plus three things that spurred his work: Merman's talent, the Fieldses' draft, and Rodgers and Hammerstein's support. Here's how Berlin recalled the events of that period, two decades after the fact:

> I read the first act again and over the weekend wrote two songs, "They Say It's Wonderful" and "Doin' What Comes Natur'lly." I then met with Dick and Oscar on Monday but was still playing it very cautiously and asked to think it over another week. Dick Rodgers, very rightly, said 'Why another week?' Having in mind the two songs I had already written, I said okay. It didn't take long to agree on terms. I was anxious to do it and Rodgers and Hammerstein wanted me to. The songs for the score came quickly and easily, looking back. I think the reason was because of the possibilities in the Fields' script, my association with Rodgers and Hammerstein, and, above all, writing songs for Ethel Merman. At a conference with Rodgers and Hammerstein in my office I sang for them for the first time "Doin' What Comes Natur'lly," "The Girl That I Marry," "They Say It's Wonderful," "You Can't Get a Man with a Gun," "I Got Lost in His Arms," "I'm an Indian Too," and I think one other. They were very enthusiastic.[21]

Rodgers recalled that Berlin came back from his weekend with three, not two, songs: "You Can't Get a Man with a Gun," "There's No Business Like Show Business," and "Doin' What Comes Natur'lly," only one of which corresponds to the songs in Berlin's story.[22] Barrett acknowledges that the number of songs he wrote that weekend "varies according to the teller," but that her father "came back with no less than three, maybe five, songs . . . the first always 'Doin' What Comes Natur'lly,'" plus "They Say

It's Wonderful," "The Girl That I Marry," and the two others that Rodgers named. "Feat enough," she added. "Or as he might say, a good weekend's work."[23]

The manuscripts in the Irving Berlin collection at the Library of Congress help to expand upon these accounts and to suggest why the song-count varies. If Berlin's precise memories of songs and order of events were sound, then the dated manuscripts came after that decisive weekend when Berlin wrote the first two, and perhaps more, songs. All of the dated material appears in a sixteen-day span from November 19 to December 4. The earliest is for a number that only Berlin mentions as part of the early batch of songs: "I Got Lost in His Arms," which appears on two melody lead sheets, one dated [Monday] November 19 and labeled "2nd," and another dated November 20. Material dated November 21 includes a lyric sheet for "I Got Lost in His Arms," a lead sheet and pencil draft of lyrics for "Moonshine Lullaby," and a lyric sheet for a song called "They Tell Me It's Wonderful," a working title that the Fieldses had planted in the act 1 draft of "Annie Oakley." What's surprising is that, of these three songs that mark the beginning of the written legacy of *Annie Get Your Gun*'s score, only "They Tell Me It's Wonderful" is identified in the Fieldses' script; the other two Berlin came up with on his own and only later found a place in the script.

By then we know that Berlin had been hooked, for Rodgers and Hammerstein quickly moved to make it public. On Wednesday, November 21, the *New York Times* announced that "Irving Berlin has come to rescue of 'Annie Oakley.'"[24] Assuming that Rodgers and Hammerstein would not release such an announcement to the *Times* until after Rodgers's final, successful efforts to convince Berlin at what he called a "Monday meeting," then that meeting would have taken place on November 19, and the legendary weekend must have been November 17–18. That would add two days to the period in which all the dated material appears, making a span of eighteen days— precisely the amount of time that Ethel Merman recalled that Berlin took to write the bulk of the score.[25] Thus the sources agree that Berlin dove into the score with remarkable energy for a man who had been so tired and diffident. Disparities persist about exactly which songs Berlin created (and in what order he created them) in that period, probably because a few songs—and perhaps all of them—stood in various stages of completion, worked out orally but not yet fully notated. But first, there was the book.

THE BOOK

Annie Get Your Gun now exists in two performing versions, one dating from 1966 and the other from 1999. Both of them represent significant revisions to the original 1946 script and score. Both have merits, but they obscure the expert dramaturgy of the Fieldses' original book and the way the script and songs addressed their historical moment.

The original book deftly balances and integrates two basic plots: a marriage plot and a show business plot. It was hardly a novel combination in musical comedy writing, but what made *Annie Get Your Gun* stand out was the quality of the book. The marriage plot revolves around the relationship of Frank Butler and Annie Oakley.

When they first meet, it's love at first sight for Annie but not for Frank, who reveals a fondness for the kind of traditional, dainty femininity that Annie clearly does not exhibit. Annie's victory over Frank in the sharpshooting contest gets the attention of both Frank and Buffalo Bill, who, by inviting her to join his Wild West, begins to weave the marriage plot to the show business plot. As they travel together (and with Annie serving as Frank's assistant) Annie and Frank grow closer. No sooner does Frank admit his love, however, than Annie rises to become the star attraction of the Wild West, thus displacing Frank and damaging his ego to the point where he leaves the show to join the competition, Pawnee Bill's Far East. As act 1 ends, then, the show business plot has opened up a rift in the relationship, and competition—between Frank and Annie, and between Buffalo Bill and Pawnee Bill—becomes the show's keynote.

In act 2 Annie has found great success in her career, but winning many medals and touring Europe leaves her unsatisfied, because she lacks love in her life and misses Frank. Moreover, the European tour turns out to have drained the finances of Buffalo Bill's venture. Returning to New York City, Bill and company find Pawnee Bill enjoying great celebrity and financial success. All are invited to a lavish party hosted by Pawnee Bill at the Hotel Brevoort. There, the plots begin to resolve. Members of Buffalo Bill's troupe propose to merge with Pawnee Bill, because, despite being broke, Buffalo Bill still enjoys greater prestige than his competitor. Combining the shows would bring both prestige and financial success to all. Annie likes the idea because it presents the possibility of reunion with Frank. That happens, too, but only after Annie and Frank stage a sharpshooting rematch. This time, however, Annie loses on purpose to preserve Frank's ego and thus ensure a happy ending to her marriage plot. The show ends, then, as cooperation and consensus trump competition.

Despite the book's expert dramaturgy, there are two problems that have clung to it, and both are integral to the show's double-plot structure. First is the notion that Annie must "lose" in the show business plot in order to "win" in the marriage plot. As Annie sings in Berlin's famous song that addresses that quandary: "You Can't Get a Man with a Gun," and that phrase, sung and spoken, recurs at key moments in the show. (The idea and title of the song were planted in the script by the Fieldses.)

Second, the catalytic figure in bringing about resolution in both plots is a Native American, the sympathetic but ultimately minstrelized figure of Sitting Bull. He speaks in the telegraphic style of stereotyped "Indian" stage dialect ("no put money in show business"), and he plays the familiarly stable, supportive role of the "stage Indian" of musical comedy days.[26] The big production number of act 1, described in the script as a "comedy Indian dance,"[27] is the ritual adoption ceremony in which Sitting Bull, aided by a large chorus of dancing Indians, adopts Annie as his daughter.

Annie's decision to lose the shooting match to win her love, and the show's characterization of Native Americans, have presented later productions with the difficult dilemma of remaining faithful to the show's flawless original structure or revising it to avoid distracting audiences from the comedic treatment of dated sensibilities. Producers and directors continue to be willing to confront that dilemma because the story, characters, and songs remain vivid and enduring. For historians and critics, meanwhile, the show's "problems" have posed rich challenges for analysis and interpretation of how it addressed its historical moment in 1946.

First, the plot trajectory traces an assimilation narrative, as Andrea Most has argued. From that perspective, Annie finds her identity, in love and work, through a talent that is portrayed as being fully realized in theatrical performance. Annie Oakley "sharpshooter" becomes not just an amateur talent developed for small change (selling small-animal meat to a hotel proprietor), but a professional role that brings great celebrity and social and financial reward.

More than that, however, Annie's story provides a comedic and historic enactment of the negotiation of women's place in the world that was occurring across America in the war and postwar years. In short, the plot may be seen as telling the story of Rosie the Riveter, the iconic image of women during World War II. Called upon to master what were seen as "masculine" assembly-line skills and enter the workforce during the war, thousands of women confronted a postwar world in which their skills were no longer welcomed in industry, and they were expected to leave their wartime jobs and retake their places as domestics, wives, and mothers when former soldiers returned to civilian lives and jobs.[28]

But what really accounts for the show's richness is that the two narrative archetypes weave together, making the whole greater the sum of its parts. The two perspectives come together because when Annie deliberately misses in the end, she is playing a *role*, highlighting that gender itself is a kind of performance.[29] That may be why the show has been increasingly viewed as proto-feminist—a view that remains in a distinct minority even as it comes closer to the sensibility of Dorothy Fields.[30] We shall see how Berlin's lyrics and music may help to focus and develop these ideas.

LYRICS

If the songs came "quickly and easily," as Berlin recalled, there may be another reason besides the ones he gave (star, script, and producers), which is that he seems to have instinctively disciplined his craft by deploying two of his favorite lyric-writing devices: the list and the antithesis. He uses these approaches with such flexibility and variety—and with such disparate musical styles—that it's easy to overlook how deeply they suffuse the score.

The list and the antithesis had been the stock-in-trade for songwriters for decades, but never had they been so consistently combined within a single show. Berlin established the pattern in the song he wrote first, "Doin' What Comes Natur'lly," inspired by Hammerstein's instant formula for writing "hillbilly" lyrics (drop the g's), and by a song cue that the Fieldses designated for Annie (to describe "her family and background"). The song comprises a roll call of Annie's extended family members—"pa and ma," Uncle Jed, Sister Sal, Grandpa Bill, Sister Lu, Cousin Nell, Sister Rose, and many more, none of whom ever appears in the show. And, in a series of vivid quatrains, Annie adds a wry comment on how each thrives (in courtship, drinking, music, petty theft, sex) without the benefit of formal education in a way that recalls the anti-Victorian "suggestive" songs of Berlin's early career:[31]

Uncle Jed has never read
An almanac on drinkin';
Still he's always on a spree
Doin' what comes natur'lly.

They are a hearty, frisky bunch:

Grandpa Bill lives on the hill
With someone he just married.
There he is at ninety-three
Doin' what comes natur'lly.

Cousin Nell appears to be an exception. For although Annie insists from the outset that "Folks like us could never fuss / With schools . . .," later she relates that Nell *did* attend school, and with notable success: "Cousin Nell can't add or spell / But she left school with honors." It remains unclear how Nell did it, but the lyrics imply that, by "doin' what comes natur'lly," she cheated.

The Uncle Jed and Cousin Nell passages, just quoted, contain one of Berlin's devices for emphasizing an antithetical relationship: the words *still* and *but*. Used as conjunctions, they signal a result that the facts do not necessarily support:

If you saw my pa and ma,
You'd know they had no learnin'.
Still they raised a family
Doin' what comes natur'lly.

Or else, in a humorous twist, the facts *do* predict the result:

Sister Sal, who's musical,
Has never had a lesson;
Still she's learned to sing off key
Doin' what comes natur'lly.

In this way, Berlin constructed "Natur'lly" by combining elements of the list song and the antithesis.

"You Can't Get a Man with a Gun," also among the batch of songs Berlin wrote in the first flush of inspiration, is a list song even more clearly structured by antithesis. Berlin builds each refrain with a series of Annie's descriptions of herself. She sums up her prowess with a gun, then, pivoting on the conjunction *but*, presents a contrasting image of her ineptness as a potential romantic partner:

I'm quick on the *trigger*,
With targets not much *bigger*
Than a pinpoint
I'm number <u>one</u>.
But my score with a *feller*
Is lower than a *cellar*—
Oh, you can't get a man with a <u>gun</u>.

The lyric structure thus mirrors the plot's basic tension: Annie's sharpshooter skills are not adaptable to seeking a mate, and Annie's embryonic rags-to-riches story clashes with the romantic demands of a musical comedy plot.[32] Yet Berlin, foreshadowing the plot's resolution, reinforces the relationship between those opposing narrative forces by writing couplets with a tightly controlled rhyme scheme: two pairs of internal rhymes (italicized above) linked by an end rhyme (underlined) and by the conjunction *but*, and closed off by a repetition of the monosyllabic title line. (The couplet's diction carries even more resonance: a near-rhyme with "score" and "lower" as well as a reverberating "-an" sound in "than," "can't," and "man."[33])

The song also features ingeniously monosyllabic punch lines that capture Annie's sense of humor, savvy, and self-knowledge: "you can't get a *hug* / from a *mug* with a *slug*," and "you can't shoot a *male* / in the *tail* like a *quail*," and "a man may be *hot* / but he's *not* when he's *shot*." Berlin sets each rhyming syllable on the downbeat for a comic overemphasis on the triple rhyme. Despite Berlin's reticence about writing a book show, the song reveals his perfect pitch for the situation. Annie might have sung a kind of wistful where-is-the-one-for-me torch song here, but it is too early. At this point in the show, comedy evokes empathy better than pathos. There will be time for a true torch song in act 2—one that also makes its point through antithesis: "I got lost / But look what I found."

Berlin develops a similar pattern in "I Got the Sun in the Morning," but the attitude and style are so different as to conceal the structural similarities in the lyrics.[34] (The title notably includes the "g" in "morning," revealing the distance Annie has come in literacy and worldly experience by the middle of act 2.) Berlin announces his approach in the first line's antithesis: "Taking stock of what I have and what I haven't." The verse sets up the expectation that Annie will make a two-column list, showing "a healthy balance on the credit side." The refrain's principal phrases begin, however, by listing items on the debit side: "Got no diamond, got no pearl," "Got no mansion, got no yacht," and "Got no checkbooks, got no banks." Each "debit" statement, however, finds its "balance on the credit side," pivoting on the word *still*, as in: "Still I think I'm a lucky girl," and "Still I'm happy with what I've got," and "Still I'd like to express my thanks." Berlin punctuates each of those phrases with the song's fundamental antithesis, "I got the sun in the morning / And the moon at night," which owes its imagery to yet another lyric-writing convention, the *Pollyanna weather song*—the device, most famously explored in "Blue Skies," that expresses a happy mood in imagery of pleasant weather.[35] The bridge takes up that contrast and sums up it in a rhyming couplet: "Sunshine gives me a lovely day, / Moonlight gives me the Milky Way." Chorus 2 preserves the pattern but omits the conjunction; by now, however, the structure is so clear the listener hardly needs the "still" to pick up on what's coming next.[36]

Berlin's starkest antithesis-driven list song appears in a song exploring another tried-and-true Broadway convention in fresh terms: the challenge duet "Anything You Can Do" for Annie and Frank. Each section of the refrain begins, like the other list songs, with a recurring phrase: "Anything you can (do, be, etc.) I can (do, be, etc.) better (or greater, etc.)," which sparks the other character to launch a fast, competitive exchange of antithetical phrases: "No you can't," "Yes I can." Berlin's papers preserve a typescript lyric sheet that contains an actual list of comparative adjectives for this song, including antithetical pairs in items 5–8:

[1] deeper
[2] lower
[3] faster
[4] writer [*sic*]
[5] brighter
[6] darker
[7] smaller
[8] bigger
[9] tougher.[37]

By now, the list technique appears to have become a short-order reflex, and the song, like many others, came with remarkable speed. Berlin drafted it in a taxicab after a meeting with Logan, Rodgers, and Hammerstein. As Logan recalled, in the meeting he had asked for a new duet for Frank and Annie, and Rodgers suggested a challenge duet. Berlin said "That's it!" and rushed out of the office. He called Logan within an hour and sang the song over the phone.[38]

Once recognized as a framework for his lyrics, the list can be found in almost every song in the show. "Colonel Buffalo Bill" is a ballyhoo that begins as a list of rhetorical questions announcing to an eager crowd the unique attractions of the Wild West show's star:

CHARLIE: Who's got the stuff that made the Wild West wild?
　　　　Who pleases ev'ry woman, man, and child?
　　　　Who does his best to give the customers a thrill?
CROWD: Who?
CHARLIE: Colonel Buff'lo Bill.

"I'm a Bad, Bad Man" introduces Frank by enumerating his illicit amorous adventures in several states in what amounts to a back-country catalog aria:

There's a girl in Tennessee
Who's sorry she met up with me.
Can't go back to Tennessee—
I'm a bad, bad man.
There's a girl in Omaha,
But I ran faster than her pa.
Can't go back to Omaha—
I'm a bad, bad man.

"I'll Share It All with You" develops the secondary romance between Tommy and Winnie by listing the qualities (instead of material possessions, which they lack) they will bring to their marriage:

My ear for music,
My feet for dancing,
My lips for kissing,
I'll share it all with you.

"My Defenses Are Down," marking the final stage of Frank's romantic conversion, has a bridge with a vivid list of character-specific similes showing how love can transform a powerful man:

Like a toothless, clawless tiger,
Like an organ grinder's bear,
Like a knight without his armor,
Like Samson without his hair.

"I'm an Indian Too," which forms the musical centerpiece of the act 1 ceremony dramatizing Annie's adoption by Sitting Bull, likewise grows from a simile-based list: "Like the Seminole, / Navajo, Kickapoo, / Like those Indians, / I'm an Indian too." The show's spiritual core, expressed in "There's No Business Like Show Business," takes off in a rapid-fire list of reasons that Annie should join the Wild West show: "The cowboys, the wrestlers, the tumblers, the clowns, / The roustabouts who move the show at dawn, / The music, the spotlight, the people, the towns, / Your baggage with the labels pasted on."[39] The refrain likewise develops a list of images extraordinary in their evocative specificity and disciplined simplicity: "Trav'ling through the country is so thrilling. / Standing out in front on opening nights. / Smiling as you watch the benches filling / And see your billing out there in lights."[40]

With a sure dramatic instinct, Berlin withholds the list technique in the show's most tender moments. Frank and Annie's song, "They Say It's Wonderful," serves

"There's No Business Like Show Business." Buffalo Bill, Charlie, and Frank (Ray Middleton) initiate Annie Oakley (Ethel Merman) into the world of professional performance in Annie Get Your Gun. Courtesy of Rodgers & Hammerstein, on behalf of the Estate of Irving Berlin.

Example 7.1. The "Merman sigh" figure.

7.1a. "They Say It's Wonderful."

It's won-der-ful,_____ it's won-der-ful,_____

7.1b. "I Got Lost in His Arms."

"There you go..._____ there you go."_____

as an apt exemplar of a type that Hammerstein had developed to perfection. In it, Berlin avoids the specificity he brings to the show's other lyrics, because Annie does not have firsthand experience of what she is singing about. Annie's bedtime song for her little brother and sisters, "Moonshine Lullaby," must create a mood more than it needs to communicate specific imagery; and her torch song, "I Got Lost in His Arms," distills her sadness over losing Frank. Berlin seems to avoid the list in songs conjuring genuine sentiment or even pathos. That Annie sings all three songs underscores Berlin's sensitivity to the need to develop her character. The two love songs ("They Say It's Wonderful" and "I Got Lost in His Arms") even share a characteristic musical trait that might be termed the *Merman sigh*—never before heard in the shows of Gershwin or Porter—comprising a three-note falling dotted-rhythm figure on a repeated word or phrase: "wonderful, wonderful" and "there you go, there you go" (see ex. 7.1).[41] If, as Merman put it, "Irving Berlin's lyrics made a lady out of me," then these are the songs that accomplished the feat. "They showed that I had a softer side," she wrote.[42] And she was glad of it: "my hard-boiled Tessie type had become a cliché character. The gangster moll, the hey-hey girl, was good in the twenties and thirties but people didn't care about her any more."[43] Ethan Mordden called Berlin's job nothing less than the "reinvention of Ethel."[44] (The job began very early in the writing process, since these are also the three songs with the earliest dated material among the surviving manu-scripts.) In other words, in the context of her whole career to this point, the Ger-shwins invented Merman, Porter defined her, and Berlin *re*fined her. He did it with music.

MUSIC

The songs suggest that what Berlin came up with stands far from the "hillbilly" or "period" score he had thought he had to write. In fact, what might be called a "hill-billy" style surfaces in only three numbers stacked close to the beginning (and at least two of them stand among the first he wrote): "I'm a Bad, Bad Man" (See ex. 7.2a), "Doin' What Comes Natur'lly" (ex. 7.2b), and "You Can't Get a Man with a Gun" (ex. 7.2c). The songs share several traits: repetitive, folksy melodies made up of diatonic scales and triadic figures, a relatively small range, and straightforward patternlike rhythms in quarter notes and half notes, with an occasional dotted rhythm for variety. Here and there are touches of the dropped-g country diction that Hammerstein called for, but Berlin does not even apply it consistently. He writes "Doin'," of course, but in the second chorus of "You Can't Get a Man with a Gun" Berlin retains the g's for the end-rhyming couplet "I'm cool, brave, and *daring*, / To see a lion *glaring*." (And in the second act, Annie sings "I got sun in the *morning*," not "mornin'"—a word that her country cousin Curly McClain *does* sing.) Once Berlin had loaded the opening with the appropriate hillbilly flavor, he seems to have been satisfied to have set the show's tone and moved onto other styles. Put another way, it's as if Berlin, having created and mastered his own brand of "hillbilly" style (as he had done with ragtime more than three decades earlier), gained the confidence to become more flexible in his approach.

Indeed, just as significant as his efforts at "hillbilly" material are the other song styles Berlin deploys. The quickstep march for Charlie's opening ballyhoo "Colonel Buffalo Bill," associates the Colonel with another turn-of-the-century showman with a military background, his contemporary John Philip Sousa. Frank's "The Girl

Example 7.2. Berlin's "hillbilly" style.

7.2a. "I'm a Bad, Bad Man."

7.2b. "Doin' What Comes Natur'lly."

7.2c. "You Can't Get a Man with a Gun."

that I Marry" links the waltz style with a vision of domesticated love—an impulse that goes back to Berlin's earliest waltzes, such as "When I Lost You." The march and waltz styles are at least apt for the period setting. More remarkable in this context are the songs that swing, which give *Annie Get Your Gun* a perhaps surprising link to the title song of Berlin's 1940 show, *Louisiana Purchase*. The opening phrase of "Moonshine Lullaby," in fact, shares several traits of the earlier song's initial gesture, including its start off the downbeat (as in Berlin's *ur*-rhythm song "Alexander's Ragtime Band"), its third-beat blue note (flat 7th), and its contour and rhythmic profile. (In a swing-style performance, the dotted-eighth / sixteenth rhythms of "Moonshine Lullaby" are functionally equivalent to the eighth notes in "Louisiana Purchase," which beg to be swung.) (See ex. 7.3.) The syncopated riffs of "I'll Share It All with You" (verse and bridge) and "I Got the Sun in the Morning" (refrain) stem from the same seed idea (ex. 7.4), derived from the cakewalk rhythm, but their melodic and harmonic contexts, as well as a slight change in rhythmic emphasis, disguise their connections.

Winnie and Tommy's other song, "Who Do You Love? I Hope," likewise grows from a riff-like phrase, with space for syncopated instrumental fills between melodic statements (ex. 7.5). "Anything You Can Do" shows beyond a doubt that Berlin had absorbed the swing style. Not only is the entire melody rooted in swing (even when singers "straighten" the rhythm) but the whole "no you can't, yes I can" argument amounts to a big-band, call-and-response out-chorus that finds itself perfectly at home in a challenge duet (ex. 7.6).

Almost all of the swing-style numbers came into the score relatively late in the writing process. We know from Logan's memoir that "Anything You Can Do" was among the last songs Berlin wrote for the score, and we also know that "I'll Share It All with You," "Who Do You Love? I Hope," and "I Got the Sun in the Morning" are never listed among the first batch. This reinforces the notion that, as Berlin grew more confident in his ability to write for a book show, he let go of the self-imposed "hillbilly" and "period" confines and embraced contemporary music, respecting an impulse that had charged his earliest songwriting efforts. In this way, *Annie Get Your Gun* joins a lineage that goes back to Berlin's first show. Although *Annie Get Your Gun*

Example 7.3. Swinglike openings.

7.3a. "Moonshine Lullaby."

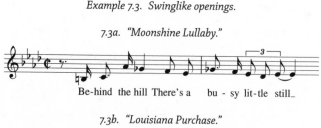

Be-hind the hill There's a bu - sy lit-tle still.

7.3b. "Louisiana Purchase."

Lou - i - si - an - a Pur - chase___

Example 7.4. Syncopated riffs.

7.4a. "I'll Share It All with You," verse.

What is mine, dear, will be yours,

7.4b. "I'll Share It All with You," refrain, bridge.

Some-day, hon - ey, I'll have mon - ey—

7.4c. "I Got the Sun in the Morning," refrain.

Got no dia - mond, got no pearl,

Example 7.5. "Who Do You Love? I Hope," refrain.

Who do you love? I hope—   Who would you kiss? I hope—

mp

Example 7.6. "Anything You Can Do," refrain.

Annie

An-y note you_ can reach, I____ can go high - er. I can sing an - y-thing high

- er than you._   Yes I can._   Yes I can._

Frank

No you can't. ___   No you can't. ___   No you can't.

could hardly be more different from *Watch Your Step*, the two shows share a similar relationship to one of their source styles: in 1945–46, swing occupied a position in American musical culture comparable to ragtime in 1914. Both styles were in their second decade of popularity, had entered the mainstream of American popular music, had been largely deracinated from their roots in black music, and would soon be considered passé.[45]

Something else puts distance between Berlin's *Annie Get Your Gun* songs and "hillbilly" or "period" songs: harmonic richness. One of Berlin's favorite voice-leading devices recurs frequently: a descending chromatic line in the bass and/or inner voices. In "You Can't Get a Man with a Gun," the melody and a chromatic inner voice even merge briefly (on the words "can't get a") as the tune moves toward a half-cadence on the phrase: "But my score with a feller / Is lower than a cellar—/ Oh, you can't get a man with a gun" (see ex. 7.7a). The insistent cakewalk rhythms in the verse of "There's No Business like Show Business" gain harmonic depth from chromatic lines in parallel thirds between the bass line and inner voice (ex. 7.7b). In the chorus, the sweeping scalar figure on "Yesterday they told you you would not . . ." moves smoothly to a melodic sequence on a falling-third figure supported by a similar parallelism between bass and inner voice on the phrase ". . . not go far, / That night you open and there you are" (ex. 7.7c). The incantatory melody of "I Got Lost in His Arms" is enriched by its molten inner voices, and by the chromatically charged harmony (founded, again, on descending chromatic voices) at the melodic climax: "And I said to my heart / As it foolishly kept jumping all around . . ." (ex. 7.7d). In "They Say It's Wonderful," Berlin incorporates a descending chromatic line into the melody itself. (In ex. 7.7e, the C-Cb-Bb descent in the refrain's main phrase, on the boldfaced syllables of "**It's** won-der-**ful, so they say**," forms part of what Allen Forte identifies as one of "two planes of melodic activity" in the song).[46] Among Berlin's most unusual and memorable harmonic notions appears in "I Got the Sun in the Morning," where the refrain begins on a dominant chord with a flatted fifth in the bass, creating an oscillating chromatic effect as the chord alternates with the tonic (ex. 7.8). Most unusual of all is the Tommy-Winnie duet "I'll Share It All with You," whose refrain begins with a series of chromatically descending parallel seventh chords (ex. 7.9), a harmonic passage so unusual that Alec Wilder finds it outside the scope of a theater or pop song—the kind of song "one writes . . . for one's friends in Jim and Andy's, the jazz musician's bar."[47]

Berlin also adds harmonic color through the familiar device of mediant modulation. The verse of "There's No Business Like Show Business," for example, suddenly shifts from C to E major on Frank's phrase "The sawdust and the horses and the smell." "Doin' What Comes Natur'lly" likewise introduces a sudden mediant shift from C to E for the words "My uncle out in Texas / Can't even write his name; / He signs his checks with X's, / But they cash them just the same." "My Defenses Are Down" modulates briefly to the mediant (from A to F major) in the bridge for the beginning of its sequence of similes. Together, harmonic richness and a swing-based rhythmic approach reinforce a fact about the plot and setting to which we'll return: behind the libretto's historical "Western" veneer stands a story saturated in the contemporary New York lives of its creators.

Example 7.7. *Descending chromatic lines in bass and inner voices.*

7.7a. *"You Can't Get a Man with a Gun."*

(*continued*)

"ANNIE OAKLEY, FIRST DRAFT"

If Berlin ignored his own considerable skill in explaining why the score came "quickly and easily," he did acknowledge the influence of the script—that "first draft" of act 1 that came into his hands soon after Kern's death. So potent was the script for Berlin that he offered to reduce his own percentage of the show's gross earnings in order to raise Herbert and Dorothy Fields's share to an equal level.[48] The script played a key role in inspiring all of his quick early work because of those "possibilities" that he mentioned. In fact, the "possibilities" came in the form of eleven numbered song cues plus suggested reprises, some with titles and some with descriptions about what the song should accomplish dramatically (see table 7.1, pp. 246–47).[49]

Under different circumstances, such cues might look like a remarkably aggressive imposition on an experienced theater songwriter like Berlin, but we must remember that when they were written, they were intended for Jerome Kern and Dorothy Fields. So the song cues were, in effect, Dorothy's notes to herself. Yet in most cases, Berlin wrote the song suggested in the first draft even though he was not its intended recipient. Indeed, the Fieldses even supplied the title in several cases, as in "You Can't Get a Feller with a Gun" and "They Tell Me It's Wonderful." Berlin adopted the titles, but in both cases characteristically replaced a two-syllable term with a monosyllable: "Man" for "Feller" and "Say" for "Tell Me."

7.7b. "There's No Business like Show Business," verse.

(continued)

Keeping in mind that by the time Berlin signed on, he was joining a project that was well under way, we can see that it posed an unusual collaborative challenge. The circumstances dictated that Berlin had to fit songs into an existing structure already worked out by the Fieldses. That did not lend itself to the kind of give-and-take that marked the Rodgers and Hammerstein collaboration, or any kind of integrated project for that matter—in this age when the term *integration* was Broadway's catchword. Some have viewed *Annie Get Your Gun* as failing to match up with the R&H model, but it is important to remember that Berlin was writing shows three decades before Rodgers and Hammerstein ever teamed up on anything, so their work never served as his chief model, although *Annie Get Your Gun* provides evidence that Berlin and the Fieldses may have been paying attention to *Oklahoma!* in particular—a connection that will be explored in greater detail below.

Coming from a songwriter whose chief successes had been in the revue, not the book show, *Annie Get Your Gun* is best construed as an aesthetic balance that adheres

7.7c. *"There's No Business like Show Business," refrain.*

Charlie

Buffalo Bill

Yes-ter-day they told you you would not go far—___ That

night you o - pen and there you are—___

(*continued*)

to Berlin's values from his earliest days: that is, simply, an approach that aims to have it both ways, preserving the individual integrity and independence of the song module and the dramatic integrity that comes from placing that module in a vivid theatrical context. That at least eleven of the show's fourteen vocal numbers can be, and have been, extracted from the show and sung alone, testifies to its success in these terms. (That rate of extraction cannot be claimed for any Rodgers and Hammerstein show, with the possible exception of *South Pacific*.)

The extant materials for the show help to throw Berlin's values into relief. In particular, looking more closely at the "Annie Oakley" first-act draft in light of the final version reveals that Berlin's numbers both filled orders in the script and drove revisions to the script, inspiring a tighter show with fewer spoken lines and fewer jokes. And they gave the show a more pointed focus on romance and show business, the twin impulses that drive the characters and the plot.

For cue number 1, in which Buffalo Bill's manager, Charlie, ballyhoos the Wild West show to an excited crowd, the Fieldses wrote "Charlie and Ensemble (in which he tells the customers what they will see in the show . . .)," and Berlin answered the call with "Colonel Buffalo Bill." Yet while the song filled an order in the script, it also inspired a notable change. In the first draft, the Fieldses gave Charlie a long speech with one-liners and some banter with his audience before the song cue. After Berlin wrote the song, however, the Fieldses tightened Charlie's speech to a crisp twenty words: "Ladies and Gentlemen, opening tonight at the Cincinnati Fair Grounds for four days only! The one and only Buffalo Bill!" Here and elsewhere, the song got to the point and better conveyed what the Fieldses had sought in words alone.

7.7d. *"I Got Lost in His Arms."*

said   to my heart   As it fool-ish-ly kept jump-ing all a - round,___

7.7e. *"They Say It's Wonderful."*

Annie

They say that   fall-ing in love is   won - der - ful,___   It's

won - der - ful,___   so they   say.___

Example 7.8. *"I Got the Sun in the Morning," refrain.*

Got   no dia - mond,   got   no pearl,__

Example 7.9. "I'll Share It All with You," refrain.

Cues 2 through 5 reveal that, already in the first draft, the Fieldses aimed to throw focus on the show's male and female protagonists, Frank and Annie, first separately and then together. Number 2 introduces Frank, and the indication "Frank and Girls" suggests that the writers chiefly wanted to establish Frank as a ladies' man. Berlin responded with "I'm a Bad, Bad Man." Number 3 introduces Annie through a song "in which she tells about her family and background." The countrified list song "Doin' What Comes Natur'lly" fit the bill. For number 4, soon after Frank and Annie meet, the Fieldses suggest a duet called "What Am I Doing?" at whose conclusion they write, "we feel that Annie has 'struck out.'" Although Berlin did not write a *duet* called "What Am I Doing?" he still drew inspiration from the libretto draft for the *solo* that he did write. In the lines leading up to the song, Frank begins to describe a vision of his ideal woman, one who is "pink and soft." The line got cut from the script when Berlin plucked it out of the dialogue, reversed the words, and used it for his song's initial simile "The girl that I marry will have to be / As *soft and as pink* as a nursery." Again, Berlin's song takes a "possibility" planted in the script and makes it vivid. Here, the situation offered another chance to write an antithesis-based list song, one that contrasts the qualities of Frank's future "girl" with the one right in front of him. But Berlin knew better in this case: by focusing entirely on Frank's vision in the song, he built antithesis into the scene. Frank exits, and Annie, now alone, sings the song that suggests she has "struck out." The Fieldses summed up the feeling in the cue phrase "You Can't Get a Feller with a Gun." Berlin, master of the monosyllable, took the "feller" and turned him into a "man."

In summary, the four-song sequence from "I'm a Bad, Bad Man" through "You Can't Get a Man"—already embedded in the Fieldses' draft—throws a decisive spotlight on

Table 7.1. From "Annie Oakley" to *Annie Get Your Gun*, act 1 cues (bold indicates songs not indicated or not specifically called for in the draft)

	"Annie Oakley," act 1 "first draft" (LC-IBC Box 69, Folder 2) Song cues in Fields script (finished by Nov. 8, 1945)	*Annie Get Your Gun*, act 1 Berlin songs (composed after mid-Nov. 1945)
1	"Charlie and Ensemble (in which he tells the customers what they will see in the show . . .)"	"Colonel Buffalo Bill"
2	"Frank and Girls (including Winnie) (Frank starts the number with Winnie. During the dance, Winnie sees Tommy, calls to him. Tommy joins the number. Winnie and Tommy exit, leaving Frank with the Girls and perhaps the dancers to finish. All exit on the dance.)"	"I'm a Bad, Bad Man"
3	"Annie. (In which she tells about her family and background. At a point in the number the Children leave. Annie finishes singing to Wilson. Both remain after song.)"	"Doin' What Comes Natur'lly"
4	"(There will be a further cue into: 'WHAT AM I DOING?') (Number IV:DUET: Annie and Frank) (At the conclusion of the number, (on stage) we feel that Annie has 'struck out!')"	**"The Girl that I Marry"**
5	"You Can't Get a Feller with a Gun!"	"You Can't Get a Man with a Gun"
	"Annie exits after the number. Now we begin a musical build for Buffalo Bill's entrance. It might be an exciting variation on Number I. . . ."	"Entrance of Buffalo Bill" ["Colonel Buffalo Bill" instrumental reprise]

(continued)

Table 7.1. (*continued*)

	"Annie Oakley," act 1 "first draft" (LC-IBC Box 69, Folder 2) Song cues in Fields script (finished by Nov. 8, 1945)	*Annie Get Your Gun*, act 1 Berlin songs (composed after mid-Nov. 1945)
6	"Quartette—Annie, Charlie, Frank, and Buffalo Bill (As they sing the Traveler closes behind them.)"	"There's No Business Like Show Business"
7	Duet "They Tell Me It's Wonderful"	"They Say It's Wonderful"
	"They Tell Me It's Wonderful" reprise	**"Moonshine Lullaby"**
8	"Winnie, Tommy, and Ensemble. The song tells a bit about the rivalry of the two cities [Minneapolis and St. Paul]. They hop from the platform and shake hands with the cityfolks. The number resolves into a dance for the ensemble, Tommy and Winnie. The two exit after the number."	**"I'll Share It All with You"**
9	"Further cue into: Number 9: Annie and Ensemble" [As Annie stares at her picture on the poster]	**"There's No Business Like Show Business" reprise (originally "Take It in Your Stride")**
10	"Tough Row to Hoe"	**"My Defenses Are Down"**
11	Annie, preceded by "Indian ritual" with "singing to the beat of several tom-toms. . . . The song is followed by a tribal dance in which Annie and Sitting Bull engage. It is done for comedy as well as production. It is a vigorous, exhausting routine."	"Ceremonial Chant," "I'm an Indian Too," and "Dance"
	"You Can't Get a Feller with a Gun!" [brief reprise]	"You Can't Get a Man with a Gun" [brief reprise]

the two protagonists, tracks the unrequited early phase of their relationship, and captures the basic conflict facing our leading lady. In the context of the act 1 first draft, Berlin's score shows that he distilled and reinforced the dramatic and comedic thrust of that sequence. Heard as distinct yet related modules, the songs heighten our expectation that the show's leading man and woman will answer the demands of comedy and ultimately get together.

As experienced script writers, the Fieldses knew that they would need to cover a set change from scene one's hotel exterior to scene two's train interior, so they inserted a number to be sung before the traveler curtain. Described in the draft simply as "Quartette" for Annie, Charlie, Frank, and Buffalo Bill, the cue says nothing about what the Fieldses intended for the number. What has just happened, of course, is that Buffalo Bill has invited Annie to join his show, and the dialogue leading into the song sharpens our sense that a whole new world is opening up for her:

> FRANK: Have you ever been away from home before?
> ANNIE: Uh-uh!
> CHARLIE: Have you ever been to a show?
> ANNIE (*Starry eyed*): Uh-uh.
> BUFFALO BILL: Have you ever seen a railroad train?
> ANNIE: No. Not never.
> (*NUMBER VI: Quartette—Annie, Charlie, Frank and Buffalo Bill*)
> (*As they start to sing the Traveler closes behind them*)

The two lines leading into the cue suggest that perhaps the Fieldses may have envisioned a train number here. The song that Berlin wrote, however, identifies the key element in that sequence and pulls it out for further elaboration, and thus the transitional "quartette" became "There's No Business Like Show Business." And the Fieldses duly adjusted the script to set up the song (stage directions deleted):

> FRANK: Have you ever been away from home before?
> ANNIE: Do I gotta leave home?
> BUFFALO BILL: Sure, we travel all over the country.
> FRANK: Have you ever been on a railroad train?
> ANNIE: Uh huh.
> FRANK: Do you know anything about show business?
> ANNIE: Show business? What's show business?

The song thus begins as an answer to a question in the dialogue, yet it remains eminently detachable and continues to be one of the show's most extractable modules.

When Annie joins the Wild West show, the plot opens up both her romantic and professional opportunities. Frank now sees Annie in a new light, and the Fieldses wrote a cue for a song called "They Tell Me It's Wonderful" to mark a new stage in their relationship. As he substituted "say" for "tell me," Berlin answered the need for a type of number in which Oscar Hammerstein II had excelled: a kind of number that might be termed the *conditional love duet*, a song in which a couple covers their attraction in a series of qualifications, as in "Make Believe" (*Show Boat*), "People Will Say We're in Love" (*Oklahoma!*), and "If I Loved You" (*Carousel*).[50] *Conditional love duet* is my term for a type of theater song in which the situation reveals that members of the putative couple (or at least one person in it) have already shown interest in the other, while there remains some reason (social, economic, previous commitment, speed of attraction) dictating that the romantic impulse cannot or should not be admitted. In the song, Berlin's phrase "they say" allows Annie to hide her feelings behind a veneer of hearsay, and Frank, who claims to know about love because he has "been there once or twice," hides his feelings by assuming the role of an instructor rather than a romancer. That idea was planted in the script, yet nothing in the script suggests the lyricism and harmonic richness that Berlin brought to the number. The result might have been more at home in an elegant 1930s Astaire-Rogers setting than in a busy railroad train headed west in the late nineteenth century. In short, while the song module fits snugly into the plot, its lyrics and music encourage extraction. Indeed, as the show continues, the numbers increasingly sound more like music in contemporary New York than turn-of-the-century Ohio or anywhere else.

Despite some telling changes, what we have seen so far is that Berlin's songs answered specific demands and cues in the script draft. In three later cues, Berlin wrote a different song in response to cues the Fieldses provided in the draft.

If we look at those spots and compare the first draft's cues with the songs that Berlin wrote, we can see more clearly how Berlin's sensibility redirected the script and characters. For example, in the summary of cue number 8, the Fieldses had suggested a song about the rivalry between the Twin Cities—perhaps conceived as a challenge number for a split ensemble in the spirit of *Oklahoma!*'s "The Farmer and the Cowman." Yet in the final script, the Fieldses reduced the twin-cities competition to a pair of signs, one saying "What are you doing in St. Paul?" The other: "Buffalo Bill opens in Minneapolis today." The reason? Here, Berlin shifted his sights from the urban landscape to two figures within it and wrote the whimsically romantic duet "I'll Share It All with You." The number focuses a musical spotlight on the secondary couple, Tommy and Winnie. Lacking material possessions, they sing about having nothing but their love to share. Berlin might well have written a simple song for such a young, naïve pair, but instead he gave them a rangy, syncopated tune over a series of chromatically descending seventh chords, as we have seen. As with "They Say It's Wonderful," the song's lyrics match character while the music invites extraction. Unlike "They Say It's Wonderful," it is a not a ballad but a rhythm song. Yet in each case, the song both suits and transcends the script's demands.

Yet another number sharpens the focus on romantic feeling in a way not suggested in the script draft. Although the script does plant the idea of Frank's romantic reversal, Berlin hones Frank's emotional shift by writing another song not indicated in the Fieldses' draft. (The first was "The Girl that I Marry.") "My Defenses Are Down" marks the complete reversal of Frank's feelings. The number helps to justify "They Say It's Wonderful" as a preparation for Frank's change but maintains a light, comic touch. We can only speculate what kind of song the Fieldses had in mind with the title "A Tough Row to Hoe." In the lines preceding the song cue in the first draft, Annie asks Frank: "Will ye watch and tell me if'n I done good?" He responds: "The audience will tell you. But, don't forget, Honey. Bull's eye every time. Ten out of ten!" And Annie answers, "What d'ye mean? TWELVE outa ten!" It is unclear what the Fieldses intended for this number, but the title and dialogue point to a song about show business, not love, perhaps a song about how hard it is to achieve perfection and to please an audience. In the final version of the script, the Fieldses ratcheted up the romantic intensity. Just before Annie goes off to perform, Frank and Annie trade hints about marriage, and Frank kisses her. These clear signs of his love prepare us for "My Defenses Are Down."

"Moonshine Lullaby," the other act 1 song that Berlin conceived without a cue in the first draft, is a special case. Although it does not develop the romance, it certainly helps to develop Annie's character. The title phrase—an ingenious, and ingenuous, spin on moonlight imagery that would otherwise be apt for a lullaby—appears at a point where the Fieldses' first draft indicates an immediate solo reprise of "They Say It's Wonderful." Berlin's choice to place "Moonshine Lullaby" here helps to round out Annie's character and gives her a more maternal relationship with her little brother and sisters. It shows that Annie does not dwell on her romantic attachment when it's time to take care of the kids. Even so, the song invites empathy for the show's love interest. It's one of those songs that revealed Merman's "softer side." By showing Annie's uniquely nurturing style, the song encourages the audience to become even more invested in a positive outcome for her blossoming romantic impulses. It also reveals Berlin again tapping the wellsprings of minstrelsy: Annie's solo gets backing vocals from a trio of black (but not blackface) helpers: a trainman, a waiter, and a porter. On the train, then, her concern for the children joins with her empathy for the Native American performers and her performance with African American support in a way that suggests that the writers saw this as a way to reveal her common touch.

Only one song that Berlin wrote in response to the act 1 draft got cut before the show's opening. It was intended for the scene in which Annie first glimpses her name and image on a poster advertising her appearance in Buffalo Bill's Wild West show. Here, in a song called "Take It in Your Stride," just before her debut, we find Annie balancing pride and humility in yet another instance of an antithesis-driven list song ("There'll be ups and there'll be downs; / There'll be smiles and there'll be frowns"). Like "They Say It's Wonderful" and "I'll Share It All with You," this number could stand on its own, and its style, a syncopated, medium-tempo swing number, begs for extraction even as it suits the show. Ultimately the song was cut in favor of a reprise of what the collaborators began to see as one of the show's potential hits: "There's No Business Like Show Business."

In general, the Fieldses' script draft—both the act 1 draft, and the draft of the later acts—is edgier than the final version. It withholds romantic development more in the style of an Astaire-Rogers film, where the principal couple's interactions are charged with a sharp, if comic, antagonism, and where, of course, Fields and Kern had already known great success with songs such as "A Fine Romance" and "The Way You Look Tonight." When Berlin came onto the project, the humor softened, the romances came into stronger focus, and *show business* became a catchword summing up the world in which the characters lived, loved, fought, and came back together.

A choice that all the collaborators seemed to have agreed upon was to strip away the old musical comedy convention of the elaborate act-1 reprise finaletto, which Berlin had used as recently as *Louisiana Purchase*. The finaletto, a keystone of 1920s musical comedy that continued to flourish in the 1930s, followed a general formula: it was an extended number developing the plot through music, in which several numbers are partially reprised, sometimes in rapid succession and with revised lyrics to fit the situation. The situation itself involved maximum confusion and an apparent mismatching of couples or a misunderstanding within the principal romantic couple. In short, the finaletto was operatically conceived, and its purpose and conventions

Annie Oakley (Ethel Merman) in show business. Courtesy of Rodgers & Hammerstein, on behalf of the Estate of Irving Berlin.

hark back all the way to Italian opera buffa of the latter half of the eighteenth century. Its deletion from *Annie Get Your Gun* represents another way that the show stripped away musical comedy formula in the post-*Oklahoma!*, postwar age. Berlin and the Fieldses preserve the substance of the finaletto without all the musico-dramatic fuss. Rather than an extended pastiche we get dialogue, underscoring, and a single line of lyric and melody of "You can't get a man with a gun" that sums up Annie's basic quandary and the show's narrative tension between professional ambition and romantic fulfillment. In *Annie Get Your Gun*, we witness Berlin abandoning the last remnant of the operatic impulse—channeled into musical comedy convention—that had fueled his musical theater work over three decades. Giving up the finaletto, indeed, manifests perhaps the principal means by which *Annie Get Your Gun*, as Ethan Mordden put it, corrects the "mistakes" of traditional musical comedy—a kind of cleansing ritual inspired chiefly by *Oklahoma!*[51]

AFTER *OKLAHOMA!*

Since the opening of *Annie Get Your Gun*, much has been made of its connections to *Oklahoma!* Yet such connections have not been overemphasized so much as they have been underexplored. By being more specific about the comparison, we might open up opportunities to explore other stylistic models and sources. Perhaps the only obvious link is the general relationship between their settings: historical, instead of contemporary, and largely non–New York—though *Annie Get Your Gun* is more urban than it has been given credit for. (Three of act 2's four scenes are set in Greater New York City.) The plots share a basic foundation: in both, two opposing forces (farmer and cowman, Buffalo Bill and Pawnee Bill) must join together for the greater good, and that larger resolution forms the backdrop for—and facilitates—the principal romance. At least a couple of songs are cousins to songs in *Oklahoma!*: "My Defenses are Down" and "It's a Scandal" both feature a principal male character with male chorus singing about being led into monogamy, though Frank and Ali Hakim have different roles in the plot, and Frank enjoys the feeling much more than Ali Hakim. And "They Say It's Wonderful" serves a purpose similar to that of "People Will Say We're in Love"—both are conditional love songs that mark a crucial moment in the principal couple's romance. One might even point to the rising scale at a prominent moment in the show's respective anthems: the bracing introduction to the song "Oklahoma" and, in "There's No Business Like Show Business," on the line "Everything about it is appealing."

Critics almost never made such specific comparisons when they repeatedly cited *Oklahoma!* as a reference point for *Annie Get Your Gun*. And if the association was prompted by the Rodgers and Hammerstein connection or by the shows' Western period flavor, no critic mentioned it. Rather, the critics seem concerned more generally to determine the extent to which *Annie Get Your Gun* matched *Oklahoma!*'s standard of *quality*. Above all, whether summoning *Oklahoma!* in order to praise or to find fault with *Annie Get Your Gun*, the reviews collectively strike a keynote of continuity: *Annie Get Your Gun* was a *successor*. The comparison began even before the show hit New York. Even though the *Philadelphia Inquirer* claimed that "it isn't another *Oklahoma!*," it still found that show to be the nearest point of comparison, and it invoked *Oklahoma!* not to render judgment but to emphasize how much *Annie Get Your Gun* depends on a star, "for some other star would be unthinkable as a successor to this Annie Oakley."[52] Ironically, that claim would be proven wrong repeatedly over the next half century and beyond.

Reviews of opening night continued to invoke *Oklahoma!*, but always with a different spin.[53] "Not since one March night in 1943, at the St. James Theatre, have I had so high a musical time on Broadway," claimed Robert Garland in the *Journal-American*. The *Herald Tribune* mentioned the connection in order to deny it: "Comparisons with 'Oklahoma!' are neither necessary nor in any sense invidious. 'Annie Get Your Gun' is all of a piece, as fresh as a daisy and a delight that is certain to become a hardy Broadway perennial." Berlin's score held up particularly well in the comparison. The *New York Enquirer* echoed that general comparison and added that "the score is the most listenable since . . . 'Oklahoma.'"[54] The *Brooklyn Eagle* was more specific: "Only Miss Merman and the music will be of advantage to those who want to compare it with the 'Oklahomas' and the 'Carousels.'" *Dance Magazine* drew a similarly sharp contrast by placing *Annie Get Your Gun* in a different genre (another theme that comes up in some reviews): "Irving Berlin . . . has written no folk opera to rival his producers' own *Oklahoma!* or *Carousel* . . . doing what naturally comes to him." It continued by making another important distinction, rarely mentioned in the *Annie Get Your Gun/Oklahoma!*

Annie Get Your Gun, *final tableau. Courtesy of Rodgers & Hammerstein, on behalf of the Estate of Irving Berlin.*

comparison: "You'll find no *Oklahoma!* folk-accented routines nor attempts at the *Carousel* kind of ballet poignancy. Agnes de Mille styles are left strictly alone, but withal, Miss [Helen] Tamiris has achieved originality and taste."[55]

The comparisons followed the show to London, where it opened in June 1947 to a "Wham reception, almost equaling that of 'Oklahoma!'"[56] And they continued to resonate during the U.S. tour, where one Chicago critic—again pointing to Berlin's work—called it "a high mark in the melodious cycle that began with 'Oklahoma,'"[57] and another noted (reinforcing the genre distinction) that "If you say that 'Oklahoma!' really isn't a musical comedy, then 'Annie' is the bull's-eye of the decade."[58] A Pittsburgh critic claimed that Annie had the "gustiness [*sic*] of 'Oklahoma'" but "is more bewitching to the eye."[59] Ultimately, the point that perhaps sticks out for its stark numerical distinction is the comparison between their initial runs on Broadway. On the occasion of the show's one thousandth performance, on October 7, 1948, several reports cited *Oklahoma!* again, since it was the only other musical to have reached that milestone. In the end, *Oklahoma!* held the record at 2,212 performances (a run that ended in May 1948, more than five years after it began). When *Annie Get Your Gun* closed on February 12, 1949, it came in second at 1,147.

THE FIELDS CONNECTION

The comparisons and contrasts between *Oklahoma!* and *Annie Get Your Gun* obscure other, equally important differences and precedents. Coming to grips with them involves shifting the context from the towering Rodgers and Hammerstein model to the lesser known but highly successful efforts of Dorothy and Herbert Fields. A quick survey of the Fieldses' work since the late 1930s reveals that many of *Annie Get Your*

Gun's key elements came into focus outside the realm of *Oklahoma!*'s measurable influence; a kind of cognitive structure had developed within Dorothy Fields's own experience to prepare that "flash" of inspiration "from God." First, after a successful stint in Hollywood that included an Academy Award for Best Song with Jerome Kern ("The Way You Look Tonight," 1936), Dorothy Fields returned to New York in 1938, got married (for the second time), and resumed writing for Broadway shows. According to one biographer, it was in this period that Fields "began thinking like a dramatist"—thinking not just about crafting her lyrics but also about how songs fit into the libretto.[60] It started with a show called *Stars in Your Eyes* (1939), starring Ethel Merman as a film diva in a satire of the Hollywood culture that Fields had just left behind. Then Dorothy became a librettist herself, co-writing a series of shows with brother Herbert: *Let's Face It* (1941), *Something for the Boys* (1943), and *Mexican Hayride* (1944). These shows had several things in common: contemporary but non-urban settings, scores by Cole Porter, and impressive runs of more than four hundred performances.

Ethel Merman figured prominently in the Fieldses' lives and works. She starred not only in *Something for the Boys*, but also in two recent Porter shows for which Herbert Fields had co-written the book with Buddy G. DeSylva: *Dubarry Was a Lady* (1939) and *Panama Hattie* (1940). Together, Porter's songs and the Fieldses' scripts helped to define Merman's stage persona: a brassy broad with a heart of gold, or as Ethan Mordden has more precisely put it: "a city girl, gutsy and funny, easily offended, fierce when crossed, but very loyal and so guilelessly unpretentious that she was constantly going up against, and ultimately either charming or defeating, various haughty aristocrats."[61] By now, in fact, Merman and Dorothy Fields were close friends, a bond strengthened not just by the success of the shows they worked on but by renewal through remarriage and family: both of them gave birth to two children, a boy and a girl, during the war years when their collaboration was at its peak.

Many of the Fieldses recent shows had followed a relatively new tendency to set musical comedy plots outside of urban New York. *Something for the Boys* used the old plot device of an inheritance to find itself on the site of the bequest: a Texas ranch (echoes of Merman's breakthrough show, *Girl Crazy*, which also dislocates its protagonist to a western ranch). *Mexican Hayride*, as its title suggests, followed its con-artist protagonist (played by the vaudeville veteran Bobby Clark) through a variety of colorful Mexican locales. These shows, produced by Michael Todd, shared with their more famous contemporary, *Oklahoma!*, a move to reopen the Southwest as a musical comedy setting. As such, both shows created opportunities for their stars to impersonate an Indian maiden—unlike *Oklahoma!*, notable for its lack of Native Americans in the very territory designated as a major reservation before it became a state. *Something for the Boys*, in fact, featured a show-stopping, pseudo-Indian duet sung by Ethel Merman and Paula Laurence in native garb: "By the Mississinewa." The *New York Times* critic Lewis Nichols called it "the funniest moment in a musical show in years."[62] No wonder the Fieldses would later want to recapture some of that song's success through a big "Indian" number that, in their act 1 "Annie Oakley" draft, called "for comedy as well as for production" (see table 7.1, no. 11). *Something for the Boys* even lent *Annie Get Your Gun* its cast-off working title, *Jenny Get Your Gun*.[63]

In 1945, however, with two solid hits in his recent past, Todd suggested something different: a story set in a Currier-and-Ives world and conjuring nostalgia for nineteenth-century Americana. In response, the Fieldses did some research and brought the Michael Todd musical back to the city, but now in a historical setting: 1870s New York. Titled *Up in Central Park*, the show blended fact and fiction in dramatizing the efforts of a newspaper reporter to expose "Boss" William Tweed and his cronies' attempts to steal money intended for the park's renovations. The score, by Sigmund Romberg, lent the proper old-world flavor and produced a romantic popular song with lyrics by Dorothy Fields: "Close as Pages in a Book."[64]

The Michael Todd connection signals a key point about how the Fieldses conceived their "Annie Oakley" show. Dorothy had first approached Todd, not Rodgers and Hammerstein, with her idea, a gesture that reveals that she saw the new show as a continuation of her recent work, not a new conception in the R&H mold, however influential that may have been on the final product. Todd, however, categorically rejected the idea with a verbal wave of the hand: "Who's gonna care about a girl who knows from nothing but guns?"[65] Only then did Dorothy approach Rodgers and Hammerstein.

In sum, there was much in Dorothy Fields's experience over the six-year period since her return to New York that prepared her "flash" of inspiration in August 1945: the new interest in developing musical comedy books, the brother-sister collaborations,

The creative team and stars of Annie Get Your Gun. *Standing,* left to right: *Joshua Logan, Irving Berlin, Richard Rodgers, Oscar Hammerstein II, Dorothy Fields, and Herbert Fields.* Kneeling: *Ray Middleton and Ethel Merman. Courtesy of Rodgers & Hammerstein, on behalf of the Estate of Irving Berlin.*

the Merman stage persona, the western settings, the Indian impersonations, and a Michael Todd production that captured a slice of nineteenth-century Americana.

Yet there were still other models and sources from which Dorothy Fields could draw her ideas. In the background stood *Show Boat*, a precedent that the Fieldses may have considered when they believed they were writing the script for Jerome Kern (and at a time when *Show Boat* was about to be revived on Broadway). The whole show-within-a-show motif, the mix of midwestern and urban settings for the onstage and backstage plot developments, the notion of show business as a metaphor for American life, touched off by an early ballyhoo number—surely Kern and Hammerstein's work of two decades earlier loomed as the Fieldses shaped the script. The *Show Boat* precedent also brings into focus significant ways in which they were determined *not* to echo it: most notably the melodramatic and racial dimensions. *Show Boat*'s lovers part under strained circumstances (the discovery of Julie's mixed blood, Ravenal's gambling debts), but *Annie Get Your Gun*'s romance follows the familiar, lighter trajectory of girl-meets-boy, girl-loses-boy, girl-gets-boy. Moreover, nowhere in *Annie Get Your Gun* do the Indians voice discontent with white culture (as did the stevedores in *Show Boat*'s startling first scene), nor do the white characters openly mistreat the Indians. The Fieldses disciplined the show to fit comfortably and recognizably into the musical comedy genre, and Berlin's songs followed suit.

Besides *Show Boat* and more recent Fields musical comedies, however, there was a historic-plot model even closer to home: the screenplay for the 1935 film *Annie Oakley*, starring Barbara Stanwyck in the title role. Dorothy and Herbert's older brother, Joseph, had received co-credit for the story idea. The film established some of the narrative elements that Dorothy and Herbert Fields developed (and rearranged). Most notable among them is Annie's deliberately missed shot during a shooting match with Frank. The real Annie Oakley did sometimes deliberately miss, *not* in order to throw a match to Frank but only "because it looks so easy if you never miss and the spectators might think there was a trick in it."[66] The story of her missing for Frank's sake enters the Annie Oakley legend only after her death but not in the first biography, *Annie Oakley: Woman at Arms*, published in 1927, a year after Oakley's death. That book describes Annie's victory in vivid detail. The missed shot incident comes through Hollywood. In the film, Annie deliberately misses after her mother quietly notes that by losing the match, Toby Walker (the name for the Frank Butler character) might also lose his job—a prospect that had resonance for the film's Depression-era audience. In the post-Depression, postwar world of *Annie Get Your Gun*, the Fieldses preserve the idea of the fictional missed shot on Frank's behalf, but now it comes at the end of the story and serves as the catalyst for sealing the story's principal romance. If, in the film, Annie's missed shot is altruistic, in the musical it is at once self-effacing and self-serving. Both portrayals suit prevailing views in the period in which they were conceived. The first suits the Depression era's emphasis on holding a job; the second reflects the postwar period's emphasis on returning women to their subservient, domestic place. In both, the woman must show deference to the man, even though her ability matches or exceeds his.[67] But in *Annie Get Your Gun* the Fieldses have it both ways by showing clearly that Annie is playing a role; that is, by losing the shooting match, she succeeds both at romance and show business.[68]

Other plot elements that the Fieldses develop from their brother's story include the romantic interest, Sitting Bull's adoption, and Annie's rise to fame—all of which come from Annie's actual biography. Yet the 1946 musical comedy script has little resemblance to the 1935 screenplay. In the film, Annie's missed shot occurs in the initial shooting match in Darke County. Further, Frank's departure from the show is motivated by failing eyesight, not jealousy about Annie's talent. Moreover, as portrayed by Barbara Stanwyck, Annie is a well-mannered young lady. The only hint of her rural upbringing is a slight drawl, not any apparent lack of education, manners, or taste. The film is a conventional, and rather bland, romantic comedy for which sharpshooting and show business remain a colorful backdrop.

NEW YORK ENTERTAINMENT

Joseph Fields's role in the show's background signals a larger issue that addresses *Annie Get Your Gun*'s fundamental differences from *Oklahoma!*, its New York roots, and its underlying postwar contemporaneity (all of which are audible in the score's swing numbers). The subject of Annie Oakley and the Wild West shows had a long-established connection to the Fields family and to show business in general. For the Fieldses, in particular, the story of Annie Oakley and Buffalo Bill's Wild West shows were part of personal experience and of family history. Their father, Lew Fields, had toured with the Weber-and-Fields troupe during the same period as the Wild West show, and the two troupes even crossed paths not far from New York, in Paterson, New Jersey. Indeed, the first scene's treatment of the subject of living quarters for the Indians may have been a family in-joke. In the script, when Charlie tells Wilson, the hotel proprietor, that "The Indians can sleep in the lobby," he reverses the actual situation Lew Fields faced some six decades earlier. In Paterson, Weber and Fields slept in the lobby and the Indians took rooms.[69]

That, then, points to another key difference between *Oklahoma!* and *Annie Get Your Gun*: for Rodgers and Hammerstein, the story and characters of *Oklahoma!* came from another script and stood far from their experience. For the Fields and Berlin, as well as for Rodgers and Hammerstein, Annie Oakley and Buffalo Bill represented important public figures that they would have witnessed and perhaps met in their childhoods or early adulthood. For Hammerstein, certainly, memories of seeing the Wild West in Brooklyn stood behind his initial enthusiasm for producing the show.[70] By the turn of the century, the whole city had a proprietary interest in Buffalo Bill and Annie Oakley. Tens of thousands of New Yorkers attended the Wild West shows performed at Madison Square Garden and other venues, indoor and outdoor, in the greater metropolitan area. It seems quite likely that the Fieldses and Berlin would have been among the spectators; at the very least, they could not have escaped hearing and reading about the troupe, as Buffalo Bill's productions stood among the grandest, most spectacular entertainments available to audiences in the late nineteenth and early twentieth centuries. Their proximity to the show comes into relief, in particular, through the location of Madison Square Garden, where the Wild West show played annually for many years. Between 1879 and 1925 the first two incarnations of the Garden stood at Fifth Avenue and Twenty-third Street, within easy walking distance of Berlin's youthful haunts, such as Jimmy Kelly's saloon on Four-teenth Street and Tin Pan Alley's turn-of-the-century headquarters along West Twenty-eighth Street. Buffalo Bill's Wild West, in short, was a paradigm of populist New York entertainment in the very period when Irving Berlin rose from Lower East Side street urchin to barroom busker and song-plugger to internationally acclaimed songwriter.

So Dorothy Fields's epiphany, and her collaborators' excitement about the pro-ject, grew from a powerful, and personal, sense of connection to New York's theat-rical history, a history that the Fields family, the Hammerstein family, Richard Rodgers, and Irving Berlin had all played central roles in shaping over several decades stretching back well before the "new age ushered" by the atomic bomb—and by *Oklahoma!* While the show plays a vital role in reasserting a connection to earlier, simpler days, paradoxically, as Andrea Most has shown, *Annie Get Your Gun* also represents as a complex example of how theatrical performance—show business—becomes an allegory of Jewish American identity.

ANNIE, SITTING BULL, AND JEWISH ASSIMILATION

The story of Annie and her siblings shares the contours of the archetypal immigrant experience—and bears a close resemblance to the trajectory of European and Rus-sian Jewish immigrant entertainers like Berlin and Lew Fields, Dorothy and Her-bert's father. At first, they speak corrupted English, are nearly illiterate, and poorly educated (they can't count higher than twenty)—all of that comes out in Annie's "Doin' What Comes Natur'lly." Annie's exceptional shooting ability is strictly func-tional at first; like Izzy Baline's singing, it's a means of survival. Later it gets more formal recognition and reward as a talent that can be displayed before a paying audi-ence. After meeting Frank, Annie becomes chiefly concerned with improving her ap-pearance by wearing nice clothes and looking "dainty," which further links Annie's experience with the immigrant concern for clothes as an external manifestation of assimilation[71]—and with traditional images of femininity. When introduced in Buf-falo Bill's show, Dolly and Winnie, dressed in "theatrical cowgirl costumes," execute a "traditional vaudeville assistant's bow" with flair. Then Annie introduces her "assis-tants" (her siblings), who try to copy Dolly and Winnie's bow. They are learning the protocol of show business, but they are obviously awkward about it. After Annie demonstrates her skill with a rifle, she is invited to join Buffalo Bill's troupe and gets her first full induction into show business through the song "There's No Business Like Show Business." In short, in this view, act 1, scene 1 dramatizes Annie's immi-gration and assimilation, and "show business" becomes a symbol and microcosm of America itself.

But Annie's journey is far from finished. Her foothold in show business is simply as an apprentice—like Berlin when he was a song-plugger. Not until the end of act 1 does she become Frank's equal, and ultimately she surpasses him as a public figure. Her feat of shooting targets from a motorcycle leads to a double conversion that confirms her assimilation: Sitting Bull, having declared his refusal to invest in show business on principle, relents after seeing Annie's marksmanship, and more than that, invites her to become his adopted daughter, a gesture sealed in "I'm an Indian Too" and the "Adoption Dance." That number-complex forms a parallel with "No Business": both are scene-ending production numbers that mark important steps in Annie's transformation.

The Indian adoption ceremony forms both a crux of the plot's Jewish-American allegory and a problematic scene that has been cut entirely for its stereotyped depictions of Native Americans. Clearly, however, the presence of Indians, and especially the presence of Sitting Bull, was essential to the show's creators. In fact, the script telescopes time to make him more of a central force in the survival and development of the Wild West show, and in Annie and Frank's romantic vicissitudes. The real Sitting Bull met Annie in 1884 and joined the show only for the 1885 season. (He was shot and killed in 1890.)[72] Yet in the musical he remains with the show for a longer period and even oversees the merger of the Buffalo Bill and Pawnee Bill troupes, which did not occur until 1909, almost two decades after Sitting Bull died.[73] The real Sitting Bull, far from investing in and developing an interest in show business, was often depressed during his short involvement with the show and did not enjoy being part of the business.[74]

As Andrea Most has shown, however, the scene—and the characterization of Sitting Bull—has more to do with theatrical tradition than with actual Native Americans, and it has strong links, in particular, with a history of theatricalized Jewish-Indian interaction almost as old as Broadway. On one hand, Sitting Bull plays the role of the traditional stage Jew-as-Indian: the chief mediator who steers the romantic plot toward its successful consummation. In this well-established convention, the Indian, as Most puts it, "fulfills an essential function in the comic plot: he ensures that romantic (New World) love triumphs."[75] On the other hand, he also plays the role of Indian-as-Jew. Andrea Most explains the disparity between the real Sitting Bull and the fictionalized Sitting Bull by arguing that the show reveals him to be "serving the same function as the Jewish comics in earlier plays who become the voice of, indeed the embodiment of, theatrical performance of the self." He is "a Jewish-style master of theatricality."[76] Indeed, in the show, Sitting Bull becomes a linchpin of the plot. In him, "[t]he Indian/Jew is no longer an outsider; he is not only an important investor in the Wild West show—he is the one character who is capable of teaching Annie how to succeed in the new world she has entered."[77] Annie, she argues, "is truly an immigrant story but the American who teaches the new immigrant how to behave in her adopted country is an Indian who acts like a Jew."[78]

Most's trenchant analysis draws more of its support from the Fieldses' script, however, less from Berlin's lyrics, and not at all from Berlin's music. Although neither Sitting Bull nor Annie (nor the actors who originally played them) were Jewish, it is interesting to note that Berlin's musical setting of "I'm an Indian Too" blends Indian and Jewish tropes in a way that amplifies Most's analysis of plot and characters: the outer voices, comprising the largely pentatonic melody and bass drone, conform to Indian musical stereotypes with nineteenth-century roots. In a sophisticated analysis of the song from a perspective deeply informed by Indianist tropes across two centuries, Michael V. Pisani has shown how Berlin's song demonstrates remarkable "fluidity with the musical syntax and accumulated rhetoric of Indianism."[79] Pisani aims

Example 7.10. *"I'm an Indian Too."*

to recapture the scene's "burlesque" quality, a quality almost entirely lost to later generations, as Pisani points out, sensitive to its potential "hurtfulness to those who endured endless suffering for merely being 'in the way.'"[80] Meanwhile, the inner voices, featuring a descending chromatic line, link the song to several other songs in the show and also, specifically, to Jewish musical stereotypes that flourished in the 1920s.[81] The song's music alone thus forms a potent embodiment of the Jewish-Indian merger (see ex. 7.10).

We cannot know whether Berlin thought about it this way, of course, but there are revealing precedents with which Berlin would have been well aware—all thoroughly enmeshed in show business and Indianist burlesque. The title even echoes a song that became a Fanny Brice specialty in the 1910s and 1920s: "I'm an Indian." In it, Brice, as one "Rosie Rosenstein," explains that although she looks the part of an Indian—with her moccasins, papoose, and feathers—she cannot conceal that she is a "terrible squaw."[82] Even farther back stands another song by Berlin himself, written in collaboration with Edgar Leslie around 1909, during a fad for Hebrew-Indian songs, called "My Father Was an Indian."[83] In it, a man named Jake Cohen, "way out in the wild and wooly West," takes off his crisp new suit (evidence of the sartorially conscious urban Jew) and dresses up "just like an Indian." When his feathers blow away, he is caught by real Indians and tries to explain his lineage to save his life, but his final line breaks the end-rhyme pattern established in the first quatrain—and reveals his true identity:

My father was an Indian,
My mother was his wife,
My uncle almost died
Until a kind judge gave him life [Joke].
My brother was the president
Of every Ind'an Club,
My sister was a chambermaid,
So that made me a Hebrew.[84]

Jake Cohen fails to assimilate where Annie succeeds. Annie's assimilation into Indian culture features much of the inept Indian impersonations by Berlin's Jake Cohen and Brice's Rosie Rosenstein, but in the show's context they are accepted as awkward steps toward true acceptance. Both Annie and Jake are eager for acceptance as Indians. Unlike Jake, however, who is bound and surrounded by fire, Annie, in the show's terms, is successfully absorbed into Indian culture. The key difference, of course, is that the later scenario has been stripped of its explicit Jewish associations, but the allegory of assimilation remains unmistakable. Also now unmistakable is the autobiographical force behind the show's conception: in it, Dorothy Fields not only dramatizes Jewish American assimilation but also the terms by which a woman may be assimilated into a male-dominated world, whether shooting or writing lyrics—and show business forms the link. The impulse for Fields's "flash" of inspiration makes even more sense from that perspective.

ANNIE IN THE WORLD

The assimilation story at *Annie Get Your Gun*'s core, like its Rosie-the-Riveter plot, marks the show's postwar, mid-century, New York vintage, but it also seems to speak to a more universal interest. As a popular postwar show, *Annie Get Your Gun* had enormous global impact, through an original cast album, a longer run in London than in New York (1,304 performances), a successful U.S. tour and television production, a film version, and productions throughout Europe, and even in the Far East, South America, and Africa. Annie superseded even *Oklahoma!* in its worldwide appeal, perhaps because the way had been paved by Buffalo Bill himself, with his extensive tours of Europe decades earlier. The show surely touched a chord of postwar nostalgia for earlier times that might well have been stronger in Europe than in America. Indeed, Annie's reception in continental Europe was especially strong—in Paris (1950), as *Annie du Far West*, Vienna (1957), and German cities (1963), where it was dubbed *Schiesslos Annie*. There, the point of reference was not musical comedy or even *Oklahoma!* but operetta, perhaps as a European way of distinguishing the show from opera.[85] The Frankfurt *Abendpost* even dubbed Berlin the "American Lehar."[86]

Two decades of continuous, international performance history culminated in a 1966 Broadway revival that brought Ethel Merman, at fifty-four, back to the title role. Her zesty performance immediately quashed "Granny Get Your Gun" jokes. Critics found the show as lively as ever—and more streamlined: gone was the juvenile romance of Tommy and Winnie (and their swinging duets), and added was a brilliant new Berlin counterpoint song: "Old-Fashioned Wedding," in which Frank and Annie present contrasting visions of their impending nuptials.

Critics who wondered if the show could survive Ethel Merman's star turn have been answered by a long parade of leading ladies, beginning with Mary Martin in the U.S. tour and 1957 television production during Martin's sassier and earthier pre–*Sound of Music* period. Reviewing what he called the "disappointing" television production, the critic Jack Gould nevertheless revealed how Martin brought a distinctively new approach to the character: "Instead of being the boisterous hick from the sticks she was more the genteel elf . . . Miss Martin's interpretation leaned to fragility rather than a decisive and authoritative zest."[87] Other notable Annie's include: Dolores Gray in the post-Broadway London production that ran for a remarkable 1,304 performances; Betty Hutton, replacing an incapacitated Judy Garland, in the 1950 film; and Ginger Rogers on a 1960 tour. The *Boston Globe* compared Rogers favorably, and vividly, to Merman—two divas who had gotten their starts in the Gershwins' *Girl Crazy* thirty years earlier. Imagining an onstage duel between Merman and Rogers, critic Kevin Kelly claimed that "Miss Rogers would shine that soft smile, cock her elbows against her Hollywood waist, flick her loose legs over her puff-blonde coiffure and step through the rhythms of 'Doin' What Comes Naturally' and, for the moment, it would be a stand-off."[88]

The 1999 Broadway revival, in a revision by Peter Stone, preserved Annie's robust, three-dimensional character at the core of an extensive revision that restored as much music as possible, including Tommy and Winnie's duets from the 1946 production and "An Old-Fashioned Wedding" from 1966. Meanwhile, it deleted or smoothed over what were by then dated Native American stereotypes and sexist implications in what was characterized as a "feminist reworking."[89] Even for those who accept that some changes needed to be made for turn-of-the-century tastes, however, we can still say that the production did not trust the material. For example, it stacked its classic song up front—with a show-within-a-show presentation of "There's No Business Like Show Business," as one and then another actor ambles onto a darkened stage that gradually awakens with an energetic full-ensemble, production-number treatment that recalled the opening of 1961's *Carnival*. As a result, the production cuts entirely the well-crafted expository numbers, "Colonel Buffalo Bill" and "I'm a Bad, Bad Man." Indeed, comparing the song stacks[90] of the show's three major U.S. productions, we can see how "Show Business" reprises serve as filler when other songs are omitted (see table 7.2).

The table also shows how the 1999 production omitted the expositional songs "Colonel Buffalo Bill" and "I'm a Bad, Bad Man" and the entire complex of Indian adoption ceremony music—severe cuts that fundamentally alter the show's pace and flow, and skew its balance. This revised production ran on Broadway for almost three years before closing on September 1, 2001; it had almost as many performances (1,045) as the original production (1,147), and then went on the road. So it stands today as one of two "official" versions of the show. The other version is what is now called the "classic" version, which is the 1966 revision.[91] That version continues to thrive, most notably in a 2011 Glimmerglass Festival production starring the Wagnerian soprano Deborah Voight, whom the *New York Times* dubbed a "Gun-Totin' Brünnhilde."[92] The coexistence of two versions, neither of which reflects the original

Table 7.2. *Annie Get Your Gun*: song order in three major productions

1946	1966	1999
Act 1		
Colonel Buffalo Bill	Colonel Buffalo Bill	There's No Business Like Show Business
I'm a Bad, Bad Man	I'm a Bad, Bad Man	—
Doin' What Comes Natur'lly	Doin' What Comes Natur'lly	Doin' What Comes Natur'lly
The Girl That I Marry	The Girl That I Marry	The Girl That I Marry
You Can't Get a Man with a Gun	You Can't Get a Man with a Gun	You Can't Get a Man with a Gun
There's No Business Like Show Business	There's No Business Like Show Business	There's No Business Like Show Business (reprise)
They Say It's Wonderful	They Say It's Wonderful	I'll Share It All with You
Moonshine Lullaby	Moonshine Lullaby	Moonshine Lullaby
I'll Share It All with You	Wild West Pitch Dance	—
Ballyhoo	—	There's No Business Like Show Business (reprise)
There's No Business Like Show Business (reprise)	There's No Business Like Show Business (reprise)	They Say It's Wonderful
My Defenses Are Down	My Defenses Are Down	My Defenses Are Down
Wild Horse Ceremonial Dance	Wild Horse Ceremonial Dance	—
I'm an Indian Too	I'm an Indian Too	—
Adoption Dance	Adoption Dance	—
You Can't Get a Man with a Gun (reprise)	You Can't Get a Man with a Gun (reprise)	You Can't Get a Man with a Gun (reprise)
Act 2		
—	—	Entr'acte: The European Tour
(I Got) Lost in His Arms	(I Got) Lost in His Arms	(I Got) Lost in His Arms
Who Do You Love? I Hope	There's No Business Like Show Business (reprise)	Who Do You Love? I Hope

(continued)

Table 7.2. (continued)

1946	1966	1999
Act 1		
I Got the Sun in the Morning	I Got the Sun in the Morning	I Got the Sun in the Morning
They Say It's Wonderful (reprise)	An Old-Fashioned Wedding	An Old-Fashioned Wedding
The Girl That I Marry (reprise)	The Girl That I Marry (reprise)	The Girl That I Marry (reprise)
Anything You Can Do	Anything You Can Do	Anything You Can Do
There's No Business Like Show Business (reprise)	There's No Business Like Show Business (reprise)	They Say It's Wonderful (reprise)
[They Say It's Wonderful (reprise)]	They Say It's Wonderful (reprise)	Finale Ultimo [There's No Business Like Show Business (reprise)]

production, marks a paradox: as the show's classic status has become more secure, its original text has become increasingly obscure and unstable.

Yet this need not be occasion for predictable laments about a loss of authenticity. The show lives on through performance, a point emphasized in a recent study by Bruce Kirle who places less emphasis on score and book as he argues for understanding musicals—even canonic ones—as always "works-in-process."[93] There was a time, as we have seen, when critics believed that *Annie Get Your Gun* could not survive Ethel Merman's performance. Yet in the 1999 production, Bernadette Peters and Reba McIntyre both put their unique stamps on the role of Annie. Peters won a Tony Award for a performance that—in the words of Ben Brantley of the *New York Times*— "radiates emotional vulnerability," whereas McIntyre's "expansive, crowd-embracing characterization" became "the most disarmingly unaffected Annie in years."[94] There are as many Annies as there have been actresses to bring her to life. As Mary Martin put it, "A fine libretto, wonderful music, a role full of vitality can make milestones in the careers of entirely different personalities in the theater. Annie was one of those roles."[95] The libretto and songs that were tailor-made for Ethel Merman have become material for an endless procession of women: something for the girls. Today, the show endures as a problematic classic that singing actresses, the theater, and the American Songbook cannot do without.

8
STATE OF THE UNION
• • •
BERLIN, LINDSAY AND CROUSE, 1950–62

He collected lots of ordinary phrases
Like "I love you, dear," and "You're for me,"
But he found that when he set them all to music,
They were just as good as poetry.
—from "Once Upon a Time Today"

On November 14, 1945, in the week that Berlin began writing the score for "Annie Oakley," a new play opened at the Hudson Theatre on West Forty-fourth Street presenting a populist vision of postwar, post-FDR American politics. In it, an airplane industry executive named Grant Matthews gets drafted to become the Republican presidential candidate. Matthews is a decent if somewhat gullible man with strong feelings about his country, whose postwar climate, he believes, has encouraged fragmentation into small interest groups. With his marriage on the rocks, Matthews wants to restore the spirit of shared sacrifice for a larger good that, he believes, ended with the war. But he finds that his presidential bid makes him feel "torn between ambition and integrity."[1] The campaign, driven by cynical, manipulative political bosses and an alluring newspaperwoman who represents the chief challenge to his marriage, forces him to say and do things that he does not believe. In the end, rather than risk compromising his ideals, Matthews abandons his presidential run and reconciles with his wife, vowing to become an active agent of American democracy, "yelling from the sidelines" and "asking questions" because, as he exclaims in the optimistic curtain line, "we've got something great to work for."[2]

The writers did several things to enhance the show's uniquely contemporary feel and comedic impact—for the *Times* critic had called the play a "comedy with a serious purpose."[3] They peppered the script with allusions to people and issues in the news, referred to Harry Truman as the incumbent, revised lines *daily* during the run of the show to keep it current (much to the delight of the cast and audience), and called for a newspaper prop—and the line referring to its headline—to be changed at every performance to reflect that day's news.[4]

The name of the play was *State of the Union*, and it would go on to win a Pulitzer Prize for its authors, Howard Lindsay and Russel Crouse, and to become a 1948 film directed by Frank Capra and reuniting Spencer Tracy and Katharine Hepburn. By the time the play appeared in 1945, Lindsay and Crouse had thrived in collaboration for more than a decade, and their well-crafted scripts would help define an intelligent style of popular theater in the middle decades of the twentieth century. The partners had been brought together almost by accident to revise the book for Cole Porter's 1934 musical comedy, *Anything Goes*. (Lindsay had contracted influenza and urged his producer to find help.) Yet their happenstance collaboration proved durable, and they stand among the very few playwrights who enjoyed consistent success writing both musical comedy books and scripts for the "legitimate" theater, most notably *Life with Father* (1939), which ran for 3,224 performances over seven and a half years and became the longest-running play in Broadway history in its time.[5] By 1959, when they co-wrote the book for *The Sound of Music*, their twenty-five-year collaboration had become the longest in American theater history.[6] Although since eclipsed in collaborative longevity by the likes of Comden and Green, and Kander and Ebb, Lindsay and Crouse still comprise one of Broadway's most long-lived, productive, and successful creative partnerships. And together, their names became so mellifluously familiar that Crouse and his wife named their daughter Lindsay Ann.

The spirit and style of *State of the Union* informed Lindsay and Crouse's two subsequent collaborations with Irving Berlin: *Call Me Madam* (1950) and *Mr. President* (1962). Both shows feature a likeable, well-meaning, and somewhat naïve American Everyman (or Everywoman) protagonist thrust into the center of a political maelstrom that tests the durability of personal relationships. Both shows, too, engage with current events and include plenty of references to people and happenings in the recent news. The musicals appeared during particularly tense periods of the Cold War, and their plots, characters, and numbers take shape within a framework of a volatile international political climate. The result is that, in Berlin's shows with Lindsay and Crouse, as in *State of the Union*, the protagonists (an ambassador and a president) are forced into roles that do not come naturally—roles they have to *learn* to perform in accordance with convention and public expectation. In other words, for these characters political engagement becomes a kind of theatrical performance. In fact, the first scenes of both *Call Me Madam* and *Mr. President* establish a gap between the protagonists' "real" nature and the roles they must adopt in political Washington. The plot trajectories of both shows—like *State of the Union*—aim to reconcile the opposing forces embodied by the main character. Both protagonists do something that brings them shame and rejection in the public sphere, but both, in the end, are recognized as important figures in international relations and are restored to a place of respect in the public eye. The thing they do to bring shame and rejection in both cases is to attempt to bridge a gap in international relations through a common touch that breaches protocol but makes a human connection. There's a pointed critique here, though a gentle one: you can't do the right thing and maintain your position.

Being musical comedies, the shows make everything right in the end: international and personal relations improve together. Yet along the way the protagonists are forced to confront their strengths and limitations. They ultimately preserve their integrity even as they suffer embarrassment and leave the public position they had sought or occupied for much of their on-stage lives—a description that ultimately fit not just the characters but also the creators. For although both shows established new heights for advanced ticket sales on Broadway thanks to the blockbuster collaboration of Berlin and Lindsay and Crouse, *Mr. President* would effectively end the Broadway careers of all three.

What brought this triumvirate together initially was not a theme, subject, plot, or character, but a real person with whom they had all previously worked: Ethel Merman. In a flash of inspiration remarkably similar to the one that Dorothy Fields had in August 1945, Howard Lindsay conceived *Call Me Madam* four years later with Merman in mind. While Merman and her family and Lindsay and his wife were all vacationing together at a hotel in Colorado, Merman recalled:

> There, one day out of the blue, came Howard's idea. . . . Howard was looking out of a window at me when he suddenly yelled, "Hey, I've got a wonderful idea for a show for you!"
>
>   "What is it?" I yelled back.
>   "Perle Mesta!" he yelled.
>   "Who's Perle Mesta?" I shouted.
>   "Tell you later," he said.
>
> . . . Later Howard said that, when he'd looked down at me, a copy of a weekly magazine with Perle Mesta's picture on it was lying next to me, and he'd said to himself, "Ethel as an ambassadress."[7]

Perle Mesta (1889–1975) was a wealthy Washington, D.C., widow and socialite whose lavish yet down-to-earth VIP parties led *Time* magazine to dub her "the capital's No. 1 hostess" soon after Truman was elected president.[8] As an early and generous supporter of Truman, she won an appointment as ambassador to Luxembourg in 1949. She had come by her wealth through inheritance from her father, an Oklahoma oil tycoon, and her marriage to George Mesta, a major manufacturer of steel-mill equipment and machinery near Pittsburgh until his death in 1925.[9] Many believed that Mesta had essentially bought the appointment, yet she took the job seriously, and moreover, it turned out that Luxembourg's steel industry was something that Mesta understood from her husband's work. When she was dismissed from the post in April 1953 after Eisenhower's election, the Grand Duchess awarded her with the Grand Cross of the Oak, a high honor in Luxembourg. By then, *Call Me Madam* had earned Ethel Merman her first Tony Award—the first of that recently established award she had been eligible to receive—and closed after a solid run of 644 performances; its film version had its premiere, ironically, just a few weeks before Mesta's dismissal.[10]

Mesta had already become something of a celebrity before Truman appointed her ambassador. The March 14, 1949, cover of *Time* featured an illustrator's rendering of the elegantly gowned and bejeweled grand dame standing before a rich, red drape partly drawn to reveal the Washington Monument as the central post in an elaborate candelabrum. The caption read: "Washington Hostess Perle Mesta." A *Time* cover is sometimes cited as Lindsay's inspiration, but Truman did not appoint Mesta until three months later.[11] By late summer, Mesta had arrived in Luxembourg, yet when Lindsay and Crouse invited Berlin in on the project around that time, Berlin, like Merman earlier, did not know who she was. Still, the concept and approach that Lindsay and Crouse laid out must have had for him a familiar ring: from *Watch Your*

Step (Vernon and Irene Castle) through *Annie Get Your Gun* (Annie Oakley), Berlin wrote shows conceived for stars based on plots that had strong links to characters and stories from real life. And like Annie, the Mesta character was a Merman role modeled on a famous American woman who had succeeded in a man's world. As he had done with the Fields siblings, Berlin would be working with a book-writing duo that had had notable previous experience writing for a Cole Porter show featuring Merman: *Anything Goes.*

Unlike the creative process in *Annie Get Your Gun*, however, the writers would write the entire book "like a straight play," Berlin noted, "strong enough to stand by itself without music, instead of a libretto with song cues," and they expected Berlin to be able to locate and place the numbers himself.[12] Another difference was the nature of the plot and protagonist. Lindsay and Crouse had a penchant for capturing the historical moment on stage, and that resonated with Berlin's long experience in revues and musical comedies that engaged with the here-and-now. Thus, the heroine, unlike Annie Oakley, was still alive and on the job in which she would be portrayed. The writers gave her a new name, Sally Adams, and slyly discouraged comparisons to an actual woman with a disclaimer, printed in the program and script, that "neither the character of Mrs. Sally Adams, nor Miss Ethel Merman, resembles any other person, alive or dead."[13] But the model for the show's protagonist was no secret. For more than a year, newspaper stories about the developing show had regularly cited Mesta as the show's inspiration; the newspaper columnist Leonard Lyons had arranged a meeting between Mesta and Merman; and another article had included a photograph of Merman, Mesta, and Margaret Truman together.[14]

For all of the connections between Mesta and her fictional counterpart, Merman tended to emphasize their differences instead. According to Merman, the show did not exactly hold a mirror up to the real Perle, who possessed

> a certain amount of dignity and class, whereas the footlight ambassadress was brassy and said anything that came into her mind. The real Perle is very intelligent and she can talk on any subject, which I couldn't do in the show. Half the time the stage ambassadress didn't know what she was talking about, but she was likable and lovable, and she pulled a lot of sympathy from the audience. That was particularly true when her prime minister boy friend walked out on her.[15]

Indeed, from the outset, the script and numbers played to the strengths of Merman's stage persona and made little effort to capture Mesta's real personality. The curtain rises in Washington, D.C., as Sally Adams is being sworn in as ambassador of Lichtenburg. She abruptly invites the gathering to her farewell party and shatters the formal mood with her blackout line, directed at Secretary of State Dean Acheson: "Hey Dean—where the hell is Lichtenburg?" The chorus then renders the party invitation ("Mrs. Sally Adams"). At the party, she appoints the young, bookish, and idealistic Kenneth Gibson, son of the wealthy businessman Henry Gibson, as her press attaché, noting that her social agility trumps her knowledge of politics, diplomacy, and Lichtenburg ("The Hostess with the Mostes'"). Democrats and Republicans may disagree, but for the common good Sally shows how they can get along ("Washington Square Dance").

The scene shifts to a public square in Lichtenburg, where the local population, led by the handsome, dignified foreign minister Cosmo Constantine, introduces the country as they await Sally's arrival ("Lichtenburg"). Although Sally has been charged to refuse requests for an American loan, diplomatic protocol soon dissolves when she meets Cosmo ("Can You Use Any Money Today?"). Cosmo, though quite taken with Sally, refuses the offer on principle, suggestively noting that there are things more valuable than money ("Marrying for Love"). Yet Lichtenburg's economic situation is so severe that its annual fair has been cancelled. Sally offers to pay for it with personal funds, since it will be like hosting "a party where you invite the whole country." The lovely Princess Maria, daughter of the Grand Duke and Duchess of Lichtenburg, launches the fair with a song and dance with her countrymen ("The Ocarina"). Sally introduces Maria and Kenneth, who is immediately attracted to the princess ("It's a Lovely Day Today"). Sally and Cosmo, meanwhile, express a deepening attraction to one another ("The Best Thing for You"). The developing romances, however, quickly hit a snag when Sally forges ahead with a U.S. loan of $100 million, and Cosmo angrily rejects it. At the same time, Maria has confessed to having clandestine meetings with Kenneth in a passageway linking the Duke's castle and the American embassy. As Kenneth is considered a "commoner" in Lichtenburg, she is forbidden to speak to him ever again. Feeling out of place and disappointed, Sally reflects ruefully on their situation ("Can You Use Any Money Today?" reprise) as the curtain falls on act 1.

Cosmo, his pride still hurt by the aid package, affirms his national pride ("Lichtenburg" reprise). An American delegation arrives to support the loan offer, and Sally responds by throwing another party ("Something to Dance About"). There, romantic hope returns to both couples. Sally and Cosmo make up, while Kenneth, though still forbidden to *speak* to Maria, realizes that they may develop their modern fairy-tale romance through *song* ("Once Upon a Time Today"). Meanwhile, the Lichtenburg officials argue the merits of American aid and call the first national election in twenty years, in which Cosmo will run against his rival on the issue of the loan. The American congressmen, puzzled by Lichtenburg's political system, discuss one they know more about, as they consider the upcoming 1952 U.S. presidential election ("They Like Ike").

Sally has asked Kenneth to respond to the U.S. State Department's investigation of complaints that she has been interfering with local politics, but Kenneth is too distracted to think about anything but Maria ("It's a Lovely Day Today" reprise), and she sings her response from outside his window. Sally enters and inquires about Kenneth's dreamy, distracted mood. As he explains with one melody, she offers some maternal wisdom with another melody in counterpoint ("You're Just in Love").

Kenneth secures from his wealthy father a promise to open a hydroelectric power plant in Lichtenburg if Kenneth can raise 10 percent of the capital. Sally offers to put up the money, which will not only allow the plant to be built but also allow Kenneth to remain in Lichtenburg and try to work out his relationship with Maria. It will also solve Cosmo's problem: "Industrialization for Lichtenburg! If that happens it doesn't matter who wins the election!" With all of their problems ostensibly solved, Cosmo and Sally confirm their love ("The Best Thing for You" reprise). But a phone call from "Harry" (President Truman) interrupts their intimate moment with the news that Sally has been relieved of her duties because of her perceived meddling in the Lichtenburg election campaign. This twist of fate has seemingly sabotaged their reconciliation. Sally and Cosmo start to say their sad goodbyes in the embassy, but Maria interrupts them by entering from the passageway. Sally warns her to leave before she is caught, but then the Duke and Duchess emerge from the passageway as well. They apologize to Sally, wish her well, and concede that she has done wonders for their country. Kenneth enters, meets the Duke and Duchess for the first time, and tells them about how the hydroelectric plant will be built a safe distance from the Hammersburg Falls and therefore will not interfere with Lichtenburg's natural beauty. He tells them, too, that he plans to marry Maria, but the gruff Duke rejects the idea. As a distraction designed to allow Kenneth and Maria to be alone, the sympathetic Duchess invites Sally to tea and then tells her husband: "Otto, remember our talk with Cosmo. For the first time in many years the people of Lichtenburg are really free. Isn't it about time the royal family was free, too?" Before exiting, the Duchess reminds Maria that, as princess, she must ask Kenneth to marry her, not vice versa. Maria does, and Kenneth responds ("It's a Lovely Day Today" reprise).

Having returned to Washington, Sally hosts a coming-home party ("Mrs. Sally Adams" reprise), but she is unhappy because she believes she has lost Cosmo, who, it turns out, has won the election. Dean Acheson tells Sally that relations between the U.S. and Lichtenburg "have never been more friendly, and they have made a magnificent gesture to show that you are persona grata." Enter Cosmo, who bestows upon Sally a medal, by order of the Grand Duke. Cosmo announces that "the Grand Duke thought it was the best thing for Lichtenburg, and—unofficially—it is the best thing for me." He kisses Sally, who begins the finale ("You're Just in Love") to which the chorus sings the counterpoint melody and the curtain falls.

The script and numbers took shape from the fusion of two plot archetypes with an added Cold War twist. One plot archetype was the Merman vehicle. As we've seen, Lindsay's initial inspiration grew from Merman's persona. He noted that he was "studying her" and that "she seems so American—raucously, good-naturedly, almost vulgarly American." So, he began "wondering how we could spot her in a foreign setting," and that led to the connection with Perle Mesta.[16] Moreover, a Merman show with a Berlin score appearing just four years after *Annie Get Your Gun* inevitably conjured associations with the earlier show. Echoes of the stage Annie Oakley are numerous in the world of Sally Adams: blunt naiveté in the face of experienced professionals; a professed lack of education and intelligence (with songs that begin "Folks are dumb where I come from" and "Please let me say from the start, / I don't pretend to be smart"); the trademark wide-eyed, open-mouthed "ga-ga" look when the heroine meets the handsome hero; the heroine's maternal efforts to facilitate the secondary romance, even when her own romantic prospects remain in limbo; the act 1 finale comprising a truncated reprise of the number she sang after meeting the hero, but sung now when her love life appears to be shattered ("You Can't Get a Man with a Gun" and "Can You Use Any Money Today?"). In both shows, too, Merman's character follows a Rosie-the-Riveter trajectory and loses her unique professional rank just before she wins the man. These were sure-fire elements of the Merman "star text" that audiences had appreciated in *Annie Get Your Gun*. In other words, the plot and characters of *Call Me Madam* took shape within the context of Merman's past roles and aspects of her stage persona.

If Merman-as-Mesta was the catalyst, however, an older plot model also informed the script: the Graustark archetype, whose roots go back a half-century to the writers' youths. As John Dizikes has explained, it had a powerful effect on American musical theater, especially operetta. Anthony Hope's novel *The Prisoner of Zenda* (1896), set in the imaginary land of Ruritania, "loosed an avalanche of Ruritanian romances in America, written by Americans."[17] Most notable among them was the Indiana native George Barr McCutcheon's novel *Graustark* and its five sequels, published between 1901 and 1927. Like Hope's Ruritania, Graustark was a mythical country situated somewhere in central Europe, a small, quaint land that time forgot. Although the proximate inspiration for Lichtenburg was obviously Luxembourg, Lichtenburg fits the description of a Graustarkian setting.

Moreover, Kenneth matches the traits of the Graustarkian hero, as described by John Dizikes: "an American, of an ordinary sort, fresh, clean, young, a believer in democracy and a go-getter, whose modern ideas and energetic ways won out over the plots of decadent, feudal-minded Graustarkians."[18] Whereas in earlier *Zenda* spinoffs, the hero rescues the princess from a villain who threatens her inheritance of the royal throne, in the Graustark novels, the hero *marries* the princess. Even though Kenneth comes from a wealthy family in America, the Lichtenburg royalty view him as a "commoner" who must be kept away from the princess. Therefore, Kenneth embodies all of the key traits of Graustark's traditional protagonist.

Sally may be seen as an older, female image of the Graustarkian hero: she strives both to save the country and to win the heart of a man who, if not a prince, is nevertheless deferential to royal authority. This is no small change from the model, however, since the Graustark series relied on men and women to play more or less stereotyped gender roles, something upset by Sally's strong character and influential wealth. Thus the Graustark archetype and the Merman plot effect a transformation of both.

Although Graustark was not mentioned in commentary on the show, it is notable that Lindsay himself had envisioned a setting in which "all the qualities that make her [Merman] a typical American would be emphasized."[19] And when the show's movie version was released, a film critic wrote of the story as if it had a familiar trajectory: "The plot [is] one of those things about an uncouth American democrat in the midst of refined European decay."[20] Graustarkian plots were decidedly old-fashioned in the postwar period, but the archetype was still a point of reference. Brooks Atkinson, in panning a new operetta in 1948, noted that the characters "are still carrying passports from Graustark, which . . . has now disappeared from the cultural atlas and need never be explored again."[21] Another *Times* critic, Lewis Nichols, in a postwar reflection on the standard operetta book, called it an "immovable object" set in Graustark.[22] Both critics clearly assumed that their readers would understand the reference without further explanation while claiming the plot type as passé.

Deploying Graustarkian plot elements for a *musical comedy* with a contemporary plot stands as Lindsay, Crouse, and Berlin's fresh contribution to the theater in 1950.[23] That they framed the plot and musical numbers within a Cold War theme makes it even more distinctive. The dual romance of the traditional musical comedy here weaves together with the dynamics of contemporary international relations. The plot's movement depends on the fundamental dichotomy printed in the script and program: "The play is laid in two mythical countries. One is called Lichtenburg, the other the United States of America." The comic tensions that drive the plot arise from the oppositions between the two countries: America/Europe, rich/poor, democracy/duchy, modern/traditional. And the lovers embody these differences. The Americans (Sally and Kenneth) fall in love with Lichtenburgers (Cosmo and Maria) who have been shaped by traditional beliefs and economic stagnation. Their romantic prospects rise and fall with the vicissitudes of diplomatic engagement destabilized by the disparity between America's wealth and Lichtenburg's (that is, Europe's) poverty.

That disparity had become a major force in postwar international relations, whose overall thrust was defined by the Marshall Plan. In his landmark speech of June 1947, just two years before *Call Me Madam* was conceived, Secretary of State George C. Marshall outlined the crucial importance of U.S. aid to a war-ravaged Europe, and he linked the promise of aid to an implicitly anti-Soviet, anti-communist message involving mutual cooperation and a respect for human rights. With an eye on the Soviet efforts to form a communist bloc in Eastern Europe, Marshall noted that the consequences of failure to rebuild European infrastructure would be "economic, social and political deterioration of a very grave character."

None of that, of course, comes out explicitly in *Call Me Madam*. Respecting the discipline and craft of musical comedy, the writers reduced the external threat to a few punch lines in song and script about "Uncle Joe" Stalin, and they turned Senator McCarthy, who had launched his red-scare efforts just a few months earlier, into a joke who could not attend a party because of laryngitis. Instead, the writers followed the money and took satirical aim at the emotional and logistical challenges of promising and delivering U.S. aid to Europe. In the process, they created Sally and Kenneth as endearing characters who also serve as vehicles to satirize sincere but misguided American impulses.

Self-awareness has crept into the Graustarkian model. In the script's terms, Sally embodies the well-meaning but naïve American belief that money is what European countries need and that it can solve all problems; her can-do directness must have appeared refreshing at time when Marshall Plan aid, though helping, tended to get tangled in bureaucratic delays. Knowledge about the country, for Sally, is distinctly secondary to goodwill, charisma, and cash. Kenneth provides an apt foil to Sally because he is studious and much more informed about the country. Kenneth's extensive knowledge, however, stands on the assumption that knowledge can solve all of the country's problems. Both of them miss the traditional values that Cosmo and Maria stand for. For Cosmo, that means integrity above all. For Maria, that means a love of beauty that all of Kenneth's knowledge and can-do problem-solving spirit seems to overlook. She knows the country's beauty and history, and he knows facts and potential for development. Kenneth's promise to build the power plant far from the Hammersburg Falls represents an effort to reconcile the tensions between (American) modern development and (European) historic natural beauty. That he accomplishes his goals through private enterprise—Sally's and his father's wealth—instead of Marshall Plan aid, and that Cosmo embraces private money instead of viewing it as an affront to his national pride, reflects a sensibility that leans toward Republican.

Berlin's score reinforces the show's oppositions by featuring American musical comedy styles for the Americans and operetta-like numbers for the Lichtenburgers (see table 8.1). The "American" tunes—built from Berlin's distillations of swing, jazz, rag, and march elements, plus one salient quotation from his own song catalogue—dominate the score, musically reinforcing the bracing impact of Sally and Kenneth. Among them, the two "Lichtenburg" numbers sound musically quaint and old fashioned. Don Walker's orchestration, re-created for the first time on a 1995 recording, reinforced the contrast by emphasizing brass and reeds in the American numbers, and foregrounding strings and the exotic sound of the ocarina in the Lichtenburg numbers.[24] Meanwhile, the show's carefully spaced ballads, also featuring string-dominated orchestrations, form a kind of expressive common ground where the couples can meet, for they lack both the vital rhythmic profile of the "American" numbers and the Old-World signifiers of the "Lichtenburg" numbers. In this context, the counterpoint song "You're Just in Love" / "I Wonder Why" stands out as unique for several reasons. The song stack shows something else at a glance. It reinforces the fact that this show is a Merman vehicle, with half of its numbers featuring Sally alone, in duet, or with chorus.

A closer look at the numbers reveals how Berlin deployed some of his songwriting trademarks in fresh ways and addressed musical comedy conventions in developing the romances through song. The "Bright Shuffle Tempo" indicated for the opening ensemble number, "Mrs. Sally Adams," follows the natural rhythms of her name and generates the swinging rhythm of the whole number, including a prominent and repeated syncopated phrase that conjures swing-era, big-band arrangements. The number establishes the show's musical tone, for it wears its Americanness proudly, not just for the rhythmic energy but also in its brief, witty quotation of "God Bless America."[25]

Sally's ensuing numbers, "The Hostess with the Mostes'" and "Washington Square Dance" establish her as the musical and comedic center of the show. "The Hostess with the Mostes'" builds from a two-bar syncopated riff, ratcheted up a perfect-fourth interval using the device Berlin had practically patented in "Alexander's Ragtime Band" (ex. 8.1). Once again, Berlin's swing style, like his earlier brand of jazz, emerges from devices with ragtime roots, yet it sounds entirely of its period, with a rhythmic suppleness in a melody that throws its weight around and an orchestration that conjures a swing-era big band.

"The Hostess with the Mostes'" represents a familiar type of number for a musical protagonist. An analog to Annie Oakley's "Doin' What Comes Natur'lly," it is a kind of I-am song in which Sally quickly summarizes her past in the verse (based on some facts of Perle Mesta's life: her inheritance of her father's oil fortunes) and then launches the refrain celebrating her party-giving talents. Here again Berlin demonstrates a perfectly chiseled conversational American English that balances sound and sense:

I'm the chosen party giver for the White House clientele, and they know that I deliver what it takes to make 'em jell, and in Washington I'm known by one and all as the hostess with the mostes' on the ball.

Table 8.1. Call Me Madam, Musical Numbers

"American" Numbers	Love Ballads	"Lichtenburg" Numbers
Mrs. Sally Adams (Chorus)		
The Hostess with the Mostes' (Sally)		
Washington Square Dance (Sally and Chorus)		
		Lichtenburg (Cosmo and Chorus)
Can You Use Any Money Today (Sally)		
	Marrying for Love (Cosmo and Sally)	
		The Ocarina (Maria and Chorus)
It's a Lovely Day Today (Kenneth and Maria)		
It's a Lovely Day Today Encore (Kenneth and Chorus)		
	The Best Thing for You (Sally)	
Can You Use Any Money Today Reprise (Sally)		
		Lichtenburg Reprise (Cosmo and Chorus)
Something to Dance About (Sally and Chorus)		
	Once Upon a Time Today (Kenneth)	
They Like Ike (Wilkins, Brockbank, and Gallagher)		
It's a Lovely Day Today Reprise (Kenneth and Maria)		
You're Just in Love (Sally)	I Wonder Why (Kenneth)	

(continued)

Example 8.1. "The Hostess with the Mostes'."

I'm the cho-sen par-ty giv - er For the White House cli-en-tele,

— And they know that I de-liv - er What it takes to make 'em jell,——

Beyond some obvious end-rhymes (*clientele / jell* and *all / ball*), the phrases contain subtler internal rhymes, such as *cho*sen and *know*, and [part]-*y giv-er* and *de-liv-er*. The passages also features subtle assonance, as in the three-syllable parallelism between "what it takes" and "Wash-ing-ton" (each hitting the letters, "w," "i," and "t" on the syllables) and the parallels between "known by one and all" and "mostes' on the ball" with their long and short "o" sounds (*known / mostes'* and *one / on*).

Sally's next song, "Washington Square Dance," is an optimistic call for bipartisanship in the form of a country dance. Like several numbers in *Annie Get Your Gun*, however, the ostensibly countrified style has a syncopated swagger. The orchestration features a touch of country fiddling, but much of the number resounds with brassy big-band music. A dance sequence is even labeled "jazzy tempo" in the score and features blues inflections and dotted rhythms (published sheet-music's approximation of swung eighths in rhythm numbers). Meanwhile, as a witty ensemble number featuring a cheerful but strong-willed Oklahoma matron striving to bring two opposing groups together at a festive occasion, "Washington Square Dance" recalls "The Farmer and the Cowman," from *Oklahoma!* Although it would be hard to find two more dissimilar American settings on the musical stage, the impulse to join together for the common good—at a time of extreme circumstances in U.S. international relations—remains strong in both.

The short punchy phrases, rhythmic vigor, witty rhymes, and material wealth projected in the show's first three numbers set up a strong contrast for our introduction to the other "mythical country" in a song titled simply "Lichtenburg." The sound of ocarinas in the orchestration imparts an archaic, folksy quality to the song's introduction, and it continues with a verse in waltz style—that signifier of traditional values in Berlin's world. In the verse, Cosmo introduces his country, emphasizing that it is "poor," "impractical," and old-fashioned. Yet as he continues the song takes on qualities of an I-am song for the male lead. Cosmo refers to himself as the head of the "Conservative-Radical" party, striking a balance that echoes Sally's effort to reconcile Democrats and Republicans. Lindsay and Crouse wrote a monologue for Cosmo that articulates his centrist political stance, supported by the waltz's musical underscoring:

> Now, there's our problem. These young people feel we should be a modern country, and so they dress in modern clothes. And I know we must find some way to be modern. That's the radical in me. And yet when I see our old couples clinging to their native dress, I feel a warmth in my heart. That's the conservative in me. And that's why the party of which I am the head is known as the Conservative-Radical.

The refrain sharpens the image of Lichtenburg's quandary with a combination of two of Berlin's prized devices, the list and antithesis, as in the lines: "Too small to be a city, / Too big to be a town" and "Too slow to please the young folk, / Too fast to please the old; / Too many who have copper pennies, / Too few who have gold." The song stops short of bathos, however, with a touch of humor on a quadruple rhyme highlighted by a rhythmic and harmonic change: "Too little to sell across the *seas*—/ B*abies* and *cheese* / Are our main indus*tries*." After Cosmo sings the first refrain, the chorus joins him for the second, making the number sound like a forlorn, contemplative national anthem. Brooks Atkinson singled it out as "a poignant song with a mature sense of deference toward modest people."[26]

"Can You Use Any Money Today?" wrenches the musical style back to Sally's brash Americanist vein. Launched by her cue line, "I'm just trying to explain our American policy," the number may be heard as a foil to "Lichtenburg"—a spitfire comic national anthem of American abundance in the postwar age of the Marshall Plan. The word *money* appears twenty times in the first refrain alone, launched by the sixfold phrase: "Money, money, money, money, money, money—" On the line "Two million, four million, six million, eight million, ten," the strong beats aptly trace a scalar ascent that matches the rising cash offer (ex. 8.2a). This device of building a melody from an expanding-interval motif was already seen, slightly modified, at the beginning of the refrain of "Lichtenburg," and will appear again in "It's a Lovely Day Today" (exx. 8.2b and 8.2c). Interestingly, it is a prominent trademark of Richard Rodgers's theater songs from "Blue Room" (*The Girl Friend*, 1926) to "The Surrey with the Fringe on Top" (*Oklahoma!*, 1943), and beyond.[27] (The refrain melody of "Lichtenburg" also bears a striking resemblance to Harold Arlen's melody for the 1934 song, "Fun to Be Fooled.")

Even as Cosmo declines Sally's brash offer, he finds himself attracted to her winsome directness. He expresses that impulse in a classic exemplar of the conditional love song, "Marrying for Love," which is placed in the analogous spot as "They Say It's Wonderful" in *Annie Get Your Gun*. Such songs rarely address marriage directly, which is the fresh twist that Berlin gives it here. Yet it remains in the abstract realm: it is "an old-fashioned *idea*" that Cosmo is "thinking of." Parrying the thrust of Sally's animated offer of wealth, Cosmo's soft ballad conjures another kind of richness: "If she must have gold, / Let it be in her hair, / Rubies, / Let them be in her lips. / Diamonds, / Let them shine in her eyes." The song at once confirms his rejection of the loan offer and his romantic interest in Sally. It is noteworthy that the film version, preserving

Example 8.2. Expanding-interval melodies.

8.2a. *"Can You Use Any Money Today?"*

8.2b. *"Lichtenburg."*

8.2c. *"It's a Lovely Day Today."*

much of the original stage production, highlights Sally's red lips and shining eyes, yet it deletes Sally's musical response—a full chorus of the song following Cosmo's exit—which completes the duet requirements of a conditional love song.

At this point, although Sally's offer of a large loan to Lichtenburg hangs in the balance, she has succeeded in personally financing the annual Lichtenburg Fair, which had been canceled due to the country's economic straits. When Princess Maria declares that "the fair is open," she cues a new song conjuring the quaintness of Lichtenburg: "The Ocarina." The piercing sweetness of a harmonizing pair of ocarinas sets the tone in the orchestration, and Berlin creates the impression of a European folk song. The melody is entirely diatonic, its rhythm comprised of lilting dotted figures devoid of the kind of shuffle and swing vocabulary of Sally's and Kenneth's numbers, and its harmony confined to four standard chords (tonic, dominant, subdominant, and supertonic). The introduction even features drone fifths, a centuries-old signifier of folk music.

But there are a few traits that bear Berlin's stamp. First, the structure of the first phrase recalls "The Army Has Made a Man Out of Me," with its diatonic melody, two-chord harmony, and threefold iteration of key word(s) from the title: "man out of me" and "ocarina," both of which suggest the popular precedent of the 1942 hit "Don't Sit under the Apple Tree" (ex. 8.3). Second, "The Ocarina" identifies the sound of an instrument as a national symbol. Heard first in the introduction to "Lichtenburg," the instrument has already been linked to the mythical European country, an apt one given that the instrument had a long history and a particularly strong connection to Europe since the nineteenth century. Given its shape, it was often referred

Example 8.3. "The Ocarina."

Dance to the mus-ic of the oc - a - ri - na, oc - a - ri - na, oc - a - ri - na,

to as a "sweet potato," to which Berlin makes reference in the refrain—"Dance to the music of the sweet potata . . . / Cheeks getting redder than a ripe tomata / Dance to the ocarina, dance." Berlin's tendency to write such songs—linking music and dance—goes back to his early years, and he wrote many songs about musical instruments (or groups of them), especially in his ragtime years, as in "Alexander and His Clarinet," "I Love a Piano," "Ragtime Violin," and "Yiddle on Your Fiddle Play Some Ragtime." Unique among this group, however, "The Ocarina" qualifies as a reflexive song—a song about the sound it makes.

In their two Berlin musicals, Lindsay and Crouse demonstrated a knack for developing their plots in a public event: the Lichtenburg Fair in *Call Me Madam*, and the Mansfield (Ohio) Fair, in *Mr. President*. Such scenes have clear dramaturgical value, as Rodgers and Hammerstein had shown in their 1945 film, *State Fair*: they open up opportunities for characters to cross paths and make important connections. They also have musical value, for Berlin found in them ways to spot important numbers. And so it happens that the fair becomes the venue that launches the show's secondary love interest and its key song. Due to disparities in social class and notions of decorum, Kenneth and Maria's initial meeting is charged with resistance, adding to the romantic spark. Sally introduces Maria to Kenneth, and Kenneth begins to convey all of his knowledge of the country. His straightforward talk at once unsettles and intrigues the Princess. "Never has any young man spoken to me like this before," she notes. "Come to think of it, never has any young man spoken to me before." She tries to dismiss him:

MARIA: You may go!
KENNETH: But I don't want to go.
MARIA: It so happens that I have many, many things to do.

That line cues Kenneth's song "It's a Lovely Day Today," a number about which Berlin's daughter aptly asked: "such a whimsical, romantic young man's song—how could someone sixty-two remember?"[28] The song's combination of syncopations and wide leaps suggest a swing-style instrumental number more than a Broadway vocal number (ex. 8.4). Meanwhile, Berlin enriched the tune with chromatically sliding harmony—giving the swing tune some harmonic depth. Its fivefold appearance suggests that the collaborators saw it as the show's potential hit. Indeed, Merman recalled that it stopped the show every night, and its reception inspired her to call for "a number with the kid."[29]

Traditional musicals sometimes offer a second love song in act 1 that takes the principal romance from conditional to confirmed. "The Best Thing for You" serves that purpose. The verse makes a seamless transition from speech to lyrical song, and its brevity typifies the efficient, rhythmically supple verses in Berlin's later songs. The chorus is a marvel of harmonic richness, beginning with a major chord on the

Example 8.4. "It's a Lovely Day Today."

It's a love-ly day to-day,___ So what-ev-er you've got to do,_____ You've got a love-ly day To do it in,___ That's true._____

seventh degree of the scale, A. Berlin had used such an unusual chord famously in "A Pretty Girl Is Like a Melody"—on the climactic line "she will *leave you* and then . . ." In both cases it appears as a rich and strange surprise, but here it is part of a deceptive cadence, leading a listener to expect one resolution but getting another. The tune actually came from Berlin's trunk. Although it sounds entirely true as a love song, Berlin had originally set it to a lyric about a modest home in New York based on the "Home, Sweet Home" archetype: "Beautiful Brooklyn," written for his unfinished 1948 show, "Stars on My Shoulders" (ex. 8.5).

Three other things about "The Best Thing for You" add to its richness. In the bridge Berlin modulates to the chord of the flat-sixth degree, unusual if not unheard of in popular song. (One famous precedent in Berlin's work was "Let's Face the Music and Dance.") The bridge features a falling melodic leap reminiscent of the "Merman sigh" in "They Say It's Wonderful" from *Annie Get Your Gun* (ex. 8.6). Finally, Berlin

Example 8.5

8.5a. *"The Best Thing for You."*

8.5b. *"Beautiful Brooklyn."*

Example 8.6. *"Merman sigh" in "The Best Thing for You," bridge.*

withholds the melodic peak for the end—on the word "a-*gree*" in measure 32 just before the short extension.

With breathtaking efficiency, two plot twists allow act 1 to end in traditional musical comedy fashion: by posing grave challenges to the relationships of the two romantic couples. Sally's "Best Thing for You" had culminated in a kiss, and in Cosmo's comment that "Darling, you have accomplished your mission. You have brought about a closer unity between us." But as Cosmo starts to kiss her again, the telephone rings, and it is "Harry" telling Sally that the U.S. loan to Lichtenburg has been approved. Sally, overjoyed, reports this to Cosmo, who is profoundly disappointed and disdains her belief that money can solve their problems. "We are waiting for your country to offer the world something more than dollars," says Cosmo. And he adds: "So long as I am Prime Minister, Lichtenburg is not for sale," and he exits. Just then, Kenneth enters and reports that since the Duke and Duchess found out about his secret meetings with Maria, she wrote a note to him and "we're never going to speak to each other again." Like Annie, Sally gets the last notes and words of the act, as she sings an empty echo of "Can You Use Any Money Today?"

By all accounts, act 2 caused the collaborators considerable problems, and two important solutions came not from Lindsay, Crouse, or Berlin but from the choreographer and the star.[30] (Merman's suggestion will be considered in its place.) When Jerome Robbins told Berlin that the ensemble needed "something to dance about," Berlin used the phrase as the keynote and title of a reflexive number in the embassy party that Sally hosts early in the act.[31] (A 2009 public television *American Masters* feature on Robbins would borrow back the title phrase.) The sprightly tune that Berlin came up with would have sounded at home in a musical comedy of two decades earlier. The principal melody of the chorus grows from the two-note secondary rag pattern yielding to a waltz on the word *waltz* (ex. 8.7), and the lyrics and dance tempo indications (e.g., "Guy Lombardo Waltz Tempo") refer to styles that were popular between the 1910s and early 1930s: fox-trot, waltz, tango, Charleston, blues, and rumba. That the number does not sound old-fashioned for 1950 Broadway provides further testimony to Berlin's ability to refresh his ragtime vocabulary long after the style itself has passed from fashion.

That Kenneth and Maria continue to be forbidden to speak to each other gives them something more to sing about. Sally's warning, "Now remember not to talk to each other," serves as the catalyst for Kenneth's ballad "Once Upon a Time Today." It marks the third "today" song in the score, and another reflexive number—that is, a song that calls attention to itself. Thus too it is another diegetic number, that is, another song recognized as such by the characters. So it represents a savvy solution to the problem of placing numbers in an integrated show. One of the challenges of the so-called integrated era was that the old show-within-a-show plot device had become passé, thus rendering it more difficult to include diegetic numbers even as the bar had been raised on weaving numbers seamlessly into the plot—a problem successfully solved most recently by *Kiss Me, Kate*. Kenneth sings this "twentieth-century fairy tale" in a way that highlights the Graustarkian nature of their romance, the challenges to be overcome when a royal falls for a commoner:

> Once there was a princess,
> Once there was a guy,
> And they fell in love one wonderful day.
> But she was a princess,
> He was just a guy,
> So there was the royal devil to pay.

Example 8.7. *"Something to Dance About."*

In time-honored Berlin fashion the song continues by reinforcing the power of song:

> They were ordered not to speak to one another,
> And they knew the sorrow that would bring;
> Still they promised not to speak to one another—
> But they didn't promise not to sing.

Berlin even injects a self-effacingly autobiographical moment into the lyrics:

> He collected lots of ordinary phrases
> Like "I love you, dear," and "You're for me,"
> But he found that when he set them all to music,
> They were just as good as poetry.

"They Like Ike" belongs among the distinctively American songs in the show, aptly enough for a number sung by the American delegation. Berlin cast the song in old-fashioned quickstep march style that he favored for comical songs with military associations in a lineage that extends from "Oh! How I Hate to Get Up in the Morning" to the *White Christmas* songs "The Old Man" (about the General) and "Gee, I Wish I Was Back in the Army." The song also reveals another way in which Berlin deploys antithesis, as the Republican congressman Wilkins leads but gets interrupted by the Democratic senators Gallagher and Brockbank reminding him not forget about "Harry." The number thus aims to strike a balance. It celebrates Eisenhower, while having the Republicans outnumbered two to one among its singers. Also, the characters refer to "the people" and to the incumbent, not themselves, as the partisans. "*They* like Ike," claims Wilkins, and "Harry won't get out," counter Gallagher and Brockbank.

Although effectively woven into the book, the song is more like a revue number than an "integrated" number. It addressed a specific, dynamic historical moment— the two years leading up to the 1952 presidential election when it had become clear that Eisenhower would be a popular Republican candidate, but when he was still publicly resisting the idea of entering politics. Although Eisenhower had been considered a strong potential candidate as soon as the war was over, he maintained his military position and so was committed to serving his commander in chief. Yet, stoked by his own denials, the prospect of Eisenhower's candidacy remained newsworthy, and *both* parties considered him an attractive figure before Truman sought and won re-election in 1948. In January 1948, the *New York Times*, in an effort to discern the military man's inscrutable politics, described him ambiguously as "probably liberal Republican like his family, somewhat tempered by military conservatism."[32] The article noted that pro-Eisenhower campaign slogans, including "I Like Ike," had already appeared on buttons. It was in that year, Berlin claimed, that he initially wrote "I Like Ike" as a campaign song, not for a show.[33] Being president of Columbia University at the time that Call Me Madam opened on Broadway on October 12, 1950, Eisenhower came to the premiere and, as Berlin put it, "seemed to enjoy it."[34] As he had done since Watch Your Step and the Music Box Revues, Berlin wrote a stage song uniquely addressing the audience in front of him at the moment of its premiere. Had the issue of Eisenhower's presidency been current in 1933, "They Like Ike" could have fit snugly among the newspaper headlines in As Thousands Cheer.

"They Like Ike" was the first number that Berlin knew would be part of act 2, but the show's biggest hit and crowd-pleaser, "You're Just in Love," was inserted very late, when Merman requested "a song with the kid" after noticing the impact of twenty-six-year-old Illinois native Russell Nype's performance of "It's a Lovely Day Today." That Berlin responded to Merman's request with a counterpoint song came about in part because of the renewed success of his first such song, "Simple Melody," in a hit recording by Bing Crosby and his son Gary.[35] Berlin spent a weekend with his assistant, Helmy Kresa, weaving some residual lines from an unused number intended for Annie Get Your Gun into one his most famous showstoppers.[36] For a song added so late in the process, during the out-of-town tryout, it is remarkably well integrated: it becomes a musical response to Maria's spectral echoes of "It's a Lovely Day Today." The lines "I hear singing and there's no one there," represent one of those signature Berlin show-tune lyrics that at once respond to a specific situation in the show and work perfectly well when the song is extracted from its original context.

The song has all the trademarks of Berlin's counterpoint songs since "Simple Melody" had appeared on the New Amsterdam stage thirty-six years earlier: a smooth ballad set against a syncopated rhythm song. Sally sings the rhythm song, and its melodic structure bears some resemblance to "Alexander's Ragtime Band" (like "Hostess with the Mostes'"). It begins with a rhythmic riff figure, which is then repeated, and then reiterated again with an extension. Berlin then ratchets up and reiterates the entire phrase at a new pitch level (this time a major third, instead of the "Alexander" pattern of a perfect fourth). (See ex. 8.8.) As Philip Furia has observed, Sally's lyric begins with a blithe swipe at psychoanalysis, a theme that Berlin's former collaborator Moss Hart had made central to his script for the 1941 musical Lady in the Dark:[37] "You don't need analyzing; / It is not so surprising / That you feel very strange but nice." The number is unique within the show's three song categories. With both ballad and rhythm song, it bridges two styles in a show where the ballads reveal no traces of the "syncopated ballad" that had long been a trademark of Berlin's style. Moreover, this is the only song that Kenneth and Sally sing together.

Emblematic of Berlin's act 2 challenges is a song list in his project files. Dated May 16, 1950, four months before the New Haven tryout, it shows that all nine of the act 1 numbers were already spotted (if not yet written, like the "opening chorus"), but that only two were in place for the second act, and only one of those ("They Like Ike") actually made it into the show (see table 8.2). A few other points are worthy of note. "Free," listed as a "possible number," was inserted into the show eventually but ultimately

Sally Adams (Ethel Merman) and Kenneth Gibson (Russell Nype) sing the counterpoint duet "You're Just in Love," which Berlin wrote because Merman wanted "a song with the kid." Courtesy of Rodgers & Hammerstein, on behalf of the Estate of Irving Berlin.

deleted because it seemed too preachy. ("Free" ended up in *White Christmas* as "Snow.") The song "A Man Chases a Girl," which also appears in the list as a "possible" number, had been composed in 1948 and intended for the unproduced show "Stars on My Shoulders." It ultimately found a place in the 1954 film *There's No Business like Show Business.* "Lichtenburg Cheese," one of just two second-act numbers that Berlin included in the May 1950 list, survives as a lyric only.[38] (It includes the memorably forced rhyme on "coma" and "aroma" to describe the cheese's impact on the brain.) The "Sophie" referred to in the list, always with Kenneth, must have been the original name of the character of Princess Maria; in the final script, it was the Grand Duchess who was named "Sophie."

Berlin's *Complete Lyrics* make it clear—with at least half a dozen full or partial lyrics for the show—that Berlin struggled to find the right tone and balance among his numbers.[39]

If the songs did not fall into place until late in the process, the writers were clear about developing situations, dialogue, and lyrics that foreground the theatrical dimensions of politics. The opening scene shows Sally giving a formal speech about improving international relations before she launches her own brand of American English. The speech recurs once again when she meets Cosmo. Likewise, in a brief scene before she meets the Grand Duke and Duchess, Sally must rehearse her movements and dialogue, in full costume, because she has trouble getting the part down.

Example 8.8. "I Wonder Why / You're Just in Love."

She appears in a "gown with a long train, opera length gloves, and the three feathers stuck in her hair . . . [and] all the Adams jewelry she can carry." The dialogue with the officious Charge d'Affaires Pemberton Maxwell follows:

MAXWELL: Are you sure you know what to do, Madam?

SALLY: I curtsey at the door. I step inside and curtsey again—why I'll never know—I go to the throne and curtsey again—for God's sake—then I hand the Grand Duke my recommendation.

MAXWELL: Your credentials!

SALLY: O.K. I hand 'em to him. Then I tell him how glad I am to be here, and he tells me how glad he is I am here. I make out I believe it. Then maybe he says sit down. In that case I tell him a couple of jokes—

MAXWELL: Please—

SALLY: I'll keep it clean. When he gets up, I get up. I curtsey again—I back to the door, and I curtsey again. And just to be sure I ain't got a chance, they make me wear this. I don't mind a train, but did they have to give me the Super Chief?[40]

Table 8.2. Song list for *Call Me Madam*, dated May 16, 1950 (LC-IBC Box 256, Folder 6)

First Act Numbers
1—Opening Chorus (This could be a concerted number in one of the guests arriving to the party after the first scene.)
2—The Hostess With the Mostes' On The Ball (Merman)
3—Washington Square Dance (Kenneth)
4—Welcome to Lichtenberg (Cosmo)
5—Can You Use Any Money Today? (Merman)
6—Marrying For Love (Cosmo)
7—The Ocarina (Sophie)
8—The Best Thing For You Is Me (Merman & Cosmo)
9—It's a Lovely Day Today (Kenneth & Sophie)
10—Reprise—The Best Thing For You Is Me (Cosmo)
Second Act
1—They Like Ike (Three Senators)
2—Lichtenberg Cheese (Merman & Entire Company)
Possible Numbers
1—Free (Merman)
It would be desirable if a situation could be found to have a number for Merman, Cosmo, Sophie & Kenneth.
Also, a duet for Sophie and Kenneth instead of the reprise of A Man Chases A Girl

Behind such a scene, it is possible to detect an inversion of the old comedic impulse to exhibit the greenhorn immigrant's awkward efforts to dress and act appropriately in the New World—an impulse seen as well in Annie's conversion from backwoods amateur sharpshooter to worldly professional performer. Merman, though not an immigrant herself, seems to have been particularly gifted at portraying such efforts.

We may even detect an effort to perform her identity during her love ballad, "The Best Thing for You." The second half of the song uses a rhetorical device to reaffirm her feelings, and she divides her identity into "myself and I." In the process Berlin extends the song form beyond the predicted thirty-two bars, to thirty-six:

Ev'ry day
To myself I say,
Point the way,
What will it be?
I ask myself,

What's the best thing for you?
And myself and I
Seem to agree
That the best thing for you
Would be me.

For his part, Cosmo also self-consciously performs his dual role as political offi-cial and lover: roles he is unable to play simultaneously. He finds himself in a quan-dary when his romantic interest in the American ambassador conflicts with his professional duty to his ducal superiors. Sally's meeting with the Duke and Duchess occurs offstage, but in the ensuing scene Maxwell itemizes her numerous breaches of protocol, and Cosmo follows by impressing upon her their seriousness: she did not adequately perform her role. He enters and, "bowing stiffly," conveys the Duke and Duchess's "deep displeasure" about the meeting. He exits and then immedi-ately returns and says: "Has that tiresome Prime Minister been here on official busi-ness? . . . Well, I'm glad he's gone. Now Cosmo is here. (*He steps towards her with open arms.*)" The script and songs continually remind us that its protagonists, not just the actors, play roles.

The show's style of political theater addressed the Cold War only obliquely. Like the script, the songs of *Call Me Madam* offer only occasional reminders of the loom-ing presence of the Soviet Union. The writers disciplined the show to avoid preachy ideology. To begin the second chorus of "Hostess with the Mostes,'" for example, Sally sings about "entertaining vodka drinkers" as one of her jobs, and concludes that "What they really need behind the iron wall / Is the hostess with the mostes' on the ball"[41]—as if a warm party could end the Cold War. "Washington Square Dance" strives to reconcile Democrats and Republicans in the spirit of presenting a united front to "our friends across the sea." It also implicitly places "Uncle Sam" and "Uncle Joe" (Stalin) in opposition to one another when Sally "calls" the dance:

Now duck for the oyster,
Dig for the clam,
But do your digging for Uncle Sam—

. . . .

Now one for the money,
Two for the show,
Three to get ready for Uncle Joe.[42]

Not long after that, in "Lichtenburg," Cosmo implicitly refers to contemporary Europe under the Soviet shadow: "While other lands / Keep changing hands, / Old Lichtenburg stays the same."

In the obvious effort to make the show current—with prominent and repeated references to Harry Truman and Truman's future rival Dwight Eisenhower (who was as yet publicly uncommitted to any party affiliation, though the song defines him as a Republican candidate)—it is possible to view the few comical references to the Soviet challenge as an escapist denial of reality, a familiar criticism of musicals and movies. For example, a party scene features multiple conversations punctuated by vaudevil-lian gag-lines, some of which fall flat, as in the following discussion between senators:

GALLAGHER: You know, Jim, as a loyal and devoted Democrat, I'm not satisfied with the Russian situation.

BROCKBANK: You think Uncle Joe's up to something crooked?

GALLAGHER: Crooked? Why, even the wool he pulls over our eyes is fifty per cent cotton.

An earlier version of the lyrics for "Something to Dance About" included the line:

Here's a note from the Russians;
Let the arguments cease.
We are tired of discussions;
Let's sit down and talk peace.[43]

Far from ignoring or underestimating the real political and international tensions that shape the plot, the collaborators rather seem to have realized that audiences needed little reminder that such tensions supplied the framework for the plot, characters, and songs. That, at least, links this show to the spirit of the revue, in which allusions to current events and people could be telegraphic or oblique because they formed the common ground on which creators and audience stood together. And making light of large-scale problems over which individuals have little or no control marks American humor from the Virginia Minstrels to Jon Stewart's *The Daily Show*.

Although the script is expertly crafted and most of the songs hold up well, new stage productions of *Call Me Madam* will always be few and far between, since the show's conception and details are so embedded in the world of America, ca. 1950. But it does survive in what the musical theater historian Miles Krueger has termed a "superior film adaptation."[44] Indeed, *Call Me Madam* is arguably the most faithful film adaptation of a Berlin stage musical, and unlike *Annie Get Your Gun*, a possible improvement on the original stage production. In this film, unlike *Annie Get Your Gun*, Merman reprised her starring role. Moreover, the film included all but two songs from the Broadway version ("Once Upon a Time Today" and "They Like Ike"), and the screenwriter Arthur Sheekman tightened the script to last a few minutes under two hours, distilling the plot to its essentials.

The film did, however, feature notable differences from the original stage production. Its release in 1953, after Eisenhower had become president, required alterations of time. So the opening credits indicate that it takes place in the "past," namely 1951, during the Truman administration, so that the interrupting phone calls from "Harry" may be preserved. Significant changes come to the secondary couple. For one thing the screenplay introduces the character of Prince Hugo as Maria's fiancé, creating added tension to Maria's forbidden romance with Kenneth. Further, by casting Donald O'Connor as Kenneth, and Vera-Ellen as Princess Maria, the filmmakers re-envisioned the secondary couple as a *dancing* couple, creating opportunities for elegant choreography—including an Astaire-Rogers-style private dance floor outside of the crowded ballroom—that had not been included in the original production. Moreover, the Kenneth/Maria romance resolves in the United States, not in Lichtenburg, as Maria comes to Sally's last party with Cosmo, after someone reports to Sally that Cosmo was traveling with a young woman (dashing Sally's hopes temporarily).

There is no talk of the hydroelectric plant. Instead Maria renounces the throne to marry Kenneth (and implicitly, to stay in the States).

Some telling changes to the score linked the film to Berlin's distinctive cavalcade musicals with plots shaped around already-popular songs rather than newly composed ones. "It's a Lovely Day Today" becomes a diegetic number that Kenneth identifies as an "American song" popular on Broadway. Two other songs came in from Berlin's existing catalog. At the party at the American embassy in Lichtenburg, Sally sings a revised version of "The International Rag," Berlin's 1913 call for unity through ragtime. For this purpose, he deleted a phrase about "Russian czars" and added a dig at the Soviets: "All Harrys, Dicks, and Tommies / And someday even commies / Will dance around / To the sound / Of the International Rag."[45] Later, O'Connor sings "What Chance Have I with Love?" from *Louisiana Purchase*—and executes a witty balloon dance to its music, rather than performing "Once Upon a Time Today." In another sequence, an orchestral segue deploys the major-sixth interval in a way that clearly demonstrates the connection between the melodies of "Lichtenburg" and "It's a Lovely Day Today." A nice touch in the film is that the reprise of "You're Just in Love" after Sally is fired reverses the roles so that Kenneth sings "You're Just in Love" and Sally sings "I Wonder Why."

Besides its fine film version, *Call Me Madam* produced a legacy that includes at least four hit songs, two phrases that became part of the American vernacular, and one campaign slogan. "Hostess with the Mostes'," "It's a Lovely Day Today," "Something to Dance About," and especially "You're Just in Love" became the show's song hits. The phrases "hostess with the mostes'" and "I Like Ike" entered the American vernacular. And of course, "They Like Ike," transformed into "I Like Ike," followed Eisenhower long after his presidency. Like Eisenhower's candidacy, the song had assumed a life of its own even before the show closed. In January 1952 Eisenhower became a candidate, winning the New Hampshire primary in March. In response, Berlin revised the lyric again as "I Like Ike." Over the next decade and a half, Berlin would revise or rewrite the song three more times, as "I Still Like Ike" (for the White House Correspondents Dinner, 1954), as "Ike for Four More Years" (for the Republican National Convention, 1956), and as "We Still Like Ike" (for an unproduced television presentation of *Call Me Madam*, 1967).[46] The song tracks Berlin's temporary political shift from Democrat (for which he had been a fervent Roosevelt supporter) to Republican during the Eisenhower years. (Despite a common misconception, Berlin did not always vote Republican in later presidential elections.)[47]

Yet one more perspective on the legacy of *Call Me Madam* is the way in which it helped set the stage for Merman's subsequent work, and, more broadly, for musical theater's later history. By depicting Merman as both a romantic lead (with Cosmo) and as a maternal figure (with Kenneth), *Call Me Madam* paved the way for musicals portraying an older woman as a strong, independent-minded heroine with romantic possibilities. As her biographer Caryl Flinn has put it, as Sally Adams "Ethel was now a good-looking *adult*."[48] When *Call Me Madam* opened, Merman was forty-two, certainly older than most female protagonists in musical theater. Yet as she aged, her compelling star power still burned bright, and writers strove to take advantage of it by conceiving musical plots featuring her as a mother of advancing age, whether widowed (*Happy Hunting*, 1956) or thrice-divorced (*Gypsy*, 1959). This marked a stark contrast from the Rodgers and Hammerstein model, in which older women, almost always widowed or otherwise unmarried, often assume the role of matronly advisors who serve chiefly to foster communal solidarity, to facilitate the romances of younger couples, and to offer earnest messages of hope.[49] Although Merman is in no sense marginal in musical theater history, her roles in the 1950s, beginning with Mrs. Sally Adams, may be seen as countercultural within the dominant style of the age.[50] But it would certainly become a model for the future, not just for *Gypsy* but for the strong, complex older women in the later musicals of Stephen Sondheim. Elaine Stritch embodies the connection. She understudied Merman for Sally Adams and later played the role in the show's national tour; at forty-five, she would be famously cast as the wise-cracking, cynical but sympathetic Joanne in Sondheim and George Furth's *Company* (1970). *Call Me Madam* thus marks a pivot at mid-century, for it bequeathed to the American musical theater a kind of character who would reappear transformed—darker, more troubled, and troubling—in the second half of the century.

MR. PRESIDENT

From Madam Ambassador to Mr. President, Lindsay, Crouse, and Berlin turned their sights to the highest office in the land. The presidency had long fascinated all three for its theatrical potential—a man playing a powerful role. In *State of the Union* Lindsay and Crouse had created a compelling protagonist who was a strong presidential candidate

Ethel Merman toasts Berlin, Howard Lindsay, and Russel Crouse around the time of Call Me Madam. *Courtesy of Rodgers & Hammerstein, on behalf of the Estate of Irving Berlin.*

but never ran for election. In *Call Me Madam*, they featured a charismatic female protagonist while the real president remained an offstage character. Berlin had already conceived, but never finished, a show titled "Stars on My Shoulders" about a former general considering a run for president. A prototype may have been *Life with Father*, depicting a strong patriarchal figure who nevertheless cannot seem to exert the kind of control to which he aspires. So *Mr. President*, which placed a fictional president center stage, may be seen as a culmination of an enduring impulse in their work. They created, in the words Berlin wrote for the opening number, a "simple American" father who "happens to be president of these United States." By focusing on the president's family relationships, they essentially envisioned "life with father" in the White House. Yet making the president the protagonist of a musical comedy ultimately conjured a burden too heavy for the script and songs to carry.

Creating *Mr. President* placed their work in a long continuum of presidential depiction in American popular culture, which included films, plays, radio portrayals, and Rodgers and Hart's 1937 presidential musical comedy, *I'd Rather Be Right*, famously starring George M. Cohan as FDR in a book by George S. Kaufman. In fact, the title they gave their work echoes the title of a series that ran on ABC radio from 1947 to 1953: *Mr. President*. A summary of the show bears a striking resemblance to the plot that Lindsay and Crouse conceived: "Each week, the president, acting out of his innate sense of justice and desire to help the American people, took an unpopular course of action . . . the show reinforced the status and power of the presidency while also humanizing the office."[51] The radio show rewarded historical knowledge by acting out a pivotal moment in an actual presidency but not identifying the president until the end. It is not known whether the writers of the musical considered the radio show in shaping their script, but it would have been hard for them to have avoided knowledge of a popular network program that had run for six years.[52] More recently, Theodore White's *The Making of the President, 1960*, had appeared in 1961 and won the Pulitzer Prize the following year, creating a new interest in behind-the-scenes glimpses of American politics.[53] But unlike the radio show and White's book, the Lindsay-Crouse-Berlin musical took pains at once to deny any resemblance to an actual president. Indeed, unlike *Call Me Madam*'s Harry Truman, the fictional chief executive of *Mr. President* could hardly have been more unlike the current president.

The timing of the show's premiere—so spot-on for *State of the Union* and *Call Me Madam*—could hardly have been less auspicious. After tryouts in Boston (beginning August 27, 1962) and Washington, D.C. (three weeks beginning September 25, 1962), *Mr. President* opened at the St. James Theatre in New York on October 20, 1962. Two days later, on October 22, 1962, President Kennedy gave an urgent speech on national television to inform the American people that the Soviet Union had begun to establish "offensive weapons of mass destruction" in Cuba. Citing the mistakes of appeasement in the 1930s as a "clear lesson," Kennedy stated his case and what he intended to do about it in the strongest possible terms. The "Cuban missile crisis speech" escalated the Cold War to the brink of nuclear war.

None of that, of course, resonated in the show. Although in some ways saturated in the present, the opening scene actually harkened back to several other Berlin shows, some of them in the distant past. Berlin's musical theater was *about* Berlin's musical theater. For example, in the manner of the opening number of *Louisiana*

Purchase and the *Call Me Madam Playbill*'s disclaimer about resemblance to anyone living or dead, the show opens with a brief Prologue featuring an actor, identified as the "Manager," offering a disclaimer denying any semblance to actual people and events. It was a sound comedic strategy, but distinctly old-fashioned. The opening goes back further than *Louisiana Purchase*, in fact, for its clearest model is the minstrel finale of the 1919 *Follies*, with an emcee-like character emerging to introduce the show. Just as in the verse of "I'd Rather See a Minstrel Show" where Eddie Cantor had rejected "the drama," "revues," and "play," here the emcee rejects any notion that the show's protagonist is modeled on real presidents: "Not the Roosevelts, / Not the Trumans, / Not the Eisenhowers, / . . . Not the Kennedys."[54] Likewise, at the end of Cantor's number the curtain had opened to reveal a spectacular set (in minstrel formation), so too the Manager ends by asking the audience to "take a glance / At a formal, dignified White House dance." The opening image—a lighted silhouette of the White House—recalls the first *Music Box Revue*'s stage representation of the theater itself. Meanwhile, no one seems to have noticed that Berlin had stolen a musical phrase from another one of his famous songs (ex. 8.9).

The show proper traces the rise, fall, and redemption of Stephen Decatur Henderson and the effect of his political vicissitudes on his wife (Nell), his son (Larry), and his daughter (Leslie)—each of whom is introduced individually during the Prologue. The story quickly violates some key tenets of musical comedy that stem from classic comedy models. Stephen and Nell Henderson are presented as ordinary and old-fashioned people. In the midst of a party dancing the Twist, Nell rejects current fads

Example 8.9

8.9a. Mr. President, *opening.*

8.9b. *"White Christmas," end of verse.*

and sings "Let's Go Back To the Waltz." The central relationship of a musical comedy, like most traditional comedy, is typically a young couple, with the adults, or the characters who are older, serving either to abet or block the aspirations of the younger ones. Exceptions might appear, as with Emile de Beque as an older romantic lead in *South Pacific*. Broadway had seen the apotheosis of youth just five years earlier in *West Side Story*, where the adults, in the end, are ultimately rendered "useless." Lindsay and Crouse, however, grew increasingly interested in developing older protagonists, making Cosmo and Sally central to *Call Me Madam*. Then, in *The Sound of Music*, they presented a "parental" couple as the romantic and liberal center of the plot, while the adolescent love of Rolf and Liesl is distinctly secondary and ultimately unfulfilled. So by creating a presidential protagonist at the end of his second term (legally unable to run again, and with, at first, no apparent aspirations beyond finishing his presidency with integrity) and by showing Henderson and his wife in a stable, resolved, and explicitly old-fashioned relationship —favoring the waltz over the Twist and longing to retire to a simple life—the veterans of Broadway recast the musical in their own image, or at least asked their audience to age with them.

Mr. President (Robert Ryan) and the First Lady (Nanette Fabray). Courtesy of
Rodgers & Hammerstein, on behalf of the Estate of Irving Berlin.

The conservative impulse driving the show appears to be reinforced by the love triangle coalescing around Henderson's daughter, Leslie. Act 1 presents her developing romance with Youssein Davar, son of the leader of an unnamed Middle Eastern country. Leslie justifies her attraction by explaining that he represents a fresh alternative to her usual choice "between the 'Ban-the-Bomb' boys and the 'Go-Go-Go-for-Goldwater' gang," a provocative attempt by the writers to steer a politically neutral course.[55] Complicating Leslie's situation is the persistent presence of two Secret Service officers, one of whom, Pat, is in love with her but believes that Leslie could not be interested in someone with his simple "Meat and Potatoes" tastes. Pat recalls being around Leslie since she had "Pigtails and Freckles"—a long way from the grown-up young woman now in his presence. It turns out, however, that Youssein, for all his charm, may be insincere and has questionable values. The first hint comes late in act 1 when Youssein tells Leslie over wine that he has spread the rumor that they are engaged, a good thing because "it's raised the spirits of the whole country." The last straw, however, does not come until act 2, after Election Day, when at a party Youssein becomes attracted to Betty, the daughter of the new president, and claims to be "neutral" about everything, for "we help both sides [America and Russia] every way we can." Leslie, now prompted by a combination of patriotism and romantic rejection, leaves the party with Pat. Youssein is revealed as a foreign opportunist whose romantic interests are driven by a need for proximity to power. (There are striking parallels between Youssein and *Sound of Music*'s Elsa Schraeder, with whom Captain von Trapp breaks his engagement upon learning that she is willing to accommodate the Nazis in order to maintain her social position.)

Leslie's private love triangle plays out in the context of Cold War politics and leads to a remarkable moment of international harmony at odds with the historical moment of its arrival on a Broadway stage—October 1962. In act 1, President Henderson's political fortunes at home depend on his decisions about a "good will" tour to several foreign countries, including the Soviet Union. The tour had been a campaign promise, so Henderson feels compelled to follow through, even though he would rather stay home. (He agonizes over the decision in the forlorn number "It Gets Lonely in the White House.") On the trip the First Couple is generally greeted with warmth in the various countries they visit ("They Love Me," sings the First Lady), but along the way the president creates an international incident in a speech where he makes a joke comparing the Russian leader to a "wild cat." Back on the plane, Henderson receives a radio message stating that he is unwelcome in Moscow due to the "resentment and indignation" sparked by his joke. The president decides to go anyway. They land in Moscow, and he gets off the plane long enough to make a brief conciliatory speech, translated by his son, Larry, who has been studying Russian, to some Soviet people gathered on the tarmac. It is a speech with a common touch in which Henderson claims that Russians and Americans are fundamentally alike. There are at least two versions of what happened next, one poignant, and one humorous. In a late "rehearsal version," the president and his son then turn back and mount the steps to the plane, and the script indicates that "at the top of the steps they turn and wave uncertainly to the Russians. Nell and Leslie join them. The Russians, slowly, hesitantly, raise their hands and wave back. Both sides break into smiles and wave toward each other with sincerity."[56] In the script currently licensed by the Rodgers and Hammerstein Organization, the president (through his son) tells a Russian man with eight children that "You're a better man than I am," and the Russians laugh and wave as the president climbs back into the plane.[57] Both versions reinforce the common humanity that Henderson wished to emphasize.

The trip, despite its brief glimpse of a thaw in the Cold War, becomes a political liability at home, and Bob Wheeler, the incumbent candidate, finds that the president's coattails may not lead him to success against the challenger, Ed Chandler. Wheeler loses, and Larry admits to punching the party chairman on television for claiming that his dad's support cost Wheeler the election. The president scolds Larry for being a poor loser, but then we learn that Wheeler, too, blames the president for his loss, specifically the trip to Moscow. In a like-son, like-father moment, Henderson claims *he* would like to punch Wheeler in the nose. Nell tries to rally the family with a light song of optimism, "Laugh It Up." In the script's rehearsal version, act 1 ends showing the president about to leave the White House with a sense of defeat, singing a brief reprise of "It Gets Lonely in the White House" much as Merman had sung a sorrowful reprise to close act 1 in *Annie Get Your Gun* and *Call Me Madam*. The creators, however, may have seen that as too pathetic, and so act 1 ends instead with a reprise of "In Our Hide-Away," showing the Hendersons relieved and looking ahead to return to private life.

Act 2 shows the former president adjusting to political retirement back in his home town of Mansfield, Ohio—shopping for groceries, keeping up with the news, attempting to write his memoirs. But he finds that the simple life he had yearned for in the White House leaves him restless and feeling sorry for himself. (The image of the retired national hero, uncertain about his future, is one that Berlin had explored before: first in the unfinished "Stars on My Shoulders," then in *White Christmas*—as if Berlin sensed that the postwar world had found him out of step with the times.) The family is invited to a reception at the White House to show, in the words of the new president's status-conscious daughter Betty, "that my father, the President, isn't mad at your father." The party, of course, results in Youssein and Leslie's breakup, and it leads Leslie to Pat, the Secret Service man who has been in unrequited love with her throughout act 1. An opportunity arises, however, when Henderson learns from a reporter that one of Ohio's senators has died, and that the governor will likely ask Henderson to finish the senator's term. But Henderson declines when he realizes the governor wants him for strictly political reasons. The governor then turns around and appoints himself as the senator. The incident stokes Henderson's patriotism, as he tells Nell, in a scene comparable to the end of *State of the Union*, that "I know this country. I know the worst of it and I know the best of it." The line leads into the big patriotic number, "This Is a Great Country." Within seconds of this flag-waver, another opportunity comes his way when Henderson learns that President Chandler is inviting him to serve in an official capacity at an international "summit meeting" in Copenhagen because, as Pat, serving as a messenger, announces, "that landing in Russia—the Russians have great respect for you, sir." The show ends as the former president goes out the door to accept the invitation and to greet Chandler with what turns out to be the curtain line: "Mr. President—." The finale ensues with a choral reprise of "This Is a Great Country."

The score, like Henderson's idealistic patriotism, has a distinctively retrospective quality for anyone who knows Berlin's work over the past five decades and sounds as decidedly old-fashioned as the characters—certainly more so than in *Call Me Madam*. It reveals Berlin relying on his own earlier models and raiding his trunk with an almost encyclopedic range of allusions and adaptations of songs and song types from the past four decades or more. Some of these are certainly the kind of clever self-referential in-jokes that Berlin frequently inserted into his early shows. "The Washington Twist," for example, rewards listeners who remembered *Call Me Madam*. As a song in which "dance" presents the double meaning of movement to music and of political gamesmanship, its concept and title resonate with "The Washington Square Dance." And its repeated reference to the president as "the host with the most" conjures memories of the best remembered lyric about the ambassador to Lichtenburg.

Most other numbers reveal devices, phrases, and styles that had worked in the past, a fact about which Berlin was open, declaring in a *New York Times* interview published six days before the show's Broadway opening that "I always use things from the past, always have, in every show."[58] "Let's Go Back to the Waltz," as it rejects the Twist, recalls "The Waltz of Long Ago" from the *Music Box Revue of 1923*, in which Grace Moore dismissed the appeal of jazz. In scene 2, when the Hendersons imagine returning to a simple life, they sing a song reminiscent of the old cozy-cottage numbers of musical comedies of the 1910s and 1920s, like Berlin's own "A Little Bungalow" in *The Cocoanuts*: "In our hide-away / Far from all the fuss / That bothers us, / We'll hide away." Later in the same scene, Nell confronts her full schedule for the following day, and expresses her dismay in a quickstep march song with series of ordinal numbers reminiscent of a device that Berlin had deployed in "The Fifth Army" for the Italian tour of *This Is the Army*: "I'd rather be the second or the third or the fourth / Or the fifth or the sixth or the seventh / Instead of the First Lady of the land." In scene 3, when Pat tries to deny his attraction to Leslie, whom he believes is much too sophisticated to be interested in a simple man like himself, he borrows a lyric from *Annie Get Your Gun*: "The girl that I marry," he sings, "Will have to be / Meat and potatoes / Potatoes and meat, / Like me." When Leslie confides in her mother that she is falling in love with Youssein, Nell sings her advice to consider how she would answer the question "Is He the Only Man in the World for Me?," the melodic phrase for which Berlin borrowed from his 1928 song "Where is the Song of Songs for Me?"[59] As the president contemplates the "good will" tour that he promised during his campaign, he sings the song "It Gets Lonely in the White House," originally intended for "Stars on My Shoulders," the unproduced 1948 project about a retired general considering a run for the presidency. Later, when the Hendersons go on their tour, Nell enjoys her celebrity in a song called "They Love Me" whose music bears a striking resemblance to the phrase "We love him" in "The Old Man"—a song performed in *White Christmas* by former soldiers of the retired General Waverly. The repeated title phrase of "Laugh It Up" also echoes a phrase from an army song: "This Is the Army, Mister Jones" (the last phrase of the refrain's "A" section). And what Berlin theater score would be complete without a counterpoint song? In *Mr. President*, Pat and Leslie argue about whether love can survive without finances in "Empty Pockets Filled with Love."

The show's patriotic finale also resonated back to several earlier Berlin songs. Much of the bouncy, syncopated refrain of the show's flag-waver "This Is a Great Country"

Example 8.10. The rhythmic basis of "This Is a Great Country."

would not have sounded out of place five decades earlier during World War I, when Berlin wrote "For Your Country and My Country," but the song's verse, with its reflection that "patriotism has gone out of fashion" could only have come in Berlin's later years. A critic called it "a successor to 'God Bless America,'"[60] but when the ensemble begins to sing it in four-part harmony, it sounds closer to Berlin's 1949 Miss Liberty's hymnlike finale, "Give Me Your Tired, Your Poor." No one commented, however, that the principal phrase's rhythm borrows its bounce from "There's No Business Like Show Business"—a perhaps coincidental, but still telling, linkage between two of Berlin's fundamental drives: love of country and love of theater (ex. 8.10).

This is not to say that the score lacks originality. Berlin wrote what may be his only twelve-bar blues number in "The Washington Twist," supported with an excellent, idiomatic orchestration by Philip J. Lang that had an early 1960s vintage in the heart of the Twist craze. It represents Berlin's last successful effort to resonate contemporary popular music on the stage—something he had done for more than half a century. One critic who clearly had no affinity for the style noted that "Berlin has written a twist song that is bearable."[61] The number that was most enthusiastically received was "The Secret Service," sung by Leslie in act 1: "the secret service makes me nervous," she claims, and she finds herself unable to pursue a romance—or to do most other things an ordinary young lady can do.[62] "They Love Me" was a big production number featuring Nanette Fabray enjoying the attention of people from all over the world. Many reviews commented on the moment Nanette Fabray emerged on the stage riding a "comic elephant"—a visual echo of Mrs. Meshbesher's dramatic entrance in the finale of Face the Music thirty years earlier. "The Only Dance I Know" was essentially a burlesque number cast in an exotic orientalized guise for the Mansfield, Ohio, fair. Such songs, however, did not prove to be enough to save the show.

Yet the show did amazing business in advanced ticket sales thanks to the stars who created it, described, in words analogous to the president himself, as the "top level of the Broadway Establishment." It included not just Berlin, returning to Broadway after a twelve-year hiatus, but also key players on the team that had a historic success with Rodgers and Hammerstein in The Sound of Music, still running on Broadway. Producer Leland Hayward's estimate of $2.5 million made it "the largest pre-opening income in the history of the Broadway theatre," the big news in the week before the Broadway opening, reported on October 14, the date that often marks the beginning of the Cuban missile crisis.[63]

By then, mixed reviews of the show itself had already begun. The Times surveyed the Boston reaction after the opening night of the tryout there. One was quoted claiming that, while "not the unqualified smash hit that had been hoped for, it has a lot of good qualities." Another noted some "amusing" parts but that it was "sometimes cornily dull." Still another simply claimed that *Mr. President* was in "dreadful shape at the present time," yet it had "at least three or four songs with the authentic lilt and magic of Irving Berlin at his ultimate best."[64]

Although Lindsay, Crouse, and Berlin undertook revisions, they did not have much effect on the critical reaction after opening night nearly two months later. "Has there ever been as dull a President as the man occupying the White House in 'Mr. President'?," asked Howard Taubman in the *New York Times*. "If so," he answered, "the nation, praise be, has survived." Recalling an important precedent for staging the American presidency, Taubman noted that the show was "mechanical in an old-fashioned way. It lacks an edge, like 'Of Thee I Sing' of hallowed memory. It has no exhilarating personal viewpoint or style, Presidential or otherwise." Taubman did single out the President Henderson's speech in Moscow as a memorable scene: "If you are prone [recte: susceptible?] to musical-comedy heroism, you will find it hard to stanch a proud tear." The only real saving grace of the show for Taubman was the "effervescent" performance of Nanette Fabray as the First Lady, who in his view saves the show from being "as diverting as a budget message."[65] The *London Times* printed a review by its unnamed "New York Dramatic Critic" claiming that "the cliché presentation of family warmth and patriotic fervor never wavers. . . . If the plot and characters are, in the American phrase, sheer 'corn,' Mr. Berlin's principal songs match them, especially 'Meat and Potatoes' (about the qualities a Secret Service man seeks in his bride) and a flag-waving tune, 'This Is a Great Country.'" The *London Times* critic did not even share Taubman's sympathetic view of the pivotal scene on the Moscow airport tarmac, calling it an "odd, foolish incident."[66]

Meanwhile, *Of Thee I Sing* had apparently been on the minds of other critics as well. (Although that show was now more than three decades old, it had seen a Broadway revival ten years earlier, in 1952.) While *Mr. President* was still in Washington, Hayward noted that critical expectations hurt the show's prospects: "For some reason—maybe it's the title and the Kennedys' being in the White House—the intellectuals come expecting a cross between 'State of the Union' and 'Of Thee I Sing.' A satire, with big jokes and 'Wintergreen for President.' Well, we're not doing a satire. We're doing a warm, human, simple story of a man who is President and his family." It was, Hayward argued, an "audience show." Berlin, likewise, went over the critics' heads and claimed that "I don't think we have a Pulitzer Prize show, a Critics Circle Award show. I do think that we have a show that audiences will love."[67] In another interview just before opening night, Berlin similarly said: "The best critic I have found . . . is the audience, and this is an audience show"—echoing not just Leland Heyward but also his own old claim that the mob is always right.[68]

Recognizing connections between the characters onstage and the creators offstage, Berlin wrote a line that Joshua Logan claimed "describes perfectly what it has been like" to develop the show under the glare of media: "I've been exposed beyond control, / Just like a goldfish in a bowl."[69] The exposure continued after the show opened and closed, much to the dismay of the illustrious collaborators. For Lindsay and Crouse, who had now authored their second misfire branded "old-fashioned" by at least one major critic, *Mr. President* marked the end of their collaboration after nearly four decades.[70] After the show closed on June 8, 1963, after just 265 performances, a *New York Times* report noted that *Mr. President* had achieved the dubious distinction of "the shortest run for the biggest advance sale in theatrical history."[71] *The Sound of Music* outlasted *Mr. President* and closed a week later, on June 15, 1963, having run for 1,443 performances. In the long view, the Broadway musical that most closely defined the Kennedy-era presidency was not *Mr. President* but rather a 1960 show set in the distant past in a legendary England, *Camelot*, which was still running when *Mr. President* opened in the fall of 1962.

The three-week Washington tryout had been a major cultural event and its opening there was perhaps the production's peak moment. Under the headline "Thousands Queue Up to Buy Tickets for 'Mr. President,'" the *Washington Post* reported that the first man to buy tickets for the show had arrived at the theater sixteen hours before the box office opened.[72] The journalist Helen Thomas noted that the capital's chic hair stylist for the elite, Jean Louis, was "booked solid for the day of the premiere."[73] And a feature story claimed that opening night "turned into one of Washington's biggest fashion shows to date," and supported its points with a half-dozen photographs of prominent women in designer gowns, including Ethel Kennedy ("Mrs. Robert F. Kennedy") and Jackie Kennedy ("Mrs. John F. Kennedy").[74] Yet another article about opening night treated it as a news event, where "the most dazzling evening's entertainment in Washington" since Kennedy's inauguration took place "off stage," as "several thousand persons jammed the streets to watch the notables filing down the red carpet and into the theater."[75]

Observers who commented on the audience noted that Washingtonians generally loved the show, confirming the creators' claims that it was an "audience show." A Los Angeles critic who witnessed the Washington tryout referred to "Laugh It Up" as a "show-stopper," and generally noted that "the audience seemed to thoroughly enjoy" the show. He further explained the reception of "They Love Me," when Nanette Fabray "rides in on an elephant a la Jackie Kennedy": "Washington audiences really eat that stuff up."[76]

A perceptive observer of the show's Washington tryout run from late September through mid-October was a thirteen-year-old boy named Frank Rich who attended several performances and wrote about them in a memoir entitled *Ghost Light*, published thirty-eight years later, after he had become well known as a theater critic and then an op-ed columnist for the *New York Times*. Rich remembered that "what entranced me most . . . was the extravagance of the scenery and costume, the men in tails, the women a rainbow of silk ball gowns, simulating the White House and all its storied occupants. . . . the show abetted my fantasy of the capital's hidden glamour."[77] By attending the production several times, each different than the last as the authors and actors adjusted the script and songs, Rich observed that the show became "a living organism, different at each performance."[78]

Rich also became eyewitness to the troubled state of the show's creators. With his standing-room-only ticket at the back of the theater, Rich observed "standing in the deep shadows at the rail a few places down were five older men, uniformly stone-faced," and he recognized them from pictures he had seen in the Washington papers: Berlin, Lindsay, Crouse, Hayward, and director Joshua Logan. "How, I wondered, watching their grim expressions, could they be unhappy even as the audience showered their show with affection?"[79] While *Mr. President* ended the stage careers of Lindsay, Crouse, and Berlin, it awakened Frank Rich's identity as a theater critic.

Although dubbed a "spectacular Broadway fiasco" (Rich would also use the word *fiasco* in his memoir), *Mr. President* apparently attracted some interest from major film companies. Director Logan reported that there would be significant changes to the plot of any film adaptation. "The emphasis . . . will transfer to the romantic subplot involving the president's daughter and her Secret Service boyfriend, with the White House occupants reduced to 'character' second leads." Logan cited Ann-Margret as an actress "who would make a wonderful president's daughter."[80] Ann-Margret was just twenty-two in 1963 and had become a star on television and films. If the idea had merit, its timing was nevertheless unfortunate. Kennedy's assassination happened just four months after the *Times* published that report, likely making it impossible for Hollywood to present a musical comedy that envisioned a member of the Secret Service in a romantic relationship with the president's daughter.

Noting that *Mr. President* opened just before the Cuban missile crisis reached its peak, and ideas for its film version were floated just months before Kennedy's assassination, superstition-prone theater people have ample reason to believe the show to be cursed. In 2001 Gerard Alessandrini, the writer of spoof-driven revues known as *Forbidden Broadway*, attempted to revive the show with updated lyrics and a script that featured characters with names like George Shrub, Jr., and Dick Brainy—making them sound like they had walked in from an old Harry B. Smith script. It opened off-Broadway in August 2001. With a plan to run for several weeks, it was to be the flagship production "in a program of new looks at Broadway flops"—but it closed within a week of its opening, and further efforts in the series, dubbed "Gong-cores" (the name a hybrid of Broadway's "Encores!" series and "The Gong Show") never materialized.[81] The celebration of flops—beginning with Berlin's most extravagant one—had again flopped, and it did so just before another national crisis.

Grand old men of the theater, Russel Crouse died in 1966 and Lindsay passed away three years later. Berlin, older than both, continued working. At seventy-eight he revised *Annie Get Your Gun* for its revival, and he continued to write songs for a variety of other purposes, notably the ongoing (but ultimately unproduced) "Say It with Music" film project. The renewed success of *Annie Get Your Gun* in 1966, and Berlin's ability to once more "reach up" and "find" a show-stopping song in "Old-Fashioned Wedding" inspired him to continue thinking up projects. His last known musical theater ideas took him back farther into the past. One was a new edition of the *Music Box Revue*. The other returned him to his American roots: "East River," a musical about life on the Lower East Side for which he wrote what was probably his last counterpoint song ("Wait until You're Married").[82] Although a stage adaptation of the film *White Christmas* appeared in 2008 and continues to tour during the winter holidays, Broadway would never again see a truly new Berlin work on the stage.

CONCLUSION

• • •

"THIS IS AMERICA"

If Broadway saw nothing new from Irving Berlin between the two Lindsay and Crouse shows, it was not for lack of effort. He had many more projects brewing in that period but none reached the stage. The singular impression these projects make is one of retrospection and nostalgia—in topic, style, and affect—sometimes marked by an overripe patriotism, and dated ethnic and racial portrayal. "Stars on My Shoulders" (1948–49) explores the postwar life of a retired general, who, feeling forgotten, considers a run for the presidency when some of his former soldiers give him a boost. Berlin wrote several scenarios and nine songs for the show, and act 1 was scripted before the project ran aground.[1] The idea and some of its songs got refracted in *White Christmas* (the retired general) and *Mr. President* (the decent, old-fashioned man in the White House). In 1955, Berlin wrote a scenario for an "all-negro show" called "Cindy Lou" intended as a Cinderella story conceived for Eartha Kitt (in the title role), Duke Ellington (as her father, the "King of Jazz"), and Ethel Waters as the fairy godmother ("a maid for a night-club singer") who helps Cindy Lou get the man of her dreams, a newly returned veteran of the Korean War.[2]

Between 1952 and 1956, Berlin also made great strides in developing a musical based on the story of the Mizner brothers, Wilson and Addison. Wilson, one of Berlin's friends in his early years, was known as a playboy, gambler, and sometime playwright. Addison became known as an architect for Florida's rich during the boom in real estate there during the 1920s. Interest in the brothers had resurfaced after the publication of Cleveland Amory's *Last Resorts* (1952), which brings out Addison's role in the Florida land boom. The initial plan, based on Amory's book and titled "Palm Beach," was to create another Merman vehicle with a script by Lindsay and Crouse.[3] When that project fell through, Berlin's attention shifted to developing a show based on another new book: Alva Johnston's *The Legendary Mizners* (1953), for which the playwright S. N. Behrman had acquired the rights. Berlin—and for one month, George S. Kaufman—joined the project, now titled "Sentimental Guy," with an eye toward a musical focusing on the brothers' vicissitudes. Behrman finished the act 1 script, and Berlin wrote at least a dozen songs for the show, but act 2 foundered, despite Berlin's earnest efforts to drive the plot scenario to the end.[4] The script made the conventional coupling of a marriage plot and a show business plot. For it, Berlin wrote yet another counterpoint song in which two characters debate the relative merits of Dallas and New York.[5] The show stalled by mid 1956. For years the rights remained unavailable, despite at least one musical theater composer's long-held desire, since reading Johnston's Mizner story at the age of twenty-two, to write a show based on it. That show finally came to fruition a half century later in Stephen Sondheim and John Weidman's off-Broadway production of *Road Show* (2008), a musical that had endured a decade of development from its first incarnation as *Wise Guys* (1999) and its second as *Bounce* (2003), which faltered during out-of-town previews.[6]

It should not come as a surprise that Berlin's late work became so retrospective. After all, almost all of his films trace a historical trajectory that amount to a kind of mythmaking about the origins and development of show business. Berlin had pioneered the cavalcade musical featuring plots grown from song seeds in the Berlin catalog: *Alexander's Ragtime Band* (1938), *Blue Skies* (1946), *Easter Parade* (1948), and *White Christmas* and *There's No Business Like Show Business* (both 1954). Each one not only packs in as many Berlin songs as possible but places show business itself at the center of the plot. Indeed, film may be seen as Berlin's chief medium for commemorating, re-creating, and preserving live performance, especially *stage* performance—whether in a theater, in a nightclub, on the radio, or on a battlefield. Berlin's films are fundamentally about theater itself, reinforcing the metatheatrical impulse behind so much of his work.

The most intriguing unfinished project of Berlin's later years is one that most clearly lays bare the link between his theatrical values and his patriotic world view. In 1956 Berlin drafted a remarkable scene titled "This Is America."[7] In it, several "immigrant couples" strip off their old-world clothes and put on "American dress of the period" while surrounded by what Berlin's scenario describes as "members of the minstrels as in 'This Is the Army, Mister Jones.'" By modeling the ritualistic opening scene of "This Is America" on the opening of *This Is the Army*, Berlin made explicit something that had been latent in his work for at least four decades since he created *Yip Yip Yaphank*, the conflation of three seemingly unrelated phenomena: American immigrant assimilation, military induction, and minstrelsy. All three, for Berlin, require wearing clothes and playing roles that allow the immigrant, the citizen, and the performer to be embraced by a larger community. A reminder of the profound impact of war on his theatrical imagination, minstrelsy here becomes the medium for Berlin's theater of war *and* peace, a theatrical style through which the immigrant becomes a citizen and the civilian becomes a soldier, and thus, for better or worse, through which both become more fully American. The lyrics, music, and scenario strike a jarring note in a period at the dawn of the era of civil rights and rock 'n' roll, when traditional minstrelsy had long been out of fashion. Its clumsy dramaturgy has nothing to recommend it for the stage, but it does stand as a vivid glimpse of the foundations of Berlin's distinctively American musical theater.

And here we have the fundamental paradox of Berlin's work and its legacy: it drew its energy from a delicate balance of laserlike focus on the current American scene and knowledge of its theatrical and musical traditions that was broad and deep—and as riddled with contradictions as the country for which he saw his work as a "mirror." At its best, Berlin's theater had perfect pitch for the sound and look of America and how it should be reflected on stage. At its worst, it resorted to hoary clichés that had their roots in the turn-of-the-century vaudeville long after they had ceased to entertain the mob whose approval he so eagerly sought.

If, as Alan Jay Lerner claimed, Berlin made American musical theater *possible*, then its ability to thrive and remain vital depends on each generation addressing that balance in a new way. But there is much more to say as we reflect on Berlin's work for the stage. Lerner did not much expand on his notion of Berlin's foundational contribution, so perhaps this is the place to sum it up.

Berlin's career traced a fundamental shift in American musical theater from the centrifugal forces of variety to the centripetal forces of the integrated musical. Yet even after integration became the catchword he insisted that musical numbers should be able to stand alone as independent songs. In expressing his disdain for the term *integration*, Berlin said, with reference to an Alan Jay Lerner show: "it wouldn't be hard to integrate any of the songs from *My Fair Lady* in another show. One of the characters gets the urge to dance all night and there you go."[8] That belief joined his aesthetic values and business instincts. Uniquely, I think, he understood and deployed the full range of musical-theatrical idioms that Americans of his generation knew. In his early years, his shows were *about* the sheer exhibition of that variety within a single show—the Dillingham shows and the *Music Box Revues* being exemplars of that impulse. As he worked with more gifted book writers from the 1920s on—Kaufman, Hart, Ryskind, the Fieldses, and Lindsay and Crouse—he learned how to channel his craft to serve the needs of plot situation while still asserting an omnivorous stylistic range. The better the books, however, the more his theatrical songwriting drew from a narrower, but deeper, well. By the 1940s, all signs of his operatic ambitions had disappeared from his scores with the exception of the counterpoint song—of which he was the undisputed master. Overt minstrelsy was gone, too, with or without blackface, after its last, sensational deployment in *This Is the Army*, and yet Merman's Annie and Sally reflect the enduring spirit of the end man in their down-to-earth common (wo)man sensibilities cracking wise at the proud and pompous. In essence Berlin re-channeled opera, minstrelsy, vaudeville, and revue so that their most potent elements became smoothly assimilated into mainstream musical comedy. Berlin's brand of musical theater, then, was all-encompassing, defying the notion of a monolithic "Broadway style." Along the way his shows became less overtly metatheatrical and reflexive but remained self-referential nevertheless. For the man who wrote "there's no business like show business" the theater itself was not just business but a redemptive form of secular religion and patriotic expression.

But it was a business, too. Berlin's contribution transcends musical, linguistic, and theatrical style. Long before the age of integration—long before "Rodgers and Hammerstein's *Oklahoma!*"—Berlin placed the songwriter's role at center stage of the musical theater enterprise with his very first show: writing the entire score himself, publishing it himself, and forbidding interpolations by other songwriters. *Watch Your Step* was a producer-and-star–driven show that came to be known as "Irving Berlin's *Watch Your Step*." Indeed, in the decades to come, many of Berlin's works for the stage and screen would carry the composer's name in their titles—signifying a grasp of branding long before Broadway's Disneyfication. In that sense, the Broadway musical may be construed still as Irving Berlin's American musical theater.

NOTES

PREFACE

1. Alan Jay Lerner, *The Musical Theatre: A Celebration* (New York: McGraw-Hill, 1986), 48.

2. Joshua Logan, "A Ninetieth-birthday Salute to the Master of American Song," *High Fidelity* 28, no. 5 (May 1978): 81.

3. The biographies include: Alexander Woollcott, *The Story of Irving Berlin* (New York: G. P. Putnam's Sons, 1925); David Ewen, *The Story of Irving Berlin* (New York: Holt, 1950); Michael Freedland, *Irving Berlin* (New York: Stein and Day, 1974); Laurence Bergreen, *As Thousands Cheer: The Life of Irving Berlin* (New York: Penguin, 1990); Philip Furia, *Irving Berlin: A Life in Song* (New York: Schirmer, 1998); Edward Jablonski, *Irving Berlin: American Troubadour* (New York: Henry Holt, 1999). Among them, Furia best captures the nature of the work in the life, with a literary flair that rises to its demanding subject. Mary Ellin Barrett, *Irving Berlin: A Daughter's Memoir* (New York: Simon and Schuster, 1994), also contains valuable biographical information and insight.

4. For a lavishly illustrated and engagingly written coffee-table book focusing on both stage and screen, see David Leopold, *Irving Berlin's Show Business* (New York: Harry N. Abrams, 2005). On lyrics, see Furia, *Life in Song*, and Furia, *The Poets of Tin Pan Alley* (New York: Oxford University Press, 1990). For musical analysis, see Alec Wilder, *American Popular Song: The Great Innovators, 1900–1950* (New York: Oxford University Press, 1972); Allen Forte, *The American Popular Ballad of the Golden Era, 1924–1950* (Princeton, NJ: Princeton University Press, 1995); and David Carson Berry, "Dynamic Introductions: The Affective Role of Melodic Ascent and Other Linear Devices in Selected Verses of Irving Berlin," *Intégral* 13 (1999): 1–62; and Berry, "Gambling with Chromaticism? Extra-diatonic Melodic Expression in the Songs of Irving Berlin," *Theory and Practice* 26 (2001): 21–85.

5. Joseph P. Swain, *The Broadway Musical: A Critical and Musical Study* (New York: Oxford University Press, 1990); Geoffrey Block, *Enchanted Evenings: The Broadway Musical from* Show Boat *to Sondheim and Lloyd Webber* (1997; repr., New York: Oxford University Press, 2009); Raymond Knapp, *American Musical Theater and the Formation of National Identity* (Princeton, NJ: Princeton University Press, 2004) and *American Musical Theater and the Performance of Personal Identity* (Princeton, NJ: Princeton University Press, 2006); Andrea Most, *Making Americans: Jews and the Broadway Musical* (Cambridge, MA: Harvard University Press, 2004); Bruce Kirle, *Unfinished Business: Broadway Musicals as Works-in-Process* (Carbondale: Southern Illinois University, 2005); and Scott McMillin, *The Musical as Drama* (Princeton, NJ: Princeton University Press, 2006).

6. See Charles Hamm, *Irving Berlin: Songs from the Melting Pot: The Formative Years* (New York: Oxford University Press, 1997); and Hamm, ed., *Irving Berlin: Early Songs, 1907–1914*. Music of the United States of America 2, Recent Researches in American Music 20, 3 vols. (Madison, WI: A-R Editions, 1994).

7. Irving Berlin, *The Complete Lyrics of Irving Berlin,* ed. Robert Kimball and Linda Emmet (New York: Alfred A. Knopf, 2001), hereafter cited as *CL*.

INTRODUCTION: IRVING BERLIN'S CENTURY

1. This capsule biography is based on my article on Berlin in *The Scribner Encyclopedia of American Lives*, vol. 2 © 1998 Gale, a part of Cengage Learning, Inc. Reproduced by permission. www.cengage.com/permissions. It draws chiefly from the following sources: Woollcott, *Story*; Bergreen, *As Thousands Cheer*; Jablonski, *American Troubadour*; Furia, *Life in Song*; Barrett, *Daughter's Memoir*; and personal communication from Mary Ellin Barrett and Linda Emmet, November 2003.

2. Berlin, "Some notes on my trip to help exploit 'White Christmas,'" unpublished typescript dated Oct. 1954, LC-IBC, Box 332.

CHAPTER 1: IRVING BERLIN'S THEATER

1. Jablonski, *American Troubadour*, 22, provides the most detailed account of Berlin's lodgings and the "near fatal" stabbing.

2. Berlin quoted in Ward Morehouse, "Sentimental Journey: Prowling with Millionaire Irving Berlin Where He Used to Sing for Pennies," *Philadelphia Bulletin*, Mar. 2, 1947. Clipping in LC-IBC Box 280, Folder 13.

3. Quoted in Furia, *Life in Song*, 8

4. Morehouse, "Sentimental Journey," and Woollcott, *Story*, 27.

5. Woollcott, *Story*, 32. In an unpublished typescript dated Oct. 1954, Berlin wrote that "George M. Cohan supplied us 'buskers' with the great special material and hit songs that made it possible for us to earn our living. I tried to write like him." Berlin, "Some notes on my trip to help exploit 'White Christmas,'" LC-IBC Box 332.

6. Berlin, "Some notes," LC-IBC Box 332.

7. Jablonski, *American Troubadour*, 22.

8. Woollcott, *Story*, 49.

9. Ibid., 66.

10. Morehouse, "Sentimental Journey."

11. Ibid. Stephen Banfield ascribes Berlin's voice to a "cantorial stage tradition," which he describes in fascinating technical detail in "Stage and Screen Entertainers in the Twentieth Century," in *The Cambridge Companion to Singing*, ed. John Potter (Cambridge: Cambridge University Press, 2000), 70.

12. *London Times*, [ca. 1910] clipping in IB Scrapbook #1, LC-IBC. The full quotation is revealing in the way it contrasts Berlin's performance style with "the blatant bellowings that we are used to," and suggests that Berlin put a new spin on ragtime songs that brought out "all their quaintness, their softness, their queer patheticalness." This leads the unidentified reviewer to invoke a stunning racial reference: "they sound, indeed, quite new, and innocently, almost childishly, pleasing, like a negro's smile."

13. At least two articles, based on separate interviews two years apart, quote Berlin using the phrase "the mob is always right": S. J. Woolf, "What Makes a Song: A Talk with Irving Berlin," *New York Times*, July 28, 1940; and S.J. Woolf, "Sergeant Berlin Re-enlists," *New York Times*, May 17, 1942.

14. Berlin, typescript in folder of correspondence with Stanley Green, 1–2. LC-IBC Box 332.

15. *Unsung Irving Berlin* (Milwaukee: Hal Leonard Corp., 1996).

16. Berlin, LC-IBC Box 332, 2.

17. Wilder, *American Popular Song*, 120.

18. The many similarities in background between Berlin and the early Hollywood producers has been explored in Jeffrey Magee, "Irving Berlin's 'Blue Skies': Ethnic Affiliations and Musical Transformations," *Musical Quarterly* 84, no. 4 (Winter 2000): 551–52.

19. Quoted in Clayton Koppes and Gregory D. Black, *Hollywood Goes to War: How Politics, Profits, and Propaganda Shaped World War II Movies* (New York: Free Press, 1987), 5.

20. Scott Eyman, *Lion of Hollywood: The Life and Legend of Louis B. Mayer* (New York: Simon and Schuster, 2005), 8.

21. *CL*, xix.

22. Quoted in "Jerome Kern Dies; Noted Composer," *New York Times*, Nov. 12, 1945.

23. Koppes and Black, *Hollywood Goes to War*, 4–5.

24. Jeffrey Melnick, *A Right to Sing the Blues: Jews, African Americans, and American Popular Song* (Cambridge, MA.: Harvard University Press, 1999), 67.

25. David A. Hollinger, *Science, Jews, and Secular Culture: Studies in Mid-Twentieth-Century Intellectual History* (Princeton, NJ: Princeton University Press), 11–14.

26. Irving Howe, *World of Our Fathers: The Journey of the East European Jews to America and the Life They Found and Made* (New York: Galahad Books, 1976), 488, for example, where he calls Jewish eclecticism "the aesthetic corollary of multilingualism, eternal wandering and *galut* [diaspora]."

27. Ronald Sanders, "The American Popular Song," in *Next Year in Jerusalem: Portraits of the Jew in the Twentieth Century*, ed. Douglas Villiers (New York: Viking, 1976), 202.

28. Mark Slobin, *Tenement Songs: The Popular Music of Jewish Immigrants* (Urbana: University of Illinois Press, 1982), 190.

29. Melnick, *Right to Sing the Blues*, 72.

30. Abraham A. Schwadron, "On Jewish Music," in *Music of Many Cultures*, ed. Elizabeth May (Berkeley: University of California Press, 1980), 287.

31. Sanders, in Villiers, *Next Year in Jerusalem*, 202.

32. For a brilliant analysis of the rhetoric of "eclecticism" around Aaron Copland, see Beth Levy, "From Orient to Occident: Aaron Copland and the Sagas of the Prairie," in *Aaron Copland and His World*, ed. Carol J. Oja and Judith Tick (Princeton, NJ: Princeton University Press, 2005), 307–49.

33. Melnick, *Right to Sing the Blues*, 76.

34. Howe, *World of Our Fathers*, 483–92.

35. Bergreen, *As Thousand Cheer*, 69; see especially Melnick's analysis of the rumor's persistence and Berlin's various efforts to deny it or joke about it, in *Right to Sing the Blues*, 114–19.

36. Quoted in Ian Whitcomb, *Irving Berlin and Ragtime America* (New York: Limelight, 1988), 15.

37. Miriam Hansen, "The Mass Production of the Senses: Classical Cinema as Vernacular Modernism," *Modernism/Modernity* 6 (Apr. 1999): 59–77; repr. in *Reinventing Film Studies*, ed. Linda Williams and Christine Gledhill (London: Edward Arnold, 2000), 332–50. Another attempt claim Berlin's realm of popular culture as Modern appears in Ulf Lindberg, "Popular Modernism? The 'Urban' Style of Interwar Tin Pan Alley," *Popular Music* 22, no. 3 (2003): 283–98.

38. Most, *Making Americans*, 7.

39. Melnick, *Right to Sing the Blues,* 65–66.

40. Herbert quoted in Russell Sanjek, updated by David Sanjek, *Pennies from Heaven: The American Popular Music Business in the Twentieth Century* (New York: Da Capo Press, 1996), 98.

41. Typescript in folder of correspondence with Stanley Green, LC-IBC Box 332, 1–2. The statement actually reads "A song much [*sic*] reach an audience."

42. Berlin, typescript in Stanley Green correspondence file, LC-IBC Box 332, 1–2.

43. Berlin, "The Secret of Song Writing," typescript in LC-IBC Box 269, Folder 2. The typescript probably dates from the 1910s.

44. Frank Ward O'Malley, "Irving Berlin Gives Nine Rules for Writing Popular Songs," *American Magazine* 90 (Oct. 1920): 36–37, 239–46.

45. Wilder, *American Popular Song,* 116.

46. Quoted in O'Malley, "Irving Berlin Gives Nine Rules," 240. He was not alone in that respect: Oscar Hammerstein II observed "the sweat pouring off of" Jerome Kern after hours of working on a song, as quoted in Stephen Banfield, *Jerome Kern* (New Haven, CT: Yale University Press, 2006), 23.

47. Berlin, typescript in correspondence with Stanley Green, LC-IBC Box 332, 2.

48. Jablonski, *American Troubadour,* 56.

49. For an account of Berlin's songwriting method in his early years (to 1914), see Hamm, *Songs from the Melting Pot,* 7–9.

50. Ibid., 9.

51. Some of the following derives from my chapter, "Ragtime and Early Jazz," in *The Cambridge History of American Music,* ed. David Nicholls (Cambridge: Cambridge University Press, 1998), 394.

52. Berlin, "Secret of Song Writing," LC-IBC Box 269, Folder 2.

53. O'Malley, "Irving Berlin Gives Nine Rules," 244.

54. Anita Loos, *The Talmadge Girls* (New York: Viking, 1978), 40–41.

55. Bergreen, *As Thousands Cheer,* 142.

56. Berlin, typescript in Stanley Green correspondence folder, LC-IBC Box 332.

57. O'Malley, "Irving Berlin Gives Nine Rules," 244.

58. Berlin, "Secret of Song Writing," LC-IBC Box 269, Folder 2.

59. Berlin, typescript in Stanley Green correspondence folder, LC-IBC Box 332.

60. Quoted, among other places, in Gordon Allison, "Irving Berlin's Forty Years of Song Writing," *New York Herald Tribune,* May 16, 1948.

61. Marjorie Rambeau, "The Story of Irving Berlin," *New York City* [*sic*] *Times,* Jan. 2, 1916. Clipping in IB Scrapbook #3 on LC-IBC microfilm.

62. Furia, *Life in Song,* 22.

63. For a more thorough discussion of "Blue Skies," see Magee, "Irving Berlin's 'Blue Skies,'" 541–52. For another close musical analysis, see Forte, *American Popular Ballad,* 87–91.

64. O'Malley, "Irving Berlin Gives Nine Rules," 243–44.

65. Berlin typescript in Stanley Green correspondence file, LC-IBC Box 332, 4

66. Hamm, *Songs from the Melting Pot,* chap. 4, esp. 140–52.

67. Frederick James Smith, "Irving Berlin and Modern Ragtime," [Dramatic?] *Mirror.* Unidentified clipping in IB Scrapbook # 1 on LC-IBC microfilm. Although the clipping bears no date, it cites Berlin's "newest song" as "Daddy Come Home," copyrighted on Dec. 16, 1913 (*CL,* 81.)

68. Quoted in Hamm, *Songs from the Melting Pot,* 90.

69. Horace Hornem [Lord Byron], *Waltz: An Apostrophic Hymn* (London: W. Clark, 1821), 14–15.

70. See Steven Baur, "'Waltz Me Around Again Willie': Gender, Ideology, and Dance in the Gilded Age," in *Musicological Identities: Essays in Honor of Susan McClary,* ed. Steven Baur, Raymond Knapp, and Jacqueline Warwick (Burlington, VT: Ashgate, 2008), 47–62.

71. Jablonski, *American Troubadour,* 45.

72. See Hamm, *Songs from the Melting Pot,* chap. 2, "Berlin and Blackface."

73. See Charles Hamm, "Genre, Performance, and Ideology in the Early Songs of Irving Berlin," in *Putting Popular Music in Its Place* (Cambridge: Cambridge University Press, 1995), 370–80.

74. Berlin, "Notes on: 'White Christmas,'" seven-page typescript "dictated" Aug. 5, 1949, LC-IBC Box 210, Folder 1.

75. On the popularity of "Uncle Tom shows" in early twentieth-century America, especially in small towns and rural areas, see Joseph Boskin, *Sambo: The Rise and Demise of an American Jester* (New York: Oxford University Press, 1986), 86. Boskin notes that people who otherwise considered theater disreputable were able to view "Tom shows" as morally acceptable.

76. [Berlin], "Thoughts on 'There's No Business Like Show Business,'" copy of three-page typescript, n.a., n.d., on regular, unmarked (non-letterhead) paper (Box 269, Folder 8, LC-IBC) The folder also includes several song lists for the production dating from 1952 on. Box 188 contains five versions of the script written between June 1952 and Feb. 1954. These "thoughts" are obviously a response to one of the earlier scripts. The combination of a vividly described scene coupled with a modest disclaimer ("random thoughts" that "I don't cling to") is typical of the many typescript scenarios and "plot treatments" scattered throughout his papers.

77. Eric Lott, *Love and Theft* (New York: Oxford University Press, 1995), 30.

78. Hamm, "The Last Minstrel Show?" in *Putting Popular Music in Its Place* (Cambridge: Cambridge University Press, 1995), chap. 17. Creative reuses of minstrel conventions in the service of cultural critique appear in Spike Lee's film *Bamboozled* (2000), Little Brother's rap concept album *The Minstrel Show* (2005), and *The Scottsboro Boys* (2010), a musical by John Kander, Fred Ebb, and David Thompson.

79. Melnick, *Right to Sing the Blues,* 45. On Jewish blackface, see also Howe, *World of Our Fathers,* 557–63; Michael Rogin, *Blackface, White Noise: Jewish Immigrants in the Hollywood Melting Pot* (Berkeley: University of California Press, 1996); and Matthew Frye Jacobson, *Whiteness of a Different Color: European Immigrants and the Alchemy of Race* (Cambridge, MA: Harvard University Press, 1998), 119–22.

80. Charles Hamm traced and logged most of the quotations in *Irving Berlin: Early Songs,* and Larry Hamberlin has thoroughly explored the paramount role of operatic music, subjects, and references in early Tin Pan Alley songs with particular emphasis on Irving Berlin; Larry Hamberlin, *Tin Pan Opera: Operatic Novelty Songs in the Ragtime Era* (New York: Oxford University Press, 2011).

81. Although this is a notion that neither Berlin nor his later interpreters seem to have recognized, it gains support from an unlikely source: a study of the nineteenth-century French composer Hector Berlioz's similar effort to channel his operatic interests into another genre. In Berlioz's *Roméo et Juliette* symphony, Jeffrey Langford noted the composer's use of "thematic superposition . . . the simultaneous

sounding of two unrelated themes, each of which had been heard separately earlier in the piece." Langford further notes that the technique is unusual for a symphony but was used regularly in operas in Berlioz's day. See Jeffrey Langford, "The 'Dramatic Symphonies' of Berlioz as an Outgrowth of the French Operatic Tradition," *Musical Quarterly* 69, no. 1 (Winter 1983): 96.

82. Hamm, *Songs from the Melting Pot*, 27–29; Robert W. Snyder, *The Voice of the City: Vaudeville and Popular Culture in New York* (New York: Oxford University Press, 1989).

83. Robert Speare, "Bill of Stars at the Victoria," Sept. 12, 1911. Clipping in IB Scrapbook #1, LC-IBC microfilm.

84. Ibid.

85. Unidentified review in IB Scrapbook #1, LC-IBC microfilm.

86. Knapp, *American Musical and the Formation of National Identity*, 122.

87. Banfield, *Jerome Kern*, 71.

88. The assumption that the relationships are heterosexual remains unspoken but is virtually universal in traditional comedy.

89. Northrup Frye, *The Anatomy of Criticism: Four Essays*, in *Collected Works of Northrup Frye*, vol. 22, ed. Robert D. Denham (Toronto: University of Toronto Press, 2006), 151–52.

90. Most, *Making Americans*, 3–4.

91. Eric Weitz, *The Cambridge Introduction to Comedy* (Cambridge: Cambridge University Press, 2009), 44.

CHAPTER 2: LEGITIMATE VAUDEVILLE: THE DILLINGHAM SHOWS, 1914–15

1. "Color and Action Fill 'Watch Your Step,'" *New York Herald*, Dec. 9, 1914; and Louis Sherwin, "The Theatre," *New York Globe*, Dec. 9, 1914, clippings in IB Scrapbook #3. While researching the Dillingham shows, I took most of my notes from reviews in the original scrapbooks housed at the Irving Berlin Music Company offices in New York. Thanks to Bert Fink for allowing me to see the original scrapbooks. The same reviews are available at LC-IBC on microfilm.

2. "Gaby Deslys in New Musical Show that Easily Wins," *New York Herald*, n.d., IB Scrapbook #2. Quoted in *Complete Lyrics*, 140. Several other opening-night reviews highlighted Sousa's appearance, although many did not, suggesting the possibility that many reviewers rushed off to meet their deadlines before the show ended. Among those who did, a few, like the those from the *Herald*, even mention it in their headlines: "Even Sousa and His Band Are Enlisted to Make Opening Performance Real Holiday Event" (*New York World*), and "Sousa Provides Band Surprise," clippings in IB Scrapbook #2. Charles Dillingham recounts the moment in his unpublished memoir, 56–57; Charles B. Dillingham Papers, NYPL Box 32.

3. Dillingham memoir, 56–57.

4. The idea of forces for and against the show comes from Foster Hirsch's discussion of Al Jolson's performances at the Winter Garden in the 1910s, in *The Boys from Syracuse: The Shuberts' Theatrical Empire* (Carbondale: Southern Illinois University Press, 1998), 146.

5. Robert Baral, *Revue: The Great Broadway Period* (New York: Fleet, 1962), 28–29.

6. Quoted in *CL*, 133, letter from Berlin to Eileen Ruby, Dec. 19, 1967.

7. Dillingham's biography is summarized in Gerald Bordman, *American Musical Theatre: A Chronicle*, 2nd ed. (New York: Oxford University Press, 1992), 196.

8. June 1915 article quoted in Margaret Knapp, "*Watch Your Step*: Irving Berlin's 1914 Musical," in *Musical Theatre in America: Papers and Proceedings of the Conference on the Musical Theatre in America,* ed. Glenn Loney (Westport, CT: Greenwood Press, 1984), 251, n. 10.

9. Performers who used vaudeville as a stepping-stone to the legitimate theater were known as "in-and-outers." See Armond Fields and L. Marc Fields, *From the Bowery to Broadway: Lew Fields and the Roots of American Popular Theater* (New York: Oxford University Press, 1993), 112. Operetta also embraced vaudevillians. M. Alison Kibler reports a 1910 review of Victor Herbert's operetta *Naughty Marietta* titled "Vaudeville Invades Comic Opera." See Kibler, *Rank Ladies: Gender and Cultural Hierarchy in American Vaudeville* (Chapel Hill: University of North Carolina Press, 1999), 202.

10. "Dillingham and Vaudeville," *Variety*, Dec. 25, 1914, 45, 47.

11. The show's original program and published score both use the phrase "Made in America." See Richard A. Norton, *A Chronology of American Musical Theater* (New York: Oxford University Press, 2002), 2:64; and Irving Berlin, *Watch Your Step* (New York: Irving Berlin, Inc., [1915]), where the phrase appears over the cast of characters.

12. In his unpublished memoir, Dillingham writes that "the first time I heard Alexander's Ragtime Band, I decided that the composer I.B. should write an entire score for me, and that was the start of 'Watch Your Step'" (72). Berlin's solo act at Hammerstein's was announced in *Variety*, Sept. 9, 1911, among the "New Acts Next Week" (16), and reviewed a week later in the Sept. 16 issue (18).

13. Anthony Bianco, *Ghosts of 42nd Street: A History of America's Most Famous Block* (New York: Morrow, 2004), 16.

14. Ibid., 15.

15. Ibid., 12–33.

16. Dillingham and company may also have been aware of a 1906 vaudeville act titled "Look, Stop, and Listen," starring the writer-actress May Tully, which received a favorable review in *Variety*, Nov. 16, 1906, 9.

17. IB Scrapbook #3 includes clippings of such spreads in the *New York Telegraph* and the *Evening Mail* as early as June 27, 1914, and continuing into July, August, and September.

18. This announcement appears in the *Telegraph, Press, Times, Sun, Herald,* and *Mail*. IB Scrapbook #3.

19. "Where Is the 'But'?" *New York Telegraph*, Nov. 19, 1914, clipping in IB Scrapbook #3.

20. Dillingham Papers, 72–73.

21. On the Irene Castle phenomenon, see Susan C. Cook, "Watching Our Step: Embodying Research, Telling Stories," in *Audible Traces: Gender, Identity, and Music,* ed. Elaine Barkin and Lydia Hamessley (Zurich: Carciofoli Verlagshaus, 1999), 177–212.

22. Reuel Keith Olin, "A History and Interpretation of the Princess Theatre Musical Plays: 1915–1919" (PhD diss., New York University, 1979), 13.

23. Ibid.

24. According to *Variety*, Oct. 17, 1914, the Castles had been making $1,600 weekly but announced that they "were tired from their dancing exertions twice daily," so they wanted to take a break but suggested they could come back for $2,500. That was refused. "Next week the dancing pair start rehearsing with Charles B. Dillingham's 'Watch Your Step' at $1,000 weekly."

25. "A Prize Beauty," *Detroit Journal*, Dec. 3, 1914, clipping in IB Scrapbook #3.

26. *New York Star*, Dec. 12, 1914, IB Scrapbook #3.

27. "Interviewing the Dog Star," *New York Times*, Dec. 20, 1914; and "The Soul Story of a Very Artistic Dog," *New York Press*, Jan. 3, 1915. The *Syracuse Herald* described the dog's stage role as "do[ing] nothing but star[ing] blandly up into its master's face" after being "commanded . . . in sepulchral tones to do various stunts," and claimed that the act was "the funniest feature of the show." Clipping in IB Scrapbook #3.

28. For example, Harold E. Stearns, "Irving Berlin's 'Syncopated Walk' from the East Side to Exclusive Residential District," *New York Press*, Dec. 20, 1914; and Marjorie Rambeau, "The Story of Irving Berlin," *New York City Times*, Jan. 2, 1916. Clippings in IB Scrapbook #3.

29. IB Scrapbook #3 includes photo spreads and feature articles in: *Opera News* (n.d.), *Vogue*, Dec. 15, 1914, and the Dec. 6, 1914, issues of the *Herald*, *World*, *Sun*, *Times*, *Telegraph*, and *Press*.

30. *Sun*, Dec. 20 and 27, 1914, IB Scrapbook #3.

31. Harry B. Smith's typescript alternately identifies her as "Violette" and "Gaby," so there appears to have been some notion of pretending she was another character. Harry B. Smith, *Stop! Look! Listen!* libretto, typescript in NYPL for the Performing Arts, Theater collection, NCOF+.

32. The original sheet music, whose cover features Deslys and Harry Pilcer doing the dance, is available at the website for the Indiana University Lilly Library's Sam DeVincent sheet music collection at: http://webapp1.dlib.indiana.edu/sheetmusic/devincent.do?c=01&p=1&id=LL-SDV-202007&s=full. Accessed June 1, 2008.

33. In its review of the show, the *Dramatic Mirror* quipped that "some one has wisely restrained Mr. Pilcer from overexerting himself, so that his effort were practically confined to demonstrating a versatility in tumbling downstairs." (Jan. 1, 1916, 9). A YouTube video of Pilcer's feat may be seen at http://youtube.com/watch?v=T_UYWy3SjVs&feature=related under the title: "Histoire de Musique-Hall Francais—Harry Pilcer Part 2." Accessed June 1, 2008.

34. On Soubrette Row, see Bianco, *Ghosts of 42nd Street*, 52.

35. Charles Darnton, "'Stop! Look! Listen! Typical Dillingham Hit," *New York World*, clipping in IB Scrapbook #2.

36. "Gaby Deslys in New Musical Show that Easily Wins," *New York World* [Dec. 26, 1915], clipping in IB Scrapbook # 2.

37. See Jablonski, *American Troubadour*, 40, and John Franceschina, *Harry B. Smith: Dean of American Librettists* (New York: Routledge, 2003), 213. For the triple bill, see Internet Broadway Database at: http://www.ibdb.com/index.php, accessed Jan. 25, 2011.

38. Bianco, *Ghosts of 42nd Street*, 74; Lewis Erenberg, *Steppin' Out: New York Nightlife and the Transformation of American Culture, 1890–1930* (Westport, CT: Greenwood Press, 1981), 61.

39. Bianco, *Ghosts of 42nd Street*, 42ff.

40. *New York Telegram*, Dec. 9, 1914, clipping in IB Scrapbook #3.

41. Bianco, *Ghosts of 42nd Street,* 53.

42. Ann Ommen van der Merwe, *The Ziegfeld Follies: A History in Song* (Lanham, MD: Scarecrow, 2009), 14–15 and 141–42.

43. See *CL,* 43.

44. Act 1 script, 6, NYPL for the Performing Arts, Theater Collection, NCOF+.

45. Act 1 script, cast of characters, n.p., NYPL, NCOF+.

46. Ethan Mordden, *Make Believe: The Broadway Musical in the 1920s* (New York: Oxford University Press, 1997).

47. James Kenneth Randall, "Becoming Jerome Kern: The Early Songs and Shows, 1903–1915" (PhD diss., University of Illinois, Urbana-Champaign, 2004), 188.

48. Norton, *Chronology,* 2:64.

49. Charles Hiroshi Garrett, *Struggling to Define a Nation* (Berkeley: University of California Press, 2008), chap. 5, "Sounds of Paradise: Hawai'i and the American Musical Imagination."

50. Act 1 script, cast of characters, n.p., NYPL.

51. Ibid., 5.

52. Ibid., 8.

53. Ibid., 26.

54. See M. Knapp, *"Watch Your Step,"* in Loney, *Musical Theatre in America,* 247.

55. Dillingham memoir, 74–75. The passage has been lightly edited for spelling and grammar.

56. "Big Audience Was Pleased by New Show," *Syracuse Post-Standard* [probably Nov. 27, 1914], clipping in IB Scrapbook #3.

57. "'Watch Your Step' Is Hilarious Fun," *New York Times,* Dec. 9, 1914, IB Scrapbook #3.

58. *New York Herald,* Sunday, Dec. 13, 1914, IB Scrapbook #3.

59. Unidentified clippings in LC-IBC Scrapbook #3. (These clippings are *not* from the *Times, World, Telegram, Herald, Variety, Dramatic Mirror,* or *Clipper.*)

60. "'Stop, Look, Listen,' New Play with Gaby Deslys as Star, Makes a Hit," *New York Telegram,* n.d., IB Scrapbook #2.

61. Darnton, "'Stop! Look! Listen!' Typical Dillingham Hit," IB Scrapbook #2.

62. Bordman, *Chronicle,* 93.

63. The numbers are based on count of 161 listings in the period 1887–1932 and take into account revivals, in Norton, *Chronology.*

64. Bordman, *Chronicle,* 93.

65. "Fritzi Scheff as Babette," *New York Times,* Nov. 17, 1903. Quoted in Bordman, *Chronicle,* 197.

66. Dillingham memoir, 72–73.

67. Burkan had represented music publishers in the conflict that resulted in the Copyright Act of 1909, and he was among several key songwriters and publishers, including Berlin, who helped to form ASCAP in 1914. See David Suisman, *Selling Sounds: The Commercial Revolution in American Music* (Cambridge, MA: Harvard University Press, 2009), 162–74 passim.

68. Letters from Nathan Burkan, attorney for Charles Dillingham, to Dillingham, Aug. 26 and Sept. 9, 1914, suggest Berlin's changing stance on the subject of interpolations. Dillingham Papers, Correspondence 1913–14, A-K, Box 10, NYPL.

69. Quoted in Hamm, *Songs from the Melting Pot,* 213; clipping in IB Scrapbook #3.

70. *Variety,* Dec. 9, 1914.

71. Norton, *Chronology,* 2:64; *Dramatic Mirror,* Dec. 16, 1914. The published score identifies the show in the same terms.

72. Hamm, *Songs from the Melting Pot,* 165.

73. Aaron Copland, "Jazz Structure and Influence," *Modern Music* 4, no. 2 (Jan. 1927): 10–11.

74. Rambeau, "The Story of Irving Berlin," IB Scrapbook #3.

75. "'Watch Your Step' Is a Castles' Night," *New York World,* Dec. 9, 1914, IB Scrapbook #3.

76. *Dramatic Mirror,* Dec. 16, 1914, IB Scrapbook #3.

77. London *Observer,* May 9, 1915, IB Scrapbook #3.

78. Unidentified clipping, IB Scrapbook #3.

79. *New York Herald,* n.d., LC-IBC Scrapbook #2. Fast pace was also characteristic of some vaudeville routines and was already known as a characteristic of the vaudeville-derived productions of Berlin's idol, George M. Cohan, as Stephen M. Vallillo has noted in "George M. Cohan's *Little Johnny Jones,*" in Loney, *Musical Theatre in America,* 234.

80. Julian Johnson, "Irving Berlin—A Restless Success," *Theater Magazine* 21 (1915): 97; clipping in IB Scrapbook #3.

81. "How to Write Ragtime Songs," *Ideas,* IB Scrapbook #1.

82. Clipping otherwise unidentified in IB Scrapbook #1.

83. Rennold Wolf, "The Boy Who Revived Rag-time," *Green Book Magazine* 10, no. 2 (Aug. 1913): 209.

84. Frederick James Smith, "Irving Berlin and Modern Ragtime," [*Dramatic?*] *Mirror,* n.d. [ca. Dec. 1913 or Jan. 1914], IB Scrapbook #1.

85. John Dizikes, *Opera in America: A Cultural History* (New Haven, CT: Yale University Press, 1993), 214. For a historical analysis of the meanings of *verismo* and how insight into how the term *verismo* applies to these and other operas, see Andreas Giger, "Verismo: Origin, Corruption, and Redemption of an Operatic Term," *Journal of the American Musicological Society* 60, no. 2 (Summer 2007): 271–315.

86. Dizikes, *Opera in America,* 323.

87. "Jazz Opera in View for Metropolitan," *New York Times,* Nov. 18, 1924; and "Berlin Calls Jazz American Folk Music; Composer Predicts It Will Eventually Be Sung in the Metropolitan Opera House," *New York Times,* Jan. 10, 1925.

88. Madame Critic, *New York Dramatic Mirror,* Dec. 16, 1914, IB Scrapbook #3.

89. Rennold Wolf, "'Watch Your Step' Best of the Year / Bigger Hit Than 'Chin-Chin,'" *Morning Telegraph* (n.d., probably Dec. 9, 1914), in IB Scrapbook #3.

90. LC-IBC Box 207, Folder 18. The "the" lacks an acute accent, but nevertheless the phrase surely refers to a tea dance, or *thé Dansant.* Either way, the phrase emphasizes contemporary dance more than ragtime per se. On the popularity of *thés Dansant*—where alcohol was served in tea cups—see Bianco, 75.

91. *New York Tribune,* probably Dec. 9, 1914, clipping in IB Scrapbook #3.

92. Louis Sherwin, "The Theatre," *New York Globe,* Dec. 9, 1914, clipping in IB Scrapbook #3.

93. "New Plays of the Week," *New York Dramatic News,* Dec. 19, 1914, clipping in IB Scrapbook #3.

94. The scene is described in Fields and Fields, *From the Bowery to Broadway*, 244–45. A photograph of the scene appears in Gerald Bordman, *American Musical Comedy* (New York: Oxford University Press, 1982), following p. 88.

95. Sherwin, "The Theatre," IB Scrapbook #3.

96. Clipping from *Syracuse Post-Standard*, n.d. [probably Nov. 26 or 27, 1914], in IB Scrapbook #3.

97. Harold E. Stearns, "Irving Berlin's 'Syncopated Walk' from the East Side to Exclusive Residential District," *New York Press*, Sunday morning, Dec. 20, 1914, clipping in IB Scrapbook #3.

98. Rambeau, "The Story of Irving Berlin," clipping in IB Scrapbook #3.

99. Irving Berlin, *Stop! Look! Listen!* manuscript piano-vocal score in Burnside Collection, NYPL for the Performing Arts.

100. Review in the *New York Dramatic Mirror*, Jan. 1, 1916, clipping in IB Scrapbook #2.

101. Sime [Silverman], "Stop! Look! Listen!" *Variety*, Dec. 31, 1915, 17.

102. "'Stop, Look, Listen,' New Play with Gaby Deslys as Star, Makes Hit," *New York Telegram* (n.d., probably Dec. 26, 1915), clipping in IB Scrapbook #2.

103. Letter of Dec. 19, 1967, from Berlin to Eileen (Mrs. Harry) Ruby, quoted in *CL*, 138.

104. Heywood Broun, "Gaby Here as Holiday Tinsel," *New York Tribune*, Dec. 27, 1914, clipping in IB Scrapbook #2.

105. Letter quoted in *CL*, 138.

106. "Dillingham Dazzles with His New Show," *Syracuse Journal*, Nov. 27, 1914, clipping in IB Scrapbook #3.

107. Edgar Smith, lyrics, and A. Baldwin Sloane, music, "Heaven Will Protect the Working Girl (A Burlesque Ballad)" (New York: Charles K. Harris, 1909). Sheet Music Consortium, http://digital.library.ucla.edu/sheetmusic/, accessed April 7, 2009. According to Gerald Bordman, this song, "the most famous song A. Baldwin Sloane ever composed," was popularized by headliner Marie Dressler in *Tillie's Nightmare*, which Lew Fields produced on Broadway in 1910. See Bordman, *American Musical Comedy*, 89.

108. Irving Berlin, "Keep Away from the Fellow Who Owns an Automobile" (New York: Waterson, Berlin and Snyder, 1912), repr. in Hamm, ed., *Early Songs*.

109. Maurice Abrahams, "He'd Have to Get Under—Get Out and Get Under (to Fix Up His Automobile)" (New York: M. Abrahams, 1913). M.I.T. Lewis Music Library, Inventions of Note Collection, http://libraries.mit.edu/music/sheetmusic/index.html, accessed May 30, 2008.

110. The term comes from Banfield, *Jerome Kern*, 40–41.

111. Larry Hamberlin, *Tin Pan Opera: Operatic Novelty Songs in the Ragtime Era* (New York: Oxford University Press, 2011), 243.

112. Burns Mantle, "'Watch Your Step' a Syncopated Revel," *New York Mail*, Dec. 9, 1914, clipping in IB Scrapbook #3.

113. Hamberlin, *Tin Pan Opera*, 243.

114. "Words and Music by Irving Berlin," clipping in IB Scrapbook #2.

115. *Detroit News*, Dec. 1, 1914, clipping in IB Scrapbook #3.

116. *Referee*, Sunday, May 9, 1915, clipping in IB Scrapbook #3.

117. *News of the World*, May 9, 1915, clipping in IB Scrapbook #3.

118. Bordman, *American Musical Comedy*, 80.

119. Bordman, *American Musical Revue* (New York: Oxford University Press, 1985), 56.

120. Leonard Bernstein, *The Joy of Music* (1959; rpt. Pompton Plains, NJ: Amadeus Press, 2004), 180. The quote is from a transcript of his telecast about "American Musical Comedy" on October 7, 1956.

121. *Variety*, Nov. 26, 1914, clipping in IB Scrapbook #3.

122. *New York Telegram*, Dec. 9, 1914, clipping in IB Scrapbook #3.

123. Wolf, "'Watch Your Step.'"

124. *Syracuse Post-Standard*, n.d., clipping in IB Scrapbook #3.

125. *New York World*, Dec. 9, 1914, clipping in IB Scrapbook #3.

126. Charles Darnton, *New York Evening World*, Dec. 1914, clipping in IB Scrapbook #3.

127. *New York Sun*, Dec. 9, 1914, clipping in IB Scrapbook #3.

128. "'Watch Your Step' Is Hilarious Fun," *New York Times*, Dec. 9, 1914, in IB Scrapbook #3.

129. "Words and Music by Irving Berlin," in IB Scrapbook #2.

130. Fields and Fields, *From the Bowery to Broadway*, 336.

131. Fields and Fields pick up the phrase and note that decades later, "'glorified vaudeville' is still a fair designation for what happens to a musical when showmanship substitutes for narrative integrity" (246).

CHAPTER 3: BERLIN'S FOLLIES, 1918–19

1. The show title's punctuation differs widely from source to source, as will be clear in the source citations throughout this chapter. The title *without punctuation*, used here, reflects the title as printed in the opening night program (as reprinted in Norton, *Chronology*, 2:155), in Berlin's typescript about the show, and in the review printed in *Variety* after opening night. *CL* (165) and David Leopold's *Irving Berlin's Show Business* (49), both completed in close association with the Irving Berlin Music Company, use commas between the words, "Yip, Yip, Yaphank," as does a review in *Theatre Magazine*, Oct. 1918, 222. A piece of sheet music reprinted in Leopold's book (49) indicates dashes, as in "*Yip-Yip-Yaphank.*" *New York Times* articles about the show regularly inserted exclamation points after each word: "Yip! Yip! Yaphank!" (articles of Aug. 25, Aug. 30 [2 articles], and Sept. 1, 1918), and yet *Times* articles of July 27 and Sept. 11, 1918, used commas instead. Three recent biographies (Bergreen, Jablonski, and Furia) print the title as *Yip! Yip! Yaphank*, without an exclamation point at the end. The manuscript score (not in Berlin's hand, but autographed by him and dated "Feb. 3, 1920") does not indicate a title (LC-IBC Box 213, Folder 7).

2. Quoted in *CL*, 165.

3. "'Yip, Yip, Yaphank' Coming," *New York Times,* July 27, 1918, 7; and "'Yip! Yip! Yaphank!' Goes On," *New York Times*, Aug. 25, 1918, 32.

4. "'Yip! Yip' to Move to Lexington," *New York Times*, Aug. 30, 1918, 9; and "What News on the Rialto?," *New York Times*, Sept. 1, 1918, 36.

5. Sime [Silverman], "Yip Yip Yaphank," *Variety*, Aug. 23, 1918, 8.

6. "'Yip! Yip! Yaphank!' Goes On," *New York Times*, Aug. 25, 1918, 32.

7. *Yip Yip Yaphank* manuscript score, LC-IBC Box 213, Folder 7; *CL*, 165–72.

8. *CL*, 165.

9. "Yaphank Actors Here," *New York Times*, Aug. 6, 1918, 24.

10. Charles M. Steele, "Say, Let's Have a Show," *Theatre Magazine*, Nov. 1918, 284; and "The Theatre and the Armed Forces," *Theater Arts*, Mar. 1943.

11. "'Yip! Yip! Yaphank!' Makes Rousing Hit," *New York Times*, Aug. 30, 1918, 7.

12. See Norton, *Chronology*, 2:146–48; "Soldiers Give a Play: 'Good-Bye, Bill' Written and Acted by Army Men," *New York Times*, Mar. 11, 1918, 9; and "Pelham Navy Boys Play in 'Biff-Bang!,'" *New York Times*, May 31, 1918, 15.

13. "Pelham Navy Boys Play in 'Biff-Bang!,'" *New York Times*, May 31, 1918, 15.

14. Sime [Silverman], "Yip Yip Yaphank," *Variety*, Aug. 23, 1918, 8.

15. "New York Cheers 'Yip, Yip, Yaphank,'" *Theatre Magazine*, Oct. 1918, 222.

16. Sime [Silverman], "Yip Yip Yaphank," *Variety*, Aug. 23, 1918, 8. All further quotations of Silverman come from this review.

17. See William J. Mahar, *Behind the Burnt Cork Mask* (Urbana: University of Illinois Press, 1999), 13. Mahar reprints twenty-five representative minstrel-show playbills of the 1843–59 period, five of which feature "wedding" numbers.

18. Norton, *Chronology*, 2:155.

19. *CL*, 169.

20. A photograph of the scene, with four black children and the "bride," appears in *Theatre Magazine*, Oct. 1918, 223.

21. "New York Cheers 'Yip, Yip, Yaphank,'" *Theatre Magazine*, Oct. 1918, 222. The description seems to have caused some understandable confusion among Berlin's biographers, two of whom interpreted the "real lady" line to indicate either Mandy or the bride (see Bergreen, *As Thousands Cheer*, 160; and Furia, *Life in Song*, 83). But the program clearly indicates that white men played those roles (Private Healy played Mandy, and Private Friend, the bride), and the "real colored picks" appeared as the bridesmaids and flower girl only in the "Ding Dong" number. For the cast member identifications based on the opening night program, see Norton, *Chronology* 2:155, and *CL*, 167.

22. *CL*, 167, indicates that the song was published as "Ever Since I Put on a Uniform," but the program listed it as "What a Difference a Uniform Will Make."

23. Information on Bevo comes from www.houblon.net, www.beerbottlecollector. com; and en.wikipedia.org/wiki/bevo. The article at houblon.net is credited to Max Rubin and *American Heritage* and dated July 7, 2002. Accessed Jan. 5, 2007.

24. *New York Times*, Oct. 15, 1917, 8.

25. *New York Times*, Mar. 25, 1918, 8.

26. There was a precedent, however, in the first edition of the *Follies* (1907), which had featured a song called "Budweiser's a Friend of Mine," Van der Merwe, *Ziegfeld Follies*, 3.

27. "New York Cheers 'Yip, Yip, Yaphank,'" *Theatre Magazine*, Oct. 1918, 222.

28. Audience members were identified in "New York Cheers 'Yip, Yip, Yaphank,'" *Theatre Magazine*, Oct. 1918, 222.

29. "'Yip! Yip! Yaphank!' Makes Rousing Hit," *New York Times*, Aug. 30, 1918, 7.

30. *CL*, 155. The song was copyrighted on Aug. 27, 1917.

31. The "war" in this case was an imagined clash between the United States and Mexico following the so-called Tampico Incident, as Ann van der Merwe has noted (*Ziegfeld Follies*, 75–76).

32. Van der Merwe, *Ziegfeld Follies*, 123.

33. Norton, *Chronology*, 2:154.

34. "New York Cheers 'Yip, Yip, Yaphank,'" *Theatre Magazine*, Oct. 1918, 223.

35. See Magee, "Ragtime and Early Jazz," 407.

36. For a critical analysis of the film's mythmaking, see George F. Custen, "I hear music and . . . Darryl and Irving Write History with *Alexander's Ragtime Band*," in *Authorship and Film*, ed. David A. Gerstner and Janet Staiger (New York: Routledge, 2003), 77–95.

37. *CL*, 169.

38. Charles Hamm, "Irving Berlin's Early Songs as Biographical Documents," *Musical Quarterly* 7, no. 1 (Spring 1993): 10–34.

39. Jablonski, *American Troubadour*, 77.

40. "'Yip! Yip! Yaphank!' Makes Rousing Hit," *New York Times*, Aug. 20, 1918.

41. In 1919 Arthur Fields made what has been described as a "number-one selling recording" of the song (*CL*, 169) that includes the following words at the end of the second chorus—another comical overreaction to the bugler's playing—which appear neither in the song's original sheet music publication nor in *CL*: *I'll sneak into his room some night, And fill his horn with dynamite, And spend the rest of my life in bed.*

Recording at http://www.archive.org/details/ArthurFields-OhHowIHateTo GetUpInTheMorning1919edisonCylinder (accessed Sept. 9, 2010).

42. "New York Cheers 'Yip, Yip, Yaphank,'" *Theatre Magazine* (Oct. 1918): 222.

43. See Norton, *Chronology*, 2:152.

44. On parodies in the *Follies* before 1918, see Van der Merwe, *Ziegfeld Follies*, 5, 11, and 105, for example. On Miller's "impressions" in the *Passing Show of 1914*, see Norton, *Chronology*, 2:55.

45. *CL*, 171.

46. On Savoy and Brennan in the 1918 *Follies*, see Van der Merwe, *Ziegfeld Follies*, 119.

47. "New York Cheers 'Yip, Yip, Yaphank,'" *Theatre Magazine*, Oct. 1918, 222.

48. Marion Spitzer, "Two Wars and Two Shows," *New York Times*, July 12, 1942.

49. Berlin letter to Abel Green, July 19, 1954, quoted in *CL*, 321–22.

50. Jablonski, *American Troubadour*, 81.

51. Berlin, letter to Abel Green, July 19, 1954, quoted in *CL*, 321–22.

52. Ibid.

53. Berlin, letter to Harry Ruby, Oct. 26, 1971, quoted in *CL*, 322.

54. Ruby, quoted in Max Wilk, *They're Playing Our Song: Conversations with America's Classic Songwriters* (1991; repr., New York: Da Capo, 1997), 275.

55. Quoted in *CL*, 169. Original manuscript in LC-IBC, Box 269, Folder 11.

56. Van der Merwe offers an encyclopedic account of the musical numbers from all of the *Follies*, so that will not be attempted here.

57. Ibid., 1.

58. The 1910 show may have included the Berlin-George Botsford song "Grizzly Bear," but this has not been confirmed. *CL*, 20.

59. See *CL*, 35–39. A fourth song, "You've Built a Fire Down in My Heart," was apparently written that year for Ziegfeld, but it is unclear whether it was performed in his show.

60. Quoted in Stanley Green, liner notes to *Ziegfeld Follies of 1919* (Smithsonian American Musical Theatre Series, Smithsonian R 009; 1977).

61. Van der Merwe, *Ziegfeld Follies*, 134.

62. See Hamberlin, *Tin Pan Opera*, chap. 4, on "Visions of Salome" in the era's Tin Pan Alley songs.

63. *CL*, 186.

64. "'Ziegfeld Follies of 1919,' Lyrics," typescript dated May 27, 1919, in LC-IBC Box 218. The script's last word is "thinking," surely a typographical error.

65. Berlin, letter to Abel Green, 1945, quoted in *CL*, 186.

66. Berlin statement quoted in *CL*, 186.

67. Berlin, letter to Abel Green, 1945, quoted in *CL*, 186.

68. Doris Eaton Travis, with Joseph and Charles Eaton, as told to J. R. Morris, *The Days We Danced: The Story of My Theatrical Family from Florenz Ziegfeld to Arthur Murray and Beyond* (Seattle: Marquand Books, 2003), 78.

69. Despite its rising trajectory to that peak, however, this verse does not qualify as one of the "verses of ascent" that the music theorist David Carson Berry has perceptively noted in several other Berlin standards. See Berry, "Dynamic Introductions: The Affective Role of Melodic Ascent and Other Linear Devices in Selected Song Verses of Irving Berlin," *Intégral* 13 (1999): 1–62.

70. "Ziegfeld Follies of 1919" script (act 2, p. 7), dated June 23, 1919, at memory. loc.gov/amen/index.html, accessed September 2010.

71. On the term *good music* in early twentieth-century America, see Mark Katz, *Capturing Sound: How Technology Changed Music* (Berkeley: University of California Press, 2004), 50–56.

72. Doris Eaton Travis, interview with author, July 16, 2009, West Bloomfield, MI.

73. In this case, the script's version ("as the *singers* filled up our ears") sounds more like Berlin than Mrs. Travis's version ("as the *music* filled up our ears"), since Berlin used the word *music* in the next line.

74. Berlin ranks among the most reflexive songwriters in the musical theater. See Michael G. Garber, "Reflexive Songs in the American Musical, 1898–1947" (PhD diss., City University of New York, 2006).

75. See Berlin's statements about the number in *CL*, 186.

76. For a perceptive analysis of Offenbach's unusual musical dramaturgy, see Heather Hadlock, *Mad Loves: Women and Music in Offenbach's "Les Contes d'Hoffmann"* (Princeton, NJ: Princeton University Press, 2000).

77. Sara M. Evans, *Born for Liberty: A History of Women in America* (New York: Free Press, 1989), 169.

78. Van der Merwe, *Ziegfeld Follies*, 4.

79. Sime [Silverman], in *Variety* 55, no. 4, June 20, 1919. 14.

80. The whole scene appears in the "Ziegfeld Follies of 1919," script (act 1, pp. 34–36), memory.loc.gov/ammen/index.html. A substantial but incomplete version of the scene is reprinted in *CL*, 184–85.

81. Stephen Banfield attributes the effect to the influence of portamento in Jewish cantillation. See Banfield, "The Voice in the Theatre," 70–71.

82. *CL*, 184.

83. The following musical dialogue does not appear in *CL*.

84. "Ziegfeld Follies of 1919" script (act 1, p. 35). In our 2009 interview, Doris Eaton Travis recalled that only end men Cantor and Williams appeared in blackface. It is possible that the staged performance departed from the script here, but nevertheless a pickanniny act in a minstrel scene would not be out of the ordinary in this period.

85. "Ziegfeld Follies of 1919" script (act 1, pp. 35–36). The script actually says "sung by piano [*sic*] by all," but this is probably a typo, as the indication actually seems to suggest singing at a soft dynamic level ("piano"), a meaning explicit in an earlier version of the script (dated May 27, 1919, in LC-IBC Box 218). It is worth noting that Van and Schenck recorded "Mandy" around the time of the production, and their performance includes a refrain otherwise undocumented but which may preserve some of the flavor of the number's climax. In it, one hums the chorus melody while the other sings a counterpoint melody, which does not appear in sheet music nor in *CL*. The recording has been reissued on *The Ultimate Irving Berlin*, vol. 2 (Pearl Gemm 0117).

86. Berlin, letter to Gus Van, of Van and Schenck, quoted in *CL*, 184: "One of the thrills of my memory is you and Joe singing 'Mandy' in the *Ziegfeld Follies of 1919*. Everyone still thinks that was the best *Follies* Ziegfeld had and the Minstrel Finale was the high spot."

CHAPTER 4: "AMERICA'S GREATEST SHOW": *THE MUSIC BOX REVUES, 1921–24*

1. It was solicited and first quoted by Woollcott, *Story*, 215.

2. "Eighteen Prospective New Theatres," *New York Times*, June 6, 1920.

3. Berlin and Harris's purchase was announced in an article titled "Still Another Theatre," *New York Times*, Mar. 15, 1920. It mentioned the name "Music Box" and noted that Berlin and Harris would take possession on May 1.

4. For example, "Music Box Theatre, Expensively Built / Cost Over $1,000,000 to Date—May Be Scaled at $4—Open in Sept." ran a subhead on a page-one *Variety* article of July 22, 1921. And a *New York Times* column, "Gossip of the Rialto," Aug. 7, 1921, similarly noted that the theater cost one million, "twice the $500,000 that was originally figured for it."

5. Jablonski, *American Troubadour*, 92.

6. Moss Hart, *Act One: An Autobiography* (New York: Random House, 1959), 300–302.

7. For a longer summary of Berlin and Harris's early acquaintance, friendship, and partnership, see Jablonski, *American Troubadour*, 91–93. Berlin himself dated the first meeting with Harris in 1906, in one of his scenarios for *Say It with Music*, LC-IBC Box 182, Folder 3

8. Hart, *Act One*, 261–62.

9. "Music Box Revue Filled with Beauty," *New York Times*, Dec. 2, 1924.

10. Useful surveys of the revue have been written by Baral, *Revue*, and Bordman, *American Musical Revue*.

11. Bordman, *American Musical Revue*, 76. Bordman surveys the Ziegfeld-age revue in chaps. 3–5.

12. Cecil Smith and Glenn Litton, *Musical Comedy in America*, 2nd ed. (New York: Theatre Arts Books, 1981), 125.

13. Lehman Engel, *The American Musical Theater, A Consideration* (n.p.: CBS Records/Macmillan, 1967), 45.

14. The claim that Broadway witnessed more new musical comedies than revues in this period emerges from counting shows billed as such in Norton, *Chronology*,2:177–285, a sample that includes all of three seasons from 1919/20 through 1921/22. The musical comedy count includes shows billed as "musical comedy," "musical farce," and "comedy with music." In this count, musical comedies outnumber revues in the period by a slim margin of 55 to 49.

15. David Walsh and Len Platt, *Musical Theater and American Culture* (Westport, CT: Praeger, 2003), 74; Bordman, *American Musical Comedy*, 82.

16. "The New Plays," *New York Times*, June 15, 1919.

17. "Theatrical Notes," *New York Times*, June 8, 1921.

18. "Theatrical Notes," *New York Times*, July 15, 1921.

19. "Collier and Bernard in 'Music Box Revue,'" *New York Times*, Aug. 20, 1921.

20. "Berlin to Act in 'Music Box Revue,'" *New York Times*, Sept. 9, 1921.

21. "Gossip of the Rialto," *New York Times*, Sept. 11, 1921.

22. Kern's comparison appears in the same letter to Alexander Woollcott in which he made the famous statement quoted at the beginning of this chapter (Woollcott, 214). For a useful overview of the *Music Box Revues* and the historiographical problems of reconstructing them, see Larry Bomback, "The Music of the *Music Box Revues*," *Musicological Explorations* 7 (Spring 2006): 51–88.

23. Van der Merwe, 126.

24. Quoted in van der Merwe, 203.

25. Norton, *Chronology*, 2:306.

26. Ibee [*sic*], "New Plays Presented within Week on B'way," *Variety* 72, no. 6, Sept. 27, 1923, 18

27. Ibid.

28. *CL*, 212–13. The musical score does not survive.

29. The following account is based on the manuscript piano-vocal score contained in LC-IBC Box 172, Folder 2.

30. "Mr. Hornblow Goes to the Play," *Theatre Magazine* (Sept. 1920): 106.

31. The passage, labeled "Mysterioso Pizzicato," appears in J. Bodewalt Lampe, ed., *Remick Folio of Moving Picture Music,* vol. 1 (New York: Jerome H. Remick, 1914), 38. The index lists the music as apt for a situation involving burglars, which is precisely how Berlin uses it here.

32. A proquest search yielded the tag line "they work while you sleep" in several Cascaret magazine and newspaper ads of the 1920–21 period (for example: *Life* 76 [Dec. 16, 1920]: 1158). A general Google search turned up multiple historical references and images for Cascarets with the same phrase.

33. IBDB Internet Broadway Database, http://www.ibdb.com/index.php, accessed July 29, 2009.

34. *CL*, 198, notes that the song was copyrighted six months before the show opened. Jablonski notes that it was "already quite popular in Manhattan" before the premiere (*American Troubadour*, 95).

35. The example represents a transcription from the manuscript piano-vocal score for the show (LC-IBC Box 172, Folder 2), not the original sheet music. There are differences: the show version includes many more expressive and articulation markings redolent of operetta and what might be called a *high-class ballad* on Tin Pan Alley. The show version also includes slightly different text.

36. Thanks to Geoffrey Block for pointing this out.

37. Also quoted in *CL*, 199.

38. Stephen Vincent Benet, "The King of the Cats," in *The Signet Classic Book of American Short Stories*, ed. Burton Raffel (New York: Signet Classic, 1985), 579.

39. Alexander Woollcott, *New York Times*, Sept. 23, 1921.

40. Jack Lait, "America's Greatest Show," *Variety* 64, no. 6, Sept. 30, 1921, 15.

41. *New York Herald*, Sept. 23, 1921, quoted in Jack P. Sederholm, "The Musical Directing Career and Stagecraft Contributions of Hassard Short 1919–1952" (PhD diss., Wayne State University, 1974), 251–52.

42. *New York Evening Telegram*, Sept. 23, 1921, quoted in Sederholm, "Hassard Short," 249.

43. Lait, "America's Greatest Show."

44. While the score's appendix of lyrics includes a full verse about Annabel Lee, the piano-vocal score does not include that section.

45. See *CL*, 190.

46. Bordman, *American Musical Comedy*, 73.

47. On the "American rage for sex farces" beginning in 1915 and extending through 1921, see Ronald H. Wainscott, *The Emergence of the Modern American Theater, 1914–1929* (New Haven, CT: Yale University Press, 1997), chap. 4 and appendix.

48. As Wainscott, 57, summarizes the typical plot line: "Through myriad misunderstandings and coincidences the playwrights manage to troop all the characters through the bedroom, trapping various people of opposite sexes in or under the bed in compromising positions."

49. Mel Gussow, "The Music Box Takes a Bow at 50," *New York Times*, Sept. 23, 1971.

50. Sime Silverman review of Sept. 11, 1911, quoted in Jablonski, *American Troubadour*, 48.

51. On this and other back-to-Dixie songs in the 1910s, see Hamm, *Songs from the Melting Pot*, 92–99.

52. Bomback, "*Music Box Revues*," 55, claims that most of the instrumental music in the score was not by Berlin.

53. Van der Merwe, 103–4.

54. The following information has been culled from programs reprinted in Norton, *Chronology*, 2:97–389.

55. Woollcott, "The Play: The Music Box Begins to Play," *New York Times*, Sept. 23, 1921.

56. New York *World*, Sept. 23, 1921, quoted in Sederholm, "Hassard Short," 253.

57. Lait, "America's Greatest Show."

58. Alexander Woollcott, "Irving Berlin Outdoes Himself," clipping in LC-IBC Scrapbook #4, music microfilm 92–20–013.

59. See, for example, the cover of "Crinoline Days," at IN Harmony, http://webapp1.dlib.indiana.edu/inharmony/welcome.do, accessed Oct. 7, 2010.

60. Bomback, "*Music Box Revues*," 65.

61. "New Music Box Revue is Dazzling," *New York Times*, Oct. 24, 1922.

62. The staging of the number and its impact on later shows is discussed in Sederholm, "Hassard Short," 253–54 and 541.

63. Lait, "America's Greatest Show."

64. A ten-page piano-vocal manuscript score of the number may be found in LC-IBC Box 173.

65. Ibee, "Plays Presented within Week on B'Way."

66. Grace Moore, *You're Only Human Once* (Garden City, NY: Doubleday, Doran and Co., 1944), 81.

67. Burns Mantle, "Berlin Songs Feature New Music Box Revue," *Daily News*, undated clipping [Dec. 2, 1924] in LC-IBC Scrapbook #4, music microfilm 92–20–013.

68. Moore, *You're Only Human Once*, 84.

69. Ibid., 85.

70. Ibee, "Plays Presented within Week on B'Way," *Variety* 72, no. 6, Sept. 27, 1923, 18.

71. See *CL*, 217.

72. Ibee, "Plays Presented within Week on B'Way."

73. John Murray Anderson, the director who staged the scene, described it in his memoir, as told to and written by Hugh Abercrombie Anderson, *Out without My Rubbers: The Memoirs of John Murray Anderson* (New York: Library Publishers, 1954), 86. In a chronicle of the revue's history, Gerald Bordman, drawing on uncited sources, describes the scene slightly differently, noting that Shaw and Moore were "dressed in white" and "sat beside white telephones on opposite sides of an otherwise darkened stage," in *American Musical Revue*, 83.

74. "The big punch of the Music Box had been class—and class . . . was the slogan for 1922." *Variety* 68, no. 10, Oct. 27, 1922, 16. The comedian Sam Bernard claimed the theater itself "stinks from class" (Gussow, "The Music Box Takes a Bow at 50," *New York Times*, Sept. 23, 1971. Robert Baral described the Music Box revues' distinctive style in similar terms as "high polish and taste" in *Revue*, 152.

75. Undated clipping labeled "Mirror" [*Daily Mirror*?] in LC-IBC Scrapbook #4, music microfilm 92–20–013.

76. The following derives from an earlier article: Jeffrey Magee, "'Everybody Step': Irving Berlin, Jazz, and Broadway in the 1920s," *Journal of the American Musicological Society* 59, no. 3 (2006): 697–732.

77. Ibee, "Plays Presented within Week on B'Way."

78. *Variety* 68, no. 10, Oct. 27, 1922, 16.

79. Woollcott, *Story of Irving Berlin*, 216.

80. Quotations from newspapers around the time of Berlin's wedding to Ellin Mackay in Jan. 1926, appear in Bergreen, *As Thousands Cheer*, 258.

81. "Jazz Opera in View for Metropolitan," *New York Times*, Nov. 18, 1924; "Berlin Calls Jazz American Folk Music; Composer Predicts It Will Eventually Be Sung in the Metropolitan Opera House," *New York Times*, Jan. 10, 1925.

82. "Diaghileff Ballet to Appear Here Soon," *New York Times*, Nov. 28, 1927.

83. An exception appears in Gary Giddins, *Visions of Jazz: The First Century* (New York: Oxford University Press, 1998), 31–44, where a full chapter on Berlin appears in the section dubbed "Precursors." Giddins provides a brisk account of Berlin's entire career, launched by a bracing summary of "Alexander's Ragtime Band" as a work that embodies "old forms made new" (31), but does not address how or why Berlin might have been construed as an actual jazz musician.

84. Bergreen, *As Thousands Cheer*, 258.

85. *The New Grove Dictionary of Music and Musicians*, 2nd ed., s.v. "Jazz" by Mark Tucker, 14:910 (London: Macmillan Publishers; and New York: Grove's Dictionaries, Inc., 2001).

86. "A World Court of Eminent Musicians Discuss 'the Ten Great Masterpieces,'" *Etude Music Magazine* (Mar. 1924): 150–52, 154. Carpenter, identified as "Eminent American Composer," lists "ten works which seem to me close to indispensable" (150). He concedes that "in the case of Berlin, the choice of this particular composition is arbitrary. Any one of a half a dozen masterpieces of the same type by this composer would serve as well. . . . Ditto in reference to the Chopin selection." In the Aug. 1924 issue of *Etude*, which focused on "The Jazz Problem," Carpenter was again consulted, and his comment linked Berlin's music—implicitly, his ragtime and jazz idioms—to the beginnings of a distinctive American music: "I am strongly inclined to believe that the musical historian of the year two thousand will find the birthday of American music and that of Irving Berlin to have been the same" (518). Statements by Carpenter and other participants in the *Etude* issue are reprinted in Robert Walser, ed., *Keeping Time: Readings in Jazz History* (New York: Oxford University Press, 1999), 41–54.

87. See Gershwin's published statements in 1926, in Robert Wyatt and John Andrew Johnson, eds., *The George Gershwin Reader* (New York: Oxford University Press, 2004), 100 (cf. p. 97). In a July 1926 article called "Does Jazz Belong to Art?," Gershwin at first identifies Jerome Kern's "They Didn't Believe Me" as the jazz song in question (97), but later, replying to a published letter to the editor, corrects himself in print by naming "Everybody Step," claiming that his initial reference to the Kern song was an error in a transcription of hastily prepared comments (100). The third commentator to publish a statement about "Everybody Step" was Isaac Goldberg, *Tin Pan Alley* (1930; repr. New York: Frederick Ungar, 1961), 281. Goldberg cites Paul Whiteman's 1921 recording of "Everybody Step" as "excellent for a number of jazz illustrations, particularly cross rhythms, tone color and spirit."

88. The first printed reference to "secondary rag" appears in Don Knowlton, "Anatomy of Jazz," *Harper's* 154, Apr. 1926, 581, where he claims to have gotten the phrase from a "negro" guitarist. The rhythmic pattern, however, already had a history dating back at least two decades, appearing in such pieces as Charles L. Johnson's "Dill Pickles" (1906) and Euday Bowman's "12th Street Rag" (1914), a popular song of its era that would become a jazz standard in years to come.

89. Two-note secondary rag may be seen as a fusion of the familiar three-note version and the cakewalk rhythm. Like the cakewalk pattern, two-note secondary rag goes back to the early twentieth century: the pattern forms the rhythmic basis of the second strain of Scott Joplin's "Pineapple Rag" (1908). See Edward A. Berlin, *Ragtime: A Musical and Cultural History* (Berkeley: University of California Press, 1980), 130–34 and 137.

90. The "blues bass" pattern, of more recent vintage than the rag-based devices, seems to date from the late 1910s or even 1920. Berlin used it in his earlier "Home Again Blues" (1920), and it recurs in prominent blues or blues-based songs of the 1920s. The ultimate source of the pattern remains unclear. It may have roots in sheet music of the 1910s, such as the four-beat left-hand pattern in the last strain of W. C. Handy's "St. Louis Blues" (1914), or in publications of Clarence Williams, as Wayne Shirley has suggested (personal communication, Mar. 2006). It may also derive from Harlem piano playing, perhaps especially the recordings and piano rolls of James P. Johnson. When Fletcher Henderson began making records with Ethel Waters in 1921, Waters recalled—in a description that matches the "blues bass" pattern identified here—"Fletcher wouldn't give me what I call 'the damn-it-to-hell bass,' that chump-chump stuff that real jazz needs," so she demanded that he study Johnson's piano rolls. Ethel Waters, with Charles Samuels, *His Eye Is on the Sparrow: An Autobiography* (1950; repr. Westport, CT: Greenwood Press, 1978), 146–47.

91. Often printed as "Everybody's Doin' It Now," the song's title appears differently on the first page of sheet music and the title page, which appears to have been the source of the discrepancy ever since. See *CL*, 40.

92. See, for example, Henry O. Osgood, *So This Is Jazz* (Boston: Little, Brown, 1926), 131, on claims that Paul Whiteman would make an "honest woman out of jazz." The imagery linking jazz and womanhood went to sometimes absurd extremes. Lawrence Gilman, reviewing the premiere of Gershwin's Concerto in F, cited Walter Damrosch's extended metaphor about "Lady Jazz" needing a "knight who could lift her to a level that would enable her to be received as a respectable member in musical circles." Gilman goes on to "amend Mr. Damrosch's engaging metaphor" with reference to "Jazzerella," a "not quite Cinderella"-like figure whom Gershwin has joined in "marriage." Wyatt and Johnson, *George Gershwin Reader*, 85–86. Melnick, *Right to Sing the Blues*, has explored the notion of jazz as embodying "a ripe but unauthorized femininity" (21).

93. See Judith Tick, "The Origins and Style of Copland's *Mood for Piano*, no. 3, 'Jazzy,'" *American Music* 20, no. 3 (Fall 2002): 282–84. As Howard Pollack has shown, John Alden Carpenter preceded Copland in quoting "Alexander's Ragtime Band" in a concert work, in his *Adventures in a Perambulator* (1914), yet it seems to have been Copland who first made its "jazzy" associations explicit. See Pollack, *John Alden Carpenter: A Chicago Composer* (1995; repr., Urbana: University of Illinois Press, 2001), 114–15.

94. Osgood, *So This Is Jazz*, 43; Copland, "Jazz Structure and Influence," *Modern Music* 4, no. 2 (Jan. 1927): 11.

95. *CL* prints it as: "*They* put a trick in it" (*CL*, 206), but the original sheet music has "Then."

96. See Hamm, *Songs from the Melting Pot*, 58–59. By 1914, when Berlin uses "walk" in songs for the legitimate stage in such as "The Syncopated Walk," the sexual overtones—so resonant in the vaudeville numbers from 1911/12 that Hamm cites—seem to be muted if not entirely silent.

97. W. Anthony Sheppard, "Strains of Japonisme in Tin Pan Alley, 1900–1930," paper presented as part of a Society for American Music session at the Musical Intersections conference, Toronto, Nov. 2, 2000. Sheppard noted a marked peak in Japanese-themed songs in 1917, which gradually declined through the 1920s.

98. "Mr. Jazz Himself" sheet music cover viewed at the website of Indiana University's Lilly Library sheet music collections, accessed Apr. 14, 2006: http://www.letrs.indiana.edu/s/sheetmusic

99. Unidentified 1924 clipping in LC-IBC Scrapbook #4, music microfilm 92-20-013.

100. *The Ultimate Irving Berlin*, vol. 2 (Pearl Gemm 0117, 2002).

101. Berlin's published lyric differs here from what his original cast sang on the recording. The published lyric reads: "So then if we don't pass our exam, / Oh, we're going to be in a jam! / Mother's going to spank us / But we don't give a damn" (*CL*, 200).

102. On popular images of black women in the 1920s, and Ma Rainey's appearance in particular, see Sandra Lieb, *Mother of the Blues: A Study of Ma Rainey* (Amherst: University of Massachusetts Press, 1981), 8, 10. On later associations between jazz and black masculinity, especially in the bebop era, see Ingrid Monson, "The Problem with White Hipness: Race, Gender, and Cultural Conceptions in Jazz Historical Discourse," *Journal of the American Musicological Society* 48, no. 3 (Fall 1995), esp. 402–6. The associations of jazz and the femme fatale/honest lady dichotomy seem to have died out by the end of the 1920s.

103. On the importance of recognizing how assumptions about gender, sexuality, and race inform jazz narratives, see Sherrie Tucker, "Big Ears: Listening for Gender in Jazz Studies," *Current Musicology* nos. 71–73 (Spring 2001–Spring 2002): 375–408.

104. Lait, "America's Greatest Show."

105. Baral, *Revue,* 15. Sheet music accessed at http://digital.library.ucla.edu (Sept. 22, 2005). On the Shimmy, its racial associations, its sexual provocativeness, and Gilda Gray's role in popularizing it, see Rebecca A. Bryant, "Shaking Things Up: Popularizing the Shimmy in America," *American Music* 20, no. 2 (Summer 2002): 168–87.

106. *Variety* 72, no. 6, Sept. 27, 1923, 18.

107. The "Lancers" referred to popular nineteenth-century dance comprising a set of five quadrilles, each in a different meter.

108. Irish–black relations were particularly tense in New York during the mid-nineteenth century, George Brown Tindall and David E. Shi, *America: A Narrative History*, 4th ed. (New York: W. W. Norton, 1996), 500. The Chinese Exclusion Act of 1882 stopped Chinese immigration for a decade and was renewed indefinitely in 1902 (ibid., 894–95).

109. Ibee, "Plays Presented within Week on B'Way."

110. Gilbert Osofsky, *Harlem: The Making of a Ghetto*, 2nd ed. (New York: Harper and Row, 1971), 17.

111. For summaries of these works, see William E. Leuchtenburg, *The Perils of Prosperity, 1914–32*, 2nd ed. (Chicago: University of Chicago Press, 1993), 205.

112. *CL*, 214.

113. Tindall and Shi, *America*, 1092–96.

114. Henry Bial, *Acting Jewish: Negotiating Ethnicity on the American Stage and Screen* (Ann Arbor: University of Michigan Press, 2005), 155.

115. Unidentified clipping by Percy Hammond, LC-IBC Scrapbook #4, music microfilm 92-20-013.

116. *New York Times*, Dec. 2, 1924.

117. Undated clipping labeled "Mirror" [*Daily Mirror?*] in LC-IBC Scrapbook #4, music microfilm 92-20-013.

118. Melnick, *Right to Sing the Blues*, 45.

119. See, for example, David Schiff, *Gershwin: Rhapsody in Blue* (Cambridge: Cambridge University Press, 1997), 90, quoting a 1924 review claiming that "Many of those who write, orchestrate, and play [jazz] are of Russian-Jewish extraction."

120. Samson Raphaelson, *The Jazz Singer* (New York: Brentano, 1925), 10.

121. Isaac Goldberg, "Aaron Copland and His Jazz," *American Mercury* 12 (Sept. 1927): 63.

122. MacDonald Smith Moore, *Yankee Blues: Musical Culture and American Identity* (Bloomington: Indiana University Press, 1985); Michael Rogin, *Blackface, White Noise*; Melnick, *A Right to Sing the Blues*; and Most, *Making Americans*.

123. Berlin, letter to Ellin Mackay, Oct. 28, 1924, quoted in *CL*, 211.

124. Barrett, *Daughter's Memoir*, 40.

125. For a full account, see *CL*, 325–26.

126. LC-IBC, Box 205, Folder 1, includes the typescript, dated Apr. 4, 1939, on which the heading reads: "NOTES ON 'SAY IT WITH MUSIC'—which is to be a sequel to ALEXANDER'S RAGTIME BAND / By Irving Berlin."

127. The typescript appears in LC-IBC Box 182, Folder 3, and the date "about 1954" appears in pencil on the first page.

128. LC-IBC Box 182 holds script drafts by Arthur Laurents (1963), Betty Comden and Adolph Green (1966), and George Wells, revising the Comden and Green version (1967). For lyrics that Berlin wrote for them, and a summary of the film's checkered history, see *CL*, 481–85.

CHAPTER 5: "AN IDEAL COMBINATION": BERLIN, KAUFMAN AND CO., 1920S–30S

1. George S. Kaufman and Ring Lardner, *June Moon*, in *Kaufman and Co.: Broadway Comedies*, ed. Laurence Maslon (n.p.: Library of America, 2004), 272.

2. *June Moon* refers to Berlin by name four times. In the play's prologue, the aspiring lyricist Fred Stevens aims to impress a girl he's just met by claiming that someone "said the boys expected me to make Irving Berlin jealous" (*Kaufman and Co.*, 202). Later the composer-pianist Paul Sears claims that "I can play as good as Berlin, and he's turned out twice as many hits as anybody" (210–11). A few minutes later, when Paul performs his new song, "Montana Moon," his wife offers the "verdict": "I don't think Berlin will kill himself" (219). Yet a third songwriter later identifies his style as being "like Berlin, only more pathetic" (263).

3. See *CL*, 236.

4. One of Kaufman's biographers claims that Kaufman's "unshakable abhorrence of sentimental scenes, whether in life itself or on the stage" was "implanted" by his mother's "constant nagging about his health and her frequent death scenes," behavioral quirks exacerbated by the loss of her firstborn son. Malcolm Goldstein, *George S. Kaufman: His Life, His Theater* (New York: Oxford University Press, 1979), 10–11.

5. Quoted from a 1960 article by Kaufman in Goldstein, 130.

6. Quoted in Goldstein, 130.

7. Quoted in Howard Teichmann, *George S. Kaufman: An Intimate Portrait* (New York: Atheneum, 1972), 92. The anecdotes, however, conceal genuine respect that Kaufman expressed for songwriters in a 1938 article, where he recalled fondly the

first time he heard "Always," when Berlin woke him up at 5 a.m. after a night of work and introduced the song to him. Kaufman, "Music to My Ears," *Stage*, Aug. 1938, 30. He may have been atoning for his earlier slight to the touchy Berlin, who "never talked about the actual writing of 'Always,'" according to Berlin's daughter, although it was "my mother's . . . wedding present." Barrett, *Daughter's Memoir*, 40.

8. For thoughtful reconsiderations of musical theater in this pre-Rodgers and Hammerstein era, see Alisa Roost, "Before *Oklahoma!*: A Reappraisal of Musical Theatre During the 1930s," *Journal of Drama and Theatre* 16, no. 1 (Winter 2004): 1–35; and Geoffrey Block, "Revisiting the Glorious and Problematic Legacy of the Jazz Age and Depression Musical," *Studies in Musical Theatre* 2, no. 2 (2008): 127–46.

9. *New York Tribune*, Oct. 8, 1933.

10. Brooks Atkinson, "After Thinking It Over," *New York Times*, Mar. 20, 1932.

11. Compare their essays in special musical issue of the theater magazine *Stage*: George S. Kaufman, "Music to My Ears," *Stage*, Aug. 1938, 27–30; and Moss Hart, "Mad about Music," *Stage*, Aug. 1938, 36–38.

12. Steven Bach, *Dazzler: The Life and Times of Moss Hart* (New York: Alfred A. Knopf, 2001), 32; and Russell Lynes, *The Lively Audience: Social History of Visual and Performing Arts in America, 1890–1950* (New York: Harper and Row, 1985), 158.

13. Hart, *Act One*, 125.

14. See Barrett, *Daughter's Memoir*, 40; Stanley Green, *The World of Musical Comedy*, 4th ed., rev. ed. (1980; repr. New York: Da Capo, 1984), 74. A rare exception, Ethan Mordden views the show as a lively entry in the "messy" world of 1920s musical comedy, in *Make Believe*, 73–75.

15. For an account from the Marxian perspective, see Stefan Kanfer, *Groucho: The Life and Times of Julius Henry Marx* (New York: Vintage, 2001), 93–101. Kanfer explores the extent to which Kaufman deserves credit for helping to create the Marx Brothers' stage (and screen) personae.

16. Morrie Ryskind, with John H. M. Roberts, *I Shot an Elephant in My Pajamas: The Morrie Ryskind Story* (Lafayette, LA: Huntington House, 1994), 69.

17. "The Cocoanuts," script in NYPL NCOF+ 80–893, labeled "as produced at the Lyric Theatre, New York City, N.Y., Dec., 1925," refers to "Henry W. Schlemmer" as the character, to "Groucho" as the performer of his songs, and to "Julius" as the speaker of his dialogue.

18. George S. Kaufman, *By George: The Collected Kaufman*, ed. Donald Oliver (New York: St. Martin's Press, 1979), 202.

19. Oliver notes that, because the published script documents opening night, the Viaduct scene does not appear because it was added after opening (Kaufman, *By George*, 202). For a brief account of its creation, see Ryskind, *I Shot an Elephant*, 62. See also Richard Anobile, ed., *Why a Duck: Visual and Verbal Gems from the Marx Brothers Movies* (New York: Darien House, 1971), 41.

20. Kaufman, *By George*, 202.

21. Mordden, *Make Believe*, 73–74.

22. Kaufman, *By George*, 209–10.

23. Ibid., 210.

24. Ryskind, *I Shot an Elephant*, 63.

25. Kaufman, *By George*, 247.

26. Kaufman, "Music to My Ears," 30.

27. Ryskind, *I Shot an Elephant*, 63.

28. "Four Nuts in 'The Cocoanuts,'" *New York Times*, Dec. 9, 1925.

29. "Ellin Mackay Wed to Irving Berlin; Surprises Father," *New York Times*, Jan. 5, 1926.

30. See Jablonski, *American Troubadour*, 324–25.

31. Hart, *Act One*, 418.

32. Ibid., 6.

33. Bach, *Dazzler*, 386.

34. See Harold Clurman, ed., *Famous American Plays of the 1930s* (New York: Dell, 1959), 17.

35. Bach, *Dazzler*, 76–77.

36. Hart, *Act One*, 263.

37. Bach, *Dazzler*, 18.

38. Ibid., 59–60.

39. Hart, quoted in Jared Brown, *Moss Hart: A Prince of the Theatre* (New York: Back Stage Books, 2006), 76.

40. *Face the Music*, "final version," photocopy of typescript in LC-IBC Box 102, Folder 2. For comparable scenes, see, for example, the openings of acts 2 and 3 in Kaufman and Hart's *Once in a Lifetime*, the opening crowd scene of Kaufman and Ryskind's *Of Thee I Sing* (which features, like *Face the Music*, a choral song), and the beginning of Kaufman and Hart's *The Man Who Came to Dinner*.

41. See Lorraine B. Diehl and Marianne Hardart, *The Automat* (New York: Clarkson Potter, 2002).

42. J. Brooks Atkinson, "Satire of Politics, Depression, and Show Business in Beautiful Musical Comedy," *New York Times*, Feb. 18, 1932.

43. Atkinson's review noted that "the droll Andrew Tombes" (in the role of Reisman) had the job of "impersonating a legendary maker of 'Follies.'"

44. See Diehl and Hardart, *Automat*, 107–8. The nickel coffee was "sacred" to the automat's regular clientele, they write, and customers were dealt a "heavy blow" when the price doubled to a dime.

45. Furia, *Life in Song*, 150.

46. *Face the Music*, "final version," photocopy of typescript in LC-IBC Box 102, Folder 2, 1–11.

47. Einstein now had celebrity status in New York, where he had just received the keys to the city from Mayor Walker in Dec. 1930. "Chronological Record for the United States in 1930," *New York Times*, Jan. 2, 1931.

48. *Face the Music*, "final version," photocopy of typescript in LC-IBC Box 102, Folder 2, 1–32.

49. Ibid.

50. Ann Douglas, *Terrible Honesty: Mongrel Manhattan in the 1920s* (New York: Farrar, Straus and Giroux, 1995), 463.

51. The "little tin box" would return to Broadway in a Bock and Harnick song by that name in *Fiorello!* (1959). For accounts of the Seabury investigation, see Herbert Mitgang, *Once Upon a Time in New York: Jimmy Walker, Franklin Roosevelt, and the Last Great Battle of the Jazz Age* (New York: Free Press, 2000); and Mitgang, *The Man Who Rode the Tiger: The Life and Times of Judge Samuel Seabury* (Philadelphia: J. B. Lippincott, 1963), esp. chaps. 9–16.

52. *Face the Music,* "final version," photocopy of typescript in LC-IBC, Box 102, Folder 2, 1–23.

53. Comments on Berlin's musical numbers are based on the piano-vocal score in LC-IBC.

54. See undated reviews of opening night in Moss Hart Scrapbook, WHS-MH: Percy Hammond, "The Theaters," *New York Herald Tribune*; Abel [Green], "Face the Music," *Variety*; and Robert Garland, "Cast and Miscast."

55. John Storm Roberts, *The Latin Tinge: The Impact of Latin American Music on the United States* (1979; 2nd ed., New York: Oxford University Press, 1999), 76–80.

56. Roberts, 83. For production details about *The Third Little Show,* see Norton, *Chronology,* 2:645.

57. Roberts notes that "Broadway fed off the immense success of Latin music, satirized it, and—particularly toward the end of the decade—contributed to it" (83). So Berlin, if not the first Broadway composer to write a Latin tune, nevertheless seems to have been ahead of the curve in bringing the style to musical theater. Berlin would also make a lighthearted jab at the Latin fad in "The Piccolino" (*Top Hat,* 1935), a song *about a song* that "was written by a Latin, / A gondolier who sat in / His home out / In Brooklyn / And gazed at the stars."

58. Reviews from *Women's Wear Daily* and *New York Times* (both published Feb. 18, 1932) quoted in Sederholm, "Hassard Short," 352.

59. *Face the Music,* "final version," photocopy of typescript in LC-IBC, Box 102, Folder 2, 1–48.

60. Ibid., 1–49.

61. Sederholm, "Hassard Short," 353 and 541.

62. Hart quoted in ibid., 353, from *New York Herald-Tribune,* Mar. 1, 1932; and in a clipping titled "Irving Berlin Wonders How It Can Happen," Moss Hart Scrapbook, WHS-MH.

63. Sederholm, "Hassard Short," 355.

64. Ibid., 355. "Irving Berlin Wonders How It Can Happen," Moss Hart Scrapbook, WHS-MH.

65. The "Face the Music" script in WHS-MH indicates the reverse.

66. Sederholm, "Hassard Short," 355–58.

67. "'Face the Music' Is Called Grandest Eyeful of Season," *Daily Mirror,* clipping in Moss Hart Scrapbook, WHS-MH.

68. Carl Rose, Dec. 8, 1928, reprinted in *The Complete Cartoons of The New Yorker,* on CD-ROM, with foreword by Robert Mankoff, 661.

69. "Acknowledgment is made to the 'New Yorker' for permission to use the phrase, 'I Say It's Spinach,'" program in Moss Hart Scrapbook, WHS-MH.

70. William A. Everett, *Sigmund Romberg* (New Haven, CT: Yale University Press, 2007), 137.

71. Examples include: "Finch' han dal vino," sung by Don Giovanni in Mozart's *Don Giovanni*; "Il segreto per esser felici," sung by Orsini in act 2 of Donizetti's *Lucrezia Borgia*; "Si colmi il calice," sung by Lady Macbeth in act 2 of Verdi's *Macbeth*; "Libiamo ne' lieti calici," sung by Alfredo and Violetta in act 1 of Verdi's *La Traviata*; "Viva, il vino spumeggiante," sung by Turiddu in scene 2 of Mascagni's *Cavalleria rusticana*; "Inaffia l'ugola!," sung by Iago in act 1 of Verdi's *Otello*; and "The Tea-Cup Brindisi" ("Eat, drink and be gay") in the finale of act 1 of Gilbert and Sullivan's *The Sorcerer.*

72. Script "final version," LC-IBC Box 102, Folder 2, 2–10.

73. [Jack] Lait, "Music Box Revue," *Variety*, Oct., 27, 1922.

74. The music and lyrics for "The Nudist Colony" appear in LC-IBC Box 97, Folder 5, and the lyrics are in *CL*, 279. *CL*, however, claims that Berlin recycled the 1922 "Crinoline Days" for this spot, even though the music and lyrics in the piano-vocal score clearly belong to a different song with the slightly different title "Dear Old Crinoline Days."

75. Sederholm, "Hassard Short," 359–60.

76. In the script's "final version," LC-IBC Box 102, Folder 2, "shouts" are indicated but the following stage direction is crossed out: "Through the blackness of the previous blackout we hear the shouts of newsboys calling: 'Extra! Extra! All about the Extra! Extra!'" (act 2, scene 7, p. 1). So it is difficult to know for certain the nature of the "shouts."

77. The *Daily Mirror* critic claimed to "remember when we ran a column by that title." "'Face the Music' Is Called Grandest Eyeful of the Season, *Daily Mirror*, clipping in Moss Hart Scrapbook, WHS-MH.

78. *Face the Music* program in Moss Hart Scrapbook, WHS-MH.

79. *Women's Wear Daily*, quoted in Sederholm, "Hassard Short," 361.

80. Wilder, *American Popular Song*, 104–5.

81. Burns Mantle, "'Facing the Music' Good: Irving Berlin and Moss Hart Take the City's Grafters for a Racketty Ride," *Daily News*, clipping in Moss Hart Scrapbook, WHS-MH.

82. Abel [Green], "Face the Music," *Variety*, clipping in Moss Hart Scrapbook WHS-MH.

83. Robert Garland, "New Revue Carries Chip on Its Shoulder," clipping from *New York World Telegram*, in Moss Hart Scrapbook, WHS-MH.

84. Lehman Engel, *The American Musical Theater: A Consideration* (New York: CBS Records and Macmillan, 1967), 67.

85. See Norton, *Chronology*, 2:613–713 (covering the four seasons from 1930–31 through 1933–34).

86. For a brisk, witty narrative of examples of the "new revue," see Ethan Mordden, *Sing for Your Supper: The Broadway Musical in the 1930s* (New York: Palgrave, 2005), 19–33.

87. Engel, *American Musical Theater*, 67; the quoted phrase comes from Mordden, *Sing for Your Supper*, 27.

88. Stanley Green, *Broadway Musicals, Show By Show*, 5th ed., rev. by Kay Green (Milwaukee: Hal Leonard, 1996), 74.

89. It would be surpassed by the revues *Hellzapoppin'* (1,404 performances) and *Pins and Needles* (1,108), and the book shows *Of Thee I Sing* (441) and *Anything Goes* (420).

90. Brooks Atkinson, "Some of the Recent Good News: Spring Invades the Times Square District—'As Thousands Cheer' an Example of the Best in Musical Revues," *New York Times*, Oct. 15, 1933.

91. Quoted in Sederholm, "Hassard Short," 377, from *New York Herald-Tribune*, Oct. 1, 1933.

92. Quoted in ibid., 378, from *New York Times*, Oct. 8, 1933.

93. Percy Hammond, "The Theaters: 'As Thousands Cheer,' A Wise and Humorous Broadway Revue," *New York Herald Tribune*, Oct. 2, 1933; Waters, "As Thousands Cheer," *Variety*, Sept. 12, 1933. This was a review of the out-of-town tryout in Philadelphia.

94. Brooks Atkinson, "The Play," *New York Times*, Oct. 2, 1933.

95. Sederholm, "Hassard Short," 381.

96. "Huge Times Sign Will Flash News," *New York Times*, Nov. 8, 1928.

97. "The Theatre: No Complaints," *New Yorker*, clipping in Moss Hart Scrapbook, WHS-MH.

98. Quoted in Sederholm, "Hassard Short," 378–79, from *New York Herald-Tribune*, Oct. 1, 1933.

99. It is attributed to an editor who worked for Dana, in Frank Luther Mott, *American Journalism, A History: 1690—1960*, 3rd ed. (New York: Macmillan, 1962), 376.

100. Norton, *Chronology*, 2:701.

101. Moss Hart and Irving Berlin, "As Thousands Cheer," photocopied script in LC-IBC, Box 72.

102. The discussion of musical numbers is based on the piano-vocal score in LC-IBC.

103. "Man Bites a Dog, So Gets into the News," *New York Times*, June 29, 1925.

104. Bach, *Dazzled*, 104; setting quoted at IBDB; http://www.ibdb.com/index.php, accessed July 31, 2010.

105. "Barbara Hutton Sails. Woolworth Heiress Leaves Count Borromeo-D'Adda on Pier," *New York Times*, Jan. 29, 1933.

106. "Huttons Meet in Paris," *New York Times*, May 20, 1933; and "Barbara Hutton Is Wed to Prince," *New York Times*, June 21, 1933.

107. *CL*, 284.

108. "Josephine Baker's Dances Forbidden," *New York Times*, Apr. 14, 1929.

109. Harry Akst and Grant Clarke, "Am I Blue," sung by Ethel Waters, May 14, 1929 (New York: Columbia 1837-D) accessed at *redhotjazz.com*, Aug. 2, 2010. Scene from 1929 film *On with the Show*, http://www.youtube.com/watch?v=FN8Yy8Rl3s&feature=related, accessed Aug. 2, 2010.

110. The way Waters *sang* the phrase (C–C–A), represented in example 5.8, varied slightly from the way it was *published* (C–D–A).

111. Nine jazz recordings of "Georgia on My Mind" appeared in the 1930–32 period. See Richard Crawford and Jeffrey Magee, *Jazz Standards on Record, 1900–1942: A Core Repertory* (Chicago: Center for Black Music Research, 1992), 26. For evidence of network radio play, see "'Georgia on My Mind' Mills Bros. Feature," *Atlanta Daily World*, Sept. 5, 1932; accessed online, July 26, 2010.

112. Richard M. Sudhalter, *Stardust Melody: The Life and Music of Hoagy Carmichael* (New York: Oxford University Press, 2002), 136–38.

113. Furia, *Life in Song*, 150.

114. Ethel Waters, with Charles Samuels, *His Eye Is on the Sparrow* (Garden City, NY: Doubleday, 1951), 221.

115. For an illuminating analysis of the song's verse and its links to the rest of the song, see Berry, "Dynamic Introductions," 16–24.

116. LC-IBC Box 72.

117. During the tour, one critic noted Lady Liberty's "blunder"—unmentioned in any other source: "I think the best of all the satire is when the Goddess of Liberty, down from her pedestal to bid bon voyage to the visiting debt commissioners, forgets the words of the 'Star Spangled Banner.'" Ralph Holmes, "'As Thousands Cheer': Brilliant Revue Sparkles with Satires of World's Great," *Detroit Evening Times* [ca. Oct. 9, 1934], Moss Hart Scrapbook, WHS-MH.

118. "Mr. Hart Takes His Dream Girl to Dinner," *Philadelphia Inquirer*, Sept. 3, 1933; Moss Hart Scrapbook, WHS-MH.

119. "Theatrical Notes," *New York Times,* May 13, 1933.

120. Waters, *His Eye Is on the Sparrow*, 222. Waters incorrectly refers to "Harlem on My Mind" as the "take-off" with Harrington, but her description fits "To Be or Not to Be."

121. All other key sources of the song—the published sheet music, *CL*, 287, and Waters's own 1954 recording—repeat "Lord." It is unknown whether Waters ever sang "God" in the original production.

122. Waters, *His Eye Is on the Sparrow,* 222.

123. John Mason Brown, "'As Thousands Cheer' New Revue on Broadway," *New York Evening Post*, clipping in Moss Hart Scrapbook, WHS-MH.

124. "The Theatre: No Complaints," *New Yorker*, clipping in Moss Hart Scrapbook, WHS-MH.

125. Mordden, *Sing for Your Supper*, 153.

126. Waters, *His Eye Is on the Sparrow*, 222.

127. Bach, *Dazzled*, 105.

128. *CL*, 155.

129. Philip Roth, *Operation Shylock: A Confession* (New York: Simon and Schuster, 1993), 127.

130. Leigh Eric Schmidt, "The Easter Parade: Piety, Fashion, and Display," *Religion and American Culture* 4, no. 2 (Summer 1994): 135–36.

131. Mott, *American Journalism*, 684.

132. "Survey of Reader Interest in Various Sections of Sunday Newspapers to Determine the Relative Value of Rotogravure as an Advertising Medium," http://memory.loc.gov/ammem/collections/rotogravures/rotoprocess.html, accessed Aug. 1, 2010.

133. See Horowitz, *American Classical Music: A History*, 363.

134. Ibid., 363.

135. Susan Smulyan, *Selling Radio: The Commercialization of American Broadcasting, 1920–1934*, chap. 5.

136. "Asserts Radio 'Ads' Disgust Listeners," *New York Times*, Jan. 14, 1931. See also Smulyan, 137, on newspaper attacks on commercialized radio.

137. Dizikes, *Opera in America*, 476; "'Mignon' Greeted by 4,000 at Opera," *New York Times*, Dec. 31, 1933.

138. Bach, *Dazzler*, 105; *New York Times*, Jan. 14, 1931.

139. *CL*, 289.

140. Brooks Atkinson, "Some of the Recent Good News: Spring Invades the Times Square District—'As Thousands Cheer' an Example of the Best in Musical Revues," *New York Times*, Oct. 15, 1933.

141. Lloyd Lewis, "A Hit at Grand," *Chicago Daily News* (ca. Nov. 7, 1934), Moss Hart Scrapbook, WHS-MH.

142. For new insights into Berlin's work with Astaire, see Todd Decker, *Music Makes Me: Fred Astaire and Jazz* (Berkeley: University of California Press, 2011).

143. Elliot Norton, "Berlin to Broadway," *New York Times*, Apr. 21, 1946.

144. Berlin, "Some notes on my trip to help exploit 'White Christmas,'" LC-IBC Box 332.

145. On the term "star text," see David Brackett, "Banjos, Biopics, and Compilation Scores: The Movies Go Country," *American Music* 19, no. 3 (Autumn 2001): 249 and 284, n. 6. Although the term originated with video and film studies, it transfers easily to stage works. Brackett notes that "star text" applies to the ways in which "aspects of the image or biography of the performer . . . may comment or expand upon aspects of character or plot" (249). In the context of discussing Gaxton and Moore, we may also add aspects of *characters* they had played before.

146. Merman, as told to Pete Martin, *Who Could Ask for Anything More?* (Garden City, NY: Doubleday, 1955), 100.

147. On the type in R&H, see Richard M. Goldstein, "'I Enjoy Being a Girl': Women in the Plays of Rodgers and Hammerstein," *Popular Music and Society* 13, no. 1 (Spring 1989): 1–8.

148. John Paxton, "Zorina: International Angel," *Stage* (July 1938): 29.

149. Ryskind, *I Shot an Elephant*, 170–71. On Ryskind's involvement in the Screen Writers Guild in its battles to be recognized as a legitimate union, which he proudly claimed as "quite an achievement in the field of labor relations" (163), see 151–63.

150. Ryskind, *I Shot an Elephant*, 208.

151. Bach, *Dazzler*, 97.

152. The document appears in LC-IBC Box 106, Folder 1. The entire scenario is reprinted in *CL*, 348–49.

153. Berlin refers here to the song "M-O-T-H-E-R: A Word that Means the World to Me," music by Theodore Morse, lyrics by Howard Johnson (New York: Leo Feist, Inc., 1915).

CHAPTER 6: MUSICAL THEATER OF WAR: *THIS IS THE ARMY*, 1942–45

1. Alan Anderson, *The Songwriter Goes to War* (Pompton Plains, NJ: Limelight Editions, 2004), 238.

2. Ibid., 238–39.

3. Ibid., 239.

4. Ibid., 242.

5. On the ways in which the creators and promoters of *Oklahoma!* strategically emphasized its novelty, see Tim Carter, *Oklahoma! The Making of an American Musical* (New Haven, CT: Yale University Press, 2007), esp. 173–74.

6. Gerald Bordman, *Chronicle*, 528.

7. For writings in which the *This Is the Army* is discussed only as film, see, for example, Clayton R. Koppes and Gregory D. Black, *Hollywood Goes to War* (New York: Free Press, 1987), 182; Thomas Doherty, *Projections of War: Hollywood, American Culture, and World War II* (New York: Columbia University Press, 1993), David Culbert, "This Is the Army," in *The Movies as History: Visions of the Twentieth Century*, ed. David W. Ellwood (Stroud, Gloucestershire: Sutton/History Today, 2000). and Benjamin L. Alpers, "This Is the Army: Imagining a Democratic Military in World War II," *Journal of American History* 85, no. 1 (June 1998): 129–63.

8. Culbert, "*This Is the Army*," 75.

9. Quoted in Barrett, *Daughter's Memoir*, 205. Statistics are recorded in a typescript dated Oct. 27, 1945, by David Supple, which is a supplement to his "'This is the Army' Detachment Statistics up to and including Aug. 28, 1945, Ulithi, Caroline Islands," LC-IBC Box 277, Folder 6.

10. Albert D. Hughes, *Christian Science Monitor* (n.d., but probably Sept. 1942), clipping in LC-IBC Scrapbooks, Microfilm 92–20013, Reel 3.

11. S. J. Woolf, "Sergeant Berlin Re-enlists," *New York Times*, May 17, 1942. Clipping in LC-IBC Berlin Scrapbooks, Microfilm 92–20013, Reel 3.

12. For example, see Henry Wallace, *The Century of the Common Man*, ed. Russell Lord (New York: Reynal and Hitchcock, 1943), 17–20; Cleveland Amory, "What We Fight For," *Atlantic Monthly*, June 1941, 687–89; Koppes and Black, 66–67. The "common man" view of the war received reinforcement from Ernie Pyle's journalism, Bill Mauldin's cartoons, and Marion Hargrove's *See Here, Private Hargrove* (New York: Henry Holt, 1942). That notion became the basis of a persistent metanarrative about World War II that remains powerful into the twenty-first century. See John Bodnar, "*Saving Private Ryan* and Postwar Memory in America," *American Historical Review* 106, no. 3 (June 2001): 805–17.

13. Alpers, "This Is the Army,"153.

14. "Army Camp Showmanship" (Nov. 27, 1940): 1, 20. See also Lynn O'Neal Heberling, "Soldiers in Greasepaint: USO-Camp Shows, Inc. during World War II" (PhD diss., Kent State University, 1989).

15. "Fort Dix (NJ) Culling Entertainers Out of Draftees Via 'Espionage' System to Solve Show Problems" (Feb. 5, 1941): 51; and "Equity Gets Supervision of Army Camp Shows" (Feb. 12, 1941): 38.

16. "Equity Gets Supervision" (Feb. 12, 1941): 38.

17. *Variety* (Mar. 19, 1941): 1, 52.

18. *Variety* (Apr. 9, 1941): 1, 44.

19. *Variety* (Apr. 23, 1941): 3, 16.

20. "Berlin Huddles on '41 Yaphank," *Variety* (May 21, 1941): 3, 10.

21. "Charge U.S. Army With Falling Down on Adequate Shows for Service Men," *Variety* (Aug. 13, 1941): 1, 25.

22. "U.S. ARMY AS NO. 1 BARNUM," *Variety* (Aug. 27, 1941): 1, 46.

23. Alpers, "This Is the Army," 153. The *Variety* articles of March and April 1941 tracking the army's growing interest in entertainment appear to offer a slightly earlier date than Alpers's claim that "By the summer of 1941, Marshall began to consider alternatives to lectures and pamphlets." Cleveland Amory's June 1941 article thus seems to have helped accelerate an effort that was already under way.

24. Letter from Berlin to U.S. War Department quoted in *CL*, 357.

25. Ezra Stone, Letter to the Editor, *Journal of American History* 74, no. 1 (June 1987): 252.

26. See Frank Coffey, *Always Home: 50 Years of the USO* (Washington, DC: Brassey's, 1991), esp. 3, 5–7, 25–28 on the origins of the USO and its activities in World War II; and Heberling, "Soldiers in Greasepaint." Camp shows were not an exclusively American phenomenon. On Japanese camp shows, see Barak Kushner, "A Most Sucessful [*sic*] 'Failure'—World War Two Japanese Propaganda" (PhD diss., Princeton University, 2002), esp. chap. 3, "'A Funny Thing Happened to Me on the Way to the Front,' Japanese Comedy and the Fifteen Year War."

27. "The Theatre and the Armed Forces," *Theater Arts* (Mar. 1943): 162 and 168.

28. "Certificate of Incorporation of This Is the Army, Inc." dated May 27, 1942, in LC-IBC Box 277, Folder 18. The three directors of the corporation were attorneys Francis Gilbert and A. L. Berman (Berlin's attorney) and John G. Paine, a representative of the American Society of Composers, Authors, and Publishers.

29. A statement by the Executive Director of Army Emergency Relief, Major General Irving J. Phillipson, appears in the *This Is the Army* "souvenir album": "Army Emergency Relief has been organized by The Army to give prompt financial help and other short-term assistance to all soldiers and their dependents who deserve help, whenever and wherever such help is needed. Relief may take the form of money, or aid in kind such as fuel, hospitalization, medical and dental care, or other emergency services such as assistance in matters of re-employment, allotments and insurance. Soldiers or their dependents can ask for help at any army post, camp or air field, or local Red Cross chapter, where full information will be available. When applying, dependents must give name, grade, serial number, organization, station or lasting mailing address of soldier." *Irving Berlin's This Is the Army* (New York: This Is the Army, Inc., 1942, 1943), 2.

30. A copy of the certificate signed by Truman appears in LC-IBC Box 278, Folder 6. Its text is reprinted in *CL*, 357. Six million is a modest figure next to the sums cited in other sources. A letter from Harry Warner to General George Marshall (n.d., but probably Nov. 1944) cites $7 million raised by the film alone (LC-IBC Box 271, Folder 36). As early as 1943, the *This Is the Army* "souvenir album" sets the amount of money raised at "a possible $12,000,000" (*This Is the Army* [New York: This Is the Army, Inc., 1942, 1943], 4). A scholarly postwar account puts the amount at $10,000,000. Lowell Matson, "Theatre for the Armed Forces in World War II," *Educational Theatre Journal* 6, no. 1 (Mar. 1954): 6.

31. Paul Fussell, *Wartime: Understanding and Behavior in the Second World War* (New York: Oxford University Press, 1988), 143. See also Alpers, "This Is the Army," 153.

32. "The Theatre and the Armed Forces," *Theater Arts* (Mar. 1943): 150.

33. For reflections on World War II as a "good war," see, for example, Michael C. C. Adams, *The Best War Ever: America and World War II* (Baltimore, MD: Johns Hopkins University Press, 1994), especially chap. 1 ("Mythmaking and the War"), and Studs Terkel, *"The Good War": An Oral History of World War II* (New York: Pantheon, 1985).

34. "The Theatre and the Armed Forces," 167.

35. "Opening of 'This Is the Army,'" LC-IBC Box 191, Folder 9.

36. The British script of the show (in a blue folder dated 1942 in LC-IBC Box 204, Folder 2) includes the scene between Bernie and Manson, with some dialogue that the film preserves and other dialogue that was not.

37. In the British script, Bernie simply states the last line and exits. The script gives no indication that the guard leads him off.

38. This kind of impersonation, as Toll puts it, showed women "with fluttering eyelashes and hearts . . . [who] flirted behind fans and forced beaux to steal kisses." Robert C. Toll, *Blacking Up: The Minstrel Show in Nineteenth-Century America* (New York: Oxford University Press, 1974) 140.

39. Ibid., 139.

40. Ibid., 144.

41. William J. Mahar, *Behind the Burnt Cork Mask* (Urbana: University of Illinois Press, 1999), 317–18.

42. *CL*, 363.

43. "Welcome Yellow Aryans," LC-IBC Box 191, Folder 3.

44. Berlin letter to Sandrich (Dec. 22, 1941) quoted in *CL*, 362–63.

45. See Joshua S. Goldstein, *War and Gender: How Gender Shapes the War System and Vice Versa* (Cambridge: Cambridge University Press, 2001), 356ff.

46. *CL*, 363.

47. LC-IBC Box 279, Folder 1. A program for the Detroit performance (Dec. 21, 1942) includes "That Russian Winter," but that song, and others about the Axis, do not appear in later programs for overseas performances.

48. Terkel, *"The Good War,"* 5.

49. Barrett, *Daughter's Memoir*, 204.

50. For example, the caption on a photo spread featuring *TITA*'s black performers in the *New York Amsterdam News* two weeks after the premiere called the show "one of the greatest song and dance shows yet to hit the Big Street" (July 18, 1942). A critic likewise praised *TITA* as "one of the greatest musical shows in this country," Dolores Calvin, "Broadway Sees and Likes Irvin [sic] Berlin's Show 'This Is the Army,'" *Chicago Defender*, July 18, 1942. See also Frank E. Bolden, "'This Is the Army' Is a Wow in Europe," *New York Amsterdam News*, Dec. 9, 1944.

51. Herman Hill, "'This is the Army' Preview Sends Herman Hill, Courier Coast Scribe," *Pittsburgh Courier*, Aug. 21, 1943.

52. Charles H. Loeb, "Our GI's in S. Pacific Fiercely Resent 'Uncle Tom' Roles," *New York Amsterdam News*, Sept. 1, 1945.

53. Ralph Warner, *Daily Worker* (July 7, 1942), clipping in IB Scrapbooks, LC-IBC Microfilm 92–20013, Reel 3.

54. On the minstrel parade, see Toll, 135–39.

55. Anderson, *Songwriter Goes to War*, 93.

56. Pittsburgh *Sun-Telegraph*, Oct. 12, 1942. Clipping in IB Scrapbooks, LC-IBC, Microfilm 92–20013, Reel 3.

57. "Soldier Actors Take Broadway by Storm in 'This Is the Army,'" *Pittsburgh Courier*, July 11, 1942.

58. Stone, "Letter to the Editor," *Journal of American History* 74 (June 1987): 252.

59. Anderson, *Songwriter Goes to War*, 78.

60. Ibid., 79–81.

61. Kathryn Shattuck, "Veteran Troupe Celebrates 'This Is the Army,'" *New York Times*, June 9, 1997,.

62. See George Murphy, with Victor Lasky, *"Say . . . Didn't You Used to Be George Murphy?"* (New York: Bartholomew House Ltd., 1970), 257.

63. The story was published on Sept. 26, 1942. Two months later, the same paper ran a page-one story again commending Berlin for racial sensitivity for what now may seem to be a surprising reason: for agreeing to delete the word *darky* from future printings of his song "Abraham," which was playing on radio and records after having recently appeared in the film *Holiday Inn*. "No song is important enough to offend a whole race," Berlin is quoted as saying. "I should never have released it had I known the epithet was objectionable." "Irvin [sic] Berlin Orders Song Word Change," *Baltimore Afro-American*, Nov. 14, 1942.

64. Shattuck, "Veteran Troupe."

65. Alpers, "This Is the Army," 146.

66. Barrett, *Daughter's Memoir,* 203.

67. The program appears in Norton, *Chronology,* 2:852. The ballet is not listed in the program as such, but the number just preceding the song in the original *TITA* program is described as "A Soldier's Dream" and includes privates, valets, a gypsy violinist, and "dream girls"—an indication that all the ingredients of his original ballet scenario appeared in the original production.

68. "Rough Outline of the HATE TO GET UP IN THE MORNING BALLET," LC-IBC Box 191, Folder 8.

69. *CL,* 368–69.

70. Ibid., 376.

71. Ibid., 369.

72. The typescript "Rules for Hostesses" and the handwritten list appear in LC-IBC Box 191, Folder 8.

73. For full lyrics, see *CL,* 362. The exchange of memos between Hal Wallis of the Hays Office and Irving Berlin occurred on Apr. 2, 1943, and both may be found in LC-IBC Box 190, Folder 5. The revised ("canoodling") line appears in *CL,* 362.

74. War Department, *Technical Manual of Field Music* (Washington, DC: War Department, Sept. 20, 1940), in LC-IBC Box 279, Folder 10.

75. Anderson, *Songwriter Goes to War,* 114.

76. Ibid., 118.

77. Lt. Herb Golden, "on leave from *Variety,*" unpublished manuscript dated Apr. 8, 1945, with stamp indicating it passed through the Office of Public Relations—U.S. Navy, Review Section, on May 5, 1945, LC-IBC Box 277. Two other unpublished reports of performances in 1945 expressed the same opinion. A letter from one Arnold Horwitt to *Variety* editor Abel Green noted that the final performance in Hawaii "seemed even better than I remembered it in New York. It was faster paced and had several new comedy bits and songs which were fine" (letter dated Oct. 24, 1945). An earlier typescript in Box 277, Folder 13, contains "Notes on interview re: THIS IS THE ARMY," Mar. 15, 1944, noted that "many . . . including Berlin" thought the overseas version was "a much better and faster show."

78. Both of these two-page typescript lists appear in LC-IBC Box 277, Folder 15.

79. The letters, dating from Aug. 1944 and Apr. 1945 are preserved in LC-IBC Box 269, Folders 21–26.

80. Berlin to Ben Washer, Aug. 15, 1944, preserved in Ben Washer's diary, LC-IBC Box 509, Folder 1.

81. Anderson, *Songwriter Goes to War,* 200.

82. Ibid., 94–95.

83. Ibid., 186.

84. Shattuck, "Veteran Troupe."

85. Anderson, *Songwriter Goes to War,* 200.

86. Ibid., 4.

87. Ibid., 74–76.

88. Ibid., 98.

89. The article was Clayton R. Koppes and Gregory D. Black, "Blacks, Loyalty, and Motion-Picture Propaganda in World War II," *Journal of American History* 72, no. 2 (Sept. 1986): 383–406.

90. Stone, "Letter to the Editor," 252–53.

91. Anderson, *Songwriter Goes to War*, 86, refers to him as a "father figure" for many.

92. Ibid., 33.

93. Ibid., 65.

94. The following summary is based on the account in Ibid., 207–28.

95. Ibid., 228.

96. Ibid., xvi.

97. LC-IBC Box 279, Folder 10.

98. LC-IBC Box 269, Folder 11.

CHAPTER 7: SOMETHING FOR THE GIRLS: *ANNIE GET YOUR GUN*, 1945–PRESENT

1. Quoted in John Crosby, "The Master—A New Show," *New York Herald Tribune*, June 4, 1962.

2. The story comes from Merman, with slight discrepancies among the retellings, in Robert Sullivan, "Ethel Merman Scores Again," *Sunday News*, May 26, 1946, who says the meeting took place on August 15, "three days" after Merman's son was born; Merman's memoir, probably more trustworthy on dates because it was around her son's birth, says it was on "August 13, 1945, two days after my son Bobby was born"; see Ethel Merman, as told to Pete Martin, *Who Could Ask for Anything More* (New York: Doubleday, 1955), 184. Merman tells a similar story, along with the "stitches" line, in her revised and updated memoir, written with George Eells, *Merman* (New York: Simon and Schuster, 1978), 138.

3. Merman reports the "flash" in *Who Could Ask for Anything More*, 183–84. Deborah Grace Winer claims that Fields had gotten the idea the night before meeting with Merman, see Winer, *On the Sunny Side of the Street: The Life and Lyrics of Dorothy Fields* (New York: Schirmer, 1997), 144. If so, Fields worked very quickly the next day, since Mike Todd—who had produced several previous Fields/Merman collaborations—was first approached about producing the show and turned it down. Only then did Fields broach the idea with Rodgers and Hammerstein. All of this happened before Fields called Merman. See also Charlotte Greenspan, *Pick Yourself Up: Dorothy Fields and the American Musical* (New York: Oxford University Press, 2010).

4. Fields quoted in Winer, *Sunny Side of the Street*, 144. The only biography of Annie Oakley available in 1945 included a photo of the medal-bedecked sharpshooter as its frontispiece. See Courtney Ryley Cooper, *Annie Oakley: Woman at Arms* (New York: Duffield, 1927). Also see three different photos (one of which duplicates that frontispiece) in the later biographies of Oakley by Glenda Riley, *The Life and Legacy of Annie Oakley* (Norman: University of Oklahoma Press, 1994), 101; and Shirl Kasper, *Annie Oakley* (Norman: University of Oklahoma Press, 1992), 168 and 239.

5. "JAPAN SURRENDERS, END OF WAR!," *New York Times*, Aug. 15, 1945.

6. Richard Rodgers, *Musical Stages: An Autobiography* (New York: Random House, 1975), 246.

7. Hammerstein had been a close friend and collaborator since the 1920s when they wrote *Show Boat* and other musicals; Fields had worked on and off with Kern since their Academy Award–winning effort for the 1936 Astaire-Rogers film *Swing Time*; and Rodgers would later refer to his early years as a "Kern worshipper" in his memoirs. See Rodgers, *Musical Stages*, 20.

8. Sam Zolotow, "Kern to Do Score for 'Annie Oakley,'" *New York Times*, Sept. 14, 1945.

9. Gerald Bordman, *Jerome Kern* (New York: Oxford, 1980), 406, offers the most detailed account of Kern's last days.

10. "Leaders in Theatre Attend Kern Rites," *New York Times*, Nov. 13, 1945.

11. Berlin got the call "a day or so" after the funeral, according to Barrett, *Daughter's Memoir*, 235.

12. Berlin quoted in *CL*, 385.

13. "Honored for 'This Is the Army,'" *New York Times*, Oct. 2, 1945.

14. Rodgers, *Musical Stages*, 248.

15. Sam Zolotow, in his theater column headlined "Richards Comedy Arriving Tonight," *New York Times*, Nov. 21, 1945, mentions "Tea Leaves," but word had been circulating about it since at least the summer, when Berlin received several letters from performers aspiring to audition for it. (The letters, the earliest pair of them dated July 17, 1945, are preserved in LC-IBC Box 269, Folder 6 [folder labeled "Box 268"]).

16. Rodgers notes Berlin's resistance to a book show in *Musical Stages*, 248.

17. Berlin quoted in *CL*, 385, 387.

18. See Berlin's statement about "Doin' What Comes Natur'lly" in *CL*, 387.

19. According to Logan, Rodgers had asked him to direct the show before the war ended. But the fact was not announced publicly until well after the end of the war. See Sam Zolotow, "'Brighten Corner' Will Open Tonight," *New York Times*, Dec. 12, 1945. For Logan's account, see *Josh: My Up and Down, In and Out Life* (New York: Delacorte, 1976), 215–16.

20. Anderson, *Songwriter Goes to War*, 63–64, 151.

21. *CL*, 385, quoting Berlin's letter to a press agent in 1966.

22. Rodgers, *Musical Stages*, 248.

23. Barrett, *Daughter's Memoir*, 235.

24. Zolotow, "Richards Comedy Arriving Tonight."

25. In Merman's words, "Then he sat down and in eighteen days he wrote ten of the best songs ever written by anybody." Merman as told to Pete Martin, in *Who Could Ask for Anything More*, 187.

26. Most, *Making Americans*, 55–65.

27. Herbert and Dorothy Fields, *Annie Get Your Gun*, production script (London: Chappell and Co. Ltd., 1952), 55.

28. Larry Stempel raises this dimension of the show in *Showtime: A History of the Broadway Musical Theater* (New York: W. W. Norton, 2010), 316.

29. Gender as performance is the resonant keynote of Judith Butler's influential book, *Gender Trouble: Feminism and the Subversion of Identity* (New York: Routledge, 1990).

30. Marshall Berman explicitly calls it "feminist," in *On the Town: One Hundred Years of Spectacle in Times Square* (New York: Random House, 2006), 155; while others raise the issue implicitly, as in Stacy Wolf, *A Problem Like Maria: Gender and Sexuality in the American Musical* (Ann Arbor: University of Michigan Press, 2002), esp. 103–4.

31. On Berlin's suggestive songs, also termed "urban novelty" songs, see Hamm, *Songs from the Melting Pot*, 54–63.

32. Later, as Andrea Most points out, Annie will get into trouble when she starts "trying to playing the starring role in [the] two competing narratives simultaneously." See Most, *Making Americans*, 145.

33. Reflecting an inconsistency in the libretto, however, some singers render "can't" as a countrified "cain't." In act 1, scene 1, for example, Annie claims she "cain't" miss a shot (27), just a few minutes after she has sung "You Can't Get a Man with a Gun." In scene 2 she asks Tommy and Winnie, "Can't ye start your own family?" (33), but later in the scene she says, "Gosh, I cain't" (38). Ethel Merman sang Berlin's "can't," but Mary Martin, who sang the role on tour and in a 1957 television production, sang "cain't." In the 1990 studio cast recording conducted by John McGlinn, Kim Criswell likewise sang "cain't" (Musical Heritage Society 13335F).

34. Did Berlin get "got" from Gershwin? The protagonist's humble acceptance in song of a modest material existence, launched by the solecism "I got," brings Ira Gershwin to mind: "I Got Rhythm" (*Girl Crazy,* 1930) and "I Got Plenty O' Nuttin'" (*Porgy and Bess*, 1935). Thanks to Geoffrey Block for noting the intriguing connection.

35. Philip Furia coined the phrase *Pollyanna weather song* in *Ira Gershwin: The Art of the Lyricist* (New York: Oxford University Press, 1996), 31.

36. Berlin wrote a third chorus that was cut. No wonder—it dispels the song's Pollyanna motif with remarkably grim tone: "Got no future, got no plan, / Things look different without a man . . ." For more on this song, see Most, *Making Americans*, 132–34.

37. LC-IBC Box 36, Folder 1.

38. Logan, *Josh*, 224.

39. In contrast to *CL*, the show's scripts (1946 and 1966) and published piano-vocal score consistently show a slightly different lyric: "roustabouts *that* . . ." and "spotlights" (plural).

40. Some of the discarded songs show the same tendencies, in using antithesis, as in "Something Bad's Gonna Happen ('Cause I Feel So Good)," and antithesis coupled with list-driven parallel construction, as in "Take It in Your Stride."

41. The dotted rhythm and falling contour on "wonderful" again conjure echoes of Gershwin, in "S'Wonderful." (Thanks again to Geoffrey Block for the observation.)

42. Merman as told to Pete Martin, in *Who Could Ask for Anything More*, 187.

43. Ibid.

44. Ethan Mordden, *Beautiful Mornin': The Broadway Musical in the 1940s* (New York: Oxford University Press, 1999), 115.

45. For a different view, see Raymond Knapp, *The American Musical and the Performance of Personal Identity* (Princeton, NJ: Princeton University Press, 2006), 213. Knapp argues that music derived from African American idioms serves as a "marker" of Annie's "'true' identity," and that this "affinity" reveals her as "marginalized" and having "difficulty fitting in." I would argue the opposite: that the swing idiom actually signals Annie's assimilation, for, by 1946, swing enjoyed a strong position in—had been assimilated into—mainstream American popular music.

46. Forte offers a sustained analysis of the song in *American Popular Ballad*, 112–16. The quoted phrase appears on 113.

47. Wilder, *American Popular Song*, 116.

48. Jablonski, *American Troubadour*, 238.

49. The draft, in a yellow folder, is in LC-IBC Box 69, folder 2.

50. In writing that has inspired this coinage, Geoffrey Block has noted "hypothetical" love in *Oklahoma!* and *Carousel*. See Block, *Enchanted Evenings*, 164 and 166.

51. Mordden, *Beautiful Mornin',* 112.

52. Linton Martin, "The Call Boy's Chat: 'Annie Get Your Gun' Hit; Ethel Merman in Top Form," *Philadelphia Inquirer*, May 5, 1946. LC-IBC Microfilm 92/20013, Scrapbook 32 (Reel 6).

53. Unless otherwise noted, these reviews appeared on May 17, 1946, the day after the opening. Unless otherwise noted, all quotations and citations have been taken from copies in the Irving Berlin scrapbooks, LC-IB Microfilm 92/20013, Scrapbook 32 (Reel 6).

54. John C. Wynne, "Curtain Time," May 27, 1946.

55. Sid Garfield, "A Word on Plays" *Dance Magazine*, Aug. 1948—date according to clipping service tag, but article is among August 1946 clippings in scrapbook, LC-IBC.

56. Clipping with dateline: "London, June 10 [1947]" in unidentified periodical, LC-IBC.

57. Basil Talbott, *Chicago American*, Nov. 5, 1947, clipping in LC-IBC.

58. Claudia Cassidy, *Chicago Daily Tribune*, Nov. 5, 1947, clipping in LC-IBC.

59. Kaspar Monahan, *Pittsburgh Press*, Mar. 16, 1948, clipping in LC-IBC.

60. Winer, *Sunny Side of the Street*, 121.

61. Mordden, *Beautiful Mornin',* 36. See also Stanley Green's description of Panama Hattie as a "brassy, gold-hearted nightclub owner." Green, *Broadway Musicals, Show By Show*, 5th ed., rev. Kay Green (Milwaukee: Hal Leonard, 1996), 111.

62. Jan. 8, 1943.

63. Robert Kimball, ed., *The Complete Lyrics of Cole Porter* (1983; repr. New York: Da Capo, 1992), 320. That title, in turn, echoed an early Tin Pan Alley song called "Johnny Get Your Gun," which Berlin's early idol, George M. Cohan, had prominently quoted in his World War I hit, "Over There."

64. Winer, *Sunny Side of the Street*, 133; Green, *Broadway Musicals*, 126.

65. Quoted in Winer, *Sunny Side of the Street*, 144. For the most extensive discussion of *Up in Central Park*, see William A. Everett, *Sigmund Romberg* (New Haven, CT: Yale University Press, 2007), 232–41.

66. Quoted in Kasper, *Annie Oakley*, 47; see also Riley, *Life and Legacy of Annie Oakley*, 21.

67. Riley, *Life and Legacy*, 210–17.

68. Most, *Making Americans*, 148–52; R. Knapp, *American Musical and the Performance of Personal Identity*, 214.

69. See Fields and Fields, *From the Bowery to Broadway*, 56–57.

70. See Hugh Fordin, *Getting to Know Him: A Biography of Oscar Hammerstein II* (New York: Random House, 1977), 243.

71. See James Heintze, *Adapting to Abundance: Jewish Immigrants, Mass Consumption, and the Search for American Identity* (New York: Columbia University Press, 1990), esp. chap. 6, "The Clothing of an American."

72. Riley, *Life and Legacy*, 148–49.

73. Kasson, *Buffalo Bill's Wild West*, 152.

74. Riley, *Life and Legacy*, 149.

75. Most, *Making Americans,* 62.

76. Ibid., 136.

77. Ibid., 139.

78. Ibid., 140.

79. Michael V. Pisani, *Imagining Native America in Music* (New Haven, CT: Yale University Press, 2005), 285–91.

80. Ibid., 291.

81. For this technique's association with Jewishness, see Magee, "Irving Berlin's 'Blue Skies,'" 547 and 549.

82. Barbara W. Grossman, *Funny Woman* (Bloomington: Indiana University Press, 1991), 112.

83. On the fad, see Grossman, *Funny Woman,* 112; and Jack Gottlieb, *Funny, It Doesn't Sound Jewish: How Yiddish Songs and Synagogue Melodies Influenced Tin Pan Alley, Broadway and Hollywood* (Albany: State University of New York and the Library of Congress, 2004), 64.

84. The lyrics are reprinted in *CL,* 15, and bracketed material and quotation marks are preserved from the original.

85. For example, see the Berlin *Tagesspiegel,* Sept. 7, 1963; Cologne-Stuttgart *Deutsche Zeitung,* Sept. 9, 1963; clippings in LC-IB scrapbooks, Microfilm 92/20013, Scrapbook 32 (Reel 6).

86. *Tagesspiegel,* Sept. 7, 1963; clipping ibid.

87. Jack Gould, "TV: Annie Get Your Gun: Mary Martin and John Raitt Are Starred in Disappointing Channel 4 Revival," *New York Times,* Nov. 29, 1957; clipping ibid.

88. *Boston Globe* (July 20, 1960); clipping ibid.

89. Ben Brantley, "Annie's Got Her Gun Again, And Hits the Clay Pigeons," *New York Times,* Feb. 9, 2001.

90. *Song stack* is derived from Ethan Mordden's useful, and satisfying literal, neologism *tune stack,* in *Make Believe,* 74. I prefer the alliterative version with "song."

91. Rodgers and Hammerstein Company website, http://www.rnh.com/show_home.asp, accessed Jan. 27, 2011.

92. Anthony Tommasini, "Gun-Totin' Brünnhilde," *New York Times,* July 18, 2011.

93. For a compelling discussion of the "problem with authenticity" in texts of musical theater works, including *Annie Get Your Gun,* see Bruce Kirle, *Unfinished Show Business: Broadway Musicals as Works-in-Process* (Carbondale: Southern Illinois University Press, 2005), esp. 36–39.

94. Ibid. Peters played the role from its opening in early 1999 to Feb. 2001. McIntyre then took over for the next few months, playing her last performance on June 23, 2001.

95. Mary Martin, *My Heart Belongs, an Autobiography by Mary Martin* (New York: Morrow, 1976), 155.

CHAPTER 8: STATE OF THE UNION: BERLIN, LINDSAY AND CROUSE, 1950–62

1. Howard Lindsay and Russel Crouse, *State of the Union* (New York: Random House, 1946), 139.

2. Ibid., 224–26 passim.

3. Lewis Nichols, "'State of the Union,'" *New York Times*, Nov. 25, 1945.

4. About the ongoing effort to change topical references in the script to keep it current, see Howard Lindsay and Russel Crouse, "Life with Lindsay and Crouse," *New York Times*, Jan. 13, 1946; and William DuBois, "Changing the 'Union,'" *New York Times*, Nov. 10, 1946. The production closed in Sept. 1947, so the writers did not have to face changes that would have been necessitated by the real presidential campaign of 1948. Yet the "acting edition" of the script invites further changes to reflect the times in which it is staged: "The political comment in this play reflects the issues of the year 1946. It would not be difficult for anyone politically informed to bring these issues up-to-date by re-writing the lines involved. This would in no way affect the structure of the play or qualify its basic story. However, if this is done there must be a program note giving credit to whoever makes these revisions and absolving Mr. Lindsay and Mr. Crouse of any responsibility for the political implications contained in the revised version." Lindsay and Crouse, *State of the Union*, Acting Edition (New York: Dramatists Play Service, 1974), [4].

5. See Gilbert Millstein, "First 25 Years of Lindsay & Crouse," *New York Times Magazine*, Nov. 22, 1959, 16.

6. Ibid., 16, 109–10.

7. Merman, as told to Pete Martin, *Who Could Ask for Anything More*, 200.

8. "The Capital: Widow from Oklahoma," *Time*, Mar. 14, 1949. Accessed online at http://www.time.com, May 8, 2010.

9. Information about the Mesta Machine Company may be found through the University of Pittsburgh Digital Library: http://images.library.pitt.edu, accessed May 8, 2010.

10. "Perle Mesta Dismissed as Luxembourg Envoy," *New York Times*, Mar. 28, 1953; Edwin Schallert, "'Call Me Madam' Opulent Entertainment Carnival," *Los Angeles Times*, Mar. 5, 1953.

11. Caryl Flinn, *Brass Diva: The Life and Legends of Ethel Merman* (Berkeley: University of California Press, 2007), 179, for example, cites the show's inspiration as a 1948 *Time* magazine article on Mesta as ambassador—a year before she was appointed. Bess Furman, "Mrs. Mesta Named Luxembourg Envoy," *New York Times*, June 22, 1949, 1; and "Perle Mesta Is Confirmed As Diplomat," *Washington Post*, July 6, 1949, 1.

12. Berlin quoted in a *Boston Post* article, in Furia, *Life in Song*, 245.

13. Quoted in Jablonski, *American Troubadour*, 268.

14. For example, see: Leonar [sic] Lyons, "The Lyons Den," *Washington Post*, Sept. 3, 1949; N.a., "Berlin Writing Show on Mesta's Life," *New York Times*, Dec. 29, 1949; J. P. Shanley, "News and Gossip on the Rialto," *New York Times*, Aug. 27, 1950; Harry Gilroy, "Musical for Merman," *New York Times*, Oct. 8, 1950. The photograph of Merman, Mesta, and Margaret Truman appears under the headline "Came to See Envoy Sail," *New York Times*, June 8, 1950. Merman recounts her meeting with Mesta similarly in both of her memoirs: Merman, as told to Pete Martin, *Who Could Ask for Anything More*, 202–3, and Merman, as told to George Eells, *Merman*, 159–60.

15. Ethel Merman, as told to Pete Martin, *Who Could Ask for Anything More*, 209–10.

16. Lindsay to Crouse, WHS-L&C Box 8, Folder 2. Also quoted in Furia, *Life in Song*, 243–44.

17. Dizikes, *Opera in America,* 212.

18. Ibid., 212.

19. Harry Gilroy, "Musical for Merman, *New York Times,* Oct. 8, 1950.

20. Robert Kass, "Film Reviews: Call Me Madam," *Films in Review* (Apr. 1953): 193.

21. Brooks Atkinson "On Musical Stages: New Season Has Brought Three Song Shows," *New York Times,* Sept. 26, 1948; Atkinson's comment referred to *Magdalena,* a new operetta with music by Heitor Villa-Lobos, lyrics by Robert Wright and George Forrest, and book by Frederick Hazlitt Brennan. In his effort to convey the work's old-fashioned Hollywood-inspired style, he noted that Wright and Forrest "wrote the lyrics and musical adaptations for most of the Jeanette MacDonald and Nelson Eddy pictures."

22. Lewis Nichols, "Prince of Song: The Operetta Book Still Clings to the Purple Robes of Royalty," *New York Times,* Sept. 16, 1945.

23. Lerner and Loewe's *Brigadoon* (1947) might be considered a prominent precedent, but it lacks the sharp class distinctions that inform the hero's marriage plot.

24. On the vicissitudes of the original orchestrations, see Rob Fisher's "Musical Notes," liner notes to *Call Me Madam* DRG 94761 (1995). The recording preserves the Encores! production at City Center, New York.

25. Berlin exploited his little bit of musical wit to favor one of his cherished causes. The columnist Walter Winchell reported that "Irving Berlin turned over all royalties on 'God Bless America' to the Boy and Girl Scouts. But he borrowed four [recte: six] notes from that song for interpolation in one of his 'Call Me Madam' tunes—so he sent them an additional $100 weekly." "Walter Winchell . . . in New York: White Light Night," *Washington Post,* Nov. 22, 1950.

26. Brooks Atkinson, "Ethel Merman as an American Envoy in 'Call Me Madam,' with Berlin's Music," *New York Times,* Oct. 13, 1950.

27. Other Rodgers melodies deploying the expanding-interval device include the bridge of "My Funny Valentine" (*Babes in Arms,* 1937), the ending of "Mister Snow" (*Carousel,* 1945), and the verse of "There's Nothin' Like a Dame" (*South Pacific,* 1949).

28. Barrett, *Daughter's Memoir,* 262.

29. CL, 434.

30. For example, see Barrett, *Daughter's Memoir,* 262–63; Furia, *Life in Song,* 245–47; Jablonski, *American Troubadour,* 267–68.

31. *CL,* 431.

32. "Eisenhower's 'No,'" *New York Times,* Jan. 25, 1948.

33. *CL,* 431.

34. Letter to Ed Sullivan, 1952, quoted in *CL,* 431.

35. Helmy Kresa, quoted in *CL,* 434.

36. The whole story, in Kresa's words, is related in *CL,* 434–35.

37. Furia, *Life in Song,* 247.

38. *CL,* 438.

39. *CL,* 435–38.

40. *Call Me Madam* (London: Irving Berlin Ltd., 1956). This British version of the script (in LC-IBC, Box 89) cites the "train" as the Golden Arrow instead of the Super Chief.

41. *CL,* 427. This chorus was deleted from the published score. Irving Berlin, *Call Me Madam* (London: Irving Berlin Ltd., 1952).

42. *CL*, 428.

43. *CL*, 431.

44. Miles Krueger, commentary on *Call Me Madam* DVD (1953; Twentieth Century Fox, 2004)

45. *CL*, 77.

46. *CL*, 433–34.

47. Personal communication from Mary Ellin Barrett and Linda Emmet, November 2003.

48. Flinn, *Brass Diva*, 185.

49. Richard M. Goldstein, "'I Enjoy Being a Girl': Women in the Plays of Rodgers and Hammerstein," *Popular Music and Society* 13, no. 1 (Spring 1989): 3.

50. Stacy Wolf vividly demonstrates that in her discussion of Merman's performance as Mama Rose in *Gypsy*. See Wolf, *A Problem Like Maria*, esp. 101–28.

51. Timothy W. Kneeland, "Radio," in *The American President in Popular Culture*, ed. John W. Matviko (Westport, CT: Greenwood Press, 2005), chap. 12, 179.

52. Thanks to Rose Rosengard Subotnik for the personal testimony that the radio *Mr. President* "was indeed a popular show. My brother and I never missed it." Communication with the author, July 13, 2011.

53. Theodore H. White, *The Making of the President, 1960*. New York: Atheneum, 1961.

54. The lyric's list of presidents appears in *CL*, 468, and is sung on the original cast album, but it does not appear in the libretto currently leased by the Rodgers and Hammerstein Organization, which indicates a copyright date of 1978. That libretto omits several references that would have been current in 1962. Thanks to Bert Fink for providing a copy of that libretto.

55. The line, another reference rooted in 1962 America, appears in the rehearsal version (LC-IBC Box 171, in act 1, scene 5, p. 37), but not in the licensed R&H libretto.

56. "Rehearsal Version" (LC-IBC Box 171), act 1, scene 11, p. 59.

57. Act 1, scene 11, p. 78.

58. Herbert Mitgang, "'Mr. President' of Tin Pan Alley," *New York Times*, Oct. 14, 1962.

59. *CL*, 263 and 471.

60. Bill Henry, "What—Another Berlin Problem," *Los Angeles Times*, Oct. 9, 1962.

61. "'Mr. President' Dull Musical Stage Show," *Los Angeles Times*, Oct. 23, 1962.

62. Thanks to Rose Rosengard Subotnik for sharing her memory of the number, whose enthusiastic reception she witnessed as early as the Boston tryout.

63. John Keating, "Popular Candidate: Spotlight Has Followed 'Mr. President's' Woes," *New York Times*, Oct. 14, 1962. On Sept. 26, the *Times* had reported a similar figure of $2.4 million in advance ticket sales "despite the somewhat unenthusiastic reviews during the Boston premiere last month." Marjorie Hunter, "'Mr. President' Seen in Capital," *New York Times*, Sept. 26, 1962.

64. "Opening in Boston for 'Mr. President,'" *New York Times*, Aug. 29, 1962.

65. Howard Taubman, "Musical Opens at the St. James Theater," *New York Times*, Oct. 22, 1962.

66. "Belle Poitrine Hits Broadway in a Musical of Little Me," *London Times*, Dec. 28, 1962.

67. Quoted in Keating, "Popular Candidate."

68. Ronald Evans, "Try Anything—If It's a Hit," *Toronto Telegram*, Oct. 20, 1962.

69. Quoted in Keating, "Popular Candidate."

70. Taubman on *Mr. President*; on their previous "old-fashioned" project (*Happy Hunting*), see Brooks Atkinson, "Theatre: Return of Ethel Merman," *New York Times*, Dec. 7, 1956.

71. Eugene Archer, "By Way of Report: Chaplin and Susskind and a 'President,'" *New York Times*, July 28, 1963.

72. Paul Schuette, "Thousands Queue Up to Buy Tickets for 'Mr. President,'" *Washington Post*, Sept. 4, 1962.

73. Helen Thomas, "Premiere Piles Up Coiffure Bookings," *Washington Post*, Sept. 24, 1962.

74. Patricia Peterson, "Fashion Steals Scene at Musical's Debut in Washington," *New York Times*, Sept. 27, 1962.

75. Marjorie Hunter, "'Mr. President' Seen in Capital," *New York Times*, Sept. 26, 1962.

76. Henry, "What—Another Berlin Problem."

77. Frank Rich, *Ghost Light: A Memoir* (New York: Random House, 2000), 184.

78. Ibid., 186.

79. Ibid.

80. Eugene Archer, "By Way of Report: Chaplin, Susskind, and a 'President,'" *New York Times*, July 28, 1963.

81. See "The Alessandrini-fied Mr. President Opens Off-Broadway Aug. 2," *Playbill.com*, Aug. 2, 2001, accessed June 10, 2010; Barbara and Scott Siegel, "Mr. President," *Theatermania.com*, accessed June 10, 2010; and Ben Brantley, "Names Change; White House Doesn't," *New York Times*, Aug. 6, 2001.

82. *CL*, 488–89; The song was published in *Unsung Irving Berlin* (Milwaukee: Hal Leonard/Irving Berlin Music Company, 1996), 75–80.

CONCLUSION: "THIS IS AMERICA"

1. Materials for "Stars on My Shoulders" may be found in LC-IBC Box 185; for lyrics see *CL*, 404–5.

2. Dated Sept. 9, 1955, the one-page typescript scenario is in LC-IBC Box 219, Folder 21.

3. See *CL*, 455, for an account of that show and Berlin's well-developed scenario, plus song list.

4. See LC-IBC Box 212 for script drafts, songs, and Berlin's "rough outline of second act as I see it."

5. For lyrics to the show, see *CL*, 450–55.

6. See Jeff Lunden, "After Years, Sondheim's 'Road Show' Pulls into N.Y." (Nov. 18, 2008), at http://www.npr.org/templates/story/story.php?storyId=97154938, accessed January 30, 2011.

7. The lyrics appear in *CL*, 464. The lyrics, music, and additional notes for the project appear in LC-IBC Box 241, Folder 44.

8. Quoted in John Crosby, "The Master—A New Show," *New York Herald Tribune*, June 4, 1962.

BIBLIOGRAPHY

ARCHIVES

NYPL   New York Public Library
          Charles B. Dillingham Papers, NYPL
LC-IBC   Irving Berlin Collection, Library of Congress
WHS-MH   Moss Hart Papers, Wisconsin Historical Society
WHS-L&C   Lindsay and Crouse Papers, Wisconsin Historical Society

MUSICAL SCORES AND LYRICS BY IRVING BERLIN

Annie Get Your Gun. London: Irving Berlin Ltd., 1947.

As Thousands Cheer. Manuscript piano-vocal score. LC-IBC.

Call Me Madam. London: Irving Berlin Ltd., 1952.

The Complete Lyrics of Irving Berlin [*CL*]. Edited by Robert Kimball and Linda Emmet. New York: Alfred A. Knopf, 2001.

Face the Music. Manuscript piano-vocal score. LC-IBC.

Irving Berlin Anthology. Milwaukee, WI: Hal Leonard.

Irving Berlin: Early Songs, 1907–1914. 3 vols. Edited by Charles Hamm. Music of the United States of America 2, Recent Researches in American Music 20. Madison, WI: A-R Editions, 1994.

Irving Berlin's This Is the Army. New York: This Is the Army, Inc., 1943.

Music Box Revue (1921). Manuscript piano-vocal score. LC-IBC.

The Songs of Irving Berlin. 13 vols. [1909–1919]. Boca Raton, FL: Masters Music, n.d.

Stop! Look! Listen! Manuscript piano-vocal score. NYPL.

Unsung Irving Berlin. Milwaukee, WI: Hal Leonard / Irving Berlin Music Company, 1996.

Watch Your Step. New York: Irving Berlin, Inc. [1915].

Yip Yip Yaphank. Manuscript vocal score, LC-IBC.

LIBRETTOS AND SCRIPTS

Fields, Herbert, and Dorothy Fields. *Annie Get Your Gun*. London: Chappell and Co., 1952.

Hart, Moss. "As Thousands Cheer." Photocopied typescript. LC-IBC.

Hart, Moss. "As Thousands Cheer." Autograph manuscript. WHS-MH.

Hart, Moss. "Face the Music." Typescripts and autograph manuscripts. LC-IBC.

Kaufman, George S. "The Cocoanuts." Typescripts. LC-IBC.

Kaufman, George S. *By George: The Collected Kaufman*. Edited by Donald Oliver. New York: St. Martin's Press, 1979.

Kaufman, George S. *Kaufman & Co.: Broadway Comedies*. Edited by Laurence Maslon. New York: Library of America, 2004.

Lindsay, Howard, and Russel Crouse. *Call Me Madam*. London: Irving Berlin Ltd., 1956.

Lindsay, Howard, and Russel Crouse. "Call Me Madam." "Very early draft." WHS-L&C.

Lindsay, Howard, and Russel Crouse. "Mr. President." "Rehearsal version." LC-IBC.

Lindsay, Howard, and Russel Crouse. *Mr. President*. New York: Rodgers and Hammerstein Organization, 1978.

Lindsay, Howard, and Russel Crouse. *State of the Union.* New York: Random House, 1946.

Lindsay, Howard, and Russel Crouse. *State of the Union.* Acting Edition. New York: Dramatists Play Service, 1974.

Smith, Harry B. *Stop! Look! Listen!* NYPL.

This Is the Army. British script. LC-IBC.

"Ziegfeld Follies of 1919." Typescript dated June 23, 1919, available at memory.loc.gov/ammen/index.html.

Books and Articles

Adams, Michael C. C. *The Best War Ever: America and World War II.* Baltimore: Johns Hopkins University Press, 1994.

Alpers, Benjamin L. "This Is the Army: Imagining a Democratic Military in World War II." *Journal of American History* 85 (June 1998): 129–63.

Amory, Cleveland. "What We Fight For." *Atlantic Monthly* 167 (June 1941): 687–89.

Anderson, Alan. *The Songwriter Goes to War.* Pompton Plains, NJ: Limelight, 2004.

Anderson, John Murray, as told to Hugh Abercrombie Anderson. *Out without My Rubbers: The Memoirs of John Murray Anderson.* New York: Library Publishers, 1954.

Anobile, Richard, ed. *Why a Duck? Visual and Verbal Gems from the Marx Brothers Movies.* New York: Darien House, 1971.

Atkinson, Brooks. *Broadway.* Rev. ed. New York: Macmillan, 1974.

Bach, Steven. *Dazzler: The Life and Times of Moss Hart.* New York: Knopf, 2001.

Banfield, Stephen. *Jerome Kern.* New Haven, CT: Yale University Press, 2006.

Banfield, Stephen. *Sondheim's Broadway Musicals.* Ann Arbor: University of Michigan Press, 1993.

Banfield, Stephen. "The Voice in the Theatre: Stage and Screen Entertainers in the Twentieth Century." In *The Cambridge Companion to Singing,* edited by John Potter, 63–82. Cambridge: Cambridge University Press, 2000.

Baral, Robert. *Revue: The Great Broadway Period.* New York: Fleet, 1962.

Barrett, Mary Ellin. *Irving Berlin: A Daughter's Memoir.* New York: Simon and Schuster: 1994.

Baur, Steven. "'Waltz Me around Again Willie': Gender, Ideology, and Dance in the Gilded Age." In *Musicological Identities: Essays in Honor of Susan McClary,* edited by Steven Bauer, Raymond Knapp, and Jacqueline Warwick. Burlington, VT: Ashgate, 2008.

Bennett, Robert Russell. *The Broadway Sound: The Autobiography and Selected Essays of Robert Russell Bennett.* Edited by George J. Ferencz. Rochester: University of Rochester Press, 1999.

Bergreen, Laurence. *As Thousands Cheer: The Life of Irving Berlin.* New York: Penguin, 1990.

Berlin, Edward A. *Ragtime: A Musical and Cultural History.* Berkeley: University of California Press, 1980.

Berman, Marshall. *On the Town: One Hundred Years of Spectacle in Times Square.* New York: Random House, 2006.

Berry, David Carson. "Dynamic Introductions: The Affective Role of Melodic Ascent and Other Linear Devices in Selected Song Verses of Irving Berlin." *Intégral* 13 (1999): 1–62.

Berry, David Carson. "Gambling with Chromaticism? Extra-Diatonic Melodic Expression in the Songs of Irving Berlin." *Theory and Practice* 26 (2001): 21–85.

Bial, Henry. *Acting Jewish: Negotiating Ethnicity on the American Stage and Screen*. Ann Arbor: University of Michigan Press, 2005.

Bianco, Anthony. *Ghosts of 42nd Street: A History of America's Most Infamous Block*. New York: William Morrow, 2004.

Block, Geoffrey. *Enchanted Evenings: The Broadway Musical from* Show Boat *to Sondheim and Lloyd Webber*. 2nd ed. New York: Oxford University Press, 2009.

Block, Geoffrey. "Revisiting the Glorious and Problematic Legacy of the Jazz Age and Depression Musical." *Studies in Musical Theatre* 2, no 2 (2008): 127–46.

Block, Geoffrey. *Richard Rodgers*. New Haven, CT: Yale University Press, 2003.

Bodnar, John. "*Saving Private Ryan* and Postwar Memory in America." *American Historical Review* 106, no. 3 (June 2001): 805–17.

Bomback, Larry. "The Music of the *Music Box Revues*." *Musicological Explorations* 7 (Spring 2006): 51–88.

Bordman, Gerald. *American Musical Comedy*. New York: Oxford University Press, 1982.

Bordman, Gerald. *American Musical Revue*. New York: Oxford University Press, 1985.

Bordman, Gerald. *American Musical Theatre: A Chronicle*. 3rd ed. New York: Oxford University Press, 2001.

Bordman, Gerald. *Jerome Kern*. New York: Oxford University Press, 1980.

Boskin, Joseph. *Sambo: The Rise and Demise of an American Jester*. New York: Oxford University Press, 1986.

Brackett, David. "Banjos, Biopics, and Compilation Scores: The Movies Go Country." *American Music* 19, no. 3 (Autumn 2001): 247–90.

Brown, Jared. *Moss Hart: A Prince of the Theatre*. New York: Back Stage Books, 2006.

Bryant, Rebecca A. "Shaking Things Up: Popularizing the Shimmy in America." *American Music* 20, no. 2 (Summer 2002): 168–87.

Butler, Judith. *Gender Trouble: Feminism and the Subversion of Identity*. New York: Routledge, 1990.

Carter, Tim. *Oklahoma! The Making of an American Musical*. New Haven, CT: Yale University Press, 2007.

Clurman, Harold, ed. *Famous American Plays of the 1930s*. New York: Dell, 1959.

Coffey, Frank. *Always Home: 50 Years of the USO*. Washington, DC: Brassey's, 1991.

Cook, Susan C. "Watching Our Step: Embodying Research, Telling Stories." In *Audible Traces: Gender, Identity, and Music,* edited by Elaine Barkin and Lydia Hamessley. Zurich: Carciofoli Verlagshaus, 1999, 177–212.

Cooper, Courtney Ryley. *Annie Oakley: Woman at Arms*. New York: Duffield, 1927.

Copland, Aaron. "Jazz Structure and Influence." *Modern Music* 4, no. 2 (January 1927): 9–14.

Crawford, Richard, and Jeffrey Magee. *Jazz Standards on Record, 1900–1942: A Core Repertory*. Chicago: Center for Black Music Research, 1992.

Culbert, David. "This Is the Army." In *The Movies as History: Visions of the Twentieth Century*, edited by David W. Ellwood. Stroud, Gloucestershire: Sutton/History Today, 2000.

Custen, George F. "I hear music and . . . Darryl and Irving Write History with *Alexander's Ragtime Band*." In *Authorship and Film*, edited by David A. Gerstner and Janet Staiger. AFI Film Readers. New York: Routledge, 2003, 77–95.

Decker, Todd. *Music Makes Me: Fred Astaire and Jazz*. Berkeley: University of California Press, 2011.

Diehl, Lorraine B., and Marianne Hardart. *The Automat*. New York: Clarkson Potter, 2002.

Diner, Hasia. *In the Almost Promised Land: American Jews and Blacks, 1915–1935*. Westport, CT.: Greenwood Press, 1977.

Dizikes, John. *Opera in America: A Cultural History*. New Haven, CT: Yale University Press, 1993.

Doherty, Thomas. *Projections of War: Hollywood, American Culture, and World War II*. New York: Columbia University Press, 1993.

Douglas, Ann. *Terrible Honesty: Mongrel Manhattan in the 1920s*. New York: Farrar, Straus and Giroux, 1995.

Engel, Lehman. *The American Musical Theater, a Consideration*. N.p.: CBS Records/ Macmillan, 1967.

Erenberg, Lewis A. *Steppin' Out: New York Nightlife and the Transformation of American Culture, 1890–1930*. Chicago: University of Chicago Press, 1984.

Evans, Sara M. *Born for Liberty: A History of Women in America*. New York: Free Press, 1989.

Everett, William A. *Sigmund Romberg*. New Haven, CT: Yale University Press, 2007.

Eyman, Scott. *Lion of Hollywood: The Life and Legend of Louis B. Mayer*. New York: Simon and Schuster, 2005.

Fields, Armond, and L. Marc Fields. *From the Bowery to Broadway: Lew Fields and the Roots of American Popular Theater*. New York: Oxford University Press, 1993.

Flynn, Caryl. *Brass Diva: The Life and Legends of Ethel Merman*. Berkeley: University of California Press, 2007.

Fordin, Hugh. *Getting to Know Him: A Biography of Oscar Hammerstein II*. New York: Random House, 1977.

Forte, Allen. *The American Popular Ballad of the Golden Era, 1924–1950*. Princeton, NJ: Princeton University Press, 1995.

Franceschina, John. *Harry B. Smith: Dean of American Librettists*. New York: Routledge, 2003.

Frye, Northrup. *The Anatomy of Criticism: Four Essays*. In *Collected Works of Northrup Frye*, edited by Robert D. Denham. Toronto: University of Toronto Press, 2006, vol. 22.

Furia, Philip. *Ira Gershwin: The Art of the Lyricist*. New York: Oxford University Press, 1996.

Furia, Philip. *Irving Berlin: A Life in Song*. New York: Schirmer, 1998.

Furia, Philip. *The Poets of Tin Pan Alley*. New York: Oxford University Press, 1990.

Fussell, Paul. *The Great War and Modern Memory*. New York: Oxford University Press, 1975.

Fussell, Paul. *Wartime: Understanding and Behavior in the Second World War*. New York: Oxford University Press, 1988.

Gabler, Neal. *An Empire of Their Own: How the Jews Invented Hollywood*. New York: Anchor Books, 1988.

Garber, Michael G. "Reflexive Songs in the American Musical, 1898–1947." PhD diss., City University of New York, 2006.

Garrett, Charles Hiroshi. *Struggling to Define a Nation: American Music and the Twentieth Century*. Berkeley: University of California Press, 2008.

Giddins, Gary. *Visions of Jazz: The First Century*. New York: Oxford University Press, 1998.

Giger, Andreas. "Verismo: Origin, Corruption, and Redemption of an Operatic Term." *Journal of the American Musicological Society* 60, no. 2 (Summer 2007): 271–315.

Goldberg, Isaac. *Tin Pan Alley*. 1930. Reprint. New York: Frederick Ungar, 1961.

Goldstein, Joshua S. *War and Gender: How Gender Shapes the War System and Vice Versa*. Cambridge: Cambridge University Press, 2001.

Goldstein, Malcolm. *George S. Kaufman: His Life, His Theater*. New York: Oxford University Press, 1979.

Goldstein, Richard M. "'I Enjoy Being a Girl': Women in the Plays of Rodgers and Hammerstein." *Popular Music and Society* 13, no. 1 (Spring 1989): 1-8.

Gottlieb, Jack. *Funny, It Doesn't Sound Jewish: How Yiddish Songs and Synagogue Melodies Influenced Tin Pan Alley, Broadway, and Hollywood*. Albany: State University of New York and the Library of Congress, 2004.

Green, Stanley. *Broadway Musicals, Show By Show*. 5th ed., Rev. Kay Green. Milwaukee: Hal Leonard, 1996.

Green, Stanley. *The World of Musical Comedy*. 4th rev. ed. San Diego: A. S. Barnes, 1980.

Green, Stanley. Liner Notes to *The Ziegfeld Follies of 1919*. Smithsonian American Musical Theatre Series. Washington, DC: Smithsonian Collection, 1977.

Greenspan, Charlotte. *Pick Yourself Up: Dorothy Fields and the American Musical*. New York: Oxford University Press, 2010.

Grossman, Barbara Wallace. *Funny Woman: The Life and Times of Fanny Brice*. Bloomington: Indiana University Press, 1991.

Hadlock, Heather. *Mad Loves: Women and Music in Offenbach's "Les Contes d'Hoffmann."* Princeton, NJ: Princeton University Press, 2000.

Hamberlin, Larry. *Tin Pan Opera: Operatic Novelty Songs in the Ragtime Era*. New York: Oxford University Press, 2011.

Hamm, Charles. *Irving Berlin: Songs from the Melting Pot: The Formative Years, 1907–1914*. New York: Oxford University Press, 1997.

Hamm, Charles. "Irving Berlin's Early Songs as Biographical Documents." *Musical Quarterly* 7, no. 1 (Spring 1993): 10–34.

Hamm, Charles. *Putting Popular Music in Its Place*. Cambridge: Cambridge University Press, 1995.

Hansen, Miriam. "The Mass Production of the Senses: Classical Cinema as Vernacular Modernism." In *Reinventing Film Studies*, edited by Linda Williams and Christina Gledhill. London: Edward Arnold, 2000, 332–50.

Hargrove, Marion. *See Here, Private Hargrove*. New York: Henry Holt, 1942.

Hart, Moss. *Act One: An Autobiography*. New York: Random House, 1959.

Hart, Moss. "Mad About Music." *Stage* (August 1938): 36–38.

Heberling, Lynn O'Neal. "Soldiers in Greasepaint: USO–Camp Shows, Inc., during World War II." PhD diss., Kent State University, 1989.

Heintze, James. *Adapting to Abundance: Jewish Immigrants, Mass Consumption, and the Search for American Identity*. New York: Columbia University Press, 1990.

Hirsch, Foster. *The Boys from Syracuse: The Shuberts' Theatrical Empire*. Carbondale: Southern Illinois University Press, 1998.

Hollinger, David A. *Postethnic America: Beyond Multiculturalism*. New York: Basic Books, 2000.

Hollinger, David A. *Science, Jews, and Secular Culture: Studies in Mid-Twentieth-Century Intellectual History*. Princeton, NJ: Princeton University Press, 1996.

Horowitz, Joseph. *American Classical Music: A History*. New York: W. W. Norton, 2007.

Howe, Irving. *World of Our Fathers: The Journey of the East European Jews to America and the Life They Found and Made*. New York: Galahad Books, 1976.

Jablonski, Edward. *Irving Berlin: American Troubadour*. New York: Henry Holt, 1999.

Kanfer, Stefan. *Groucho: The Life and Times of Julius Henry Marx*. New York: Vintage: 2001.

Kasper, Shirl. *Annie Oakley*. Norman: University of Oklahoma Press, 1992.

Kasson, Joy S. *Buffalo Bill's Wild West: Celebrity, Memory, and Popular History*. New York: Hill and Wang, 2000.

Katz, Mark. *Capturing Sound: How Technology Changed Music*. Berkeley: University of California Press, 2004.

Kaufman, George S. "Music to My Ears." *Stage*, August 1938, 27–30.

Kibler, M. Alison. *Rank Ladies: Gender and Cultural Hierarchy in American Vaudeville*. Chapel Hill: University of North Carolina Press, 1999.

Kirle, Bruce. *Unfinished Business: Broadway Musicals as Works-in-Process*. Carbondale: Southern Illinois University Press, 2005.

Knapp, Margaret. "*Watch Your Step*: Irving Berlin's 1914 Musical." In *Musical Theatre in America*, edited by Glenn Loney. Westport, CT: Greenwood Press, 1984, 245–52.

Knapp, Raymond. *American Musical Theater and the Formation of National Identity*. Princeton, NJ: Princeton University Press, 2004.

Knapp, Raymond. *American Musical Theater and the Performance of Personal Identity*. Princeton, NJ: Princeton University Press, 2006.

Kneeland, Timothy W. "Radio." In *The American President in Popular Culture*, edited by John W. Matviko. Westport, CT: Greenwood Press, 2005.

Koppes, Clayton R., and Gregory D. Black. "Blacks, Loyalty, and Motion-Picture Propaganda in World War II." *Journal of American History* 72, no. 2 (Sept. 1986): 383–406.

Koppes, Clayton R., and Gregory D. Black. *Hollywood Goes to War: How Politics, Profits, and Propaganda Shaped World War II Movies*. New York: Free Press, 1987.

Lampe, J. Bodewalt, ed. *Remick Folio of Moving Picture Music*. Vol. 1. New York: Jerome H. Remick, 1914.

Langford, Jeffrey. "The 'Dramatic Symphonies' of Berlioz as an Outgrowth of the French Operatic Tradition." *Musical Quarterly* 69, no. 1 (Winter 1983): 85–103.

Leopold, David. *Irving Berlin's Show Business*. New York: Harry N. Abrams, Inc., 2005.

Lerner, Alan Jay. *The Musical Theatre: A Celebration*. New York: McGraw-Hill, 1986.

Levy, Beth E. "From Orient to Occident: Aaron Copland and the Sagas of the Prairie." In *Aaron Copland and His World*, edited by Carol J. Oja and Judith Tick. Princeton, NJ: Princeton University Press, 2005, 307–49.

Lieb, Sandra. *Mother of the Blues: A Study of Ma Rainey*. Amherst: University of Massachusetts Press, 1981.

Lindberg, Ulf. "Popular Modernism? The 'Urban' Style of Interwar Tin Pan Alley," *Popular Music* 22, no. 3 (2003): 283–98.

Logan, Joshua. *Josh: My Up and Down, In and Out Life*. New York: Delacorte, 1976.

Loos, Anita. *The Talmadge Girls*. New York: Viking, 1978.

Lott, Eric. *Love and Theft: Blackface Minstrelsy and the American Working Class*. New York: Oxford University Press, 1993.

Lynes, Russell. *The Lively Audience: A Social History of the Visual and Performing Arts in America, 1890–1950*. New York: Harper and Row, 1985.

Magee, Jeffrey. "'Everybody Step': Irving Berlin, Jazz, and Broadway in the 1920s." *Journal of the American Musicological Society* 59, no. 3 (Fall 2006): 597–632.

Magee, Jeffrey. "Irving Berlin's 'Blue Skies': Ethnic Affiliations and Musical Transformations." *Musical Quarterly* 84, no. 4 (Winter 2000): 537–80.

Magee, Jeffrey. "Ragtime and Early Jazz." In *The Cambridge History of American Music*, edited by David Nicholls. Cambridge: Cambridge University Press, 1998, 388–417.

Mahar, William J. *Behind the Burnt Cork Mask*. Urbana: University of Illinois Press, 1999.

Martin, Mary. *My Heart Belongs, an Autobiography by Mary Martin*. New York: Morrow, 1976.

Marx, Groucho. *Groucho and Me*. 1959. Reprint. New York: Da Capo, 1995.

Mast, Gerald *Can't Help Singin': The American Musical on Stage and Screen*. Woodstock, NY: Overlook Press, 1987.

Matson, Lowell. "Theatre for the Armed Forces in World War II." *Educational Theatre Journal* 6, no. 1 (March 1954): 1–11.

McMillin, Scott. *The Musical as Drama*. Princeton, NJ: Princeton University Press, 2006.

Melnick, Jeffrey. *A Right to Sing the Blues: Jews, African Americans, and American Popular Song*. Cambridge, MA: Harvard University Press, 1999.

Meredith, Scott. *George Kaufman and His Friends*. Garden City, NY: Doubleday, 1974.

Merman, Ethel, as told to George Eells. *Merman*. New York: Simon and Schuster, 1978.

Merman, Ethel, as told to Pete Martin. *Who Could Ask for Anything More*. New York: Doubleday, 1955.

Miller, Jordan Y., and Winifred L. Frazer, eds. *American Drama between the Wars: A Critical History*. Boston: Twayne Publishers, 1991.

Mitgang, Herbert. *The Man Who Rode the Tiger: The Life and Times of Judge Samuel Seabury*. Philadelphia: J.B. Lippincott, 1963.

Mitgang, Herbert. *Once Upon a Time in New York: Jimmy Walker, Franklin Roosevelt, and the Last Great Battle of the Jazz Age*. New York: Free Press, 2000.

Monson, Ingrid. "The Problem with White Hipness: Race, Gender, and Cultural Conceptions in Jazz Historical Discourse." *Journal of the American Musicological Society* 48, no. 3 (Fall 1995): 396–422.

Moore, Grace. *You're Only Human Once*. Garden City, NY: Doubleday, Doran and Co., 1944.

Moore, MacDonald Smith. *Yankee Blues: Musical Culture and American Identity*. Bloomington: Indiana University Press, 1985.

Mordden, Ethan. *Beautiful Mornin': The Broadway Musical in the 1940s*. New York: Oxford University Press, 1999.

Mordden, Ethan. *Coming Up Roses: The Broadway Musical in the 1950s*. New York: Oxford University Press, 1998.

Mordden, Ethan. *Make Believe: The Broadway Musical in the 1920s*. New York: Oxford University Press, 1997.

Mordden, Ethan. *Sing for Your Supper: The Broadway Musical in the 1930s*. New York: Palgrave, 2005.

Most, Andrea. *Making Americans: Jews and the Broadway Musical*. Cambridge, MA: Harvard University Press, 2004.

Mott, Frank Luther. *American Journalism, A History: 1690–1960.* 3rd ed. New York: Macmillan, 1962.

Murphy, George, with Victor Lasky. *"Say . . . Didn't You Used to Be George Murphy?"* New York: Bartholomew House, 1970.

Norton, Richard. *A Chronology of American Musical Theater.* 3 vols. New York: Oxford University Press, 2002.

Olin, Reuel Keith. "A History and Interpretation of the Princess Theatre Musical Plays: 1915–1919." PhD diss., New York University 1979.

O'Malley, Frank Ward. "Irving Berlin Gives Nine Rules for Writing Popular Songs." *American Magazine* 90 (October 1920): 36–37, 239–46.

Osgood, Henry O. *So This Is Jazz.* Boston: Little, Brown, 1926.

Osofsky, Gilbert. *Harlem: The Making of a Ghetto.* 2nd ed. New York: Harper and Row, 1971.

Pisani, Michael V. *Imagining Native America in Music.* New Haven, CT: Yale University Press, 2005.

Pollack, Howard. *John Alden Carpenter: Chicago Composer.* 1995. Reprint. Urbana: University of Illinois Press, 2001.

Randall, James Kenneth. "Becoming Jerome Kern: The Early Songs and Shows, 1903–1915." PhD diss., University of Illinois, Urbana-Champaign, 2004.

Raphaelson, Samson. *The Jazz Singer.* New York: Brentano, 1925.

Rich, Frank. *Ghost Light: A Memoir.* New York: Random House, 2000.

Riley, Glenda. *The Life and Legacy of Annie Oakley.* Norman: University of Oklahoma Press, 1994.

Rourke, Constance. *American Humor: A Study of the National Character.* 1931. Reprint. Introduction and bibliographical essay by W. T. Lhamon Jr. Tallahassee: Florida State University Press, 1986.

Roberts, John Storm. *The Latin Tinge: The Impact of Latin American Music on the United States.* 2nd ed. New York: Oxford University Press, 1999.

Rodgers, Richard. *Musical Stages: An Autobiography.* New York: Random House, 1975.

Rogin, Michael. *Blackface, White Noise: Jewish Immigrants in the Hollywood Melting Pot.* Berkeley: University of California Press, 1996.

Roost, Alisa. "Before *Oklahoma!* A Reappraisal of Musical Theatre during the 1930s." *Journal of Drama and Theatre* 16, no. 1 (Winter 2004): 1–35.

Rosen, Jody. *White Christmas: The Story of an American Song.* New York: Simon and Schuster, 2007.

Roth, Philip. *Operation Shylock: A Confession.* New York: Simon and Schuster, 1993.

Ryskind, Morrie, with John H. M. Roberts. *I Shot an Elephant in My Pajamas: The Morrie Ryskind Story.* Lafayette, LA: Huntington House, 1994.

Sanjek, Russell, updated by David Sanjek. *Pennies from Heaven: The American Popular Music Business in the Twentieth Century.* New York: Da Capo, 1996.

Sanders, Ronald. "The American Popular Song." In *Next Year in Jerusalem: Portraits of the Jew in the Twentieth Century,* edited by Douglas Villiers. New York: Viking, 1976, 197–219.

Schiff, David. *Gershwin: Rhapsody in Blue.* Cambridge: Cambridge University Press, 1997.

Schmidt, Leigh Eric. "The Easter Parade: Piety, Fashion, and Display." *Religion and American Culture* 4, no. 2 (Summer 1994): 135–64.

Schwadron, Abraham A. "On Jewish Music." In *Music of Many Cultures,* edited by Elizabeth May. Berkeley: University of California Press, 1980.

Sears, Benjamin, and Bradford Conner. "Reconstructing Lost Musicals." *Music Reference Services Quarterly* 10, nos. 3–4 (2007): 67–77.

Sederholm, Jack P. "The Musical Directing Career and Stagecraft Contributions of Hassard Short 1919–1952." PhD diss., Wayne State University, 1974.

Slobin, Mark. *Tenement Songs: The Popular Music of Jewish Immigrants.* Urbana: University of Illinois Press, 1982.

Smith, Cecil, and Glenn Litton. *Musical Comedy in America.* 2nd ed. New York: Theatre Arts Books, 1981.

Smulyan, Susan. *Selling Radio: The Commercialization of American Broadcasting, 1920–1934.* Washington, DC: Smithsonian Institution Press, 1994.

Snyder, Robert W. *The Voice of the City: Vaudeville and Popular Culture in New York.* New York: Oxford University Press, 1989.

Stempel, Larry. *Showtime: A History of the Broadway Musical Theater.* New York: W. W. Norton, 2010.

Stone, Ezra. Letter to the Editor. *Journal of American History* 74 (June 1987): 252–53.

Subotnik, Rose Rosengard. "Shoddy Equipment for Living? Deconstructing the Tin Pan Alley Song." In *Musicological Identities: Essays in Honor of Susan McClary,* edited by Steven Bauer, Raymond Knapp, and Jacqueline Warwick. Burlington, VT: Ashgate, 2008.

Sudhalter, Richard M. *Stardust Melody: The Life and Music of Hoagy Carmichael.* New York: Oxford University Press, 2002.

Suisman, David. *Selling Sounds: The Commercial Revolution in American Music.* Cambridge, MA: Harvard University Press, 2009.

Swain, Joseph P. *The Broadway Musical: A Critical and Musical Survey.* 2nd ed. Lanham, MD: Scarecrow Press, 2002.

Teichmann, Howard. *George S. Kaufman: An Intimate Portrait.* New York: Atheneum, 1972.

Terkel, Studs. *"The Good War": An Oral History of World War II.* New York: Pantheon, 1985.

"The Theatre and the Armed Forces." *Theatre Arts* (March 1943): 149–68.

Tick, Judith. "The Origins and Style of Copland's *Mood for Piano,* no. 3, 'Jazzy,'" *American Music* 20, no. 3 (Fall 2002): 277–96.

Tindall, George Brown, and David E. Shi. *America: A Narrative History.* 4th ed. New York: W. W. Norton, 1996.

Toll, Robert C. *Blacking Up: The Minstrel Show in Nineteenth-Century America.* New York: Oxford University Press, 1974.

Travis, Doris Eaton, with Joseph and Charles Eaton, as told to J. R. Morris. *The Days We Danced: The Story of My Theatrical Family from Ziegfeld to Arthur Murray and Beyond.* Seattle: Marquand Books, 2003.

Tucker, Mark. "Jazz." *New Grove Dictionary of Music and Musicians.* Vol. 14. 2nd ed. London: Macmillan; and New York: Grove's Dictionaries, 2001.

Tucker, Sherrie. "Big Ears: Listening for Gender in Jazz Studies." *Current Musicology* nos. 71–73 (Spring 2001–Spring 2002): 375–408.

Vallillo, Stephen M. "George M. Cohan's *Little Johnny Jones.*" In *Musical Theatre in America,* edited by Glenn Loney. Westport, CT: Greenwood Press, 1984, 233–44.

Van der Merwe, Ann Ommen. *The Ziegfeld Follies: A History in Song*. Lanham, MD: Scarecrow, 2009.

Wainscott, Ronald H. *The Emergence of the Modern American Theater, 1914–1929*. New Haven, CT: Yale University Press, 1997.

Wallace, Henry. *The Century of the Common Man*. Edited by Russell Lord. New York: Reynal and Hitchcock, 1943.

Walser, Robert, ed. *Keeping Time: Readings in Jazz History*. New York: Oxford University Press, 1999.

Walsh, David, and Len Platt. *Musical Theater and American Culture*. Westport, CT: Praeger, 2003.

Waters, Ethel, with Charles Samuels. *His Eye Is on the Sparrow: An Autobiography*. 1950. Reprint. Westport, CT: Greenwood Press, 1978.

Weitz, Eric. *The Cambridge Introduction to Comedy*. Cambridge: Cambridge University Press, 2009.

Wertheim, Albert. *Staging the War: American Drama and World War II*. Bloomington: Indiana University Press, 2004.

Whitcomb, Ian. *Irving Berlin and Ragtime America*. New York: Limelight, 1988.

White, Theodore H. *The Making of the President, 1960*. New York: Atheneum, 1961.

Wilder, Alec. *American Popular Song: The Great Innovators, 1900–1950*. New York: Oxford University Press, 1972.

Wilk, Max. *They're Playing Our Song: Conversations with America's Classic Songwriters*. 1991. Reprint. New York: Da Capo, 1997.

Winer, Deborah Grace. *On the Sunny Side of the Street: The Life and Lyrics of Dorothy Fields*. New York: Schirmer, 1997.

Wolf, Stacy. *A Problem like Maria: Gender and Sexuality in the American Musical*. Ann Arbor: University of Michigan Press, 2002.

Woollcott, Alexander. *The Story of Irving Berlin*. New York: G. P. Putnam's Sons, 1925.

Wyatt, Robert, and John Andrew Johnson, eds. *The George Gershwin Reader*. New York: Oxford University Press, 2004.

DISCOGRAPHY

Annie Get Your Gun. [Original 1946 Cast] MCA Classics MCAD-10047. 1990.

Annie Get Your Gun. 1957 NBC Live Recording. With Mary Martin and John Raitt. Broadway Classics #19. Angel ZDM 0777 7 64765 2 0. 1993.

Annie Get Your Gun. An Original Cast Recording. RCA Victor. 1966. 1988.

Annie Get Your Gun. EMI Records / Musical Heritage Society 513335F. 1991.

As Thousands Cheer. World Premiere Cast Recording. Varese Sarabande VSD-5999. 1998.

Call Me Madam. Encores! Cast Recording. DRG 94761. 1995.

Everybody Step: Irving Berlin's Music Box Revues and Other Songs from 1921–1925. Oakton Recordings. 2004.

Face the Music. Encores! Cast Recording. DRG-CD-94781. 2007.

Louisiana Purchase. 1996 Original New York Cast Recording. DRG 94766. 1996.

Miss Liberty. Original Broadway Cast. Sony Broadway. [1949] 1991.

Mr. President. Original Broadway Cast. Sony Broadway SK 48212. [1962] 1992.

Music Box Revues, 1921–1924. American Classics. 2005.

This Is the Army. Recorded by the Original All-Soldier Cast. Decca B0000831–02. [1942] 2003.

This Is the Army. The Original Soundtrack Recording. Hollywood Soundstage 4009.

The Ultimate Irving Berlin. Original Cast Recordings. Two Volumes. Pearl GEM 0116 and 0117. [Vol. 1: 1910–1916; Vol. 2: 1917–1927]

Watch Your Step. Off Broadway Cast. Original Cast OC-6009.

Yip! Yip! Yaphank! American Classics. 2010.

Ziegfeld Follies of 1919. Smithsonian Collection R 009. 1977.

ACKNOWLEDGMENTS

Writing this book paralleled two key aspects of Berlin's career: longevity and collaboration. The seeds were planted long before I realized they would grow into a book, when I served as an editor of Charles Hamm's hefty three-volume edition of Irving Berlin's early songs. Working on that project was like getting paid for taking a year-long seminar with a master scholar. I played and studied every bar of words and music, and I learned a lot from two people, the scholar and the songwriter, who thereafter visited my dreams. Without Charles, who passed away while I was correcting proof, this book simply wouldn't exist.

On the basis of an essay about "Blue Skies," the series editor Geoffrey Block invited me to write a book about Berlin and the musical theater. I was pleased but also naively skeptical that the subject warranted an entire book. Geoffrey patiently parried my protests, and I relented. Together, Hamm, Block, and Berlin himself made me feel as if this project found me rather than the other way around, and for that, I'm grateful. Geoffrey has remained the book's champion in the twelve years since our first discussion about it. He has perceptively read chapter drafts, answered many questions, re-read chapters, then read the whole manuscript and delivered copious and deeply informed commentary along the way, all of which reflected the mind of a meticulous and prolific scholar.

Oxford's Norm Hirschy has been a dream of an editor from proposal to production—offering wise advice and listening, reading, commenting, connecting, encouraging, and reassuring all the way. Thanks (again) to production editor Joellyn Ausanka and copyeditor Mary Sutherland for the care with which they reviewed all aspects of the book and steered it efficiently toward publication. I also appreciate the expertise of the designer, Caroline McDonnell, and the marketing point-person, Samara Stob, for what they did to prepare the book to go out into the world.

I'm grateful to many other scholars, students, teachers, writers, musicians, and friends for substantial support and insights that came in many forms: Alan Anderson, Amy Asch, Katie Baber, Stephen Banfield, Jim Barrett, Amy Beal, Bruce Brown, Tim Carter, Paul Charosh, Richard Crawford, Todd Decker, Rachel Ee, George Ferencz, Philip Furia, Charlotte Greenspan, Larry Hamberlin, Dawn Harris, Eve Harwood, Desiree Hassler, Ellie Hisama, Sheryl Kaskowitz, Ashley Klingler, Cynthia Lauer, Esther Lee, Eric Levin, Beth Levy, Robert McNeily, Carol Oja, Ellen Peck, Jody Rosen, Wayne Shirley, Jeff Taylor, Ann Ommen van der Merwe, Justin Vickers, Chris White, and Stacy Wolf. Thanks, too, to the dynamic duo of Ben Sears and Brad Conner, Berlin experts both, who shared recordings and knowledge. Thanks especially to Todd Decker and Tim Carter for making perceptive comments on parts of the manuscript early on, and to Rose Rosengard Subotnik for a close and empathetic reading of the entire manuscript that led to a cleaner, sharper final product. I'm grateful that Philip Furia, whose books have taught me a lot about how to read and hear Berlin's songs, also read the entire manuscript and offered valuable suggestions.

Several graduate students at Indiana and Illinois—some now long finished with their degrees, for this book developed on two campuses through two jobs—did valuable legwork in tracking down sources: Dan Batchelder, Kunio Hara, Alison Mero,

Peter Schimpf, Holly Holmes, and Aaron Ziegel. Holly and Aaron deserve special recognition for preparing the musical examples as well. Aaron, in particular, performed countless tasks across several years of the project with delightful efficiency, musicality, and meticulousness.

A big research assist came from the other end of the generational span. On a warm July day in 2009 the former *Ziegfeld Follies* dancer Doris Eaton Travis, then 105 years old, welcomed me to her home in a Detroit suburb and shared her memories of the 1919 production. I am deeply grateful that she gave her time—and especially that she sang unpublished lyrics from memory into a recording device. Thanks, too, to her nephew Joe Eaton, who arranged the interview, sat with us while we talked, and dug up a videotape of Mrs. Travis dancing Berlin's "Mandy" number at the New Amsterdam Theatre, proving that she still had the goods after hitting the century mark. She passed away less than a year later on May 11, the date that Berlin marked his birthday. I'm sorry she did not live to see the results of a project for which she promised to help "in any way that I can."

At the Library of Congress, many staff members shepherded materials from the archives to my desk. Thanks to Ray White, Dee Gallo, and Walter Zvonchenko for help above and beyond the call of duty. Archivists who helpfully fielded questions and requests for illustrations include Rick Watson (Harry Ransom Research Center), Thomas Lisanti and Jeremy Megraw (New York Public Library), Robbi Siegel (Museum of the City of New York), Chamisa Redmond (Library of Congress), and Rosemary Cullen (Brown University).

Staff members of the Rodgers and Hammerstein Organization and Irving Berlin Company, now under the auspices of Imagem Music Group, were enormously helpful in answering questions, fulfilling requests, and ensuring accuracy in lyric quotations. Special thanks, above all, to Bert Fink, and also to Ted Chapin, Robin Walton, Carol Cornicelli, Bruce Pomahac, and Sebastian Fabal, and to Berlin's eldest daughter, Mary Ellin Barrett, who over the years has shown a keen interest in scholarly analysis of her father's life and work and, through Bert Fink, communicated useful information.

To Christopher Hart and Anne Kaufman: thank you for the personal contact along with permission to include excerpts from the works of Moss Hart and George S. Kaufman. I have been an admirer of your fathers' works since appearing in a high school production of *You Can't Take It with You*, and it's been delightful to learn about their collaborations with Berlin. Thanks also to Tim Crouse, who perceptively reviewed and commented on quotations from his father's work, along with David Grossberg and Jeremy Nussbaum for facilitating permissions requests.

Financial support and gifts of time came from the National Endowment for the Humanities, the Indiana University President's Arts and Humanities Initiative, the University of Illinois Center for Advanced Study, and grants from that university's Fine and Applied Arts Research and Creative Activity fund and the Research Board. Without that support, this prairie-state scholar could not have made so many trips to the Library of Congress.

To paraphrase Oscar Hammerstein II, by your children you'll be taught. My daughter, Ellen, and son, Miles, often sat patiently, and often impatiently, nearby, at home, in cafes, and in bookstores while I wrote. They also made comments at key moments that focused my thinking. Ellen and I were riding in the car listening to the soundtrack of the film *Enchanted*, a witty, reflexive twist on the Disney princess musical with songs by Stephen Schwartz and Alan Mencken. The film's finale, "Ever Ever After," came on, and Ellen said that she liked the song because it could fit into many other shows. The comment stuck with me because it was a perfect summary of Irving Berlin's ideas about musical theater. I'm grateful to Miles for his perceptive comment about "musicals where people sing for no reason," which encouraged my search for the reasons people sing in Berlin's shows. This project shifted into a new gear after he was born, so it's apt to say that Miles grew up with the book—faster than the book, it seemed to me. Meanwhile, like Ellen, he seems to be growing up with a tendency to say it with music.

My brother Rich deserves special thanks for coordinating visits to Washington, D.C. (one of them with his son, Kevin), with mine, which made several of my research trips to the Library of Congress more lively and enjoyable. He is a constant source of humor and wisdom, a model of persistence, and a great friend. Alan and Monika Magee added another layer of familial support, asking perceptive questions, offering encouragement, and even traveling about two hundred miles to attend one of my Berlin talks.

My parents, Joyce and Richard Magee, earn the book's dedication for a lifetime of love and support—and because musical theater has marked key moments of our shared lives. As teenagers in Bucks County, Pennsylvania, their courtship developed while attending musicals at the Lambertville Music Circus in New Jersey. Years later, in sickness and in health, they came to see me in high school musical productions. They also took me and Rich to our first Broadway musical and have been stalwart audience members for Ellen's stage performances as well. They were the first to read this book's manuscript from beginning to end—an unexpected gift.

And now it can be told: Every day I am grateful to be both husband and colleague to Gayle Magee—loving supporter, perceptive and aptly skeptical reader, proud Canadian, and devoted mother and wife with a gift for creating time and space to do my best work.

CREDITS

"I Love to Sit By the Fire" by Irving Berlin
© Copyright 2001 by The Estate of Irving Berlin
© Copyright Renewed. International Copyright Secured.
All Rights Reserved. Reprinted by Permission.

"I Say It's Spinach (And the Hell with It)" by Irving Berlin
© Copyright 1932 by Irving Berlin
© Copyright Renewed. International Copyright Secured.
All Rights Reserved. Reprinted by Permission.

"I'll Share It All with You" by Irving Berlin
© Copyright 1946 by Irving Berlin
© Copyright Renewed. International Copyright Secured.
All Rights Reserved. Reprinted by Permission.

"I'm a Bad, Bad Man" by Irving Berlin
© Copyright 1946 by Irving Berlin
© Copyright Renewed. International Copyright Secured.
All Rights Reserved. Reprinted by Permission.

"I'm an Indian, Too" by Irving Berlin
© Copyright 1946 by Irving Berlin
© Copyright Renewed. International Copyright Secured.
All Rights Reserved. Reprinted by Permission.

"I'm Getting Tired So I Can Sleep" by Irving Berlin
© Copyright 1942 by Irving Berlin
© Copyright Renewed. International Copyright Secured.
All Rights Reserved. Reprinted by Permission.

"I'm the Guy Who Guards the Harem (And My Heart's In My Work)" by Irving Berlin
© Copyright 1919 by Irving Berlin
© Copyright Renewed. International Copyright Secured.
All Rights Reserved. Reprinted by Permission.

"In Our Hide-Away" by Irving Berlin
© Copyright 1962 by Irving Berlin
© Copyright Renewed. International Copyright Secured.
All Rights Reserved. Reprinted by Permission.

"International Rag, The" by Irving Berlin
© Copyright 1913 by Irving Berlin
© Copyright Renewed. International Copyright Secured.
All Rights Reserved. Reprinted by Permission.

"Interview, An" by Irving Berlin
© Copyright 2001 by The Estate of Irving Berlin
© Copyright Renewed. International Copyright Secured.
All Rights Reserved. Reprinted by Permission.

INDEX

double song. *See* counterpoint song

"Down to the Folies–Bergere," 42

"Drinking Song," 23, 174–75, 178

Dumont, Margaret, 26, 152, 153, 154, 156

Easter Parade (film), 7, 66, 120, 1810, 193, 302

"Easter Parade" (song), 6, 7, 10, 18, 31, 191–92, 194, 199

Easter parades, 191–92

"East River," 23, 300

Eaton, Doris. *See* Travis, Doris Eaton

Eaton, Mary, 156

eclecticism, 12–13, 307n26

Eisenhower, Dwight D., 7, 222, 282–83, 287, 288, 289

"Elegy" (Massenet). *See* classical instrumental music references in Berlin's shows

Ellington, Duke, 301

Emmet, Linda (daughter), 6

"Empty Pockets Filled with Love," 23, 296

Engel, Lehman, 179

"Ephraham Played upon the Piano," 30, 83

Erlanger, Abe, 36, 37

"Everybody's Doing It Now," 60–62, 97, 130, 132–33, 155

"Everybody Step," 5, 17, 65, 73, 129–37, 138, 139, 140, 141, 143

"Everyone in the World (Is Doing the Charleston)," 155

"Everything in American Is Ragtime," 34, 40

Fabray, Nanette, 293, 298

Face the Music, 6, 20, 23, 97, 149, 150, 152, 154, 155, 158–78, 195, 201, 297. *See also individual song titles*

"Fair Exchange," 118–19

Faust. *See* operatic references in Berlin's shows

Faye, Alice, 147, 194

Feldman, Bert, 4

Ferber, Edna, 150, 152

Fields, Dorothy, xiii, 194, 226, 227, 228, 231, 241, 253–58, 261, 267, 303

Fields, Herbert, xiii, 226, 227, 228, 241, 253–58, 303

Fields, Joseph, 256, 257

Fields, Lew, 56, 67, 257

Fields, W.C., 45, 79

"Fifth Army Is Where My Heart Is, The," 203, 219, 220, 296

Fifty Million Frenchmen, 185

"Fifty Million Frenchmen (Can't Be Wrong)," 185–86

"Fine Romance, A," 250

Fiorello!, 329n51

"First Lady of the Land, The," 296

Flinn, Carol, 289

Florodora, 42, 58, 60, 75, 85, 214

"Flower Garden of My Heart," 97, 170

Follies. *See Ziegfeld Follies*

Follies (Sondheim), 97

Follow the Fleet, 6, 194

Fontanne, Lynn, 209

"Fools Fall in Love," 197

Ford, Gerald, 7

Ford, Henry, 25

Forte, Allen, 240

"For Your Country and My Country," 18, 297

Foster, Stephen, xi, 186

"Free," 283–84, 286

Friend, Howard, 72

Frohman, Charles, 36

Frye, Northrup, 31

"Funnies, The," 189

"Fun to Be Fooled," 276

Furia, Philip, 20, 163, 187, 283, 305n3, 341n35

Garland, Judy, 7, 262

Gaxton, William, 195, 196

genre, 25–33, 34–37, 43, 67–68, 103–4, 303

"Georgia on My Mind," 186

Gershwin, George, xiii, 3, 26, 129, 143, 148–49, 150, 168, 186, 194, 195, 197, 236

Gershwin, Ira, 26, 111, 148–49, 150, 194, 195, 341n34